JAZZ

The First 100 Years

ENHANCED

3rd

EDITION

JAZZ

ENHANCED 3rd EDITION

The First 100 Years

Henry Martin
Rutgers University

Keith Waters
University of Colorado

Australia • Brazil • Canada • Mexico • Singapore • United Kingdom • United States

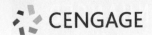

Jazz: The First 100 Years, **Enhanced**
Third Edition
Henry Martin, Keith Waters

Product Director: Monica Eckman

Product Manager: Sharon Adams Poore

Senior Content Developer: Kathy Sands-Boehmer

Associate Content Developer: Erika Hayden

Senior Product Assistant: Rachael Bailey

Media Developer: Liz Newell

Marketing Manager: Jillian Borden

Senior Content Project Manager: Corinna Dibble

Senior Art Director: Linda May

Manufacturing Planner: Julio Esperas

IP Analyst: Jessica Elias

IP Project Manager: Farah Fard

Production Service and Compositor:
Cenveo Publisher Services

Text Designer: Roy Neuhaus

Cover Designer: Rokusek design

Cover Image: Peter Willi /SuperStock;
© 2014 Artists Rights Society (ARS),
New York / ADAGP, Paris

For product information and technology assistance, contact us at
**Cengage Customer & Sales Support, 1-800-354-9706
or support.cengage.com.**

For permission to use material from this text or product, submit all requests online at **www.cengage.com/permissions.**

Library of Congress Control Number: 2014947989

Student Edition:
ISBN-13: 978-1-305-09186-3
ISBN-10: 1-305-09186-8

Loose-leaf Edition:
ISBN-13: 978-1-305-65197-5
ISBN-10: 1-305-65197-9

Cengage
200 Pier 4 Boulevard
Boston, MA 02210
USA

Cengage is a leading provider of customized learning solutions with employees residing in nearly 40 different countries and sales in more than 125 countries around the world. Find your local representative at: **www.cengage.com.**

To learn more about Cengage platforms and services, register or access your online learning solution, or purchase materials for your course, visit **www.cengage.com.**

For Barbara and Gene

Brief Contents

Listening Guide Tracks   *Inside front cover*

Preface   xix

About the Authors   xxiv

Intro   **Jazz Basics   3**

1   **Roots   23**

2   **Early Jazz   57**

3   **Morton, Bechet, Armstrong, and Beiderbecke   83**

4   **1920s Jazz in New York and Europe   103**

5   **The Swing Era   131**

6   **Swing-Era Bands and Stylists   163**

7   **The Bebop Era   191**

8   **The 1950s and New Jazz Substyles   223**

9   **The 1960s Avant-Garde   259**

10   **Mainstream Jazz: Into the 1960s   285**

11   **Jazz-Rock, Jazz-Funk Fusion   321**

12   **Jazz Since the 1980s   345**

Notes   376

Glossary   382

Selected Readings   391

Selected Discography   395

Selected Jazz DVDs and Videos   398

Credits   402

Index   406

Audio Primer Tracks   *Inside back cover*

Contents

Listening Guide Tracks   *Inside front cover*

Preface   xix

About the Authors   xxiv

Introduction / Jazz Basics   3

Hearing *Form* in Jazz   4
   The 32-bar AABA song form   5
   The aab Blues Form   8

More on Rhythm   10

More on Melody   10

More on Harmony   12

Timbre and Texture   14

Dynamics and Articulation   14

Jazz Instruments   15
   Wind Instruments   15
   String Instruments   16
   Percussion Instruments   16
   The Piano   17

More on the Blues   17
   The Blues Scale   18

Jazz Performance Terms   18

Ways of Listening to Jazz   19
   ■ Insider's Guide to . . . The Blues Scale   19
   Key Terms   20

Chapter 1   Roots   23

African American Music in the Nineteenth Century   23

Sources of Musical Diversity   24

The Preservation of African Traditions   25

LISTENING GUIDE: "Kasuan Kura" **28**

Track 1

LISTENING GUIDE: "Daniel" **29**

Track 2

European Music in the Nineteenth Century   29

Instrumentation, Form, and Harmony   29

Written Versus Head Arrangements   31

Early African American Music   31

The Character of Early African American Music   31

Christianity, the Ring Shout, Spirituals, and Work Songs   33

LISTENING GUIDE: "Dere's No Hidin' Place Down Dere"   **34**

Track 3

Blue Notes and Syncopation   35

Minstrelsy   36

Ragtime   38

Scott Joplin   40

LISTENING GUIDE: "Maple Leaf Rag" (excerpt)   **41**

Track 4

James Scott   43

Joseph Lamb   43

Artie Matthews   43

Ragtime's Relationship to Jazz   44

LISTENING GUIDE: "Maple Leaf Rag" **45**

Track 5

The Blues   46

W. C. Handy   47

Blues Form   48

Pioneers of the Delta Blues   49

LISTENING GUIDE: "Love in Vain" **50**

Track 6

Bessie Smith   51

LISTENING GUIDE: "Backwater Blues" **52**

Track 7

Characteristics of Early Jazz Singing   53

Boogie-Woogie and Other Forms of the Blues   53

Exam Review Questions   54

Key Terms   54

Chapter 2 Early Jazz   57

The Shift from Ragtime to Jazz   57

New Orleans   60

How Did Jazz Arise in New Orleans?   62

Buddy Bolden   63

The Evolution of the Jazz Band   64

Early Jazz Instruments and Their Players   65

Cornet   65

■ Insider's Guide to . . . Early Jazz Performance Terms   65

Trombone   66

Clarinet   66

Bass/Tuba   67

Guitar/Banjo   67

Drums   67

Piano   68

The Exodus from New Orleans   68

The Migration North   70

The Roaring Twenties   71

The Chicago Jazz Scene in the Late 1910s and Early 1920s   72

The Advent of Jazz Recording   72

The ODJB and the First Jazz Recording   73

LISTENING GUIDE: "Tiger Rag"   **75**
Track 8

King Oliver and the Creole Jazz Band   77

LISTENING GUIDE: "Dippermouth Blues"   **78**
Track 9

The Evolution of Improvisation   80

Exam Review Questions   81

Key Terms   81

Chapter 3 Morton, Bechet, Armstrong, and Beiderbecke   83

Jelly Roll Morton   83

Sidney Bechet   86

LISTENING GUIDE: "Grandpa's Spells"   **87**
Track 10

Louis Armstrong   89

Armstrong's Classic Style   90

Armstrong in the Later 1920s   90

LISTENING GUIDE: "Cake Walking Babies (from Home)"   **91**
Track 11

LISTENING GUIDE: "West End Blues"   **94**
Track 12

The Chicagoans and Bix Beiderbecke   96

LISTENING GUIDE: "Singin' the Blues"   **99**
Track 13

Exam Review Questions   101

Key Terms   101

Chapter 4   1920s Jazz in New York and Europe   103

Tin Pan Alley   106

The Harlem Renaissance   106

Harlem Stride Piano   108

Eubie Blake   109

James P. Johnson   109

LISTENING GUIDE: "Carolina Shout"   **111**
Track 14

Fats Waller   112

Art Tatum   113

LISTENING GUIDE: "Tiger Rag"   **115**
Track 15

Paul Whiteman and George Gershwin   116

Beginnings of the Big Bands   117

Fletcher Henderson   118

Duke Ellington's Early Career   120

LISTENING GUIDE: "East St. Louis Toodle-Oo"   **123**
Track 16

Jazz in Europe   124

LISTENING GUIDE: "Tiger Rag"   **128**
Track 17

Exam Review Questions   129

Key Terms   129

Chapter 5   The Swing Era   131

Social Upheavals in the 1930s   131

A Decade of Swing   133

The Big Band in the Swing Era   135

Instrumentation, Technique, and Arrangement   135

■ Insider's Guide to . . . Big-Band Terms   136

LISTENING GUIDE: "Down South Camp Meeting"   **137**

Track 18

The Changing Role of the Rhythm Section   139

Territory Bands   140

The Original Blue Devils   141

Kansas City   142

Mary Lou Williams and The Clouds of Joy   142

Count Basie   143

LISTENING GUIDE: "Mary's Idea"   **144**

Track 19

■ Insider's Guide to . . . Jazz Performance Terms   146

LISTENING GUIDE: "Every Tub"   **147**

Track 20

Benny Goodman: King of Swing   150

Goodman's Later Career   153

LISTENING GUIDE: "Down South Camp Meeting"   **153**

Track 21

Ellington After the Cotton Club   154

Building on the Band   155

Changes for the Better   156

The 1940s   158

LISTENING GUIDE: "Ko-Ko"   **158**

Track 22

Exam Review Questions   160

Key Terms   161

Chapter 6   Swing-Era Bands and Stylists   163

Influential Big Bands of the Swing Era   163

Cab Calloway   163

Jimmie Lunceford   165

Chick Webb   165

The Casa Loma Orchestra   166

Mckinney's Cotton Pickers   166

Tommy and Jimmy Dorsey   167

Glenn Miller   167

Artie Shaw   168

Louis Armstrong and His Orchestra   168

LISTENING GUIDE: "Swing That Music"   **169**
Track 23

■ Technique and Technology: Trombone Technique   170

World War II and The "All-Girl" Bands   171

LISTENING GUIDE: "Vi Vigor"   **172**
Track 24

Swing-Era Stylists   173

Benny Goodman   173

LISTENING GUIDE: "Down South Camp Meeting"   **174**
Track 21

Coleman Hawkins   175

Lester Young   176

LISTENING GUIDE: "Body and Soul"   **177**
Track 25

LISTENING GUIDE: "Every Tub"   **178**
Track 20

Roy Eldridge   180

Jack Teagarden   180

Earl Hines   180

Teddy Wilson   181

Jimmy Blanton   182

Jo Jones   183

Gene Krupa   183

Charlie Christian   183

LISTENING GUIDE: "Swing to Bop (Topsy)"   **184**
Track 26

Benny Carter   186

Billie Holiday   187

LISTENING GUIDE: "Body and Soul"   **188**
Track 27

Summary of the Features of Swing   188

Exam Review Questions   189

Key Terms   189

Chapter 7   The Bebop Era   191

The War Years and the 1940s   192

Revolution Versus Evolution   192

Characteristics of the Bebop Style   194

▪ Insider's Guide to . . . A Contrafact: Dizzy Gillespie's "Groovin' High"   195

The Historical Origins of Bebop   196

The Early Forties: Jamming at Minton's and Monroe's   196

Big Bands in the Early 1940s   197

Bebop Moves to Fifty-second Street   198

The Architects of Bebop   199

Charlie Parker   199

LISTENING GUIDE: "Salt Peanuts"   **201**
Track 28

LISTENING GUIDE: "Ko Ko"   **203**
Track 29

Dizzy Gillespie   207

Latin Jazz   208

LISTENING GUIDE: "Manteca"   **209**
Track 30

Bud Powell   210

LISTENING GUIDE: "Tempus Fugit"   **211**
Track 31

Thelonious Monk   213

▪ Technique and Technology: Monk and Metric Displacement   214

LISTENING GUIDE: "Four in One"   **215**
Track 32

Other Bebop Artists   217

J.J. Johnson   217

Fats Navarro   217

Dexter Gordon   217

Bop-Style Big Bands of the Late 1940s   219

Woody Herman   219

Claude Thornhill   219

Exam Review Questions   220

Key Terms   221

Chapter 8 The 1950s and New Jazz Substyles   223

Jazz and the New Substyles   224

▪ Technique and Technology: Technological Advances in the 1950s   226

Cool Stylists   227

Miles Davis and *Birth of the Cool*   227

LISTENING GUIDE: "Jeru"   **228**
Track 33

Gerry Mulligan and Chet Baker   229

The Modern Jazz Quartet   230

LISTENING GUIDE: "Versailles (Porte de Versailles)"   **231**
Track 34

Dave Brubeck   233

LISTENING GUIDE: "Blue Rondo à la Turk" (excerpt)   **234**
Track 35

Stan Getz   236

LISTENING GUIDE: "The Girl from Ipanema"   **237**
Track 36

Lennie Tristano   238

Jazz on the West Coast   239

Third-Stream Music   240

Piano Stylists   241

Hard Bop and Funky/Soul Jazz   243

Art Blakey and the Jazz Messengers   243

LISTENING GUIDE: "Moanin'" (excerpt)   **244**
Track 37

Horace Silver   245

Clifford Brown–Max Roach Quintet   246

Sonny Rollins   247

LISTENING GUIDE: "Powell's Prances"   **247**
Track 38

Charles Mingus   249

LISTENING GUIDE: "Hora Decubitus"   **250**
Track 39

Miles Davis in the 1950s   252

▪ Insider's Guide to ... What Is Modal Jazz?   254

LISTENING GUIDE: "So What" (excerpt)   **255**
Track 40

Exam Review Questions   257

Key Terms   257

Chapter 9 **The 1960s Avant-Garde** **259**

Ornette Coleman and Free Jazz   261
  LISTENING GUIDE: "Street Woman" **264**
  Track 41

John Coltrane   265
  Overview of Coltrane's Career   265
  Early Years   266
  Hard Bop with Miles Davis   266
  Coltrane's Classic Quartet   268
  LISTENING GUIDE: "Acknowledgement" **270**
  Track 42
  Coltrane and the Avant-Garde   271
  Eric Dolphy   272

Avant-Garde Jazz and Black Activism   273
  Archie Shepp   274
  ■ Issues of Race: Voices of Discontent   274
  Albert Ayler   275
  LISTENING GUIDE: "Ghosts: First Variation" (excerpt) **276**
  Track 43
  Black Activism and the Avant-Garde Today   277

Cecil Taylor   277

Sun Ra   279

Chicago: AACM, the Art Ensemble of Chicago,
and Anthony Braxton   280

Black Artists Group and the World Saxophone Quartet   281
  Exam Review Questions   282
  Key Terms   283

Chapter 10 **Mainstream Jazz: Into the 1960s** **285**

Vocalists in the 1950s and 1960s   285
  Ella Fitzgerald   286
  Sarah Vaughan   287
  LISTENING GUIDE: "Take the A Train" (excerpt) **287**
  Track 44
  Cool Singing in the 1950S: The Big Band Legacy   289

Joe Williams   289

Vocalese: Eddie Jefferson and Lambert, Hendricks, and Ross   289

LISTENING GUIDE: "Lullaby of Birdland"   **290**
Track 45

Frank Sinatra   292

The Big Bands Persevere   292

Count Basie and The New Testament Band   293

LISTENING GUIDE: "Corner Pocket"   **293**
Track 46

Duke Ellington After 1950   295

LISTENING GUIDE: "Sunset and the Mockingbird"   **296**
Track 47

Thad Jones–Mel Lewis Big Band   298

Miles Davis in the 1960s   298

LISTENING GUIDE: "E.S.P."   **301**
Track 48

Pianists   302

Bill Evans   302

LISTENING GUIDE: "Autumn Leaves" (excerpt)   **304**
Track 49

Herbie Hancock   306

Chick Corea   307

Keith Jarrett and ECM Records   308

LISTENING GUIDE: "The Windup" (excerpt)   **309**
Track 50

Funky/Soul Jazz   311

Cannonball Adderley   312

The Blues In Funky/Soul Jazz   312

Jimmy Smith and Jazz Organists   312

LISTENING GUIDE: "Mercy, Mercy, Mercy"   **313**
Track 51

LISTENING GUIDE: "James and Wes" (excerpt)   **315**
Track 52

Guitarists   315

The Hard Bop Legacy in the 1960s   316

Blue Note Records   316

Lee Morgan and Freddie Hubbard   317

Wayne Shorter   317

Joe Henderson   318

Other Blue Note Artists   318

Exam Review Questions   318

Key Terms   319

Chapter 11 / Jazz-Rock, Jazz-Funk Fusion   321

Elements of Jazz-Rock and Jazz-Funk Fusion   321

The Synthesizer   322

The Role of the Electric Guitar   323

The Character of Seventies Fusion   323

The Appeal of Rock and Funk   324

The Fusion Music of Miles Davis   326

LISTENING GUIDE: "It's About That Time/In a Silent Way" (excerpt)   **326**

Track 53

Other Fusion Pioneers   329

Lifetime   330

Mahavishnu Orchestra   330

Herbie Hancock and *Headhunters*   *331*

LISTENING GUIDE: "Phenomenon: Compulsion"   **332**

Track 54

Chick Corea and Return to Forever   334

Weather Report   336

LISTENING GUIDE: "Birdland"   **338**

Track 55

Pat Metheny   340

Other Fusion Bands: The Brecker Brothers and Steps   341

Exam Review Questions   342

Key Terms   343

Chapter 12 / Jazz Since the 1980s   345

Classicism and the Jazz Repertory Movement   347

Complete Jazz-Recording Reissues   347

Jazz Pedagogy   348

Jazz Repertory   349

Wynton Marsalis   349

LISTENING GUIDE: "Express Crossing"   **351**

Track 56

The Blakey Alumni   353

Big Bands   356

LISTENING GUIDE: "Hang Gliding" (excerpt)   **357**

Track 57

The Popular Connection 359

Digital Technology 359

Smooth Jazz 359

LISTENING GUIDE: "Softly, As in a Morning Sunrise" **360**
Track 58

Acid Jazz and Hip Hop 361

The Mass Market: Radio and the Internet 362

Neo-Swing 362

The Avant-Garde, World Music, Crossover, and Jazz to Come 362

Jazz and Feminism 363

Jazz Abroad 363

Latin Jazz: The Afro-Cuban Tradition, The Caribbean, and Salsa 364

LISTENING GUIDE: "Guataca City (To David Amram)" **365**
Track 59

Crossover, Postmodernism, and World Music 366

LISTENING GUIDE: "Salt Peanuts" **368**
Track 60

Directions for Crossover Jazz 370

LISTENING GUIDE: "Solitude" **370**
Track 61

LISTENING GUIDE: "Falsehood" **373**
Track 62

The Future of Jazz 374

Exam Review Questions 375

Key Terms 375

Notes 376

Glossary 382

Selected Readings 391

Selected Discography 395

Selected Jazz DVDs and Videos 398

Credits 402

Index 406

 Audio Primer Tracks *Inside back cover*

Preface

IN THE FIRST AND SECOND EDITIONS of *Jazz: The First 100 Years*, our goal was to provide college students with a text that presented a fresh overview of jazz history and focused greater attention on jazz since 1970. We tried to stimulate fresh thinking about the jazz canon by including recordings that complement rather than duplicate the selections in the *Smithsonian Collection of Classic Jazz*. In addition to the book's primary concern—the development of jazz and its most important artists—our first, second, and third editions related the music to relevant aspects of social and intellectual history, including the Harlem Renaissance in the 1920s and black activism in the 1960s. Finally, we included the most up-to-date information possible, taking advantage of the fine scholarly work on jazz that has appeared during the past several years.

In this third edition with enhanced media resources, our goal has been to facilitate interactive learning. It is important to stress, however, that our original conception of the text, its overall organization, and its philosophy have remained the same through all three editions, and that this enhanced media edition largely preserves the text of our third edition (with updates where necessary). Our chronological presentation of jazz history preserves the customary divisions of the music into stylistic periods because we feel that this is the clearest method of introducing the material. Nonetheless, throughout the text we continue to acknowledge and emphasize that many (if not most) artists have produced significant work beyond the era in which they first came to public attention.

As with any history, we sometimes must stray outside the time frame of a given era to complete the narrative of a certain artist. For the most part, however, an individual is generally treated in the era in which he or she exerted the most influence. The two main exceptions to this practice are Miles Davis and Duke Ellington. Although Ellington was prominent and influential throughout his career, he played an especially important role in early jazz and the swing era (Chapters 4 and 5), as well as in 1960s mainstream jazz (Chapter 10). Davis exerted considerable influence on the disparate styles of 1950s cool jazz, 1960s mainstream jazz, and 1970s jazz-rock, so his story is related in Chapters 8, 10, and 11, to clarify these distinct contributions.

Using the Text

The text is divided into the Introduction on Jazz Basics and twelve chapters; for a one-semester class, an instructor should cover approximately one chapter per week. The text can also support a two-semester class. Instructors may wish to finish with Chapter 7 in the first semester; in this case the first semester presents jazz from 1900 to 1950, and the second semester covers jazz from 1950 to the present. Within each chapter the material is organized through main headings and subordinate headings, which should help the instructor to maximize the use of class time and (in smaller classes) coordinate discussion according to the most important topics. Because the book combines a historical narrative with broader summaries of stylistic features, the instructor is free to use and shape the given material.

Features

▶ This book features a historical focus on the evolution of significant trends, key figures, and the changing role of instrumental and improvisational style. It also includes relevant ideas in twentieth-century U.S. social and intellectual history, including the Harlem Renaissance and the countercultural movements of the sixties. Many issues related to contemporary U.S. political and social history appear in the photographs and their extended captions. One-third of the book chronicles jazz since 1960, giving a balanced and nuanced view of significant trends and performers of the 1960s through the 2000s.

▶ Current scholarly and critical work is reflected throughout as the text takes into account some of the groundbreaking jazz research of the previous three decades. The presentation attempts to illuminate and amplify current historical and musical controversies rather than assert unqualified truths.

▶ Jazz guitarists and jazz vocalists, their techniques, and their contributions to the history of jazz (not always considered in other texts) are covered throughout.

▶ A new, **magazine-like design** helps bring jazz to life, including "pull quotes" that capture the spirit of the times and of the artists.

▶ **Glossary terms** are now boldfaced in the text and their definitions gathered, for ease of reference, on the page.

▶ **Listening Guides** with a new The Main Point preview and clear within-text references, as well as detailed timings keyed to events in the music and the work's overall form, are included for each of the sixty-two musical selections.

Sarah Vaughan, "Lullaby of Birdland"

▶ **New marginal icons** cue pieces that are available for additional listening and download on the text's preselected Spotify and YouTube playlists, located on the text website (see Supplements below).

▶ **Boxes** with the themes "Technique and Technology," "Issues of Race," and "Insider's Guide to…" provide enrichment material on such diverse topics as jazz transcriptions and the sociocultural background of jazz.

▶ **Timelines** at the beginning of each chapter put the chapter's musical and historical developments in chronological context.

▶ **Exam Review Questions** and **Key Terms** at the end of each chapter help students prepare for tests on the chapter's material.

▶ At the end of chapters introducing a new style, the text includes **tables comparing jazz styles**, which appear in interactive form on the text website.

▶ Additional resources include a new Introduction to Jazz Basics; instructive end Notes; a Glossary of key terms; Selected Readings for further research; Selected Jazz DVDs and Videos, listing extensive sources for viewing and further study; and a comprehensive Index.

What's New in the Third Enhanced Edition

▶ MindTap, available on the book's website, offers interactive learning aids that will enable students to explore the book's main ideas creatively. See below for more on this feature.

▶ An expanded Introduction, Jazz Basics, discusses such general topics on musical fundamentals as rhythm, melody, harmony, the instruments of jazz, and standard musical terminology—using George Benson's "Softly, As in a Morning Sunrise" as an illustrative example. The Introduction also includes listening examples throughout that are keyed to the Audio Primer Tracks, indicated by the Audio Primer 🅟 logo.

▶ We decreased the total number of music examples in order to make the text more accessible to both music majors and nonmusic majors.

▶ We have expanded the coverage of women in jazz, including "all-girl" big bands and Maria Schneider as well as singers Sarah Vaughan, Peggy Lee, Chris Connor, Anita O'Day, and Ella Fitzgerald.

▶ We have also expanded the coverage of Latin jazz, now including new selections "The Girl from Ipanema," with Stan Getz and Astrud Gilberto; and "Guataca City (To David Amram)," with Paquito d'Rivera.

▶ Chapter 1 includes additional information about Robert Johnson.

▶ Chapter 3 focuses on the major figures of early jazz—Jelly Roll Morton, Sidney Bechet, Louis Armstrong, and Bix Beiderbecke—with expanded new material on Bechet.

▶ Chapter 4 follows the establishment of early jazz with the emergence in New York of Tin Pan Alley, the Harlem Renaissance, the stride pianists, Fletcher Henderson, and Duke Ellington. There is also expanded material on James P. Johnson.

▶ Chapter 5 features additional coverage of the social upheavals of the Depression and of race relations during the 1930s. Coverage of Duke Ellington's and Count Basie's work during the 1950s is now consolidated in Chapter 10.

▶ Chapter 6 includes new material on Louis Armstrong during the swing era and expanded coverage of Charlie Christian.

▶ Chapter 7 begins with a new introduction to the war years and the 1940s in general, then expands its treatment of Charlie Parker.

▶ Chapter 8 opens with an introduction to the culture of the 1950s, then proceeds to expanded coverage of the Modern Jazz Quartet and of Stan Getz and bossa nova. Vocalists of the 1950s and 1960s have now been consolidated in Chapter 10 on mainstream jazz of the 1950s–60s.

▶ Chapter 10 now surveys some of the significant mainstream jazz vocalists (especially Ella Fitzgerald and Sarah Vaughan) and examines the legacy of big bands, with particular focus on the bands of Count Basie and Duke Ellington.

▶ Chapter 11 features much expanded coverage of 1970s fusion.

▶ In Chapter 12 we continue to treat the increasing number of women and non-Americans making major names in jazz and include selections by Maria Schneider as well as Paquito D'Rivera. We also update the material and include a selection by Vijay Iyer that demonstrates the continuing connections jazz is making with music of other cultures.

Supplements

▶ The **Audio Primer tracks,** prepared by the authors, are included on the course website (see below). These tracks demonstrate basic musical concepts (such as scales, syncopation, blues, rhythm changes, inside/outside playing, and so forth) as well as the instruments of jazz (the four principal saxophones, trumpet and trombone with different mutes, electric and acoustic guitars, the different sounds of the drum set, and so on). In-text references are indicated by the Audio Primer 🅟 logo. Where appropriate, the definitions of Key Terms in the text refer to the Audio Primer so that students can hear musical examples of what is being defined. For Audio Primer contents, see the inside back cover of this textbook.

▶ **Active Listening Guides**. This edition includes, as a part of the course website, online, interactive Active Listening Guides. These Active Listening Guides feature full-color interactive and streaming listening guides for every selection discussed within the text, along with listening quizzes, background information, and printable PDF Listening Guides.

▶ **MindTap Course Website**. MindTap combines readings, multimedia, activities, and assessments into a singular learning path, guiding students through their course with ease and engagement. Included within this MindTap course are interactive Chapter and Listening quizzes, streaming music, active Listening Guides, and Spotify and YouTube playlists.

▶ A download card, which replaces the three CD set, includes all the piece of music discussed within the book and are keyed to the Listening Guides in the text. For a full list of downloads see the inside front cover of this textbook.

Changes to the Download Tracks

The recordings selected for the download card represent a general overview of jazz in the twentieth century. The text includes a Listening Guide for each track, containing commentary that highlights aspects of form, instrumentation, and improvisation. In making our selections, we followed these criteria: the recordings should be representative of the artists' work generally; the recordings should be well known, unless there is reason to include something more obscure; and the choice and the arrangement of the selections should work aesthetically.

This third enhanced edition includes numerous new selections (some excerpted):

▶ "Love in Vain"—Robert Johnson

▶ "Cake Walking Babies (from Home)"—Clarence Williams's Blue Five (with Armstrong and Bechet)

▶ "Carolina Shout"—James P. Johnson

▶ "Every Tub"—Count Basie and His Orchestra

▶ "Down South Camp Meeting"—Benny Goodman and His Orchestra

▶ "Ko-Ko"—Duke Ellington and His Orchestra

▶ "Swing That Music"—Louis Armstrong

▶ "Topsy (Swing to Bop)"—Charlie Christian at Minton's

▶ "Ko Ko"—Charlie Parker

▶ "Tempus Fugit"—Bud Powell

▶ "Versailles"—Modern Jazz Quartet

▶ "Blue Rondo à la Turk"—Dave Brubeck Quartet

▶ "The Girl from Ipanema"—Stan Getz

▶ "Take the A Train"—Ella Fitzgerald

▶ "Lullaby of Birdland"—Sarah Vaughan

▶ "Corner Pocket"—Count Basie

- ▶ "Sunset and the Mockingbird"—Duke Ellington
- ▶ "E.S.P."—Miles Davis
- ▶ "The Windup"—Keith Jarrett
- ▶ "Mercy, Mercy, Mercy"—Cannonball Adderley
- ▶ "James and Wes"—Wes Montgomery
- ▶ "Phenomenon: Compulsion"—John McLaughlin
- ▶ "Birdland"—Weather Report
- ▶ "Hang Gliding"—Maria Schneider
- ▶ "Guataca City (To David Amram)"—Paquito d'Rivera
- ▶ "Solitude"—Herbie Hancock
- ▶ "Falsehood"—Vijay Iyer

Acknowledgments

The first edition of *Jazz: The First 100 Years* began as an expanded second edition of Martin's *Enjoying Jazz* (Schirmer Books, 1986) but quickly developed into a comprehensive jazz history text. We acknowledge the wise guidance of the staff at Schirmer Books in overseeing the early development of the first edition of *Jazz: The First 100 Years*. We also thank Javier Gonzalez, who checked discographical and biographical information for the first edition.

For the second edition we benefited from the advice of Latin jazz expert Christopher Washburne in our discussion of Latin jazz and in the selection of "Manteca." We thank Charles Turner, who went beyond the call of duty in locating "Daniel" and "Dere's No Hidin' Place Down Dere." Both Sherrie Tucker and Janna Saslaw provided expert advice on women in jazz, and we thank them for their thoughtful critiques of our additional material and the suggestion of "Vi Vigor." Thanks also to Rosalind Cron for her photo of the International Sweethearts of Rhythm. We thank Craig Wright for the selection "Kasuan Kura" from his text *Listening to Music* (6th ed., Cengage).

For the third edition, we benefited from the advice of Ricky Riccardi on Louis Armstrong; Joshua Berrett for comments on Duke Ellington's "East St. Louis Toodle-Oo"; Alexander Stewart for a correction to the form of "Weather Bird"; Bob Waters for suggestions on Sarah Vaughan; Graeme Boone for advice on Steve Coleman's "Salt Peanuts"; David DeMotta for comments on Latin jazz; Robert Morris and David Claman for insights on the relationship between jazz and Indian music; and Bob Palmieri, Paul Brady, Evan Perri, and David McGillicuddy for advice on Pat Metheny and the extended guitar techniques of John McLaughlin.

The environment and support provided by the Special Interest Group in Jazz (SMT-Jz) of the Society for Music Theory have helped make this book a reality. Many thanks to the members of SMT-Jz who encouraged us to pursue this project initially and offered suggestions throughout the development of all three editions.

We thank Clark Baxter, former publisher for music at Cengage Learning, who originally encouraged us to write the third edition. We owe Clark and his colleagues a tremendous debt for their tireless work in uncovering the photographs, sheet music covers, and other pictorial material used in the text.

We thank Sharon Adams Poore, Product Manager at Cengage, for encouraging us to proceed with the third enhanced media edition. Discussions with her resulted in several ideas that helped make the book's resources more appealing. We thank Kathy Sands-Boehmer, senior content developer, who reviewed the text in detail to make sure it was balanced and suggested several improvements. She was a pleasure to work with in every way. We would also like to thank Jillian Borden, marketing manager; Erika Hayden, associate content developer; Liz Newell, media developer; Corinna Dibble, senior content project manager; and Linda May, senior art director.

For the Audio Primer, many thanks to the excellent Denver-based musicians who agreed to perform on it. They include Rich Chiaraluce, Mark Harris, Bill Kopper, Ron Miles, Todd Reid, and Ken Walker. We would also like to thank our assistant engineers, Ty Blosser, Jerry Wright, and John Romero. A special thanks to Joe Hall, who was the principal engineer as well as the trombonist. Thanks also to Paul Rinzler for creating the Active Listening Tools, to Paul Brady for editing the Active Listening Guides, and to Maya Whelan, who helped develop the MindTap materials.

We thank Tom Laskey of Sony Music Custom Marketing Group, who obtained the rights for the download music tracks. Tom's patience and resourcefulness in locating the best possible audio sources for each selection were admirable.

We would also like to thank the readers engaged by Cengage Learning to critique the manuscript for the third edition. We gained excellent insights and suggestions from Larry Dwyer, University of Notre Dame; Keith Pawlak, University of Arizona; Emmett G. Price, Northeastern University; Doug Reid, Shoreline Community College; Teri Roiger, State University of New York, New Paltz; and David Wakeley, Spokane Falls Community College.

We profited enormously from the suggestions of readers of the first and second editions, and thank them profusely: John Fremgen, University of Texas, Austin; Wayne E. Goins, Kansas State University; John R. Harding, University of North Carolina, Charlotte; Mark Mazzatenta, University of North Carolina at Greensboro; Brian Moon, University of Arizona; John Murphy, University of North Texas; Cara Pollard, Texas Tech University; Tom Wolfe, University of Alabama; and Bret Zvacek, Crane School of Music, SUNY Potsdam.

We must especially single out Carl Woideck of the University of Oregon and Lewis Porter of Rutgers

University–Newark for special consideration. Each of them read the text with exceptional thoroughness. They offered alternative ideas, vigilantly pointed out errors, and sometimes questioned interpretations. Carl's suggestions for the download music tracks were invaluable. Both Lew's and Carl's advice and suggestions inform many sections and are too copious to acknowledge adequately here.

We would like to thank David Cayer and Lewis Porter for timely advice on our initial selection of jazz videos. Rob Duboff worked to refine the list into final form and wrote many of the video descriptions.

Our historical and analytical insights are profoundly indebted to the explosion of recent first-rate scholarly and critical studies on jazz. Many have proven invaluable, including (but not limited to) Lewis Porter's excellent studies of Lester Young and John Coltrane, Mark Tucker's work on Duke Ellington, Scott DeVeaux's writings on bebop, Stuart Nicholson's book on jazz-rock fusion, Sherrie Tucker's work on the all-women bands of the swing era, and Enrico Merlin's material on Miles Davis's electric period. We would like to thank Tom Riis for his input on late-nineteenth-century American music in general and Robert Sadin for insight into the experience of conducting "Express Crossing." Our thanks go to Vijah Iyer for comments on his recording "Falsehood." Bill Kirchner offered excellent advice in the early stages of the process, as did Greg Dyes, formerly of the University of Colorado, and Michael Fitzgerald. Brian Fores's unpublished master's thesis on John Zorn contributed material not available elsewhere. John Galm, Travis Jackson, Eric Charry, and Steve Pond provided insights into the retention of African music in the United States and helped us clarify the summary of African music in Chapter 1.

The graduate students in the master's degree program in jazz history and research at Rutgers University–Newark read earlier drafts of many sections and provided valuable feedback; we thank them for their time and comments. We also thank Steve Lindeman and Sam Miller for several corrections. We particularly acknowledge the staff of the Institute of Jazz Studies at Rutgers University–Newark: Dan Morgenstern, Ed Berger, and Vince Pelote were extremely generous with their time and advice. Dan and Ed have since retired, and we wish them the best.

Finally, we would especially like to acknowledge the personal and endless support of Barbara Fiorella and Gene Hayworth. Each managed to deal with the authors' individual whims, predilections, peccadilloes, and other personal idiosyncrasies with humor, understanding, and continuing encouragement. The term *significant other* is clumsy, but for each of us there truly is no one more significant. We are extraordinarily fortunate to have our lives so enriched. We dedicate this book to Barbara and Gene.

About the Authors

Henry Martin is a professor of music at Rutgers University–Newark. With a Ph.D. from Princeton University and degrees from the University of Michigan and Oberlin Conservatory, he has pursued a dual career as a composer-pianist and a music theorist specializing in jazz and the Western tonal tradition. Martin's compositions (published by Margun Music and Evensong Music, Media, and Graphics) have won several awards, including the 1998 Barlow Endowment International Composition Competition and the National Composers Competition sponsored by the League of Composers–International Society for Contemporary Music. Albany Records released his *Selected Piano Music* CD in 2010 (TROY1171, with performances by Hilary Demske), and Bridge Records released his *Preludes and Fugues* CD in 2004 (Bridge 9140, with Martin performing).

Martin teaches in the master's degree program in jazz history and research at Rutgers–Newark, the country's only program granting a degree in jazz scholarship. He is a co-editor of the *Journal of Jazz Studies*, which is published online by the Rutgers University Libraries. He is the author of *Charlie Parker and Thematic Improvisation* (Scarecrow Press, 1996) and *Enjoying Jazz* (Schirmer Books, 1986). Scarecrow also published his *Counterpoint* in 2005. Martin has published numerous articles on music theory in such journals as *Perspectives of New Music*, the *Journal of Music Theory*, and *In Theory Only*. He is also the founder of the Special Interest Group in Jazz, an organization of music theorists devoted to advancing scholarship in jazz theory.

Keith Waters is a professor of music theory at the University of Colorado at Boulder. He received a Ph.D. in music theory from the Eastman School of Music, a master of music degree in jazz piano from the New England Conservatory of Music, and a bachelor of music degree in applied piano from the University of North Carolina–Greensboro. He is the author of the award-winning book, *The Studio Recordings of the Miles Davis Quintet, 1965-68* (Oxford University Press, 2011), and *Rhythmic and Contrapuntal Structures in the Music of Arthur Honegger* (Ashgate, 2002). He has published articles on Herbie Hancock, Booker Little, Miles Davis, Wayne Shorter, and Keith Jarrett as well as on other topics related to jazz analysis and improvisation.

As a jazz pianist, Waters has performed in jazz festivals and clubs throughout the United States and Europe, appearing in such venues as the Blue Note and the Village Corner in New York City, and Blues Alley and the Kennedy Center in Washington, DC. He has performed in concert with numerous jazz artists, including James Moody, Bobby Hutcherson, Eddie Harris, Chris Connor, Sheila Jordan, Keter Betts, Buck Hill, and Meredith D'Ambrosia. He has recorded for VSOP Records, and his playing has been featured in *Jazz Player* magazine.

▶ The authors welcome suggestions for subsequent editions. Comments may be e-mailed to the authors:

Henry Martin
martinh@andromeda.rutgers.edu

Keith Waters
keith.waters@colorado.edu

JAZZ

ENHANCED

3rd

EDITION

The First 100 Years

Jazz Basics

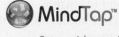

Start with a quick
warm-up activity.

Today, WE HEAR MUSIC EVERYWHERE. IT IS SO PERVASIVE
that we sometimes don't realize that we're hearing it. Music forms the background to
movies, television shows, Internet websites and games, retail stores, elevators, airport
lounges, doctors' offices, and so on. Some of us walk around listening to iPods; others
keep radios and televisions on in their homes to accompany other activities, and of
course much of the sound they provide is music. What this means is that we often take
the presence of music for granted. When music forms the focus of our attention, however, it becomes foreground rather than background activity, and we have the opportunity to listen carefully rather than carelessly. Careful listening helps us appreciate and
enjoy the music more fully.

This Introduction will give you the basic vocabulary you need to talk about jazz.

Our goal in this Introduction is to describe some of the underlying musical
ideas in jazz and define its elements so that you will be able to appreciate and
enjoy jazz more fully. This Introduction will also give you the basic vocabulary
you need to talk about jazz. We will begin with a track from the historical selections that accompany this book and throughout will also refer to the ⊕ Audio
Primer tracks that are available on the companion website. These latter tracks
demonstrate fundamental principles, the most common jazz instruments, and
basic ideas of form.

To help you master all this new terminology, some key terms are shown in **bold**
when they first come up in text; this means that the term's definition appears on the
page of its first usage, in the Glossary at the back of the book, and as one of the Key
Terms at the end of the chapter.

Hearing *Form* in Jazz

What do we do when we listen to jazz? Just what are we hearing? Let's begin with the recording (Track 58) of George Benson's recording of "Softly, As in a Morning Sunrise." First, listen to the entire track, and try to hear its different sections (parts of the music) and recognize the instruments that are playing. You may recognize the track as an example of "smooth jazz," a kind of jazz heard frequently in elevators, dentists' offices, and other venues that are attempting to create a relaxed overall mood. You may be used to hearing singing in the music you like, so you should note that there is no singing on this track. Although there are many important jazz singers, much jazz is what we call **instrumental music**, which lacks vocals. You probably have heard smooth jazz, but you may have not listened to it carefully before. Let us analyze what you are hearing in more detail.

Play "Softly, As in a Morning Sunrise" again from the beginning. As the track begins, you will hear the music

What else can you hear in the Benson track from time 0:08 to 0:22? For one thing, you may have found yourself tapping your hand or foot to the recording. In most of the world's music you can feel a steady pulse to which you may clap your hands, tap your foot, or dance. That pulse is

In much of jazz (and in other music as well), the drummer keeps the beat.

known as the **beat**. In much of jazz (and in other music as well), the drummer keeps the beat. However, even music without drums (such as a solo piano performance) may still project a strong beat, although there is no drummer "keeping time" or "keeping the beat." Thus, a beat is something that may be abstract, because its presence isn't always as obvious as a drumbeat. In the Benson track, we hear the beat most clearly in the drum sounds, most of which are created electronically.

A beat is an instance of what in music we call **rhythm**. Jazz is especially known for its rhythm, but rhythm

Listen to Track 3 of the ⓐ Audio Primer, on which you will hear a melody played on the piano—first without chords, then with chords.

seem to grow from the beginning of the track until time 0:08 when the melody begins. Benson, the featured electric guitarist, enters at 0:08 and plays the **melody** in the foreground of the music. Listen, in particular, to the melody from 0:08 through 0:22. The building blocks of the melody, heard in Benson's guitar, are called *notes* or *tones*. Later in this section we will consider several other musical terms that will help you understand the various aspects of melody.

In addition to hearing Benson play the melody on the guitar, we hear other sounds. The sum total of all the different sounds you hear produces the **texture** of the music. We hear this particular texture as dominated by electronic sounds, including the sound of Benson's electric guitar, which is the featured element in the texture. What other elements of the texture of the accompaniment can you distinguish? You might, for example, notice there is an electronic bass part that provides a lower-range foundation to the sound.

There are also mid-range **chords** (groups of notes, to be discussed later) that were probably produced by a synthesizer, a device that creates sounds electronically. There are also *percussion* sounds that include drums, finger snaps, and so on. Together, these sounds provide a background accompaniment to the *lead* part heard in Benson's electric guitar. Jazz styles can be identified, at least in part, by their textures, so learning to recognize the sounds of the instruments making up the texture narrows down the style.

pervades all music. When notes follow each other in time, they are necessarily in some kind of rhythm, so we can think of rhythm as the experience of music through time.

Our innate attraction to music may have developed through the experience of rhythm even before birth: our perception of our mothers' heartbeats while we were still in the womb. After birth, our first actual experience of music may have been our mothers' singing the lullabies that calmed us as infants and lulled us to sleep. In listening to our mothers' lullabies, we experience the overwhelming power of music and its effect on our emotions from the very beginning of life.

Instrumental music is music that lacks vocals.

Melody is the sequential arrangement of the notes of the scale into a coherent pattern.

The **texture** of music arises out of the sum total of all the different sounds you hear—the number and kind of instruments playing and the manner in which they are being played.

A **chord** is a group of three or more notes played simultaneously and acts as the basic unit of **harmony**.

Beat is a steady pulse, such as a heartbeat, and an instance of **rhythm**, the experience of music through time.

Tempo is the speed of the music's beat, ordinarily ranging from forty to two hundred beats per minute.

Meter is the organization of music into regular groups of beats representing strong and weak pulses. In **duple meter**, the music alternates between two pulses—one strong and one weak (ONE-two, ONE-two)—or, in a common form of duple meter, the music features four pulses—the first pulse receiving the strongest accent and the third pulse an accent stronger than two and four (ONE-two-three-four). In **triple meter**, two weak pulses separate a single strong pulse (ONE-two-three, ONE-two-three). Most music has meter.

A **bar** or **measure** represents each instance of the meter.

Form describes how we organize music in time by dividing a work into individual units called sections. Each **section** contains a set of measures and divides further into sets of measures called **phrases**. We label a section with a capital letter of the alphabet (A, B, C, and so on) and label a phrase with a lowercase letter (a, b, c)—a system that allows us to describe a work's musical form in abbreviated fashion.

The beat of music is roughly equivalent to the human heartbeat, normally around seventy-two beats per minute. The speed of music's beat, its **tempo**, ranges from somewhat slower to considerably faster but within the same

Most jazz uses duple meter.

basic range: from about forty beats per minute to about two hundred beats per minute. Slower tempos tend to be moodier and more contemplative, whereas faster tempos are livelier. The Benson track features what we might call a "medium tempo"—not too slow or too fast.

In music, beats are organized according to meter. **Meter** arises from regular patterns of strong and weak pulses or beats. When we feel the music alternating between two pulses—one strong and one weak (ONE-two, ONE-two)—the meter is called **duple**; when two weak pulses separate single strong pulses (ONE-two-three, ONE-two-three), the meter is called **triple**. Meter can also be *irregular* when the strong pulses occur unpredictably. Most jazz, however, uses duple meter. The Benson track is in a particularly common form of duple meter in which we can count a fairly brisk ONE-two-THREE-four, ONE-two-THREE-four, and so on through the track. Each instance of ONE-two-THREE-four

is called a **bar** or **measure**. We refer to such bars or measures as being in "4/4 time," an idea discussed more fully later in this Introduction when we treat rhythm in more depth.

In the Benson example, let's begin counting ONE-two-THREE-four at time 0:08 and continue through time 0:22. What do you notice happens at the second time unit? You

Four-bar phrases and eight-bar sections are very common in jazz.

may have noticed that the melody begins to repeat. That is, during 0:22–0:36 Benson repeats the tune he first played in 0:08–0:22. When we notice parts of pieces repeating, we begin to recognize what we call musical **form**.

The 32-bar AABA song form

Musical form is the term we use to describe how the music is organized in time. In counting ONE-two-THREE-four from 0:08 through 0:22 in the Benson track, we would repeat "ONE-two-THREE-four" eight times. We say, then, that the melody has *eight bars* or *eight measures* before it repeats. These eight bars denote an important musical unit, typically present in jazz performances, that is called a **section**. The eight-bar section is a self-contained musical grouping. We often think of it as divided into two 4-bar **phrases**. Four-bar phrases and eight-bar sections are very common in jazz, though other measure groups are possible. Benson then repeats the same melody from 0:22 to 0:36, in which we hear another eight bars.

Notice that at time 0:37 the music changes; that is, new material begins. We can label the initial eight bars (the first section) of the piece as A. Because the material repeats from 0:22 to 0:36, the piece, so far, can be described as AA. In general, to develop an awareness of form, you should try to recognize where the music begins to repeat. We often describe the form of a musical work by labeling its sections, frequently with the letters A, B, C, and so on, although some musicologists use lowercase letters. Letters can stand for small units, such as phrases, as well as much longer parts of compositions and performances.

In general, to identify the basic form of a piece of music, count the number of bars that create self-contained, clearly different sections. The easiest way to count bars is to keep track of them systematically through

To develop an awareness of form, try to recognize where the music begins to repeat, and count the number of bars that create self-contained, clearly different sections.

the beat of the music. For example, to count bars of 4/4 time, you should count as follows:

ONE-two-three-four (1st bar)

TWO-two-three-four (2nd bar)

THREE-two-three-four (3rd bar)

FOUR-two-three-four (4th bar)

FIVE-two-three-four (5th bar)

SIX-two-three-four (6th bar)

(and so on)

As you near the end of a phrase (often, four bars) or a section (often, eight bars), listen to how the music creates a **cadence**, where the musical elements combine to create a feeling of closure or ending to that phrase or section. The cadence enables the preceding part of the music to feel self-contained. The more important the sectional division, the more conclusive will be the cadence that helps create that closure.

What of the material from the beginning of the track until 0:08? This brief beginning to the piece sets up Benson's entrance with the melody and is called the piece's **introduction**. We can extrapolate the beat backward from the beginning of the first A section to the beginning of the piece. In so doing, we notice that although the bass hasn't yet entered and beat is not as clear as it will become, the Introduction is four bars long. Hence, we can describe the piece thus far as follows:

Introduction	0:00–0:07	(4 bars)
A	0:08–0:22	first melody (8 bars)
A	0:22–0:36	first melody repeats (8 bars)

We pointed out above that the music changes at 0:37. The new music that we hear is different from the music we called A, so let's call it B. If we then begin counting bars at 0:37, we will notice that eight bars of music will pass by before the A part returns, at 0:52. At the point when the A returns, it also continues for eight bars.

Introduction	0:00–0:07	(4 bars)
A	0:08–0:22	first melody (8 bars)
A	0:22–0:36	first melody repeats (8 bars)
B	0:37–0:51	new, second melody, different from A (8 bars)
A	0:52–1:06	first melody returns (8 bars)

The presentation of the melody can thus be described as AABA, with each section eight bars long, for a total of 32 bars. This is the form of the melody, or original song. As will become evident throughout this text, the **32-bar AABA song form** is one of the most common in jazz. This form, in fact, pervades American popular music, especially songs written before 1950. Sometimes, the A section

is called the **head**; the B section is known as the **bridge**. Even though this Benson recording is from 2004, the song

The 32-bar AABA song form is one of the most common forms in jazz.

was actually written in the 1920s and is characteristic of pre-1950s popular music.

Almost all jazz before the 1950s is based on symmetrical sections with the numbers of bars occurring in multiples of four, the common phrase length. We typically find sections of eight or sixteen bars that combine to create larger groups of thirty-two bars. After 1950, symmetrical forms continue to dominate jazz performance, but irregular forms become more common.

Sometimes, in AABA form, if a section repeats but is modified, the repeated section may be denoted by **primes**

A common texture in jazz is that of the piano trio.

added to the section letter: AA′BA″ shows that the initial A section returns twice but is modified, first in one way (A′), then in another (A″).

There are other instances of 32-bar AABA songs included with this text and on the ⊕ Audio Primer. Listen, for example, to Track 10 of the ⊕ Audio Primer. You should note that this example is not smooth jazz. Rather, you should be able to distinguish three instruments: piano, bass, and drums. We heard a bass in the Benson recording, but the bass on this ⊕ Audio Primer example is known as an acoustic bass.

Toward the end of this chapter, we will briefly describe the principal jazz instruments, including the acoustic bass. You should also recognize the piano and drums.

A **cadence** occurs at the end of a section or phrase and creates a feeling of closure. It can also refer to a common closing chord progression.

An **introduction** occurs at the beginning of a piece and sets up the entrance of the melody and first section.

The **32-bar AABA song form** presents the melody in four sections labeled A, A, B, and A, each section eight bars long, for a total of 32 bars.

The term **head** describes the A section or principal melody of a song; **bridge** describes the B section.

A **prime** added to a section letter indicates that a section repeats but in modified form.

A **piano trio** is a performance group made up of piano, bass, and drums. Another form of the piano trio features piano, bass, and guitar.

Harmony defines a **chord**, generally a group of three or four notes played simultaneously.

The essence of jazz, **improvisation** or an *improvised solo* refers to a performance technique in which the improviser or soloist spontaneously creates a melody that fits the form and harmony of the piece.

> Linking chords together successively in music provides a flow of harmony that serves as an accompaniment to a melody and adds richness and context to it.

Together, these three instruments comprise a texture that is common in jazz and is known as a **piano trio**.

The tempo in this recording is faster than what we heard in the Benson recording, so when you count ONE-two-THREE-four, TWO-two-THREE-four, and so on, you will have to count more quickly. In particular, listen to the bass notes: your counting should coincide with the bass notes. If you count through the track, you will note that the recording's form can also be described as AABA. Although the pianist (coauthor Keith Waters) is not playing a melody that you can hum as a tune, you should be able to hear that he is playing basically the same material in the eight-bar A sections and something different during the B section. We will return to issues of form later in this chapter to describe some items in greater detail. Because the pianist does not seem to be playing a melody on Track 10 of the 🅟 Audio Primer, what, in fact, is he playing? We have briefly described two of the three elements of Western music as rhythm and melody. The third element is more abstract, but essential to many forms of Western music, including most jazz: harmony. The pianist is playing **chords**, which are groups of notes that represent what we call **harmony**.

Linking chords together successively in music provides a flow of harmony that often serves as accompaniment to a melody and adds richness and context to it. In Western music a singer often performs a song's melody while the accompanying instruments play chords that provide harmony. The piano has long been the basic instrument of Western music because it can function as a kind of one-man band in which the performer can provide melody and harmony simultaneously: a player's right hand can play the melody while the left hand plays chords that provide harmony. Listen to Track 3 of the 🅟 Audio Primer, on which you'll hear a melody played on the piano—first without chords, then with chords.

If you replay the Benson track (Track 58), you will notice that the sustained electronic sounds that provide a background to Benson's melody are in fact chords. In that

> Listen again to Track 3 of the 🅟 Audio Primer on which you'll hear a melody played on the piano—first without chords, then with chords.

track, the chords appear in the electronic keyboard parts, whereas in Track 10 of the 🅟 Audio Primer, you can hear the pianist playing the chords on the acoustic piano.

We noticed earlier that in the Benson track, we hear the melody presented as AABA from 0:08 until 1:07. What happens next in the music after 1:07? Benson continues to play, with a similar background texture, but we no longer hear the melody that we identified as A. Instead, Benson is playing what we call an **improvisation** or *improvised solo*. That is, he is playing spontaneously rather than repeating the melody of "Softly, As in a Morning Sunrise." What Benson improvises, however, is not formless, because the other instruments continue to provide the form and harmony of the original song. When the song was first written, the composer created a sequence of chords to accompany the melody. Jazz musicians typically think of these chords as something that can be isolated from the melody of the song. Some of the players, then, provide a background texture by playing the song's chords, which frees another player, an *improviser* or *soloist*, to create a spontaneous melody that fits

> Much of what happens in jazz occurs in this format: a soloist improvises melodically to a harmonic and rhythmic background supplied by other players in the group.

these chords. Much of what happens in jazz occurs in this format: a soloist improvises melodically to a harmonic and rhythmic background supplied by other players in the group. We can hear now that Benson's "Softly, As in a Morning Sunrise" follows a 32-bar AABA form followed by an improvised solo.

Introduction	0:00–0:07	(4 bars)
A	0:08–0:22	first melody (8 bars)
A	0:22–0:36	melody repeats (8 bars)
B	0:37–0:51	new, second melody, different from A (8 bars)
A	0:52–1:06	first melody returns (8 bars)
Improvised Solo	1:07–	spontaneous creation of melody to fit song's chords

If we return to the recording on Track 10 of the ⊕ Audio Primer, we hear the pianist playing the chords to a notably important song, "I Got Rhythm," which was written by George and Ira Gershwin in 1930. Jazz musicians were so comfortable with the harmony of this song that they used it often as the basis of their improvisations. As such, the harmony, abstracted from the song, has itself a name: **rhythm changes**. This name derives from the "rhythm" of the song title "I Got Rhythm" and "changes" as a shortened form of "chord changes," a term used to designate the harmony of a song. Because the song first appeared in 1930, many composers have since written melodies on the harmonies of rhythm changes. One particularly well-known example is the theme song to *The Flintstones*. If you know this tune, you should try singing it to yourself and following the form. Again, as with the other elements that we've introduced here, a further

The Flintstones
"TV theme"

discussion of concepts relating to harmony follows later in this chapter.

The aab Blues Form

In addition to the 32-bar AABA form that is so common in jazz, there is another singularly important form that appears throughout the music's history, **blues form**. Blues is actually simpler than 32-bar AABA form because it has only one section, which appears in a 12-bar format. Listen to Track 7, which features the legendary blues singer Bessie Smith, accompanied by pianist James P. Johnson. After a 2-bar Introduction, you should be able to count twelve bars before the melody begins to repeat with a different lyric.

Although the blues is based on a single 12-bar form that typically repeats through a blues performance, that 12-bar form itself typically divides into three 4-bar units, or phrases. Listen to Smith sing the first line at 0:04: "When it rains five days, and the sky turns dark as night." Smith then repeats this lyric with a similar melody at 0:13. Finally, at 0:23, Smith sings a different lyric to conclude the presentation of the melody. (See the Listening Guide for this song in Chapter 1 when we return to its discussion on Track 7.)

In fact, this format is known as the **12-bar aab blues form**, in that the singer typically repeats the first line of the lyric. (We'll use lowercase a and b to distinguish these phrases from the capital letters that we use to denote sections.) The b line typically provides a line of lyric that answers or explains the a line, and often rhymes it. In many blues tunes, the melodies of the two a phrases and b phrases are virtually identical. If so, the phrases are distinguished by the lyrics and their placement in the form as either the first, second, or third phrase.

When a song is performed, we call a single presentation of it a **chorus**. Thus, when Smith starts to repeat the melody at 0:32, she is beginning to sing the second chorus of the song. If you listen to the entire track, you'll notice that her performance consists of seven blues choruses, each one of them twelve bars. In each of these choruses you should be able to hear the aab form of the lyric.

Rhythm changes is a term derived from the form and harmony (or chord changes) of the song "I Got Rhythm."

The **blues form** is a single, 12-bar section that repeats throughout the song and typically divides into three 4-bar phrases. The classic blues featured an aab lyric pattern that fit regular chord changes.

The **12-bar aab blues form** is one in which the singer typically repeats the first line (a) of the lyric in the second line (aa) and in the third line—the b line—supplies a lyric that answers or explains the a line and often rhymes it (aab).

A **chorus** is a single presentation of a song.

Strophic is a term used to describe a musical work that has repeated choruses.

Blues harmony features a standard set of chord changes.

Classic **ragtime form**, borrowed from the European march form, contains three or four sections, called strains, of 16 bars each.

To hear another example of a classic blues performance with repeated aab choruses, listen to Track 6, which features Robert Johnson singing and accompanying himself on guitar. After a brief Introduction (0:03–0:12), you

There are other forms too that appear in jazz but are somewhat less common than the blues form and the AABA form. Especially significant in ragtime and early jazz is what is called **ragtime form**. Based on a European form heard in the march and other musical genres, this form is particularly important to the music's early history and will be described in Chapter 1. Further, in addition to 32-bar AABA form there is another 32-bar form common in jazz, known as ABAC. It should be noted, however, that jazz composers do not always restrict themselves to these forms but create their own as part of the process of composition. Nonetheless, so much jazz depends on the 32-bar forms and the 12-bar blues that you should

> Jazz often features music in which choruses are repeated, either with improvisation or different lyrics.

should be able to follow Johnson's performance of four blues choruses.

As we have seen in the Smith and Johnson recordings, a blues performance often consists of repeated choruses in which the melody remains largely the same, but the lyrics change for each chorus. We also noticed that in the Benson song, the AABA structure was repeated, but during the first chorus Benson played the melody of the song, and in the second chorus improvised. Jazz often features music in which choruses are repeated, either with improvisation or with different lyrics. In general, music that features repeated choruses is called **strophic**. Much jazz, therefore, features strophic structures.

In addition to the 12-bar chorus and repeating chorus format that make up the Smith performance of "Back Water Blues," the song also features a standard **blues harmony**, that is, a set of chord changes that are important and reappear in numerous jazz performances. We will describe these chord changes in the more detailed section on the Blues later, but to hear them in a jazz piano trio, in which there is no melody present, listen to Track 11 of the 🅟 Audio Primer. There you will hear the pianist, accompanied by bass and drums, play the chord changes of two choruses of the blues emphasizing its harmony. As in the example of rhythm changes on Track 10, follow the form of Track 11 by counting ONE-two-THREE-four, TWO-two-THREE-four, and so on at each of the bass notes, the instrument marking the beat. Note, also, that because the pianist is playing the harmony of the blues, but no melody, the aab lyric structure that we heard with Bessie Smith and Robert Johnson is not present.

> So much jazz depends on the 32-bar forms and the 12-bar blues that you should practice counting the bars until you are comfortable following them.

practice counting the bars until you are comfortable following them.

Learning to follow the forms of the 32-bar AABA song and the 12-bar blues will help you hear jazz more deeply and understand what the musicians are working with: what skills they've had to master and the various freedoms and constraints that characterize the different jazz styles. Although this Introduction provides you with the basics of these forms, you should practice following the forms with the Listening Guides that appear throughout this text for each of the historical tracks. There is a popular misconception that what jazz musicians play is formless. This is surely not the case, as should be clear from the examples discussed so far.

Our Introduction to jazz has shown that it has three essential elements (which indeed underlie much Western music): rhythm, melody, and harmony. A fourth element—and our emphasis so far in this chapter—is form, which is related to rhythm because it is basically the temporal organization of the music. For the remainder of this chapter, we will describe these elements in greater detail and relate them to the musical keyboard and basic music notation. The Introduction continues with a

> Jazz, indeed most Western music, has four essential elements: rhythm, melody, harmony, and form.

description of the instruments most commonly heard in jazz performance groups, then concludes with a brief summary of significant jazz performance terms.

More on Rhythm

Earlier in this chapter, we described the idea of duple meter. Meter, which is common in virtually all jazz, is represented in musical notation by what we call the **time signature**. Music Example I-1 shows a *music staff* (the five horizontal lines) with a *treble clef* followed by a time signature, in this case 4/4, the most common of all time signatures, and an example of duple meter. The top 4 means that there are four beats in a *measure*, or *bar*, of the music; the bottom 4 means that a certain note, called a *quarter note* (♩) receives one beat. The bars are separated by vertical lines (called *barlines*) running continuously through the staff. The four quarter notes correspond to the four beats in the bar. In a bar of 4/4 time, we feel structural, or stronger, *accents* on the first and third beats, as shown by the accents above those notes in Music Example I-1. The music is generally organized in reference to those beats. The weaker beats (2 and 4) may receive dynamic, or secondary, *accents* because drummers, as well as people who clap their hands to the music, may emphasize them as well.

The second bar of Music Example I-1 shows two notes (♩) that are *half notes*, and each receives two beats. The third bar shows one *whole note* (𝅝), which fills the whole measure by receiving the full four beats. The fourth bar shows eight *eighth notes* (♪) that receive one-half beat each. The fifth bar shows sixteen *sixteenth notes* (♬), each of which receives one-quarter beat. These types of notes are the most common in jazz, although even smaller note values that further subdivide the beat are often heard at slow tempos (because there is more space for players to fill between the slowly occurring beats). Beats can also be divided into threes, but we won't discuss that topic here.

The disruption of regular meter, an important musical effect that is very common in jazz, is known as **syncopation**. Syncopation occurs when the weaker portions of a metrical grid unexpectedly receive stronger accents. Music that normally includes syncopation ends up sounding static or stiff without it. To hear the effect of removing syncopation from a familiar piece that features

it, listen to Track 4 of the 🅟 Audio Primer. Notice how flat and uninteresting the ragtime excerpt is when the syncopation is removed from the rhythm.

More on Melody

Melody may be the most familiar of all musical elements. We usually think of melody as consecutive single notes that are usually singable. Jazz musicians often refer to melodies as *tunes*, without implying that they are trite. What gives melody its identity are the distances between the successive notes. The distance between any two notes is called an **interval**. Of particular importance is a crucial interval called the **octave**, in which notes vibrate in a 2:1 ratio. When notes do this, they sound exactly the same but higher or lower from each other. We acknowledge this property by giving notes that are an octave apart the same name: do and do, re and re, and so on. You can hear the sound of an octave for yourself by singing the first few words of "Take Me Out to the Ball Game" or "Somewhere Over the Rainbow." The first two notes of each song are an octave apart.

The property of notes being higher or lower is referred to by the word **pitch**, as in "a low pitch" or "a high pitch." For example, women's voices typically have a higher pitch than men's. Musical notes are sometimes called pitches.

We name the notes of music by using the letters of the alphabet and arranging them into **scales** that are organized by the octave. *Scale* is from the Italian *scala*, or

---

The **time signature** is a symbol that appears on a music staff. It consists of two numbers, one on top of the other, that together indicate the music's meter.

Syncopation, very common in jazz, is the disruption of regular meter and occurs when the weaker notes of the designated meter receive unexpectedly stronger accents, as in the second and fourth beats in 4/4 meter receiving stronger accents.

An **interval** is the distance between any two notes.

An **octave** is an interval of eight notes, in which the notes sound exactly the same but are higher or lower than each other, as in the first two notes of "Take Me Out to the Ball Game."

Pitch refers to a note's sound relative to its place higher or lower on the music scale.

The **scale**, derived from the Italian word for ladder, arranges notes into a series of octaves, the individual notes of which are labeled A, B, C, D, E, F, G, and repeat in ascending or descending order.

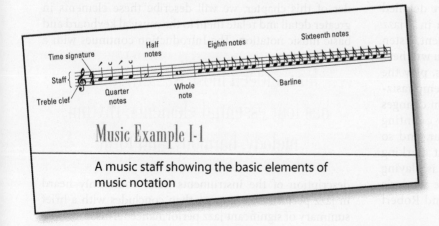

Music Example I-1

A music staff showing the basic elements of music notation

The **sharp** symbol ♯ raises the pitch of a given note by one half-step.

The **flat** symbol ♭ lowers the pitch of a given note by one-half step.

The **tonic** is the first note of a given scale and forms the "center of gravity" to which all the other notes in the scale relate.

"ladder," because the notes move up and down by step, as on a ladder. Notes that are immediately next to each other in a scale are thus said to be a "step" apart. In the music of Western culture, the note names are given the first seven letters of the alphabet: A, B, C, D, E, F, and G. The next note of this ascending scale would again be A, but this new A would be an octave higher than the original A. This second A is the eighth note above the initial A, which explains the origin of *octave* from the Latin *octo*, or "eight." To hear examples of scales, listen to Track 1 of the Audio Primer, in which different scales are played on the piano.

As the diagram in Music Example I-2 makes clear, the seven basic notes, A to G, correspond to the white keys of the piano keyboard. There are five additional notes that are variants of the seven basic white-key notes and are arranged as the black keys of the keyboard. These black keys are normally named relative to the white keys. For example, a black key just to the right of C is called C♯, or C sharp. The **sharp** symbol raises the pitch of C by one half-step. The same black key falls just to the left of D, so it has the additional name of D♭, or D flat. The **flat** symbol lowers the pitch of D by one-half step. It isn't necessary for us to get into the complex issues of why musical notes can have more than one name (the white keys can assume different names as well), but you should be aware that

the black keys are usually called sharps or flats depending on their relationship to adjacent white keys. Together, these twelve notes, repeating in lower and higher versions related by the octave, form the basis of Western music.

In Music Example I-2 we also see *music notation*, a system that represents the notes of Western music on a *music staff*. Each line and space on the staff corresponds to a white key on the keyboard. Flats and sharps on the same lines and spaces refer to the black keys. The *treble clef* and *bass clef* (also called the G and F clefs) indicate which notes correspond to higher or lower positions on the staff. In piano and keyboard writing, the staff with the F (bass) clef usually corresponds to music played by the left hand and is lower in pitch, whereas the G (treble) clef usually corresponds to the higher music played by the right hand.

Scales in Western music are combinations of white and black keys, ascending and descending. The simplest scale—one that is often taught first—is the C major scale, which consists of the white keys only and is named after the note C, which is the *tonic* of the scale. The **tonic** is of primary importance to the scale, forming a "center of gravity" to which all the other notes in the scale relate. (The use of tonics gives rise to the sense of *key*, or *tonality*, which we discuss in the following section on harmony.)

The notes of the scale merely ascend and descend. But to create melodies, which are much more interesting, we arrange the notes of the scale into coherent patterns. Melodies are made coherent by the use of patterns that combine predictability on the one hand and surprise on the other. Too much predictability is boring, whereas too much surprise can be incoherent. Jazz musicians often base their playing on *songs*, which generally consist of notes coherently arranged in a melody. We saw earlier in this chapter that jazz musicians also create spontaneous melodies, a process called *improvisation*, which is part of the essence of jazz. The education of any jazz musician includes learning to create improvised melodies that are coherent and emotionally engaging.

As we saw earlier, melodies are usually divided into *phrases*: self-contained subgroups that are often four bars long and sung in one breath. Think of "The Star-Spangled Banner." Its first phrase would be "Oh, say, can you see by the dawn's early light." At that point in singing it, you would probably want to take a breath. Similarly, "Take Me Out to the Ball Game" would probably have an opening phrase of "Take me out to the ballgame, take me out with the crowd."

The building blocks of the phrases that constitute melodies are scales in which successive notes are often a single step, or note, apart. You can hear such steps in the familiar Irving Berlin songs "White Christmas" and "God Bless America." The first phrase in each song is built on *stepwise notes*, notes moving in the small increments known as *steps*. Interestingly, the first phrase of "The Star-Spangled Banner" is

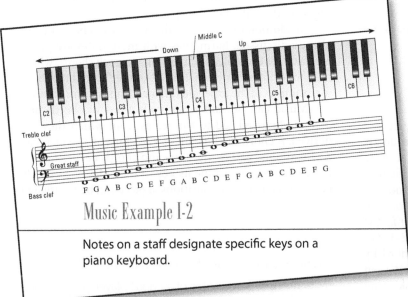

Music Example I-2

Notes on a staff designate specific keys on a piano keyboard.

In the same way that the sun acts as the center of gravity for our solar system, the tonic forms the center of gravity for all the notes in a given scale.

built, not on stepwise notes, but on *leaps* or *skips*, intervals between notes that are larger than steps. Leaps give rise to harmony, the third fundamental of music.

Different cultures have different notes and scales. Because jazz is a Western music (although a significant part of its history is non-Western), most of its notes, scales, phrases, and other musical building blocks are Western in origin.

More on Harmony

We saw earlier that harmony, another important feature of Western music, underlies much jazz. Melodies frequently use stepwise notes, whereas harmony is based on notes that are a leap or skip apart. We can create a simple harmony by taking a scale and playing every other note in groups of three or four notes. If we play these blocks of three or more notes simultaneously, we have *chords*, the basic units of harmony. In a C major scale (C–D–E–F–G–A–B–C), we create a C major **triad**, a three-note chord, by playing C–E–G, that is, by skipping over D and F. We can also create a D minor triad by playing D–F–A, or skipping over E and G. In similar fashion, we can build numerous

triads by including the black keys and beginning on various keys, both white and black.

When we move through the notes of a chord one note at a time, up or down, the result is an **arpeggio**, the individual notes of a chord played in sequence, a word deriving from the Italian for "harp."

In addition to the triads (the most basic chords) we've already discussed, harmonies with more notes are possible. Jazz, for example, often exploits *seventh chords*, which have four notes. Listen to Track 2 of the Audio Primer for examples of the arpeggios created from seventh chords.

Music can be said to be collections of chords and melodic lines related to the scales from which they are derived. A chord can be built on each note of a given scale. As mentioned earlier, the scale and chords occurring in a piece of music determine its **key**. If the notes of a melody keep the same relative positions, a piece can be *transposed*

A **triad** is a three-note chord, the most basic chord.

An **arpeggio** is the notes of a chord played in sequence rather than simultaneously.

The **key** refers to the **tonality** of a piece of music as determined by the scales and chords that the piece uses. If, for example, a work uses the C scale (a scale that starts on the note C), the work is said to be in the key of C. A key may take a major or minor form, as indicated by its scale.

Tonality is a Western musical system in which pieces are organized according to harmony within some key or with respect to some central pitch. Western tonality rests on a system of twenty-four major and minor keys.

Slash notation is a method of showing the harmonies (or "chord changes") in jazz and popular music. Each slash in a measure denotes a beat. The arranger places chords over the slashes to show the beats on which the harmonies change. (See Music Examples I-4 and I-5 for examples.)

A **chord progression** describes the sequence of chords, usually within a composition.

Harmonic substitution allows the alteration of the original chord progression by the use of new chords that function similarly to the original chords.

---

from one key to another without changing the nature of the musical piece. This is often done for a vocalist whose best singing range is higher or lower than that of the published sheet music. For example, "The Star-Spangled Banner" begins with the notes G–E–C–E–G–C in the key of C. The same song can be transposed to occur in twelve different keys, each corresponding to a different note on the keyboard.

The musical keys that are derived from the notes of the keyboard have two common forms: *major* and *minor*. There is the key of C major, the key of C minor, the key of B♭ major, the key of B♭ minor, and so on. Melodies in a major key are traditionally considered "happier" or more

upbeat. Those in a minor key tend to have a "sadder," more somber mood. When composers write songs or when jazz improvisers create melodies spontaneously, they work within the key system of twenty-four major and minor

> The three most important harmonic functions are "tonic," "dominant," and "subdominant," which correspond to the I, V, and IV chords.

keys, the basis of Western **tonality**. In later jazz (from the 1950s on), a system called *modality* both extends and partially supplants the major-minor system.

As shown in Music Example I.3, Roman numerals are often used to designate a chord's place in the key that contains it. In general, each of the seven notes of the scale can take a Roman numeral that helps specify what that chord does in the context of the scale's key. The set of chordal usages for a given chord in a key is referred to as its *function*. The three most important harmonic functions are "tonic," "dominant," and "subdominant," which correspond to the I, V, and IV chords. We will refer to these chords and functions throughout the book.

The chordal element of jazz is so pervasive that a system of **slash notation** describing chords has become standard in most jazz styles, as shown in Music Example I.4. The slashes stand for beats, so that in a 4/4 bar we see four slashes, one for each beat of the bar. Above the staff and over the slashes are symbols that specify the chords. A jazz musician, reading the line, would understand that a chord is activated on a particular beat whenever a new chord appears over a slash. Further, if a chord does not appear over a slash, then the previous chord is understood to remain in effect. Thus for the first two beats (slashes) of the example, the chord is Cmaj7 (called "C major-seventh"). The next two beats (that is, beats 3 and 4 of the first bar) are harmonized by an Am7 chord (called "A minor-seventh").

Sequences of chords used in music are typically not random, but based on standard conventions. Such chordal sequences are called **chord progressions** or simply **progressions**. The word *progression* implies that the chords have direction and are not random.

Another feature of jazz harmony is called **harmonic substitution**. The original chord

> When improvisers adapt their melodic improvisations to the underlying chords, they are said to be playing inside. When the melody and harmony don't quite match, the improviser is playing outside.

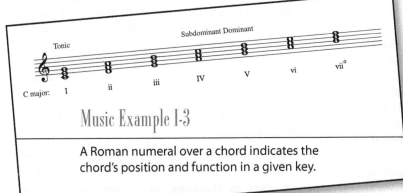

Music Example I-3

A Roman numeral over a chord indicates the chord's position and function in a given key.

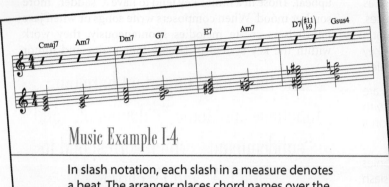

Music Example I-4

In slash notation, each slash in a measure denotes a beat. The arranger places chord names over the slashes to show the beats on which the harmonies change.

in which they are being played. Textures can be described as thick or thin, high or low, fast or slow. A thin texture, for example, has few notes and/or instruments, such as a human voice singing without accompaniment. A thick texture may have many notes and/or instruments, such as a large symphony orchestra with all members playing. Some very flexible instruments, such as a piano, can by themselves project many different textures.

To focus on the texture when you listen to music, ask yourself:

▶ What instruments am I hearing? Can I distinguish them?

▶ How are they being played? (Lots of notes, few notes, fast, slow, soft, loud, high, low, and so on.)

progression is altered by using new chords that function similarly to the original chords. On Track 6 of the Audio Primer you can hear a standard jazz chord progression (ii7-V7-I, using the Roman numeral designation) modified by the use of *extensions* (extra notes added to the chord) and *substitution*. (The chord substitution used here is the *tritone substitution*, which was popularized during the bebop era, beginning in the 1940s.)

When improvisers choose to adapt their melodic improvisations to the underlying chords, they are said to be playing *inside*. When the melody and harmony don't quite match, the improviser is playing *outside*. Listen to Track 8 of the Audio Primer to hear the difference between inside and outside playing.

Although there's much more that could be said about rhythm, melody, and harmony, the material here should help you understand most of the references in the text. There are other elements of music beyond these basics, however. We explore them next.

Timbre and Texture

Although rhythm, melody, and harmony are the fundamental aspects of Western music, there are important secondary qualities too, which are important to music's total effect. Among these we note that the specific quality of the sound of a given instrument is its **timbre** (TAM-ber), or tone color. For example, the timbre of a violin is quite different from the timbre of a trumpet or the timbre of a friend's voice.

The *texture* of music, as described at the beginning of this chapter, is what you hear at any given moment: the combination of instruments playing and the manner

Dynamics and Articulation

Music ranges from very soft to very loud. This is most obvious when you listen to recorded music: you can make the playback louder or softer just by turning the volume control up or down.

However, musical sounds themselves have subtly varying degrees of softness and loudness within the same performance. The notes of a melody would sound very mechanical if all were played at the same volume. The way performers vary the softness and loudness of the notes they play greatly affects their performances and their emotional impact on listeners. The softness and loudness of musical sounds are referred to as **dynamics**.

Notes can be *attacked*, or played, in numerous ways. We refer to the ways that notes are played as **articulation**. For example, the articulation of notes proceeding smoothly from one to another is **legato**. Short, detached notes are **staccato**.

Dynamics and articulation are often included in the overall category of *expression*, because the way a performer varies the dynamics and the articulation of notes greatly affects the overall expressiveness of that performance.

Jazz styles can be identified, at least in part, by their textures, so learning to recognize the sounds of the instruments producing the texture narrows the field.

Timbre is the specific quality of sound in a given instrument or voice.

Dynamics in music address the volume of sound, from very soft to very loud.

Articulation refers to the manner in which notes are played, as in **legato**, a smooth movement through a series of notes, or **staccato**, short detached strikes on notes in a series.

Wind instruments produce sound from players' breaths and divide into two families: **brasses** and **reeds**. For brass instruments, a player buzzes the lips into a cup-shaped mouthpiece to create sound; for reed instruments, the player blows through or across a reed that is attached to the mouthpiece to create the sound.

Small Tom / Fotolia

Paylessima / Dreamstime.com

Jazz Instruments

Just like those in a modern symphony orchestra, the musical instruments used in jazz are grouped into families based on their construction and function. Their characteristic sounds and playing techniques are all demonstrated in the ⓟ Audio Primer.

Wind Instruments

Wind instruments, whose sounds are created by players' breaths, are normally divided into two families: **brasses** and **reeds**. In brass instruments, the sound is created by players buzzing their lips into a cup-shaped mouthpiece. In reed instruments, the players blow through or across a reed, which is attached to the mouthpiece, to create the sound.

Among the brasses, the most important jazz instrument is the *trumpet*. Its close cousin, the *cornet*, is common in early jazz and sounds like a trumpet but is mellower and more restrained. Another trumpet-like instrument is the *flugelhorn*, which sounds even mellower than the cornet.

The trumpet can be played open—that is, without mutes—or with various types of mutes. The characteristic sound of the open trumpet is heard on Track 12 of the

ⓟ Audio Primer. Mutes are placed into the trumpet bell (the flared end of the horn) to change its timbre. Cup and harmon mutes are demonstrated on Tracks 13–15 of the ⓟ Audio Primer.

After the trumpet, the *trombone* is the most important jazz brass instrument. Like the trumpet, it can be played open or with mutes, as heard on the ⓟ Audio Primer. Track 22 demonstrates a trombone with an open sound and Track 23, with a cup mute. The growl sound on Track 24 is a common brass technique that can also be performed on the trumpet. The tailgate effect of Track 25

Three different mutes used to change the sound made by the trumpet: the Harmon mute, cup mute, and straight mute

Lightpro / Dreamstime.com

Billyfoto / Dreamstime.com

Lebedinski / Dreamstime.com

Pferd / Dreamstime.com

is sometimes heard in Dixieland jazz; it is created by moving the slide while holding a note, a feature technically called a **glissando**.

The *saxophone* is the most important reed instrument in jazz. There is a whole family of saxophones in various sizes. The most common saxophones are heard on Tracks 16–19 of the Audio Primer, ranging from high (soprano sax) to low (baritone sax).

The *clarinet* is a reed instrument that was more common than the saxophone in early jazz. The clarinet has receded in popularity since its heyday in the 1930s but has recently made a comeback. Tracks 20 and 21 of the Audio Primer display two common clarinet stylizations: the swing-style music of the 1930s and the kinds of lines heard in the Dixieland jazz of the 1920s.

© iStockphoto.com/Mac Miller

Clarinet

String Instruments

The most commonly used **string instruments** in jazz are the guitar, electric and acoustic, and the acoustic bass. The *acoustic bass* should be distinguished from its cousin, the horizontal electric bass guitar, which is more common in rock and jazz-rock. The acoustic bass was originally played without amplification but now is usually amplified. The acoustic bass is commonly heard in the jazz ensemble but can be heard alone on Track 43 of the Audio Primer. There, it *walks*—that is, the player provides a note for each beat in mostly stepwise fashion. You also heard a walking bass in Tracks 10 and 11 of the Audio Primer, where we suggested you count the form by noting that the beats coincide with the bass notes.

Acoustic bass

The *guitar* comes in both electric and acoustic versions, demonstrated on Tracks 36–42 of the Audio Primer. The older acoustic guitar was very much a rhythm instrument in classic jazz because it played chords on each beat, an

effect heard on Track 36 of the Audio Primer. The acoustic guitar was not very loud, but in a small-group setting it could play occasional melodies, as heard on Track 37. Track 38 features bossa nova–style acoustic guitar, a sound that became popular in the 1960s.

The electric guitar was developed during the 1930s. The use of the amplifier enabled it to be heard in any setting. The early sound of the electric guitar is featured on Track 39 of the Audio Primer; this is the basic sound associated with the jazz electric guitar in non-rock settings. After rock and roll became popular in the 1950s and 1960s, the electric guitar underwent a sonic revolution. Electronic effects were introduced that radically augmented the sounds the instrument could produce. Some of these sounds, typical of jazz-rock and jazz-funk fusion, can be heard on Tracks 40–42.

Percussion Instruments

Drums are examples of **percussion instruments**—instruments that are generally struck with either the hand or a stick or mallet. The *drum set* is like a piano in that the drummer can play a number of instrumental parts simultaneously. Unlike a piano, however, drums cannot play specific pitches to create chords.

Let's summarize the percussion instruments most commonly found in the drum set, demonstrated on solo Tracks 26–35 of the Audio Primer. (To describe playing the various instruments of the drum set, we assume a right-handed, right-footed drummer; this arrangement is sometimes reversed for drummers who favor their left side.)

Track 26 showcases the *snare drum*, usually played with the left hand (if the right hand is otherwise keeping the beat). Tracks 27 and 28 feature high and low tom-toms, which can be played with either hand. The *bass drum* (Track 29) is sometimes articulated on each beat of the bar, especially in older jazz. It is played by the right foot, using a pedal. The *ride cymbal* (Track 30) is usually played with the right hand. The track features what is called a swing beat. The *hi-hat* (Track 31) consists of a pair of cymbals, top and bottom. It is usually played by the left foot pedal, which closes and opens the cymbal pair, thus producing a "chick" sound. The top cymbal of the hi-hat can also be played by hand, usually the right, with a stick. Track 32 shows the simultaneous foot pedal

Guitar

© iStockphoto.com/Jake Holme

MM/Fotolia

A **glissando** is the sound created by moving the slide of the trombone while holding a note, in jazz known as the tailgate effect. The notes are slurred directly from one to another, producing a continuous rise or fall in pitch.

String instruments produce sound from a player plucking, strumming, or striking strings drawn over a voice box.

Percussion instruments are those struck with either the hand or a stick or mallet.

The **rhythm section** is a part of a jazz band that provides the rhythmic pulse, harmonies, and bass line. It may include any of the following: piano, guitar, bass, or drums. Early jazz bands sometimes included banjo and tuba in place of the guitar and bass.

The **lead** or **front-line instruments** in a jazz ensemble are usually melodic (playing one note at a time) and are often featured at the front of the stage.

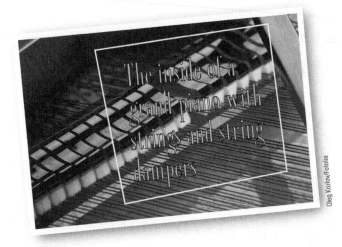

The inside of a grand piano with strings and string dampers

Oleg Kozlov/Fotolia

Drum set

© iStockphoto.com/istockphoto

instrument because hammers with felt tips strike tautly stretched strings to produce the instrument's sounds. The keys of the piano keyboard, when depressed, activate the hammers to strike the strings. Because the keys can be operated independently by the pianist's ten fingers to produce simultaneous sounds, the piano can play both melody and harmony. In fact, solo piano can mimic a larger ensemble because of the piano's ability to fill the functions of numerous instruments. Larger pianos, called *grand pianos*, have longer strings, resulting in a richer, more powerful sound than upright pianos.

In the jazz ensemble, the piano is often grouped with other instruments (banjo or guitar, bass, and drums) to provide a backup accompaniment to the primary instruments playing the melody (cornet or trumpet, trombone, clarinet, or saxophone). This backup subgroup of the ensemble is called the **rhythm section**.

As we saw in the first part of this chapter, Tracks 10 and 11 of the 🅐 Audio Primer feature a common jazz ensemble called a *piano trio*, which usually consists of piano, acoustic bass, and drum set. (A somewhat less common piano trio consists of piano, bass, and guitar.)

and hand playing of the hi-hat, which produces a familiar swing rhythm sound. Crash cymbals (Track 33) add color and accents to the drum texture; they are most commonly played by the right hand. On Track 34 all the drum set parts are combined into a swing beat; try to distinguish the different sounds made by each instrument in the set.

The piano has long been the basic instrument of Western music because the pianist can provide melody and harmony simultaneously, the right hand playing the melody while the left hand plays chords that provide harmony.

Finally, Track 35 shows how the drum set can be played with wire brushes instead of sticks. This creates a lighter, softer sound but one that can still generate considerable rhythmic drive.

The Piano

The *piano*, developed in the early 1700s, soon became the most common of all Western instruments. (Electronic keyboards and guitars may be overtaking the piano more recently.) It is a combination string-percussion

A piano trio is essentially a rhythm section without **lead** instruments.

More on the Blues

As we saw earlier in this Introduction, blues form (the kind most commonly used by jazz musicians) consists normally of twelve bars comprising three

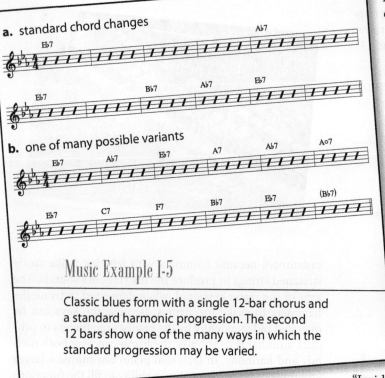

Music Example I-5

Classic blues form with a single 12-bar chorus and a standard harmonic progression. The second 12 bars show one of the many ways in which the standard progression may be varied.

4-bar phrases. Music Example I.5a shows a classic form with a single 12-bar chorus and a typical harmonic progression. The harmonic progression of the blues is quite regular, but there are many possible variants, one of which is shown in Example I.5b. One of the most significant harmonic moves of the blues is to the IV chord of the key at m. 5.

As we saw earlier in this chapter, the melody and lyric corresponding to the 12-bar chorus of the classic blues is aab, with the ends of the a and b phrases often rhyming. This form is ideal for improvisation because the singer can think ahead for an answering third phrase during the repetition of the first. Adding to the ease of improvisation, each a and b phrase usually falls within the first two or three bars of each four-bar phrase. The concluding part of each phrase can be filled with a response from the instrumental accompaniment while the singer ponders the next phrase.

Early blues was less regular than the 12-bar format. Because folk musicians 0ften perform very informally, simplifying the harmony, embellishing the melody, and freely interpolating extra bars, country blues exhibited great flexibility of form. Once we reach the classic blues of the 1920s, however, we can represent the blues form as a single 12-bar chorus with a strict basic harmonic progression. Within the framework of standard chord changes, we can construct variants. As pointed out earlier, Track 11 of the 🅟 Audio Primer demonstrates two choruses of blues changes in a piano trio format.

The Blues Scale

Earlier we discussed the major scale but referred to the use of other scales in jazz. One particular form often heard in jazz is the **blues scale**, which incorporates notes commonly heard in blues melodies. Some of these notes, not part of the major scale, are called *blue notes*. (See box "Insider's Guide to the Blues Scale.") In many instances, these blue notes suggest pitch inflections or slurred pitches rather than discrete pitches. If, however, we consider blue notes as discrete pitches, we can construct a blues scale, as shown in Music Example I.6.

Sometimes the traditional blues scale has incorporated other pitches. For example, the jazz style known as bebop featured a flatted fifth (conventionally spelled as F♯, as in Music Example I.6, rather than G♭), a note that can take on the quality of a blue note. More generally, it is possible to inflect any note of the scale in such a way that it becomes a blue note, but the blue third and seventh are by far the most pervasive.

Jazz Performance Terms

Tracks 44–49 of the 🅟 Audio Primer summarize the material we have discussed so far in this Introduction. They feature a jazz quintet performing the basic blues form. As we describe these tracks, let's define a few other important jazz terms.

On Track 44 we hear the first blues chorus. As pointed out earlier, each time a band or soloist plays through the complete changes of a song or of a given chord progression, it is called a chorus. For this first chorus, all we hear is the bass player walking and accompanied by the drums. Count the bars of the chorus to follow the 12-bar blues structure.

Continuing to Track 45, the band adds the pianist comping chords for the group's second chorus.

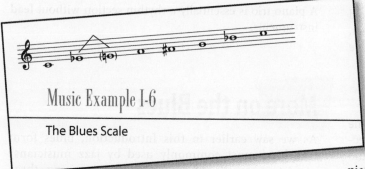

Music Example I-6

The Blues Scale

A **blues scale** is a form of scale that incorporates the principal notes used in the blues. Most often, 1–♭3 – 4– ♯4 – 5–♭7. Listen to the second scale played on Track 1 of the Audio Primer.

Comping refers to a technique in which a pianist or guitarist plays a chord progression in a rhythmically irregular fashion.

Solo breaks or **breaks** are moments during a jazz performance in which the rhythm instruments stop playing while the soloist continues.

Common since the swing era, **trading solos**—specifically called trading twos, trading fours, and trading eights—are improvisational jazz formats that create climactic moments in performances. In trading twos, for example, each soloist improvises for two bars before the next soloist takes over for two bars.

In classic **call-and-response**, a single voice or instrument states a melodic phrase—the call—while a group of voices or instruments follows with a responding or completing phrase—the response.

Stop time describes a performance technique in which the rhythm section punctuates distinct beats, often to accommodate a soloist's improvisation between the band's chords.

A **riff** is a short melodic idea, usually one to two bars long, that repeats as the core idea of a musical passage.

Comping, probably derived from *accompany* or *complement*, is a technique of playing in which a pianist or guitarist provides chords that follow the chord progression, but in a rhythmically irregular fashion.

For the third chorus (Track 46), the trumpet player takes solo breaks on bars 1–2, 5–6, and 9–10. **Solo breaks** are moments in which the rhythm stops while the soloist remains featured.

On the fourth chorus (Track 47), the trumpet player and the saxophonist trade twos. *Trading twos, trading fours,* and *trading eights* are improvisational formats in jazz, common since the swing era. In trading twos, for example, each soloist improvises for two bars before the next soloist takes over for two bars. Any number of soloists may participate, but two to four are most typical. **Trading solos** are often used to create climactic moments in performances. It is also an example of **call-and-response**, a common technique in which players take turns answering one another. In classic call-and-response, a single voice or instrument states a melodic phrase—the *call*—while a group of voices or instruments follows with a responding or completing phrase—the *response*.

Stop time is featured on the fifth chorus (Track 48). In **stop time**, the rhythm section or band punctuates distinct beats, often to accommodate a soloist's improvisation between the band's chords. Here stop time provides a background texture to the saxophone solo.

For the sixth and final chorus (Track 49), the trumpet player provides a background riff while the saxophonist continues to solo. A **riff** is a short melodic idea, usually one to two bars long, which is repeated as the core idea of a musical passage.

Ways of Listening to Jazz

In this Introduction, we have focused on some of the basics necessary for listening to music analytically. Analytical listening is an important skill that can broaden your understanding of how jazz works. We don't always listen analytically, though—nor should we. Sometimes we can simply move to the groove or close our eyes and let the sounds wash over us. The enjoyment of music need

Insider's Guide to...

The Blues Scale

The use of blue notes in African American music is complex.* Some scholars have suggested that blue notes refer to pitch inflections or slurred pitches rather than discrete pitches. For example, Gilbert Chase writes that "it is not the flatted third [or any other lowered interval of the scale] as such, but rather this ambivalent, this *worried* or slurred tone that constitutes the true 'blue note.'"† Others suggest the presence of a **blues scale** that incorporates natural as well as "neutral" thirds and sevenths.

Sometimes the blues scale has incorporated other pitches. For example, the jazz style that evolved in the 1940s, *bebop*, features extensive use of a flatted fifth, which can take on the quality of a blue note. More generally, it is possible to inflect any note of the scale in such a way that it becomes a blue note, but the blue third and seventh are by far the most pervasive.

---

* For this and the following points, we are particularly indebted to William Tallmadge's article "Blue Notes and Blue Tonality," *The Black Perspective in Music*, 12, no. 2 (1984): 155–164.

† Gilbert Chase, *America's Music: From the Pilgrims to the Present*, 2d ed. rev. (New York: McGraw-Hill, 1966), 453.

not always be an intellectual activity, but even when it is appreciated purely emotionally, understanding its technical bases can heighten the experience. We cannot emphasize this point too strongly: analytical listening strengthens music's emotional impact by letting you get more inside

> ## Analytical listening strengthens music's emotional impact by letting you get more inside the notes.

the notes. After studying the historical examples presented in this book, you should step back and listen again just for pure enjoyment. Your increased expertise will make the experience more fulfilling.

Although much of the focus on listening in this book is through analysis and commentary, jazz (in fact, all music) can be appreciated even more through an understanding of its relationship to culture, not just through analysis of its technical bases. This more sociological approach to understanding is emphasized by **ethnomusicology**, the study of music in a cultural context. In many cultures, for example, music is used to accompany religious ceremonies or social rituals that mark such significant milestones as births, weddings, and deaths. There are

times when we wish to approach music from a technical perspective; analytical listening can help us best in these "internal" considerations of the music. At other times, when we wish to focus on its larger-scale import—that is, its reception, function, and value to a society—both the historical and the ethnomusicological approaches are more appropriate. Although historical events may influence musical creation directly, more often history provides a general context, what has been called a *zeitgeist*, a spirit of the times. By recalling important events and moods in history, we can better appreciate how the jazz produced at that time came about. The social commentary that extends through this book should help you understand how the historical context set the stage for the musical creation.

What's remarkable about music is that its richness encompasses all these multiple perspectives, ranging from the analytical, to the music-historical, to the ethnomusicological. The best jazz, like the best music, binds society together, unites us as a people, and furnishes us with a powerful means of artistic communication and cultural understanding.

Ethnomusicology is the study of music in a cultural context.

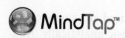 MindTap™

Test Yourself on Key Concepts with an additional Chapter Quiz on the text website.

Key Terms

Test your knowledge of the Introduction's key terms by defining the following. If you can't remember the meaning of a term, refresh your memory by looking up the boldfaced term in the chapter, turning to the Glossary at the back of the book, or working with the flashcards at the text website.

12-bar aab blues form 8

32-bar AABA song form 6

arpeggio 12

articulation 14

bar 5

beat 4

blues form (as aab phrases) 8

blues harmony 9

blues scale 19

brasses 15

bridge 6

cadence 6

call-and-response 19

chord 4

chord progression 13

chorus 8

comping 19

duple meter 5

dynamics 14

ethnomusicology 20

flat (♭) 11

form 5

front-line instruments 17

glissando 15

harmonic substitution 13

harmony 7

head 6

improvisation 7

instrumental music 4

interval 10

introduction 6

key 12

lead instruments 17

legato 14

measure 5

melody 4

meter 5

octave 10

percussion instruments 16

phrase 5

piano trio 7

pitch 10

prime 6

ragtime form 9

reeds 15

rhythm 4

rhythm changes 8

rhythm section 17

riff 19

scale 10

section 5

sharp (♯) 11

slash notation 13

solo break 19

staccato 14

stop time 19

string instruments 16

strophic 9

syncopation 10

tempo 5

texture 4

timbre 14

time signature 10

tonality 13

tonic 11

trading solos 19

triad 12

triple meter 5

wind instruments 15

Published in 1900, this sheet-music cover celebrates the birth of the twentieth century with the latest inventions, many of them American. The artist implies that Americans will continue to invent, and the evolution of jazz proved him correct.

Roots

1

Start with a quick warm-up activity.

THE ROOTS OF JAZZ LIE IN ITS AFRICAN, EUROPEAN, AND even Caribbean musical traditions. Although the precise contributions of various cultures and subcultures remain controversial, jazz would not have come into being without their blending. This much is clear: jazz arose not in Africa, not in Europe, and not in the Caribbean, but in the United States, thanks to the importation of nonnative musical elements into the dominant European culture of U.S. society. Because African and European cultures have contributed the most to jazz, we begin with a brief examination of these cultures and the elements that they contributed.

African American Music in the Nineteenth Century

The story of African American music in the nineteenth century can be told only partially. It is the story of the stevedores on the wharves of Savannah, the tobacco pickers in the Piedmont of North Carolina, the cotton pickers on the plantations of rural Alabama, the worshipers at the camp meetings in Kentucky, the Methodist ministers of Philadelphia, the oarsmen of the Sea Islands in South Carolina, the dance hall performers of New York, the riverboat minstrels on the Mississippi, and the conservatory-trained musicians of Boston. Most of their music was not written down but transmitted orally from musician to musician. Except for a few collections of **transcriptions**, the only tangible sources of information are diaries, letters, newspapers, and novels, as well as paintings and pictures—but these do not always depict African American music clearly or reliably.

African American Ring Shouts (Track 2)
    1868 – Scott Joplin, Kid Ory, and Buddy Bolden born
      African American Spirituals (Track 3)
      African American Field Hollers
        1885 King Oliver born
          —New York City's Tin Pan Alley, the heart of the U.S. song-publishing and
            sheet music business, begins to flourish
          —Ragtime developing
        1890 Jelly Roll Morton born
        1897 Sidney Bechet born
        1899 Scott Joplin publishes "Maple Leaf Rag" (Track 4)
          —Duke Ellington born
        1900–1917 Ragtime flourishing
          —Jazz developing
         1901 Louis Armstrong born
         1903 Bix Beiderbecke born
         1904 Count Basie born
         1905 Earl Hines born
         1909 Benny Goodman born
          —Lester Young born
          1917–1930 Ragtime declining
          —Jazz flourishing

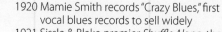

            1920 Mamie Smith records "Crazy Blues," first
              vocal blues records to sell widely
            1921 Sissle & Blake premier *Shuffle Along*, the
              first black Broadway musical
            1927 Bessie Smith records "Backwater Blues"
              (Track 7)

                    1937 Robert
                        Johnson
                        records "Love
                        in Vain" (Track 6)

Jazz

| 1860 | 1900 | 1910 | 1920 | 1930 |

1863 President Abraham Lincoln issues Emancipation Proclamation freeing the slaves
1865 American Civil War ends
1869 First Transcontinental Railroad built in United States
    —U.S. President Andrew Johnson impeached by the House, cleared by the Senate
  1876 Founding of baseball's National League
    1882 Electricity powers homes, cities, streetcars, and subways
      1898 Spanish-American War
        1900 Boxer Rebellion in China
          1903 Wright brothers complete first plane flight
          1905 First Russian revolution
           —Eugene Debs founds the Industrial Workers of the World (IWW)
          1909 Heredity found to be linked to chromosomes

Historical Events

Sources of Musical Diversity

Countless, mostly nameless, individuals contributed to a rich African American musical heritage before, during, and after the Civil War. This diverse musical culture varied over time and from region to region. There were clear musical differences between the North and the South; among the East, Midwest, and West; between urban and rural areas; and before and after the Civil War. Despite these distinctions, the African American heritage provided a foundation for jazz when it began to develop around the end of the nineteenth and the beginning of the twentieth centuries.

To **transcribe** a piece of music is to write in standard European musical notation what the listener, or transcriber, hears. The transcriber's notated version is called the **transcription**. Transcriptions of the same piece of music can vary widely, depending on the quality of the original sound source, the skill of the transcriber, and what the transcriber chooses to include in the notation.

Christianity and gained literacy and early emancipation, they were less likely to preserve their African traditions. In contrast, larger plantations in the Southeast, dependent as they were on large numbers of slaves who lived together in separate quarters, made it possible for some African traditions to survive more intact. Furthermore, many owners encouraged slaves to perform their music as well as to learn European musical styles.

The Preservation of African Traditions

When we look at the preservation of African musical traits in the New World, several questions arise: What characteristics of African music took root on American soil? How were they preserved, and how were they adapted? More specifically, which of these elements influenced jazz?

Most slaves came to the New World from the tribes of western, sub-Saharan Africa. These tribes exhibited numerous and varying musical cultures in the eighteenth and nineteenth centuries. Although these cultures were not studied much at the time, we can assume that the same musically significant traits that exist today in these regions also characterized African music in the eighteenth and nineteenth centuries and therefore must have been part of the musical culture of U.S. slaves. As

A transcription—the written (or notated) version of the musical sounds (or notes) the listener hears.

Pedro Antonio Salaverría Calahorra/Dreamstime.com

Much of this musical heritage emerged from African music and culture. The earliest slaves came to the New World in the beginning of the seventeenth century, and the tyranny of slavery continued for more than two hundred

Although "slave music is . . . rapidly passing away, it may be that this people who have developed such a wonderful musical sense . . . will produce a composer who could bring a music of the future out of this music of the past."

~Thomas P. Fenner, 1875

years. Uprooted from their homelands, especially from the rain forests of the west coast of Africa—including Senegal, the Guinea coast, and the Niger Delta—the slaves witnessed the destruction of their families and the elimination of their well-defined social structures. Nonetheless, many West African musical traditions persevered and ultimately blended with American and western European traditions.

Geography strongly influenced the degree to which African slaves preserved their musical traditions. In regions where whites lived separately from African Americans, slaves tended to retain their African traditions. For example, the relative inaccessibility of the coastal Sea Islands of Georgia and South Carolina allowed the resident Gullah blacks to preserve several musical as well as linguistic elements from African culture, some of which survive to this day (see later in this chapter the shout "Daniel," Track 2). But in the northeastern United States, where farms were relatively small and the number of slaves fewer, blacks and whites interacted more often. As blacks in the North converted to

such, we need to examine twentieth-century African musical cultures to see which musical features likely contributed to jazz.

Above all, traditional African music plays an important social function: it accompanies work, forms an essential part of religious and social events, and is often accompanied by dance. Thus African music is highly functional. Writing in 1952, Richard Waterman identified five characteristics shared by the various tribes that distinguish their functional music cultures from the European tradition:[1]

▶ **Metronomic sense**. African musicians tend to maintain a steady, underlying pulse throughout a performance. The regularity of the beat can be compared to a *metronome*, a mechanical device that enables

---

Metronomic sense is a steady rhythmic pulse, often associated with drums and with music from Africa.

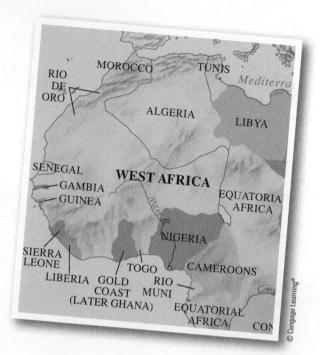

CABIN AND PLANTATION SONGS. 235

In dat great gittin=up Mornin'.

This song is a remarkable paraphrase of a portion of the Book of Revelations, and one of the finest specimens of negro "Spirituals." The student who brought it to us, and who sings the Solos, has furnished all that he can remember of the almost interminable succession of verses, which he has heard sung for half an hour at a time, by the slaves in their midnight meetings in the woods. He gives the following interesting account of its origin :

"I have heard my uncle sing this hymn, and he told me how it was made. It was made by an old slave who knew nothing about letters or figures. He could not count the number of rails that he would split when he was tasked by his master to split 150 a day. But he tried to lead a Christian life, and he dreamed of the General Judgment, and told his fellow-servants about it, and then made a tune to it, and sang it in his cabin meetings."　　　　J. B. TOWE.

I'm a gwine to tell you bout de comin' ob de Sav-iour; Fare-you-well,

Fare-you-well. I'm a gwine to tell you 'bout de com-in ob de Saviour;

Fare-you-well, Fare-you-well. Dar's a bet-ter day a comin'; Fare-you-well,

Fare-you-well; When my Lord speaks to His Fa-der; Fare-you-well,

Fare-you-well. Says Fa-der, I'm tired o' bear-in', Fare-you-well,

Photo courtesy of the Morgan Collection

From *Cabin and Plantation Songs* as sung by students of the Hampton Normal and Agricultural Institute of Virginia—now Hampton Sydney University—and published by G. P. Putnam's Sons in 1875 at the height of Reconstruction following the Civil War. To raise money for their college, the Hampton students toured the country with this collection of songs. In his introduction Thomas P. Fenner, head of Hampton's music department, noted that although "slave music is … rapidly passing away, it may be that this people who have developed such a wonderful musical sense in their degradation will, in their maturity, produce a composer who could bring a music of the future out of this music of the past." Note the use of black dialect in the lyrics, a feature of much African American music of the time.

musicians to maintain a steady beat while practicing. The dancers' motions generally show the pulse.

▶ *Overlapping call-and-response.* In **call-and-response**, a solo vocalist sings one line (often improvised), then a group responds. In African traditions, the group response tends to overlap the original solo part.

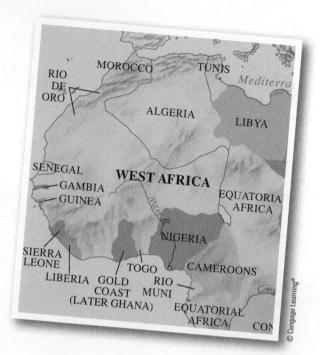

© Cengage Learning®

West Africa in 1914

▶ *Off-beat phrasing of melodic accents.* This is the unexpected accenting of weaker notes within the melody, or what many scholars describe as **syncopation**.

▶ *Dominance of percussion.* In African music, percussion instruments are plentiful and used more widely than melodic ones, with some exceptions. The melodic instruments themselves are sometimes played percussively.

▶ **Polyrhythm.** This is an intricate web of rhythms heard among the different parts.

Call-and-response is a musical procedure in which a single voice or instrument states a melodic phrase—the call—and a group of voices or instruments follows with a responding or completing phrase—the response.

Syncopation is the disruption of regular meter that occurs when the weaker notes of the designated meter receive unexpectedly stronger accents, as in the second and fourth beats in 4/4 meter receiving stronger accents. For an illustration, see Music Example 1-2, third measure (page 15), and listen to Track 4 of the 🅿 Audio Primer. The Joplin phrase is played first with syncopation, as it was written, then without.

Polyrhythm is an intricate web of rhythms heard among the different parts.

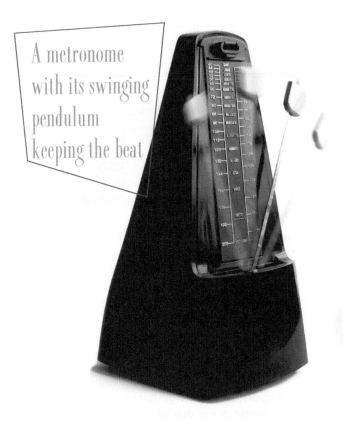

A metronome with its swinging pendulum keeping the beat

Rodho/Dreamstime.com

that most actively worked to convert slaves to Christianity; so throughout most if not all of the American South, slave owners outlawed drums, thus eliminating a fundamental percussive element of West African music.

Lacking drums, the slaves adapted in ingenious ways. They used stringed instruments in a percussive manner. They added percussion by clapping and stamping, for example, when performing the **ring shout** in religious worship. Finally, *patting juba* (clapping, stamping, and slapping thighs) provided percussive dance accompaniment, frequently without any other instruments. (See the Listening Guide for Track 2, "Daniel," performed by the Georgia Sea Island Singers.)

The survival of polyrhythm is more difficult to trace. In African music, percussion parts are typically played

Call-and-response patterns, nearly universal in West African culture, formed the basis of work songs and spirituals in the United States and became a significant component of blues and jazz.

on different drums and rattles, each with its own rhythm, creating a complex overlay of contrasting patterns. African Americans did not retain this practice in the United States, mostly because of the proscription against drums. Instead they expressed percussive rhythm in syncopated melodies and **cross-rhythms**. In this way African rhythmic complexity survived in African American music.

Meter in music is a rhythmic pattern arising from regular groupings of two or three beats. These define, respectively, duple or triple meter. Most music with a steady pulse has meter.

Polyphony describes music with at least two distinct and simultaneous melodic lines. Another name for a polyphonic texture is **counterpoint**.

The **ring shout**, originally derived from African religious practice, was a rhythmic dance performed in a circle. Worshipers moved counterclockwise while singing spirituals and accompanying themselves by clapping and stamping. The worshipers ingeniously circumvented the prohibition against dancing—strictly speaking, to lift and cross the feet—by shuffling. Some historians describe the ring shout as contributing the essence of African song, dance, and spirit to African American music.

Cross-rhythms refer to the performance of simultaneous and contrasting rhythms, such as patterns with duple and triple groupings. By superimposing one rhythmic pattern on another, we create a cross-rhythm. Cross-rhythms are sometimes called polyrhythms.

We should probably consider these five traits as general principles that inform much of West African music, and we hear them in "Kasuan Kura" from present day Ghana, Africa, Track 1, discussed in the Listening Guide. Although the first four attributes of African music are fairly straightforward, polyrhythm is more complex. The rhythmic layering of the different instruments in an African ensemble is typically founded on a single ground beat, usually in duple or triple **meter**. Africans themselves often think of their music's rhythm as projected along a time line in which patterns may be based on large numbers of beats, perhaps as many as twelve. In addition, many of the rhythms arising from this layering can seem independent, though they are not played separately. Thus African music is often described as rhythmically **polyphonic**.

Although there is no way to be sure, we assume that these five traits were generally true of African music in the eighteenth and nineteenth centuries; certainly, many of these elements appear in African American music today. Religious and secular music retained the metronomic sense. Call-and-response patterns, nearly universal in West African culture, formed the basis of work songs and spirituals in the United States and became a significant component of blues and jazz. African American music in the nineteenth century retained the off-beat phrasing of melodic accents, a key characteristic that became part of the jazz tradition.

African slaves brought their tradition of drumming to the United States. Slave owners, however, suspected that the drums allowed slaves to communicate over long distances. Moreover, drumming and dancing were forbidden by Methodists and Baptists, the Protestant denominations

LISTENING GUIDE

"Kasuan Kura"

Track 1

The People of Dagomba, Ghana: "Kasuan Kura." Field recording (Ghana) by John Miller Chernoff.

The Main Point   Listen for these characteristics of West African music: the dominance of percussion in the dondon and gongon drums; the steady pulse; the call-and-response between the leader accompanied by dondons and the chorus accompanied by gongons; the occasional off-beat phrasing; and the complex polyrhythm.

Along with Track 2, this recording is an example of a *field recording*, a recording that folklorists and ethnomusicologists make on-site with performers in their cultural settings. An advantage of field recordings for folk material is that scholars are able to capture the works in context. The performers themselves, who very likely are not professionals, may be more comfortable in their familiar surroundings than in formal recording studios. As a result, we are likely to obtain freer, less self-conscious performances. A disadvantage of such recordings is that audio quality may suffer. Still, it is certainly better for us to glimpse these pieces in their usual settings.

The Dagomba live in northern Ghana in West Africa and are known for their sophisticated oral culture. Indeed, oral culture has served the role of professional historian. "Kasuan Kura," for example, is a *praise-song*, telling the story of an honored ancestor. His name forms the "answer" in this call-and-response format.

We first hear *dondons*, or talking drums, whose pitch can be varied by pulling on leather thongs that connect the two drumheads on each drum. We also hear *gongons* in the ensemble. These are larger drums that have a string stretched over the drumhead to produce a rattle as the drum is played. As the performance develops, the rhythmic relationships between the different types of drums and the singing grow more complex.

0:00	Dondons begin the excerpt, followed closely by gongons. The feeling of the beat is irregular at first, then becomes more regular as the voices enter.
0:12	Voices enter with call-and-response figures. Notice that the response figures remain roughly the same, as is usually the case with a chorus. This type of chorus singing is called *heterophonic*—there is a kind of spontaneous harmony, but not a European-oriented chord progression. A *groove*, or repeating rhythm pattern, underlies the performance, but the dondons engage in a conversation with the lead singer. That is, both dondons and gongons accompany the calls, but usually only gongons accompany the responses.
1:24	The drumming becomes more intense, as does the singing of the leader. Nevertheless, the singers continue with roughly the same answering figures.

Listen to this music in an animated Active Listening Guide available at the text website.

Clearly, rhythm played a prominent role in defining the African musical aesthetic, so it became crucial in shaping the African American musical aesthetic as well.

We might best consider the five attributes of African music as merely a beginning point for understanding a very rich and complex musical heritage. Nevertheless, writers have continued to examine how African approaches to music making have been retained in African American music—a crucial issue in understanding the African roots of jazz. In discussing the relationship between West African and African American music, one writer states:

The approach to metrical organization with cross-rhythms as the norm, the percussive technique of playing any instrument resulting in an abundance of qualitative accents, the density of musical activity, the inclusion of the environmental factors as part of the musical event, the propensity for certain "buzzylike" musical timbres—all these are African features which have been consistently maintained in Afro-American music.[2]

LISTENING GUIDE   Track 2
"Daniel"

Georgia Sea Island Singers: "Daniel" (traditional). New World Records 278. Field recording by Alan Lomax, 1960. Willis Proctor, leader; Bessie Jones, Jerome Davis, John Davis, Peter Davis, Joe Armstrong, Henry Morrison, Ben Ramsay.

The Main Point   This ring shout—a call-and-response between the leader calling the lyric and the chorus responding with "Daniel" or "O, Daniel"—accompanies a highly energetic circle dance. Listen for the rhythmic, percussive handclapping that replaces the drums of "Kasuan Kura" and provides a syncopated accompaniment.

The Sea Islands are located off the coast of the eastern United States, extending from Maryland to Florida. Because of their isolation from much of the rest of the country through the mid-twentieth century, these areas featured a vibrant black culture—sometimes called *Gullah*—with a remarkably close connection to its African roots.

The piece begins directly (0:00) with the leader and his call. The leader is shadowed by another singer who sometimes sings along with him. The choral response approximates a major triad that suggests the influence of Western tonality.

Because the form of the piece is undifferentiated (other than the changing lyric of the call), there are no timing cues in this Listening Guide. Instead, the piece develops the story, with each line repeated by the lead singer, followed by the response of the other singers. (Sometimes a line is repeated three times for a total of four calls.) This abbreviated form creates much intensity and drive and is appropriate for the highly energetic circle dance that the music of the ring shout accompanies.

Listen to this music in an animated Active Listening Guide available at the text website.

European Music in the Nineteenth Century

The European tradition remains embedded in jazz. Indeed, as we examine the range of jazz history, we find that even in its earliest days a particular mix of European and African elements often characterized a specific jazz substyle. Here we look at the main contributions of European music to jazz: instrumentation, form, and harmony, and arrangements.

Instrumentation, Form, and Harmony

Many elements of the European tradition contributed to the formation of early jazz. The instruments of early jazz are virtually all European. The **front line** and the **rhythm section** of a typical early jazz band included the following:

MELODY	RHYTHM
Trumpet or cornet	Piano (melodic also)
Clarinet	String bass or tuba
Trombone	Guitar or banjo
	Drums

The saxophone, although occurring in early jazz, was not as common as the clarinet. The banjo, which lost favor in subsequent jazz styles, was very common in early jazz and has African roots, although theories about its specific origins are controversial.

The **front line** described the lead (melody) instruments in early jazz bands and usually included trumpet (or cornet), trombone, and clarinet. The saxophone came later to jazz.

The **rhythm section** in early jazz bands included three or four players on drums, bass or tuba, and one or more chordal instruments (piano, banjo, or guitar). (Listen to Tracks 44 and 45, of the 🅟 Audio Primer to hear a modern rhythm section. Track 44 has bass and drums; Track 45 adds the piano.)

A **countermelody**, like an obbligato, is a secondary melody that accompanies the main melody. A countermelody is generally heard in the trombone or a lower voice, has fewer notes than the obbligato, and is often improvised. (Listen to Track 7 of the 🅟 Audio Primer; the piano enters in the middle register with a countermelody.)

Obbligato is a term borrowed from classical music to describe a complementary melodic part played along with the main melody as a necessary, or expected, addition. In early jazz, obbligato parts were often florid, usually played by the clarinet, and sometimes improvised. (Listen to Track 21 of the 🅟 Audio Primer to hear an obbligato-like clarinet melody.)

AABA comprises an eight-bar theme (A) played twice. A contrasting melody (B) follows, also usually eight bars long, before the A theme returns. Quite often the second and third A sections will vary slightly.

In the **ABAC song form**, each section is, again, usually eight bars. Musicians often speak of the "first half" of the tune (AB) and the "second half" (AC).

European song form became especially prominent as jazz matured through the 1920s. The two basic formats, **AABA** and **ABAC**, that were described in the Introduction have been mainstays of the music ever since. In each of these forms, the A section may be called the *head* (although this term is more commonly applied to the

> In most jazzlike musical textures, the melody plays on top of the harmony. The accompanying rhythm instruments—piano, banjo, or guitar—provide the backup chords to the primary melodic instruments—cornet or trumpet, trombone, clarinet, or saxophone.

original melody as a whole), and the B section the *bridge*. (Two older terms for the B section, *channel* and *release*, are now uncommon.) We point out examples of these forms later when we analyze specific pieces.

Despite the prominence of rhythm as a key ingredient of African music, the basic instruments of the jazz drum set—snare drum, bass drum, and cymbals—are those of the European marching band. Pioneering drummers in

> Despite the prominence of rhythm as a key ingredient of African music, the basic instruments of the jazz drum set—snare drum, bass drum, and cymbals—are those of the European marching band.

early jazz bands created the drum set by arranging these instruments so that one person could play them all at once. Modern additions to the basic drum set—gongs, wind chimes, hand drums, and so on—come from cultures the world over.

The European marching or brass band also contributed instrumentation that served as a model for many early jazz bands, and we hear it in the basic textural layout of the cornet (or trumpet) lead melody, the trombone **countermelody**, and the clarinet **obbligato**.

In addition to instrumentation, the most significant European contributions to jazz are its form—that is, the basic layout of the music—and harmony. As described in the Introduction, a great deal of the jazz repertory maintains the 8-, 16-, and 32-bar symmetrical sections of European popular song, dance music, and marches. These symmetrical forms provide large-scale paths through the music and tell us where we are in the composition. We discuss march form, which influences the pre-jazz style known as ragtime, later in this chapter.

We can think of form as large-scale rhythm because it marks off periods of time. In general, there are several different levels of rhythmic activity in a jazz piece, from the note-to-note progression, to the overall form of a work. Examining these levels clarifies the mixture of the African and European traditions:

▶ At the note-to-note level, we hear clear African influences: accents fall in unexpected places, the music shows syncopated movement, and unusual vocal and instrumental timbres are evident.

▶ At the level of meter and phrase, we hear both European and African tendencies. The harmonic flow is European in origin, yet the syncopation, cross-rhythms, and call-and-response forms are largely of African origin.

▶ Finally, at the level of form, the European influence is strongest in such features as sectional structure, tonality, and instrumentation.

European harmony is based on chords built on each step of a given scale. These chords, the progressions among them, and the scales that define them give rise to musical keys. It is this European model that defines much of jazz form and its use of harmony.

In most jazzlike musical *textures*, the melody is an overlay, that is, it plays on top of the harmony. The accompanying rhythm instruments (piano, banjo, or guitar) provide the backup chords to the primary melodic instruments (cornet or trumpet, trombone, clarinet, or saxophone). (Listen to Track 3 of the ⏺ Audio Primer to hear a melody played without chords, then with chords.)

A constant dialogue between the written (European) and improvised (African) traditions runs throughout jazz history.

Early African American Music

Throughout the eighteenth and nineteenth centuries, African American music drew on both European and African characteristics and appeared in both sacred and secular settings. This music was communal and woven into the daily rituals of life. The notion of the professional musician was largely unknown (a characteristic typical of folk music), as was the separation between performer and audience that we know today.

Written Versus Head Arrangements

Jazz groups with large numbers of players usually require arrangements. **Arrangers** are responsible for the final sound of the performance of a piece because they work up all the required elements: form, chord voicings, introductions, codas, and so on. The arranger provides the players with the written music, called *parts*, which they may practice at rehearsal. This concept of musical performance comes largely from the European tradition.

The arranger usually provides the rhythm players with **slash notation** in written arrangements, but he or she may specify the parts more precisely when necessary. Arrangers often use slash notation to designate passages of improvisation, usually for the soloists.

One alternative to the written arrangement is the **head arrangement**, that is, a musical plan and form worked up by the players themselves, who create their own parts. Less common than the traditional written arrangement, especially for larger groups, the head arrangement relates conceptually more to the African tradition than to the European. Head arrangements were probably common in jazz through the late 1930s because there was less turnover in band personnel and players had more time to rehearse. Since then written arrangements became standard. As we see in a later chapter, some well-known bands, such as the Count Basie Orchestra in its early days, were defined in part by head arrangements.

A constant dialogue between the written (European) and improvised (African) traditions runs throughout jazz history. Whereas the African musical tradition was oral, jazz band members performing written arrangements must be able to read their parts. Some jazz players learned to play "by ear" but then joined bands for which they needed to learn to read music. Such stories are especially common in early jazz.

The Character of Early African American Music

Contemporary transcriptions of nineteenth-century African American folk music emerged slowly in the second half of the century. Three white scholars collaborated in 1867 to produce the first published collection: *Slave Songs of the United States*. With this collection we see an attempt to translate into European musical notation the African American music that had, up until that point, been performed and transmitted orally. The process of transcription made clear how different African American and European performance practices were. Transcription also made clear the limitations of European musical notation for African American music.

The early transcribers frankly admitted to the difficulty of notating African American music. One of them, Lucy McKim Garrison, pointed to the problem of accurately rendering the vocal effects and the rhythmic qualities:

> It is difficult to express the entire character of these negro ballads by mere musical notes and signs. The odd turns made in the throat, and the curious rhythmic effect produced by single voices chiming in at

An **arranger** plans the form of a band's performance and often notates the parts for the different instruments.

Slash notation is a method of showing the harmonies (or "chord changes") in jazz and popular music. Each slash in a measure denotes a beat. The arranger places chords over the slashes to show the beats on which the harmonies change. (See Music Examples I-4 and I-5 in the Introduction chapter for examples.)

A **head arrangement** is a musical plan and form worked up orally by the players themselves in rehearsal or on the bandstand.

different irregular intervals, seem almost as impossible to place on the score as the singing of birds or the tones of an Aeolian Harp.[3]

Garrison's comments describe a number of performance practices. The technique of vocal ornamentation, referred to by some writers as "trimming" and what Garrison calls "the odd turns made in the throat," points to a flexibility of interpretation and perhaps even alterations in vocal timbre. Garrison also describes the overlapping call-and-response pattern: the "curious rhythmic effect produced by single voices chiming in at different irregular intervals." Although the transcriptions in the book suggest single-line melodies, Garrison implies that nonunison singing occurred in the original performances that either were not or could not be notated.

Another transcriber discusses the inability of the European notational system to represent other African-derived performance practices:

> Tones are frequently employed which we have no musical characters to represent. Such, for example, is that which I have indicated as nearly as possible by the flat seventh … The tones are variable in pitch, ranging through an entire octave on different occasions, according to the inspiration of the singer.[4]

The last sentence points to a significant feature of the music—an emphasis on improvisation, in which pitch choices may be made or altered "according to the inspiration of the singer."

Transcriptions are at best only an approximation of actual practice. In 1899 Jeanette Robinson Murphy noted that she had followed "old ex-slaves, who have passed away in their tasks, listened to their crooning in their cabins, in the fields, and especially in their meeting houses, and again and again they assured me the tunes they sang came from Africa."[5]

She noted, for example, that in certain collections of transcriptions, nothing indicated to the singer

that he must make his voice exceedingly nasal and undulating, that around every prominent note he must place a variety of small notes, called "trimmings," and he must sing notes not found in our scale; that he must on no account leave one note until he has the next one well under control. He might be tempted … to take breath whenever he came to the end of a line or verse!

Five generations of a South Carolina slave family in an 1862 photo taken during the Civil War.

Library of Congress Prints and Photographs Division LC-B8171-152-A]

But … he should carry over his breath from line to line and from verse to verse, even at the risk of bursting a blood vessel. He must often drop from a high note to a very low one, he must be very careful to divide many of his monosyllabic words into syllables.… He must intersperse his singing with peculiar humming sounds…[6]

Murphy has described here many of the vocal elements commonly heard in blues singing.

Although the music that evolved was rooted in the African tradition, it soon took on European elements. Slaves who were called on as musicians to entertain whites at dances and balls came to know the European tradition. Classified advertisements in newspapers of the period referred to slaves as highly skilled players on European instruments. An advertisement from as early as 1766 called attention to a slave proficient on the French horn; other advertisements announced slaves' skills on the violin or fife.

We know very little about African American music before the eighteenth and early nineteenth centuries. Songs and instrumental pieces passed from one individual to another almost completely through an oral tradition in which performers sang and played by ear.

Photo courtesy of the Morgan Collection

This picture of a black debutante on the cover of the Sunday Musical Supplement of the *Denver Times*, March 24, 1901, appears to be an unusual item for the time. As we shall see, photos or drawings of white composers and performers were invariably featured on sheet music covers, but not until the 1950s did depictions of black or female composers regularly appear.

problems. We can be sure, however, that where black performers and composers were active a strand of authenticity resided. The vigorous, unsentimental tunes of 1840s minstrelsy, only rarely identified with known black composers, present persistent syncopations, asymmetrical note groups, and the call-and-response pattern. These features all point to the retention of African elements, although the evidence for direct African provenance is slim.

The presence on the minstrel stage of African and Afro-American instruments—drums and banjos—and of strong black characters drawn from American folklore—John Henry and his kin—confirms a unique black influence, in comparison with other ethnic groups, on the development of minstrelsy.[16]

One of the most famous minstrel figures was James Bland (1854–1911), a black performer who gained international fame in minstrelsy and who composed several famous songs, including "Carry Me Back to Old Virginny"

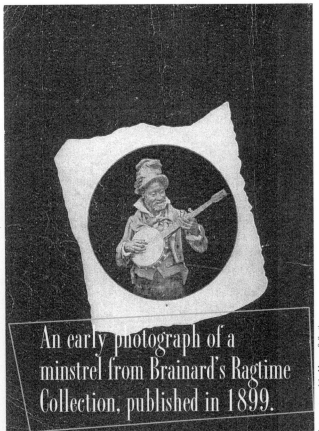

An early photograph of a minstrel from Brainard's Ragtime Collection, published in 1899.

Photo courtesy of the Morgan Collection

and "Oh, Dem Golden Slippers." Many of the most famous songs of the first professional U.S. songwriter, Stephen Foster (1826–1864)—including "Oh! Susanna," "Old Folks at Home" (aka "Swanee River"), "De Camptown Races," and "My Old Kentucky Home"—were minstrel-type songs that incorporated black dialect.

Despite the initial exclusion of blacks from minstrelsy and the later pejorative portrayals of blacks, minstrel shows introduced many whites to black

Among the most memorable black dances was the cakewalk, which achieved considerable popularity with whites.

music; provided employment for black actors, dancers, and musicians; and helped popularize various black dances. Among the most memorable dances was the **cakewalk**, which achieved considerable popularity with whites. Bert Williams, a well-known black entertainer and

A **cakewalk** is a dance involving an exaggerated walking step. In exhibitions of cakewalking, the most talented couple won a cake at the end of the evening. The cakewalk may have been an imitation of the way members of white "high society" comported themselves.

Ragtime is an African American musical genre that flourished from the late 1890s through the mid-1910s and is based on constant syncopation in the right hand often accompanied by a steady march bass in the left hand. Associated now primarily with piano music, ragtime was originally a method of performance that included syncopated songs, music for various ensembles, and arrangements of nonragtime music. Scott Joplin was ragtime's most famous composer.

dancer in the early twentieth century, taught the dance to Edward VII of England.

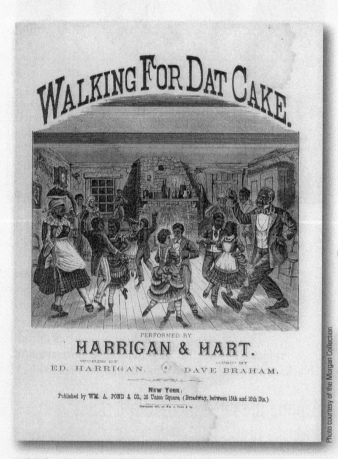

Published in 1877, this sheet music is an early reference to the cakewalk. Here is a portion of the lyrics:

'Twas down at Aunty Jackson's,
there was a big reception
Of high-tone colored people
full of sweet affection.
Such singing and such dancing,
we made the ceiling shake,
The cream of all the evening
was a'walking for dat cake.

Notice that although the art is not that skillful, it appears to be an honest attempt to capture the dance without undue caricature.

In the late nineteenth century, minstrelsy was replaced by *vaudeville*, a touring entertainment form similar to minstrelsy but without self-contained troupes. Vaudeville often included much ethnic humor that we would now regard as offensive, but its stereotyping of African Americans was

> Great vaudeville performers, such as blues singer Bessie Smith, helped popularize jazz in its early years.

less overt than in minstrelsy. Great vaudeville performers, such as blues singer Bessie Smith (discussed later in this chapter), helped popularize jazz in its early years.

Urban musical theater also developed out of minstrelsy. Turn-of-the-century New York developed a flourishing black theater community that included composers Bob Cole, James Weldon Johnson, Ernest Hogan, and Will Marion Cook. They built many of their works on African American themes, and their songs served as precursors to ragtime. With the decline of minstrelsy, many composers turned to ragtime and vaudeville. Yet the composers just listed also continued to work in black musical theater and greatly contributed to the rising consciousness of African American culture. Will Marion Cook (1869–1944), as we see in Chapter 4, took one of the first protojazz ensembles to Europe as early as 1919.

Ragtime

Legend has it that the 1893 World's Columbian Exposition (a kind of World's Fair) in Chicago marked the beginning of the popular fascination with **ragtime**. For the first time, thousands of Americans heard a new type of music associated with black, itinerant piano players. Adapting African polyrhythms to piano, these players developed the use of syncopation that would become one of ragtime's central features. (An example of the adaptation of polyrhythms to the piano is shown in our discussion of "Maple Leaf Rag" later in this chapter.)

"Syncopation," Irving Berlin maintained, "is nothing but another name for ragtime."[17] As a sober observer of the *London Times* said, "In American slang to 'rag' a melody is to syncopate a normally regular tune."[18] The traditional ragtime piano figures, which often pivot around fixed notes, may have been taken from banjo playing. In time, Scott Joplin and other ragtime composers would formalize the genre to create the works that we now call "classic ragtime." The overall form of the classic rag usually comprised three or four 16-bar sections called *strains* and was borrowed from the march (and other multiple strain forms of the time).

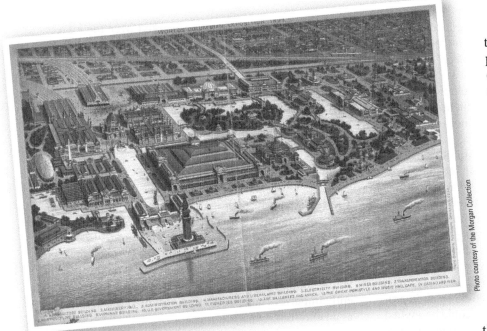

A bird's-eye view of the World's Columbian Exposition (May 1 to October 31, 1893, in Jackson Park, Chicago), where many Americans first heard ragtime. The exposition occupied 664 acres, with a frontage of 1½ miles on Lake Michigan, and cost an estimated $25 million to build, an enormous amount of money at a time when many workers earned $1 a day or less.

During its heyday, however, ragtime was not strictly associated with piano music. Early ragtime probably derived from songs taken from minstrel shows and urban musical theater. Although many of these songs were unsyncopated, the early ragtime pianists worked up arrangements for solo piano or for piano and voice. The syncopated manner in which these songs were performed came to be described as "ragged time" or ragtime.

Although the idea of "ragging" melodies was first associated with songs and solo piano, ragtime was quickly taken up by bands. In the late nineteenth century, brass bands were extremely common throughout the country and sometimes acted as a locality's cultural focus. A small city might have three or four bands; an average town usually had at least one. In larger cities, such as New Orleans, there were numerous bands, both black and white, that competed through concerts, funerals, dances, parades, and other venues. The southern black bands served as training ensembles for many early jazz musicians and often performed marches from the white repertory

> As ragtime grew in popularity, the practice of ragging marches—especially those by John Philip Sousa—became common.

(see Chapter 2). As ragtime grew in popularity, the practice of ragging marches—especially those by John Philip Sousa—became common. (Sousa, the country's premier march composer, was not especially fond of ragtime but did include it in his band concerts.) Not only were the sectional design and the key relationships of classic ragtime taken from marches, but many

Beginning in the 1890s and lasting two decades, ragtime swept the nation. The success of ragtime was unparalleled. It was especially significant because, for the first time, a specifically black musical genre entered and dominated the U.S. mainstream. The music was not only wildly popular, but it was also commercially successful. Entrepreneurial fortunes were made as publishing houses for

> Beginning in the 1890s and lasting two decades, ragtime swept the nation. For the first time, a specifically black musical genre entered and dominated the U.S. mainstream.

ragtime compositions sprang up throughout U.S. towns and cities. The first manual of ragtime performance, *Ben Harney's Ragtime Instructor*, appeared in 1897. Two years later "Maple Leaf Rag"—Scott Joplin's second published rag—became the most celebrated ragtime composition for piano.

ragtime composers also named some of their rags "marches" or indicated "march tempo" as the speed and rhythm of the work.

Proficient ragtime pianists were expected to improvise ragtime versions of popular songs; and in the Ragtime

Championship of the World Competition, held in New York in 1900, the three semifinalists were required to improvise a version of the popular period piece "All Coons Look Alike to Me." (This song is not as racist as its title suggests. Written by black composer and entertainer Ernest Hogan, the lyric depicts a black woman lamenting the loss of her lover; because other black men do not interest her, they all "look alike.")

Ragtime versions of other types of music were also popular. *Ben Harney's Ragtime Instructor* included syncopated versions of hymns and folksongs. Patriotic songs were not immune; several pianists featured syncopated versions of "The Star-Spangled Banner" in their repertories. In another practice, called "ragging the classics," performers created ragtime renditions of classical compositions—Felix Mendelssohn's "Wedding March" was a particular favorite.

These practices show that ragtime could be an *improvised* music—a performance practice that could be applied to any well-known melody—as well as a written art form. It is possible too that the more improvised performance practice came first. Although many players improvised,

the masters of classic ragtime worked over their pieces with much attention to compositional detail. Aside from Scott Joplin, whose life and work we examine, the finest classic ragtime composers included Tom Turpin, whose "Harlem Rag" (1897) may be the earliest ragtime masterpiece and the first rag published by a black composer; James Scott; Joseph Lamb; and Artie Matthews.

Scott Joplin

The solo piano rags of Scott Joplin became the pinnacle of the classic ragtime canon. Born in 1868 in Texarkana, Texas, Joplin studied music with several local teachers, the most significant of whom was Julius Weiss, a musician born in Germany. Weiss was impressed enough with the young Joplin to give him free music lessons and apparently imparted "an appreciation of music as an art as well as an entertainment."[19]

A well-known photograph of Scott Joplin, ca. 1900, dressed to reflect the respectability that he sought for his music.

Courtesy Frank Driggs Collection

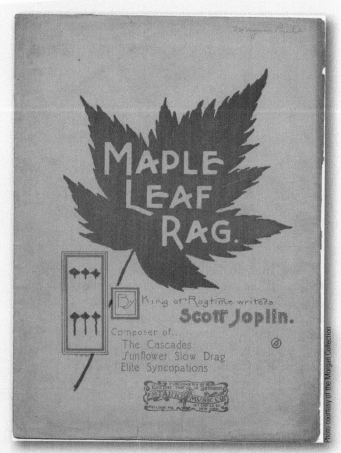

Photo courtesy of the Morgan Collection

An early edition of "Maple Leaf Rag" by Scott Joplin, the "King of Ragtime writers," published in 1899. The sheet music cover advertises more-recent Joplin rags. Notice that the Stark Music Co. bills itself as "publishers of ragtime that is different" but does not show a picture of "King" Joplin on the cover—a cautious omission that was to continue for the next several decades.

A picture of John Stark from an article that appeared in Melody, A Monthly Magazine for Lovers of Popular Music, October 1918. The writer reported, "It was (Stark) who discovered Scott Joplin, who put on paper for the first time the genius of that wonderful composer of classic ragtime." In fact, Stark was not Joplin's first publisher, although his publications established Joplin's supremacy.

Photo courtesy of the Morgan Collection

Piano rolls are cylinders of rolled paper punched with holes. When fed through a properly equipped **player piano**, the holes activate hammers that play the piano automatically.

A **player piano** is a piano equipped with a mechanism that allows it to play piano rolls.

It is thought that Joplin left home around 1885 or so and worked as an itinerant musician in the Midwest, but there is no direct evidence. In 1891 he became a member of the Texarkana Minstrels and was probably present at the 1893 World's Fair in Chicago.

After the World's Fair, Joplin stopped in St. Louis then continued on to Sedalia, Missouri, where he settled in 1895. It was in Sedalia that he composed "Maple Leaf Rag," named after the Maple Leaf Club, a black social organization that Joplin may have joined. "Maple Leaf Rag" was enormously successful, allowing the composer to live comfortably after its publication in 1899 by John Stark, a music store owner in Sedalia trying to capitalize on the rising popularity of ragtime. Stark went on to build one of the most prestigious publishing houses for what he called "classic ragtime." Remarkably, he offered Joplin a publishing contract for "Maple Leaf Rag" that included a penny royalty for each copy sold. This was a generous arrangement at the time: although such contracts are commonplace now, a fair agreement between a white publisher and a black artist was virtually unheard of in the 1890s. The fame Joplin achieved through "Maple Leaf Rag" increased the sales of his other rags. We discuss Joplin's recording of "Maple Leaf Rag" on **piano roll** in the Listening Guide for Track 4.

LISTENING GUIDE
"Maple Leaf Rag" (excerpt)

Track 4

Scott Joplin: "Maple Leaf Rag" (Joplin). Connorized piano roll 10265. April 1916. Joplin, piano.

The Main Point As in most ragtime piano works, in "Maple Leaf Rag" we hear the left hand keeping time with bass notes and chords while the right hand plays a syncopated melody. Its jaunty rhythms were characteristic of the best ragtime compositions.

The marchlike form of "Maple Leaf Rag" is AABBACCDD, with each section called a *strain*. The excerpt on Track 4, with only the AAB strains, is from a piano roll performed by Scott Joplin himself. Many of the great pianists of the teens and twenties recorded piano rolls, including Scott Joplin, James P. Johnson, Eubie Blake, Thomas "Fats" Waller, and George Gershwin. The rolls, however, could not reproduce dynamics and phrasing adequately, and tempo depended on how fast the roll was fed through the piano. Hence the "recordings" of piano rolls are not accurate guides to the players' styles.

In the past several years, the use of electronic technology has vastly improved the performance of piano rolls, and remarkably lifelike versions of piano-roll performances by George Gershwin, for example, are now available.

Composed and notated for publication, Scott Joplin's "Maple Leaf Rag" quickly became a ragtime classic.

A strain

0:00 The opening A strain is 16 bars long, as is customary for ragtime works. The left hand keeps time and provides the harmony while the right hand plays syncopated "ragged" melodies. The basic two-bar thematic idea is as follows:

The right-hand melody exhibits the pivoting pattern possibly derived from banjo technique. The repeated E♭ octaves recur every three sixteenth notes, as shown by the dotted eighth notes above the staff marking off that regularity. This dotted-eighth-note emphasis on E♭ in the right hand creates a cross-rhythm relative to regular eighth notes in the left hand. Moreover, the left hand does not simply alternate bass note with chord but instead projects an A♭–A♮–B♭ rising bass line with yet another rhythm, as shown under the left-hand staff, thus adding further complexity to the opening thematic idea.

A strain repeats

0:22 The A strain repeats.

B strain

0:44 The left hand becomes more regular in the B strain, usually alternating a bass note with a chord, while the right-hand part becomes more active and moves to a higher register on the piano. Moreover, the right-hand melody, instead of just pivoting around the E♭ octave as in the opening of the A strain, now descends, beginning on E♭ and emphasizing octaves that extend the dotted-eighth-note cross-rhythm first heard at the beginning of the piece:

Listen to this music in an animated Active Listening Guide available at the text website.

Possibly as a result of his earlier classical study with Weiss, Joplin sought to elevate ragtime to an art form. His published ragtime compositions artfully combined the African American tradition with techniques, forms, and principles derived from European music.

Joplin relocated in St. Louis in 1901, following Stark, who had moved his publishing business to the larger city. In addition to writing piano rags, Joplin began incorporating ragtime within larger, more classically oriented musical forms, including the ballet *Ragtime Dance* and two operas. The first of these operas, *A Guest of Honor* (1903), is now lost.

In 1907 Joplin moved to New York. Interestingly, around this time Stark also established a presence for his publishing company there, but differences must have developed between the two men. Joplin began placing his work with other publishers, and he sometimes published his pieces himself. He spent the last years of his life working on his second opera, *Treemonisha*. Unable to interest publishers in this large-scale venture, Joplin eventually published the piece himself in a piano/vocal edition in 1911. Sadly, Joplin spent his final years trying to mount *Treemonisha*, but its only performance, in 1915, was unsuccessful. Meanwhile Joplin grew increasingly ill with

A player piano with its white piano roll.

C Squared Studios/Photodisc/Getty Images

(1921). Note that this third title speaks of Scott's antipathy to the rapidly rising popularity of jazz. Scott eventually moved to Kansas City in 1914, where he became a music teacher, a theater organist, and eventually a bandleader.

The opening of Scott's "Troubadour Rag" (1919) shows the use of *dotted rhythms*, a feature of late ragtime that is a link to early jazz styles (see Music Example 1-3).

James Scott, "Broadway Rag" (published 1922)

Music Example 1-3

© Cengage Learning®

what may have been complications of syphilis compounded by the bitterness of the reaction to *Treemonisha*. He died in New York in 1917 at the age of only forty-nine.

Joplin's attempts to merge large-scale European classical forms with jazz, as we shall see, continued with the works of jazzmen James P. Johnson and Edward "Duke" Ellington. Joplin's music returned to vogue in the 1970s with the success of the movie *The Sting*, which featured several of Joplin's rags, including "The Entertainer."

Scott Joplin, "The Entertainer" (published 1902)

The opening of Scott's "Troubadour Rag" (1919) shows the use of dotted rhythms, a feature of late ragtime that is a link to early jazz styles.

James Scott

Often considered second only to Scott Joplin as a classic rag composer, James Scott (1886–1938) was born in the small town of Neosho, Missouri, where he began studying piano as a child. His talent and dedication transcended the early absence of a piano in his home, and his study included sight-reading. By the time he was a teenager, he was living in Carthage, Missouri, and "plugging" songs for a living. **Song pluggers** promoted songs for music publishers by performing them for potential buyers. He published his first rag, "A Summer Breeze—March and Two Step," when he was seventeen.

Scott later established a relationship with John Stark, Scott Joplin's publisher, and continued to write exceptional rags, including "Frog Legs Rag" (1906), "Ragtime Oriole" (1911), and "Don't Jazz Me—Rag (I'm Music)"

Joseph Lamb

Originally from Montclair, New Jersey, Joseph Lamb (1887–1960) was a white composer fortunate enough to meet Scott Joplin in New York in 1907. Joplin took an interest in the younger man's work and helped him secure a publishing agreement with Stark. Among Lamb's finest rags are "Ethiopia Rag" (1909) and "Ragtime Nightingale" (1915). The latter is especially striking—a lush, romantic composition with a rich harmonic conception.

Artie Matthews

Artie Matthews (1888–1959) worked for the Stark Publishing Company, where he published his own material and worked up arrangements for composers unable to notate their own pieces. He is best remembered for a series of "Pastime" rags, numbered 1 to 5, which are daring

In the 1920s a **song plugger** was someone who performed a song, usually at a music store, to encourage people to buy the sheet music.

Photo courtesy of the Morgan Collection

A disproportionately small number of women worked as instrumentalists—as opposed to vocalists—in early jazz. Still, several women published successfully, among them Nellie W. Stokes (here, 1906), Adaline Shepherd, and Charlotte Blake.

Although the ragtimers must have improvised to some extent, evidence is generally lacking; in recorded ragtime multiple strains often repeat their melodies verbatim. In part this may have been because fairly well-known

After 1913 jazz—or at least the use of the term—began to gain in popularity over ragtime.

ensembles were the first to record and were expected to perform a "straight" version—the version they had made popular. More-informal ragtime was surely improvised at least in part because so many of its practitioners played by ear.

As further evidence of the ragtime/jazz symbiosis, both forms were persistently associated with dancing. Published ragtime pieces frequently listed dances for the work: the cakewalk, the two-step, the slow drag, and the march. From this we can argue not only that jazz replaced ragtime but also that ragtime at a later stage *became* early jazz. We can also argue the other side—that ragtime and jazz were distinct. According to this reasoning, a stricter, more vertical sense of rhythm characterized ragtime performance, whereas jazz rhythm was looser and more fluid. Furthermore, jazz incorporated more improvisation as a matter of course. Without further evidence, the debate remains open.

After 1913, jazz—or at least the use of the term—began to gain in popularity over ragtime.

The works of the classic ragtime composers showed a shift toward simpler, sometimes fewer, syncopations. The use of dotted rhythms became commonplace, bringing about what the scholar Edward A. Berlin described as the "erosion" of classic ragtime.[20]

Berlin offers three hypotheses for this new rhythmic convention of dotted rhythms:

▶ Composers were reflecting the performance practice of pianists, who were already interpreting eighth notes (♪♪) as dotted eighth–sixteenth notes (♪.♪).

▶ Composers were looking for ways to revitalize the hackneyed rhythmic figures of ragtime.

▶ Ragtime composers were writing music to accompany new dances, such as the fox trot and the turkey trot, which came to prominence after 1910.

in their use of unusual musical materials. "Pastime Rag No. 4" (1920) uses "wrong note" cluster harmonies in the right hand. "Pastime Rag No. 5" (1918), published before No. 4, shows the dotted-rhythm influence of late ragtime.

Ragtime's Relationship to Jazz

Was *ragtime* just another name for early jazz? The boundaries between them were certainly never fixed. Whatever their differences, ragtime and early jazz influenced each other mightily during the early twentieth century, as the following time line shows.

1885?–1900	1900–1917	1917–1930
Ragtime developing almost entirely improvised	**Ragtime flourishing** written and improvised	**Ragtime quickly declining**
	Jazz developing largely improvised	**Jazz flourishing** largely improvised, also written

Eubie Blake
"Sounds of Africa"
("Charleston Rag")
(1921)

Whatever their origins, the use of dotted rhythms provided one of the links from ragtime to the more fluid rhythmic language of early jazz. Recordings of jazz-oriented treatments of ragtime compositions—such as Lemott Ferdinand Joseph "Jelly Roll" Morton's interpretation of Joplin's "Maple Leaf Rag"—made clear the practice of "swinging" the eighth notes, that is, playing them either as dotted eighth–sixteenth notes or as triplets. (See Listening Guide for Track 5, Jelly Roll Morton's performance of "Maple Leaf Rag.") The decline of ragtime paralleled, or gave rise to, early jazz styles that made greater use of these looser rhythms and reduced the consistent ragtime syncopations.

Additionally, the style of solo jazz piano known as *stride* evolved directly from ragtime. Stride pianists used

LISTENING GUIDE   Track 5
"Maple Leaf Rag"

Ferdinand "Jelly Roll" Morton: "Maple Leaf Rag" (Joplin). Library of Congress Recordings Disc 1654A ("Morton Style"). Washington, DC, June 1938. Morton, piano.

The Main Point   In contrast to the metronomic pulse heard in ragtime, this early jazz version of "Maple Leaf Rag" from Jelly Roll Morton has a looser rhythm, a more swinging feel, and incorporates more improvisation by departing frequently from the written version of the piece—all characteristics of jazz.

Comparing this Jelly Roll Morton version with Scott Joplin's piano roll version (Track) provides a fascinating glimpse into the shift from ragtime (Joplin) to early jazz (Morton). Not only is Morton's version slower but it is also much lighter. Morton's left hand is highly active, with syncopated melodic ideas that might be played by a trombone in the front line of a New Orleans band. Throughout you can hear Morton keeping time by tapping his foot.

Introduction

0:00   In contrast to the Joplin version, Morton includes an introduction. This eight-measure introduction is taken from the second half of the A strain.

A strain

0:11   The A strain begins. Listen for the difference in rhythmic feel compared with the Joplin version. The A strain is played only once (perhaps because eight measures of it have already been heard in the introduction).

B strain

0:33   As in the A strain, the B strain is played only once here. Notice the active left hand throughout.

A strain returns

0:54   Morton embellishes the return to the A strain, compared with what he played at the beginning of the piece (0:12). The left hand plays less of the traditional ragtime style (alternating bass and chord), saving that for the following C strain.

C strain (trio)

1:15   Morton plays this section in a hotter, more driving style. Listen for the more consistent ragtime left hand that alternates bass note and chord.

1:36   C strain repeats.

Listen to this music in an animated Active Listening Guide available at the text website.

Blues is an African American folk music that appeared around 1900 and exerted influence on jazz and various forms of U.S. popular music.

left-hand techniques similar to those of ragtime but treated the melodic right hand in a freer manner with added blues elements (as we see in Chapter 4). Pianists James P. Johnson, Thomas "Fats" Waller, William "Count" Basie, and Edward "Duke" Ellington were brought up in this style of piano playing, which owes its origins to ragtime but which clearly became part of the jazz tradition.

The Blues

The addition of **blues** to ragtime helped create jazz. More precisely, ragtime—both in its classic piano form and in songs and marches "ragged" by ensembles—gradually metamorphosed into jazz. It did so through an internal evolution alongside the infusion of the blues. Because the addition of this final ingredient was so significant, some claim that improvising with authority and passion in the jazz tradition requires the ability to play the blues well.

An active musical genre to this day, the blues has roots in the nineteenth century. By the 1870s and 1880s, the diverse, formerly African slaves living in the United States had become African Americans and, thanks to emancipation, were now free citizens. The blues—from spirituals and work songs, through hollers and shouts—celebrated black entrance into a world less repressive, less harsh, and more optimistic—but also far more uncertain, still tragic, and full of deprivation. The unique character of the blues projected sadness, guilt, and sometimes despair, but also humor and bawdiness. Ironically, the blues could express joy, although this was less characteristic of the form as a whole.

The origins of the blues can be traced to the African American secular and sacred music of the late nineteenth century. The classic form of the genre, however, coalesced from its various antecedents rather suddenly at the dawn of the twentieth century; not until shortly after 1900 do examples of *blues forms*, or written descriptions of what sounds to our ears like the blues, surface. As we described in the Introduction, the classic blues featured an aab lyric pattern that fit regular chord changes:

> *The blues is a lowdown, achin' heart disease,*
> *The blues is a lowdown, achin' heart disease,*
> *It's like consumption, killin' you by degrees.*[21]

Where and how was the blues first performed? The music was originally vocal, usually accompanied by guitar, piano, or harmonica (although instrumentalists also played the blues). In the country blues tradition, singers often accompanied themselves. Groups of performers would gather informally in what were known as jook

> *The blues—from spirituals and work songs, through hollers and shouts—celebrated black entrance into a world less repressive, less harsh, and more optimistic—but also far more uncertain, still tragic, and full of deprivation.*

joints, barrelhouses, honky-tonks, or chock houses. These were simple, wooden structures with a bar for drinking, perhaps a floor for dancing, and a few stools and tables. The "bandstand" might consist of a battered piano in the corner—used not only for the blues but also for ragtime. The musicians themselves were often nonprofessionals who substituted improvised, homemade instruments for the real thing: a washboard played with a thimble became a snare drum; a jug blown on became a bass. The audience added clapping, call-and-response lines,

> The addition of blues to ragtime helped create jazz.

and encouragement. From such humble beginnings grew what was to become one of the greatest and most influential folk traditions of the United States.

Although local variations and styles of the blues proliferated throughout the country, the Mississippi Delta and Texas spawned the greatest number of early blues singers. As first performed by these folk artists, the blues

Frenchies Bar, a jook joint at an all-purpose destination in the Deep South of the 1930s: crossroads store, bar, gas station, and jook joint with a beat-up piano.

The library of congress

was free in form, befitting its origins in the African American vernacular tradition. Many of the early blues singers sang about a life of pain and despair and of the need to endure. Indeed the great authority of their performances arose from vivid descriptions of tragic hardship yielding to the necessity of song. Among the great country blues performers were Charley Patton and Robert Johnson, whom we discuss in more detail below.

neighborhoods of urban centers, particularly New York. Throughout the 1920s recording companies such as OKeh, Paramount, and Vocalion released numerous blues and blues-oriented vocal music.

Until the end of the 1920s at least, many great jazz musicians worked as accompanists for blues singers. Record companies called on cornetists such as Louis Armstrong and Joe Smith, pianists such as Fletcher Henderson

> Mamie Smith made the first significant vocal blues recording, "Crazy Blues," for OKeh/Phonola records in 1920. Within a few weeks, it sold more than 75,000 copies in Harlem alone and precipitated the blues craze and a demand for music by and for blacks.

Unfortunately, the earliest recordings of the blues were not made in any quantity until the 1920s. By then the country blues form had acquired the professional sound of the classic blues as heard in the works of such artists as the incomparable Bessie Smith. Many of the best-known blues performers from the 1920s got their start in vaudeville, where most of the blues singers were women. These performers often recorded with jazz musicians, although blues singers were soon to be differentiated from jazz singers as such. Still, through their recordings we can view the blues as the first jazz vocal style. One of the earliest of the notable blues singers to record was Ma Rainey, although she did not make the first blues record.

and James P. Johnson, and many others to make blues recordings. Later the *Dixieland* style adapted various blues vocal techniques. Certainly, the interaction between the instrumentalists and the singers on these early blues recordings brought to bear a significant blues influence on instrumental jazz.

> Ultimately, we can trace the story of the blues from its country origins in field hollers, spirituals, and folk ballads through the jook joints, circuses, minstrel shows, and vaudeville stages and finally to the center of U.S. songwriting in New York's Tin Pan Alley.

Ultimately, we can trace the story of the blues from its country origins in field hollers, spirituals, and folk ballads through the jook joints, circuses, minstrel shows, and vaudeville stages and finally to the center of U.S. songwriting in New York's *Tin Pan Alley*. No other artist more embodied the professional emergence of the blues than the composer and collector of several notable blues compositions, W. C. Handy.

Gertrude "Ma" Rainey (1886–1939) worked in minstrel shows with her husband, Will. She went on to record prolifically in the 1920s, often with jazz musicians rather than to her own accompaniment in the country blues manner. Compared with her protégée, Bessie Smith, Rainey was fairly limited in technique; her vocal lines were often quite similar to one another. Nonetheless, she bridged country blues and the classic blues with performances that were effective in their deeply felt honesty.

Mamie Smith made the first significant vocal blues recording, "Crazy Blues," for OKeh/Phonola records in 1920. Within a few weeks, it sold more than 75,000 copies in Harlem alone and precipitated the blues craze and a demand for music by and for blacks. *Variety* noted that "colored singers and playing artists are riding to fame and fortune with the current popular demand for 'blues' disk recordings."

These recordings, known as **race records**, targeted black audiences that had expanded in the black

W. C. Handy

As a youngster William Christopher Handy (1873–1958) was lucky to receive a solid education in his hometown of Florence, Alabama. He was at first discouraged from pursuing music by his father, a minister, who told him, "Son, … I'd rather see you in a hearse. I'd rather follow you to the graveyard than to hear that you had become a musician."[22] Nonetheless, music became Handy's overwhelming interest. He learned some formal music theory and soon was playing with various bands despite plans to attend college.

A **race record** was an early recording, usually of jazz or blues and typically performed by and marketed to African Americans.

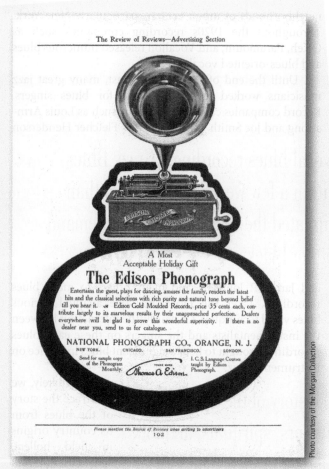

Edison first patented his phonograph in 1877 as an "Improvement in Speaking Machines" and later realized its advantages for music. In this advertisement from 1904, notice (at the base of the horn) the revolving metal cylinder that carried the recorded sound.

Handy's band work eventually took him to Memphis, where in 1909 he wrote the first genuine blues to be published, "Memphis Blues" (published 1912); he then followed its success with the most famous blues tune of all: "Saint Louis Blues" (1914). A key aspect of "Saint Louis Blues" is its section with a Latin rhythm, possibly derived from the habanera and related to the tango. Use of this rhythm recalls Handy's fascination with Cuban music and again underlines the significance of Caribbean influences in establishing jazz. Latin rhythms in general divide the beat into two even halves (rather than the uneven rhythm of swing).

After composing a third key blues tune, "Beale Street Blues," in 1916, Handy moved to New York with his Orchestra of Memphis and began promoting his music-publishing business, working to popularize the blues and devoting himself to the cause of black music and its recognition. Acknowledging the folk sources he drew on for his blues tunes, Handy eventually became known as the "father of the blues"—an overstatement but one that does

> Among the pioneers of country blues was Charley Patton, a singer and guitarist who played with a bottleneck slide— the glass neck of a liquor bottle run across the fret board to give a sliding or whining sound.

suggest his significance to the genre. He also recorded; among his early records were "The Snaky Blues" (1917) and "Livery Stable Blues" (1917)—the latter a cover of the hit by the Original Dixieland Jazz Band (see Chapter 2). With Handy's popular works, the various forms of the blues became standardized into the 12-bar format and as such provided an interesting contrast to the looser performance practices of the original country blues.

Blues Form

It is difficult to ascertain precisely how country blues influenced early jazz. Jazz evolved as a more instrumental music. Instruments such as the cornet, trombone, and clarinet preferred the "flat side" of the key range (that is, F, B♭, and E♭).

In a significant early job, he became a cornet soloist with Mahara's Minstrels in 1896, a group he would later direct.

It was with the Minstrels that Handy toured the country and became a professional. The Minstrels' trip to Havana in February 1900 dramatizes the connections between ragtime, the blues, and the music of the Caribbean. In his autobiography Handy writes, "The music of the island intrigued me. I never missed the concerts of the one-hundred-piece Havana Guards Band." Handy also sought out "the small, shy bands that played behind closed shutters on dark out of the way streets … These [bands] fascinated me because they were playing a strange native air, new and interesting to me. More than thirty years later I heard that rhythm again. By then it had acquired respectability in New York and had acquired a name—the Rumba."[23]

> "I'd rather follow you to the graveyard than to hear that you had become a musician."
> ~ Reverend Handy to his son W. C.

Country blues was more vocal. Its most common instrument was the guitar, and guitarists naturally preferred sharp keys, such as G, D, or A, which fit the open strings the *blues form* as a single 12-bar *chorus* with a strict basic harmonic progression.

Sometimes a verse introduces the chorus, much like the verse in a Tin Pan Alley song. As mentioned in the Introduction, because the lyric too follows a sharply defined format, each *a* and *b* phrase in *aab* blues form usually encompasses 4 of the 12 bars. This form is ideal for improvisation because the singer can think ahead for a rhyming third phrase during the repetition of the first. Adding to the ease of improvisation, each a and b phrase usually falls within the first two or three bars of each four-bar phrase. The concluding part of each phrase can be filled with a response from the instrumental accompaniment while the singer ponders the next phrase.

> (a) I was with you, ba-by, when you did not have a dime.
> (a) I was with you, ba-by, when you did not have a dime.
> (b) Now since you've got plenty mon-ey, you have brought your good gal down.

Pioneers of the Delta Blues

The Mississippi Delta was a particularly fertile area for growing cotton (thus supporting large plantations worked primarily by African Americans)—and creating blues music.

In the early twentieth century, several extremely talented performers surfaced in this region, each influencing the other. Thanks to the popularity of blues on records, we can hear many of these performers today.

Robert Johnson
"Cross Road Blues"
(1936-1937)

Among the pioneers was Charley Patton, a singer and guitarist who played with a bottleneck slide—the glass neck of a liquor bottle run across the fret board to give a sliding or whining sound. Patton's intense vocal style and original songs were widely copied.

A guitarist younger than Patton and more popular among blues revivalists and rock-and-roll musicians is Robert Johnson, one of the important Mississippi Delta blues artists. Born in 1911 in Hazlehurst, Mississippi, Johnson died in Greenwood, Mississippi in 1938. Legend surrounds Johnson not only because he died so young (at age 27), but also because so little is known about him. Reminiscences of him generally

Composer W. C. Handy published this 1916 edition of "Saint Louis Blues." Unlike most composers of the time, Handy retained copyright and started his own publishing company. Notice that the music hall performer (later, the recording artist) was invariably pictured on early sheet music. The cityscape in the background is St. Louis; notice the riverboat approaching the bridge. The large cube in the foreground is a bale of cotton among cotton plants.

of the instrument well. With such disparate preferences, how much or how often did these two genres interact during the formative years of jazz? *Exactly* how blues catalyzed the earliest forms of jazz and ragtime remains controversial and is not likely to be settled because all the forms were predominantly oral between about 1890 and 1910. The influence of blues, however, is clear.

> According to legend, Johnson met a large man at a crossroads, who showed him how to tune and play the guitar. The man was the devil, and as a result of their meeting Johnson became an outstanding musician but lost his soul.

Because folk musicians often perform very informally—simplifying the harmony, embellishing the melody, and freely interpolating extra bars—country blues exhibited great flexibility of form. Once we reach the classic blues of the 1920s, however, we can represent mention that he was very shy. He was said to have "made a pact with the devil" to learn to play the blues. According to legend, Johnson met a large man at a crossroads who showed him how to tune and play the guitar. The man was the devil, and as a result of their meeting Johnson became an outstanding musician but lost his soul.

Johnson composed many songs that have become rock favorites, including "Love in Vain" and "Crossroads." In the 1990s Johnson's complete recordings,

reissued on CD, sold more than a quarter million copies, much to the surprise of the music industry. Clearly, Johnson's music holds strong appeal for a new generation of listeners. (See the Listening Guide for Track 6, "Love in Vain.")

The Rolling Stones
"Love in Vain"

LISTENING GUIDE   Track 6
"Love in Vain"

Robert Johnson: "Love in Vain" (Johnson). Vocalion 4630. Dallas, TX, June 20, 1937. Johnson, guitar and vocal.

The Main Point   In "Love in Vain," we hear the power and affective sensibility that is at the heart of the blues. Although the aab form tells us enough of the story to sympathize with and understand Johnson's pain, he never lets his emotions get the better of him. Despite the bleak sadness of the final chorus, the song allows Johnson to work through his separation from Willie Mae.

An important attraction of Johnson's songs is their combination of concrete imagery with situational ambiguity. That quality may have been a reason why his songs were frequently taken up by rock artists, and it is a quality we can hear in "Love in Vain."

Particularly noticeable on Johnson's recordings is his skill in accompanying himself. Here he not only keeps the rhythm going with regular chords that articulate most of the beats, but also adds melodic answering figures without interrupting the regular beat.

Introduction—2 beats + 3 bars

0:00	Count this piece in a moderately slow four beats to the bar. Note that the piece begins with Johnson speaking to the recording engineer with a line that sounds like "I wanna go on with our next one myself." He begins to play his guitar introduction at 0:02. If you start counting "three, four" then "one" (the downbeat), as Johnson begins to play, you will be correctly oriented to the form when Johnson begins his first chorus.

1st chorus

0:13	"Love in Vain" begins with the lyric "And I followed her to the station with her suitcase in my hand." This line is the *a* line of the *aab* form.
0:22	As Johnson finishes the line, he answers it with a guitar figure. Johnson then repeats line *a* (0:24) but varies its melody.
0:30	The answering figure in the guitar is more extensive than the first figure and includes a dominant-tonic chord progression that appears throughout the song (0:32–0:33). The idea of answering the vocal lines with guitar figures continues through the performance.
0:35	The *b* line follows with "Well, it's hard to tell, it's hard to tell when all your love's in vain—all my love's in vain." The lyrical ambiguity here is compelling: just what is it that's hard to tell? Is it the reason she's leaving him? The repeat of the title lyric "all my love's in vain" is especially deft, as it sets up the second chorus of the tune during the final bars of the first chorus. This pattern of using the "love in vain" tag line continues through the performance of the different choruses.

2nd chorus

0:47 The second chorus continues the story with the train rolling up to the station. Notice the poignancy of the situation: he looks her in the eye but doesn't tell us how she reacts or if she says anything.

1:08 The *b* line answers the *a* line with emphases on the emotional words "lonesome" and the rhyme at the end of the line: "cry." The tag line "all my love's in vain" sums up the situation and ends the chorus.

3rd chorus

1:20 The story continues with the train leaving the station. Johnson notes two lights at the end of the train and equates the blue light to his "blues" and the red light to his "mind." The blue light may symbolize the power of the blues, helping to calm the red light of Johnson's mental turmoil. Because we cannot be sure, the ambiguity remains.

4th and final chorus

1:53 In the fourth and final chorus, Johnson turns to a kind of **scat singing** as a wordless cry, which he alternates with the woman's name, which we learn is Willie Mae. The performance ends with the summation of "all my love … 's in vain" with a pause for emphasis before the last two words.

 Listen to this music in an animated Active Listening Guide available at the text website.

Bessie Smith

In the early 1920s, before microphones, blues singers establishing their reputations needed volume and projection. Of all the fine blues singers of this period, the most beloved and probably most important was Bessie Smith (1894–1937). The richness and breadth of her tone are evident even on her oldest recordings.

Bessie Smith
"Lost Your Head Blues" (1926)

Ma Rainey's greatest protégée, Smith was a member of Rainey's Rabbit Foot Minstrels and frequently appeared in traveling vaudeville shows before embarking on a solo career. Her first blues recordings for Columbia, "Down-Hearted Blues" and "Gulf Coast Blues," were hits in 1923, but by the end of the decade her popularity waned as classic blues vocalists found themselves less in demand. Her star eclipsed, she began to work in minor musical shows that toured the country. She was on such a tour when she died in a car crash in Clarksdale, Mississippi. With Smith's work we can begin to detect the qualities that later differentiated the jazz, pop, and blues vocal idioms. (See the Listening Guide for Track 7, Bessie Smith's "Backwater Blues.")

Scat singing is a jazz vocal style in which the soloist improvises using made-up or "nonsense" syllables.

An elegant publicity portrait of Bessie Smith at about age thirty. Later images of Smith showed her dressed more flamboyantly, in keeping with her vocal power and musical standing as "empress of the blues."

Photo courtesy of the Morgan Collection

LISTENING GUIDE   Track 7
"Backwater Blues"

Bessie Smith and James P. Johnson: "Backwater Blues" (Smith). Columbia 14195-D. New York, February 17, 1927. Smith, vocal; Johnson, piano.

The Main Point   The form and the performance of this blues song could not be simpler, but the power of Bessie Smith's vocal expression is clear throughout. Johnson's accompaniment provides a steady and beautifully wrought commentary to Smith's story.

After a two-bar introduction, the song unfolds in seven choruses of aab 12-bar blues. As you did with the Johnson recording and with the help of the timing cues, you should practice counting 12-bar choruses, with four beats to the bar, to determine where each chorus begins and ends.

James P. Johnson was Bessie Smith's favorite accompanist. Their superb performance of "Backwater Blues" is one of their finest joint efforts.

Introduction—2 bars

0:00   Count this piece in a moderate four beats to the bar. Johnson provides a rolling introductory vamp before Smith comes in for her first chorus.

1st chorus

0:04   Smith's phrases generally fill the first two bars of each four-bar phrase. Johnson fills the remaining two bars. The first chorus sets the scene with its depiction of five days of rain in aab form.

2nd chorus

0:32   The song turns more personal. Note the despair of the line "Can't even get outta my door."

3rd chorus

1:00   The story continues with the description of the boat picking up Smith with her clothes to escape the flood.

4th chorus

1:28   A return to the nature description of the first chorus.

1:34   Note how Johnson's expressive bass answers Smith's phrases and helps depict the storm.

5th chorus

1:54   A return to the personal as Smith looks down on her flooded house.

6th chorus

2:21   "The blues" calls Smith to reflect on her loss.

7th chorus

2:49   Complete despair: Smith "can't move no more." Johnson ends the piece without a tag or any extra musical statement.

Listen to this music in an animated Active Listening Guide available at the text website.

Characteristics of Early Jazz Singing

In the performances of "Love in Vain" and "Backwater Blues," we can point to three features of blues vocal style that will remain characteristic of subsequent jazz singing:

▶ Loosely constructed phrasing

▶ Off-beat, syncopated placement of notes and lyrics

▶ Use of slides, blue notes, and other vocal embellishments

First, in jazz singing, the phrasing of the song must be loose. For example, sometimes the phrase may begin on the downbeat; at other times it may begin as a pickup, that is, at the end of the preceding bar. This practice of varying the placement of the phrase relative to the beat gives

> Of all the fine blues singers of this period, the most beloved and probably most important was Bessie Smith.

a free quality to the performance and contrasts with the on-the-beat feel of non-jazz singing. In later styles, beginning in the 1930s, such singers as Billie Holiday delayed the placement of the melody as much as a full bar. Slight delays and embellishments, as heard in Smith, are typical of twenties blues singing. The loose placement of the phrase has become an element heard in much popular-song singing in our own time.

Second, jazz and blues singing is characterized by the off-beat, syncopated placement of principal notes and their lyrics. Jazz singing epitomizes the freedom of loose phrasing allied with inventive syncopation.

Third, jazz and blues singers use slides, blue notes, and other melodic pitch inflections and ornaments. Although these features appear in all popular singing, they are especially prominent in the blues. In general, constant modification and the embellishment of various phrases play significant roles in distinguishing jazz and blues singing from pop singing, which is usually less ornamental.

With the popularization of the blues in the 1920s, composers began to write songs in the 12-bar blues style. Blues artists began to differentiate themselves from jazz artists, although connections between jazz and blues have remained and artists from each genre still frequently perform together.

Boogie-Woogie and Other Forms of the Blues

During the 1920s blues pianists of the South and the Southwest developed a driving style of piano playing that became extremely popular throughout the country. **Boogie-woogie** remains a pivotal jazz-related genre—a piano form of the blues based on propulsive, repeating bass figures that usually maintain regular eighth notes through each bar. The bass figures would repeat, usually every two, four, or eight beats. Music Example 1-4 shows a two-beat pattern and an eight-beat (or two-bar) pattern. Over these driving left-hand figures, the player would improvise blues choruses in the right hand.

Among the significant boogie-woogie pianists of the 1920s and 1930s were Jimmy Yancey (1898–1951) and Meade "Lux" Lewis (1905–1964). Lewis's "Honky Tonk Train Blues," recorded in 1927, was a powerful and influential exemplar of the style.

Meade "Lux" Lewis
"Honky Tonk Train Blues" (1927)

Such songs as "In the Mood" (Garland) and "One O'Clock Jump" (Basie) were in fact blues tunes with riffs based on the melodic figures of the boogie-woogie pianists. Later, in such songs as "Rock Around the Clock" (Freedman-DeKnight) and "Blue Suede Shoes" (Perkins), we can hear blues harmony, form, and phrasing. These

---

Boogie-woogie is a form of blues piano playing in which the performer maintains a driving eighth-note rhythm in the left hand while improvising blues figures in the right hand.

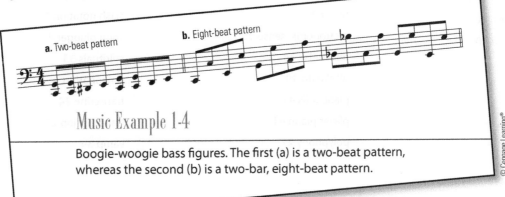

Music Example 1-4

Boogie-woogie bass figures. The first (a) is a two-beat pattern, whereas the second (b) is a two-bar, eight-beat pattern.

© Cengage Learning®

features of early rock and roll offer evidence of its evolution from the blues and R&B (rhythm and blues).

In addition to the standard 12-bar blues form, by far the most common in jazz, there are 8- and 16-bar forms whose harmonic structures are somewhat more unpredictable. Although modern composers have written blues tunes with highly irregular structures, much classic blues retains the simpler 12-bar, rhyming lyric structure.

With ragtime's popularity waning in the late teens and the blues thriving as a separate genre, the necessary conditions were in place for jazz to become the primary musical medium of popular culture. The next two chapters examine this breakthrough, which largely takes place during the late teens and 1920s and is fully completed by the 1930s.

Exam Review Questions

Use these questions and the materials on the text website to help you understand and pass tests on the content of this chapter.

1. How do the African and European musical traditions differ? Contrast both the musical and the cultural qualities.

2. In what ways was ragtime fresh and innovative?

3. What are some of the characteristics of the blues? How do these characteristics relate to the African tradition? How do the vocal styles of Robert Johnson and Bessie Smith differ?

4. What are the main differences between ragtime and the blues?

5. In what ways can ragtime be seen as a blend of the African and European traditions?

6. How did ragtime and the blues each contribute to the formation of early jazz?

7. Should ragtime be considered an early form of jazz or a distinct genre of music? Cite arguments for both positions.

 MindTap™

Test Yourself on Key Concepts with additional Chapter Quizzes and Listening Activities on the text website.

Key Terms

Test your knowledge of this chapter's key terms by defining the following. If you can't remember the meaning of a term, refresh your memory by looking up the boldfaced term in the chapter, turning to the Glossary at the back of the book, or working with the flashcards at the text website.

AABA song form **30**

ABAC song form **30**

arranger **31**

blue note **35**

blues **46**

boogie-woogie **53**

cakewalk **37**

call-and-response **26**

countermelody **30**

counterpoint **27**

cross-rhythms **27**

front line **29**

head arrangement **31**

meter **27**

metronomic sense **25**

minstrelsy **36**

obbligato **30**

piano rolls **41**

player piano **41**

polyphony **27**

polyrhythm **26**

race record **47**

ragtime **38**

rhythm section **29**

ring shout **27**

scat singing **51**

slash notation **31**

song plugger **43**

spirituals **33**

syncopation **26**

transcribe **24**

transcription **23**

vamp **34**

DAWN OF THE CENTURY

XX CENTURY.

MARCH & TWO STEP

BY E.T. PAULL.

PUBLISHED BY E.T.PAULL MUSIC Co. 46 WEST 28th ST.

PHILADELPHIA, PA.
M.D. SWISHER.

NEW YORK

LONDON, ENG.
W. PAXTON & Co.

CHICAGO, ILL.
F.J.A. FORSTER Co.

SPRINGFIELD, MASS.   PHILADELPHIA, PA.
A.H. GOETTING.   JOS. MORRIS.

NEW YORK.
CROWN MUSIC CO.

TORONTO, CAN.
CANADIAN-AMERICAN MUSIC CO. LTD.

NEW YORK.
NEW YORK MUSIC SUPPLY CO.

NEW YORK.
ENTERPRISE MUSIC CO.

BOSTON, MASS.
COUPON MUSIC CO.

Copyright. MDCCCC. By E.T. Paull

SOLO. 5

SIMP. 4

FOUR HANDS. 10

LITH.BY ANDEN & CO. RICHMOND VA.

A WAR SONG WITH THE SPIRIT OF '17
WE'LL HAVE PEACE ON EARTH AND EVEN IN BERLIN

WORDS BY
JAS. A. FLANIGAN
MUSIC BY
THOS. J. FLANAGAN

REFRAIN

Just a million strong, we're goin' to march along
To fight for Liberty
We'll play Yankee Doodle, on the Kaiser's noodle
When we reach Old Germany.
And the Sons of dear Old Glory
Have never failed to win.
And when the boys begin to shout
Kaiser Wilhelm this way out
We'll have peace on earth
And even in Berlin.

At the same time that jazz was developing, the United States, led by President Woodrow Wilson,
entered World War I (1914–1918) to "make the world safe for democracy." This sheet music
cover from 1917 captures the dominant artistic style and ardent patriotism of those years.

5

PUBLISHED BY
THE **THOMAS J. FLANAGAN MUSIC CO.**
SYRACUSE ———— NEW YORK

Early Jazz

IN THIS CHAPTER WE EXPLORE JAZZ AS IT BECAME A mainstream music in the late teens and early twenties, particularly in and around the cities of New Orleans and Chicago. Despite controversies surrounding the origins of jazz, which this chapter considers, the city of New Orleans figures prominently in any discussion of the music's early history. After we discuss the emergence of various jazz-based styles in New Orleans and other areas of the country, we consider changes in the use of instruments. Much of what made early jazz exciting was the innovative way players approached traditional instruments, producing effects that were considered tawdry by traditionalists but brilliant and creative by early jazz fans.

The Shift from Ragtime to Jazz

New Orleans is popularly considered the birthplace of jazz, but the entire picture is much more complex and has produced a significant and ongoing controversy among historians. Some contend that jazz crystallized in New Orleans; others argue that jazz-like styles were evolving throughout the country but that New Orleans musicians were the first to break through with the Dixieland style. Both positions are partially true. During the teens and twenties, in a decisive step toward the emergence of jazz, some prominent New Orleans musicians and therefore jazz styles moved to Chicago. But jazz styles also developed in other urban centers such as New York and Kansas City. In fact, jazz styles developed wherever musicians, encouraged by the spontaneous performance practices of ragtime and turn-of-the-century popular music, took jazzlike liberties.

For example, in his groundbreaking study *Early Jazz*, Gunther Schuller interviews George Morrison, an African American violinist who discusses playing jazz in Denver, Colorado, around 1920. Morrison mentions Benny Goodman (not the famous clarinetist), a musician who "was a violinist and he improvised just [as] I did on the violin.

1900–1917 Ragtime flourishing
—Jazz developing
1908 Cornetist Freddie Keppard forms band using the Dixieland combination
    1915 Billie Holiday born
    1917 New Orleans musicians begin leaving the city, many to settle in Chicago where New Orleans style
       flourishes
      —Original Dixieland Jazz Band (ODJB) records first jazz record, "Livery Stable Blues"
      —Dizzy Gillespie born
      —Thelonious Monk born
   1917–1930 Ragtime declining
      —Jazz flourishing
      1918 ODJB records "Tiger Rag" (Track 8)
      1919 Sidney Bechet receives glowing review from Ernest Ansermet
         1920 Charlie Parker born
         1920s Chicago jazz style develops
         1921 James P. Johnson records "Carolina Shout" (Track 14)
        —Sissle & Blake premier *Shuffle Along*, the first black Broadway musical
        1922 Louis Armstrong joins King Oliver's Creole Jazz Band in Chicago
        1923 Jelly Roll Morton makes first interracial recording with the New Orleans
           Rhythm Kings (NORK)
        —Jelly Roll Morton records "New Orleans Blues"
        —Ellington becomes established in New York
        —King Oliver's Creole Jazz Band records "Dippermouth Blues" (Track 9)
           1924 Bix Beiderbecke records "Jazz Me Blues" with the Wolverines

Jazz

| 1910 | 1920 | 1930 |

Historical Events

1910–1920 More than 65,000 blacks emigrate from the southern states to
      Chicago alone
1914 Outbreak of World War I
1915 Charlie Chaplin stars in *The Tramp*
   —Einstein devises general theory of relativity
1916–1919 Nearly half a million blacks moved north
  1917 United States enters World War I
    —Czar abdicates as Lenin and Bolsheviks seize power in Russia
    1918 End of World War I
      1919 Prohibition (18th Amendment) outlawing the sale of alcoholic
        beverages throughout the country enacted (repealed 1933)
      —League of Nations founded
      —Commercial airplane service begins, between London and Paris
        1920 Commercial radio broadcasting begins
          —19th Amendment giving women the right to vote is ratified
        1921 Pablo Picasso paints *Three Musicians*
        1922 Revolution in Italy brings Fascists to power
        —T. S. Eliot publishes "The Waste Land"
        —James Joyce publishes *Ulysses*
          1924 Stalin becomes Russian dictator
          1925 F. Scott Fitzgerald publishes *The Great Gatsby*
           —beginning of electrical recording
          1926 Ernest Hemingway publishes *The Sun Also Rises*
          1927 *The Jazz Singer*, first movie with sound, ushers in talking movies
           —Television transmission realized
           —Charles Lindbergh completes first solo flight across the Atlantic
           —Adolf Hitler publishes *Mein Kampf*
            1929 Stock market crash
              —William Faulkner publishes *The Sound and the Fury*
              1930 Penicillin discovered
                —Grant Wood paints *American
                  Gothic*
                —Cyclotron developed in United
                  States

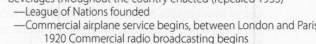
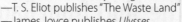

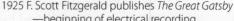
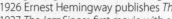
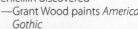

And we had piano players who improvised on the piano. That's what we did up in those mining towns."[1] This and other examples show that improvisation did not proceed from the New Orleans tradition alone. Thus, whereas some historians define early New Orleans style as the beginning of jazz, others define it as the first jazz style to achieve national prominence.

The origins of the word *jazz* are also murky. The word first appeared in print in 1913 in the baseball column of a San Francisco newspaper, where it seems to have meant "pep" or "energy." The word gained currency by 1917, especially after the first recording labeled as jazz (from the Original Dixieland Jazz Band, to be discussed shortly). Its variable spelling was noted by a writer for the *New York Sun* in 1917:

> Variously spelled Jas, Jass, Jaz, Jasz, and Jascz. The word is African in origin. It is common on the Gold Coast of Africa and in the hinterland of Cape Coast Castle.... Jazz is based on the savage musician's wonderful gift for progressive retarding and acceleration guided by his sense of "swing."[2]

In fact, the etymology of the word *jazz* is even more obscure than the writer suggests. Some have pointed to a French origin from the verb *jaser*, which means to chatter or gossip; others have said that the word is a synonym for sexual intercourse. It is unlikely that the origins of its name will ever be precisely determined.

Use of the term *jazz* was controversial when it was fairly new. In 1924 Meyer Davis, a radio broadcaster, held a contest to rename *jazz*; out of 70,000 suggestions, the winner was *syncopep*,[3] which obviously did not catch on. Other attempts to revise the name or concept also failed. Thus the term *jazz* remains with us today.

The boundaries between ragtime and jazz were considerably blurred between 1910 and 1920. A lack of agreement over the meanings of both terms added to the confusion. Historians such as Lawrence Gushee have suggested that their usage was regional. To the New Orleans musicians who were performing before 1920, jazz was nothing more than "just a fashionable, Northern name for

New Orleans instrumental ragtime."[4] For example, one of the leading early jazz saxophonists from New Orleans, Sidney Bechet, consistently used the term *ragtime* throughout his life to refer to the type of music he played.

Around 1920, musicians performed and wrote compositions that highlighted the ambiguity of the ragtime-to-jazz shift. Older New Orleans musicians played "jazz" based on the formal structure of ragtime. For example, many of Jelly Roll Morton's works, such as "King Porter Stomp" or "Grandpa's Spells," maintained a ragtime architecture: multiple 16-bar strains, with the trio (the C strain) modulating to the subdominant. Many of the works played by King Oliver's Creole Jazz Band, one of the first important New Orleans groups to record, also follow ragtime form. The stride pianists also maintained a close connection to the ragtime form and much of its performance practice (see Chapter 4).

In the early 1920s, musicians began moving away from the ragtime format. Instead of relying on multiple 16-bar strains, they took the popular songs that emerged from publishing houses, record companies, and musical theater and used them as vehicles for jazz—casting them primarily in a 32-bar AABA format. In addition, many of the New Orleans and Chicago musicians made the 12-bar blues a staple of the repertory. Jazz musicians such as Louis Armstrong and Fletcher Henderson accompanied blues singers on recordings as well. Lawrence Gushee summarizes these changes:

> Also obvious in the years after World War I was a shift from tunes with many articulated sections (several strains differing in character and often in key, along with introductions, transitions, interludes, codas) to the verse-chorus format, with the verse often disappearing in instrumental performance. The older pieces were routines that had to be played as such; the newer ones were repetitions of a chord progression that cried out for elaboration and enlivening through ingenious arrangement or solo extemporization.[5]

While improvisation thrived in urban areas throughout the country, jazz musicians from New Orleans were especially skilled in "elaboration" or "extemporization." At

The cover of the *Gem Dance Folio* from 1920 displays photographs of the composers of 1919's hit songs. Notice that jazz is in quotes, indicating that the word was not yet in common usage. Notice too that this cover is integrated by race and gender. Interestingly, we have forgotten the names of most of these composers, but not Clarence Williams (shown bottom right), an important pianist, composer, and music publisher.

the same time, these pioneers, both black and white, incorporated elements of the blues tradition in their treatment of ragtime forms. The kind of jazz played by the basic New Orleans jazz group became popularly

> The kind of jazz played by the basic New Orleans jazz group became popularly known as Dixieland jazz or Dixieland.

known as **Dixieland jazz** or **Dixieland**. It has the following characteristics:

▶ Typical instrumentation of cornet, clarinet, trombone, piano, banjo, and drums (string bass or tuba optional)

▶ The cornet, clarinet, and trombone as the *front line*

▶ Improvised ensemble sections, with the first cornet taking the lead and the other instruments providing countermelodies and accompaniments

▶ **Collective improvisation**, with the members of the front line often improvising their parts simultaneously.

▶ A driving 4/4 meter, with emphasis on the beat.

▶ A "hot" style, with exuberant performances by all the musicians.

▶ Simple rhythm-section parts with all the rhythm instruments articulating the beat.

The evolution of the standard Dixieland ensemble took place in New Orleans, and so it is probably more accurately described as New Orleans style. The next section describes the fertile musical environment of the Crescent City.

New Orleans

By all accounts music was omnipresent in New Orleans during the first two decades of the twentieth century. Anecdotes and remembrances by those who were there describe a constant flood of outdoor and indoor social events, nearly all of which required music. Groups such as the Eagle Band, the Magnolia Band, the Imperial Band, the Superior Band, and the Olympia Band supplied music for nighttime dancing and often performed on horse-drawn bandwagons during the day to advertise a dance that night. Sit-down orchestras such as John Robichaux's nine-piece band performed sophisticated schottisches and quadrilles for dancing.

The legendary red-light district of Storyville, the section of town set off for legalized prostitution in 1897, flourished until its closing by the U.S. Navy Department in 1917. Storyville's bordellos provided steady employment for pianists. The bars and sporting houses of "the District," as Storyville was known to musicians, hired dozens of bands. Clarinetist Louis "Big Eye" Nelson recalled that the four saloons on the corner of Iberville and Franklin had

---

Dixieland is a popular term for the jazz style that originated in New Orleans and flourished in the late 1910s and 1920s. The Dixieland jazz band often had a front line (of trumpet or cornet, trombone, and clarinet) accompanied by a rhythm section (of piano, guitar or banjo, bass, and drums). Also called **New Orleans jazz**.

Collective improvisation is the term often applied to the simultaneous improvising of the New Orleans (Dixieland) jazz ensemble. The term may also be used to describe free jazz performances that include simultaneous improvisation.

eight bands among them, and the saloons "changed bands like you change underclothes."[6]

Enshrined in the history of New Orleans jazz are the *brass bands*. They played for street parades, carnivals,

> "There were a lot of string trios around playing street corners, fish frys, lawn parties, and private parties. The piano players like Drag Nasty, Black Pete, Sore Dick, and Tony Jackson were playing the whorehouses."
> ~Pops Foster

Another participant, bassist Pops Foster, described the explosive musical activity in the city:

> There were always twenty-five or thirty bands going around New Orleans. There was all kinds of work for musicians from birthday parties to funerals. Out at the lake [Lake Pontchartrain] they had some bands in the day and others at night; Milneberg was really jumping. There were a lot of string trios around playing street corners, fish frys, lawn parties, and private parties. The piano players like Drag Nasty, Black Pete, Sore Dick, and Tony Jackson were playing the whorehouses. In the District there were the cabarets, Rece's, Fewclothes, Huntz & Nagels, and Billy Phillips who had the best bands. Some bands played dances in mild dairy stables and the bigger name ones played the dance halls like the Tuxedo

> The street brass bands provided the training ground for early jazz musicians: Joe Oliver was part of the Onward Brass Band, while Louis Armstrong was a member of the Tuxedo Brass Band.

> Dance Hall, Masonic Hall, Globes Hall, and the Funky Butt Hall. The bands played picnics out at the lake; they played excursions on the riverboats and for the trains. The restaurants like Galatoires on Dauphine Street had bands. On Chartres Street there was Jackson Square Gardens where they had two or three bands going. There were tonks like Real Tom Anderson's at Rampart and Canal, and Tom Anderson's Annex at Iberville and Basin Street. Out in the country, like Breakaway, Louisiana, or Bay St. Louis, Mississippi, you played dances, fairs, picnics, and barbecues. We had plenty of fun together and there was music everywhere.[7]

lawn parties, and picnics. Although they emerged out of the tradition of military march music performed by reading musicians, these bands altered this tradition in significant ways. Whereas many marches such as John Philip Sousa's "Washington Post March" were written in 6/8 time and performed as written, a tradition developed of "ragging" (syncopating) the marches, or performing them in a ragtime 2/4 meter and improvising. Edmond Hall, who began playing around 1915, stated that "in the very early days of brass bands, in the '90s and even before, the music was mostly written—I mean in the kind of band my father played in. As time went on, there was more improvising."[8] In all likelihood these early forms of improvisation consisted of ornamentation of the melodies and perhaps some basic countermelodies.

The influence of brass bands and early jazz dance bands was probably reciprocal. Historian William J. Schafer suggests that the brass band influenced jazz bands in three ways: repertory, instrumentation, and technique. More specifically, the roles of the instruments in the brass band, in which the cornet performs the melody, the clarinet plays piccolo-like elaborations, and the trombone provides an independent voice of harmony notes and glissandi, suggest an origin for the front line of Dixieland instrumentation.[9]

The jazz bands also probably influenced the brass bands. Brass bands most likely made their styles hotter

> "The jazz played after New Orleans funerals didn't show any lack of respect for the person being buried. It rather showed their people that we wanted them to be happy."
> ~Warren "Baby" Dodds

by adopting the improvised syncopated style of the dance bands. At any rate the relationship between jazz and brass bands is difficult to disentangle because many of the same

Creoles of Color were people of mixed black and white ancestry. Until the late nineteenth century, they enjoyed more freedom and were better educated than the general black population. Musicians from this group generally had classical training and could read musical scores.

---

musicians played for both groups. The street brass bands provided the training ground for early jazz musicians: Joe Oliver was part of the Onward Brass Band, while Louis Armstrong was a member of the Tuxedo Brass Band. Jelly Roll Morton, although better known as a pianist and a composer, claimed to have organized brass bands and to have played both trombone and drums.

In their role in New Orleans funerals, brass bands made a prominent contribution to jazz lore. New Orleans had numerous fraternal organizations—clubs, lodges, and benevolent associations—that would pay for the funerals of their members and provide a band to accompany the funeral procession to and from the burial site, which was often a mausoleum because underground burials were not permitted in the swampy Louisiana lowlands. Band members usually earned between $2 and $2.50 per funeral. Accompanying the casket on the way to the burial, the band played dirges. But when returning from the graveyard, the band would unmuffle the drum and launch into up-tempo, jazzlike popular compositions.

One of New Orleans's most renowned drummers, Warren "Baby" Dodds (1898–1959), described this tradition:

> Of course we played other numbers coming back from funerals. We'd play the same popular numbers that we used to play with dance bands. And the purpose was this: as the family and people went to the graveyard to bury one of their loved ones, we'd play a funeral march. It was pretty sad, and it put a feeling of weeping in their hearts and minds and when they left there we didn't want them to hear that going home. It became a tradition to play jazzy numbers going back to make the relatives and friends cast off their sadness. And the people along the streets used to dance to the music. I used to follow those parades myself, long before I ever thought of becoming a drummer. The jazz played after New Orleans funerals didn't show any lack of respect for the person being buried. It rather showed their people that we wanted them to be happy.[10]

How Did Jazz Arise in New Orleans?

Two general theories have arisen to explain the origins of jazz in New Orleans. The "uptown/downtown" theory holds that the mixing of uptown-dwelling black musicians with downtown-dwelling Creoles of Color created a catalyst for New Orleans jazz.

Creoles of Color were people of mixed black-and-white ancestry who throughout the nineteenth century enjoyed a privileged status over the blacks. These Creoles of Color (as distinguished from the Creoles who were

French-speaking people of white ancestry) formed a professional, skilled class and were usually well educated. Some Creoles of Color even owned slaves. Most of the Creoles of Color lived in downtown New Orleans in what is now known as the French Quarter. By comparison the blacks of New Orleans lived uptown above Canal Street and were primarily unskilled workers. Throughout the 1880s, however, the whites enacted increasingly restrictive legislation against the Creoles of Color and

> New Orleans jazz arose from the combination of the European musical tradition from the Creoles of Color and the African tradition from the black musicians.

gradually reduced their status. By 1894 the segregation code removed the final legal distinctions between Creoles of Color and blacks, and from that point on Creoles of Color were segregated along with blacks.

The "uptown/downtown" theory, then, maintains that jazz emerged after 1894 out of the musical chemistry between Creoles of Color and blacks. Although the musicians among the downtown Creoles of Color were conservatory trained in the European classical tradition, with many of them playing in the French opera orchestras of New Orleans, the uptown black musicians received far less musical training. Because the black musicians often did not read music, they relied on memorization and, significantly, improvisation. The Creoles of Color thus performed in a more refined, sophisticated style (sometimes called "sweet" or "dicty" by the musicians), whereas the black musicians played in a rougher, improvised style (called "hot" or "ratty"). *New Orleans jazz* arose from the combination of the European musical tradition from the Creoles of Color and the African tradition from the black musicians.

A second theory suggests that the rougher, improvised music gradually *replaced* that of the more refined style. According to this "generational" theory, an earlier generation of reading Creole musicians, such as clarinetists Lorenzo Tio and Alphonse Picou and trumpeter Manuel Perez, taught and were followed by a newer generation of musicians who played in a hotter style. The novelty of ragtime and the changes in social dance styles brought about a demand for this style, which evolved into jazz. As more jobs of this type became available for musicians, even the trained Creole musicians who could read music were forced reluctantly to switch to the more popular (and lucrative) style. Some Creole musicians born after the 1894 segregation laws, such as Sidney Bechet, were not primarily reading musicians and performed only in the rougher style.

Another layer of complexity in the development of New Orleans style is the continuing influence of Caribbean music. Jelly Roll Morton, whose work we discuss in Chapter 3, was quoted as saying, "In fact, if you can't manage to

> "If you can't manage to put tinges of Spanish in your tunes, you will never be able to get the right seasoning, I call it, for jazz."
> ~Jelly Roll Morton

put tinges of Spanish in your tunes, you will never be able to get the right seasoning, I call it, for jazz."[11]

The so-called *Spanish tinge* provided by Latin beats has always been part of the jazz tradition, as discussed in Chapter 1. But aside from jazz pieces with specific Latin rhythms, the syncopated patterns associated with early jazz may themselves have originated in the Caribbean. For example, musicologist Christopher Washburne identifies Caribbean *clave* rhythmic patterns in early jazz: "The frequency of these rhythms in early jazz suggests that the Caribbean influence was so tied to its developmental stages that the rhythms became part of the rhythmic foundation of jazz."[12] We return to the issue of Latin jazz when treating the music of the 1940s, the period in which it becomes especially prominent.

Buddy Bolden

Many of the New Orleans musicians attributed the genesis of the rougher, improvised style to a single person: black cornetist Charles "Buddy" Bolden. Bolden never recorded, but he may have had a considerable influence on the emerging jazz style. Baby Dodds, for instance, wistfully described the generational change between the older music readers and the younger improvisers of his time:

> Bolden cause all that.... He cause these younger Creoles, men like [Sidney] Bechet and [Freddie] Keppard, to have a different style altogether from the old heads like [Lorenzo] Tio and [Manuel] Perez. I don't know how they do it.... Can't tell you what's there on the paper, but just play the hell out of it.[13]

Bolden was born in 1877. A plasterer by trade (although he also owned a barbershop), he formed a band around 1895 that performed throughout New Orleans in the saloons of Storyville, in the dance halls, and in the parks. Said to be heard for several miles, the volume of Buddy Bolden's horn was legendary. Cornetist Peter Bocage claimed that Bolden "was powerful. Plenty of power. He had a good style in the blues and all that stuff."[14] By 1901 Bolden's band included cornet, clarinet, valve trombone, guitar, double bass, and drums. He developed as a player through the 1890s and achieved his greatest influence around 1905, leading a band that performed in

> Said to be heard for several miles, the volume of Buddy Bolden's horn was legendary.

numerous venues throughout New Orleans. Bolden was a heavy drinker, and his bouts of insanity led to his institutionalization in 1907. He died in a state institution in Jackson, Louisiana, in 1931.

Bolden's style of improvisation was based on "ragging" the melodies. As Wallace Collins noted, "He'd take

Buddy Bolden and his band, ca. 1900. *Standing left to right:* Jimmie Johnson, bass; Buddy Bolden, cornet; Willie Cornish, valve trombone; Frank Lewis, clarinet; *seated left to right:* Brock Mumford, guitar; Willie Warner, clarinet. This famous photograph has been the subject of controversy, with various writers claiming that some of the players are holding their instruments incorrectly. Musicians have been known to do this as a practical joke.

A **"lick"** or **formula** is a worked-out melodic idea that fits a common chord progression.

A **saxophone** is a single-reed instrument made of brass that is common in all jazz styles except New Orleans (*Dixieland*). The saxophone comes in many sizes and ranges. (Listen to Tracks 16–19 of the ⓐ Audio Primer to hear the four most common saxophones.)

one note [of the original] and put two or three to it."[15] This technique is similar to what clarinetist Alphonse Picou described when he said that the rising jazz style was made up of "additions to the bars—doubling up on notes—playing eight or sixteen for one."[16] Bolden was particularly remembered for playing the blues, and henceforth this folk idiom, imported from the Mississippi Delta, became a primary source for New Orleans musicians. Blues then became closely allied with jazz and the jazz repertory. Clarinetist Louis "Big Eye" Nelson even averred that blues "is what cause the fellows to start jazzing."[17]

Was Bolden the first New Orleans jazz musician, the first hot jazz cornetist? That is probably impossible to answer. Banjoist Johnny St. Cyr claimed that Bolden inserted the same "hot **lick**" in each of his compositions but that other bands, such as the Golden Rule Band, were playing in a hotter style. Clearly Bolden's six-piece band, along with his use of a ragged, improvised style and reli-

> In New Orleans style the lead cornet dominates while the other instruments play parts similar to accompaniments.

ance on the blues, strongly influenced an emerging New Orleans jazz style, instrumentation, and repertory. Even so, it was probably the next generation of musicians, those born around 1890, who solidified the New Orleans jazz style. According to Jelly Roll Morton, cornetist Freddie Keppard formed the "first Dixieland combination" in

The Evolution of the Jazz Band

Jazz ensembles evolved from different types of groups, including dance bands, brass bands, and string bands. As pointed out earlier, numerous ensembles featured three horns (usually trumpet, trombone, and clarinet) and three rhythm players (drums, bass/tuba, and a chordal instrument such as piano, banjo, or guitar). Naturally, there were exceptions. For example, King Oliver's Creole Jazz Band featured the two cornets of Joe "King" Oliver and Louis Armstrong. And even though we associate the tuba with the bass voice in early jazz, the string bass was also common because it blended better with the violins of the New Orleans string bands. We even see a string bass in the only extant picture of the Buddy Bolden group (see page 63). The tuba was useful for outdoor work, of course, but much jazz was performed indoors, in which the string bass was generally adequate and provided more-subtle support. The string bass gradually supplanted the tuba in jazz in the 1920s, rendering the latter instrument uncommon by the early 1930s.

By the end of the 1920s, some dance bands had as many as twelve or more players. **Saxophones** became common in these larger bands. In fact, the use of the saxophone in jazz in the late twenties was an adaptation of its presence in earlier dance bands.

Although earlier pre-jazz bands probably featured melodies played in unison, perhaps by clarinet and violin, the jazz style moved toward polyphonic improvisation in which the horns improvised simultaneously, creating an intricate web of rhythmic and melodic activity.

As defined in Chapter 1, *polyphony* describes distinct, simultaneous parts. Applying the term to the collective improvisation of the New Orleans ensemble, however, would be slightly inaccurate. Normally, *polyphony* refers to equally important parts or melodies, but in New Orleans style the lead cornet dominates the ensemble texture while the other instruments play parts similar to accompaniments.

The jazz ensemble frequently used the technique of *breaks*, in which the band stops and allows a soloist to play

> The jazz ensemble frequently used the technique of breaks, in which the band stops and allows a soloist to play alone … "Without breaks and without clean breaks and without beautiful ideas in breaks, you don't even need to think about doing anything else, you haven't got a jazz band and you can't play jazz."
> ~Jelly Roll Morton

1908 when Keppard rearranged his band, dropping violin, bass, and guitar and adding pianist Bud Christian to the already-present Dee Dee Chandler on drums, Edward Vincent on trombone, George Bacquet on clarinet, and Keppard on cornet.

alone in time. In his discussions of jazz, Jelly Roll Morton made it clear how fundamental breaks were: "Without breaks and without clean breaks and without beautiful ideas in breaks, you don't even need to think about doing anything else, you haven't got a jazz band and you can't play jazz."[18]

Breaks not only featured soloists but also provided textural relief from the busy sound of collective improvisation. As the soloists' improvisational prowess increased through the 1920s, collective improvisation became less frequent, especially in the highly competitive urban musical centers of Chicago and New York.

Early Jazz Instruments and Their Players

The development of the standard Dixieland ensemble—front line: cornet/trumpet, trombone, and clarinet; rhythm: piano/banjo/guitar, bass, and drums—was one of the key contributions of New Orleans jazz. Moreover, thanks to the talents of individual musicians, the role of each instrument grew and changed. The removal of the

> The development of the standard Dixieland ensemble—front line: cornet/trumpet, trombone, and clarinet; rhythm: piano/banjo/guitar, bass, and drums—was one of the key contributions of New Orleans jazz.

violin, which sometimes played in unison with the clarinet, allowed for the simultaneous improvisation of the front line. The piano could be used in indoor performances, but outdoor performances usually required a guitar or banjo. By about 1915 the banjo eclipsed the guitar as the accompanying string rhythm instrument.

Cornet

The **cornet** in early jazz bands usually carried the melody. In addition, the cornet adapted to jazz by incorporating techniques such as **glissandos**, "half-valve effects," and the use of a variety of **mutes** and stopping devices. How a player combined these effects helped define the specific attributes of that player's style. Although originally one of the primary jazz horns, the cornet was surpassed during the 1920s by its close relative, the *trumpet*.

Because the cornet was the principal lead instrument of the New Orleans style, many cornet players became bandleaders. For example, Manuel Perez (1871–1946) led the Onward Brass Band and the Imperial Orchestra from 1903 to 1930. He was known not as a hot player, but as a "military man [who] played on a Sousa kick" and "a great street-parade trumpet player."[19] Unfortunately, Perez and many of the other early players never recorded during the peak of their popularity.

Freddie Keppard (1890?–1933) was another notable player who went unrecorded during his prime performing years. Leader of the Olympia Orchestra around 1906,

---

The **cornet** is a medium-range brass instrument much like a trumpet but with a larger bore and hence a mellower sound. Heard mostly in New Orleans and Chicago jazz in the 1920s where, like the trumpet, it was a lead instrument.

A **glissando** is a technique whereby the notes are slurred directly from one to another, producing a continuous rise or fall in pitch.

Mutes are devices played in or over the bells of brass instruments to alter their tone. Different mutes create different kinds of effects, but a muted horn will usually be less brilliant than an "open" one. (Listen to Tracks 13–15, 23, and 24 of the ⓐ Audio Primer to hear examples of muted brass sounds.)

Insider's Guide to . . .

Early Jazz Performance Terms

A **break** occurs when the band stops playing for a short period of time—usually one or two bars—to feature a soloist. When the band or rhythm section punctuates beats, it is said to be playing in **stop time**. Often a band will play in stop time while the soloist improvises breaks during and between the band's chords. (Listen to Tracks 46 and 48 of the ⓐ Audio Primer to hear breaks and stop time.)

A **tag** is a short, coda-like section added to the end of a composition to give it closure.

Jazz performances would frequently build to an exciting, climactic chorus, usually performed by the entire ensemble, called a **shout chorus**. The shout chorus was often the final chorus of the performance, in which case it might also be called an **out-chorus**.

Staccato is the technique of playing short detached strikes on notes in a series. The opposite of staccato is **legato**, the technique of playing notes smoothly in a connected manner.

The **trombone** is a lower brass instrument that changes pitch by means of a slide. (There is also a less common valve trombone that works largely like a lower-pitched trumpet.) In New Orleans jazz, it typically provides countermelodies to the trumpet lead. It is also an important jazz solo instrument. (Listen to Tracks 22–25 of the Audio Primer to hear examples of trombone playing.)

Tailgate trombone refers to the New Orleans style of playing trombone with chromatic glissandos. The trombonist would play in the back—on the tailgate—of the New Orleans advertising wagons when the bands traveled during the day to advertise their upcoming dances. (Listen to Track 25 of the Audio Primer to hear an example of tailgate trombone.)

The **clarinet** is a single-reed woodwind instrument. (Listen to Tracks 20 and 21 of the Audio Primer to hear examples of the clarinet.)

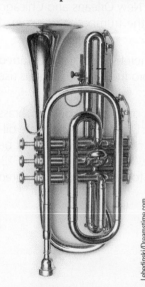

he was considered one of the best New Orleans cornetists. Mutt Carey claimed that Keppard had "New Orleans all sewed up."[20] He became established as a New Orleans musician between 1906 and 1914, then spent years on the road and performed in vaudeville. He finally settled in Chicago in the 1920s. Rumored to have turned down the opportunity to make the first jazz recording, Keppard eventually recorded in Chicago in 1926. By then his health was in decline, and his best playing lay behind him. Recordings such as his "Stockyards Strut" give evidence of crisp **staccato** playing strongly influenced by ragtime.

Buddy Petit (1897–1931) was another legendary player who, unlike Keppard, never recorded. Despite gigs with Jelly Roll Morton in California and a few other tours, he was primarily a New Orleans player who remained mostly in that area.

Trombone

The instrumental technique of the **trombone** underwent rapid developments through the end of the 1920s. Well suited to jazz phrasing, the instrument allowed the chromatic motion of blue notes and bent notes. In the traditional collective improvisational style of New Orleans,

the trombone would play countermelodies, bass pitches, and harmony, often sliding from one pitch to the next. The New Orleans style of playing with chromatic glissandos was known as **tailgate trombone**, a term possibly derived from the trombonist's position at the back—the tailgate—of the bandwagon driven around to advertise that evening's dance. Among the prominent early New Orleans trombonists were Edward "Kid" Ory (1890–1973) and Honore Dutrey (1894–1935). The latter's performance

Paylessima/Dreamstime.com

of "Snake Rag," recorded with King Oliver's Creole Jazz Band, provides a clear example of tailgate trombone playing. (Listen to Track 25 of the Audio Primer to hear examples of tailgate trombone.)

Clarinet

Although the earlier New Orleans Creole clarinetists Lorenzo Tio Sr. (1866–1920), Lorenzo Tio Jr. (1893–1933), and Alphonse Picou (1878–1961) were known as readers rather than improvisers, they taught many of the first generation of jazz clarinetists, including Sidney Bechet, Omer Simeon (1902–1959), Barney Bigard (1906–1980), and Albert Nicholas (1900–1973). These players developed a more blues-based style of playing that became part of the New Orleans tradition. Most of the musicians played the standard B♭ **clarinet**, although some players, such as George Lewis (1900–1968) preferred the E♭ soprano clarinet favored by some of the older clarinetists.

Two of the most important New Orleans clarinetists who moved to Chicago were Johnny Dodds (1892–1940) and Jimmie Noone (1895–1944). Dodds was part of King Oliver's band at the Lincoln Gardens. Dodds played and recorded not only with Oliver but also with many of the famous New Orleans players in Chicago, including Freddie Keppard, Louis Armstrong and Hot Five and Hot Seven, and Jelly Roll Morton. Although

© iStockphoto.com/Marc Miller

Lebedinski/Dreamstime.com

occasionally marred by technical flaws, Dodds's blues-inspired playing was highly emotional and characterized by a **vibrato** slightly below pitch. A more technically proficient player, Jimmie Noone had studied in New Orleans with Lorenzo Tio Jr. and probably Sidney Bechet; he then toured with Freddie Keppard's band. While in Chicago, Noone had also taken classical training with Franz Schoepp and developed a sound technique in every register of the instrument. He had a strong influence on later clarinetists; the great swing-era player Benny Goodman singled out Noone as an important predecessor. (Listen to Tracks 20 and 21 of the 🅟 Audio Primer to hear examples of the clarinet.)

Bass/Tuba

A bass instrument was commonly used in ragtime groups as early as the 1890s. In these groups players often doubled on tuba and string bass, using **tuba** for marching bands and **bass** for "sit-down" groups. Discographies often refer to a "brass bass"; this instrument could be a tuba, sousaphone, or helicon—the latter two being variations on the tuba. The only known photograph of Buddy Bolden's band (see page 63) shows the string bass player, Jimmie Johnson. Initially, the bass was bowed, not plucked, because the bowed bass was typical of New Orleans string bands. In general, the bass provided the basic harmonic accompaniment of roots and fifths of chords. The New Orleans bassists usually played on the first and third beats of the 4/4 meter but occasionally marked all four beats or used stop time. Note that a bass was not always used in the early bands; for example, in several King Oliver and Armstrong recordings, and in the recordings of the Original Dixieland Jazz Band, the piano and the banjo supply the bass notes. Although bass and tuba players were not featured prominently, some New Orleans players became well known, such as Wellman Braud (1891–1966), who eventually performed with Duke Ellington.

Guitar/Banjo

As with the bass, the **guitar** or **banjo** was primarily an accompanying rather than a solo instrument. The player usually strummed every four beats or else syncopated the meter by playing on beats 2 and 4 of the bar. Sometimes a more involved accompaniment (eighth-note triplets, for example) was played. One of the best-known New Orleans banjo guitarists was Johnny St. Cyr (1890–1966), who recorded with both Louis Armstrong and Jelly Roll Morton.

Drums

The **drum** set evolved when players organized a variety of marching-band instruments so that they could be played by a single, seated percussionist. Early on some players used a foot pedal with a drum almost twice the size of the bass drums used today. The *bass drum* marked the first and third beats of a 4/4 measure (sometimes all four beats), which coincided rhythmically with the bass or tuba. For sound effects, woodblocks and cowbells were attached to the bass drum. In addition there were *tom-toms, cymbals* controlled by a foot pedal, and a *snare drum*

© iStockphoto.com/Andresr

mounted on a stand directly in front the player. A suspended cymbal was used for highlighting and accents; a common ending of compositions involved quickly dampening this cymbal by grasping it with, usually, the left hand. The *hi-hat*—two parallel cymbals that closed by means

---

Vibrato is a method of varying the pitch frequency of a note, producing a wavering sound. A vibrato brings a note to life. Heard mostly on wind instruments, strings, and vocals.

The **tuba** is a low brass instrument that sometimes provided the bass part in New Orleans (*Dixieland*) and Chicago-style jazz.

The **bass** is a low-pitched stringed instrument and one of the members of the rhythm section in a jazz band. (Listen to Track 43 of the 🅟 Audio Primer to hear an acoustic bass.)

A **guitar** is a string instrument played as either a lead instrument (through picking) or a rhythm instrument (through chord strumming). It can be acoustic or amplified. (Listen to Tracks 36–42 of the 🅟 Audio Primer to hear examples of acoustic and electric guitars in different settings.)

A **banjo** is a stringed, strummed instrument that often provided the chords in New Orleans (*Dixieland*) and Chicago-style jazz.

Drums Backbone of the jazz rhythm section.

The **piano** is the principal Western keyboard instrument. In jazz it functions as a solo instrument and as part of the rhythm section (usually with bass and drums and sometimes added guitar or banjo).

of a foot pedal—was not used until the 1930s. Usually, a drummer used drumsticks, although such players as Zutty Singleton (1898–1975) recorded with brushes in the late 1920s. Singleton's accompaniment patterns often stressed the second and fourth beats on temple blocks or woodblocks. (Prior to the mid-twenties, drummers sometimes recorded with just woodblocks and cymbals because the vibrations of the bass drum could potentially knock the needle off its groove during acoustic recording.)

Ragtime drumming was often indebted to military patterns, and such patterns were taken over by the early jazz drummers. You can hear these techniques in early recordings by Antonio "Tony" Sbarbaro (1897–1969) with the Original Dixieland Jazz Band. In one technique known as "double drumming," the snare was placed at an angle to the bass drum so that the player could hit the bass drum first, then quickly hit the snare. In early jazz style, as typified by Baby Dodds and Zutty Singleton, the drummer often improvised patterns to correspond with the soloist, with beat divisions of eighth notes and triplets. (Listen to Tracks 26–35 of the 🅟 Audio Primer to hear different drums and cymbals.)

Piano

In a jazz band, the **piano** supplied an accompaniment, often consisting of bass notes and chords, which together provided a backup rhythm. Because it was self-contained, the piano also appeared in a wide range of other milieus, from the staid Victorian living room to the Storyville brothel. As such the piano—a one-person entertainment system—was perhaps the most important instrument of the early twentieth century.

© istockphoto/Rhienna Cutler

Many of the early jazz band pianists also worked as solo entertainers in bars, brothels, restaurants, and at New York *rent parties*, which we discuss in Chapter 4. So-called piano professors entertained the clientele and sometimes pimped for the women in brothels.

Among the many interesting and unsung pianists associated with the New Orleans tradition was Lil Hardin (1898–1971), who played with King Oliver (discussed shortly) and Louis Armstrong, whom she married in 1924. Although not remembered for her work as a solo pianist, Hardin occasionally showed herself to be a superb accompanist, as in the clarinet-piano duo with Johnny Dodds in Hardin's own composition "Sweet Lovin' Man." Hardin herself recalled that her role was not as a soloist:

> It wasn't the style during the King Oliver days for the pianist to play many solos.... Sometimes I'd get the urge to run up and down the piano and make a few runs and things, and Joe [Oliver] would turn around and look at me and say, "We have a clarinet in the band."[21]

The Exodus from New Orleans

During the late teens, many of the best New Orleans musicians began leaving the city. It has been traditionally thought that the 1917 closing of Storyville, the well-known red-light district, cut down employment opportunities for New Orleans musicians, causing their departure, but this factor has probably been overstated. In fact, many musicians left earlier. In 1914 the Original Creole Band, which included Freddie Keppard on cornet, Bill Johnson on bass, and George Bacquet on clarinet, played Los Angeles and for the next four years was booked on vaudeville

The exodus of New Orleans jazz musicians was part of a much larger trend known as the Great Migration. Nearly half a million blacks moved north between 1916 and 1919, the largest internal migration in the history of the United States.

circuits throughout the country. Similarly, Sidney Bechet first left New Orleans in 1914, playing "dances, shows, one-night stands, and dime stores all over Texas with pianist-composer Clarence Williams"[22] before moving on to Chicago, New York, and Paris. Jelly Roll Morton spent much time in California before moving to Chicago. Others stayed closer, departing the city for brief periods.

In 1901 John Streckfus launched the first riverboat designed exclusively for the excursion trade along the Mississippi River and its tributaries. Without cabins or staterooms for overnight passengers, these paddleboats, like the *Natchez* above, assigned the space to large dance floors and bandstands. Wintering in New Orleans and traveling north to St. Paul in the summer, excursion boats offered short trips of a day, an afternoon, or an evening to as many as 3,000 passengers who wanted to dine, dance, and travel on the river in opulent settings. A musician himself, Streckfus launched the first steamboat to employ a New Orleans band in 1911. The New Orleans bands that stayed in New Orleans rather than join the exodus and found regular employment— $35.00 a week in the 1920s—playing for dance excursions on the riverboats were the Sam Morgan Jazz Band, Oscar Celestin's Original Tuxedo Jazz Orchestra, and Ed Allen's Gold Whispering Band. The Morgan band was especially popular for its consistent dance tempo.

Players could work the midwestern towns up the Mississippi by playing on the riverboat lines.

Musicians were probably drawn away from New Orleans by the allure of the road or the steadier employment in bigger cities. Trombonist Kid Ory, whose New Orleans band had included many of the top musicians in the city (such as Louis Armstrong, King Oliver, Jimmie Noone, and Johnny Dodds), left for Los Angeles in 1919. (Ory's 1922 Los Angeles recording as the leader of Spikes' Seven Pods of Pepper was the first record cut by a black New Orleans band.) Additionally, white bands such as the Brown Brothers, the New Orleans Rhythm Kings, and

Chicago jazz was a type of New Orleans–style jazz created by Chicago musicians in the 1920s. It merged the group sound of New Orleans bands with the emerging improvisational style and solo emphasis pioneered by Louis Armstrong in the context of larger bands.

Toby Adamson/Photolibrary

the Original Dixieland Jazz Band caught the spotlight of national recognition after leaving New Orleans.

Chicago had the strongest pull. Joe Oliver moved to the city in 1918, bringing with him such first-rate New

> Kid Ory's 1922 Los Angeles recording as the leader of Spikes' Seven Pods of Pepper was the first record cut by a black New Orleans band.

Orleans musicians as trombonist Honore Dutrey, drummer Baby Dodds, and clarinetist Johnny Dodds. In 1922 Oliver sent for Louis Armstrong to come up from New Orleans to join the band; and in Chicago Oliver's Creole Jazz Band became the leading exponent of the New Orleans jazz tradition.

Other players who had left New Orleans earlier eventually migrated to Chicago. Freddie Keppard came through Chicago in 1918, and Kid Ory left Los Angeles to join King Oliver's Dixie Syncopators in 1924.

Many New Orleans musicians, of course, chose to stay in the Crescent City. Some, like cornetist Chris Kelly, never recorded. Kelly was legendary during the twenties for his blues playing and his rendition of "Careless Love," which, it was claimed, moved men to tears and women to tear off their clothes. Other musicians who remained did record. Oscar "Papa" Celestin and his Original Tuxedo Jazz Orchestra recorded on OKeh Records in 1925. Celestin's career lasted from 1910 until his death in 1954; his New Orleans bands included many of the finest musicians in the city, including Mutt Carey, Louis Armstrong, and Alphonse Picou. In 1927 Columbia recorded Sam Morgan's Jazz Band in New Orleans. Many of Morgan's musicians were born around 1890; because they never left the city, their recording preserves a New Orleans sound perhaps purer than those of players who made their mark outside New Orleans. Nevertheless, the two saxophones in the group indicate a change in instrumentation that was taking place throughout the twenties, and Morgan's loose-swinging group is aided by the virile four-to-the-bar bass playing of Sidney Brown. Throughout the twenties and thirties, New Orleans jazz was eclipsed by later developments that altered the musical style and instrumentation, although some of its repertory was retained.

The 1940s saw a revival of New Orleans jazz and the discovery (or rediscovery) of many of the original players. In conducting research for their 1939 book *Jazzmen*, Bill Russell and Fred Ramsey were directed by Louis Armstrong to trumpeter Bunk Johnson. Johnson had traveled and played throughout New Orleans during the first three decades of the century, but because of dental problems he had stopped performing in 1934 and worked as a field laborer. After his rediscovery Johnson recorded throughout the 1940s. He claimed that he had originally played with Buddy Bolden in 1895, but these claims have now been called into question because of a possible late birth date. With the New Orleans revival, several of the players present in New Orleans during the inception of jazz—including Jimmie Noone, Baby Dodds, and Sidney Bechet—enjoyed a "second career" of performing and recording.

New Orleans jazz is still played today. There are entire periodicals devoted to Dixieland, and numerous players specializing in the style continue to find work. In 1961, Preservation Hall was established in New Orleans to focus attention on the city's contributions to the founding of jazz. The Preservation Hall Jazz Band continues to tour worldwide and is probably the most prominent ensemble devoted to keeping the New Orleans tradition alive.

As mentioned earlier, the New Orleans style flourished in Chicago during the late teens and early twenties, when many New Orleans musicians relocated to the Windy City. Among the most famous were King Oliver and Louis Armstrong, both of whom had a major and lasting impact on jazz history. Many of the jazz musicians who acquired national recognition in Chicago during the 1920s were from New Orleans, but there were indigenous players from Chicago and the Midwest as well. Thus the evolving Dixieland style of the mid-twenties has been called **Chicago jazz**.

The Migration North

The exodus of New Orleans jazz musicians was part of a much larger trend known as the *Great Migration*, in which many blacks abandoned rural life in the South for urban life in the North. The most compelling reason behind the Great Migration was probably the availability of city jobs that paid a fair wage. For example, Henry Ford invented the automobile assembly line in 1914 and needed workers to build the first mass-produced automobile—his Model T Fords. He guaranteed $5 a day—an astonishing wage at the time. Other manufacturing industries also required manpower to meet production demands arising from U.S. participation in World War I. As a result of opportunities like these, nearly half a million blacks moved north between 1916 and 1919, the largest internal migration in the history of the United States.

Between 1910 and 1920, more than 65,000 blacks emigrated from the southern states of Louisiana, Mississippi, Alabama, Arkansas, and Texas to Chicago alone. Most northern cities developed black sections because whites refused to have blacks as neighbors. The presence of blacks and black neighborhoods changed the urban entertainment industry across the country. In Chicago, for example, the entertainment community responded enthusiastically to the resulting demand for black music: cabarets and nightclubs sprang up along the South Side and created a glittering urban nightlife full of music for listening and, especially, dancing.

The newly transplanted black population could spend an evening dancing, seeing floorshows, and hearing live music at any number of dance halls. Chicago's so-called *black-and-tan clubs* allowed more interracial mingling than did the clubs in New York. Whites could take in the nightlife, and—important to the development of Chicago

> Whites could take in the nightlife, and—important to the development of Chicago jazz—white musicians could hear the black bands.

jazz—white musicians could hear the black bands. South Side clubs such as the Elite #1 held up to 400 customers. According to one newspaper account, "The entertainers and the orchestra always hit it up pretty lively during evening hours."[23]

In 1914 the Dreamland Cafe opened with a capacity of 800 people. Even larger was the Royal Gardens Cafe, later renamed the Lincoln Gardens, on Thirty-first Street. This club, where King Oliver's Creole Jazz Band performed nightly, sported a huge spotlighted mirror ball suspended from the ceiling and reflecting glittering light over the dancers. Other clubs that hosted live music during the

1920s include the Plantation Cafe, allegedly controlled by the Capone syndicate, and the Sunset Cafe, just across the street from the Plantation.

The enactment in 1919 of the Prohibition Amendment to the Constitution, which outlawed the sale of alcoholic beverages throughout the country, in effect encouraged connections between nightlife and the underworld. Because Chicago was one of the principal centers of organized crime in the 1920s, Prohibition did little to curtail the nightlife or the consumption of alcohol in South Side bars and cabarets. Instead, organized crime expanded its smuggling and distribution networks to satisfy the demand for liquor. Despite alcohol's illegality, it was easily available in nightclubs, cabarets, and **speakeasies**, in which most of the jazz players of the time found ready employment.

The Roaring Twenties

In addition to Prohibition and the maturing of jazz, the 1920s was also a period in which postwar exuberance led to a rapidly climbing stock market. American industrial might, first glimpsed in World War I, assured the country

> The Jazz Singer, the first "talking" film, appeared in 1927.

a place among the major players in the world of nations. With Germany in economic chaos following the war, Adolf Hitler began his ten-year rise to power with the "Beer Hall Putsch" of 1923. Lindbergh's solo flight across the Atlantic Ocean in 1927 dramatized the airplane's ability to shrink the world. After the high-flying 1920s, the stock market crash of October 1929 dramatically ushered in the Great Depression years of the 1930s.

Hollywood continued its dramatic growth, particularly after *The Jazz Singer*, the first "talking" film, appeared in 1927. Electronic media began to dominate information technology as commercial radio broadcasting, begun in 1920, became an important source of music, news, and talk for many. The ubiquity of radios and phonographs by the end of the decade signaled recorded music's takeover of the commercial at-home market, beginning the slow demise of published sheet music and amateur live music performance.

A **speakeasy** was a Prohibition-era nightclub in which liquor was sold illegally.

In 1927, Warner Bros. produced the first "talkie," *The Jazz Singer*. Although hailed as the first full-length sound picture, it was actually a mostly silent film with Al Jolson song sequences. The first all-singing film was *Broadway Melody* (1929).

The influence of jazz extended to literature. Writers such as F. Scott Fitzgerald captured the feeling of the Jazz Age in fine stories and novels, particularly *The Great Gatsby* (1925). African American poet Langston Hughes was extremely interested in jazz, which he championed as an expression of authentic black culture, and he sought to depict jazz in poems that reflected the jazz life and the experience of the music. Meanwhile, modernism was exemplified by T. S. Eliot in *The Waste Land* and James Joyce in *Ulysses*, both from 1922.

The Chicago Jazz Scene in the Late 1910s and Early 1920s

Chicago's many performance opportunities attracted New Orleans musicians. Through extended engagements at cabarets and dance halls, they transplanted their music

to a much more sophisticated venue. No longer were the musicians playing for street parades, fish fries, and the small saloons and wooden dance halls of New Orleans. Abandoning the open-air, folksy quality of New Orleans

> The Juvenile Protection Agency urged that fast tempos would eliminate "immoral," slower dances like the toddle and the shimmy.

music, they adapted to the urbane musical professionalism of Chicago. The extended engagements and higher level of musical competition produced two important results:

▶ The creation of distinct ensembles with their own characteristic arrangements

▶ The development of individual, improvisational skill

The competition on the Chicago scene required a higher level of virtuosity from the players than before. Up-tempo compositions were expected. Banjoist St. Cyr recalled that "the Chicago bands played only fast tempo … the fastest numbers played by old New Orleans bands were slower than … the Chicago tempo."[24] In the push for moral respectability in Prohibition-era Chicago, organizations such as the Juvenile Protection Agency urged that fast tempos would eliminate "immoral," slower dances like the toddle and the shimmy. As such, even the more respectable **sweet** white dance orchestras cultivated brisk tempos.

The New Orleans musicians who had relocated in Chicago were among the first given the opportunity to record jazz. Because of the documentation of their music, we can hear what early **hot** jazz sounded like and get a sense of what excited its listeners in the late 1910s.

The Advent of Jazz Recording

Sound recordings began as a novelty and were not taken very seriously at first because their primary function in the late teens and early twenties was to publicize a band's live performances. As quality improved and dissemination broadened, however, recordings became a decisive step

---

Sweet bands played less syncopated, slower pieces, such as ballads and popular songs.

Hot bands featured faster tempos and dramatic solo and group performances, usually with more improvisation than sweet bands had.

Courtesy Albert Haim

A famous photograph, taken on February 18, 1924, of the Wolverines at the Gennett Records recording studio in Richmond, Indiana. Note the acoustic, bell-shaped horns centered on the rear wall; these would pick up the sound of the band playing and transfer it to the master 78 rpm recording. The engineer would achieve a recording balance by placing the band personnel at various distances from the acoustic horns. *Left to right:* Min Leibrook, Jimmy Hartwell, George Johnson, Bob Gillette, Vic Moore, Dick Voynow, Bix Beiderbecke, and Al Gandee.

toward national prominence for artists and the popularizing of their work. They also became the most important evidence for later historians trying to present a coherent story of jazz. Yet, because bands that were physically present near the recording centers of New York and Chicago would naturally have had the opportunity to record first, such recordings taken out of context may present historians with a distorted view of how early jazz crystallized.

Until 1925, recordings were made acoustically instead of electrically. Musicians played into a large horn with a tapered end that connected to a cutting stylus. This stylus cut a groove into wax that covered a disc or cylinder. With this somewhat crude process, sound reproduction is poor by modern standards, but we must be thankful for the recordings we have. Jazz was the first musical genre to be so documented in its entirety.

The placement of the musicians also affected recording balances. For example, louder instruments needed to be located farther away from the recording apparatus so as not to overpower the softer instruments. According to some sources, the drums had to be placed at a distance because their dynamic range upset the acoustic recording devices. The recordings of James Reese Europe, however, featured a reasonable drum sound as far back as 1914, and drums were recorded with considerable presence in 1919.

By 1925 the advent of electric recording had improved sound fidelity. This method used microphones to capture the sound. At the standard speed of 78 rpm (revolutions per minute), recordings were normally about three minutes long for each selection and remained so until long-playing records (LPs with 33 1/3 rpm) appeared in the late 1940s.

Changes from ragtime to jazz appeared on recordings beginning around 1914. James Reese Europe's Society Orchestra, based in New York, performed music influenced by ragtime. Europe's orchestra accompanied

the dance team of Irene and Vernon Castle, who demonstrated several new dances—the fox trot, tango, and maxixe. Europe's 1914 recordings feature ragtime numbers, often played with violin lead, that seem well planned and well worked out. By the time of Europe's 1919 recordings of the 369th Infantry ("Hell Fighters") Band, improvised

In early 1917 Victor Records released the first jazz record, a performance by the Original Dixieland Jazz Band (ODJB) led by cornetist Dominic James "Nick" LaRocca.

breaks within the multiple-strain compositions show the growing influence of the New Orleans style. (Recall Morton's comment about breaks being a defining quality of jazz.)

The ODJB and the First Jazz Recording

According to legend, cornetist Freddie Keppard was the first New Orleans jazz musician given the opportunity to record. He turned down the offer for fear that others would steal his music. Instead, in early 1917 Victor Records released as the first jazz record a performance by the Original Dixieland Jazz Band (ODJB) led by cornetist Dominic James "Nick" LaRocca. The ODJB recorded two pieces, "Livery Stable Blues" and "Dixie(land) Jass

Original Dixieland Jazz Band, "Dixie Jass Band One-Step" (1917)

Band One Step." The former included humorous barnyard effects, with clarinetist Larry Shields crowing and cornetist LaRocca imitating a horse's whinny. A white band from New Orleans, the ODJB achieved popularity performing at Schiller's Cafe in Chicago and Reisenweber's Restaurant in New York. The group, which included Shields, LaRocca, Tony Sbarbaro on drums, Eddie Edwards on trombone, and Henry Ragas on piano, brought the New Orleans style to national prominence. The brash and energetic barnyard effects of these pieces made jazz synonymous with novelty or slapstick music. The ODJB may also be the first band in U.S. history to generate the mass popularity that made its members stars.

After the ODJB's appearance at Reisenweber's, the band recorded prolifically through 1923 and helped

This 1911 advertisement for different models of the Victor-Victrola appeared in an issue of the *Literary Digest*, which tells us something about who Victor thought purchased phonographs. Inventor Emile Berliner used a 7-inch-diameter disc (rather than Edison's cylinder) and, together with Eldridge Johnson, formed the Victor Talking Machine Co., later to become RCA Victor with its famous *Nipper* logo. Notice the prices at a time when the average yearly income was $950 and consider how they compare with today's price of a smart phone.

The Original Dixieland Jazz Band (ODJB) formed in 1916 and published this song in 1921. Notice the jazz band instruments and the billing that ODJB gives itself: "Creators of Jazz." Sheet music promoted individuals or bands by featuring their publicity photographs.

spread the jazz craze outside the United States. We discuss in the following Listening Guide their 1918 recording of the "Tiger Rag." They appeared in London in 1919—even performing for the royal family—then afterward in Paris. During the mid-twenties the group broke up, but they tried a comeback in 1936. Although they made several recordings for Victor, they never fully reestablished themselves.

Original Dixieland Jazz Band, "Skeleton Jangle" (1918)

Part of the novelty of early jazz bands such as the ODJB rested with the public's perception of a performance built on completely spontaneous improvisation. Bands played up their inability to read music and increased the

LISTENING GUIDE   Track 8
"Tiger Rag"

Original Dixieland Jazz Band: "Tiger Rag" (LaRocca). Victor 18472. New York, March 25, 1918. Dominic James "Nick" LaRocca, cornet; Eddie "Daddy" Edwards, trombone; Lawrence "Larry" Shields, clarinet; Henry W. Ragas, piano; Antonio "Tony" Sbarbaro, drums.

The Main Point   Performed by the group that made the first jazz recording, "Tiger Rag" originated in the oral tradition of New Orleans music and became what is probably the most famous traditional jazz composition. Listen for the instruments of the early jazz band and how they interact in typical New Orleans style.

This ODJB recording of 1918 is one of the most famous of the early recordings and very much helped popularize the piece. (To highlight its continuity in the jazz tradition, this is the first of several performances of "Tiger Rag" on our recorded music program.) At the same time, it was one of the hit records that helped make the ODJB well known.

A strain—8 bars, repeated

0:00   Without introduction the piece begins right at the A strain for the opening eight-bar section. The instruments all play together, with the cornet taking the lead. The key is B♭ major.

0:08   Repeat of the eight-bar A strain.

B strain—8 bars

0:15   The second strain acts as a kind of bridge between the repeated A strain and the return of the A strain. This second strain is in stop time; that is, the accompanying instruments play short repeated chords behind the soloist. The clarinet offers glissandos during the breaks in the rhythm.

A strain—8 bars

0:23   Repeat of the A strain.

C strain—32 bars as C1 and C2

0:31   At the C strain, the music changes key. As is typical in rags, marches, and other music associated with traditional jazz, the music moves to the subdominant (IV, that is, E♭ major). The strain features clarinet breaks throughout and is divided into two equal 16-bar sections, C1 and C2.

0:46   Beginning of the second part of the C strain (C2), which is also 16 bars. In C2 the chord progression changes, but the music remains in the same key and finishes with a conclusive cadence.

D strain—32 bars, 1st chorus

1:01   The D strain is the most famous of the "Tiger Rag" sections. The music changes key again: this time to A♭ major, the subdominant of the preceding E♭ major. The strain divides into 16 + 16. The first time through the strain, all the instruments play together, but you may be able to hear Sbarbaro's extra syncopated hits to the woodblock. The end of the first 16-bar half is punctuated by a clarinet break.

1:17   Second half of the D strain.

D strain—32 bars, second chorus

1:31   The cornet and the trombone join in a repeated figure that provides a background to the more freewheeling clarinet riding above them. Again this first half ends with a clarinet break. The cornet-trombone figure anticipates the "Hold that tiger!" melody that will be featured in the third chorus.

1:47 The second half of the D strain. Toward the end of the strain, the trumpet and the trombone join the clarinet in a drive to the cadence as a conclusion to the chorus.

D strain—32 bars, 3rd chorus

2:02 For the D strain, third time, the trombone is featured with the famous lip glissando down to the low note (the tonic A♭) that initiates the chorus lyric ("Hold that tiger!"), which is played instrumentally by the cornet and the clarinet. Yet again the clarinet marks the halfway point of the chorus with a break.

2:18 The second half of the D strain. Toward the end of the strain, the trumpet and the trombone again join the clarinet in a drive to the cadence as a conclusion to the chorus.

D strain—32 bars, 4th (out-) chorus

2:33 For the out-chorus (or final chorus, also here a shout chorus), the band picks up the intensity and improvises together. The cornet begins with a repeated, syncopated three-note figure. The clarinet again marks the halfway point of the chorus with a break.

2:48 The second half of the out-chorus. At its conclusion a short tag is added.

 Listen to this music in an animated Active Listening Guide available at the text website.

mystique of the new genre. For example, LaRocca quipped, "I don't know how many pianists we tried before we found one who couldn't read music."[25] Despite the band's ostensible musical naiveté, they played repeated sections of compositions virtually note for note. A comparison of alternative versions of the same compositions reveals that the ODJB played the same arrangements consistently for years.

Even James Reese Europe's orchestra maintained a pose of musical illiteracy, despite the fact that they were all highly trained players. As William Howland Kenney points out:

> Orchestra leader James Reese Europe, in order to maintain the illusion of the "naturally gifted" black musician, would rehearse his band on stock arrangements, leave the scores behind, and, when taking requests for these thoroughly rehearsed tunes, ask customers to whistle a few bars, and then "confer" with the musicians "in order to work it out with the boys."[26]

In the early 1920s, numerous white bands in the tradition of the ODJB—such as the Louisiana Five, the Original New Orleans Jazz Band (with pianist Jimmy Durante), and the New Orleans Rhythm Kings (NORK)—issued recordings with the spirit and the instrumentation of the ODJB. Many of these sides helped establish the Dixieland repertory. "Tin Roof Blues," recorded by the NORK for Gennett Records on March 13, 1923,

is an early example of the excellence of some of these white groups. The rise of dance as a social craze augmented Dixieland's popularity and brought about a proliferation of jazz-influenced dance-band records by small groups as well as hotel-ballroom orchestras.

The year 1923, a seminal time for instrumental jazz recording, witnessed releases by King Oliver's Creole Jazz Band—the first recordings by a black New Orleans Jazz Band in Chicago. Gennett was setting out to enlarge its catalog of race records, and Oliver's band traveled from Chicago to Richmond, Indiana, to record nine numbers. (Drummer Baby Dodds later recalled that the band recorded all nine tunes in one day because none of them had a place to stay in Richmond.) In that same year, recording with the New Orleans Rhythm Kings, Jelly Roll Morton produced the first interracial jazz record. The band recorded several of Morton's own works, including "Wolverine Blues" and "Mr. Jelly Lord."

These early recordings led to the wide dissemination of jazz on an international scale and allowed musicians

King Oliver's Creole Jazz Band, "Snake Rag" (1923)

King Oliver's Creole Jazz Band, "Working Man Blues" (1923)

New Orleans Rhythm Kings, "Tin Roof Blues" (1923)

anywhere to imitate the solo and ensemble styles of New Orleans. Aspiring jazz musicians could now model themselves not only on local players but also on famous

These early recordings led to the wide dissemination of jazz on an international scale and allowed musicians anywhere to imitate the solo and ensemble styles of New Orleans.

players' recordings; as a result, records helped break down or weaken regional differences in jazz. Dispersed through phonograph players, jukeboxes, and eventually radio broadcasts, jazz became an international phenomenon. Throughout the 1920s the music evolved rapidly through both live performances and countless recordings.

King Oliver and the Creole Jazz Band

Known as "King" in New Orleans for his outstanding cornet playing, Joe Oliver arrived in Chicago in 1918 and brought the flourishing of New Orleans music there to a climax. In 1920 he put together his own band, which played in California before returning to Chicago in 1922, and began an extended engagement at the Lincoln Gardens in June. Billed as King Oliver's Creole Jazz Band, the group featured first-rank New Orleans players: Johnny Dodds on clarinet, his brother Baby Dodds on drums, Honore Dutrey on trombone, and Bill Johnson on double bass and banjo. The pianist, Lil Hardin, was from Memphis, Tennessee. Oliver augmented his group when he sent for cornetist Louis Armstrong a month into the Lincoln Gardens engagement.

The band recorded prodigiously—forty-three sides for the OKeh, Columbia, Gennett, and Paramount labels in 1923 alone. These recordings are some of the earliest and best works in the history of jazz. Some of Oliver's numbers were recorded more than once, either on the same recording date or at one of the later sessions. The band recorded "Snake Rag," "Working Man Blues," "Riverside Blues," three versions of "Mabel's Dream, "and "Dippermouth Blues" twice, one version of which we discuss in the Listening Guide for Track 9. These selections were mostly original compositions by Oliver, Armstrong, and Hardin but also included works by New Orleans musicians A. J. Piron and Alphonse Picou. The group also recorded such New Orleans **standards** as "High Society," originally made famous by Picou's clarinet performance of the florid piccolo part in the trio section.

Oliver's fine personal performances greatly influenced the jazz cornet style of the times. He altered the sound of his instrument with mutes, often creating a wah-wah effect. In addition to mutes, he used cups and glasses to change the horn's tone. When Armstrong joined them, the group became renowned for the breaks that both cornetists seemingly improvised. According to a famous anecdote, Oliver in fact would silently finger the upcoming break so Armstrong could play along with him "spontaneously." "Snake Rag" features perhaps the best of these two-cornet breaks.

The group performed in a tightly knit fashion, with collective improvisation among the melody instruments. They recorded a roughly even number of fast three-strain rag-format compositions, medium popular songs with a verse/chorus form, and slow blues tunes. Lawrence Gushee found that Oliver's group played in three principal tempos, reflecting these three compositional types:[27]

▶ Fast/ragtime tempo at about 196–212 beats per minute

▶ Medium/pop-song tempo at about 144–180 beats per minute

▶ Slow/blues tempo at about 108–128 beats per minute

The recordings are probably at best only an approximation of the group's live performances. For example, Baby Dodds was required to keep time on woodblocks instead of playing his usual drums. Certainly the roughly three-minute length of the recordings did little to capture the group's live sound—one listener described a live performance of "High Society" that ran to forty minutes! Although such reports are likely exaggerated, the band's live improvisations must have lasted longer than what we

According to a famous anecdote, Oliver in fact would silently finger the upcoming break so Armstrong could play along with him "spontaneously."

hear on their recordings. It is unfortunate that we cannot hear precisely how they did it.

Reviewing "Dippermouth Blues," we find that the following New Orleans characteristics are evident:

▶ Typical instrumentation of cornet(s), clarinet, trombone, piano, banjo, and drums

Unlike the vast majority of popular music, a **standard** outlasts its contemporaries and enjoys a long-lasting place in current repertories. "I Got Rhythm," for example, is a standard written by George and Ira Gershwin in 1930.

LISTENING GUIDE

Track 9

"Dippermouth Blues"

King Oliver's Creole Jazz Band: "Dippermouth Blues" (Oliver). Gennett 5123. Richmond, Indiana, April 6, 1923. Joe "King" Oliver, leader and cornet; Louis Armstrong, cornet; Johnny Dodds, clarinet; Honore Dutrey, trombone; Lil Hardin, piano; Bill Johnson, banjo and vocal break; Warren "Baby" Dodds, drums.

The Main Point   "Dippermouth Blues" is one of King Oliver's finest recordings. As in the "Tiger Rag" performance by the Original Dixieland Jazz Band, the instruments perform in the contrapuntal style that typifies New Orleans jazz. It also features what is probably King Oliver's most influential cornet solo, copied by many cornet and trumpet players throughout the 1920s. At the beginning of the first chorus of this solo (1:22), notice the use of the blue third and the tonic in a motive reminiscent of an early jazz source, the field holler.

The New Orleans style is apt to sound cluttered, even a little chaotic at first, because of the thickness of the sound and the exuberance of its hot style. After several listenings, however, the three or four lead instrumental parts of the ensemble grow clearer and their distinct functions within the dense texture begin to separate.

When the entire New Orleans ensemble plays, the cornet carries the main melody. In Oliver's band, Louis Armstrong (playing second cornet) either harmonized the lead or added a **countermelody**—a separate line that runs in counterpoint to the main melody. The trombone played a countermelody below the cornets, much like a melodic bass line, while the clarinet played an obbligato above the cornets. The obbligato, usually containing more notes than the cornet parts, was often quite virtuosic. The rhythm section in Oliver's band consisted of piano, banjo, and drums. In "Dippermouth Blues" the entire performance is structured as a series of 12-bar blues choruses that are arranged for various combinations of instruments.

Introduction

0:00   "Dippermouth Blues" begins with a four-bar introduction. The lead instruments all play an introductory figure together.

Ensemble—1st 2 choruses

0:05   After a short pause, the main body of the piece begins. The rhythm section initiates a driving, on-the-beat pattern. Both the first and second choruses are played in classic New Orleans fashion: the horns' functions are separated as described above, while the rhythm-section parts are accompanimental.

0:20   The second chorus begins.

Clarinet solo—2 choruses

0:35   The clarinet solo plays two choruses in stop time; the rhythm instruments and the accompanying horns play a simple figure to accompany the soloist. The stop time figure heard in "Dippermouth Blues" consists of repeated groups of three chords, one on each beat, with a pause on the fourth beat.

0:51   The second chorus begins.

Ensemble—1 chorus

1:07   The entire ensemble plays a single chorus.

King Oliver cornet solo—3 choruses

1:22   Oliver's famous three-chorus solo follows, accompanied by the other instruments in rhythm, not stop time as was heard during the clarinet solo. Oliver builds his solo very slowly through the three choruses. His use of a mute on his cornet gives the sound a wah-wah effect. The inclusion of the other horns during Oliver's improvisation typifies early New Orleans style, where at times all the instruments continue playing through the entire performance, even the solos. (In later small-group jazz, the horns usually lay out during each other's solo, except for occasional additional riffs.)

In Oliver's first chorus, he states a basic, syncopated motive made up of the blue third (E♭) and the tonic (C). A comparison between this motive and an early field holler might show the influence of black folk music on jazz.

1:37   At Oliver's second chorus, he extends the motive to include a higher G.

1:52   For the climactic third chorus, he further extends the motive from G to include a high A. The systematic development of the motive through the three choruses is logical and emotionally satisfying.

Ensemble—Final chorus

2:08   During this final ensemble chorus, the drummer plays more heavily, increasing the feeling of drive.

2:23   The group adds a tag—a final two bars—to this final chorus.

 Listen to this music in an animated Active Listening Guide available at the text website.

▶ Improvised ensemble sections, with the first cornet on the lead melody and the other instruments providing countermelodies

▶ Hot style, with exuberant performances by all the musicians

▶ Driving 4/4 meter, with emphasis on the beat

▶ Simple rhythm-section parts, with all the rhythm instruments articulating the beat

Through its recordings and live performances, King Oliver's Creole Jazz Band was profoundly influential, with a highly integrated ensemble sound that was more than the sum of its parts. Hoping to become jazz musicians, white teenagers were sometimes permitted into the clubs and became infatuated by the level of musicianship. Banjoist Eddie Condon attested to the powerful influence of the band when he and cornetist Jimmy McPartland heard them at the Lincoln Gardens:

> Oliver and Louis [Armstrong] would roll on and on, piling up choruses, with the rhythm section building the beat until the whole thing got inside your head and blew your brains out.... McPartland and I were immobilized; the music poured into us like daylight running down a dark hole.[28]

A **countermelody** is a separate line that runs in counterpoint to the main melody.

Joe "King" Oliver and his Creole Jazz Band pose in their studio in Chicago ca. 1922. The band, which had a life span of just four years, was one of the most influential early jazz bands, and it became the launching pad for Louis Armstrong's brilliant career. *Left to right:* Johnny Dodds, clarinet; Baby Dodds, drums; Honore Dutrey, trombone; Louis Armstrong, second cornet; Joe Oliver, lead cornet; Lil Hardin, piano; and Bill Johnson, banjo.

Bettmann/Corbis

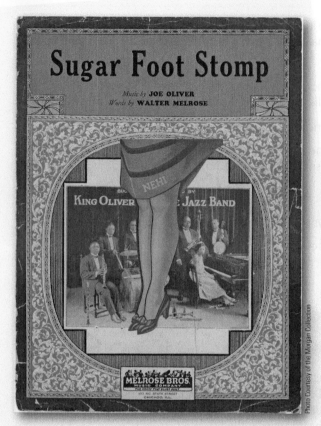

Photo Courtesy of the Morgan Collection

Published in 1926 in Chicago, this sheet music for Joe Oliver's "Sugar Foot Stomp" performed by King Oliver's Creole Jazz Band advertises Nehi stockings for women. Using the same daguerreotype as the previous studio portrait, but with the advertisement obscuring two members of the band—one of them, the young Louis Armstrong—this image may represent the one and only time that Lil Hardin upstaged her famous husband.

The degree to which Oliver's band kept intact a "pure" New Orleans style of playing is controversial. Although

> "Oliver and Louis [Armstrong] would roll on and on, piling up choruses, with the rhythm section building the beat until the whole thing got inside your head and blew your brains out."
> ~Eddie Condon

many considered the Creole Jazz Band the leading exponent of New Orleans–style jazz, at least one observer suggested that Oliver's playing had altered by adapting to the more refined requirements Jof Chicago audiences. Edmond Souchon, a guitarist and writer on New Orleans jazz, had heard Oliver play both in New Orleans and later in Chicago.

After hearing Oliver's band in 1924, Souchon noted a change:

> He was now "King," the most important personage in the jazz world, surrounded by his own handpicked galaxy of sidemen.... By the time Oliver had reached Chicago and the peak of his popularity, his sound was not the same. It was a different band, a different and more polished Oliver, an Oliver who had completely lost his New Orleans sound.[29]

Although Souchon's opinion can be questioned, it seems reasonable that Oliver's style evolved to some extent while he worked in Chicago. Moreover, Souchon may have heard Oliver late in 1924, after the departure of the entire Creole Jazz Band. Bill Johnson, Dutrey, and the Dodds brothers had already left the previous year, and Louis Armstrong and Lil Hardin left in the middle of 1924. Most likely, Souchon was describing Oliver's performance with a group later to be called the Dixie Syncopators, a ten-piece band with a reed section of two to three saxophones and arrangements that reflected a smoother and more refined commercial dance-band sound. The group, also called the Savannah Syncopators, included several New Orleans veterans—Kid Ory, Barney Bigard, Albert Nicholas, Paul Barbarin, and Bud Scott—but its sound and its style were more modern overall than that of the earlier Oliver group. The band's version of "Sugar Foot Stomp," recorded in 1926 for the Vocalion label, was in fact a remake of "Dippermouth Blues." Thus the late-1920s recordings of King Oliver show the trend toward more-arranged jazz, which progressed through the decade.

The Syncopators held the gig at the Plantation Cafe until the club was bombed in 1927, a victim of gangland violence. After a two-week stint at the Savoy in New York, the band broke up, but Oliver remained in the city. Ailing with gum problems that affected his playing, he continued to record and play as a leader, but his final recording took place on February 18, 1931. Despite his success in Chicago during the 1920s, Oliver's popularity had waned. After touring with a ten- and eleven-piece band for the next five years, he worked as a pool hall janitor in Savannah, Georgia, and died there of a stroke in 1938.

The Evolution of Improvisation

When listening to jazz in our own day, the audience often (rightly) assumes that spontaneous inspiration guides the players in their solos so that what they play varies even if the same song or arrangement is performed. It is important to distinguish this later conception of jazz improvising from what occurred in early jazz. Listening to alternate takes of early jazz recordings confirms that "improvised" solos were in fact often worked out and repeated from take to take. Soloists most likely duplicated their efforts in live performance as well. Nonetheless, as the twenties proceeded, the hot style that helped differentiate early jazz from ragtime became improvisationally freer.

The 1920s also show a general shift from melodic to harmonic improvisation. At the beginning of the decade, so-called improvised solos sometimes adhered to the melody of the composition, embellishing it occasionally. By the end of the decade, soloists were developing improvisational methods that reflected the harmonic framework of the composition.

Chicago became a hotbed of jazz thanks to the regular performances of New Orleans groups like King Oliver's. Jelly Roll Morton, another transplanted New Orleans native, also achieved his biggest success in Chicago. But despite the great popularity of the New Orleans style, collective improvisation was rapidly becoming passé as innovators claimed attention. The most important of these was Oliver's former student, Louis Armstrong. He in turn influenced a group of young, white, midwestern jazz fans who converged on the city. One of them, Bix Beiderbecke, was a cornet player with a distinctive, bell-like tone that would help him become a jazz legend. We examine Morton, an important soloist and the first important jazz composer-arranger;

saxophonist Sidney Bechet, possibly the first jazz musician to be recognized as first-rate by the musical establishment; and Armstrong and Beiderbecke, the most important jazz cornet players of the 1920s, in the next chapter.

> The development of individual soloists and their improvisational expertise gradually shifted the focus away from collective improvisation to jazz that heightened the importance of the individual player.

The development of individual soloists and their improvisational expertise gradually shifted the focus away from collective improvisation and the ensemble to jazz that heightened the importance of the individual player. As jazz historian Martin Williams wrote, this made jazz "a soloist's art."[30]

Exam Review Questions

Use these questions and the materials on the text website to help you understand and pass tests on the content of this chapter.

1. Was jazz born in New Orleans, or was the New Orleans style the first jazz style to capture wide attention?

2. Compare and contrast the two theories regarding Creole participation in the creation of the New Orleans style.

3. Describe the makeup of the Dixieland jazz ensemble. What are the roles of the different instruments?

4. In what ways can Chicago be considered the center of jazz in the early 1920s? What was Chicago's relationship to New Orleans?

5. What are the key stylistic components of the early New Orleans jazz ensemble as typified by King Oliver's Creole Jazz Band? Discuss instrumentation, repertory, and the role of each instrument within the ensemble.

 **MindTap**

Test Yourself on Key Concepts with additional Chapter Quizzes and Listening Activities on the text website.

Key Terms

Test your knowledge of this chapter's key terms by defining the following. If you can't remember the meaning of a term, refresh your memory by looking up the boldfaced term in the chapter, turning to the Glossary at the back of the book, or working with the flashcards at the text website.

banjo 67

bass 67

break 65

Chicago jazz 70

clarinet 66

collective improvisation 60

cornet 65

countermelody 78

Creoles of Color 62

Dixieland 60

drums 67

formula 64

glissando 65

guitar 67

hot bands 72

legato 66

lick 64

mute 65

New Orleans jazz 60

out-chorus 65

piano 68

saxophone 64

shout chorus 65

speakeasy 71

staccato 66

standard 77

stop time 65

sweet bands 72

tag 65

tailgate trombone 66

trombone 66

tuba 67

vibrato 67

Louis Armstrong
AND HIS CONCERT GROUP

SATCHMO THE GREAT

The ebullient Louis Armstrong. A great entertainer who appeared in nearly fifty films. Armstrong remains among the two or three most significant jazz artists ever. "Satchmo" was one of Armstrong's nicknames, coined in 1932 by a magazine editor during Armstrong's first trip to Europe. It was a shortened version of "Satchelmouth," an earlier nickname of Armstrong's that referred to the size of his mouth. When Armstrong toured for the State Department later in his career, he was nicknamed "Ambassador Satch."

Morton, Bechet, Armstrong, and Beiderbecke

3

Start with a quick warm-up activity.

IN THIS CHAPTER WE EXAMINE THE LIVES AND WORKS of four of the most acclaimed jazz musicians of the 1920s: Jelly Roll Morton, Sidney Bechet, Louis Armstrong, and Bix Beiderbecke. Although Armstrong was fortunate to have a long career, honored as one of the greatest and most influential of all jazz musicians, the careers of Morton and Beiderbecke were briefer and represent promise not entirely fulfilled. In particular, Beiderbecke's sad death at age twenty-eight helped spark his legendary status, whereas Morton was largely unsuccessful during the last decade of his life. Bechet was honored greatly in his lifetime and, working with many top musicians and groups, made many superb recordings. Unfortunately, he was never part of an ensemble that remained active long enough to enable him to create a body of work with a distinctive identity.

Jelly Roll Morton

One of the most influential New Orleans musicians of the 1920s was both a fine pianist and the first important composer-arranger in jazz: Ferdinand Joseph "Jelly Roll" Morton (1890–1941). A pool hustler, braggart, and ladies' man, he often made his living

A fine pianist, "Jelly Roll" Morton was the first important composer-arranger in jazz.

from gambling and pimping, which were far more lucrative than playing the piano. He was also a Creole of Color (discussed in Chapter 2) with a mixed ethnic background that included both black and white culture.

1919 Sidney Bechet receives glowing review from Ernest Ansermet
1920 Charlie Parker born
1920s Chicago jazz style develops
1921 James P. Johnson records "Carolina Shout" (Track 14)
—Sissle & Blake premier *Shuffle Along*, the first black musical on Broadway
1922 Louis Armstrong joins King Oliver's Creole Jazz Band in Chicago
1923 Jelly Roll Morton makes first interracial recording with the New Orleans Rhythm Kings (NORK)
—Jelly Roll Morton records "New Orleans Blues"
—Ellington becomes established in New York
—King Oliver's Creole Jazz Band records "Dippermouth Blues" (Track 9)
1924 Bix Beiderbecke records "Jazz Me Blues" with the Wolverines
—Armstrong joins Fletcher Henderson band in New York
—Bud Powell born
1925 Bechet & Armstrong record "Cake Walking Babies (from Home)" with Clarence Williams's Blue Five (Track 11)
—Fletcher Henderson records "Sugarfoot Stomp"
—Louis Armstrong records "Heebie Jeebies"
1926 Jelly Roll Morton records "Grandpa's Spells" (Track 10)
—John Coltrane born
—Miles Davis born
1927 Trumbauer and Beiderbecke record "Singin' the Blues" (Track 13)
—Ellington at the Cotton Club
—Ellington records "East St. Louis Toodle-Oo" (Track 16)
1928 Louis Armstrong & His Hot Five record "West End Blues" (Track 12)
1929 Fats Waller records "Handful of Keys"
1930 Ellington has first hit
—Ornette Coleman born

Jazz

1910   1920   1930

Historical Events

1910–1920 Out of 500,000 blacks emigrating north, more than 65,000 settle in Chicago
1919 Prohibition (18th Amendment) outlawing the sale of alcoholic beverages throughout the country enacted (repealed 1933)
—Commercial airplane service begins, between London and Paris
1920 Commercial radio broadcasting begins
—19th Amendment giving women the right to vote is ratified
1921 Pablo Picasso paints *Three Musicians*
1922 Revolution in Italy bring Fascist Party to power
—T. S. Eliot publishes "The Waste Land"
—James Joyce publishes *Ulysses*
1924 Stalin becomes Russian dictator
1925 F. Scott Fitzgerald publishes *The Great Gatsby*
—beginning of electrical recording
1926 Ernest Hemingway publishes *The Sun Also Rises*
1927 *The Jazz Singer*, first movie with sound, ushers in talking movies
—Television transmission realized
—Charles Lindbergh completes first solo flight across the Atlantic
—Adolf Hitler publishes *Mein Kampf*
1929 Stock market crash
—William Faulkner publishes *The Sound and the Fury*
1930 Penicillin discovered
—Grant Wood paints *American Gothic*
—Cyclotron developed in United States

From 1907 to 1923, Morton traveled around the country, leading bands and playing solo gigs, often remaining a few months in each city. After bumming around Texas, Mississippi, Oklahoma, and Arkansas, by 1914 he had reached Chicago. From late 1917 to 1922, he worked on the West Coast and in Tijuana, but he returned to Chicago and settled there in 1922. It was in the Windy City that Morton was to have his most spectacular successes.

Morton cut classic recordings in Chicago, mostly of his own compositions. They included superb piano solos and the best-arranged ensemble numbers of early jazz. In his ensemble work, principally with the Red Hot Peppers

Jelly Roll Morton at the piano (back right) during his last recording session on September 14, 1939—a session that included back row, l to r: Wellman Braud (bass, not shown), Claude Jones (trombone, partially cut off), Sidney De Paris (trumpet), Zutty Singleton (drums); front row, l to r: Sidney Bechet (soprano sax), Albert Nicholas (clarinet), Albert "Happy" Caldwell (tenor sax), and Lawrence Lucie (guitar). Compare this photograph to the photograph of the Wolverines' acoustic studio on page 73. Notice that by 1939, studio recording included electronic microphones (signified by the wires that are visible and Morton's vocal mike), which allowed the players to sit in the studio much as they would sit in live performances. Prior to electronic microphones, a player sat closer or farther from the recording horn depending on his or her instrument's characteristic volume (the trumpet being fundamentally louder than the guitar, for example). Also by 1939, the players divided into the reed and brass sections that, as we will see, typified the big band formations that would follow 1920s jazz styles.

Charles Peterson/Hulton Archive/Getty Images

Stride piano is a school of jazz piano performance based on a moving left-hand accompaniment alternating bass notes and chords with an appropriate right-hand figuration pulling or tugging at the left hand.

Swing is a generic term for the jazz and much popular music of the mid-thirties through the mid-forties.

on recordings of the mid-twenties, Morton shows a deft awareness of the balance between improvisation and worked-out arrangement. Because of this gift, Morton was undoubtedly the finest composer-arranger in early jazz and remains among the best in jazz to this day.

The wide variety of music Morton performed points to the complexity of early jazz evolution. In a series of interviews recorded by folklorist Alan Lomax in 1938 for the Library of Congress,[1] Morton discussed and played not only rags, blues, and stomps but also selections from light opera, popular songs, and dances such as quadrilles. Morton also claimed to have invented jazz in 1902. Although this is an exaggeration, his performance of "Maple Leaf Rag" (Track 5) demonstrates the liberties that most early improvising pianists took with written compositions and provides convincing evidence that Morton was among the cutting edge of ragtime and early jazz musicians. Like James P. Johnson (whom we discuss in Chapter 4), Morton was among the first pianists to transform the traditional ragtime figures into a more linear jazz style.

Morton's solo piano recordings for Gennett Records in 1923 and 1924 remain classics, equal in quality to the sides he was soon to record with the Red Hot Peppers. Morton played with an orchestral conception—his left-hand lines often sounded more like the trombone part in the brass band than simple piano accompaniment. Significantly different from the Harlem **stride** of James P. Johnson and Fats Waller, Morton's style is less virtuosic, although some recordings, such as "Perfect Rag," show that he could be dazzling when he wished.

Jelly Roll Morton, "The Pearls" (1927)

Morton's "King Porter Stomp" became one of the best-known tunes of the big-band era. "The Pearls," inspired by a waitress at the Kansas City Bar in Tijuana, where Morton worked in 1919, is one of his most elegant and enduring compositions.

Morton's solo recordings demonstrate his superb ability to separate the rhythms of his hands: in the remarkable cross-rhythms of "New Orleans Blues," Morton maintains a "Spanish tinge" left hand while the right hand soars freely in complex rhythms of five notes in the time of four, seven notes in the time of six, and so on. Another of Morton's best "Spanish tinge" pieces is "Mamanita" (1924). These performances represent early examples of the fusion of Latin music and jazz, a trend we explore in Chapter 7.

Morton's recordings with the Red Hot Peppers are among the greatest small-group jazz produced in the 1920s. In addition to "Grandpa's Spells," which we discuss here in the Listening Guide for Track 10, some of his best pieces include "Black Bottom Stomp," "Dead Man Blues," "Original Jelly Roll Blues," "Wild Man Blues" (copyrighted as co-composed with Louis Armstrong but probably composed by Morton himself), "The Pearls," "Mr. Jelly Lord," and "Wolverine Blues." Other fine Peppers recordings were arrangements, such as Mel Stitzel's "The Chant." During the 1930s, unable or unwilling to update his style to **swing**, Morton commanded less and less attention. When he died in 1941, relatively few people remembered him.

Jelly Roll Morton, "Black Bottom Stomp" (1926)

As one of the great characters in jazz history, Morton inspired a controversial Broadway show in the mid-1990s called *Jelly's Last Jam.* The show dramatized Morton's background as a Creole of Color who sought to deny the importance of his black heritage.

It is in fact true that Morton took pains to emphasize his French ancestry, but *Jelly's Last Jam* displayed an anachronistic understanding of the complexities of racial relations. One of the greatest musicians in jazz history

> "Without breaks and without clean breaks and without beautiful ideas in breaks … you can't play jazz."
> —Jelly Roll Morton

was reduced to a bigoted stereotype on the basis of late-twentieth-century attitudes and ethnic pride. Although the difficulties of racial issues in jazz are dramatized by Morton's multiethnic background, his contribution to jazz must be considered on its own merits and in its own time period. Race and authenticity in jazz are complex topics, issues that we will consider further in future chapters.

Sidney Bechet

One of the most important New Orleans players to emerge nationally in the 1920s was Sidney Bechet (Beh-SHAY, 1897–1959). As pointed out in Chapter 2, most of the early woodwind players played clarinet; however, the saxophone did appear during the early jazz period. Bechet began as a clarinetist, but he took on the soprano saxophone as his primary instrument and became one of its early virtuoso soloists.

Bechet's style on both clarinet and soprano saxophone was unique and unforgettable. The sound was rich

LISTENING GUIDE   Track 10
"Grandpa's Spells"

Jelly Roll Morton's Red Hot Peppers: "Grandpa's Spells"—Take 3 (Morton). Victor 20431. Chicago, December 16, 1926. George Mitchell, cornet; Edward "Kid" Ory, trombone; Omer Simeon, clarinet; Ferdinand "Jelly Roll" Morton, piano, arranger, leader; Johnny St. Cyr, guitar; John Lindsay, bass; Andrew Hilaire, drums.

The Main Point   Jelly Roll Morton was the first important jazz composer-arranger. In "Grandpa's Spells," Morton ingeniously mixes various combinations of his players to give the arrangement a surprisingly wide range of textures, despite using only seven musicians in roughly three minutes of music.

Recall Morton's insistence that for a piece to be considered jazz, it must have breaks. "Grandpa's Spells" uses breaks throughout, both to contrast solo textures with the full band and to mark off pivotal moments in the overall form. With these wonderfully varied textures and solo breaks, "Grandpa's Spells" is among Morton's finest compositions and one of his best arrangements for the Red Hot Peppers.

Introduction—4 bars of G7 establishing key of C major

0:00   The band begins with a rising scale of parallel chords in quarter notes, which establishes a bright tempo. (Count one beat per rising chord.) The overall G7 harmony also projects the key of C major, which is confirmed as the A section begins on the tonic harmony.

1st A strain—16 bars, 4 + 4 + 4 + 4, guitar breaks alternating with full band

0:04   Because the piece follows ragtime form quite precisely, we will call its 16-bar sections "strains." The A strain begins with stop time for the first four bars: the band plays chords to accompany St. Cyr's guitar breaks in the lower register of his instrument. For the next four bars, the entire band improvises.

0:13   The second half of this A strain repeats the same 4 + 4 format.

2nd A strain—16 bars, 4 + 4 + 4 + 4, cornet breaks alternating with full band

0:23   Cornetist Mitchell now plays the breaks in a repeat of the A strain format. For the first half of this strain, cornetist Mitchell begins with a rising C major triad; in the second half, he inverts the figure into a descending C major triad.

0:32   Second half of this A strain begins.

1st B strain—16 bars

0:41   For the B strain, first time, Morton maintains the 16-bar regularity but changes its format from that of the A strains. For the B strain's first half, Morton uses the full band for six bars, followed by

0:48   a piano break for two bars.

0:50   For the second half, Morton maintains the full band for the entire eight bars. The use of the full band for eight bars sets up a major change of texture for the second B strain.

2nd B strain—16 bars, clarinet solo

0:50   For the second B strain, Morton varies the texture dramatically: a Simeon clarinet solo in the lower register.

1:06   Simeon has a break in bars 7 and 8

1:08   Simeon on clarinet plays the entire second half of the B strain without a break. The cornet comes in with a short commentary on the clarinet solo during the last bar of the strain.

Return of the A strain—16 bars

1:17   Another change of texture: a trombone solo for two bars followed by just bass and drums for two bars. The full band follows for four bars.

1:26   The second half of this A section follows the same 2 + 2 + 4 textural layout.

1st C strain—16 bars, modulation to key of F major

1:35   As is customary in ragtime form, the C strain moves to the key of the subdominant, in this case F major. Again, Morton changes the texture dramatically: a 16-bar cornet solo with the cornet muted.

2nd C strain—16 bars, clarinet solo

1:54   The second C strain is given over to a clarinet solo. Simeon plays entirely in the higher register of the instrument, thus contrasting his first solo.

3rd C strain—16 bars, piano and clarinet

2:12   The third C strain features Morton on piano for its first half. The quick grace notes leading into high-register chords are a prominent feature of Morton's piano style in general.

2:16–2:18   Listen for the intense syncopation occurring here.

2:21   Second half of this C strain, Simeon returns on clarinet, only now in the lower register. This lower, quieter moment both contrasts his previous upper-register solo and helps dramatize the following out-chorus.

4th C strain—16 bars, out-chorus

2:30   After the sparser and quieter textures of the first three C strains, the entire band returns for an exuberant out-chorus.

Coda—2 bars

2:48   For the short coda, the texture of the opening A section returns: the guitar in the lower register accompanied by band chords.

Listen to this music in an animated Active Listening Guide available at the text website.

and woody, modulated by a quick and surprisingly wide vibrato. On the clarinet Bechet tended to be demure, but on the soprano sax he was more experimental and free-wheeling. On either instrument, the opulence of tone and passionate vibrato combined to create an intense expressiveness that made him one of the two or three most notable and renowned soloists of the 1920s. Furthermore, Bechet insisted on equal time for the clarinet, refusing to let the trumpet keep the lion's share of attention in the Dixieland ensemble.

> Bechet's opulence of tone and passionate vibrato combined to create an intense expressiveness that made him one of the two or three most notable and renowned soloists of the 1920s.

Bechet was possibly the first jazz musician to be recognized as first-rate by the musical establishment. In one of the most famous pronouncements in jazz history, Swiss conductor Ernest Ansermet hailed a 1919 performance of Bechet's in Europe by referring to him as an "artist of genius."[2] Some historians interpret Ansermet's recognition of Bechet as evidence that Europeans accorded jazz respectability before Americans at home did. The actual story is more complex because numerous U.S. critics throughout the 1920s wrote of the greatness of jazz. Still, the Ansermet review is

Frank Driggs/Frank Driggs Collection/Getty Images

Fifteen years after they recorded "Cake Walking Babies (from Home)," Sidney Bechet (holding his soprano sax), Clarence Williams (pianist), and Louis Armstrong (cornet) pose together at the Decca Recording Studios in New York City, May, 1940.

after joining Oliver and the Creole Jazz Band in Chicago in 1922. He recorded his first solo with Oliver, "Chimes Blues," on April 6, 1923. (Armstrong's "Dippermouth Blues" performance with King Oliver's Creole Jazz Band on Track 9, is discussed in Chapter 2.) Although the band was certainly doing very well commercially, by 1924 it was clear that Armstrong, encouraged by his wife, Lil Hardin, was ready to direct his own career:

> I never did try to overblow Joe at any time when I played with him. It wasn't any showoff thing like a youngster probably would do today. He still played whatever part he had played, and I always played "pretty" under him. Until I left Joe, I never did tear out. Finally, I thought it was about time to move along, and he thought so, too.[3]

Once Armstrong left Oliver, he played a brief stint at the Dreamland Cafe with Ollie Powers, a vocalist and drummer. Then, late in the summer of 1924, Armstrong left for

Armstrong had an overwhelming influence on his contemporaries.

New York to take over (on cornet) the third trumpet **chair** in Fletcher Henderson's band. This second apprenticeship with Henderson on the East Coast earned Armstrong growing national attention as the leading hot cornet player in the country. Not only was Armstrong the strongest soloist in Henderson's band, but his New Orleans style of improvisation was also influencing the other band members and raising the bar for hot jazz in New York. In addition to work with Henderson, Armstrong performed on numerous freelance recordings, often with blues singers—a full panorama of gigs that enabled his classic style to develop quickly.

significant because it came from one of the most notable musicians in Europe and probably represented the first praise of a jazz musician for high artistic quality in a jazz performance.

Returning to the United States in the early 1920s, Bechet made significant recordings with Louis Armstrong in groups organized by pianist-composer and music publisher Clarence Williams. Among these are two recordings of "Cake Walking Babies (from Home)," the second of which appears as Track 11. (See the Listening Guide for this title following the discussion of Louis Armstrong who joined Bechet on this recording.) Although Bechet was more established than Armstrong in the early 1920s, the latter's emerging excellence created a tension in the band that led to such fine recordings as the two versions of "Cake Walking Babies (from Home)" and "Mandy, Make Up Your Mind" (1924). For the remainder of his life, Bechet worked with numerous groups, including his own New Orleans Feetwarmers in 1932. Bechet played frequently in Europe and eventually settled in Paris in 1951.

Louis Armstrong

Louis Armstrong was born in New Orleans on August 4, 1901 (not July 4, 1900, as Armstrong himself thought). He spent an impoverished childhood first with his mother, Mayann, and then, from age thirteen, at the Colored Waifs' Home, where he played cornet in the band. He soon befriended Joe "King" Oliver, who became his mentor, and Armstrong later replaced him in the Kid Ory group when Oliver left New Orleans for Chicago in 1918. Armstrong continued to develop alongside his mentor

Chair refers to each member of a section, as in first trumpet chair, first trombone chair, and so on.

A **motive** is a short melodic fragment used as the basis for improvisation or development.

Terminal vibrato is a vibrato added to the end of a sustained note.

Armstrong had an overwhelming influence on his contemporaries. Max Kaminsky captured something of Armstrong's effect:

> I felt as if I had stared into the sun's eye. All I could think of doing was to run away and hide till the blindness left me…. Above all—above all the electrifying tone, the magnificence of his ideas and the rightness of his harmonic sense, his superb technique, his power and ideas, his hotness and intensity, his complete mastery of his horn—above all this, he had the swing. No one knew what swing was till Louis came along.[4]

Armstrong's Classic Style

Not only did Armstrong revolutionize cornet playing, but he also stands as the single most powerful, individual, and influential voice in early jazz. Although Armstrong's playing was deliberately restrained in his 1923 recordings with Oliver, his later recordings attained ever-higher levels of musical, artistic, and technical advancements as the decade progressed.

Around 1927 or 1928, Armstrong switched from cornet to the more brilliant and penetrating trumpet, which helped showcase his newfound virtuosity. He extended the upper register of the instrument, cultivating a three-octave range with dazzling technical proficiency.

Armstrong's playing showed an inventive improvisational skill, and his ability to create coherent musical relationships conveyed a dramatic depth and pacing. Armstrong had the ability to present a staggering variety of **motives**—short melodic fragments used as the basis for improvisation or development—even within a single solo. Yet, although careful listening may reveal several evolving patterns of coherence, the impression remains one of continually shifting ideas.

Why was Armstrong's the most powerful individual voice in early jazz? Among the most important factors were the following:

▶ Armstrong had instrumental virtuosity. Technically, he was head and shoulders above other trumpeters of his generation.

▶ He emphasized logical, brilliant solo improvisation. Armstrong was able to create coherent musical relationships and convey them with dramatic depth and pacing.

▶ More than his peers, Armstrong had an ability to generate swing in his playing. He did this through the following techniques:

■ Unequal eighth-note rhythms that implied an underlying 2 + 1 triplet organization

■ Unexpected accents that were largely off the beat within the melodic line

■ Control over the placement of the notes just before or after the beat

■ **Terminal vibrato** to add excitement and "movement" to notes at the ends of phrases

Armstrong in the Later 1920s

After a year with the Henderson band, Armstrong returned to play at Dreamland in Chicago in 1925. The pace of Armstrong's performing and celebrity increased: he played movie houses with the Erskine Tate Orchestra early in the evening before moving to Dreamland for late-night sets. A particularly fine recording with Tate's ensemble is "Stomp Off, Let's Go" (1926).

Erskine Tate's Vendome Orchestra "Stomp Off, Let's Go" (1926)

Armstrong also began recording under his own name after returning to Chicago. Interestingly, the groups he recorded with were not working bands but session musicians pulled together for the recordings. With these recordings Armstrong gradually departed from the collective

> Armstrong gradually departed from the collective improvisation of the New Orleans style, as heard in King Oliver's Creole Jazz Band, and altered it to feature a succession of solos with his own work as the climax.

improvisation of the New Orleans style, as heard in King Oliver's Creole Jazz Band, and altered it to feature a succession of solos with his own work as the climax.

With his gradual abandonment of the collective improvisation of the New Orleans tradition, Armstrong redefined jazz as an art in which the individual solo voice became the most significant aspect of the performance. In structuring his recordings to feature himself, Armstrong became perhaps the first jazz artist in which virtuoso display was a major aspect of his persona. Thus, through his legacy and his awe-inspiring technical ability, he virtually initiated the concept of the star soloist in jazz.

The first recordings of Louis Armstrong and His Hot Five, one of the groups assembled for recording, were cut on November 12, 1925, for OKeh Records. In addition to Armstrong on cornet and Hardin on piano, the musicians

LISTENING GUIDE
Track 11

"Cake Walking Babies (from Home)"

Clarence Williams's Blue Five: "Cake Walking Babies (from Home)" (C. Williams-C. Smith-H. Troy). OKeh 40321. New York, January 8, 1925. Clarence Williams, piano, leader; Armstrong, cornet; Charlie Irvis, trombone; Sidney Bechet, soprano saxophone; Buddy Christian, banjo; Eva Taylor, vocal.

The Main Point   In this fine example of classic New Orleans jazz we hear Armstrong teamed with the superb clarinetist-soprano saxophonist Sidney Bechet, a fellow New Orleans musician. This may be Armstrong's first acclaimed solo, a foretaste of the brilliance that was to become his hallmark.

"Cake Walking Babies (from Home)" has a front line consisting of cornet, trombone, and soprano saxophone (the latter in place of the more common clarinet), and a rhythm section of piano and banjo. Throughout the piece, the horns project the contrapuntal textures that exemplify New Orleans jazz. The song was co-written by Clarence Williams (1893–1965), who was also the leader on the record date. Williams co-wrote one of the most important early jazz hits, "Royal Garden Blues," and although we now mostly remember him as an entrepreneur, publishing and promoting works by black composers, he also made several recordings such as this one, performing as a pianist with bands assembled for studio sessions. Eva Taylor, the vocalist on this recording, was Williams's wife and appeared on many recordings with her husband. Note also that in 1925 a reference to cakewalking was certainly tongue in cheek, as this fad was some 20 years out of date.

While Armstrong was performing with the Fletcher Henderson band in New York, he had ample opportunity to moonlight on numerous record dates. It was through sessions such as these that the young Armstrong's reputation grew, gaining valuable professional experience by having to adapt to a wide variety of performance milieus. This recording marks the second time Armstrong performed "Cake Walking Babies" within a span of two weeks; he had recorded it previously on December 24, 1924, with Bechet and Williams, under the band name Red Onion Jazz Babies. Although Armstrong plays effectively on both recordings, he is dazzling in this second effort, where he steals the thunder from Bechet, who may have been the more dominating player in the earlier Red Onion session.

First chorus—ABAC as 16 + 24 structure

0:00   The recording should be counted in a moderate 2/4 time with two banjo chords per beat, that is, four banjo chords per bar. It begins without introduction in a classic New Orleans texture: Armstrong on the lead melody with Bechet and Irvis filling in contrapuntally. Without drums, the players rely on banjoist Christian and pianist Williams to provide the record's driving rhythm. The form of this opening statement is 16 bars + 24 bars, that is, the customary 32-bar ABAC form is extended by eight bars in its second half.

Verse—16 bars to introduce vocal

0:40   Here the group presents an introduction to Eva Taylor's vocal. This introduction is probably the song's "verse," a section that introduces the better-known part of the song, the "chorus." This latter word is probably why we refer to jazz musicians' cycling through the form as "choruses."

2nd chorus—Taylor vocal

0:55   The vocal features Eva Taylor's rendition of the song's chorus, in which a spirited cakewalk is described. Listen to how the soprano saxophone and trombone embellish figures around Taylor's melody. Armstrong, during this chorus, either does not play or plays very quietly, as prominent trumpet figures would crowd the song's melody. You can hear Armstrong re-enter as Taylor holds out her last word, "home."

3rd chorus—featuring breaks by Bechet

1:34   For the third chorus, Armstrong re-enters on the lead melody and the band returns to the standard New Orleans three-horn texture.

1:48   A two-bar break for Bechet. Armstrong plays demurely during this chorus, so as not to detract from Bechet's breaks.

1:58–2:06   More elaborate soprano saxophone breaks follow with the band providing a *stop-time* accompaniment with downbeat accents every two bars. Bechet demonstrates a fine mix of control and agility in his breaks.

4th chorus—featuring Armstrong's soaring lead

2:14   Although Armstrong is deliberately understated in the third chorus, he takes over here for the final chorus with a wonderful display of brilliance and emotion. Notice his focus on the higher register of the cornet, as compared to his third chorus. His breaks in this chorus parallel Bechet's in the previous chorus.

2:28   Armstrong's first break is particularly wild, with unexpected and syncopated leaps between the upper and middle registers of the cornet. His final breaks are stunning too, with surprising turns of phrase, blue notes, considerable virtuosity, and exciting high notes. The final chorus concludes without coda or tag.

 Listen to this music in an animated Active Listening Guide available at the text website.

Scat singing is a jazz vocal style in which the soloist improvises with nonsense syllables.

Louis Armstrong & His Hot Five, "Gut Bucket Blues" (1925)

Louis Armstrong & His Hot Five, "Heebie Jeebies" (1926)

included New Orleans players Johnny St. Cyr on banjo, Johnny Dodds on clarinet, and Kid Ory on trombone. The most interesting cut from the session may be "Gut Bucket Blues," in which Armstrong jovially introduces the band and begins to establish his stage personality as an entertainer.

The same band recorded again the following year on February 26. This session included the Hot Five's first major hit: "Heebie Jeebies," a vocal number for Armstrong in which he sang **scat**—nonsense—syllables over the chord changes. Although untrue, jazz mythology claims that Armstrong was

forced to make up the syllables when his lyric sheet dropped to the floor. This record helped establish Armstrong as a vocalist in addition to a cornetist.

A notable, forward-looking recording that showcases Armstrong's emerging solo virtuosity is "Cornet Chop Suey," also from the February 26 session. In this vibrant, well-balanced performance, Armstrong shines through from beginning to end—particularly on the breaks—with an apt mixture of the improvised and what was likely planned. His playing here anticipates much of the swing-era phrasing to follow in the 1930s. Thus in these recordings Armstrong remained part of the band, acknowledging the communal, polyphony-based New Orleans jazz idea, but at the same time he loosened and heated up jazz phrasing through virtuosic brilliance and unprecedented technical command. Jazz would never be the same.

Armstrong also began a musical association with pianist Earl Hines that would have lasting repercussions. Armstrong had met Hines shortly after the pianist had left

Louis Armstrong & His Hot Five "Cornet Chop Suey" (1926)

In the 1926 Hot Five recordings Armstrong remained part of the band, acknowledging the communal, polyphony-based New Orleans jazz idea, but at the same time he loosened and heated up jazz phrasing through virtuosic brilliance and unprecedented technical command. Jazz would never be the same.

Louis Armstrong and His Hot Five, left to right: Johnny St. Cyr, (banjo), Edward "Kid" Ory (trombone), Louis Armstrong (trumpet), Johnny Dodds (clarinet), and Lillian Hardin (piano) in New Orleans. Lil Hardin, now married to Armstrong, encouraged the young trumpeter to take charge of his own career. Seen here at about age twenty-four, note Armstrong's serious demeanor, although other photos of him at this time show him in more-informal poses. Within a few years, he would become a consummate entertainer.

In the meantime Armstrong continued to use pianist Lil Hardin for the most important records of that year. His band the Hot Seven, which was the Hot Five augmented by Pete Briggs on tuba and Baby Dodds on drums, went into the studio for several sessions in May 1927 that included "Chicago Breakdown," "Potato Head Blues," and "S.O.L. Blues," among others. Later that year Armstrong recorded nine sides with the Hot Five in September and December. The latter session is especially notable for the versions of "Savoy Blues," "Struttin' with Some Barbecue," and "Hotter Than That." These recordings also marked a switch to the new technique and the increased fidelity of electrical recording.

Louis Armstrong & His Hot Five, "Potato' Head Blues" (1927)

Louis Armstrong & His Hot Seven, "Struttin' with Some Barbecue" (1927)

Hines, meanwhile, had joined Jimmie Noone's five-piece band at the Apex Club; he would later record with Noone in the spring of 1928.

The 1928 collaborations between Hines and Armstrong spotlighted the two as among the leading jazz instrumentalists of the day. Hines became well known for his "trumpet style" piano; that is, he would apply the

> The 1928 collaborations between Earl Hines and Louis Armstrong spotlighted the two as among the leading jazz instrumentalists of the day.

Pittsburgh for Chicago in 1924; by mid-1926 both men were doubling in Carroll Dickerson's band at the Sunset Cafe and in Erskine Tate's orchestra at the Vendome Theater. In Hines, Armstrong found a peer. Both had developed a level of musical virtuosity far above their contemporaries, and both were willing to take improvisational chances. Hines was an easterner who had trained in the classics and absorbed stride and blues-based piano. Armstrong's roots were more informal, grounded in the predominantly oral tradition of New Orleans and King Oliver's band. Together they created a combination that produced some of the era's most exciting jazz records. Eventually, Armstrong took the leadership of Dickerson's band and made Hines the musical director.

Hines and Armstrong first recorded together in 1927, but their primary collaborations came the following year.

melodic style developed by Armstrong to improvised lines on the piano. Hines could even mimic Armstrong's terminal vibrato with an octave tremolo when holding out notes.

Working primarily within a six-piece ensemble, Armstrong and Hines included alumni from the Carroll Dickerson Savoy Orchestra: Fred Robinson on trombone, Jimmy Strong on clarinet, Mancy Carr (not Cara, as seen in old discographies) on banjo, and Zutty Singleton on drums. Their June–July recordings in the summer of 1928 were released as Louis Armstrong and His Hot Five, the last of Armstrong's Hot Five recordings, and included "Fireworks," "Skip the Gutter," and "West End Blues." The last piece is often seen as the peak of Armstrong's output in the 1920s—and we discuss it here in the Listening Guide for Track 12.

LISTENING GUIDE
"West End Blues"

Louis Armstrong and His Hot Five: "West End Blues" (Williams-Oliver). OKeh 8597. Chicago, June 28, 1928. Armstrong, trumpet and vocal; Fred Robinson, trombone; Jimmy Strong, clarinet; Earl Hines, piano; Mancy Carr, banjo; Zutty Singleton, drums.

The Main Point: Among Armstrong's many great recordings from the middle and late 1920s, "West End Blues" has long been considered a first among equals—a masterpiece of twentieth-century music. Armstrong's startling opening cadenza announces a new level of bravura and technical display in jazz performance. The piece also features Armstrong's scat vocal in a deeply felt duet with clarinetist Strong. Pianist Earl Hines, moreover, demonstrates Armstrong-like fluidity that reveals a strong musical personality.

The flashy exuberance of Armstrong's solos contrasts dramatically with the playing of the rest of the group but remains effective because of its structural and emotional affinity with the song itself. Armstrong also avoids literal repetition, preferring instead to move forward with new variations on previous figures, different ways of developing the material at hand. In addition to fine solos by the other performers, Armstrong's final trumpet chorus bears a surprisingly close thematic relationship to the cadenza as well.

Opening cadenza—Armstrong solo

0:00   The opening cadenza, ebullient, forceful, and eloquent, builds to the powerful high C before the brilliant run that eventually winds down to a low A♭ and the long chord held by the whole band. The high C in measure 4 is followed by a high B♭; this association of C and B♭ is one that Armstrong will use throughout the solo along with a motive (F♯–G–B♭), which makes its first appearance between bars 1 and 2.

1st chorus—12-bar blues as head

0:15   The first chorus, the *head,* is played by Armstrong with answering and accompanying parts in the clarinet and the trombone. The melody begins with the motive. At the end of the chorus, the rising triplets recall measures 3 and 4 of the cadenza, thus connecting the introduction and the head quite remarkably. Note that in the cadenza (measure 4), the triplets rise to C, but at the end of the first chorus they rise to B♭—an interesting association between these pitches. Because the drums and the banjo are inaudible throughout much of the recording, the piano's regular on-the-beat chords often seem to be the sole rhythmic accompaniment.

2nd chorus—Robinson trombone solo

0:50   The second chorus features Robinson's trombone solo, during which the drums are finally heard in a kind of clip-clopping rhythm.

3rd chorus—Duet between Strong and Armstrong

1:24   The third blues chorus is a duet between Strong on clarinet and Armstrong improvising vocal responses as scat. Armstrong demonstrates the use of call-and-response by answering the clarinet with similar phrases.

4th chorus—Hines piano solo

1:58   Next follows a piano solo, unaccompanied, from Hines. Although the clarinet and trombone playing on this recording help maintain the somber, bluesy mood, the technical levels of these players scarcely compare to Hines and Armstrong.

5th chorus—Full band performing out-chorus and coda

2:32   The band joins in for the final chorus, featuring Armstrong's soaring lead. Armstrong enters with the motive we first heard in the opening cadenza. The long high B♭ on the downbeat of the chorus is the same pitch that ended the first chorus, thus establishing a large-scale continuity between the trumpet statements at the beginning and the end of the piece. The B♭–A♭–G♭–E♭ figure that is repeated five times in measures 5 and 6 is the same figure that began the long cadenza at measure 5 of the introduction. The high C in measure 6 that Armstrong leaps to can be heard as connecting to the high B♭ also leapt to in measure 8.

2:55   The final chorus concludes with a series of wistful, pensive piano runs that introduce a short coda, with Armstrong again playing the lead. Notice that Armstrong's last two notes before the cadencing E♭ in measure 13 are C and B♭—this time in a lower register. Drummer Singleton gets in the last word with his *clip-clop* tag.

   Listen to this music in an animated Active Listening Guide available at the text website.

We can summarize the features of "West End Blues" as follows:

▶ Typical Dixieland instrumentation of trumpet, clarinet, trombone, piano, banjo, and drums

▶ Some group improvisation in which the trumpet carries the lead, accompanied by trombone and clarinet countermelodies

▶ Horn solos accompanied by the rhythm section

▶ Use of call-and-response

▶ Frequent use of expressive blues elements: slurs, slides, **blue notes**, and so on

▶ Use of instrumental breaks

Armstrong's general stylistic traits observable in "West End Blues" include the following features:

▶ Exuberant, fiery tone

▶ Use of the full range of the trumpet

▶ Blues inflections

▶ Impetuous, emotional projection

▶ Perfectly balanced range of rhythmic values (long notes versus short notes)

▶ Ingenious motivic connections

▶ Wide vibrato, especially at the end of held notes (terminal vibrato)

▶ **Inside** playing with use of blues scale

With Hines and the Dickerson musicians, the 1928 Hot Five recordings clearly showed Armstrong's departure from the New Orleans format of the earlier Hot Five and Hot Seven records. Dickerson's band at the Savoy was using the arrangements of Bill Challis, Don Redman, and Fletcher Henderson, and these Hot Five recordings revealed more of the small big-band format than the collective improvisational Dixieland style. Furthermore,

Armstrong by now had switched to trumpet permanently, imparting an even greater brilliance and flair to these sides.

The same group recorded again in December 1928, and the records were released as Louis Armstrong and

> Around 1927 or 1928, Armstrong switched from cornet to the more brilliant and penetrating trumpet, which helped showcase his newfound virtuosity.

His Orchestra. Armstrong sang on "Basin Street Blues," which, though not a blues composition, would become a Dixieland standard. Several cuts from the sessions included Don Redman on saxophone, who had played with Armstrong in Fletcher Henderson's band in New York. Redman arranged "No One Else but You" and "Save It, Pretty Mama." Alex Hill wrote and arranged "Beau Koo Jack," another superb number. Thus in Armstrong's evolution through the 1920s we see an increasing focus

A **blue note** is a bent, slurred, or "worried" note. It most often occurs on the third of the scale, but any note can be made "blue" by varying its intonation in a blues or jazz performance.

Jazz musicians are said to be playing **inside** when their melodic lines favor the principal notes of the harmonies. The more players depart from the notes of the harmonies, the more they are said to be playing **outside**. These terms are most commonly associated with modern jazz. (Listen to Track 8 of the 🅰 Audio Primer to hear examples of inside and outside playing.)

A **chart** is a common term for a jazz band arrangement.

Chicago jazz merged the group sound of white, New Orleans bands with the emerging improvisational style and solo emphasis pioneered by Armstrong in the context of larger bands.

on arrangement and larger ensembles. From the evenly distributed, collective improvisation of King Oliver—the essence, perhaps, of New Orleans style—we can witness

> It was a mere duo performance — "Weather Bird" —that precisely captured the improvisational art of the music and forecast the direction in which jazz would eventually turn.

a progression through an increasing emphasis on solo playing to well-arranged works in which the **chart** would build to Armstrong's climactic chorus.

Louis Armstrong & Earl Hines, "Weather Bird" (1928)

Yet it was perhaps a mere duo performance that precisely captured the improvisational art of the music and forecast the direction in which jazz would eventually turn. Amid the six- and seven-piece groups, Armstrong and Hines found time to record "Weather Bird," a three-strain composition written by Joe Oliver. Armstrong had recorded the tune with King Oliver's Creole Jazz Band in 1923 as "Weather Bird Rag," but now the duo version saw Armstrong and Hines take great improvisational liberties with the tune, engaging in fanciful flights and harmonic departures—a sort of cat-and-mouse improvisation that was both playful and ingenious. The rhythmic interaction between the players was remarkable. At times it seemed as though the beat were in danger of being lost, but this illusion merely showed their wonderful control of the time. Nor was the form ever abandoned; rather, the players kept to the three-strain framework of Oliver's original version but expanded it to A1 B1 B2 A2 Interlude C1 C2 C3 coda.

Hines and Armstrong parted ways in early 1929, shortly after these sessions concluded. Hines went on to establish a major career as both a soloist and a bandleader. Armstrong struck out for New York with Dickerson's band, landing a gig at Connie's Inn for himself, and for the band a role on Broadway in *Hot Chocolates*, a show with music

by Fats Waller and Andy Razaf. Armstrong's great success at singing "Ain't Misbehavin'," which would become one of Razaf and Waller's most popular songs, hinted at

> Armstrong's singing became almost as important as his trumpet playing.

a gradual transformation of the traditional New Orleans jazz cornetist into an internationally famous entertainer. Armstrong's singing became almost as important as his trumpet playing. At the same time, his influence helped promote the interpretation of American popular song in jazz—as both trumpeter and vocalist.

We pick up Armstrong's story again in Chapter 6. Although there is insufficient space to detail his long career after 1930, we should note that he remains one of the most significant and prominent jazz musicians, every bit as important in the dawning swing era of the 1930s as the younger musicians who followed his example. Armstrong was to remain a force in jazz for decades to come.

The Chicagoans and Bix Beiderbecke

Transplanted black New Orleans players in Chicago gave early jazz its strongest impetus, but the music soon attracted white musicians as well. During the twenties, as Chicago-based white players flocked to clubs such as the Lincoln Gardens to hear their idols Joe Oliver and Louis Armstrong play, the city provided a training ground for musicians cultivating a Chicago style. Listening to the original New Orleans players, a second generation of jazz instrumentalists fashioned their own improvisational and group styles. These players are collectively known as the *Chicagoans* and epitomize what has been called **Chicago jazz**.

These musicians included native Chicagoans as well as players from other parts of the country, drawn by the

> Although the Austin High Gang's most significant performing and recording would take place after the twenties and in New York, the group helped articulate and define the notion of Chicago jazz.

magnetic pull of Chicago's jazz world. Though Eddie Condon, Elmer Schoebel, William "Wild Bill" Davison,

Bix Beiderbecke, Hoagy Carmichael, Rod Cless, and Frank Trumbauer were born in the Midwest outside of Chicago, many of them subsequently became associated with and made their careers in that city.

The relatively affluent suburb of Austin, on the far west side of Chicago, fostered the most influential group of musicians. Collectively known as the Austin High Gang, the players included Jimmy McPartland on cornet, his brother Dick McPartland on guitar, Bud Freeman on tenor saxophone, Frank Teschemacher on clarinet, Dave North on piano, and Jimmy Lannigan on bass. It is primarily this group, together with banjoist Eddie Condon, drummer Dave Tough, and William "Red" McKenzie, who became the self-styled Chicagoans. Although the Austin High Gang's most significant performing and recording would take place after the twenties and in New York, the group helped articulate and define the notion of Chicago jazz.

Before hearing Oliver and Armstrong, the Chicagoans had learned from the recordings of the white, sweet, dance bands and the Original Dixieland Jazz Band (ODJB). A more significant influence was the New Orleans Rhythm Kings (NORK), a white band made up of New Orleans and midwestern musicians (introduced in Chapter 2). To a certain extent, the NORK based their instrumentation and repertory on the ODJB's performances, but they were somewhat more successful at transforming the ragtime syncopations of the ODJB into a looser, more swinging approach. The NORK's extended engagement at the Friar's Inn in Chicago allowed

contrast to the virtuosic flamboyance of Louis Armstrong, Beiderbecke had developed a style marked by introspection and refinement. Contemporaries strove to pinpoint Beiderbecke's restrained and uniquely lyrical sound: Mezz Mezzrow (born Milton Mesirow) stated that every note

> Possibly the deepest influence on the Chicagoans came from a cornet player born in Iowa in 1903, who received his earliest musical experiences in Chicago: Leon Bix Beiderbecke.

sounded "like a pearl" and stood out "sharp as a rifle crack." Hoagy Carmichael described it as a mallet hitting a chime; to Eddie Condon, Bix's sound came out "like a girl saying yes."[6]

Bested only by Armstrong, Bix Beiderbecke was the second-leading voice on the cornet during the 1920s. Whereas Armstrong used differing timbres, a wider range, and consistent vibrato as expressive devices, Beiderbecke's sound had a more even timbre, a narrower range, and a straight tone, with only occasional vibrato. Beiderbecke's unique tone color resulted partly from unusual trumpet fingerings, in which higher **partials** were sounded in a

> Whereas Armstrong used differing timbres, a wider range, and consistent vibrato as expressive devices, Beiderbecke's sound had a more even timbre, a narrower range, and a straight tone, with only occasional vibrato.

teenage Chicagoans to hear them; their records, originally released under the name Friar's Society Orchestra, exercised enormous influence on fledgling Chicago jazzmen.

Cornetist Jimmy McPartland described how they learned from the NORK:

> What we used to do was put the record on—one of the Rhythm Kings', naturally—play a few bars, and then all get our notes. We'd have to tune our instruments up to the record machine, to the pitch, and go ahead with a few notes. Then stop! A few more bars of the record, each guy would pick out his notes and boom! we would go on and play it. Two bars, or four bars, or eight—we would get in on each phrase and then play it all. . . . It was a funny way to learn, but in three or four weeks we could finally play one tune all the way through—"Farewell Blues." Boy, that was our tune.[5]

Possibly the deepest influence on the Chicagoans came from a cornet player born in Iowa in 1903, who received his earliest musical experiences in Chicago: Leon Bix Beiderbecke. (Bix was his given name, not a nickname.) In

lower overtone series. He also emphasized the ninths and thirteenths of the chords in his playing.

Although often associated with Chicago, Beiderbecke actually performed there infrequently. He began playing cornet in his hometown of Davenport, Iowa. With the exception of a few piano lessons, he was largely self-taught as a musician and learned by playing along with recordings of the ODJB. His parents, unhappy about his jazz playing, sent him to Lake Forest Military Academy outside Chicago in 1921. But Beiderbecke's gigs and frequent trips into the city to hear the NORK created an alarming truancy rate, and he was expelled from the academy the following year. His dismissal freed him to become a full-time professional musician; he played gigs on an excursion steamer in Lake

A **partial** (overtone) is a series of higher notes that occurs when a note is sounded and that contributes to the timbre of the original pitch. These higher notes are based on mathematical relationships to the original note, known as the fundamental.

Michigan, at fraternity parties on campuses, and throughout the Midwest with a group of players who gradually became known as the Wolverines.

The Wolverines,
"Jazz Me Blues"
(1924)

In February 1924, like King Oliver's Creole Jazz Band the year before, Beiderbecke and the Wolverines traveled to the Gennett Records studio in Richmond, Indiana, to make their first recording. (See page 73 for a photograph of this session.) The session yielded "Fidgety Feet" and "Jazz Me Blues." Few solos rank higher for their elegance and simplicity than Beiderbecke's on "Jazz Me Blues." Not a single note could be changed without detracting from the lyrical quality of its melodic line. The

> ## Few solos rank higher for their elegance and simplicity than Beiderbecke's on "Jazz Me Blues."

technical performance was exquisite and confident, yet it also expressed a cool reticence captured by no other major trumpet player except possibly Miles Davis some thirty years later.

The Wolverines recorded later that year, eighteen sides in all. "Tiger Rag" and "Royal Garden Blues" had been recorded earlier by the ODJB and the NORK, but Beiderbecke's playing was becoming tinged with the blues he had undoubtedly been hearing from Joe Oliver and Louis Armstrong. "Big Boy" captured Beiderbecke's piano playing.

Beiderbecke was beginning to have an impact on the jazz world. Cornetist Red Nichols reproduced Beiderbecke's solo from "Jazz Me Blues" verbatim on a dance-band arrangement. Rex Stewart also recorded Beiderbecke's "Singin' the Blues" solo note-for-note. Jimmy McPartland knew Beiderbecke's solos well enough that McPartland left his Austin High group, the Blue Friars, to take over Beiderbecke's chair when Beiderbecke left the Wolverines.

When Beiderbecke left the group, he headed back to the Midwest from Manhattan, where the Wolverines had been playing. He picked up some jobs with Jean Goldkette, a Detroit-based bandleader, and in 1925 joined one of Goldkette's bands in St. Louis under the leadership of Frank Trumbauer. In the company of high-caliber musicians such as Trumbauer, who played C-melody saxophone (an instrument pitched between the alto and tenor saxophones in range), and Charles "Pee Wee" Russell on clarinet, Beiderbecke's playing deepened. His reading improved, and he played piano more frequently. Frank Trumbauer (1901–1956) was a significant white jazz player of the 1920s and one of the few who played the C-melody saxophone. He became closely associated with Beiderbecke and significantly influenced Lester Young, the swing saxophone great, whom we discuss in Chapter 6.

The well-known Bix Beiderbecke portrait from the Wolverines' publicity photograph of 1923.

Although the Goldkette group was a dance band, Beiderbecke experimented with its arrangements by introducing some of the harmonic procedures of French classical impressionism—often to the chagrin of the ballroom manager. Beiderbecke did no recording during this time but instead played gigs, did jam sessions, and indulged his legendary drinking habit.

In 1926 Trumbauer and Beiderbecke graduated to Goldkette's first-string New York band, which recorded prolifically for the next year or so. The following year Beiderbecke also recorded with an orchestra under the direction of Trumbauer that included mostly members of the Goldkette band. After the latter group folded in September 1927, both Beiderbecke and Trumbauer, along with arranger Bill Challis, moved to the famous Paul Whiteman band, Beiderbecke's last major ensemble. Unfortunately, the recordings made with the large Whiteman band contain only brief cornet solos by Beiderbecke.

Frankie Trumbauer & His Orchestra (with Bix Beiderbecke),
"Mississippi Mud"
(1928)

Frankie Trumbauer & His Orchestra (with Bix Beiderbecke),
"Riverboat Shuffle"
(1927)

Beiderbecke's recordings of 1927 made a lasting impact. His solo on "Singin' the Blues," recorded with Trumbauer's band and which we discuss here in the Listening Guide for Track 13, was widely imitated by other

> Beiderbecke's melodic ideas seemed to grow logically and organically from one into the other, giving the impression of improvisation as a unified whole — what Lester Young later referred to as "telling stories."

players and later arranged by Fletcher Henderson. Challis's arrangement on "Ostrich Walk" showed Beiderbecke to great advantage; this number by the ODJB was remarkable for the way it mixed written material for the saxophones with the spontaneity of the Dixieland ensemble. Beiderbecke's fine up-tempo work on "Clarinet Marmalade," also from the ODJB repertory, was satisfyingly precise.

Beiderbecke also recorded as bandleader—under the name Bix and His Gang—including re-recordings of the Wolverines' "Royal Garden Blues" and "Jazz Me Blues." A unique item in the Beiderbecke catalog that was recorded by

Bix Beiderbecke holding his cornet, at the Club New Yorker, September 1927, the same year he recorded "Singin' the Blues" (Track 13) and four years before he died at the age of twenty-eight.

LISTENING GUIDE   Track 13
"Singin' the Blues"

Frank Trumbauer and His Orchestra: "Singin' the Blues" (Robinson-Conrad). OKeh 40772. New York, February 4, 1927. Trumbauer, C-melody (or alto) saxophone, leader; Leon Bix Beiderbecke, cornet; Bill Rank, trombone; Jimmy Dorsey, clarinet; Paul Mertz, piano; Eddie Lang, guitar; Chauncey Morehouse, drums.

The Main Point   Containing a famous Beiderbecke solo—in fact, one of his first solos to become widely known—"Singin' the Blues" exemplifies much of Beiderbecke's brilliance: his lyrical, mellow tone, rhythmic variety, and melodic subtlety.

The ensemble for this recording, under the nominal leadership of Frank Trumbauer, was assembled from the Jean Goldkette band specifically for the session. Trumbauer was well known for his work on the rare C-melody saxophone, an instrument pitched between the alto and the tenor saxophones in range, but his solo on "Singin' the Blues" may have been played on alto. This solo, equally as famous as Beiderbecke's chorus at the time, greatly impressed and influenced Lester Young, who was said to keep a copy in his saxophone case. We also hear a brief Jimmy Dorsey solo on clarinet. He and his brother, Tommy, best known as a trombonist, became two important bandleaders in the 1930s. Among the other musicians, Eddie Lang was a pioneering guitarist who often recorded with violinist Joe Venuti.

Introduction—4 bars

0:00   For the introduction the horns present block chords, accompanied only by the drums.

1st chorus—32 bars as 16 + 16, for Trumbauer

0:07   The first chorus features Trumbauer on the C-melody (or alto) saxophone, accompanied only by Lang on guitar. The sweet, unforced quality of his playing contrasted with the heaviness of much twenties saxophone playing.

0:31   A break occurs in the last two bars of the solo's first half.

0:35   The second half of the solo.

0:42   We hear a particularly nice moment in Trumbauer's descending arpeggio, answered by a descending harmonic minor scale by Lang (0:43). After this there occur several other moments in which Lang answers Trumbauer, all the while continuing to keep time.

0:59   Trumbauer's break at the end of the second half ushers in Beiderbecke's chorus.

2nd chorus—32 bars as 16 + 16, for Beiderbecke

1:02   For the second chorus, Beiderbecke is featured, accompanied yet again by guitarist Lang only. Although Beiderbecke's lyricism is a hallmark of his cornet style, the actual melody he improvises has a surprising number of leaps. Beiderbecke is seeking interesting notes to play atop the chords: extensions and altered tones. Attention to melodic detail is frequently observable in Beiderbecke's solos, giving them a sense of carefully wrought design.

1:27   As with Trumbauer's chorus, Beiderbecke concludes the first half with a break.

1:31   Second half of the chorus.

1:33   Notice that the three repeated on-the-beat notes echo the repeated on-the-beat notes heard during the break (1:27), another example of attention to detail that helps make Beiderbecke's style so elegant.

1:47   Paralleling the interplay between Lang and Trumbauer in the saxophonist's solo, both players play diminished-chord arpeggios in the opposite direction—a remarkable and beautiful moment in the solo that was probably spontaneous.

3rd chorus—32 bars with the whole band and Dorsey clarinet solo

2:00   The entire band enters with a free, almost New Orleans–style, group improvisation for the first eight bars of the first half of the chorus.

2:13   For the second eight bars of the first half of the chorus, Dorsey is featured on clarinet, accompanied by piano and guitar only.

2:25   He ends his solo with a break.

2:28   Beiderbecke's commanding cornet entrance sets up the piece's climax, consisting of the song's second half.

2:45   Lang's solo break—yet another diminished-chord arpeggiation—provides a textural contrast to the strong ending by the entire ensemble.

Listen to this music in an animated Active Listening Guide available at the text website.

the artist himself is his solo piano composition "In a Mist." This piece reflects the hazy harmonic texture of French impressionism, especially the use of **whole-tone scales** and dominant ninth/sharp eleventh chords. Challis notated "In a Mist," along with Beiderbecke's other piano works "Candlelights," "Flashes," and "In the Dark," and published them as a piano suite.

Beiderbecke's drinking caused a rapid deterioration in his health, and he died in 1931 at age twenty-eight. Although

The **whole-tone scale** consists only of whole steps, thus making it impossible to form major or minor triads. There are only two whole-tone scales: C–D–E–F♯–G♯–B♭ and D♭–E♭–F–G–A–B. They have no notes in common. The scale is often associated with French twentieth-century composers such as Claude Debussy. (Listen to Track 1 of the 🅿 Audio Primer; the whole-tone scale is the fifth scale played.)

largely unknown to the general public, Beiderbecke's legacy among musicians was profound. Other cornetists such as Jimmy McPartland, Red Nichols, Rex Stewart, and Bobby Hackett directly imitated Beiderbecke's playing. His improvisations, which emphasized diatonic pitches and upper chordal extensions such as ninths and thirteenths, affected musicians of all instruments. His melodic ideas seemed to grow logically and organically from one into the other, giving the impression of improvisation as a unified whole—what Lester Young later referred to as "telling stories." To many who idealized Beiderbecke's brief life, he served as the tragic hero of the Jazz Age, a romantic symbol of the Roaring Twenties. He became the model for Dorothy Baker's novel *Young Man with a Horn*.

"Singin' the Blues" is an excellent example of the brilliance of Bix Beiderbecke. His performance is both a wonderful solo on its own terms and representative of certain aspects of his general style:

▶ Concentration on the middle register

▶ A lyrical, mellow tone

▶ Rhythmic variety

▶ Extreme subtlety of melodic continuation

▶ Restrained use of blue notes

▶ Small but compelling emotional compass

▶ Little use of vibrato

▶ Inside playing

Beiderbecke seemed to synthesize all that Chicago had to offer New Orleans bands and styles in the twenties. He merged the tradition of the white New Orleans bands such as the ODJB and the NORK with the emerging solo emphasis pioneered by Armstrong in the context of larger bands. He helped solidify a Dixieland repertory, a group sound, and an improvisational style that the Chicagoans kept alive for the next several decades. Hundreds of later bands maintained the Dixieland tradition, and it continues to this day.

Exam Review Questions

Use these questions and the materials on the text website to help you understand and pass tests on the content of this chapter.

1. How do the varied textures of Morton's "Grandpa's Spells" show the ingenuity of Morton's composition and arranging?

2. How did Louis Armstrong revolutionize the role of the soloist in jazz? What are the key aspects of his style?

3. How did Armstrong's approach to music change in the 1930s? Discuss his relationship to the larger world of popular culture.

4. How does Bix Beiderbecke's style compare with Armstrong's?

5. With which important bands did Beiderbecke perform?

 MindTap™

Test Yourself on Key Concepts with additional Chapter Quizzes and Listening Activities on the text website.

Key Terms

Test your knowledge of this chapter's key terms by defining the following. If you can't remember the meaning of a term, refresh your memory by looking up the boldfaced term in the chapter, turning to the Glossary at the back of the book, or working with the flashcards at the text website.

blue note **95**

chair **89**

chart **96**

Chicago jazz **96**

inside playing **95**

motive **90**

outside playing **95**

partial **97**

scat singing **92**

stride piano **86**

swing **86**

terminal vibrato **90**

whole-tone scale **100**

LEW FIELD'S PRODUCTION
THE MIDNIGHT SONS

WRITTEN BY
GLEN MAC DONOUGH

COMPOSED BY
RAYMOND HUBBELL

BROADWAY

THE MIDNIGHT SONS

MY FIREFLY LADY	60
A SOUBRETTE'S SECRET	60
YANKEE HONEYMOON	60
PRINCE O'DREAMS	60
EILY RILEY	60
TRUE BLUE	60
CARMEN, THE SECOND	60
LITHOGRAPH LAND	60
A COLLEGE EDUCATION	60
THE CYNICAL OWL	60
THE WIDOW OF TWENTY-NINE	60
ANYTHING CAN HAPPEN IN NEW YORK	60
MAGGIE, YOUR ROAST IS BURNING	60
JUST CALL ME BILL	60
THE LITTLE MARY GARDENERS	60
PONY BALLET	60
MARCH	60
KISSES INTERMEZZO	60
WALTZES	60
SELECTION	75
VOCAL SCORE	1.00
	2.00

STARMER

In this scene from the early twentieth century, Broadway nightlife in New York City is as lively at midnight as it is now. Formal dress was customary, the men in elegant eveningwear—white-tie tuxedos with top hats—the women in gowns and bonnets. On the left is an open-air taxi, and above it is a trolley—both common modes of transportation then. The theater showing The Midnight Sons, featuring the song by the same name, can be seen at the left edge of the picture.

STAGED BY
NED WAYBURN

CHAS. K. HARRIS
NEW YORK CHICAGO
CANADIAN-AMERICAN MUSIC CO. LTD. TORONTO, CANADA
ALF. REES & SON
LONDON AND SYDNEY

1920s Jazz in New York and Europe

4

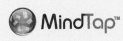
WHILE THE NEW ORLEANS JAZZ DIASPORA
was revolutionizing music in Chicago, a vibrant black population in New York—
centering on the neighborhood of Harlem—was helping make jazz an important
cultural force and the voice of a new, educated black class. The earliest manifesta-
tions of New York jazz were in the society bands and military bands, such as those
of James Reese Europe—bands that were identified with syncopation and the new
ballroom dance music. Meanwhile, ragtime and stride pianists such as Eubie Blake,
James P. Johnson, and Fats Waller introduced jazz rhythms to Broadway shows and
laid the foundation for swing and subsequent jazz piano styles. Bandleaders such
as Fletcher Henderson codified new arranging techniques and instrumentations
that planted the seeds for the big-band jazz of the 1930s. One of these bandleaders
was a young pianist originally from Washington, DC: Duke Ellington. Achieving
national prominence while in residence at Harlem's Cotton Club in the late 1920s,
Ellington would become one of the most important bandleaders and composers in
the history of jazz.

Because New York was already the media and entertainment capital of the country,
bands or artists needed to gain acceptance and promotion there to achieve a national
presence. The major figures of New Orleans—Louis Armstrong, King Oliver, Sidney
Bechet, and Jelly Roll Morton—eventually came to the Big Apple. Bix Beiderbecke
spent his last productive years in the city with Paul Whiteman's band, and many of
the Chicagoans earned their reputations in Manhattan. As we saw in Chapter 3 with
Louis Armstrong's 1924 tenure with the Henderson band, the hot, improvisational
New Orleans–Chicago school strongly influenced the New York musicians. Even so,
New York eventually became the center of jazz largely through the innovations of
Henderson, Ellington, and the stride pianists indigenous to the East Coast. Thus, while
horn players were the focus of jazz in Chicago through the 1920s, the most significant
jazz musicians in New York were pianists.

1920 Mamie Smith records "Crazy Blues," first vocal blues records to sell widely
—Charlie Parker born
1921 Sissle & Blake premier *Shuffle Along*, the first black Broadway musical
—James P. Johnson records "Carolina Shout" (Track 14)
1922 Louis Armstrong joins King Oliver's Creole Jazz Band in Chicago
—Ellington becomes established in New York
—King Oliver's Creole Jazz Band records "Dippermouth Blues" (Track 9)
1924 Bix Beiderbecke records "Jazz Me Blues" with the Wolverine Orchestra
—Armstrong joins Fletcher Henderson band in New York
—Bud Powell born
1925 Bechet & Armstrong record "Cake Walkin, Babies (from Home)" with Clarence Williams's Blue Five (Track 11)
—Fletcher Henderson records "Sugarfoot Stomp"
—Louis Armstrong records "Heebie Jeebies"
1926 Jelly Roll Morton records "Grandpa's Spells" (Track 10)
—John Coltrane born
—Miles Davis born
1927 Trumbauer and Beiderbecke record "Singin' the Blues" (Track 13)
—Ellington at the Cotton Club
—Ellington records "East St. Louis Toodle-Oo" (Track 16)
—Bessie Smith records "Backwater Blues" (Track 7)
1928 Louis Armstrong & His Hot Five record "West End Blues" (Track 12)
1929 Fats Waller records "Handful of Keys"
1930 Ellington has first hit
—Ornette Coleman born
1931 Ellington gives last performance at the Cotton Club
1933 Art Tatum records "Tiger Rag" (Track 15)
1934 Django Reinhardt & the Quintette du Hot Club de France records "Tiger Rag" (Track 17)
—Fletcher Henderson records "Down South Camp Meeting" (Track 18)
1937 Robert Johnson records "Love in Vain" (Track 6)

Jazz

1910   **1920**   **1930**

Historical Events

1914 Outbreak of World War I
1915 Charlie Chaplin stars in *The Tramp*
—Einstein devises general theory of relativity
1917 United States enters World War I
—Czar abdicates as Lenin and Bolsheviks seize power in Russia
1918 End of World War I
1919 Prohibition
—Treaty of Versailles signed
—League of Nations founded
—Commercial airplane service begins, between London and Paris
1920 Commercial radio broadcasting begins
—Nineteenth Amendment ratified, giving women the right to vote
1921 Pablo Picasso paints *Three Musicians*
1922 Revolution in Italy, Fascists take over
—T. S. Eliot publishes "The Waste Land"
—James Joyce publishes *Ulysses*
1924 Stalin becomes Russian dictator
1925 F. Scott Fitzgerald publishes *The Great Gatsby*
—Beginning of electrical recording
1926 Ernest Hemingway publishes *The Sun Also Rises*
1927 *The Jazz Singer*, first movie with sound ushers in talking movies
—Television transmission realized
—Charles Lindbergh completes first solo flight across the Atlantic
—Adolf Hitler publishes *Mein Kampf*
1929 Stock market crash
—William Faulkner publishes *The Sound and the Fury*
1930 Penicillin discovered
—Grant Wood paints *American Gothic*
—Cyclotron developed in United States

From 1917, when the Original Dixieland Jazz Band (ODJB) performed at New York's Reisenweber's Restaurant, to 1931, when Duke Ellington gave his last performance at Harlem's Cotton Club, jazz had matured. Despite its musical prowess, the ODJB's success in New York owed much to its on-stage antics and comical barnyard effects; and in the public's eye, jazz was synonymous with novelty and slapstick. Duke Ellington described this public perception of jazz in his early years:

> When I began my work, jazz was a stunt, something different. Not everybody cared for jazz and those that did felt it wasn't the real thing unless they were given a shock sensation of loudness or unpredictability along with the music.[1]

Throughout the 1920s Ellington and many others helped change this perception. Although the music continued

While horn players were the focus of jazz in Chicago through the 1920s, the most significant jazz musicians in New York were pianists.

to develop as entertainment, particularly as dance music, players improved technically. Jazz earned a seal of approval from notable musicians in Europe. European composers—including Maurice Ravel, Darius Milhaud, Ernst Krenek, and Arthur Honegger—incorporated jazz elements into their orchestral concert works. Promoters and practitioners, in both Europe and the United States, began presenting jazz as serious and sophisticated entertainment rather than as the comical stepchild of vaudeville.

Of course segregation remained the norm in the music business. It was not possible for black and white musicians to perform together in public, although a few recordings were made with mixed-race bands—such as the 1923 sessions of the NORK with Jelly Roll Morton (Chapter 2). Given the separation of the races, it was perhaps inevitable that seminal black contributions to the music were sometimes overlooked, particularly in the early 1920s. Nonetheless, Henderson, Ellington, and the stride pianists continued to define a cosmopolitan jazz style, fusing elements of the New York commercial and Broadway scene with the hot improvisation of the New Orleans musicians. At the same time, Paul Whiteman, George Gershwin, and fine white ensembles, such as the various groups led by trumpeter Red Nichols, guitarist Eddie Lang, and violinist Joe Venuti, helped popularize jazz to the white mainstream.

Thus by the end of the 1920s, New York became the leading center of jazz, a position it still occupies today. Moreover, much of the work of the New York–based artists helped set the stage for swing music in the 1930s. At the same time, jazz began a more concerted partnership

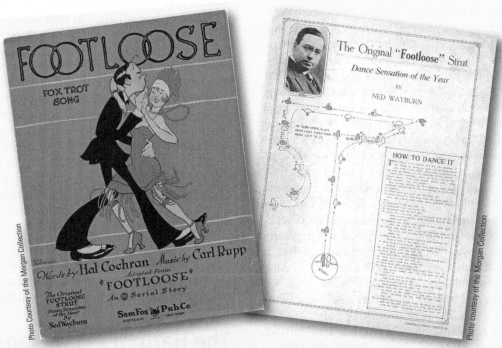

The Roaring Twenties was a time of dance crazes. The Charleston and the lindy hop were significant, but most of the dances were short-lived—including the "Footloose" strut from 1925. On the back of the sheet music for "Footloose" are the diagram and instructions for "How to Dance It." Ned Wayburn, the choreographer, appears to have given this eccentric creation his most sober attentions.

Tin Pan Alley is the collective name applied to the major New York City sheet music publishers. Tin Pan Alley flourished from the late 1800s until the mid-twentieth century.

A **song plugger** was someone who performed a song, usually at a music store, to encourage people to buy the sheet music.

From roughly 1921 to 1928, the **Harlem Renaissance** was a period of outstanding artistic activity among African Americans. The movement was centered in Harlem in New York City.

---

with the growing forces of the mass media, which were centered in New York, particularly Tin Pan Alley, the heart of the U.S. song-publishing and sheet music business.

Tin Pan Alley

Tin Pan Alley began to flourish in the late nineteenth century and experienced major growth through promoting ragtime. In the early 1920s, its popular songs provided many of the vehicles for jazz performance, a legacy that continued for decades. Tin Pan Alley pioneered mass-marketing and aggressive sales techniques in the popular-music industry, techniques that still define the business today. The district eventually consolidated on West Twenty-eighth Street in Manhattan. As part of their sales strategy, Tin Pan Alley promoters actively plugged songs by hiring pianists to play, sing, and hawk the latest tunes at the publishers' offices. Customers would wander down the street, in and out of the publishing offices, in search of the sheet music for songs that caught their ears. In the days before air conditioning, publishing companies kept the windows and doors open during the warm months, and the sounds of all the **song pluggers** playing simultaneously on upright pianos led to a street cacophony that sounded like the banging of tin pans.

Many musicians—from George Gershwin to Fletcher Henderson—got their start as song pluggers, playing and singing the constant stream of newly written popular songs that flowed from Tin Pan Alley. New York had become the heart of the nation's recording industry, and jazz musicians such as cornetist Red Nichols and guitarist Eddie Lang earned much of their living from recording Tin Pan Alley songs for the gradually expanding record industry.

Most of the songwriters of Tin Pan Alley were white, but there was a significant black presence early on. Bob Cole wrote the popular "Under the Bamboo Tree" in 1902, and Chris Smith wrote his classic "Ballin' the Jack" in 1914. W. C. Handy relocated from Memphis to New York in 1917 to promote the sheet music sales of his blues tunes. Handy's championing of black music in general, coinciding with the stupendous popularity of jazz-oriented black

Visible in this 1905 view of 28th Street between New York City's 5th & 6th Avenues—"Tin Pan Alley," the center of song publishing and the sheet music business—are the Jerome H. Remick & Company and the still extant William Morris Agency. Based in Detroit, Jerome H. Remick & Company began in 1898 with the acquisition of the floundering Whitney-Warner Music Publishing and became a leader on Tin Pan Alley, with hundreds of Remick Song Shops across the country. Working out of this office, its staff writers, among them George Gershwin from 1914 to 1917, composed hundreds of hits influencing popular music styles from ragtime through the golden age of 1920s music, from "Dill Pickles Rag" and "Black and White Rag," through "Moonlight Bay" and "Bye Bye Blackbird" to "42nd Street" and "I Only Have Eyes For You." With Jerome Remick's health failing in 1929, Warner Bros., producer of the first talking picture, acquired the firm, including its catalogue and composers, as a music publishing outlet for its films.

musicals on Broadway in the early twenties, was symptomatic of the dramatic growth of African American culture in New York known as the Harlem Renaissance.

The Harlem Renaissance

In New York's African American community, the growing acceptance of jazz paralleled the rise of the **Harlem Renaissance**.[2] Harlem in the 1920s became the central locale for black artists, writers, and musicians and the engine of a self-confident black artistic consciousness. The primary shapers of the Harlem Renaissance "aspired to high culture as opposed to that of the common man, which they hoped to mine for novels, plays, and symphonies."[3] For example, writers Langston Hughes and Zora Neale Hurston, painter Aaron Douglas, and composer William Grant Still gravitated to Harlem as the primary center of African American culture.

As pianist Eubie Blake pointed out, music was central to the Harlem Renaissance.[4] Historians often date the beginning of the Harlem Renaissance to the opening of Noble Sissle and Eubie Blake's show *Shuffle Along*, which opened in 1921 and ran to 504 performances. Other shows quickly followed, including Maceo Pinkard's *Liza* (1922) and James P. Johnson's *Runnin' Wild* (1923). Black musical theater on Broadway flourished during the 1920s—from two to five productions were initiated each year.

For many of the key figures of the Harlem Renaissance, the concert stage was the appropriate place for musical performance. Singers Marian Anderson (Track 3) and Paul Robeson performed spirituals in concert; the National Association of Negro Musicians initiated concerts and

recitals. As early as 1918, Will Marion Cook had taken his Southern Syncopated Orchestra, which included Sidney Bechet, to play concert venues in England; and during the twenties and thirties, Cook became a pivotal figure in establishing recital performances for African American

> Harlem in the 1920s became the central locale for black artists, writers, and musicians and the engine of a self-confident black artistic consciousness.

performers and composers and served as a mentor to many of the younger black musicians. Black classical composers sought to incorporate African American music into larger concert forms. William Grant Still stated that his role was "to elevate Negro musical idioms to a position of dignity and effectiveness in the field of symphonic and operatic music."[5] Such goals exercised a powerful impact on many of the Harlem jazz players, particularly James P. Johnson and Duke Ellington, who themselves soon merged jazz with concert music and classical forms.

Harlem and jazz were inextricably bound. Harlem-based jazz musicians Duke Ellington and Fletcher Henderson became the two primary black bandleaders, developing their bands through nightly performances at all-white nightclubs. White musicians such as Artie Shaw, Benny Goodman, and Paul Whiteman frequented these clubs, and classical composers Darius Milhaud and Aaron Copland heard the bands and listened closely.

In addition to nightclub performances, **rent parties** allowed many of the Harlem jazz pianists to develop their techniques. These were "funky, down-home affairs," writes Samuel Floyd:

> As far as creativity is concerned, such affairs served as the proving ground for the pianists. Dominating this creative world were James P. Johnson, Willie "The Lion" Smith, Thomas "Fats" Waller, Luckey Roberts, and Duke Ellington. It was in this world that these and other musicians honed their artistic tools and worked out their ideas for presentation in the world of show business.[6]

The Harlem Renaissance and the coincident rise of jazz in New York City during the 1920s contributed to the spirit of excitement and creativity that changed

Noble Sissle appears on the cover of his composition published in London in 1929. Sissle and Eubie Blake wrote the first all-black Broadway musical, *Shuffle Along*, a huge success in 1921.

A **rent party** was an informal gathering held to raise money for rent or groceries. At such parties musicians would often gather and perform, sometimes in competition with one another.

Courtesy Morgan Collection/Robbins Music Corp. Used by permission Warner Bros. Publications Inc/Image Courtesy Morgan Collection

Published in 1932 in New York, this sheet music aptly captures the energy and high style of the Harlem Renaissance that attracted so many to its nightlife. Patrons, black and white, came to listen and dance to the great jazz bands.

jazz from a curiosity to a phenomenon. Many musicians helped secure jazz as a music of cultural and artistic significance. Among them was a group of pianists known as the Harlem Stride school.

Harlem Stride Piano

Around World War I, New York became the center of a type of piano playing that developed out of ragtime but took on techniques that led to a high degree of virtuosity. This early jazz style, called **stride piano**, evolved at the same time as the musical developments in New Orleans and Chicago. It embodies the transition from ragtime to jazz; indeed, stride energized ragtime with greater flash, speed, incorporation of blues elements, and improvisational variations that were sometimes planned. The development of ragtime into stride parallels the hectic pace of American life during and after World War I, with stride's energy mimicking the speed of the assembly line, the automobile, the telephone, and the airplane.

Fundamentally, stride playing described the left hand's "striding" up and down the keyboard, with a bass note or an octave played on the first and third beats of the 4/4 measure, alternating with a midrange chord on the second and fourth beats. Various stride players cultivated their own flashy techniques and trademarks as well. At rent parties in Harlem, at the Jungles Casino on West Sixty-second Street, and in the piano competitions known as **cutting contests**, pianists James P. Johnson, Luckey Roberts, Willie "The Lion" Smith, and Richard "Abba Labba" McLean emerged as the best players in the highly competitive New York scene. Scholars sometimes call this stride style the eastern school to distinguish it from midwestern styles, but the regional influences overlap so that we cannot always distinguish them. In any event, while centered in Harlem, stride piano boasted fine players working throughout the Northeast and as far south as Washington, DC.

Harlem stride linked ragtime to swing by featuring elements of both; its melodies floated effortlessly between angular ragtime rhythms and smooth

> The development of ragtime into stride parallels the hectic pace of American life during and after World War I, with stride's energy mimicking the speed of the assembly line, the automobile, the telephone, and the airplane.

swing. Even the music of later Harlem pianists, such as Fats Waller, continued to exhibit connections to ragtime in both melodic style and left-hand rhythm. Stride bass formed the basis for many solo jazz piano styles.

The stride pianists took their repertory from reworkings of popular show tunes and traditional ragtime pieces as well as classical compositions played in a ragtime style. In addition, several prominent stride pianists began composing their own works.

Stride piano is a school of jazz piano performance based on a moving left-hand accompaniment alternating bass notes and chords with an appropriate right-hand figuration pulling or tugging at the left hand.

A **cutting contest** is a music competition in which players try to surpass, or "cut," one another in the brilliance of their improvisations.

Eubie Blake

Eubie Blake (1883–1983), who began his career as a pianist in Baltimore's bars and brothels, recorded in 1917 a version of his brilliant "Charleston Rag" on a piano roll. (A recording of the piece, issued as "Sounds of Africa," followed in 1921.) Blake later claimed that he wrote the work, which was extremely forward looking, in 1899, the same year Joplin's "Maple Leaf Rag" was published. If so, it would be evidence of an advanced ragtime style emerging on the East Coast around the same time as New Orleans jazz.

Blake was an important pianist and composer who, with lyricist Noble Sissle, wrote *Shuffle Along* (1921), the most successful black musical of the twenties. The same year that Blake recorded his piano roll of "Charleston Rag" (1917), James P. Johnson issued **piano rolls** of his compositions "Caprice Rag" and "Stop It." Johnson would take the ragtime-stride style to a new level.

James P. Johnson

James P. Johnson was born in 1894 in New Brunswick, New Jersey, and raised in Jersey City and New York. Though essentially a stride and popular composer-pianist,

James P. Johnson
"Riffs" (1929)
"Snowy Morning Blues" (1927)

he had a strong classical background, was heavily involved in Broadway theater (particularly during the 1920s), and always remained interested in concert music. Most of his life was spent working in Atlantic City, New York, and other cities along the East Coast, although he also toured extensively on the vaudeville circuit and even played in England. A multifaceted musician, Johnson became known as "father of stride piano" for his particularly strong legacy as a composer and performer.

As a teenager, Johnson developed his style from playing dance music at clubs in the Jungles, the black section of New York's Hell's Kitchen in the West Sixties. At the Jungles Casino, he played for transplanted southern workers, many of them black merchant seamen from Savannah and Charleston; those from the Georgia Sea Islands were called "Gullahs" and "Geechies." These patrons demanded the country dances that they had heard growing up in the South, and this provided the origin for one of Johnson's most famous compositions:

> The Gullahs would start out early in the evening dancing two-steps, waltzes, schottisches; but as the night wore on and the liquor began to work, they would start improvising their own steps and that was when they wanted us to get-in-the-alley, real low-down. Those big Charleston, South Carolina, bruisers

The "father of stride piano," James P. Johnson excelled as a pianist and as a composer of Broadway musicals and concert works. In the late 1940s he correctly predicted that future jazz musicians would need to be fluent in various jazz styles.

would grab a girl from the bar and stomp-it-down as the piano player swung into the gut-bucketiest music he could.

It was from the improvised dance steps that the Charleston dance originated. All the older folks remember it became a rage during the 1920s and all it really amounted to was a variation of a cotillion step brought to the North by the Geechies. There were many variations danced at the Casino and this usually caused the piano player to make up his own musical variation to fit the dancing. One of James P. Johnson's variations was later published as a number called "The Charleston."[7]

Piano rolls are cylinders of rolled paper punched with holes. When fed through a properly equipped **player piano**, the holes activate hammers that play the piano automatically.

Johnson wrote "Charleston" for the Broadway musical *Runnin' Wild*. His playing and compositions were celebrated for the way they combined ragtime with elements of blues and jazz, a combination Johnson had been working with since around 1913.

Johnson's most famous stride composition was "Carolina Shout," which appeared on piano rolls twice before Johnson recorded it to disc. The piano rolls show an evolution of the piece that culminates in the performance we examine here, the 1921 studio recording (see Listening Guide, Track 14), and the follow-up performances show that Johnson conceived of the piece as "set." That is, he

player piano mechanism of "Carolina Shout" and fitting his fingers to the rising and falling keys.

Johnson also recorded "Harlem Strut" and "Keep off the Grass" in 1921, works that contain similar virtuosic devices. Johnson's technique and inventiveness were prodigious. His playing seemed to absorb all the tricks of the other piano "ticklers," from Eubie Blake to Luckey Roberts. Johnson discussed his musical growth in a later interview:

I was starting to develop a good technique. I was born with absolute pitch and could catch a key that a player was using and copy it, even Luckey's. I played rags

> ## "Those big Charleston, South Carolina, bruisers would grab a girl from the bar and stomp-it-down as the piano player swung into the gut-bucketiest music he could."
> ## —Willie "The Lion" Smith

deviated but slightly from this recording. A probable reason for this is that stride showpieces, such as "Carolina Shout," are technically difficult; the performer can create a better effect (and avert potential disaster) with material practiced in advance and perfected. Of course, Johnson probably took more liberties with the piece when performing under informal circumstances.

An interesting issue in the classification of stride repertory is that there is apparently not much improvisation. As shown by the similarity of his different recordings of the

very accurately and brilliantly—running chromatic octaves and glissandos up and down with both hands. It made a terrific effect.

I did double glissandos straight and backhand, glissandos in sixths and double tremolos. These would run other ticklers out of the place at cutting sessions. They wouldn't play after me. I would put these tricks in on the breaks and I could think of a trick a minute. I was playing a lot of piano then, traveling around and listening to every good player I could. I'd steal their breaks and style and practice them until I had them perfect.[9]

> ## It can be argued that stride style has a closer connection to ragtime than to more spontaneously conceived hot jazz.

Johnson did more than just play brilliant solo piano. He also recorded with blues singers Bessie Smith (Track 7) and Ethel Waters, and he composed *Runnin' Wild*, his first Broadway musical. The show was a hit, with 213 performances, and Johnson continued to compose music for the stage through 1947. A true child of the Harlem Renaissance, he composed large-scale concert works that placed elements of jazz and African American music in classical

work, it seems clear that Johnson worked out his variations previously rather than invent them spontaneously.[8] As we saw in Chapter 1, some classic piano ragtime composers also discouraged improvisation, and thus it can be argued that stride style has a closer connection to ragtime than to more

> ## A true child of the Harlem Renaissance, James P. Johnson composed large-scale concert works that placed elements of jazz and African American music in classical forms and models.

forms and models. *Yamekraw* (1927), for example, was written for piano and orchestra and premiered at Carnegie Hall with Fats Waller as the soloist. Other orchestral works include Johnson's *Harlem Symphony* (1932), which concludes with a variation on the

spontaneously conceived hot jazz. Moreover, stride's use of the multistrain form with modulation to the subdominant continues ragtime formal procedures.

"Carolina Shout" served as a test piece for players attempting virtuosic stride; in fact, the young Duke Ellington claimed to learn the style by slowing down the

hymn "I Want Jesus to Walk with Me," and a piano concerto entitled *Jassamine* (1934). Johnson suffered several strokes in the 1940s but continued to play and record up to a final recording with Sidney Bechet in 1950. A stroke in 1951 left him unable to play, and he died in 1955.

LISTENING GUIDE   Track 14
"Carolina Shout"

James P. Johnson: "Carolina Shout" (Johnson). OKeh 4495. New York, October 18, 1921. Johnson, piano.

The Main Point   Exemplifying classic stride style and form, "Carolina Shout" requires greater virtuosity than ragtime. In the A strain, listen for the seesaw pattern in the melody, a feature often present in stride performances. Also beginning in the A strain repeat but continuing throughout, listen for the disruption of the standard left-hand pattern of bass notes, which creates a cross-rhythm—a hallmark of Johnson's style.

Johnson conceived of "Carolina Shout" as a jazz composition with sections that might undergo future development but would not serve as new passages for improvisation. Its strains are composed rather than improvised variations on previously heard strains.

Introduction—4 bars

0:00   The four-bar introduction sets up the A strain to follow. It begins with a series of accented, syncopated chords, typical of the stride style with its incorporation of blue notes.

A1 strain—16 bars

0:05   Johnson's first 16-bar A strain features a gradually descending melodic line in G major with an up-and-down "rocking" melodic pattern. In the left hand we hear the march bass pattern, largely alternating bass notes on the first and third beats with chords on the second and fourth beats. This may be varied by a more "walking" style left hand with bass octaves on all four beats.

As is typical for a ragtime (or stride) 16-bar strain, the A strain features four phrases grouped into two eight-bar groups (or *periods*). The beginnings of the first three phrases are identical:

0:05   1st phrase

0:10   2nd phrase

0:15   3rd phrase

0:19   The 4th phrase introduces harmonic and melodic variation as the material proceeds to cadence.

A2 strain—16 bars—repeat

0:24   On the repeat Johnson embellishes the right-hand melody with a variation that begins a third higher. This varied melody has an even more pronounced "seesaw" shape than the first A strain.

0:26   Listen for the disruption of the left-hand bass at the strain's second bar. Rather than keep the standard left-hand pattern with bass notes on strong beats one and three and chords on weaker beats two and four, Johnson varies the pattern by putting consecutive bass notes on beats one and two, then a chord on beat three, creating a cross-rhythm. The stride players of the day referred to this practice as a "backbeat" or "change-step." (This use of the word "backbeat" should not be confused with a wholly different meaning of the word: a drummer's heavy accenting of beats two and four.)

B strain—16 bars

0:44   The B strain begins with a relatively static melodic idea, the right-hand arpeggiating G major and C major chords for the first two bars over a regular march bass.

0:47   Beginning here with the use of a backbeat and continuing through the B section, Johnson surprises us by presenting rhythmic and harmonic contrasts to the straightforward pattern he established in the first two bars.

C1 strain—16 bars

1:03   The C strain breaks out of the tightly wound B strain into a shout: a call-and-response, with the call in the higher register answered by music in the midrange of the keyboard.

C2 strain—16 bars

1:22   Johnson repeats the C strain with minor variations.

D strain—16 bars (Trio)

1:40   In the subdominant key C major, featuring chords with blue notes, this strain is the "trio" of the piece (in keeping with stride's roots in ragtime form). Listen for the repeating harmonic pattern, or **vamp**, that supports Johnson's previously composed variations.

E strain—16 bars–bridge between D and F strains

1:59   The E strain recalls the shout-like material heard in the C strain with a call-and-response pattern between a higher right-hand melody and a syncopated response in the left hand.

F strain—16 bars (variant of D strain)

2:17   The harmonic progression of the D strain returns. Johnson plays a variation on it that involves yet another call-and-response: here, a higher melody in the right hand is answered by an alternation of the hands in the lower register of the piano.

Coda—4 bars

2:35   The beginning of the coda finds Johnson jumping far out of the key of C major (in fact, to E♭9 and A♭ chords), then returning for a C major ending.

 Listen to this music in an animated Active Listening Guide available at the text website.

Fats Waller

James P. Johnson's student, Thomas "Fats" Waller (1904–1943), achieved even greater fame and renown than Johnson himself. Although Waller became better known as a humorous entertainer, his virtuosity on the piano was unparalleled. Before meeting Johnson, Waller at age fifteen had been the organist at Harlem's Lincoln Theatre. Under Johnson's tutelage he began to excel as a stride pianist. With the help of his mentor, Waller established himself in the New York musical world and began recording piano rolls in 1922. The same year he recorded for OKeh Records, doing two sides as a piano soloist and working with blues singers Sara Martin and Alberta Hunter.

Like Johnson, Waller was a fine songwriter who wrote such classics as "Squeeze Me," "Honeysuckle Rose," "Black and Blue," and "Ain't Misbehavin'." Also like Johnson, Waller composed for the Broadway stage, working with lyricist Andy Razaf on the 1928 musical *Keep Shufflin'* as

well as on *Hot Chocolates* (1929), which had Louis Armstrong as a singer and soloist.

Waller was the first significant jazz musician to record on the pipe organ, an instrument not especially disposed to the sharp attacks of jazz phrasing. Despite his unparalleled keyboard prowess, Waller ultimately succeeded in the public eye as a popular singer and entertainer: his witty asides often called attention to the emptiness of the disposable pop songs he was increasingly called on to play.

Nevertheless, Waller's solo piano recordings are among the high points of stride piano. The piano works written and recorded between 1929 and 1934—"Handful of Keys," "Smashing Thirds," "Numb Fumblin'," "Valentine Stomp," "Viper's Drag," "Alligator Crawl," and "Clothes Line Ballet"—keep alive

---

A **vamp** is a repeated melodic or harmonic idea. In jazz, its predictability makes it easier for the performer to devise variations or improvise new ideas.

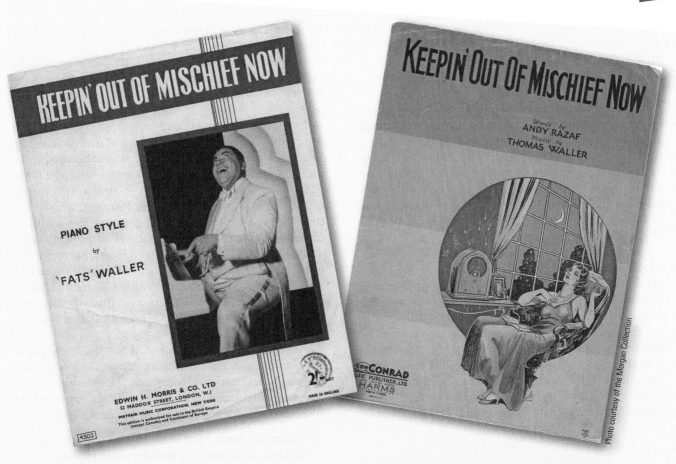

Photo courtesy of the Morgan Collection

By the 1930s jazz had become a mainstream entertainment that was gradually integrating U.S. culture. But although black and white jazz artists performed for black and white audiences, white acceptance of the work of black composers came slowly in the United States. Notice that the British sheet music cover of Fats Waller's "Keepin' out of Mischief Now" carried a picture of Fats Waller, while the U.S. edition did not.

Fats Waller
"Handful of Keys"
"Numb Fumblin'" (1929)

many of Johnson's techniques while projecting an eloquent swing regardless of tempo. Much of his fluency derived from his large hands: pianist George Shearing compared shaking hands with Waller to "grabbing a bunch of bananas."[10]

"Handful of Keys" is a tour de force of effortless up-tempo stride playing, and it became a test piece for other stride pianists. It most particularly recalls James P. Johnson and classic stride while at the same time blending it with the looser feel of swing. The piece connects to the ragtime tradition as well because of three factors:

▶ The marchlike form with a trio in the subdominant key

▶ The composed rather than improvised character of the sectional melodies

▶ The stride accompaniment

The striding left-hand racing along at such a fast tempo testifies to Waller's technique and the virtuosity of the Harlem stride style itself.

Art Tatum

Art Tatum was certainly one of the most prodigious virtuosos in jazz history. Blind in one eye and visually impaired in the other, Tatum was trained in the classics in his native Toledo, Ohio, where he was born in 1909. He learned to read music in Braille. He forged a piano style marked with dazzling runs, lightning-fast arpeggios, and an impeccable stride technique derived from Fats Waller. Tatum's repertory drew primarily on popular songs, such as "Tea for Two" and "Willow Weep for Me." While retaining the melody of the tune, he would recast the harmonic structure, substituting more-advanced chromatic harmonies for the original chords. As a solo pianist and also with trios, quartets, and larger bands, Tatum made more than 600 recordings that testify to his unerring technique and creative fluency.

Rubato is a technique in which performers take liberties with a steady pulse by speeding up or slowing down the musical flow.

Tatum elevated the technique of jazz piano to new heights of excellence—beyond what anyone had thought possible. Although his basic touch was light, his sense of rhythm was extraordinarily secure and provided a swinging foundation to his work that pianists everywhere envied. Moreover, his imaginative treatment of popular melodies and his sense of chordal enrichment influenced and inspired the newly emerging bebop scene of the early 1940s.

In his justly famed performance of "Tiger Rag," which continues our discussion of this piece (see Listening Guide, Track 15), Art Tatum's virtuosity is astounding. Recorded at his first session in March 1933, the recording established Tatum's supremacy in the highly competitive world of New York solo piano. In this performance we hear the harmonies (particularly his use of extensions, the 9, #11, and 13 qualities on the chords) that made Tatum a major influence on bebop harmony, as we discuss in Chapter 7. Interestingly, Bix Beiderbecke used chords such as these in his piano composition "In a Mist" (1927),

but Tatum incorporates them into what is more obviously a jazz context.

Tatum won the admiration of jazz musicians and the public alike for his renditions of light classical pieces in a virtuoso format and at unbelievably fast tempos. His arrangements frequently made use of **rubato** (rhythmically flexible) introductions that moved into up-tempo interpretations based on the rhythms of stride and swing. The arrangements and instrumentation of his trio, which included bassist Leroy "Slam" Stewart and guitarist Lloyd "Tiny" Grimes, were inspired by the piano trio format of Nat "King" Cole. Pianist Oscar Peterson, who was in turn inspired by Tatum, would continue the tradition. Moreover, Tatum's reharmonizations of popular tunes vastly expanded the vocabulary of jazz harmony. He influenced not only such pianists as Duke Ellington and Teddy Wilson but also saxophonists Coleman Hawkins and Charlie Parker. In fact, Tatum's virtuosity may very well have been the decisive influence on Parker's emerging bebop style.

Tatum's musical personality had two sides—the popular virtuoso and the after-hours pianist. Listeners often remarked that his best playing took place during sessions that sometimes lasted all night long. Tatum expanded the vocabulary of stride and swing piano in four significant ways:

▶ *Timing of chords.* Most stride and swing pianists played octaves, single notes, or perhaps tenths on the first and third beats and three-note or four-note chords on the second and fourth beats, but Tatum sometimes played full, richly voiced chords on all four beats.

▶ *Runs.* Whereas many stride and swing pianists used embellished runs to connect melodic phrases, Tatum used these runs more consistently and elaborately.

▶ *Rapidity.* Swing and stride pianists always featured impressive dexterity and speed, but Tatum's playing was the most dazzling.

▶ *Harmony.* Although jazz piano had been slowly developing more-sophisticated harmonies, including extended chords and nondiatonic progressions, Tatum was the most harmonically advanced of any of his contemporaries.

In the 1950s, record producer and jazz impresario Norman Granz produced a voluminous number of Tatum's recordings that advanced Tatum's career. Sadly, Tatum died in 1956, probably due to the effects of alcoholism. Still we are lucky that his art was documented with exceptional thoroughness, and it has inspired jazz pianists ever since.

Many pianists from the heyday of stride piano kept the tradition alive well past the

Virtuoso pianist Art Tatum in a publicity still from the 1940s.

Art Tatum
"Cocktails for Two" (1934)
"Get Happy" (1940)

LISTENING GUIDE Track 15

"Tiger Rag"

Art Tatum: "Tiger Rag" (LaRocca). Brunswick B13164-A. New York, March 21, 1933. Tatum, piano.

The Main Point   From the adventurous nature of his harmonies reminiscent of impressionist composers Claude Debussy and Maurice Ravel, to his incredibly fast tempo that invites a variety of left-hand textures, Tatum's creative genius and technical skill elevated the technique of jazz piano.

From the beginning, we hear a virtuoso performance. Although an introduction normally establishes the key and sets the tempo and the mood of a piece, Tatum's introduction is "out of time." Consequently, the fast tempo of "Tiger Rag" comes as a surprise. Furthermore, while the key is in B♭ major—standard for "Tiger Rag" and the key of the original ODJB recording—Tatum's harmonies are not standard in B♭ major. They are nonfunctional and imply no key at all! The opening progression of G♭9(#11) to E9(#11) to D7(#11) moves down first by a whole step, then jumps to A♭ maj7, which is not closely related to any of the first three chords. In the third bar, the G♭–E–D chord progression repeats, but the chord qualities are modified.

Although this performance can be considered an example of stride piano, and Tatum incorporates a striding left hand from time to time, he sustains this texture only toward the end of the performance.

Introduction

0:00   The introduction is played freely ("out of time"). Rather than set the tempo, mood, and key of what follows, this introduction works as a contrast, but, as will become clear, Tatum does not abandon this material completely.

A strain—8 + 8

0:14   Tatum's statement of the A strain hints at the original melody. A calm left-hand part largely alternates the tonic and dominant notes of the key.

0:20   On the repeat of the eight-bar A strain, Tatum is already embellishing the melody with added runs in the right hand. Note that the entire 16-bar A strain is played in only ten seconds!

B strain—8 bars

0:25   The second strain—the bridge between the repeated eight-bar A strain and its return—offers a change of texture. Just as the original ODJB recording featured stop time in this section, Tatum imitates this procedure with stop time punctuations in his left hand. The right hand, meanwhile, creates an arching melody that first runs up the keyboard and then back down to complete the strain.

A strain—8 bars

0:30   Repeat of the A section with the original left-hand texture.

C strain—24 bars as 16 + 8

0:35   The music changes key to the subdominant (E♭ major) at the C strain. The original ODJB recording featured breaks. Again, Tatum follows tradition with breaks that are blistering descending runs in the right hand.

0:40   For the first time in the piece, we hear a conventional stride texture as the left hand drives the rhythm home after the conclusion of the breaks (right-hand runs).

0:44   Yet another break for an upward run to conclude the first half of the C strain.

0:46   Tatum shortens the second half of the C strain to eight bars. He accomplishes this by moving more quickly to the concluding chord progression of the C strain. He also returns to the more conventional stride texture to create a contrast with the texture of the upcoming D strain. (This shortening of the C strain becomes quite common in other recordings.)

D strain—32 bars, 1st chorus

0:50 In the famous D strain, Tatum deconstructs the melody by reducing the "Hold that tiger!" tune to a syncopated chordal punctuation over continuous running eighth notes in the left hand. The strain normally divides into 16 + 16, and the first time through the strain Tatum maintains the form.

1:01 In the second half of the D strain, Tatum deviates by returning to the impressionistic chordal material that we heard in the introduction. The effect is to create a marvelous contrast in color to the straightforward tonic-dominant harmonies that characterize the piece as a whole.

D strain—32 bars, 2nd chorus

1:12 After the deviation from the piece's harmonies at the end of the first performance of the D strain, the return to tempo and a driving left-hand stride rhythm create terrific swing in Tatum's second D strain. The continuous eighth notes that we heard in the left hand of the first D strain are converted to a right-hand line of similar texture.

1:23 Tatum blurs the form of the D strain here by beginning a complex right-hand run two measures before the beginning of the D strain's second half. The accented note in the left hand is the actual point where the second half of the strain begins. The end of the chorus features another return of the impressionistic harmonies leading to a sustained dominant.

D strain—31 bars, 3rd chorus

1:33 For the D strain, third time, Tatum changes the texture yet again. Here the right hand repeats a syncopated rhythm on high chords while the left hand walks in octaves. The end of the first half features a break at 1:42.

1:44 For the second half of the D strain (third time), Tatum returns to a stride texture as he builds the excitement further. Moving into the fourth strain without changing the texture, Tatum truncates the form by a bar, adding yet more urgency and drive to the concluding fourth chorus.

D strain—32 bars, 4th (out-) chorus

1:54 For the out-chorus, Tatum repeats brilliant descending runs in his right hand over the driving left-hand stride texture. A break at measure 15 (2:03) creates a smooth flow into the second half of the out-chorus.

2:04 The second half of the out-chorus begins with the break begun two bars earlier. Tatum builds strongly into the ending of the piece, in which a descending run brings the fireworks to an unexpectedly quiet but effective conclusion.

 Listen to this music in an animated Active Listening Guide available at the text website.

twenties and thirties. In addition to Johnson and Waller, Willie "The Lion" Smith and Luckey Roberts perpetuated the Harlem solo piano style. Eubie Blake, already discussed as an important predecessor to Johnson and Waller as both a pianist and a composer, enjoyed a comeback in 1969 at the age of eighty-six. Stride piano was the developmental core of the playing of such pianists as Duke Ellington, Earl Hines, Teddy Wilson, and Count Basie, although these players quickly departed from a pure stride style. Still, later pianists—Johnny Guarnieri, Ralph Sutton, Dick Wellstood,

and Dave McKenna—studied and kept alive the Harlem piano tradition.

Paul Whiteman and George Gershwin

The elevation of jazz's status during the 1920s—and its increased popular appeal—owed a particular debt to

"Does Jazz Put the Sin in Syncopation?"
—*Ladies Home Journal*, 1921

Library of Congress

Experiment in Modern Music," the concert's grand finale featured the premiere of George Gershwin's *Rhapsody in Blue*, which Whiteman had commissioned. The composer appeared as the piano soloist. With its opening chromatic slide for clarinet, its use of blue notes, and its syncopated rhythms, *Rhapsody in Blue* placed on the concert stage the devices and rhetoric of jazz that Gershwin had enthusiastically absorbed from black Harlem musicians.

Whiteman had commissioned *Rhapsody in Blue* after hearing Gershwin's earlier jazz-influenced work, the one-act opera *Blue Monday*. Gershwin was a well-known composer of popular song and musical theater prior to

> Gershwin's folk opera Porgy and Bess (1935), based on a drama about southern black Americans and infused with elements of jazz and the blues, is arguably the best twentieth-century American opera.

Rhapsody in Blue. After its success, however, he turned his energy to jazz-based concert works and became increasingly preoccupied with the integration of jazz and classical music. He subsequently composed several concert works with jazz elements, including *Concerto in F* (1925). The second of his *Preludes for Piano* (1926) and the orchestral work *An American in Paris* (1928) employ the 12-bar blues structure. Gershwin's most ambitious work was his

the energies of several white musicians and composers. Paul Whiteman became the most successful American bandleader during this period, in part by incorporating jazz elements into an orchestral format. Whiteman referred to his music as "symphonic syncopation" and devised lush, colorful, and complicated arrangements, often more suitable for listening than for dancing. Whiteman's renown led to his label, "king of jazz," and in 1930 he appeared in a film by that name. Whiteman's recordings of "Whispering" and "Japanese Sandman" from 1920, the year he came to New York, sold more than a million copies. The success of these records marked the beginning of the demise of sheet music for the popular market and, in its stead, the simultaneous rise of recordings.

Whiteman has often been neglected or disparaged by jazz historians, largely because his form of jazz was far removed from that music's wellsprings in black culture. His very name may have also prompted the negative judgments

> The success of Paul Whiteman's recordings of "Whispering" and "Japanese Sandman" marked the beginning of the demise of sheet music for the popular market and, in its stead, the simultaneous rise of recordings.

of his music and reputation among some later historians. Yet for many in the 1920s, he was seen as embodying the best of what jazz had to offer: catchy tunes (understood by the public as jazz) in clever arrangements, played by superb musicians. His widely admired style influenced the concert jazz works of both Duke Ellington and James P. Johnson, in both form and instrumentation.[11] Solo improvisation was not a major factor in these works, however, which served to distance Whiteman from the interests of jazz historians in later eras. More recently, his significance is being acknowledged as historians redress the balance.

As Whiteman put it, he was attempting "to make a lady out of jazz" when he took jazz out of the nightclub and into the concert hall. His most celebrated concert took place in New York's Aeolian Hall on February 12, 1924. Entitled "An

folk opera *Porgy and Bess* (1935), based on a drama about southern black Americans and infused with elements of jazz and the blues. It is arguably the best twentieth-century American opera. Because of the general popularity of his tunes, their syncopated melodies, and their numerous performances by jazz musicians, Gershwin was called "the jazz composer" by the press in the 1920s and 1930s.

Beginnings of the Big Bands

In earlier chapters we discussed the New Orleans and Chicago traditions in which groups tended to be roughly five to seven players. In such bands the front-line combination of cornet, trombone, and clarinet featured one instrument

A **big band** is a large jazz ensemble typically including three to four trumpets, three to four trombones, four to five reeds (saxophones and doublings), and rhythm (typically piano, guitar, bass, and drums).

A **section** is a group of related instruments in a big band; three trumpets and three trombones might form the brass section.

A **head arrangement** is a musical plan and *form* worked up orally by the players themselves in rehearsal or on the bandstand.

Staccato is the technique of playing short detached strikes on notes in a series.

Fletcher Henderson with his band in New York in 1924. Henderson (seated at piano) and Louis Armstrong on trumpet (center, back). The saxophonists are (left to right): Coleman Hawkins, Buster Bailey, and Don Redman (alto).

per function: cornet (or trumpet) with the lead, trombone with a lower counterpoint or countermelody, and clarinet with an upper obbligato.

The **big band** featured a **section** of instruments for each instrument in the New Orleans–style band: a section of trumpets, a section of trombones (particularly after about 1930), and a section of reeds (as saxophones or clarinets). In general, the use of sections required either written or **head arrangements** worked out in rehearsal because it was difficult to be completely spontaneous with a larger number of players.

The evolution of the early big band is a matter of some controversy in jazz history. Who was the first bandleader to use a saxophone section? Recent scholarship suggests that the Art Hickman band, a San Francisco–based group, may have been the first to use two saxophones as a "proto-reed section" in 1919.[12] Bands led by Paul Whiteman and Fletcher Henderson continued to pioneer band division into four sections (trumpets, trombones, reeds, and rhythm), but the early history of the big band remains murky. If the actual course of innovation remains unclear, it is likely that the major New York–based groups, such as the Whiteman and Henderson ensembles, solidified the use of big-band sectional formulas and textures for the 1930s.

Fletcher Henderson

Fletcher Henderson arrived in New York in 1920. The twenty-two-year-old came from Atlanta (where he had

Fletcher Henderson & His Orchestra
"The Stampede" (1926)

received a degree in chemistry from Atlanta University) and began to work as a song plugger for W. C. Handy's Pace-Handy Music Company, one of the first and most successful black publishing companies. When Pace left Handy to form Black Swan Records, Henderson moved as well and began playing piano and forming bands for the new company. As the blues phenomenon hit its peak, Henderson

recorded with dozens of blues singers, including Bessie Smith, Ma Rainey, and Ethel Waters. Henderson's recordings with Ethel Waters became the bestsellers of the Black Swan catalog. Touring with Waters, Henderson at one point unsuccessfully tried to lure Louis Armstrong into Waters's band.

In the meantime Henderson had formed his own band and played at the Club Alabam for six months before moving in 1924 to the Roseland Ballroom at Broadway and Fifty-first Street. Roseland maintained a whites-only policy for clientele but had recently decided to feature both white and black bands after the success of A. J. Piron's group from New Orleans. With arranger and reed player Don Redman as musical director, Henderson's band developed a repertory that alternated written ensemble sections with the improvised solos of saxophonist Coleman Hawkins and cornetist Joe Smith.

Shortly after the band opened at Roseland in 1924, Louis Armstrong left Chicago to join Henderson as third trumpet and the featured hot soloist. Armstrong's technique, sound, and ideas had developed rapidly in his preceding two years with King Oliver, and his solo style and rhythmic sense revolutionized the Henderson band's sound. The group's somewhat stiff **staccato** rhythms loosened into Armstrong's more swinging, propulsive, and smooth style, which affected the sound of the soloists as well as of the entire ensemble. Their recordings of "Shanghai Shuffle," "Go 'Long Mule," and "TNT" reveal some of the energy that Armstrong introduced. At the same time, New Orleans clarinetist Buster

Bailey left King Oliver's band and joined Henderson, creating a reed section of three players; the addition of trombonist Charlie Green to the trumpets gave the band a total of four brass players.

As a hot jazz dance band, the Fletcher Henderson Orchestra earned increasing popularity. "Sugar Foot Stomp," a reworking of King Oliver's "Dippermouth Blues" with Armstrong paraphrasing the original Oliver solo, became a popular hit. In 1925 the trade publication *Orchestra World* crowned Henderson "king" of the black orchestra leaders. Even after Armstrong left the group and returned to Chicago, the band continued to develop and mature. It hosted an arsenal of top-notch soloists, including saxophonist Coleman Hawkins, trumpeter Rex Stewart, and trombonist Jimmy Harrison.

Although several arrangers shaped the sound of the Henderson band, Don Redman had a particularly important role, helping create many of the techniques that would be used by bands for years to follow. In some cases Redman altered preexisting **stock arrangements** to improve or personalize them. Redman's arrangements and modifications not only heightened the distinction between improvised and written sections but also made skillful use of the contrast between brasses and reeds. He alternated brass and reed sections in call-and-response fashion or set one section to play background figures behind another. Henderson's recording of "Alabamy Bound" contained another characteristic device of Redman's: the clarinet trio.

A high point of Redman's work for Henderson during this period was his arrangement of "Copenhagen." Working from a stock arrangement, Redman transformed the original into a highly effective vehicle for the band. The written portions alternate sections of the full ensemble, trumpet trio, and clarinet trio. When Armstrong solos over a 12-bar blues structure, he works within the New Orleans style of collective improvisation but also has a forward-looking rhythm-section accompaniment. The three-minute composition is a tour de force in which Redman seems to summarize the collective developments in jazz while predicting its future direction.

In 1927 Don Redman left Henderson's band to become the arranger for McKinney's Cotton Pickers. Henderson then began arranging for his group himself, turning out excellent charts that highlighted the band's capabilities. Some, such as his arrangement of Jelly Roll

Fletcher Henderson & His Orchestra
"Copenhagen" (1924)

> Fletcher Henderson's band with its careful chemistry of ensemble and solo passages and its ensemble writing designed to sound like hot solo improvisations formed a crucial link to the big band sound of the succeeding swing era.

Morton's "King Porter Stomp," were based on **riff** ideas that the band contributed.

The Henderson band featured other writers and soloists who would become important in jazz. Alto saxophonist Benny Carter began contributing arrangements in 1930. Carter would go on to become one of the finest composer-arrangers in jazz as well as a premier saxophone stylist (see Chapter 6). Trombone technique was advancing as well, as various players became more proficient as soloists. Jimmy Harrison (1900–1931), for example, who recorded with the Fletcher Henderson Orchestra, earned the nickname "father of swing trombone."

Ultimately, Henderson could not sustain his band. He lost many of his players to other groups and, because of his poor management skills, was often unable to pay those who remained. Many band members were heavy drinkers, which contributed to a general decline in quality; they were, in Duke Ellington's words, "probably one of the partyingest bands that ever was."[13] Financial difficulties forced Henderson to sell his arrangements. In 1934 Benny Goodman bought many of them; ironically, Goodman, as a successful white bandleader, brought Henderson's music to more people than Henderson himself ever had. Henderson became the staff arranger for Goodman between 1939 and 1941 but returned to lead his own bands until his death in 1950.

Historically, Henderson's band of the twenties and early thirties formed a crucial link to the succeeding swing era. With its careful chemistry of ensemble passages and solo playing, the group played a fundamental role in the development of the big band. Moreover, Henderson's ensemble writing was often designed to sound like the hot solo improvisations it surrounded, bringing about a swinging style of ensemble playing. This would soon become the signature sound of the

---

A **stock arrangement**, or **stock**, was an arrangement created and sold by a publishing company to bandleaders. In some cases stocks were generic and unimaginative; at other times the arrangements were quite effective. Bands performed stocks to keep up with the latest hit songs. They would either play them as given or modify them to work with their bands' individual styles.

A **riff** is a short melodic idea, usually one to two bars in length, that is repeated as the core idea of a musical passage. Sometimes different band sections will trade riffs in a call-and-response format, often over changing harmonies. Usually rhythmic and simple, the riff also can provide a swinging background for an improvising soloist. (Listen to Track 49 of the ⏺ Audio Primer to hear a trumpet playing a background riff in a small-group context to back up the tenor soloist.)

big bands as they jumped to unprecedented popularity in the 1930s. We return to Henderson in Chapter 5 to explore one of the band's swing-style compositions.

Duke Ellington's Early Career

When Duke Ellington originally put together a big band in New York, he modeled it on Henderson's successful group.[14] Although Henderson's band was much better known during the 1920s, Ellington's unique combination of musicianship, compositional skill, professional savvy, and aristocratic persona eventually made him perhaps the most celebrated bandleader and composer in the history of jazz.

Born in Washington, DC, on April 29, 1899, Edward Kennedy Ellington began studying piano at the age of seven. As a teenager he developed an interest in stride piano and began performing publicly. During this period he earned the nickname "Duke" for his aristocratic deportment and tasteful dress. In places like Washington's Howard Theater, Ellington could have heard such groups as James Reese Europe's Clef Club Orchestra and Will Marion Cook and his Southern Syncopated Orchestra, stride pianists such as Luckey Roberts, and the musical revues of Eubie Blake and Noble Sissle. The Howard Theater also held performances of concert music, some of which drew on themes from the history of African Americans. These performances likely provided an early prototype for Ellington's later extended compositions—*Symphony in Black* and *Black, Brown and Beige*—which dealt with similar themes. After high school Ellington formed his own band in Washington: the Duke's Serenaders.

Ellington moved to New York in March 1923 to play with Wilbur Sweatman (1882–1961), a clarinetist who was a major jazz recording artist for Columbia Records in the early 1920s. Gigs were scarce at first. Ellington remained briefly before returning to Washington, but later that year he moved permanently to New York with his band, the Washingtonians: Sonny Greer on drums, Otto Hardwick on saxophone, Elmer Snowden on banjo, and Arthur Whetsol on trumpet. The band became regular performers at the Hollywood Cafe. Though Snowden initially led the band, Ellington replaced him as leader early in 1924, and the Hollywood Cafe changed its name to the more down-home Kentucky Club.

During their earliest days, the Washingtonians represented a typical downtown dance band that was probably more sweet than hot. One change in the band's personnel, however—the addition of cornetist Bubber Miley—

In Duke Ellington the black performer's progression from minstrel buffoon to serious artist became complete—as we see here in a publicity photograph of the elegant Ellington at about age thirty.

Photo courtesy of the Morgan Collection

straight mute he created a "growling" style of playing that entirely altered the sound of the band, and Miley became the featured soloist. "Our band changed its character when Bubber came in," Ellington acknowledged. "He used to growl all night long, playing gutbucket on his horn. That was when we decided to forget all about the sweet music."[15]

James "Bubber" Miley (1903–1932) became a cornerstone of Duke Ellington's early band. Miley's mute playing, which incorporated both the straight and cup varieties, owed a debt to King Oliver as well as to New York–based cornetist Johnny Dunn. The growling sound formed the basis of Ellington's "jungle" effects, a key feature of the band's Cotton Club performances that was adopted by subsequent

> Ellington earned his nickname "Duke" for his aristocratic deportment and tasteful dress while still in high school in Washington, DC.

A **plunger** is a type of mute derived from a plumber's sink plunger. The rubber cup is held against the bell of the instrument and manipulated with the left hand to alter the horn's tone quality.

had far-reaching consequences. Not only was Miley a hot player, but with his use of the **plunger** mute and the

Ellington trumpeters and trombonists. Although not particularly distinctive, the Washingtonian' earliest recordings do capture Miley's "gutbucket" sound. In works such as "Choo Choo (I Gotta Hurry Home)" and "Rainy Nights" (both from 1924), Miley uses the cup mute and his left hand

Much of Ellington's music in the late 1920s and early 1930s was created for floorshows at the Cotton Club. The club's jungle decor enhanced the exotic atmosphere, and the band exploited the brass section's growl techniques to create the "jungle sound" in such compositions as "East

> James "Bubber" Miley "used to growl all night long, playing gutbucket on his horn. That was when we decided to forget all about the sweet music."
> —Duke Ellington

to alter the sound of the instrument. Ellington historian Mark Tucker suggests that "Miley's power comes not from volume or speed but from his subtle coloring of individual notes and his ability to create and sustain a mood. . . . Miley was a different kind of hot trumpeter from the brilliant and rhythmically daring Armstrong."[16]

The growling style of brass playing was not restricted to the cornet: as the group gradually expanded to a ten-piece band during its four-year tenure at the Kentucky Club, with additions to the group such as Harry Carney on baritone saxophone, Rudy Jackson on clarinet and tenor saxophone, Wellman Braud on bass, Fred Guy on banjo, and trombonists Charles Irvis and, later, Joe "Tricky Sam" Nanton. These latter two players also cultivated the gutbucket sound on their instruments. (Listen to Track 24 of the Audio Primer to hear an example of plunger-and-growl technique on the trombone.)

In the second half of the 1920s, trombone players began to cultivate a solo approach over the ensemble role they had played earlier. The duet between Nanton and Juan Tizol (1900–1984) in Ellington's 1931 recording of

> Much of Ellington's music in the late 1920s and early 1930s was created for floorshows at the Cotton Club.

"Creole Rhapsody" is probably the earliest recorded trombone duet in jazz.

While the growling style of brass playing underlay the so-called jungle sound, there were other components as well, such as the use of tom-toms and other drums that implied "exotic" music of Africa. Pictures of Ellington's drummer, Sonny Greer, from the late 1920s show not only unusual drums but also gongs, chimes, and other interesting percussion far removed from the standard drum kit. Ellington's pieces that conveyed the "jungle sound" also tended to favor the minor mode over the major mode—the latter being preferred by far in the jazz of the era. (The exotic implications of the minor mode can be traced back to ragtime.) Finally, the grooving aspects of the rhythm in general also recalled aspects of African music.

St. Louis Toodle-Oo," "The Mooche," "Jungle Nights in Harlem," and "Echoes of the Jungle." The costumes of the dancers as well as the stage sets augmented the jungle motif. When we consider the importance of Ellington's floorshows at the Cotton Club, Louis Armstrong's starring role on Broadway with *Hot Chocolates*, and the several shows written by James P. Johnson, it is apparent that jazz in New York was allied to musical theater, all part of the larger artistic ferment of the Harlem Renaissance.

Throughout his career Ellington melded his players' individual sounds with the color of the entire band. Each

The Cotton Club—at Lenox Avenue and 142nd Street in Harlem—was famous for its extravagant floorshows. *Rhyth-mania*, with dances by Clarence Robinson, was one of them.

musician contributed to the group's distinctive timbre, enhanced by Ellington's own stride-based piano style. Many of the band's compositions were clearly collaborative efforts. "East St. Louis Toodle-Oo," "Creole Love Call," and "Black and Tan Fantasy" are among Ellington's early masterpieces, relying on the blues for form or feeling and featuring Miley and Nanton.

Under the management of Irving Mills, Ellington and the band enjoyed increasing prestige. Mills began touting Ellington as the leader of the "foremost dance band in America."[17] Mills's hyperbole soon proved true. After the band moved from the Kentucky Club to Harlem's Cotton Club in 1927, Ellington quickly became one of the leading national figures of jazz. At the Cotton Club, the band played music for dancing, vocalists, and elaborate floorshows to a well-heeled, after-theater crowd. With a ride from Broadway to Harlem, white patrons could feel the slightly risky thrill of enjoying black entertainment in a black neighborhood while remaining part of an all-white audience.

In addition to nightly performances at the Cotton Club, Mills generated high-visibility appearances for the band: backing Florenz Ziegfeld's *Show Girl*, accompanying French singer Maurice Chevalier at the Fulton Theatre, performing in films, and playing on radio broadcasts. The popular response to a 1930 broadcast of Ellington's composition "Dreamy Blues" led Mills to retitle the song and provide a lyric for what would become one of Ellington's most famous compositions: "Mood Indigo." With the addition of Barney Bigard on clarinet, Johnny Hodges on saxophone, Freddie Jenkins on trumpet, Juan Tizol

> With a ride from Broadway to Harlem, white patrons could feel the slightly risky thrill of enjoying black entertainment in a black neighborhood while remaining part of an all-white audience.

> Throughout his career Ellington melded his players' individual sounds with the color of the entire band. Each musician contributed to the group's distinctive timbre, enhanced by Ellington's own stride-based piano style.

on trombone, and—replacing Bubber Miley—Charles "Cootie" Williams on trumpet, Ellington's Cotton Club Orchestra now had twelve players.

The band's four years at the Cotton Club served as "a prolonged workshop period."[18] Nightly performances for thirty-eight months allowed Ellington the freedom to develop the band's musical identity, to highlight the individual players,

and—most important—to experiment with unusual instrumental combinations and colors. Ellington began creating larger extended compositions. Shortly before his tenure at the Cotton Club ended in 1931, Ellington recorded two versions of "Creole Rhapsody," a composition that took up two sides of a 78 rpm record. This was a substantial departure from the standard three-minute, one-sided jazz recording. The six-minute extended composition operated as a **suite** in miniature, making use of tempo changes and passages in free tempo and heralding a new compositional direction for Ellington. In later years Ellington would write several suites, such as *The Queen's Suite* and *The Far East Suite*. (We examine a portion of *The Queen's Suite* in Chapter 10.)

In the heady atmosphere of the Harlem Renaissance, Ellington's manager Mills sought to portray Ellington not merely as a bandleader and a songwriter but as "a great musician who was making a lasting contribution to American music."[19]

> "Every one of my song titles is taken principally from the life of Harlem."
> —Duke Ellington

Ellington's work was taking on elements of "mood" or "character" pieces, many with African American themes. As Ellington noted:

> Our aim as a dance orchestra is not so much to reproduce "hot" or "jazz" music as to describe emotions, moods, and activities which have a wide range, leading from the very gay to the somber. . . . Every one of my song titles is taken principally from the life of Harlem. . . . [I look] to the everyday life and customs of the Negro to supply my inspiration.[20]

Ellington's big band was an expression of his artistic vision. He composed original works that drew on the individual skills of his musicians. Band members felt that they were given an opportunity to express their own talents while playing Ellington's unique music. Unlike in other bands, members would often work with Ellington for years, sometimes

---

A musical form of the classical European tradition, a **suite** most often denotes a piece containing several sections, each with distinctive melodies and moods. The sections may be related thematically. Often composers will extract the most popular or most effective sections from extended works, such as operas and ballets, to create a suite for concert performance.

decades, enabling them to absorb his style as he continued to develop. As we explore in Chapter 5, Ellington, as a composer, spokesperson, and bandleader, would be a central force in the ongoing evolution of jazz to a serious art form.

A key aspect of Ellington's style is his inclination to employ mixed instrumental groupings, as we explore in Chapter 5. For this reason his scoring is often harder to identify on first hearing, and his textures differ from those of

> As a composer, spokesperson, and bandleader, Ellington would be a central force in the ongoing evolution of jazz to a serious art form.

most other ensembles. Moreover "East St. Louis Toodle-Oo" is conceived as a jazz composition, not an arrangement of a popular tune (see Listening Guide, Track 16).

Ellington continually strived for distinctive timbres and a unique overall sound. A tone we might call "brooding," as heard in "East St. Louis Toodle-Oo," is the product of multiple factors:

▶ Atypical use of bowed string bass

▶ Solos that feature growling, "jungle sound"

▶ Dark, muted timbres

▶ Thick chord voicings

▶ Interplay of major and minor keys

Duke Ellington & His Orchestra
"The Mooche" (1928)

Another fine work of Ellington's from the later twenties is "The Mooche," whose form can be summarized by the following schema:

A B	C1	D1 D2	C2	A B
C minor	E♭ major	E♭ minor	E♭ major	C minor
8-bar blues	12-bar blues	12-bar blues	12-bar blues	12-bar units

"The Mooche" has a kind of "arch form," a symmetrical structure that builds to the middle (the D1–D2–E♭ minor blues) and then reverses, to end with the beginning. Very little of this arrangement features solo improvisation; the

---

LISTENING GUIDE
"East St. Louis Toodle-Oo"

Track 16

Duke Ellington and His Orchestra: "East St. Louis Toodle-Oo" (Ellington-Miley). Victor 21703. New York, December 19, 1927. Edward Kennedy "Duke" Ellington, leader, piano, arranger; James "Bubber" Miley, Louis Metcalf, trumpets; Joe Nanton, trombone; Otto Hardwick, Harry Carney, Rudy Jackson, saxophones and clarinets; Fred Guy, banjo; Wellman Braud, bass; Sonny Greer, drums.

The Main Point With its Ellington trademark of richly voiced chords, "East St. Louis Toodle-Oo" is a fine example of the Ellington band's style in the late 1920s. Listen for trumpeter Miley's growling effect that is a main component of Ellington's "jungle sound." The somewhat mournful quality of the piece can be attributed in part to the string bass which, when bowed, adds an eerie somberness to the dark chord voicings of the band. Given the underrecorded presence of the drums, the beat is often audible only in the banjo strumming the backbeats and in the occasional piano chords flavoring the more lightly scored sections.

Jazz historian Joshua Berrett interprets the moodiness of "East St. Louis Toodle-Oo" with a striking image:

> For me the piece is a remarkable evocation of some kind of memory or image Ellington must have presumably had of the atmosphere surrounding a ring shout. The instruments are very much in the "talking/moaning" mode throughout this piece. The very first sound one hears suggests the moaning and groaning of a group as they shuffle at a slow deliberate pace around in a circle. The solos of Miley, Carney, Nanton, et al., can be heard as "preaching" to the group.[21]

Introduction

0:00   The piece begins with an eight-bar introduction consisting of richly voiced chords in the saxophones, piano, and bass. These chords form the background for Miley's subsequent trumpet solo. The baritone saxophone, the lowest saxophone part, is played somewhat louder than the other saxophones and imparts an earthiness to the chords.

Trumpet solo—AABA

0:14   The trumpet solo by Miley captures the "jungle sound" for which he and the band as a whole were famous. Miley's use of mute creates the growling effect that is a main component of the "jungle sound." His ability to bend notes is an especially memorable feature of the piece. Saxophone chords accompany the A sections.

0:43   In the B section, a muted trombone takes over the accompaniment.

Baritone saxophone solo—CC

1:12   In this next section, baritone saxophonist Carney contrasts the somber mood with an almost jaunty solo in the major mode. Carney's solo divides into two C sections with a break in the middle. The second C section has a two-bar extension at the end.

Trombone solo—CC

1:45   Nanton's trombone solo, although identical in form to Carney's baritone saxophone solo, features the muted growling sounds first heard with trumpeter Miley (0:14–1:13).

Clarinet solo—AA

2:18   A return of the thick opening chords forms the background for the clarinet solo, which begins with growling in the lower register. Later in the solo, the upper register is explored as well with no loss of intensity or mood.

Ensemble—CC

2:46   The first ensemble passage of the arrangement follows the clarinet solo, built on the harmony and the form of the baritone saxophone solo. As in that solo, this section is in two parts, with a break between them.

Return of A section

3:18   Rounding off the arrangement, Miley returns with an eight-bar reprise of the A section, accompanied by the saxophones and the trombones.

 Listen to this music in an animated Active Listening Guide available at the text website.

formal sections engage the players in a series of calls-and-responses between either the brass or reed section and the soloist, or soloist and soloist.

Jazz in Europe

That Europeans quickly embraced jazz was not surprising. From 1900 to 1920, they welcomed ragtime as the first musical genre distinctive to the United States and were as excited by it as Americans themselves. Certainly, ragtime and related forms of music, such as black musical theater, flourished in Europe soon after their establishment in the States. African American music, for example, was heard in London as early as 1903, when *In Dahomey*, a black musical that featured Bert Williams, brought the *cakewalk* to England. James Reese Europe's 369th Infantry "Hell Fighters" Band toured France in 1918 and was extremely popular. Even concert-music composers such as Igor Stravinsky and Maurice Ravel incorporated aspects of ragtime into their pieces. Stravinsky in

particular wrote *Ragtime for Eleven Instruments* in 1918 and *Piano-Rag-Music* in 1919; and one of his best-known ballets, *L'Histoire du soldat* (1917), featured a ragtime movement.

Jazz spread through Europe as quickly as ragtime had. In particular, during the years of transition from ragtime to early jazz, several American jazz artists and groups performed in Europe, which helped promote interest in both Great Britain and the Continent. Most significant was a tour by Will Marion Cook's Southern Syncopated Orchestra, which featured Sidney Bechet as a soloist and occasioned the rave review from Ernest Ansermet discussed in Chapter 3. The band launched its 1919 European tour in London. Eventually, because of difficulties with the band's personnel, Cook returned to the United States in 1920. Groups formed from members of the Southern Syncopated Orchestra, however, and continued to gig around Europe, in particular bands associated with Cook's drummers, Buddy Gilmore and Benny Peyton. The latter included Bechet in his ensemble. Both Gilmore and Peyton seem to have worked in many of Europe's major cities in the early

Bert Williams in prescribed vaudevillian blackface appears on the cover of this sheet music published in 1920 for Broadway's *Ziegfeld Follies*. "Moonshine" is home-brewed liquor.

1920s, and Peyton continued to lead his own groups in Europe throughout the twenties and thirties.

> ## The ODJB was the model most often followed by the earliest European groups, particularly in England.

Not only did Americans perform jazz in Europe, but they also taught their craft. Early on, "European musicians

Ted Heath, a trombonist who later led an English big band, performed with Cook's orchestra as it toured the Continent. Heath later wrote, "In particular, Buddy Gilmore, the drummer, went out of his way to teach us something about the different approach and techniques necessary for jazz."[23]

Other European musicians quickly tried their hand at the music. London-based pianist Billy Jones, for example, performed with the ODJB in the early 1920s. Indeed the ODJB was the model most often followed by the earliest European groups, particularly in England: "Prominent among those imitators who went on to transform a passing fad into the beginnings of an identifiable national style was Lew Davis, who heard the ODJB and took up the trombone, eventually joining the brothers Sid and Harry Roy in a quartet called The Lyricals."[24] Davis took jazz groups with European players on tour to Scandinavia and Belgium as early as 1921.

In 1926 Fred Elizalde, a pianist and composer born in the Philippines, formed a jazz band with his brother Manual while he was studying at Cambridge University; the Quinquaginta Ramblers was one of the first native British jazz bands. By 1927 Elizalde was leading a British-American band at London's Savoy Hotel, which included the fine American instrumentalists Joseph "Fud" Livingston (saxophone/clarinet) and Adrian Rollini (bass saxophone). Given its personnel, the band probably approximated the sound of the twenties Red Nichols groups, which had made some of the most popular small-group recordings of the era.

Following the lead of Will Marion Cook, other formal jazz orchestras toured Europe in the 1920s, including the white ensembles directed by Art Hickman and Paul Whiteman and a black group under the direction of Sam Wooding. Whiteman was in Great Britain in 1923 and toured the Continent in 1926. Wooding was one of the bandleaders most responsible for interesting Germans, as well as other Europeans, in jazz.

Sam Wooding (1895–1985), originally from philadelphia, established himself as a pianist and a bandleader first in Atlantic City, New Jersey, then in New York clubs in the early 1920s. He left the States with the revue *Chocolate Kiddies* in 1925 bound for Berlin, where his group became the first American jazz orchestra to record in Europe. He soon toured the Soviet Union and South America, thanks

> ## Sam Wooding was one of the bandleaders most responsible for interesting Germans, as well as other Europeans, in jazz. He left the States with the revue Chocolate Kiddies in 1925 bound for Berlin, where his group became the first American jazz orchestra to record in Europe.

on both sides of the English Channel were working alongside their American counterparts."[22] For example,

to the reputation the show achieved in Berlin. Among the fine musicians who performed with Wooding were

Adolphus "Doc" Cheatham (cornet) and Garvin Bushell (woodwinds). Bushell, in one of the most revealing of early jazz memoirs, recalls their reception in Berlin:

> Opening night at the Admiral's Palace the reception was very good. The audience whistled and hollered "Bravo." At first we thought they were screaming at us, "Beasts, beasts!" Then we learned they were calling out "Bis! Bis!" for encores. Most of the numbers had to take several encores. "Mit Dir" ["With You"], sung by Lottie Gee, took about three, and "Jig Walk"—they just couldn't get over that.[25]

"Jig Walk" was in fact a tune by Duke Ellington with a "Charleston" dance rhythm. As pointed out earlier, the rhythm and its associated dance step were popularized by James P. Johnson's 1923 "Charleston."

Germany's first indigenous jazz band with a significant reputation was the Weintraub Syncopators, which was formed in 1924 under the leadership of Stefan Weintraub (1897–1981). By 1928 they had recorded such tunes as "Up and at 'Em" and "Jackass Blues" and later appeared in the 1930 film (with Marlene Dietrich) *Der blaue Engel* (*The Blue*

> "At first we thought they were
> screaming at us, 'Beasts, beasts!'
> Then we learned they were calling
> out 'Bis! Bis!' for encores."
> —Garvin Bushell

Angel). As in England, jazz in Germany was a tremendous success, not only with touring Americans and native jazz groups but also with concert musicians influenced by the trend. Ernst Krenek wrote *Jonny spielt auf* (roughly, "Johnny Strikes Up the Band") in 1927—an opera that featured an African American protagonist. Alban Berg, one of the finest concert composers of the early twentieth century, called for an off-stage jazz band in his opera *Lulu* (1934).

Jazz in Germany was compromised by the rise of Adolf Hitler and the Nazi Party, which assumed leadership in 1933. Under the policies of Nazi propaganda director Joseph Goebbels, the party attempted to promote an art

of its association with Jewish culture, particularly through prominent songwriters (Irving Berlin and George Gershwin, for example) and popular music entrepreneurs.

What is particularly surprising is that jazz groups toured the Soviet Union as early as 1926. During the 1910s Russia had warmed to ragtime, although less enthusiastically than the rest of Europe. After the Russian Revolution in 1917, jazz created a serious dilemma for Soviet officials as news of it and the first ODJB recordings filtered to the new state. On the one hand, it was a "music of the people" that arose from the folk culture of African Americans, victims of discrimination in a U.S. society structured around race and class. When viewed in this way, jazz was largely compatible with communist ideals. On the other hand, especially in its popularization, jazz was a product of Western capitalism and mass marketing—both anathemas to Soviet officials more interested in cultivating the "purer" arts, those more in keeping with the ideals of Russian folk history (not to mention a tasteful disinterest in the bottom line).

Jazz received its greatest initial impetus in the Soviet Union from a tour of *Chocolate Kiddies*, the revue backed by Sam Wooding's group that was such a success in Berlin. Beginning in February 1926, the troupe toured the Soviet Union for three months. "Much to our amazement," Wooding reported, "our Russian engagements were the best in all Europe."[26] Among other things, the revue generated interest in the Charleston. Another important American jazzman to tour the Soviet Union soon after Wooding was drummer Benny Peyton, mentioned earlier in connection with Will Marion Cook.

Again, once the fire of jazz was lit, native Russians reacted enthusiastically:

> The Chocolate Kiddies had scarcely left Leningrad in 1926 than young Leningrad pianist Leopold Teplitsky set sail for America to study the new music in its native habitat. Teplitsky's mission was to master the techniques of American jazz, buy up stock arrangements and all the necessary musical instruments, and then put all this to use in a new jazz orchestra for the city of Lenin's Revolution.[27]

Teplitsky did in fact launch a jazz orchestra in Leningrad. Other Soviet jazz musicians followed in the 1920s, including Boris Krupyshev and Georgi Landsberg, who together founded the Leningrad Jazz Orchestra in the winter of

> Beginning in February 1926, the Chocolate Kiddies troupe toured the Soviet
> Union for three months. "Much to our amazement," Sam Wooding reported,
> "our Russian engagements were the best in all Europe."

and a music that supposedly reflected Aryan, pan-Germanic associations. Cultural products that failed to qualify were labeled "degenerate." Jazz was considered degenerate not only because of its African American roots but also because

1928–29. Another group, the Astoria Kids, played the Astoria Hotel around the same time. One of the best-known Soviet jazz musicians before World War II was bandleader and pianist Alexander Tsfasman, a stride stylist "reminiscent of James

P. Johnson."²⁸ Despite the difficulties of acquiring many of the instruments associated with jazz (in particular, saxophones), jazz continued to thrive in the USSR—sometimes sanctioned officially but ever present as an underground activity.

In many ways Paris may have been the European metropolis most receptive to developing a native jazz scene, possibly because of the affinity between its cabaret culture and jazz nightlife as it developed in the United States during the 1910s and early 1920s. An American associated with the Paris jazz scene early on was Louis Mitchell (1885–1957), a black drummer and close friend of James Reese Europe. After working with Europe and forming one of the earliest U.S. jazz bands, around 1918 Mitchell organized Mitchell's Jazz Kings, a group based in Paris from the late teens until about 1925. The group included cornetist Cricket Smith, who had been an important member of Europe's band. Sidney Bechet may have performed with the group from time to time.

Certainly, jazz in Paris received a major boost from Josephine Baker's hit show, *La Revue Nègre*. Baker was a flamboyant African American singer and dancer whose revue

opened in 1925. Its jazz-based accompaniment was provided by an orchestra under the leadership of Claude Hopkins (1903–1984), a pianist who later directed a very popular

> Paris may have been the European metropolis most receptive to developing a native jazz scene, possibly because of the affinity between its cabaret culture and jazz nightlife as it developed in the United States.

black jazz group in the 1930s. Baker's show was a scandalous sensation, with erotic costumes, sensual dancing, and jungle motifs that were a forerunner of Ellington's floorshows at the Cotton Club some two years later.

Probably the most significant indigenous band to emerge from the early Paris jazz scene was the Quintette du Hot Club de France. The Hot Club itself, under the direction of jazz critic Hugues Panassié, was formed in 1932 as a place for jazz enthusiasts to gather. The organization then expanded by presenting concerts, at first with American players but soon featuring French jazz musicians. The result was the club's signature group, the Quintette du Hot Club de France, a band formed in 1934 and featuring violinist Stéphane Grappelli (1908–1997) and guitarist Jean Baptiste "Django" Reinhardt (1910–1953). We hear one of their recordings on Track 17, a performance of "Tiger Rag."

Reinhardt was a guitar phenomenon. From a Manouche (French gypsy) background, Reinhardt was raised in a gypsy settlement near Paris. In the mid-twenties he worked commercially in the Paris area and developed a reputation for technique and style. His skill and control were all the more amazing because he was burned in a fire in 1928 and was unable to use two of the fingers on his left hand. By common consent he was Europe's first truly outstanding jazz musician—with his own, identifiable style that made a critical impact on other guitarists. In Woody Allen's 1999 movie, *Sweet and Lowdown*, the main character is a 1930s American jazz guitarist who is haunted by the fact that Reinhardt will always be the better guitarist.

Stéphane Grappelli enjoyed a long career as one of the world's great jazz violinists. He was largely self-taught and worked in both dance bands and movie theaters throughout the 1920s. From around 1927 he began more jazz-oriented work. After leaving the Quintette du Hot Club de France in 1939, he worked in England with pianist George Shearing. His later associations with jazz musicians took him throughout the world. When he died in 1997, he was honored as one of the great musicians in jazz.

Jimmie Lunceford on the cover of a French magazine announcing a forthcoming concert by Benny Carter. Back in the States, Lunceford and his band played at Harlem's Savoy Ballroom, which occupied the second floor of a building that ran the entire block of Lenox Avenue from 140th to 141st streets. As the place where everyone went to dance, it was one of the earliest integrated clubs.

LISTENING GUIDE
"Tiger Rag"

Django Reinhardt and the Quintette du Hot Club de France with Stéphane Grappelli: "Tiger Rag" (LaRocca). Ultraphone AP-1423. Paris, December 1934. Grappelli, violin; Reinhardt, Roger Chaput, Joseph Reinhardt, guitars; Louis Vola, bass.

The Main Point   This performance of "Tiger Rag" by the Quintet du Hot Club de France provides interesting points of comparison with the original ODJB of Track 8 (discussed in Chapter 2), and the Art Tatum recording on Track 15 (in this chapter). In contrast to the exciting but earthy playing of the ODJB, Reinhardt on guitar and Grappelli on violin display deft, fleet virtuosity that recalls Tatum. It is remarkable how thoroughly both soloists absorbed the jazz idiom, although as Europeans they did not participate in the U.S. jazz scene. This strings-only performance (without customary horns, piano, and drums) provides a remarkable textural contrast to the standard New Orleans ensemble of the ODJB "Tiger Rag."

A strain—8 bars, repeated

0:00   As in the ODJB introduction, the piece begins right at the A strain for the opening eight-bar section. Grappelli on the violin has the principal melody, with Reinhardt on guitar harmonizing the dexterous melodic line in a lower register. Note how much faster the performance is compared with the ODJB's. Such virtuosity is more reminiscent of the Tatum performance.

0:06   Repeat of the eight-bar A strain.

B strain—8 bars

0:12   The second strain does not quite feature the stop time chorus we heard with the ODJB because the bass continues to walk. Nevertheless, the effect of the stop time is similar because the ensemble strongly accents the measures' downbeats.

A strain—8 bars

0:18   Repeat of the A section.

C strain—24 bars as C1 (16) and C2 (8)

0:24   For the C strain's first half, Grappelli's melodic line contains the piece's first blue notes. The first half of the strain also features brilliant instrumental breaks throughout, the first two for Reinhardt, the third for bassist Vola.

0:30   Grappelli's double-stops (two notes at a time) are exciting and add a new textural element.

0:36   For the second half of the strain, the music finishes with a conclusive cadence. (Compared with the ODJB performance, the group truncates to eight bars this second half of the C strain.)

D strain—32 bars, 1st chorus

0:43   The strain begins with a Reinhardt solo. His bluesy bent and held-out notes provide an effective contrast to the busy virtuosity of the C strain. (An interesting question for the D strain: Do we miss the ODJB trombone glissandos leading to the "Hold that tiger!" figure?)

0:54   After returning to faster notes, Reinhardt ends the first half of the strain with a break.

0:56   Second half of the D strain with a melodic figure that arpeggiates a seventh chord,

0:59   Reinhardt holds a note by using a tremolo, an effect created by rapidly moving the pick up and down on the string.

D strain—32 bars, 2nd chorus

1:08   For the second chorus, Grappelli solos.

1:20   His break features a brilliant arpeggio on a diminished-seventh chord.

1:21	The second half of Grappelli's solo features a nice change to triplets (a feeling of three notes per pulse) at 1:29.

D strain—32 bars, 3rd chorus

1:34	A stop time bass solo for the first half, with the guitars providing downbeat accents every two bars. A loud tremolo in the guitars sets up the second half of the D strain.
1:47	The second half of the D strain. Here the band phrases together in a passage planned to prepare the out-chorus. Loud guitar accents usher in the final chorus (1:59).

D strain—32 bars, 4th (out-) chorus

2:00	For the out-chorus, the band picks up the intensity under Grappelli's exciting final solo.
2:12	Grappelli's break signifies the end of the first half.
2:13	The second half of the out-chorus. At its conclusion a descending chromatic chord progression broadens into the final chord.

 Listen to this music in an animated Active Listening Guide available at the text website.

Django Reinhardt and Stéphane Grappelli are only two of the first-rate musicians who emerged in Europe during the late 1920s. Although there is insufficient space for us to examine other fine artists, it is important to note that significant bands and musicians continued to flourish outside the United States, not only in the 1920s but also in the 1930s as jazz metamorphosed into a style that by mid-decade was popularly called *swing*. We explore the jazz of the 1930s in Chapters 5 and 6.

Exam Review Questions

Use these questions and the materials on the text website to help you understand and pass tests on the content of this chapter.

1. How did the center of jazz shift from Chicago to New York in the late 1920s?

2. How did the Harlem Renaissance contribute to the growing sense of black history and accomplishments?

3. In what ways can stride piano be considered a jazz style growing out of ragtime? Who were the best-known stride pianists of the 1920s?

4. What leaders and arrangers contributed to the foundations of big-band style in the 1920s?

5. What were some of the stylistic features of twenties big-band writing?

6. Describe Duke Ellington's early career. What characteristics distinguished Ellington's music from that of the other big bands?

7. Describe some of the early jazz developments in Europe taking place concurrent with those in the United States.

Test Yourself on Key Concepts with additional Chapter Quizzes and Listening Activities on the text website.

Key Terms

Test your knowledge of this chapter's key terms by defining the following. If you can't remember the meaning of a term, refresh your memory by looking up the boldfaced term in the chapter, turning to the Glossary at the back of the book, or working with the flashcards at the text website.

big band **118**

cutting contest **108**

Harlem Renaissance **106**

head arrangement **118**

piano rolls **109**

player piano **109**

plunger **120**

rent party **107**

riff **119**

rubato **114**

section **118**

song plugger **106**

staccato **118**

stock arrangement (stock) **119**

stride piano **108**

suite **122**

Tin Pan Alley **106**

vamp **112**

MOONGLOW

BY WILL HUDSON • EDDIE De LANGE • IRVING MILLS

FEATURED BY *Ina Ray* HUTTON

The all-women band—in this case, Ina Ray Hutton and Her Melodears—was still a novelty in 1934, when this song was published. The group did not survive, but the song became a hit for the Benny Goodman Quartet and has since become a jazz standard.

and her MELODEARS

The Swing Era

Start with a quick
warm-up activity.

FROM ROUGHLY 1935 TO 1945 **SWING** DOMINATED the popular music of the United States, the only time that any type of jazz achieved such mainstream success. Adoring fans idolized the top players and made the most successful bandleaders rich. The big-band era had arrived.

This chapter presents the **big bands** in the context of their time. Andy Kirk's Twelve Clouds of Joy was an important territory (regional) band from Kansas City that featured Mary Lou Williams, an excellent pianist and arranger who carved out a major career in an era unreceptive to women as jazz musicians. After examining the growth of the territory bands, we turn to three of the most influential big bands: the Count Basie Orchestra from Kansas City and the Benny Goodman and Duke Ellington bands from New York. Complementing Mary Lou Williams, in Chapter 6 we examine a well-known women's big band, the International Sweethearts of Swing. We also check in on Louis Armstrong in Chapter 6, and hear him in a big-band context.

Of all the leaders of big bands, Goodman achieved the greatest mainstream success, although Basie and Ellington probably contributed the most significant elements to the big-band style. All three musicians enjoyed long and influential careers that extended beyond the swing era.

Social Upheavals in the 1930s

The Great Depression dominated life in the 1930s, causing massive unemployment and general domestic hardship. Harburg and Gorney's well-known song "Brother, Can You Spare a Dime?" (1932) captured the general mood. The Depression extended to Europe and in Germany was certainly a factor in Adolf Hitler's election as chancellor of Germany in 1933. Hitler's aggressive foreign policy through the mid-thirties culminated in Germany's invasion of Poland (1939) and the beginning of World War II. In the

Jazz

1931—Armstrong records "When It's Sleepy Time Down South"
1932—Ellington records "It Don't Mean a Thing"
1935—Benny Goodman's stupendous success at the Palomar Ballroom in Los Angeles
—Goodman records "King Porter Stomp"
1936—Lester Young plays with Count Basie
1937—Height of swing era
—Goodman, Basie, Ellington extremely popular
—Basie records "One O'clock Jump"
—Ellington records "Caravan"
—Benny Goodman Quartet records "Avalon"
1938—Benny Goodman at Carnegie Hall
—Goodman records "Undecided"
1939—Beginnings of bop at Monroe's Uptown House in Harlem
—Charlie Christian plays with Benny Goodman
—Glenn Miller records "In the Mood"
1940—Ellington records "Concerto for Cootie"
—Artie Shaw records "Star Dust"
1941—Ellington records "Take the 'A' Train"
1942—Beginnings of New Orleans Dixieland revival
—Big bands depleted by draft
—Recording ban imposed by the American
Federation of Musicians (AF of M)

1930   1935   1940

Historical Events

1931—Depths of Depression; bank failures
1933—Hitler elected chancellor of Germany
—Franklin Roosevelt inaugurated
1935—Congress passes Social Security Act
1936—Spanish civil war
1937—Japan declares war on China
—Picasso, *Guernica*
1938—Hitler annexes Austria to Germany
—Volkswagen produces first Beetle
1939—World War II begins
—Steinbeck, *The Grapes of Wrath*
—Margaret Mitchell, *Gone with the Wind*
1940—Roosevelt becomes
first three-term president
—Hemingway, *For Whom the Bell Tolls*
—Plutonium, first nonnatural element
1941—United States enters
WWII after the bombing of
Pearl Harbor
—*Citizen Kane*
—First jet plane
—*Casablanca*
1943—First nuclear reactor

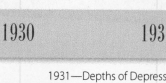

United States, Franklin Roosevelt was elected president in 1932, promising a "new deal" for the American people. Roosevelt's policies included a more active governmental role in trying to counter the effects of the Depression. For example, Congress passed the Social Security Act in 1935 to help guarantee income to retired citizens. Also significant for nightlife and the coming boom in swing music was the repeal of Prohibition in 1933.

Despite the difficult economic times, popular music flourished in the early 1930s, with composers turning out some of the greatest standards of the repertory, such as "I Got Rhythm," "Body and Soul," "How Deep Is the Ocean," "The Song Is You," and many others taken up by jazz musicians.

In concert music, major works included Bartók's *Second Piano Concerto* (1933) and Berg's *Violin Concerto* (1935). Inspired by events in the Spanish Civil War, Picasso created perhaps the most impressive painting of

Swing is the generic term used for the jazz music and much popular music of the mid-thirties through the mid-forties.

A **big band** is a large jazz ensemble typically including three to four trumpets, three to four trombones, four to five reeds (saxophones and doublings), and rhythm (typically piano, guitar, bass, and drums).

> "Dancing to swing was central to their courtship style. Young people danced—at first the fox-trot, then the so-called jitterbug dances which arose in the mid- to late-1930s—in huge, often elaborate dance palaces, in hotel restaurants and ballrooms, in high school gyms and, perhaps most of all, in living rooms to swing music from radios and record players."
> ~James Lincoln Collier

the decade, *Guernica* (1937). Among the classic novels was Steinbeck's *The Grapes of Wrath* (1939), which in part chronicled the effects of the Depression.

A Decade of Swing

Swing music was a phenomenon. Between 1935 and 1945, it became the popular music of a generation. Speaking for the generation that came of age between the beginning of the Great Depression and the end of World War II, James Lincoln Collier remembers the following:

> Swing was theirs alone. Dancing to swing was central to their courtship style. Young people danced—at first the fox-trot, then the so-called jitterbug dances which arose in the mid- to late-1930s—in huge, often elaborate dance palaces, in hotel restaurants and ballrooms, in high school gyms and, perhaps most of all, in living rooms to swing music from radios and record players. By means of the new "portable" radios their music went with them everywhere: on woodland picnics, to beaches, summer houses, skating ponds, big city parks. These people not only danced to swing, they ate to it, drank to it, necked to it, talked to it, and frequently just listened to it. It was everywhere.[1]

As Ivie Anderson sang in Duke Ellington's band, "It Don't Mean a Thing (If It Ain't Got That Swing)."

In 1930 only one-third of U.S. households had radios; by 1935 two-thirds of all homes had them. Similarly, the number of jukeboxes jumped from 25,000 in 1933 to 300,000 in 1939.

In 1932 when the song was released, however, *swing* was only an insider's term. Duke Ellington even had to explain in 1933 that his orchestra and a few others "exploited a style known as 'swing' which is Harlem for rhythm."[2] But within a few years the term—and the music—dominated popular culture.

As the 1930s progressed, more people had access to the music. Radios, increasingly more affordable, broadcast the big bands from ballrooms and hotels in the major cities. In 1930 only one-third of U.S. households had radios;

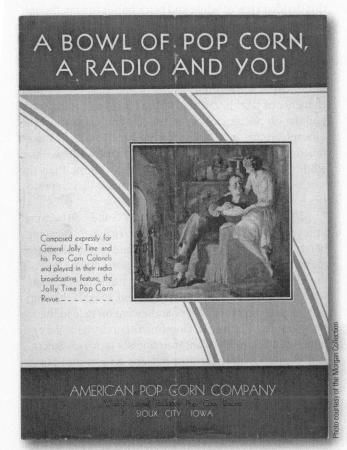

This cover of Jolly Time Popcorn sheet music—written for a 1930 radio commercial—offered a comforting image of the simple life and an American variation on the familiar formula for true contentment: "a jug of wine, a loaf of bread, and thou." The popcorn came in two varieties, with hulls and without.

Hot bands were jazz bands that featured fast tempos and dramatic solo and group performances, usually with more improvisation than **sweet bands** that played relatively less syncopated and slower pieces, such as ballads and popular songs.

by 1935 two-thirds of all homes had them. Similarly, the number of jukeboxes jumped from 25,000 in 1933 to 300,000 in 1939. The dramatic growth of the recording and radio industries changed popular music forever. No longer did people have to sing or play an instrument to enjoy music whenever they wished. Furthermore, musical success came from the numbers of records sold, not just prestigious live engagements.

It is impossible to sort out all the reasons why both white and black audiences demanded to hear, more than any other style, the **hot** jazz music of the 1920s pioneered by black bands. At the beginning of the 1930s, Duke Ellington and Fletcher Henderson, with their enlarged bands, were becoming the primary interpreters of swing music; many of the white bands, such as the Guy Lombardo band, played in a sentimental, **sweet** style. We should not carry this divided view of white and black bands too far, though. The repertory of the black bands was never exclusively hot jazz: some of their arrangements qualified as sweet music, and Ellington's Cotton Club revues and Jimmie Lunceford's shows always included novelty and show numbers. By the same token, some white bands of the early 1930s used elements of jazz. In particular, the Casa Loma Orchestra, popular on college campuses, was another of the most significant groups in establishing big-band swing. It mixed raucous up-tempo works with sentimental waltzes. Thus, while the black bands featured more hot music than the white bands did, all the bands widely varied their repertories—it was necessary for survival.

By the middle of the decade, Benny Goodman became known as the "king of swing" after rising to dizzying heights playing many of Fletcher Henderson's arrangements. Goodman's success was contagious. By the end of the 1930s, there were more than 200 name bands, each with star soloists. Often the prominent soloists, having begun their careers in other bands, went on to lead their own groups. Clarinetist Goodman, trumpeters Harry James and Bunny Berigan, trombonists Jack Teagarden and Tommy Dorsey, drummer Gene Krupa, and pianists Duke Ellington and Count Basie—all formed their own bands. Each had a distinctive sound:

> You could hear all types of swing bands: the hard-driving swing of Benny Goodman, the relaxed swing of Jimmie Lunceford, the forceful Dixieland of Bob Crosby, the simple, riff-filled swing of Count Basie, the highly developed swing of Duke Ellington, and the very commercial swing of Glenn Miller.[3]

When we listen today to the music that the more commercial swing bands played in their heyday, we would not consider much of it to be jazz. Continuing a trend from the 1920s, many bands often avoided outright

> Almost all of the bands had singers—invariably called "girl" singers and "boy" singers, whatever their age—and vocal music constituted a sizeable portion of any band's song list.

improvisation. They might work out the solo (or improvisational) sections in advance and play them identically night after night—often because listeners expected the same improvisations they heard on the recordings. Many of the bands continued to churn out sentimental ballads along with up-tempo swing. And almost all of the bands had singers—invariably called "girl" singers and "boy" singers, whatever their age—and vocal music constituted a sizeable portion of any band's song list. Many of the singers who later became famous on their own began

Fletcher Henderson, pictured on the cover of this sheet music, created memorable arrangements for Benny Goodman and helped spur his popularity.

their careers singing with swing bands: Frank Sinatra, for example, got his start with the bands of Harry James and Tommy Dorsey, and Peggy Lee started out with Benny Goodman.

Another aspect of 1930s popular culture that related in part to swing was commercial movies. Although the film industry had been expanding since the start of the twentieth century, the advent of film with sound—the *talkies* of the late 1920s—fueled its rapid advance. Film with sound formed a natural alliance with popular music,

> While it lasted, swing defined a golden age of jazz, a time when great musicians and first-rate bands produced outstanding music and brought jazz its greatest popular acclaim.

and out of this marriage two important genres were born: the short film (*soundie*) often featuring an artist performing a song (an early version of the music video), and the full-length feature film, often produced by a major studio and sometimes portraying the history of an artist or a band. With the latter take heed: Hollywood might romanticize—even distort—an artist's biography to create what the film's producers considered a more interesting plot. Beginning in the late 1920s, soundies of many jazz artists became available, while the most popular artists and big bands appeared in larger-scale productions. We describe Louis Armstrong's pioneering presence in the movies in Chapter 3. (See "Selected Jazz DVDs and Videos" at the back of this text.)

The swing boom continued unabated through the early 1940s, but from 1942 began to decline during World War II (1941–1945). Gasoline rationing and the shortage of tires made touring difficult to schedule or prohibitively expensive for bands that needed to travel extensively for live performances, and the wartime draft emptied the bands of key players. The decline of nightlife made it more expensive to spotlight the bands, and many of the singers who began with bands gained success on their own. At the end of 1946, eight of the most famous groups disbanded either temporarily or permanently—including those of Benny Goodman, Jack Teagarden, Harry James, Woody Herman, Tommy Dorsey, and Benny Carter—and the swing boom came to an end.

Beyond the societal upheavals that hastened the end of the swing era, swing itself was largely exhausted as a popular jazz style—the public wanted something new. But while it lasted, swing defined a golden age of jazz, a time when great musicians and first-rate bands produced outstanding music and brought jazz its greatest popular acclaim.

Paul Whiteman and his band, who had appeared in the 1930 Universal film *King of Jazz*, featured another dance fad called "Crazy Walk" in 1933; it did not endure.

The Big Band in the Swing Era

Instrumentation, Technique, and Arrangement

The dance orchestra and the large jazz ensemble became all but synonymous during the swing era. The lindy hop—also called the jitterbug—was a frenetic and virtuosic dance that required an up-tempo, hot jazz sound. As discussed in Chapter 4, the big band evolved for the most part from the dance orchestra, but during the 1920s the hot rhythm and improvisation of the Dixieland jazz players gradually transformed these orchestras. We have seen how bandleader Fletcher Henderson and his talented arranger, Don Redman began developing the big-band style. Other popular bands, such as the relatively mainstream Jean Goldkette and Paul Whiteman orchestras, incorporated jazz improvisation and spread the influence of large bands. These groups, along with the band of Art Hickman, spurred the development of the typical big

The **rhythm section** is a subgroup of the jazz ensemble, composed of banjo or guitar, bass, drums, and often the piano; it provides accompaniment for the primary instruments playing the melody. Early jazz bands sometimes included banjo and tuba in place of the guitar and bass. Listen to Tracks 44 and 45 of the  Audio Primer to hear a modern rhythm section; Track 44 has bass and drums; Track 45 adds the piano.

Antiphony is the trading of melodic figures between two different sections of the band; it is a more formal musical term for *call-and-response*. Antiphony implies an equal division of the musical forces rather than an answering response to a leading call. (Listen to Track 47 of the Audio Primer: the trumpet and the saxophone, by trading twos, engage in a form of antiphony.)

band into an ensemble using four instrumental divisions or sections:

▶ Trumpets (listen to Tracks 12–15 of the Audio Primer)

▶ Trombones (with trumpets and trombones grouped together as the *brass*) (listen to Tracks 22–25 of the Audio Primer)

▶ Woodwinds, usually called *reeds* (saxophones and related instruments) (listen to Tracks 16–21 of the Audio Primer)

▶ The **rhythm section**, frequently consisting of piano, guitar, bass, and drums (listen to Tracks 26–43 of the Audio Primer)

The demands on the musicians playing in a big band differed significantly from those placed on small-group players. The extensive library, or book, of arrangements that all big bands developed required that the musicians be skilled in reading parts. Playing with a big-band section required that musicians blend with similar instruments, that is, that they play together with precision and constant attention to intonation and balance. (See the box "Big-Band Terms.")

Big-band arrangements formed the basis of the swing-era repertory. The most creative arrangers of the period—Don Redman, Duke Ellington, Fletcher Henderson, Eddie Sauter, Sy Oliver, and Benny Carter—successfully and creatively balanced written ensemble sections with sections for improvised solos that showed off the star players in the bands. These arrangers skillfully used the band's various resources—for example, by setting off the brass section from the reed section or by writing a brass or reed accompaniment behind the soloist. One characteristic technique that arrangers used involved **antiphony**, particularly the antiphonal alternation of different sections of the band. An example of this occurs in Fletcher Henderson's celebrated 1935 arrangement of Jelly Roll Morton's "King Porter Stomp" in which Henderson first gives the figure to the brass in the pickup and measures

Fletcher Henderson & His Orchestra
"King Porter Stomp"
(1935)

Insider's Guide to...

Big-Band Terms

A band's **library**, or **book**, is its collection of arrangements or pieces. Arrangements are often called **charts**. These are usually songs but may also include larger-scale works. A library is necessary for big bands, but smaller groups may also have one.

A **section** of a big band is a group of related instruments; three trumpets and three trombones might form the brass section.

Musicians with good **intonation** are said to be playing "in tune." That is, the players know how to make small adjustments in the pitch of their instruments as they play so that they match the pitches of the other players in the section.

Balance refers to a section's ability to blend. In a well-balanced section, none of the players will be too soft or too loud relative to the others.

An often-heard term for each part in a section is **chair**, as in first trumpet chair, first trombone chair, and so on.

The player who usually takes the melody or top part in a section is called the **lead player**; that is, the lead player occupies the first chair of the section. Within a given section, the lead player will usually be slightly louder than the other players in a correct balance.

A band depends, in particular, on the lead chair or first trumpet player of the trumpet section. The **lead trumpet** must be a dominating player, capable of precision, power, and control of the high register.

The **jazz chair** of a section may be a player hired especially for improvisational fluency. For example, Bix Beiderbecke occupied the jazz trumpet chair in the Paul Whiteman band, as did Bubber Miley in the Ellington band.

A player who is neither a lead player nor a featured soloist is usually called a **sideman**.

2 and 4, and then to the reeds in measures 1, 3, and 5. This typical passing back and forth of the figure between brass and reeds continues the use of the **call-and-response** patterns that we first heard in vocal music. Henderson's "Down South Camp Meeting" (Listening Guide, Track 18) also illustrates antiphony. Henderson created an especially fine composition and arrangement in "Down South Camp Meeting," which, like "King Porter Stomp," later became a huge hit for Benny Goodman (Track 21).

One of the many reasons why big bands enjoyed such popularity was their focus on the hit songs of the day. The bands developed a symbiotic relationship with the

---

Call-and-response A musical procedure in which a single voice or instrument states a melodic phrase—the *call*—and a group of voices or instruments follows with a responding or completing phrase—the *response*.

LISTENING GUIDE

Track 18

"Down South Camp Meeting"

Fletcher Henderson and His Orchestra: "Down South Camp Meeting" (Henderson). Decca 213. New York, September 12, 1934. Henderson, piano, leader, arranger; Henry Allen, Irving Randolph, Russell Smith, trumpets; Keg Johnson, Claude Jones, trombones; Buster Bailey, clarinet; Hilton Jefferson, Russell Procope, clarinets, alto saxophones; Ben Webster, tenor saxophone; Lawrence Lucie, guitar; Elmer James, bass; Walter Johnson, drums.

The Main Point   In this recording of "Down South Camp Meeting," which predates Benny Goodman's more famous version that we examine later in this chapter (Track 21), we can hear many of the swing-style techniques discussed in this chapter—particularly antiphony, the trading of melodic figures between two different sections of the band. Note that there is little solo improvisation in the arrangement—only one 24-bar solo by trumpeter Henry Allen. The focus instead is on the big band itself, that is, on the composition, Henderson's arrangement, and the overall performance.

Introduction—4 bars

0:04   Count this piece as either a fast four beats to the bar or a moderate two beats to the bar. The introduction features a syncopated figure played by the entire ensemble; the prevailing harmony is G7 (extended to the thirteenth), which as a dominant sets up the A section in C major.

A section—8 bars as 4 + 4 in C major

0:05   The saxophone section has the syncopated melody, sustained notes that are attacked just before the beat. We can hear in the lead saxophone that the second-to-last note of each four-bar unit is a blue third, which contributes a hot, blues-tinged quality typical of up-tempo swing pieces. In the fourth bar of each four-bar unit, the brass answer antiphonally.

B section—8 bars as 4 + 4 in A minor

0:14   In the contrasting B section, brass and saxophones reverse roles: the brass take the lead, and the saxophones answer. The downbeat note of the lead trumpet in each four-bar unit is the blue fifth, E♭, of A minor. Thus the blue third (E♭) of C major in the A section is reinterpreted as the blue fifth (E♭) of A minor in the B section. The relative minor, A minor, offers a tonal contrast to C major.

A section—8 bars as 4 + 4

0:23   The A section returns with minor embellishments to the principal melody.

Trumpet solo—ABA as 8 + 8 + 8

0:32   The ABA framework just presented serves as a background for an Allen trumpet solo. The saxophones sustain chords as an accompaniment.

0:42	Allen alludes to the original melodic idea of the B section in the B section of his solo.
0:52	Return to the A section of the solo.

Transition—8 bars

1:01	In this transitional and modulating section, hear the antiphonal saxophone and trumpet solos. Saxophones and trombones accompany with sustained chords, which crescendo as they are held. The harmonic progression features a circle of fifths of dominant chords: C7, F7, B♭7, and E♭7, each held for two bars. The chord progression serves to set up A♭ major for the following section.

C section—CCDC as 8 + 8 + 4 + 8 in A♭ major

1:10	The C section is analogous to the trio in the older ragtime- and march-influenced jazz of the 1920s, although here the key is not the subdominant but the distant key of A♭ major, or ♭VI relative to the opening key of C major. The saxophones have the melody for the most part. The C section (first eight bars, or C) features a swinging tune with an E♭7 (V7) chord for the first four bars, resolving to an A♭ (I) chord for the second four bars. We can hear the use of C♭, or the blue third of A♭ major, as a key part of the tune.
1:29	The bridge of the C section, D, is an irregular four bars and is syncopated to provide a contrast to the relative rhythmic regularity of the C section's main theme, which contains many on-the-beat and accented quarter notes.
1:33	The return of the C section's main theme (C) is modified to create a more conclusive cadence.

C section—CCDC as 8 + 8 + 4 + 8, repeated

1:43	The brass take the melody for the first two C sections. There are some modifications and embellishments to the C theme, which we first heard in the saxophones.
2:01	The saxophones take the bridging D theme, which is also modified from its first presentation. These small changes indicate the care Henderson took to enhance the effectiveness of the arrangement.
2:06	Return to the C section.

Transition—4 bars

2:15	An antiphonal transitional section on an A♭7 chord sets up the following section, a second "trio" in D♭ major. Note the call-and-response between the brass and the reeds (with lead clarinet).

E section—8 bars, played 4 times in D♭ major

2:19	A new timbre complements a new melody and key: the melody is now played by a clarinet trio in a fairly low register. The first note of the lead clarinet is F♭, the blue third of D♭ major. Thus, Henderson continues the idea of featuring blue notes as key elements of his themes. The section is played four times.
2:38 & 2:48	The third and fourth times, the clarinets play an octave higher. The brass answer the short phrases in the reeds antiphonally.

Tag—1 bar

2:56	A short tag consisting of rising *tutti* chords—syncopated off the beat—extends the E section by a bar.

Listen to this music in an animated Active Listening Guide available at the text website.

publishers of Tin Pan Alley and would vie to be the first to perform and record the best new songs. Similarly, the publishers would try to interest the most popular bands in their latest efforts. The result was a steady stream of hit songs that the public enjoyed and their favorite bands personalized. For an extremely popular song, different groups would compete with arrangements that varied from quite similar to very distinctive.

During the course of writing a chart, arrangers often took liberties with the melodic and rhythmic structure of the original song and reworked it into swing style. Frequently, they syncopated melodies to give them the rhythmic character of an improvised jazz solo. This swing-style melody made the transitions from written sections to improvised-solo sections more seamless.

Territory bands and the groups in and around Kansas City favored the *head arrangement* (discussed in Chapter 2), which band members fashioned by ear during rehearsal or performance, working out their own parts or suggesting parts to one another. These arrangements were often simple and riff oriented, lacking the variety of textures available to arrangers working with printed scores. Although head arrangements were associated with the Kansas City bands, it should be noted that more-formal written arrangements were equally common with them.

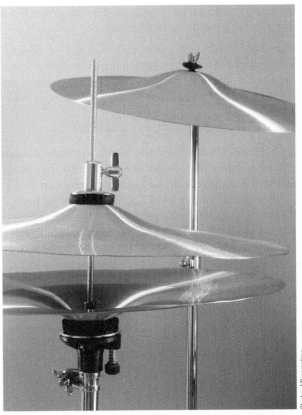

Clockey | Dreamstime

The Changing Role of the Rhythm Section

The rhythm section largely generated the hard-driving swing that propelled the ensemble and improvised sections of the bands. In the big-band era, expectations of the *rhythm section*—piano, guitar, bass, and drums—changed.

pianist from a timekeeping role. Pianists could play fewer notes and were able to accompany soloists by playing syncopated chordal figures.

The drummer's role changed considerably after the hi-hat became a part of the drummer's set. The hi-hat,

> The drummer's role changed considerably after the hi-hat became a part of the drummer's set. Instead of keeping the pulse in the bass drum, swing drummers used the hi-hat to create a more subtle propulsion that could drive an entire big band.

Responding to innovations in the design of instruments and changes in musical taste, these instruments performed differently during the swing era than they had before. During the 1920s either the tuba or the string bass provided the rhythmic underpinning for the band, but the bass gradually superseded the tuba. In addition, the bass or tuba player was expected to play either on beats 1 and 3 or on all four beats of the measure. By the mid- to late thirties, however, the bass player often played consistently on all four beats, creating the **walking bass** sound. The four-beat walking bass then freed the

introduced in 1927, consisted of two face-to-face cymbals that the drummer controlled with a foot pedal. The pedal closed the cymbals with a *chick* sound. (Listen to Track 31 of the 🅟 Audio Primer to hear this sound; Track 32 exemplifies a swing beat played on the hi-hat.) Instead of keeping the pulse in the bass drum, swing drummers such as Walter Johnson of Fletcher Henderson's band and Jo Jones

In performing a **walking bass**, the bassist articulates all four beats in a 4/4 bar. The bass lines often follow scale patterns, avoiding too many disruptive leaps between notes. The walking bass is common in jazz, heard in all styles since becoming firmly established during the swing era. (Listen to Track 43 of the 🅟 Audio Primer to hear a walking bass.)

© Jake Holmes/iStockphoto.com

A **territory band** played and toured a region around a major city that served as a home base.

A **standard** song, unlike the vast majority of popular music, outlasts its contemporaries and enjoys a long-lasting place in current repertories. "I Got Rhythm," for example, is a standard written by George and Ira Gershwin in 1930.

---

of Count Basie's band used the hi-hat to create a more subtle propulsion that could drive an entire big band. Soon other drummers learned to keep the pulse on the hi-hat. Often the drummer would close the pedal on beats 2 and 4, slightly accenting these beats in relation to the first and third beats. In addition, by the mid- to late thirties, many drummers used the bass drum on all four beats, as exemplified by Gene Krupa's work with Benny Goodman, especially on what Goodman called his up-tempo "killer-diller" numbers.

By the end of the 1920s, the guitar gradually replaced the banjo in the rhythm section. Philadelphia-born guitarist

> By the end of the 1920s, the guitar gradually replaced the banjo in the rhythm section. The introduction in 1936 of the electric guitar allowed the guitarist to be heard in a large group and take on an improvisational role.

Eddie Lang (1902–1933) helped spur this change. Lang contributed to the historic Beiderbecke-Trumbauer recordings—we heard him on "Singin' the Blues," Track 13—and recorded with Red Nichols, Jean Goldkette, and Paul Whiteman, as well as with violinist Joe Venuti. Advances in recording technology and the use of the arched-top guitar allowed the instrument to be audible in recordings and performances. With his single-line solos, Lang helped define guitar as a solo instrument and may have influenced the developing style of Django Reinhardt (see Chapter 4). He used rich harmonies in accompaniments, often by alternating single notes with chords.

As the swing era evolved, guitarists started playing four chords to the measure, giving a slight accent to the second and fourth beats. The introduction in 1936 of the electric guitar allowed the guitarist to be heard in a large group. The electric guitar also enabled the performer to take on an improvisational role in a large ensemble rather than merely providing accompaniment. (Listen to Tracks 36–42 of the Audio Primer to hear examples of acoustic and electric guitars in different settings.)

Territory Bands

The rise of swing took place gradually over time and across the country. While New York bands of the late 1920s and early 1930s were developing the swing style, many of the midwestern and southwestern **territory bands** were contributing to its evolution. From St. Louis to Denver, between Texas and Nebraska, in towns such as Omaha, Oklahoma City, and Salina, territory bands abounded. Centering themselves on a regional capital, territory bands toured their regions and played dance halls and theaters for one-night or multiweek engagements. Many of the bands covered a lot of territory:

> Jumps of 800 or 1,000 miles between engagements were not uncommon, and, among the less affluent orchestras, these trips were made by passenger car, with perhaps a truck carrying the instruments and arrangements, if any. Accounts of panic trips, with twelve musicians crammed into a single automobile, and a man or two hanging onto the running board or fender, are encountered in interviews dealing with the Depression years.[4]

Many members of territory bands were not music readers. Players and soloists sometimes relied on head arrangements and their own improvisational skills. Although the bands featured the blues and simple riff-oriented charts, arrangements of popular **standards** were common as well, although these tended to be less complicated than, say, the works of Redman and Henderson.

The territory bands had rivalries, some friendly and some not; and legendary "battles of the bands" in the

> "Accounts of panic trips, with twelve musicians crammed into a single automobile, and a man or two hanging onto the running board or fender, are encountered in interviews dealing with the Depression years."

dance halls show a fierce competitive spirit that helped improve the bands' sounds. Many significant players of the swing era—Coleman Hawkins, Ben Webster, Herschel Evans, Lester Young, Buster Smith, and Count Basie—received their earliest training in these bands.

Alfonso Trent, Terence T. Holder and His Clouds of Joy, and Troy Floyd were three of the leading Texas-based territory bands. Floyd's orchestra—which consisted

Territory bands proliferated as they responded to local popular demand generated by radio. Among them were Art Landry and His Call of the North Orchestra and Gage Brewer's Versatile Radio Orchestra—which "delighted thousands during the International Petroleum Exposition at Tulsa in 1936."

Troy Floyd & His Plaza Orchestra
"Shadowland Blues"
(1928)

of two trumpets, one trombone, three saxophones, and a rhythm section of banjo, piano, and drums—made some rare recordings in 1928 and 1929. Two of them, "Dreamland Blues" and "Shadowland Blues," were head arrangements and revealed the popularity of blues in Texas. The George Morrison Orchestra played most of the dance hall engagements in Denver, Colorado. Among Morrison's sidemen were several players who would later become bandleaders themselves, including Andy Kirk and Jimmie Lunceford.

> "The biggest upset we ever had in our life…happened to be in Sioux City, Iowa…and it was a battle of bands between Page and Jesse Stone."

The Original Blue Devils

In Oklahoma City, Walter Page's Original Blue Devils emerged in 1925 and within the next five years became one of the most respected territory bands. The group relentlessly recruited many of the best players; at different times Page's bands featured tenor saxophonist Lester Young, bassist Walter Page, trumpeter-vocalist Oran "Hot Lips" Page, trombonist-guitarist Eddie Durham, pianist William "Count" Basie, and vocalist Jimmy Rushing. In the battles of the bands, Page's group competed fiercely. Rival bandleader Jesse Stone described an upset he received at the hands of the Blue Devils:

Walter Page's Blue Devils
"Blue Devil Blues"
(1929)

The biggest upset we ever had in our life…happened to be in Sioux City, Iowa…and it was a battle of bands between Page and Jesse Stone. We got up on the stand first because we were considered like a house band there. We played there regularly. Well, we started out with some of our light things, little ballads. And the guys [the Blue Devils] hit right off the reel, *wham*, and they didn't let up all night long. They had a tough band.

They were just sharper, cleaner, more powerful, and they had more material, which was an upset to us because we had five arrangers, including myself. How could anybody have more material than we had? We had a book about that thick, you know, all arrangements. These guys came in with *three* books. Three books the same thickness.[5]

Unlike the players of many regional bands, the members of Walter Page's Blue Devils could read scores. They also competed with the Bennie Moten band out of Kansas City. When the Blue Devils outplayed Moten's band, Moten solved the problem by hiring the star players of the Blue

> In all of the Midwest, only
> Kansas City seemed immune to the
> Depression.

Devils. Basie, Jimmy Rushing, and several others joined the more lucrative Moten band. Following a disastrous tour that left them stranded in West Virginia, the rest of the Blue Devils then joined Moten in Kansas City, forming

> Like the gunfighters of the Wild West the local Kansas City
> musicians issued challenges to well-known players, such as Coleman
> Hawkins and Cootie Williams, who were passing through town.
> Legend has it that musical battles sometimes lasted twelve hours.

the nucleus of what would later become the Count Basie Band. But the Blue Devils' relocation into Kansas City was part of a larger trend. During the Great Depression, dance hall jobs for the territory bands dwindled, and many of the players made their way to Kansas City.

Kansas City

As William Saunders recalled, in discussing the Kansas City scene in the late 1920s:

> We listened. We didn't have radios or television to interrupt us.... That developed the Kansas City style because you would hear in a cluster and the style just developed between your ideas coming in here from Texas and Oklahoma and possibly Nebraska and Colorado, and there's a fusion of all those ideas together, and over a period of years and a period of sessions it became obvious as the Kansas City style.[6]

In all of the Midwest, only Kansas City seemed immune to the Depression. Music flourished. In 1935 there were more than 300 Kansas City clubs with live music. Jam sessions took place nightly; musicians spoke of leaving a session and returning several hours later to find the band still jamming on the same tune. Like the gunfighters of the Wild West—or stride pianists at the rent parties of New York—the local Kansas City musicians issued challenges to well-known players, such as Coleman Hawkins and Cootie Williams, who were passing through town. Legend has it that musical battles sometimes lasted twelve hours. Night owls could hear blues singer Big Joe Turner and pianist Pete Johnson at the Sunset Club, Count Basie's band at the Reno Club, and the arrangements of pianist Mary Lou Williams with Andy Kirk's Twelve Clouds of Joy.

In part, corruption in city government protected Kansas City from the Depression. Between 1926 and 1939, city alderman Tom Pendergast and his machine dominated the city, making certain that gambling, liquor, and prostitution were readily available. Although Pendergast himself had no interest in music, his practices allowed nightlife and live music to flourish.

One Kansas City band that achieved national recognition was Andy Kirk's Twelve Clouds of Joy. Like most of the bands of the swing era, they played both hot and sweet jazz. Originally from Dallas, the band migrated to

Kansas City after dismissing its prior leader, Terrence Holder, in 1928. Led by Kirk, who played bass saxophone and tuba, the group featured pianist Mary Lou Williams, an accomplished musician who created many of the band's arrangements. The Clouds of Joy first recorded in 1929 but scored a string of hits for the Decca label between 1936 and 1945, including "Until the Real Thing Comes Along."

Andy Kirk & His Twelve Clouds of Joy
"Until the Real Thing Comes Along" (1936)

Mary Lou Williams and The Clouds of Joy

Mary Lou Williams (1910–1981) was a remarkably fine pianist and composer, a superb musician who emerged from the swing era with a unique career. She remains

The remarkable career of pianist, composer, and arranger Mary Lou Williams spanned five decades.

techniques of Don Redman, but she combined Redman's East Coast sound with a down-home Kansas City feel to create her own sensibility. As can be heard on "Mary's Idea," she was rhythmically experimental, creating sections that would even disguise the meter through syncopation and odd phrase lengths. This phrasing offered an interesting respite from the symmetrical regularities based on the four-bar unit. She was one of the first arrangers to experiment with chord voicings, particularly in the late 1930s and early 1940s.

In addition to creating musical arrangements, Williams built a strong career in composition. The New York Philharmonic performed part of her *Zodiac Suite* in 1946. Though her work reflects mostly the late 1920s and the swing era, Williams befriended many of the jazz modernists in the 1940s and absorbed aspects of their style. As such she continued to develop as both a composer and a pianist, eventually writing bebop-style arrangements for the Dizzy Gillespie band. In the 1950s her strong religious interests led her to compose many sacred works. She remained active through the 1970s, eventually teaching at Duke University.

Count Basie

By 1932 Bennie Moten's band included many of the finest players in Kansas City. Moten was already well established.

not only one of the most important women in jazz history but also one of the very few women of her time able to develop a notable career in jazz at all. Prominent as both a pianist and an arranger-composer, she was the person primarily responsible for the sound of the Andy Kirk band and its hits in the 1930s. Although she left the Clouds of Joy in 1942, she continued to provide excellent arrangements for the major bandleaders of the era: Duke Ellington, Benny Goodman, Earl Hines, and Tommy Dorsey.

Andy Kirk & His Twelve Clouds of Joy (with Mary Lou Willams)
"Little Joe from Chicago" (1938)

As a swing pianist, Williams was a unique stylist with a light, sure touch and a legato right hand. She was always tasteful, creating a fine musical effect with less flashy bravado than many other swing players. She also incorporated stride and boogie-woogie elements into her work—the latter evident on "Little Joe from Chicago," which can be heard both with the Kirk band (1938) and as a piano solo (1939).

Williams's arranging style was equally tasteful and often adventurous. Early on she absorbed the arranging

Nine years earlier he had recorded several blues numbers with his six-piece group, including "Elephant's Wobble" and "Crawdad Blues." The size of the band grew along with its national reputation, and the group's final recording session of 1932 featured three trumpets, two trombones, three saxophones, and four rhythm-section players. An accom-

Bennie Moten's Kansas City Orchestra
"Prince of Wails" (1932)

plished pianist himself, Moten hired Bill Basie as a second pianist. Basie and trombonist-guitarist Eddie Durham contributed arrangements, such as "Toby," "Moten Swing," and "Prince of Wails," which featured fine solos by Ben Webster, Hot Lips Page, and Bill Basie. "Prince of Wails" is an especially interesting virtuoso number that shows off Basie's northeastern roots in stride piano. Moten's death in 1935 left one of the most outstanding bands in Kansas City without a leader; after breaking up temporarily, the group was reassembled by Basie, who became its leader.

Basie's band gained a national reputation as an outfit capable of playing swing with equal measures of drive and relaxation. Additionally, it was remarkably long-lived; Basie managed to keep his group together until his death in 1984, and it continued to perform under different leaders

LISTENING GUIDE

Track 19

"Mary's Idea"

Andy Kirk and His Twelve Clouds of Joy: "Mary's Idea" (Williams). Decca 2326. New York, December 6, 1938. Kirk, director; Harry Lawson, Clarence Trice, Earl Thomson, trumpets; Ted Donnelly, Henry Wells, trombones; John Harrington, clarinet, alto and baritone saxophones; John Williams, alto and baritone saxophones; Earl Miller, alto saxophone; Dick Wilson, tenor saxophone; Mary Lou Williams, piano, arranger; Ted Robinson, guitar; Booker Collins, bass; Ben Thigpen, drums.

The Main Point   "Mary's Idea" is just one of the many superb charts Mary Lou Williams wrote for the Andy Kirk band. In them she deftly combines a solid understanding of swing-era conventions with sufficient experimental curiosity to produce works of uncommon interest and effectiveness.

Introduction—4 bars

0:00   The four-bar introduction consists of a vamping figure in the saxophones, doubled by the bass and the piano. The vamping figure is atypically chromatic, incorporating the half steps surrounding the fifth-scale degree, B♭. The drummer provides a clear example of a swing beat on the hi-hat cymbals; you can hear the foot pedal closing the cymbals on the second and fourth beats of each bar.

A section—8 bars, repeated

0:06   The brass enter with a theme in counterpoint to the saxophone vamp. Note how well the different sections combine in counterpoint. The trumpet melody is almost entirely off the beat, while the saxophone vamp mixes on- and off-the-beat notes.

0:15   The saxophones answer the brass in the last two bars of the A section (first time).

B section—Bridge, 8 bars

0:28   The saxophones take over the lead for the first four bars of the bridge.

0:35   The last four bars are a trombone solo, which provides further textural contrast and variety.

A section—8 bars

0:40   The A section returns with brass lead and saxophone vamp. The music is modified in both brass and reeds to create a more definitive cadence.

0:50   The lead trumpet, in particular, moves down to the tonic through the blue third, G♭.

Trumpet solo—16-bar AA as 8 + 8

0:51   An improvised trumpet solo over the A-section material.

1:01   The saxophones answer at the end of the first eight bars.

1:13   The entire band answers at the end of the second eight bars.

Piano solo—16-bar BA as 8 + 8

1:15   Williams takes over the solo at the B-section bridge and continues on to the final A section. Her spare melodic style contrasts with the busy virtuosity of the stride stylists. Nevertheless, you can detect a remnant of the stride left hand, which occasionally follows the march-bass pattern. Her right-hand melody is elegant, with occasional blues licks fitted in.

1:32   She finishes her solo with runs of syncopated virtuosity.

1:35   In the last two bars of the section, the saxophones usher in the clarinet solo.

Clarinet solo—14 bars as 8 + 6

1:38   The clarinet solos over a new harmonic progression. The combination of muted brass and clarinet is refined and attractive. The final two bars are elided into a break that develops into an interlude.

Interlude—5 bars

1:58   The complex syncopation of the interlude imposes a 3/4 rhythmic pattern on the 4/4 bars. The section ultimately can be measured as five 4/4 bars, but this is clear only after the next section, a climax, has begun. This is one of Williams's fine experimental twists.

Climactic development—16 bar AA as 8 + 8

2:05   The climax features extensive syncopation over the final four bars of the eight-bar unit. There is again the implication of a 3/4 pattern imposed on the 4/4 meter. On the whole the section develops material from the opening A section.

2:17   These eight bars, a wonderful and experimental development of the opening idea, repeat.

B section—8 bars

2:28   A trombone solo for the first four bars of the B section provides a satisfying release from the dislocating syncopation of the preceding section.

2:34   The whole band enters for the second half in a crescendo leading to the last A-section statement.

A section—6 bars

2:39   A reprise of the A section as first heard. The "missing" two bars that would complete an eight-bar section are elided into the coda to become its beginning.

Coda—8 bars

2:48   The opening vamp begins the coda and continues for four bars.

2:54   The last four bars transform the opening material into a final cadence.

 Listen to this music in an animated Active Listening Guide available at the text website.

The young Count Basie on a one-cent publicity postcard from Music Corporation of America.

Photo courtesy of the Morgan Collection

afterward. Led by Basie's nearly imperceptible cues and nods at the piano, the band played with incredible rhythmic drive and exuberance. During the 1930s and 1940s, the band's book was based on blues and riff compositions—a legacy of their origin as a territory band. Basie became famous for his understated solos—a few well-placed chords or a simple repeated lick that propelled the band. Like a finely calibrated machine, the band's infectious swing drove such compositions as "Jumpin' at the Woodside" and Basie's signature song, "One O'Clock Jump."

The Count Basie Orchestra
"One O'Clock Jump" (1937)

William Basie was born in Red Bank, New Jersey, in 1904. He learned many of his piano skills by hearing Fats Waller play piano and organ in Harlem, and he made his living touring the Theatre Owners Booking Association (TOBA), the largest black vaudeville circuit. In 1927, while touring with a singer named Gonzelle White, the show broke up and left Basie stranded in Kansas City. He remained in town and worked with the Blue Devils and Moten's band. After Moten's death Basie's nine-piece Barons of Rhythm picked up Moten's engagement at the Reno Club and played for floorshows and dancing every night from nine until four or five the next morning.

The band's break came when record producer John Hammond heard them broadcast from the Reno Club over an experimental shortwave radio station, W9XBY. Hammond went to Kansas City in 1936 and was overwhelmed. He later wrote:

> Basie became almost a religion with me and I started writing about the band in *Down Beat* and *Melody Maker*. … My first night at the Reno in May, 1936, still stands out as the most exciting musical experience I can remember. The Basie band seemed to have all the virtues of a small combo, with inspired soloists, complete relaxation, plus the drive and dynamics of a disciplined large orchestra.[7]

Hammond convinced the Music Corporation of America (MCA), a major booking agency, to sign the group that fall. The band expanded to thirteen players (five brass, four saxes, and four rhythm), making it the size of the popular Benny Goodman big band and allowing the group to play theaters and dance halls. The big band issued its first recordings for Decca in 1937.

Much of the band's appeal came from the exuberant drive of the rhythm section (see box "Jazz Performance Terms"). The combination of Basie on piano, Walter Page on bass, Jo Jones on drums, and Freddie Green on guitar drove the band brilliantly, at all tempos and levels of volume and energy. Despite his roots in Harlem stride piano, Basie developed a freer, less cluttered, more up-to-date accompaniment style. Although he would often keep time by alternating left-hand bass note and right-hand chord in what is called **swing-bass**, Basie's sparse and light playing anticipated bebop piano styles in which the timekeeping role was left to the guitar, bass, and drums. (Swing-bass is very similar to the stride-style bass we heard in James P. Johnson, but played more lightly.) Page's walking bass and Freddie Green's regular guitar strumming worked with Jo Jones's timekeeping on the hi-hat and stated all four beats to the measure.

Pianist Teddy Wilson wrote:

> The Basie rhythm section was a completely new sound at the time. Musicians took a great deal of notice of it. … Jo Jones was playing with open cymbals, not choking them like other drummers, plus a very light bass drum and his particular use of the sock [hi-hat] cymbal.… [Walter Page] created quite a stir among the bass players with his use of the G string—the high string on the bass violin—in a 4/4 rhythm, playing very high notes with … sparkling crisp chime-like notes from Basie's piano.[8]

Swing-bass is the stride-derived practice of alternating bass note and midrange chord on every beat.

Insider's Guide to …

Jazz Performance Terms

Rhythm changes are the harmonies of the George and Ira Gershwin song "I Got Rhythm" (1930). (The final two-bar tag of the original song is omitted, so a symmetrical 32-bar AABA plan results.) The **bridge** in rhythm changes consists of two-bar harmonies following a circle-of-fifths pattern that returns to the tonic. For example, if rhythm changes are performed in B♭, the harmonies of the eight-bar bridge are D7 (two bars), G7 (two bars), C7 (two bars), and F7 (two bars). The F7, as the dominant of the tonic B♭, leads back to the A section. Extremely popular since the 1930s, rhythm changes are still commonly used by

jazz musicians for improvisation and composition. (Listen to Track 10 of the 🎧 Audio Primer to hear an example of rhythm changes.) Trading twos, trading fours, and trading eights are improvisational formats in jazz, common since the swing era. In trading fours, for example, each soloist improvises for four bars before the next soloist takes over for four bars. Any number of soloists may participate, but typically two to four. Trading solos is often used to create climactic moments in performances. (Listen to Track 47 of the 🎧 Audio Primer to hear an example of trading twos.)

The Basie rhythm section established the archetypal sound of the swing rhythm section. It became the standard that other bands emulated. Not only was it swinging

> Unfettered by the more complicated arrangements of the urban Northeast groups, the Basie band's top-flight soloists had ample freedom.

and propulsive, it generated its energy through control and nuance rather than heavy-handed grandstanding.

Unfettered by the more complicated arrangements of the urban Northeast groups, the Basie band's top-flight soloists had ample freedom. Lester Young's light tenor saxophone sound provided a wonderfully cool pastel contrast to the red-hot swing of recordings such as "Lester Leaps In" and "Roseland Shuffle." Herschel Evans, a veteran of the territory bands of Troy Floyd and Bennie Moten, provided a contrast to Young's airy sound. Evans's tenor style derived from Coleman Hawkins's brash and vibrato-laden sound. Young and Evans developed a friendly rivalry, and

their contrasting styles play to excellent advantage in Basie's recording of "Swinging the Blues."

A prime example of Basie's mid-thirties swing style, "Every Tub" (see Listening Guide, Track 20) highlights some of the features that made the Basie band unique:

▶ Emphasis on up-tempo jazz and improvisation instead of sweet dance music

▶ Fine balance between ensemble riffing and uninhibited swinging solos

▶ First-rate personnel, including some of the finest improvisers of the day

▶ Focus on improvisation that provides the soloists with the opportunity for personal statements within a big-band framework

As we have seen, the standard structure for a song in this era was 32 bars, typically in AABA or ABAC form. "Every Tub" deviates from this norm; its first two choruses are ABA. A possible reason for the modification of the AABA form here was to fit the piece into the (roughly) three minutes of playing time on the 78 rpm record. Despite the deviation, "Every Tub" mostly follows rhythm changes choruses.

LISTENING GUIDE
"Every Tub"

Track 20

Count Basie and His Orchestra: "Every Tub" (Durham-Basie). Decca 1728. New York, February 16, 1938. Bill "Count" Basie, piano, leader; Buck Clayton, Ed Lewis, Harry Edison, trumpets; Eddie Durham, Benny Morton, Dan Minor, trombones; Earl Warren, Jack Washington, alto saxophones; Herschel Evans, Lester Young, tenor saxophones; Freddie Green, guitar; Walter Page, bass; Jo Jones, drums; Eddie Durham, arranger.

The Main Point   In addition to showcasing Lester Young on tenor saxophone and Count Basie on piano, this recording features a trumpet solo by Harry "Sweets" Edison and an additional tenor saxophone solo by Herschel Evans that contrasts with Lester Young's work. Among the significant attractions of the early Basie big band was its combination of exciting big-band swing with uncluttered arrangements that allowed the band's soloists to shine.

The overall feel of "Every Tub" preserves a jam session atmosphere, in part because the arrangement is based on the chord progression known as *rhythm changes* (see box "Jazz Performance Terms"). As a result, in live performance a simple stage direction from Basie could allow his players to extend their solos. The simplicity of the arrangement can be seen in its layout—six choruses of rhythm changes with only three deviations: an introduction, a four-bar interlude, and a coda.

The Basie band recorded for Decca from 1937 to 1939 and made many of the recordings that helped bring the band to national attention. Trombonist Eddie Durham, an arranger for Basie, embodied the Basie band sound and his arrangement of this piece shows his skill. Harry "Sweets" Edison (1915–1999), who had recently joined the band, became a major swing-era trumpet stylist with a bright, distinctive sound. And we return to Young's influential solo style in Chapter 6.

Introduction—8 bars

0:00 The introduction consists of an active chord progression that establishes the tonality of the piece. The bright tempo typifies up-tempo swing style, in which the beat can be counted in two ways: (1) the accented ensemble chords at the beginning as a (medium) two beats per bar; or (2) the ensemble chords as beats 1 and 3 and with a (rapid) four beats per bar. In either case, the ensemble accents the chords in the first and third bars while Young's saxophone improvisations fill bars two and four.

1st chorus—Young tenor saxophone solo (ABA)

0:08 Young begins with an improvised solo backed by a rhythmic riff on a repeated chord in the brass (rather than a statement of the melody that we normally hear in the first chorus of a big-band chart).

0:16 At the B section, the brass lay out and Young plays a long eighth-note line that divides the eight bars unevenly into 6 + 2. This cutting across the grain of the 4 + 4 division of the eight-bar section helped develop Young's reputation for new directions for improvisation.

Also listen for here for Basie at the piano comping, that is, providing punctuated chords rather than a steady beat.

0:24 At the return of the A section the brass re-enter with the single-chord rhythmic pattern, while Young finishes his improvisation.

2nd chorus—Basie piano solo (ABA)

0:32 Basie's solo exemplifies his classic style. Notice how sparingly he plays and his focus on the higher register. A pleasing feature of Basie's uncluttered playing is that we can hear all the parts of his classic rhythm section clearly: Green's guitar chords, Page's walking bass, and the beat maintained on the hi-hat by drummer Jones.

0:40 The B section occurs.

0:47 Toward the end of Basie's final A section, he simply alternates two notes (D♭ and G) in a rhythmic pattern (0:50) that sets up his final lick.

Interlude—trumpets and drums (4 bars)

0:55 The trumpets, accompanied by drummer Jo Jones on the hi-hat, play a riff to set up Edison's third-chorus solo.

3rd chorus—Edison trumpet solo (AABA)

0:59 Edison reverts to the more customary AABA form for his full-chorus solo.

1:07 The second A section. During the A sections, the saxophones accompany Edison with an exciting rhythmic riff.

1:15 For the B section, Edison holds a single note (D), occasionally rearticulating it rhythmically before finally moving to a blue-note D♭ (1:21). This technique of holding a single note through chord changes was associated with Edison's style.

1:21 A thrilling *crescendo* (swell) in the band at 1:21 leads to the final A section.

4th chorus—full band (AA)

1:30 For the first time, the band is featured without the soloist. Listen to how the riff in the brass is answered by a riff in the saxophones, setting up a call-and-response as the thematic material.

1:38 The second A section for the band.

4th chorus—Basie piano solo (B)

1:46 Basie's minimalist piano during the fourth-chorus bridge provides textural contrast to the busy sound of the alternating band riffs in the fourth-chorus A sections.

4th chorus—full band (A)

1:54 The band re-enters with the call-and-response riffs heard in the earlier A sections.

5th chorus—full band (AA)

2:02 The band continues with a new set of riffs on the first half of the rhythm changes form. In fact, this exuberant chorus features three separate riffs interacting rhythmically: trumpets, trombones, and saxophones. The trumpet riff develops from the brass riffs that opened the piece behind the early Young tenor solo (0:10). The saxophone riff in this section might be understood as the piece's main thematic material. The interaction among the trumpets, saxophones, and trombones is ingeniously written by Durham: busy, yet clearly differentiated and swinging.

2:08 Accented cymbal crashes introduce the second A at 2:10.

5th chorus—Evans tenor saxophone solo (B)

2:17 A contrast to the sound of Lester Young is the fuller, more traditional sound of Herschel Evans. Listen to his more pronounced vibrato as compared to the sound of Young.

5th chorus—full band (A)

2:26 The band returns with riffs from the earlier A sections of this chorus.

6th chorus—full band (AA)

2:33 As the sixth chorus beings, the band continues with the same riffs heard in the fifth chorus.

2:41 The second A begins. As a result of the continuation into the sixth chorus, we hear three uninterrupted A sections of this riff combination.

6th chorus—Edison trumpet solo (B)

2:49 For the fifth-chorus bridge, Edison's trumpet returns with the idea he played earlier: a rhythmic iteration of the note D. This time, however, he deviates from it more quickly, proceeding with a logical and satisfying continuation and return to the A section.

6th chorus—full band (A)

2:57 A return to the A-section riffing among the band's three sections.

Coda—full band and Young (8 bars as 4 + 4)

3:05 The band moves to a climactic riff to set up Young's final solo flourish (3:09) before a two-bar wrap-up.

 Listen to this music in an animated Active Listening Guide available at the text website.

The Basie band continued to record into the 1940s despite the loss of many of its key players. Herschel Evans died in 1939; Lester Young left Basie the following year to form his own group. Walter Page and Jo Jones, two of the mainstays of the rhythm section, also left. Nevertheless, the band continued to thrive and maintained strong soloists: tenor player Don Byas filled Young's chair; and tenor saxophone player Jean-Baptiste "Illinois" Jacquet, a former member of Lionel Hampton's band, and trombonist J. J. Johnson both joined the band in 1945.

The big band broke up temporarily in 1950, during which Basie led a small group for about two years. In 1952, however, he reformed the big band with updated personnel, including Joe Newman (trumpet), Marshal Royal (alto saxophone), and Eddie "Lockjaw" Davis (tenor saxophone). To fans the reformed group became known as the "New Testament" band, and the 1930s–1940s group became the "Old Testament." We return to Count Basie in Chapter 10 to consider a piece from one of his later groups.

Benny Goodman: King of Swing

For many people the name Benny Goodman is synonymous with swing. His record sales and performances helped usher in the swing craze of the 1930s; for more than a decade, the "king of swing" enjoyed incredible heights of popularity. Members of his band became near cult figures. With his flashy playing and ever-present grin, Gene Krupa, Goodman's drummer, was a popular idol; trumpeter Harry James was one of the best-known brass players of the period; pianist Teddy Wilson became one of the era's most emulated pianists; and Lionel Hampton helped popularize the vibraphone as a jazz instrument.

Goodman was born on May 30, 1909, to an extremely poor immigrant family in Chicago. Coming of age in the early 1920s, Goodman associated with a group of inner-city musicians from the gritty and mostly poor immigrant

> *Members of the Benny Goodman band became near cult figures.*

sections of the city. Of these players Benny Goodman and Gene Krupa would become leading performers during the subsequent swing era. Other inner-city Chicago players included Muggsy Spanier, Art Hodes, Mezz Mezzrow, Floyd O'Brien, Volly de Faut, Joe Sullivan, Vic Berton, and Joe Marsala.

Goodman began learning the clarinet at age ten, when he played with a boy's band at a local synagogue. He eventually developed a prodigious technical foundation on the instrument while studying with Franz Schoepp, one of the most distinguished classical clarinet teachers in the country at the time. Schoepp's students included not only performers with the Chicago Symphony but also jazz players Buster Bailey and Jimmie Noone. A child prodigy, Goodman gave his first public performance in 1921, imitating clarinetist Ted Lewis; soon after, he started playing dances with members of the Austin High Gang (see Chapter 3).

In 1925 Goodman joined Ben Pollack's band and in 1928 made his way to New York. He was not only an excellent sight reader but also a strong, hot improviser, and he developed a busy career playing on studio recordings, on radio broadcasts,

Benny Goodman and His Orchestra (with Billie Holiday)
"Riffin' the Scotch"
(1933)

and in pit bands on Broadway. As a studio sideman, Goodman made nearly 500 recordings between 1929 and 1934.

Although these were not all jazz, he did cut sides with jazz players Red Nichols, Bix Beiderbecke, Jack Teagarden, and Fats Waller. He also led two numbers, "Your Mother's Son-in-law" and "Riffin' the Scotch," notable for being the first, if tentative, recordings of singer Billie Holiday.

In 1934 Goodman formed his own big band, featuring vocalist Helen Ward. The radio series *Let's Dance* hired them as the hot band, allowing Goodman to purchase topflight arrangements. For example, Fletcher Henderson provided the charts for "Sometimes I'm Happy," Jelly Roll Morton's "King Porter Stomp," and "Down South Camp Meeting." Edgar Sampson, the arranger for Chick Webb's band, contributed "Don't Be That Way" and "Stompin' at the Savoy."

While he was getting his big band off the ground, Goodman jammed with pianist Teddy Wilson at a private party; this led to a recording with Wilson and drummer Gene Krupa of four sides: "After You've Gone," "Body and Soul," "Who," and "Someday Sweetheart." Although Goodman's dance band was a big band, he also adopted the idea of a "band within a band" that featured a small group—first a trio, then a quartet—for performances that incorporated more improvisation than the big band did.

Although interracial bands had recorded prior to Goodman's band, Goodman's small group—with black musicians Teddy Wilson and Lionel Hampton—was the first well-known interracial band to perform live concerts. In addition to the three highly individual musical

> *As a result of the widespread publicity of the Goodman trio as an interracial band-within-a-band, Goodman has been recognized as a pioneer in helping break down social barriers between blacks and whites.*

personalities, the lack of a bass pegged the sound of the group. Wilson's swing-bass left hand coupled with Krupa's drumming provided the group's rhythmic backbone. The Goodman trio (and later quartet) records were among the key small-group recordings of the 1930s. As a result of the widespread publicity of the Goodman trio as an interracial band-within-a-band, Goodman has been recognized as a pioneer in helping break down social barriers between blacks and whites.

As in other social institutions—baseball most prominently—the story of racial relations in jazz mirrored the troubles of American society in general. In Chapter 1 we noted that race was a complex factor in American music as far back, at least, as the minstrel era of the early nineteenth century. Both black and white minstrel troupes, in characteristic blackface, performed throughout the nineteenth century at a time when integrated groups would have been unthinkable. As vaudeville supplanted minstrelsy in the late nineteenth century, the passage of strict segregation laws continued to bar mixed-race bands from appearing in public. Indeed, the "black-and-tan clubs" in the 1920s show that even audiences remained largely segregated through the first decades of the twentieth century. More typically, Ellington's clientele at the Cotton Club in the late 1920s was white, for example. For bands to have been publicly integrated in the 1920s would have been inconceivable.

Once recordings became a factor in American music, however, the situation changed slightly, and it is possible that mixed-race recording set a precedent for integrated ensembles to perform live. Because it was impossible for

> "Goodman always insisted that the agent should take the band in its entirety or not all, and we played all the jobs."
> ~Teddy Wilson

The Benny Goodman Quartet with left, Lionel Hampton (vibraphone), left center, Teddy Wilson (piano), center, Benny Goodman (clarinet), and right, Gene Krupa (drums) in the 1937 film, *Hollywood Hotel*, a Busby Berkeley musical.

a record buyer to know the race of the performers on a record, there were instances of blacks and whites "passing" for each other on early jazz recordings. As discussed earlier, the most celebrated early integrated recordings in jazz found the Creole Ferdinand "Jelly Roll" Morton sitting in with the white New Orleans Rhythm Kings on July 17, 1923, for Gennett Records in Richmond, Indiana.

In the later 1920s, mixed-race recordings became slightly more common. One particularly significant session, which featured the upcoming stars black pianist Fats Waller and white trombonist Jack Teagarden, took place on September 30, 1929. The resulting cuts were issued as Fats Waller and His Buddies. It is remarkable for the era that Waller received top billing on a session with white musicians.

Once Benny Goodman determined that he would appear in public with black pianist Teddy Wilson, it was clear that the success of their joint appearances greatly depended on Wilson's calm, professional demeanor. In those days of outright racism, Wilson could have endangered his life if he confronted any audience members who taunted him. About a year after Goodman hired Wilson, he also took on black vibraphonist Lionel Hampton. Wilson is remarkably understated in his description of the menacing situation in which he and Hampton found themselves:

> So it is to Benny Goodman that the credit must go to for hiring me, a Negro, against the advice of his booking agents. By doing so he in fact took a gamble on his career.... Of course there were incidents, and I know Benny had to put his foot down many times on this issue when it came to bookings, often without either Lionel or I knowing. Goodman always insisted that the agent should take the band in its entirety or not all, and we played all the jobs.[9]

Goodman's hiring of Wilson and Hampton resembled the later integration of major-league baseball in 1947, when Brooklyn Dodgers owner Branch Rickey signed Jackie Robinson. In a famous story, Rickey began lecturing Robinson on the importance of ignoring the screaming fans and the abusive teammates. At last Robinson erupted, "Mr. Rickey, do you want a ballplayer who's afraid to fight back"? Rickey replied, "I want a player with guts enough not to fight back."[10]

A hardworking musician and perfectionist, Goodman maintained exacting standards for the band. His extensive rehearsals required, as Goodman stated, "good musicians, a blend of tone, and uniform phrasing."[11] During his career he earned a reputation as an unyielding taskmaster. He became infamous for what musicians called "the Goodman ray"—a hostile glare so unnerving that it drove some of his musicians to quit the band. Nevertheless, the rigorous musicianship he required of the band helped Goodman rise to the top of the competitive music business.

National Baseball Hall of Fame Library/Major League Baseball
Platinum/MLB Photos via Getty Images

Benny Goodman's inclusion of Wilson and Hampton in his Quartet resembled the later integration of baseball when Brooklyn Dodgers owner Branch Rickey signed Jackie Robinson. Here, Brooklyn Dodgers infielder and slugger Jackie Robinson poses with teammates (l to r) Johnny "Spider" Jorgensen, Harold "Pee Wee" Reese, and Eddie Stanky, on the steps of the Dodgers dugout during Robinson's first official game on April 15, 1947, Opening Day in Brooklyn, New York.

When *Let's Dance* ended in May 1935, Goodman took his band on the road, heading west. The group's reception was decidedly lukewarm in many towns, particularly in Denver, Colorado, but the group had a triumphant performance at the Palomar Ballroom in Los Angeles on August 21. According to Goodman, the band began by playing their more conservative and commercial arrangements to a listless and unresponsive crowd, but once the group launched into their hot repertory the audience came alive. As Goodman told it:

> To our complete amazement, half of the crowd stopped dancing and came surging around the stand. It was the first experience we had with that kind of attention, and it certainly was a kick. That was the moment that decided things for me. After travelling 3,000 miles, we finally found people who were up on what we were trying to do, prepared to take our music the way we wanted to play it. That first big roar from

the crowd was one of the sweetest sounds I ever heard in my life—and from that time on the night kept getting bigger and bigger, as we played about every good number in our book.[12]

Goodman soon realized that the difference in time zones between California and New York helped account for his overwhelming success. On his radio broadcasts from the East Coast, Goodman reserved his hot numbers until later in the evening, and these exciting swing arrangements reached California during prime time and thrilled younger listeners.

In the years following the success at the Palomar Ballroom, Goodman's fame reached phenomenal heights. Goodman added West Coast vibraphonist Lionel Hampton to his trio, and the quartet recorded the song "Moonglow," which became a hit. The CBS radio broadcast *Camel Caravan* hired the Goodman band, and a wildly enthusiastic audience applauded his 1937 performances at New York's Paramount Theater.

> On his radio broadcasts from the East Coast, Goodman reserved his hot numbers until later in the evening, and these exciting swing arrangements reached California during prime time and thrilled younger listeners.

Goodman's celebrated Carnegie Hall performance the following January brought together his big band, his small group, and guest stars from Duke Ellington's and Count Basie's bands. This concert included one of Goodman's most famous numbers, "Sing, Sing, Sing," an extended minor-key composition that featured Gene Krupa in a series of drum solos and included a duet with Goodman on clarinet and Krupa on tom-toms.

Goodman hired only the strongest players and improvisers, and at one time or another his band featured many of the important players of the swing era, including trumpeters Bunny Berigan and Harry James as well as pianists Jess Stacy and Mel Powell. At the request of John Hammond, Goodman took on guitarist Charlie Christian in 1939. During Christian's all-too-brief career (see Chapter 6), he was one of the leading improvisers of the period and revolutionized jazz guitar playing.

In the early 1940s, Eddie Sauter wrote arrangements for the Goodman group, earning it the nickname the "Sauter band" for some of the most ambitious jazz arrangements of the era, such as "Benny Rides Again" and "Clarinet à la King." Pianist Mel Powell also contributed arrangements. After 1942, when Sauter left, Goodman tried to stave off the downturn in swing-band popularity by returning to a simpler style but to no avail. Semiretirement followed in 1946 while he considered what to do next.

Goodman's Later Career

The *bebop* revolution—a modern jazz development of the early 1940s discussed in Chapter 7—intrigued Goodman. Despite his occasional negative comments on the style, he admired the work of saxophonist Wardell Gray and trumpeter Fats Navarro. In 1948 Goodman experimented, first with a seven-piece group, then with a bebop-styled big band. Goodman produced some interesting work, including a Chico O'Farrill arrangement of "Undercurrent Blues." Ultimately, though, Goodman remained most at home in the swing style of his youth and early maturity. When his fans did not respond positively to his experimentation, Goodman ended his flirtation with bebop in 1949. For the remainder of his long life, he led small groups ensconced in swing and, occasionally, big bands assembled for specific events.

There is no question that Goodman set clarinet style in the 1930s. It has been said that his perfect conception of swing style on the clarinet made him a difficult act for other players to follow. Hence, after Goodman, the clarinet declined as an instrument of modern jazz; only in recent

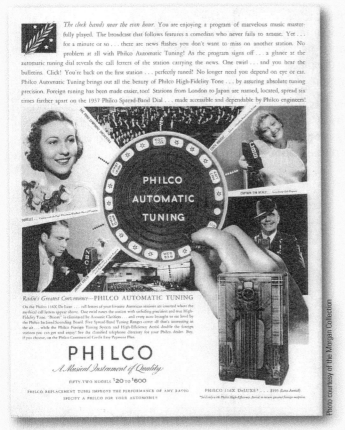

The advent of radio spread the sounds of jazz around the country. This advertisement for the Philco radio appeared in 1936 on the back of *Etude Magazine*. Notice the prices—from $20 to $600.

LISTENING GUIDE   Track 21
"Down South Camp Meeting"

Benny Goodman and His Orchestra: "Down South Camp Meeting" (Henderson). Victor 25387. Los Angeles, August 13, 1936. Goodman, clarinet, leader; Manny Klein, Pee Wee Erwin, Chris Griffin, trumpets; Red Ballard, Murray McEachern, trombones; Hymie Schertzer, Bill DePew, alto saxophones; Art Rollini, Dick Clark, tenor saxophones; [Jess Stacy, piano;] Allan Reuss, guitar; Harry Goodman, bass; Gene Krupa, drums; Fletcher Henderson, arranger.

The Main Point   We heard this Fletcher Henderson piece and arrangement earlier on Track 18. The contrast between the recordings is instructive. The only formal difference in the arrangement is that Goodman takes a clarinet solo in place of the Henry Allen trumpet solo. Otherwise, the timings of the corresponding sections are reasonably close. Side-by-side comparison, however, will show that the Goodman performance is slightly slower and hence longer, by some twenty seconds.

Although the Goodman recording was made only about two years after the Henderson, there had been advances in recording technology and a noticeable improvement in sound quality. In the Goodman, we can hear more detail.

The difference in performance styles is perhaps more difficult to pin down. The Henderson has the "easier swing," an understated nonchalance that is highly attractive. The Goodman performance is tighter. The musicians play more crisply, more accurately, more as a unit, lending the arrangement greater power and finesse. Yet, the comparative tightness of the Goodman can also be viewed negatively: the piece comes across aggressively, as if the players were out to show off their skill, and with a swing that is slightly more mechanical.

"Down South Camp Meeting" is one of Goodman's early hits from a superb and extensive library of recordings. (*Note:* An unsolved mystery surrounding this session is why Jess Stacy, Goodman's pianist, does not play.) The following chart reviews the sections and their timings. An analysis of the work can be found in the Listening Guide to the Henderson performance (page 137), and in Chapter 6 we discuss Goodman's solo.

0:00	Introduction—4 bars
0:05	A section—8 bars as 4 + 4 in C major
0:15	B section—8 bars as 4 + 4 in A minor
0:25	A section—8 bars as 4 + 4
0:35	Clarinet solo—ABA as 8 + 8 + 8
1:05	Transition—8 bars
1:15	C section—CCDC as 8 + 8 + 4 + 8 in A♭ major
1:51	C section—CCDC as 8 + 8 + 4 + 8, repeated
2:26	Transition—4 bars
2:32	E section—8 bars, played four times in D♭ major
3:11	Tag—1 bar

 Listen to this music in an animated Active Listening Guide available at the text website.

years has its popularity begun to recover. That Goodman was the consummate swing stylist was perhaps best shown by his difficulties adapting to bebop.

Goodman continued to perform until his death in 1986. He undertook several overseas tours, playing in

> There is no question that Goodman set clarinet style in the 1930s.

the Far East and South America, and he appeared at the U.S. pavilion of the Brussels World's Fair in 1958. During the height of the cold war in 1962, he traveled to the Soviet Union. With his classical training, he maintained a remarkably high degree of commitment to musicianship and clarinet technique, and he frequently performed classical works in addition to jazz. He recorded and performed works by Mozart, Debussy, and Stravinsky, and he commissioned works by contemporary concert composers Béla Bartók, Aaron Copland, and Paul Hindemith.

Ellington After the Cotton Club

Duke Ellington may have been dismayed during the mid-thirties when the commercial success of such leaders as Benny Goodman and Glenn Miller eclipsed the popularity of his own band, but Ellington's perseverance paid off. When he died in 1974, it was as one of the world's most distinguished jazz artists. The recipient of numerous musical and international honors, Ellington served for many as the paramount figure in the history of jazz.

Ellington's artistry was wide ranging. Known for his prodigious output of music, his command of arranging and orchestration detail, and his expansive musical creativity, Ellington established his excellence while crisscrossing the globe under a hectic and seemingly incessant touring schedule. As the title to one laudatory biography concluded (using a phrase that was in fact associated with Ellington), he was "beyond category."[13] Still, we can identify five areas and subgroupings of his compositions and arrangements:

▶ Original popular songs such as "Solitude" and "Don't Get Around Much Anymore"

▶ Arrangements of popular songs by other composers

▶ Shorter big-band works other than songs, such as "Sepia Panorama" or "Harlem Airshaft"

▶ Feature compositions for particular members of the band, such as "**Concerto** for Cootie" (featuring trumpeter Cootie Williams)

▶ Larger-scale works, divided into three categories:

  ▪ Extended works for the band, such as *Black, Brown, and Beige*

  ▪ Suites, such as *The Queen's Suite*, a selection of which we examine in Chapter 10

  ▪ Religious works, such as the *Sacred Concerts*

After leaving the Cotton Club, Ellington toured widely. The band traveled to Europe in 1933, playing to enthusiastic crowds and attracting critical attention in the British press. This was a pivotal moment in the evolution of jazz in Europe because the Ellington ensemble was heads and shoulders above the groups that traveled there in the 1920s. (Louis Armstrong was also in Europe twice in the early 1930s, demonstrating his revolutionary jazz showmanship.)

Without interrupting his busy touring schedule, Ellington became increasingly successful as a composer writing in the American popular-song tradition—usually 32-bar AABA compositions. "Sophisticated Lady," first recorded in 1933, was unusual in that the A sections of the composition (measures 1–16 and 25–32) were in the key of A♭, whereas the B section or bridge (measures 17–24) was a half step away in the key of G major. The song became a classic. Others followed, such as the popular "In a Sentimental Mood." "Prelude to a Kiss," with its sinuous chromatic melody, was first recorded as an instrumental and played by two of the principal soloists of the group: trombonist Lawrence Brown and saxophonist Johnny Hodges.

Following the death of his mother, with whom he was extremely close, Ellington wrote in 1935 the extended musical composition "Reminiscing in Tempo," by far his most ambitious work to date. Thirteen minutes long, the piece covered four record sides. Critical reaction to the composition was more negative than positive, but Ellington had shown growth as a composer. In particular, the work is remarkably spare in its use of motivic material, restricting itself largely to a basic thematic idea and a secondary idea, their accompaniments, and the transitions, which Ellington develops deftly.

Duke Ellington
"Reminiscing in Tempo" (1935)

A sinuous accompanying line in eighth notes forms the secondary thematic idea, but it has no definitive statement. "Reminiscing in Tempo" also uses unusual phrase lengths of seven, ten, and fourteen measures; requires little improvisation; and often adopts straight rather than swing eighth notes. These features help form a bridge from jazz to the world of classical composition and result in a hybrid that was uniquely Ellington's.

Another important extended work was "Crescendo in Blue" and "Diminuendo in Blue," companion pieces written in 1937 and occupying both sides of a 78 rpm record. Like "Reminiscing in Tempo," this longer work, rooted in the blues form and tradition, uses little improvisation.

Building on the Band

Because Ellington was determined to build on the strengths of the individual band members, much of the band's distinctive character came from its players, and collaborations with the band proved significant. Ellington noted in 1937 that some of his works were composed "almost by unanimous inspiration while the orchestra was gathered together for a practice session. New ideas are merged at each meeting, and each man contributes to the offerings of the other."[14]

This tendency to borrow ideas from his sidemen led to the infamous remark by trombonist Lawrence Brown: "I don't consider you a composer. You are a compiler."[15] Brown was going too far, of course, but the remark reveals the tensions that can develop in a band when creativity among all the players is constantly encouraged.

As part of his desire to work with his band's strengths, Ellington wrote with particular players in mind. A number of his compositions feature individual musicians showing off their strengths. For example, Ellington displayed Cootie Williams's multifaceted trumpet playing in the celebrated "Concerto for Cootie," the first theme of which became "Do Nothin' Till You Hear from Me," a hit song in 1943. "Clarinet Lament," based on the harmonic progression of the standard song "Basin Street Blues," exhibited the playing of Ellington's New Orleans–born clarinetist Barney Bigard. For trumpeter Rex Stewart, who left Fletcher Henderson to play with Ellington from 1934 to 1943, Ellington wrote "Boy Meets Horn." And with his trombonist from San Juan, Puerto Rico—Juan Tizol—Ellington co-composed the exotic Latin-tinged song "Caravan." Ellington's work provided the perfect vehicle for his players; commentators noted that his sidemen often faltered in their playing and careers once they left the band.

Consistently ranked among the best alto saxophonists of the swing era, Johnny Hodges (1907–1970) became a stalwart of Ellington's band. Born in Cambridge, Massachusetts, Hodges played both alto and soprano saxophone.

A **Concerto** is a concert composition featuring a soloist accompanied by an orchestra or a larger ensemble.

Duke Ellington at the piano at the Cotton Club in New York City, 1930, surrounded by members of his Cotton Club Orchestra. With Juan Tizol (5th from left) Ellington wrote "Caravan"; for Johnny Hodges (7th from left) Ellington wrote "Jeep's Blues"; Cootie Williams (2nd from right) inspired Ellington's "Concerto for Cootie"; and Barney Bigard (3rd from right) inspired Ellington's composition "Clarinet Lament."

Frank Driggs Collection/Archive Photos/Getty Images

He developed a blues-inflected style that owed a debt to Sidney Bechet, with whom he had studied and performed before joining Ellington in 1928. Except for a brief departure between 1951 and 1955, Hodges remained with Ellington for four decades. Nicknamed "Jeep" and "Rabbit," Hodges was considered the leading soloist of the Ellington band in the mid-thirties, and he became its highest-paid member. Other bandleaders acknowledged Hodges's status as a soloist. For example, Hodges and his bandmates Cootie Williams and Harry Carney played in the jam-session portion of Benny Goodman's Carnegie Hall concert of 1938.

Hodges's playing was particularly prominent in many of the small-group recordings made during the late 1930s. A seven-piece group formed from members of the Ellington band made several records, many of which achieved commercial success—for example, the composition "Jeep's Blues" became a jukebox hit. Hodges's ballad performances were said to be aphrodisiacal: The wife of one of the Ellington musicians reputedly warned, "Don't leave me alone around Johnny. When I hear him play, I just want to open up the bedroom door."[16]

Changes for the Better

Toward the end of the 1930s, Ellington made several radical changes. He broke with Irving Mills, who had been his manager and business partner for more than a decade. Mills had also written the lyrics for many of Ellington's compositions, such as "It Don't Mean a Thing (If It Ain't Got That Swing)," "Sophisticated Lady," and "Mood Indigo," although some of his claims for creative input on this material are dubious. (Before we blame Mills, we should point out that Ellington was not unhappy with this arrangement. Mills was Ellington's partner, and it was, and remains, a common practice in popular music to use songwriting credits to fulfill business arrangements.) Upon ending his partnership with Mills, Ellington signed with the William Morris Agency. He also left Columbia Records and by 1940 was recording for RCA Victor.

On the heels of a successful 1939 European tour, Ellington took on several new players and entered one of the most intensely fertile periods of his career. With the addition of tenor saxophonist Ben Webster (1909–1973), Ellington's saxophone section increased to five players. From Kansas City, Webster was a big-toned, breathy player whose style had been influenced by Coleman Hawkins. Having performed with Bennie Moten and Andy Kirk in the early 1930s, Webster had played an integral role in the Kansas City scene. When Webster came to New York in 1934, he played with Fletcher Henderson, Cab

Duke Ellington & His Famous Orchestra
"Cotton Tail" (1940)

Calloway, and Benny Carter, and—for a brief period between 1935 and 1936—Ellington's band; he came on board as a full-time member of Ellington's band at the end of 1939. Webster energized the group with his solos on both ballads and swing numbers. "Cotton Tail," for instance, offers an electrifying display of his solo ability. The harmonic structure of "Cotton Tail," based on the chords to "I Got Rhythm," provides the vehicle for Webster's solo, which alternates between eighth notes and longer notes and is filled with Webster's trademark devices. Along with Coleman Hawkins and Lester Young, Webster was one of the outstanding tenor saxophone stylists of the swing era.

Ellington also added Jimmy Blanton on bass in 1939. The virtuosity of this twenty-year-old from Chattanooga, Tennessee, revolutionized jazz bass playing. Creating a driving sense of swing while walking the bass, Blanton was the first bass player to become a proficient soloist in his own right. Taken with Blanton's playing, Ellington recorded a series of duets with the bassist, such as "Pitter Panther Patter," that show Blanton's remarkable agility. In his first studio outing with the full band, Ellington featured Blanton in opening and closing solos on "Jack the

Bear." Blanton was a fine improviser, but his virtuoso abilities led Ellington to write specific parts for him as well.

Finally, Ellington took on a diminutive pianist born in Dayton, Ohio. Initially hired as a second pianist and an assistant arranger, Billy Strayhorn (1915–1967) developed a remarkably close musical relationship with Ellington that lasted nearly three decades. Strayhorn quickly began contributing compositions for the band, including one of the group's theme songs, "Take the A Train." Strayhorn's collaborations with Ellington were so intertwined in coauthored works that scholars have only recently begun to untangle where Ellington's contributions left off and Strayhorn's began. Nicknamed "Sweet Pea," Strayhorn had

Most of his works are linear compositions, that is, they typically have some sense of thematic and harmonic development as well as a network of interrelationships between the various musical elements. … Before developing an interest in jazz, Strayhorn said, he studied "the three B's—Bach, Beethoven, and Brahms."[17]

In addition to bringing his own musical skills to the table, Strayhorn studied the elements of Ellington's style that had specifically contributed to the success of the composer and his band. What Strayhorn discovered was a unique quality of Ellington's that Strayhorn called the "Ellington effect":

> "Each member of the band is to him a distinctive tone color and set of emotions, which he mixes with others equally distinctive to produce a third thing, which I like to call the Ellington effect."
> ~Billy Strayhorn

a background in European classical music and theory. Some of his tunes—such as "Chelsea Bridge" and his bittersweet paean to drinking, "Lush Life"—owed a debt to Debussy. Strayhorn scholar Walter van de Leur summarizes his style as follows:

> Part of Strayhorn's musical language drew on fin de siècle composers such as Debussy and Ravel, especially in terms of orchestral colors and the use of nonfunctional harmonies. But his command of musical architecture was rooted in older classical techniques.

Each member of the band is to him a distinctive tone color and set of emotions, which he mixes with others equally distinctive to produce a third thing, which I like to call the Ellington effect. Sometimes this mixing happens on paper and frequently right on the bandstand. I have often seen him exchange parts in the middle of a piece because the man and the part weren't the same character.[18]

The A train is an express subway that runs through New York City up to Harlem and northern Manhattan. Reputedly, Strayhorn wrote the song after receiving directions from Ellington on how to get to his house by subway that began, "Take the A Train…"

A **pedal point** is a sustained or repeated bass note or drone played to accompany a melody; it is also called a pedal tone.

Another distinctive feature of Ellington's sound was his characteristic cross-sectional voicings. Although

Duke Ellington & His Orchestra
"Blue Light" (1939)

Ellington would certainly make rich use of the antiphonal effects common in big-band arranging (sections engaging in call-and-response), at other times he would mix instruments from different sections—sometimes also with mutes and unusual registers—to create a complex, uncanny color. At the beginning of the second chorus of "Blue Light," a work from 1938, we hear a choir comprising a clarinet in the low register, a muted trombone in the high register, and a muted trumpet

as lead, with a plucked string bass.[19] Not only are the four instruments from different sections, but the registration is unusual with the clarinet voiced below the brass while the trombone takes the middle part in the upper register. Moreover, Ellington's chord voicings in "Blue Light" are unusual, another feature of Ellington's music that gives it much of its character. The first chord is especially striking: it is probably a form of G7 with a blue third (B♭) and a thirteenth (E)—a remarkable voicing by any measure and very unusual in 1939.

The 1940s

The forties were a varied time for Ellington and the band. Relatively ignored in the polls during the 1930s, the group now achieved national prominence, winning the *Esquire* poll in 1945 and taking the *Down Beat* polls in 1942, 1944, 1946, and 1948. Ellington began receiving considerable royalties for many of his compositions, such as "Don't Get Around Much Anymore," "I'm Beginning

---

LISTENING GUIDE   Track 22
"Ko-Ko"

Duke Ellington and His Famous Orchestra: "Ko-Ko" (Ellington). Victor 26577. Chicago, March 6, 1940. Edward Kennedy "Duke" Ellington, leader, piano, and arranger; Wallace Jones, Cootie Williams, trumpets; Rex Stewart, cornet; Joe "Tricky Sam" Nanton, Lawrence Brown, trombones; Juan Tizol, valve trombone; Johnny Hodges, Otto Hardwick, alto saxophones; Barney Bigard, clarinet, tenor saxophone; Ben Webster, tenor saxophone; Harry Carney, baritone saxophone; Fred Guy, guitar; Jimmy Blanton, bass; Sonny Greer, drums.

The Main Point   Among the many great recordings the Ellington band made in 1940, "Ko-Ko" is an especially exciting work. Based on the blues, its imaginative textural contrasts showcase the virtuosity of the group. Its form is straightforward: seven blues choruses and an introduction that returns as a coda. But instead of using simple melodic material and developing it through orchestration and solo improvisations, "Ko-Ko" generates its thematic content sequentially, each new instrumental section seeming to grow out of the previous one. The work draws its emotive power from densely stacking the instrumental groups in the climactic sections and contrasting them with passionate solo statements. An experimental work, "Ko-Ko" is aesthetically more demanding in its aggressive and dissonant harmonies than virtually any other big-band piece of the era.

Note: Ellington's "Ko-Ko" should not be confused with a well-known 1945 Charlie Parker composition, spelled "Ko Ko," which we examine in Chapter 7.

Introduction—Pickup + 8 bars

0:00   A short tom-tom figure leads to the introductory section, eight bars of jabbing trombone chords over a **pedal point** played by baritone saxophonist Carney. The pedal point becomes a rhythmic vamp.

1st chorus—12-bar blues in E♭ minor

0:12   Accompanied by a walking bass and a more regular rhythm, the main theme is played by valve trombonist Tizol in a call-and-response format with the saxophones. Here the main blues theme is put through a familiar harmonization, but with a twist: the blues is in minor, relatively rare for the swing era. Interestingly, this theme does not appear again in the piece. Note that Ellington does not comp at the piano, but rather adds accented notes toward the end of the chorus.

2nd chorus

0:31   The first of two choruses featuring trombone soloist "Tricky Sam" Nanton. Using the plunger mute, Nanton plays lines that almost sound like a human voice saying "ya-ya." The rest of the brass back him with punctuated chords, whose off-the-beat phrasing helps maintain the tension. The "oo-ah-oo-ah" sound of these chords is produced by alternately covering and uncovering the bell of the horn with the left hand.

3rd chorus

0:49   Nanton continues his trombone solo, now moving to a higher register, while the punctuated brass chords continue. The "ya-ya" sound returns toward the end of his solo as he returns to the middle register of the trombone.

4th chorus

1:06   The saxophone section takes the lead in this chorus while the brass continue chordal punctuations in a new pattern. Ellington's piano has been sparse until this point, but here he plays aggressive chords and virtuosic runs that sweep through much of the range of the keyboard. What make the runs sound unusual is their use of the *whole-tone scale*, a group of notes that are linked consecutively by whole steps.

5th chorus

1:25   The fifth chorus consists of the first *tutti* passage of the piece (the whole band performing). Thematically related to the first blues chorus, this *tutti* nevertheless avoids any literal restatement of the riffs first heard there. The harmonies heard are dissonant, with notes not customarily found in these chords.

6th chorus

1:43   The choruses continue to grow in drama and intensity. Here, the instrumental sections answer one another, creating a rising texture. These are interrupted by Blanton bass breaks (beginning at 1:46), providing a vivid contrast to the dramatic sectional writing. Blanton's hard plucking and rhythmic intensity project a great deal of passion. The use of the bass for these solo breaks is a masterly orchestrational idea: our attention is transferred to an instrument rarely used then for such solos, but without the expected loss of energy.

7th chorus

2:01   After the solo bass breaks, the last *tutti* section (a kind of *shout chorus*) climaxes an intensity that has been unrelenting so far. Here the instrumental sections join together to create blocks of sound that follow logically from the previous *tutti* sections. For this climactic shout chorus, listen to the biting dissonance of the chords. Drummer Greer moves to heavy accents on the *backbeats* (beats two and four in a bar) to increase the intensity still further. Ending the piece at such a feverish level without any letup or release of energy would perhaps have sounded melodramatic. Hence Ellington adds a coda.

Coda—8 + 4-bar Tag

2:19   For the coda, Ellington first returns to the introduction, which, in contrast to the previous climactic passage, now seems quite cool. Ellington could then have guided the piece to a modest conclusion, but instead he adds a quickly rising four-bar tag, in which the intensity of the previous *tutti* sections returns for a final statement.

    Listen to this music in an animated Active Listening Guide available at the text website.

to See the Light," and "Do Nothin' Till You Hear from Me." He also recorded many of his finest compositions, such as "Harlem Airshaft" and "Ko-Ko."

"Ko-Ko" is certainly one of the most original jazz recordings of the era. Ellington's new aesthetic is suggested by the emotional depth and forthrightness evident throughout the piece, in which the listener is compelled to accept the music on its own strikingly original terms. Surprisingly, "Ko-Ko" is in E♭ minor, a difficult key with six flats. This key is rare for jazz of any era although we should note that black-note keys are sometimes heard in early jazz, because the black notes of the keyboard create a *pentatonic scale* (discussed in Chapter 1). Perhaps this extreme key held more emotional resonance for Ellington than more routine keys. Though recorded at the height of the swing era, "Ko-Ko"'s intensity and uncompromising emotional directness suggest the innovations in the nascent bebop era, whose exponents at this time were just beginning their experiments.

"Ko-Ko" also shows how Jimmy Blanton developed a greater role for the bass: rather than simply keep time, he plays prominent solo breaks that show off his dexterous technique. Among other innovations, Blanton developed a facility in the higher register of the instrument, which, until then, had been relatively neglected. The higher register is particularly useful for projecting the melody, which was important for solos before routine amplification of the instrument in the latter half of the 1960s.

The years also witnessed an increased turnover in players: Ellington's sidemen were attracting offers from competing bands; other players were lost to the wartime draft. Tenor saxophone player Ben Webster left in 1943 to lead his own small group. The more modern clarinetist Jimmy Hamilton replaced Barney Bigard. Cootie Williams left Ellington for Benny Goodman's band in 1940 and was replaced by trumpeter, violinist, and singer Ray Nance. Trombonist Juan Tizol joined Harry James's band, and another Ellington trombonist, Joe "Tricky Sam" Nanton, died of a stroke in 1946. Bassist Jimmy Blanton died of tuberculosis in 1942 at the tragically young age of twenty-three; the young Oscar Pettiford filled the bass chair between 1945 and 1948. Trumpeter William "Cat" Anderson, capable of trumpet screams in the very highest registers, played with the band from 1944 to 1947.

In 1943 Ellington began an annual series of concerts at Carnegie Hall. In addition to featuring his songs and hits, he composed and premiered large-scale concert works. These were often based on themes of African American culture and history. The first concert, on January 23, 1943, included a performance of his *Black, Brown, and Beige: A Tone Parallel to the History of the Negro in America*. This was an ambitious three-movement tone poem that traced the history of African Americans through the story of an African named Boola who is brought to the United States as a slave. Unfortunately, many critics panned the work; as a result, Ellington performed only sections in later concerts, especially "Come Sunday" from the opening "Black" movement. Because critics had called the work "formless," Ellington offered suites in later Carnegie Hall concerts; these shorter musical vignettes better suited Ellington's writing style. In many of the works that followed *Black, Brown, and Beige*—such as *New World a-Comin'*, *Liberian Suite*, and *Deep South Suite*—we see Ellington continuing the Harlem Renaissance tradition of celebrating in concert compositions the history and the achievements of African Americans.

By the 1950s the heyday of the swing era was long gone, and it was becoming increasingly difficult for Ellington to keep his band together. The early 1950s were difficult years for Ellington, as we shall see when we pick up Ellington's later years in Chapter 10.

Exam Review Questions

Use these questions and the materials on the text website to help you understand and pass tests on the content of this chapter.

1. What are some of the specific features of big-band writing? Cite instrumentation, the role of the instrumental sections, and overall form.

2. How did Kansas City provide a foundation for swing? Cite specific bands and aspects of their styles. Among the significant bands associated with Kansas City were territory bands. What were they, and how did they function?

3. In what ways was Benny Goodman's nickname, "king of swing," appropriate? In what ways was it inappropriate?

4. How did the bands of Count Basie and Duke Ellington differ? Further, how do the differences between Ellington and Basie as musicians and bandleaders help account for the different personalities of their bands and music?

 MindTap™

Test Yourself on Key Concepts with additional Chapter Quizzes and Listening Activities on the text website.

Key Terms

Test your knowledge of this chapter's key terms by defining the following. If you can't remember the meaning of a term, refresh your memory by looking up the boldfaced term in the chapter, turning to the Glossary at the back of the book, or working with the flashcards at the text website.

antiphony **136**

balance **136**

big band **131**

book **136**

bridge **146**

call-and-response **137**

chair **136**

chart **136**

concerto **155**

hot bands **134**

intonation **136**

jazz chair **136**

lead player **136**

lead trumpet **136**

library **136**

pedal point **158**

rhythm changes **146**

rhythm section **136**

section **136**

sideman **136**

standard **140**

sweet bands **134**

swing **131**

swing-bass **146**

territory band **140**

trading twos (fours, eights) **146**

walking bass **139**

The saxophone section of a big band

Swing-Era Bands and Stylists

6

MindTap™

Start with a quick warm-up activity.

THE BASIE, GOODMAN, AND ELLINGTON BANDS WERE perhaps the most important of the big-band era, but numerous other groups, both black and white, contributed to the excitement and the verve of swing. Many sidemen in the big bands became famous in their own right, and audiences idolized them. Their performing styles formed the roots of jazz music to come. Some of the big-band performers left their original bands to lead their own groups—a few successfully, but many less so. Some players, such as Coleman Hawkins, worked largely as "singles"—stars who performed at clubs throughout the country and worked with local rhythm sections. This chapter begins with the primary big bands (other than Basie, Goodman, and Ellington) and concludes with the best-known individual stylists, particularly those who affected subsequent directions in jazz.

Influential Big Bands of the Swing Era

During the 1930s, the hub of the music industry remained in New York, as it had in the 1920s. The recording industry was centered there, and radio stations widely broadcast the big bands as they played in popular ballrooms and dance halls. The more successful bands, such as those of Jimmie Lunceford and Cab Calloway, alternated extended performances in the dance halls of Harlem with engagements on the road. Lunceford's group was legendary for its ability to keep up a hectic schedule touring across the country.

Cab Calloway

Cab Calloway (1907–1994) was one of the most popular and colorful bandleaders to emerge during the 1930s and 1940s. His flamboyant vocal style and exuberant scat singing earned him the nickname the "hi-de-ho man," after one of his songs. Calloway noted in

1930—Casa Loma Orchestra records "Casa Loma Stomp"
1931—Cab Calloway and the Missourians record "Minnie the Moocher"
1934—Chick Webb records "Stompin' at the Savoy"
—Dorsey Brothers Orchestra formed
1935—Benny Goodman's stupendous success at the Palomar Ballroom in Los Angeles
1936—Lester Young plays with Count Basie
—Louis Armstrong records "Swing That Music" (Track 23)
—Goodman records "Down South Camp Meeting" (Track 21)
—Jimmie Lunceford and His Orchestra record "Organ Grinder's Swing"
1937—Height of swing era
—Goodman, Basie, Ellington extremely popular
1938—Benny Goodman at Carnegie Hall
— Artie Shaw records "What Is This Thing Called Love?"
1939—Beginnings of bop at Minton's Playhouse and Monroe's Uptown
House in Harlem
—Charlie Christian plays with Benny Goodman
—Coleman Hawkins records "Body and Soul" (Track 25)
—Glenn Miller records "In the Mood"
—Ella Fitzgerald takes over Chick Webb band
1940— Artie Shaw records "Star Dust"
1941— Billie Holiday and Eddie Heywood and His Orchestra
record "All of Me"
1942—Beginnings of New Orleans Dixieland revival
—Big bands depleted by draft
—Recording ban imposed by the American
Federation of Musicians (AFM)

Jazz

1930   1935   1940

1931—Depths of Depression; bank failures
1933—Hitler becomes chancellor of Germany
—Franklin Roosevelt inaugurated
1935—Congress passes Social Security Act
1936—Spanish civil war
1937—Japan declares war on China
—Picasso, *Guernica*
1938—Hitler annexes Austria to Germany
—Volkswagen produces first Beetle
1939—World War II begins
—Steinbeck, *The Grapes of Wrath*
—Margaret Mitchell, *Gone with the Wind*
1940—Roosevelt becomes first three-term president
—Hemingway, *For Whom the Bell Tolls*
—Plutonium, first nonnatural element
1941—United States enters war after bombing of Pearl
Harbor
—*Citizen Kane*
—First jet plane
—*Casablanca*
1943—First nuclear reactor

Historical Events

his biography that his "favorite scat singer has always been Louis Armstrong."[1] Indeed, he followed in Armstrong's footsteps and became famous as an entertainer with a singing style that was infectious, outgoing, and crowd pleasing.

With his band, the Missourians, Calloway took over the house gig at the Cotton Club after Ellington's band departed. The Missourians played there six months of the year and toured the other half.

Hits such as Calloway's 1931 "Minnie the Moocher" earned the band wide popularity. They also appeared in several films, including *The Big Broadcast* (1932), *The Singing Kid* (1936), and *Stormy Weather* (1943). Calloway's band included several excellent players: he helped launch the careers of tenor saxophonists Ben Webster and Leon "Chu" Berry, bassist Milt "The Judge" Hinton, and trumpeters Jonah Jones and Dizzy Gillespie.

Everett Collection

Bill "Bojangles" Robinson, Lena Horne, and the "hi-de-ho man," Cab Calloway, in a movie "lobby card" promoting *Stormy Weather*. The movie's title song would become Horne's signature song.

Jimmie Lunceford

The Cotton Club also featured another popular big band, led by Jimmie Lunceford (1902–1947). Audiences expected not only a variety of music but a *show*, and Lunceford's band was known for its onstage antics, with the musicians waving their derby hats or their horns in the air.

Lunceford studied music in high school in Denver under Wilberforce Whiteman, Paul Whiteman's father, and graduated from Fisk University with a degree in music. He organized a band in Memphis in the late 1920s and brought it to New York in 1933, where audiences quickly noted its rigorous and rehearsed professionalism.

Although Lunceford's band had fine soloists, the group was better known for its charts. Lunceford hired several top arrangers—Will Hudson, pianist Eddie Wilcox, altoist Willie Smith, and trombonist-guitarist Eddie Durham—who contributed several pieces. Early hits included Hudson's "Jazznocracy" and "White Heat." The band also performed novelty numbers as well as sweet arrangements and hot instrumentals in the manner of the Casa Loma Orchestra, an influential white band. Lunceford himself wrote an experimental riff piece entitled "Stratosphere."

The Lunceford band got a boost when trumpeter Sy Oliver (1910–1988) began arranging for them in 1934, creating what became known as the Lunceford style. Oliver became one of the best-known arrangers of the swing era. One of his popular charts for Lunceford was "Organ Grinder's Swing" (1936). (Oliver's later riff tune "Opus One" [1943] was a big hit for the Tommy Dorsey band.) Part of what made the Lunceford sound distinctive was Oliver's insistence that the rhythm section play in a two-beat style, with the first and third beats receiving more emphasis than the second and fourth; this is often accomplished by having the bass player and the drummer's bass drum play on only the first and third beats.

Not all the rhythm players liked the Lunceford style, as the band's drummer Jimmie Crawford recalled:

> Sy would say "Drop it in two," and I'd maybe show I didn't agree with him, and so he'd say, "What's wrong with two beats?" and I'd answer, "Well, there are two beats missing, that's all." I felt that if you were really going home in those last ride-out choruses, then you should really go home all the way, full steam and stay in four-four instead of going back into that two-four feel again. Oh yes, Sy and I would have some terrific arguments all right, but then we'd kiss and make up right away.[2]

No band equaled Lunceford's commercial showmanship. He continued directing the group until his death in 1947.

Chick Webb

Like the Cotton Club, Harlem's Savoy Ballroom provided a premier jazz spot for listening and dancing during the 1930s. The house band was led by drummer Chick Webb. A childhood accident in Baltimore, where he was born in 1909, had left Webb handicapped and hunchbacked, but he became one of the most influential drummers of the

Jimmie Lunceford and His Orchestra, "Organ Grinder's Swing" (1936)

early swing period. All the swing-era drummers idolized Webb and were astonished by his four-bar drum breaks in "Clap Hands, Here Comes Charlie" and his solos on temple blocks during "In a Little Spanish Town." Although most of Webb's breaks and fills were brief, he recorded longer drum solos on "Harlem Congo" and "Liza."

Drummer Buddy Rich recalled:

> Chick Webb was startling. He was a tiny man with this big face and big stiff shoulders. He sat way up on a kind of throne and used a twenty-eight-inch bass drum which had special pedals for his feet and he had those old goose-neck cymbal holders. Every beat was like a bell.[3]

Webb recorded in the early 1930s, including a version of "Heebie Jeebies," the song Louis Armstrong had made a hit six years earlier. Webb's version, arranged by Benny Carter, was the last recording of trombonist Jimmy Harrison, one of the most significant trombone players of the 1920s and early 1930s, who greatly advanced the technique of the instrument (see the box "Trombone Technique," on page 170). Webb's band of the early thirties also included John Kirby, a bassist and tuba player who had gotten his start with Fletcher Henderson. Kirby later led one of the successful small bands of the big-band era.

Webb took on arranger and saxophonist Edgar Sampson, who contributed two compositions that later became anthems of the swing era: "Stompin' at the Savoy" and "Don't Be That Way." Although Webb's band recorded them, these pieces went on to greater fame when Benny Goodman recorded them in 1938.

In the famous battles of the bands that took place at the Savoy in the thirties, Webb's loyal audience awarded victories to Webb over such groups as Benny Goodman's and Count Basie's bands. Webb also discovered and launched the career of sixteen-year-old vocalist Ella Fitzgerald, whose recording with Webb of "A-Tisket, A-Tasket" sold widely. Fitzgerald took over Webb's band after the leader's early death in 1939.

Chick Webb Orchestra, "Stompin' at the Savoy" (1934)

The Casa Loma Orchestra

One of the rare bands not to have a leader, the Casa Loma Orchestra functioned as a cooperative. This white group was founded in 1929 from members of a Jean Goldkette band—the Orange Blossoms—that had been based in Detroit. The Casa Loma Orchestra developed an enormous following on college campuses. Many of its up-tempo arrangements forecast the formulas and styles of the mid-thirties swing bands. The key writer and arranger for the Casa Loma Orchestra was banjoist Gene Gifford (1912–1970).

> Chick Webb "sat way up on a kind of throne and used a twenty-eight-inch bass drum which had special pedals for his feet and he had those old goose-neck cymbal holders. Every beat was like a bell."
>
> —Buddy Rich

Gifford wrote striking material for the band, particularly "Casa Loma Stomp," in which the call-and-response between the band sections was exciting and very well executed. Another particularly fine arrangement from Gifford was "Black Jazz."

Casa Loma Orchestra, "Casa Loma Stomp" (1930)

McKinney's Cotton Pickers

Another well-known cooperative band was a black midwestern group formed initially by Jean Goldkette in Ohio and Detroit: McKinney's Cotton Pickers. The Cotton Pickers may have influenced Gifford's work with the Casa

Loma Orchestra; the two bands have some striking traits in common, including rhythmic figures.

Don Redman left Fletcher Henderson's group in 1927 to become the music director of the Cotton Pickers. He and trumpeter John Nesbitt (1900?–1935) divided the arranging duties. Nesbitt's arrangements, in particular, distinguished the band's sound, and he contributed such forward-looking charts as "Put It There" and "Stop Kidding." Like the Casa Loma Orchestra, McKinney's Cotton Pickers anticipated many of the stylistic devices of the swing-era orchestra. Later such superb arrangers and players as Benny Carter, Coleman Hawkins, and Fats Waller would briefly join the group.

Tommy and Jimmy Dorsey

The Dorsey brothers were among the most popular swing-era bandleaders. Hailing from Shenandoah, Pennsylvania, Tommy (1905–1956) was a trombonist and Jimmy (1904–1957) was a saxophonist and clarinetist. The brothers led largely parallel early careers, working their way up the jazz-band pecking order in the 1920s. Eventually, they came to work with both the Goldkette bands and Paul Whiteman. In 1934 they cofounded the Dorsey Brothers Orchestra, but after a public dispute in 1935 Tommy left to organize his own group. Each band achieved tremendous popularity during the height of the swing era in the late 1930s. Tommy's band launched young vocalist Frank Sinatra.

The Dorseys were fine instrumentalists. Jimmy influenced pioneering saxophonist Lester Young. Although less influential as a jazz stylist, Tommy was known for the velvety elegance of his ballad work on trombone. Of the two bands, Tommy's probably featured the more inventive and interesting jazz charts. Among the excellent jazz arrangers associated with Tommy Dorsey's band was Sy Oliver, who had written superb works for both Jimmie Lunceford and Benny Goodman. The Dorsey brothers reunited briefly from 1953 to 1956 and hosted their own television show, on which a young singer named Elvis Presley made his first network appearance.

Glenn Miller

Glenn Miller's band was among the most famous of the swing era. Like many of the most acclaimed white groups, it was more strongly rooted in the popular music of the times than in jazz.

Miller (1904–1944) was born in Clarinda, Iowa, and raised in Fort Morgan, Colorado. A trombonist, he played with local orchestras and briefly attended the University of Colorado. In 1924 he joined Ben Pollack's band on the West Coast and eventually journeyed to New York with Pollack in 1928. Miller remained in New York and, like Benny Goodman and so many others, worked as a freelancer, mostly

Bandleader Glenn Miller's appearance (1939) reflects the careful polish that went into his music and made it so popular to a wide audience.

doing studio work. In 1937 he organized his first band but failed to attract much attention. Miller's second group, however, became well-known thanks largely to a major booking in 1938 at the Glen Island Casino in New Rochelle, New York, which led to other gigs and radio broadcasts that brought the band national attention.

In support of the war effort, Miller joined the U.S. Air Force in 1942 to form a band to entertain troops. In 1944 he flew from England to Paris to see about bookings for the group. Mysteriously, the plane never landed, and no trace of wreckage was found. Miller's plane most likely crashed in the English Channel.

Like the Dorsey brothers' bands, Miller's group is remembered more for its arrangements than its soloists. A taskmaster like Goodman, Miller created ensembles that were known for being very well rehearsed. His most important jazz soloist was probably cornetist Bobby Hackett (1915–1976), a player with an expressive lyricism that recalled the elegance of Bix Beiderbecke. Among Miller's most famous hits were

Glenn Miller and His Orchestra, "In the Mood" (1939)

"In the Mood," "Tuxedo Junction," and "String of Pearls." In the latter piece, Hackett fashioned a solo so strong that it has come to be thought of as part of the tune itself. "In the Mood" became one of the most popular pieces of the swing era and remains popular today.

Artie Shaw

Artie Shaw was among the most interesting of the white bandleaders to achieve celebrity during the swing era. He was, for instance, the only clarinetist to rival Goodman in popularity, yet his noteworthy personal life brought him as much fame as his musical accomplishments. With eight marriages, Shaw was as celebrated for his love life as for his music; his string of wives included movie stars Ava Gardner and Lana Turner. His celebrated "retirements" also attracted much publicity: Shaw would often express resentment against the popular-music business and disband his ensembles, only to return to performing after a short hiatus.

Born in New York City in 1910, Shaw grew up in New Haven, Connecticut. There he performed with the Johnny Cavallaro band, then from 1927 until 1929 he worked in Cleveland. In the late 1920s, Shaw relocated to New York, worked as a freelancer, and informally studied jazz with Willie "The Lion" Smith.

Shaw's interest in classical music strongly affected his approach to leading and organizing bands. For example, in 1936 he formed his first band; incredibly, it consisted of a string quartet, Shaw, and a rhythm section. Recording for Brunswick in 1936, Shaw augmented the band with a trumpet, trombone, tenor saxophone, and singer. As might be expected for such an unconventional group, its records were not major sellers. In 1937 Shaw reorganized his band with more-conventional instrumentation. His breakthrough came when he recorded Cole Porter's "Begin the Beguine" in 1938 and created one of the most popular recordings of the late thirties.

Artie Shaw and His Orchestra, "What Is This Thing Called Love?" (1938)

Shaw was an outstanding clarinetist. Technically accomplished, he was a less swinging player than Goodman, but he featured outstanding control and melodic suavity, especially in the highest registers of the instrument. His polish comes through on the highly varied band arrangements that would showcase his talents.

Shaw was something of an iconoclast in the jazz world. He broke the color barrier by briefly employing Billie Holiday as a singer with his band. Touring the South became difficult, however, and Shaw was forced to let the singer go. She made one recording with the band, "Any Old Time," in 1938. One of Shaw's most respected groups, organized in 1944, included trumpeter Roy Eldridge; their record "Little Jazz" became famous. "Lucky Number," arranged by Ray Conniff in 1945, was another interesting record, with a solo by Eldridge. A more unusual and progressive work, "Similau," was arranged by George Russell and recorded in 1949. Shaw continued to work occasionally through the 1980s, and he died in 2004.

Louis Armstrong and His Orchestra

As the swing era dawned in the 1930s, Armstrong's new manager, Joe Glaser, helped further Armstrong's persona as a featured attraction. He spent more and more time fronting big bands. He appeared frequently in Hollywood films, such as *Going Places* (1938) and *Cabin in the Sky* (1942), and became the first African American with a major radio program. Armstrong's stardom did not compromise his musicality, however. His many superb performances included solo features on "Star Dust" and "When It's Sleepy Time Down South," both from 1931. "Sleepy Time" became a trademark Armstrong number. Also noteworthy were the driving virtuosity of "Swing That Music" from 1936 (Listening Guide, Track 23), surely one of the most exciting recordings of Armstrong's career, and the high-spirited "Jubilee" from 1938.

Armstrong was thirty-five when he recorded "Swing That Music" and was perhaps in his technical prime as a trumpeter. Armstrong's youthful vigor at this point in his life allowed him to play solos that were technically beyond the reach of most jazz trumpeters of the era and thrilled his audiences. We can only imagine how the nonstop touring, where he might play this piece and other demanding solos night after night, would take its toll. Although Armstrong's excellence as a player certainly continued through the latter part of his career, we are fortunate to be able to hear him in works such as this, with the command, presence, and brilliance of his youthful maturity.

When the big-band era began to wane during World War II, Armstrong was well positioned to appear again with smaller groups. This profile fit his early work as a New Orleans Dixieland cornetist, so he was able to take full advantage of the New Orleans revival in the 1940s. He played with a group known as the All Stars, which included a reunion with Earl Hines as well as the fine

When Armstrong saw television film of a white mob angrily protesting the right of young black children to attend a white school in Little Rock, Arkansas, he lost patience and insisted that President Dwight D. Eisenhower enforce federal law regarding integration.

LISTENING GUIDE Track 23
"Swing That Music"

Louis Armstrong and His Orchestra: "Swing That Music" (Horace Gerlach, Louis Armstrong). Decca 866. New York, May 18, 1936. Louis Armstrong, trumpet, vocal, leader; Leonard Davis, Gus Aiken, Louis Bacon, trumpets; Jimmy Archey, Snub Mosley, trombones; Henry Jones, Charlie Holmes, alto saxophones; Bingie Madison, Greely Walton, tenor saxophones; Luis Russell, piano; Lee Blair, guitar; Pops Foster, bass; Paul Barbarin, drums.

The Main Point Written to feature Armstrong's vocal at the beginning and bravura trumpet playing at the end, the piece exemplifies the driving jazz of the swing era. The piece became famous for its repeated high concert Cs (high Ds on the B♭ trumpet) that set up the final ascent to the high E♭ that ends the piece.

Because Armstrong's solo is so exciting, we are apt to forget how artfully it is planned. Notice how he begins his four-chorus solo with the melody and gradually moves away from it. By the time he reaches his final chorus, the "melody" is not much more than repeated high Cs. Armstrong may have been influenced by European opera, in which spectacular high notes, particularly for sopranos or tenors, are often showstoppers.

1st chorus—Theme (band) in 32-bar ABAC form

0:00 It is probably easiest to count this piece in half time, with two beats per bar. By this reckoning, the theme is in 32-bar ABAC form. The second half of the form (bar 17, repeat of the A) begins at 0:12.

2nd chorus—Theme (Armstrong vocal)

0:24 Armstrong's vocal chorus. Second half of the form begins at 0:36.

3rd chorus—Saxophone soli

0:49 The saxophone section plays a variation on the melody in harmony. (**Soli** in big-band charts often designates a part of the piece written to feature an instrumental section in harmony.) Notice that the first half of the chorus features intricate writing for the players, whereas the second half (1:02) has a more sustained melody for contrast. During the last two bars of the chorus, the harmony is modified for a key change. The piece had so far been in C major; it now moves to E♭ major. C major was probably chosen initially to fit Armstrong's vocal range, while the modulation up to E♭ was planned for the brilliant solo ending.

Armstrong's 1st solo chorus

1:13 Armstrong begins by playing the melody. As the first half of the chorus comes to an end, he starts departing from the melody. At the second half (1:26), his playing is more improvisational, but with continuing references to the melody. For example, the phrase he plays at 1:29–1:32 sounds the lyric "swing that music."

Armstrong's 2nd solo chorus

1:37 As Armstrong begins his second chorus, he moves to a higher register of the instrument. At the second half of this chorus (1:49), his playing becomes yet more abstract, as he hits high notes and "falls off." Nevertheless, we can still detect references to the original melody at 1:53–1:58. At the end of the chorus, he sustains a high B♭ (1:59) to build the excitement.

Armstrong's 3rd solo chorus

2:00 In Armstrong's third chorus, his playing becomes more abstract still. We catch glimpses of the melody (for example, 2:17–2:21), but Armstrong largely moves between (concert) high B♭s and high Cs. Armstrong had introduced his third chorus with a sustained B♭; he now introduces his final chorus with an even higher note: C.

Armstrong's 4th solo (shout) chorus

2:25   For the final shout chorus, the abstraction of the melody is complete, now reduced to the famous, shouted high Cs. Notice how the spaces between the high Cs narrow and become more irregular at the second half of the chorus (2:37) to increase the excitement still more. At the end of the chorus, Armstrong moves from the high C to D, then to the tonic E♭ for the breathless (and breathtaking) end of the piece.

 Listen to this music in an animated Active Listening Guide available at the text website.

Soli in big-band charts often designates a part of the piece written to feature an instrumental section in harmony.

trombonist Jack Teagarden. (See the box "Trombone Technique.") With the All Stars, Armstrong combined a return to his New Orleans roots with his established showmanship. The band's numerous live performances generally followed set routines, but often featured outstanding musicianship and exciting playing. Armstrong continued to record during this period as well, including remakes of several of the pieces that established his reputation as a young man.

By the 1950s Armstrong's career had peaked, but he continued to work as hard as ever, touring the country and the world. One of his defining moments came as a result of the *Brown* v. *Board of Education* Supreme Court decision of 1954, which outlawed segregation. When segregated schools in the South were ordered to integrate in 1957, Governor Orval Faubus of Arkansas was among the prominent officials who resisted integration. Armstrong at the time was on tour in Grand Forks, North Dakota. When he saw television film of a white mob angrily protesting the right of young black children to attend a white school in Little Rock, Arkansas, he lost patience and insisted that President Dwight D. Eisenhower enforce federal law regarding integration. Sometime later, Eisenhower did in fact send troops to Little Rock to ensure desegregation of

Louis Armstrong as a mature artist. Note the handkerchief dangling from his left hand: this was one of his most recognizable trademarks, similar to Michael Jackson's white glove.

Photo courtesy of the Morgan Collection

the schools. It is possible that Armstrong's outrage at the treatment of the schoolchildren influenced Eisenhower's decision.

Technique and Technology

Trombone Technique

Trombone technique had greatly advanced since the days of the New Orleans tailgaters. One of the earliest trombonists to attain a high level of virtuosity was Irving Milfred "Miff" Mole (1898–1961), whose recordings with Ernest "Red" Nichols had a profound effect on later trombonists. James Henry "Jimmy" Harrison (1900–1931) also helped advance trombone technique during the 1920s, particularly during his assocation later in the decade with the Fletcher Henderson band. Jack Teagarden (1905–1964), originally from Vernon, Texas, arrived in New York in the late twenties. With his rich, full-toned sound and his effortless virtuosity, Teagarden became one of the finest trombonists in jazz. (For more on Teagarden, see the section later in this chapter.)

Throughout the 1950s, Armstrong was an ambassador for U.S. goodwill during the cold war with the Soviet Union, with the State Department sponsoring many of his tours. In 1959 he suffered a heart attack, which forced him to cut back his performances—especially the physically exhausting, bravura trumpet playing he was known for in the 1930s and 1940s. Despite declining health he continued working through the 1960s, though featured more as a singer than as a trumpeter. In fact, Armstrong played gigs right through 1971, the year he died on July 6.

Armstrong was a musical revolutionary in his youth and one of the two or three most important jazzmen ever. He also became a symbol of twentieth-century popular culture. Even as late as the mid-sixties, he had a hit song with a recording of "Hello, Dolly"—a number that became much associated with Armstrong during the years of his final performances. Amazingly, Armstrong had a Top 10 record in every decade from the 1920s to the 1960s—a span of fifty years.

World War II and The "All-Girl" Bands

The focus of jazz history is usually on male musicians, although there have been significant contributions by women. Jazz histories typically mention innovative female pianists and singers, such as Lil Hardin, Mary Lou Williams, Bessie Smith, Billie Holliday, Ella Fitzgerald, and Sarah Vaughan, yet many jazz histories ignore female musicians who were respected in their day but who played instruments more associated with men. These include trumpet players Valaida Snow and Dolly Jones, trombonist Melba Liston, saxophonist Vi Redd, and drummer Paula Hampton.

Recently, however, historians and scholars have attempted to describe women's participation in jazz to a greater degree. Sherrie Tucker's *Swing Shift: "All-Girl" Bands of the 1940s*[4] highlights the role of women musicians during World War II. Using oral histories and interviews, Tucker details a number of the all-women bands (invariably called "all-girl" bands in the press) that sprang up prior to and during the war years, including the International Sweethearts of Rhythm, the Prairie View Co-Eds, and the Darlings of Rhythm.

One reason for the increased visibility of these bands was that the number of male bands dwindled because many of those players had been drafted into the army. Thus the female musician became the counterpart to "Rosie the Riveter," the figure who symbolized the women working in the factories to support the war effort while the men were fighting overseas. Many female jazz bands existed before the war, however, and many of their musicians had established careers as early as the 1920s. In fact, some of the most popular female groups, such as the bands of Ina Ray Hutton and Rita Rio, broke up even before America entered the war. Tucker shows that the visibility of these all-women bands during the war years often led to heated debates in the jazz press as to whether women could—or should—play jazz.

The saxophone section of the International Sweethearts of Rhythm in 1944. *Clockwise from lower left:* Grace Bayron (tenor), Helen Saine (alto), Rosalind "Roz" Cron (lead alto), Violet Burnside (tenor), and Willie Mae Wong (baritone).

The groups encountered not only gender discrimination but also racial prejudice. Traveling and performing in the South led to many difficult circumstances for the all-women bands. During this time of the Jim Crow segregationist laws, it was illegal in the South for blacks and whites to eat, work, or travel together. Whites and blacks had to use separate bathrooms and water fountains. Some all-women groups like the International Sweethearts of Rhythm were primarily African American but often had one or two white musicians with the band, who then had to try to pass as black by using dark makeup to avoid being arrested. The group members talked about outwitting the police when traveling through the South. In one incident a band member recalled, the police discovered several white musicians on the bandstand. The group was asked to follow the police in their car to the station. When the musicians discovered that they were driving past the hotel at which they were staying, they quickly dropped off the white musicians and continued on to the station without them. The police, unable to make any arrests because there were now no white musicians present, had to let the women go.

Violet Burnside (1915–1964) was a featured soloist with the International Sweethearts of Rhythm. She joined the band in 1943 after working with various all-women groups, including the Dixie Rhythm Girls and the Harlem Play-Girls. In 1949 she formed her own group, again working with all-female personnel. In the 1950s she led bands mostly in the Washington, DC, area, where she settled. "Vi Vigor" (see Listening Guide, Track 24) is a swinging showcase for Burnside.

LISTENING GUIDE
"Vi Vigor"
Track 24

International Sweethearts of Rhythm: "Vi Vigor" (King). Victor 40-0146-A. New York, October 14, 1946. Rae Lee Jones, leader; Anna Mae Winburn, conductor; Johnnie Mae "Tex" Stansbery, Ernestine "Tiny" Davis, Nora Lee McGhee, Flo Dreyer, trumpets; Julia Travick, Helen Jones, Ima Belle Byrd, trombones; Violet Burnside, Colleen Murray, Myrtle Young, Willie Mae Wong, Jacqueline Dexter, saxophones; Jackie King, piano; Carlene Ray, guitar; Edna Smith, bass; Pauline Braddy, drums.

The Main Point   A showcase for saxophonist Violet Burnside. Although the scoring is in the big-band tradition, the phrasing shows hints of bebop, which in 1946 was continuing to grow in popularity.

Introduction—4 bars

0:00   The full band on an introduction with syncopation that is influenced by bebop. The aggressive trumpet lead line gives way to the trombone section, in which the three players enter one note at a time on a held chord.

Head—32-bar rhythm changes

0:04   First A section. The first four-bar phrase is played by the saxophones; the brass take over the lead for the second four bars while the saxophones play a countermelody.

0:12   Repeat of the A section. A modification at the end of the section allows the saxophones to complete the section with the lead line.

0:20   The B section features Burnside. Note how she fits her phrases between the aggressive entrances of the brass. This kind of "getting in the way" of the soloist is another feature of the recording that is characteristic of the aggressive feel of bebop.

0:27   The third A section is rather like the second, but Burnside closes the section with a brief melodic solo.

Interlude—8 bars

0:35   Interlude by the full band to set up the Burnside chorus.

Burnside solo 1st chorus—32-bar rhythm changes

0:44   Burnside solo, first A. For this section the brass phrases quietly in full chords. We get to hear more of Burnside by this point; her style, like that of many tenor players of the era, recalls Lester Young and Ben Webster, yet it is uniquely hers.

0:52   Second A section. The texture from the first A section continues.

0:59   In the bridge the brass provide stabbing chords on the downbeat of every other measure.

1:07   Third A section. The sustained chords from the first A sections return.

Burnside solo 2nd chorus—32-bar rhythm changes

1:15   First A section. The texture simplifies to just the rhythm section accompanying Burnside. She turns to the lower register at this point, not having to worry about being heard.

1:23	Second A section, with continuing accompaniment by the rhythm section only. Burnside returns to using the full register of the horn.
1:31	In the bridge the full band returns to back Burnside for the first half. The second half of the bridge uses the simpler texture.
1:39	Third A section. Again, the simpler texture with rhythm section only.

Burnside solo 3rd chorus—32-bar rhythm changes

1:47	First A section, added countermelody in trombones and saxophones. Here Burnside builds a passionate statement with blue notes over the trombones.
1:55	In the second A section, the trombones and the saxophones continue their counterline, but Burnside moves to the middle register.
2:03	Bridge, just the rhythm section.
2:11	Third A section; the counterline returns.

Burnside solo out-chorus with band—32-bar rhythm changes

2:19	The band returns behind Burnside's intense playing and shouting in the upper register with prominent blue notes.
2:27	Second A section. The busy textures continue, with Burnside moving to blueslike phrases in the middle register.
2:35	Bridge. The background texture is lightened somewhat here, with Burnside continuing the intensity.
2:43	For the final out-chorus A section, Burnside provides a wonderfully passionate counterpoint to the band. The piece ends with a cadencing phrase for Burnside, answered by a full chord in the band.

Listen to this music in an animated Active Listening Guide available at the text website.

Numerous other bands achieved great popularity in the swing era, including groups led by Benny Carter, Gene Krupa (both discussed later in this chapter), Charlie Barnet (1913–1991), Harry James (1916–1983), Boyd Rayburn (1913–1966), and Bob Crosby (1913–1993). As the swing era waned in the 1940s, other big bands rose to popularity, but such groups never enjoyed the celebrity of the earlier bands. Significantly, these later groups tried to incorporate the breakthroughs of the bebop revolutionaries.

Swing-Era Stylists

Here we look at the various styles of the most celebrated swing-era performers and composer-arrangers. All contributed greatly to the sound we call "swing." We discuss the following artists:

▶ Clarinet: Benny Goodman

▶ Saxophone: Coleman Hawkins and Lester Young

▶ Trumpet: Roy Eldridge

▶ Trombone: Jack Teagarden

▶ Piano: Earl Hines and Teddy Wilson

▶ Bass: Jimmy Blanton

▶ Drums: Jo Jones and Gene Krupa

▶ Guitar: Charlie Christian

▶ Composing/arranging: Benny Carter

▶ Singing: Billie Holiday

Benny Goodman

In Chapter 5, we contrasted the Benny Goodman 1936 big-band recording of "Down South Camp Meeting" (Listening Guide, Track 21) with Fletcher Henderson's original, and promised to examine Goodman's solo in some greater detail. Of all the jazz clarinet styles, Goodman's perhaps best balanced melodic control and outright swinging. Goodman's hot style featured an exquisite sense of timing and a clear articulation of the chord changes.

LISTENING GUIDE
"Down South Camp Meeting"

Track 21

Benny Goodman and His Orchestra: "Down South Camp Meeting" (Henderson). Victor 25387. Los Angeles, August 13, 1936. Goodman, clarinet, leader; Manny Klein, Pee Wee Erwin, Chris Griffin, trumpets; Red Ballard, Murray McEachern, trombones; Hymie Schertzer, Bill DePew, alto saxophones; Art Rollini, Dick Clark, tenor saxophones; Allan Reuss, guitar; Harry Goodman, bass; Gene Krupa, drums; Fletcher Henderson, arranger.

The Main Point Goodman's solo on "Down South Camp Meeting" is a fine example of his swing clarinet style. As pointed out in Chapter 5, the solo follows an ABA format rather than the more usual AABA. We examine each section of his solo in turn.

A section—8 bars as 4 + 4

0:35   Goodman enters in the high register with a short melodic idea that moves down to the tonic note C at the beginning of the third bar. Goodman then prepares the second half of the A section with a **pickup** (0:39).

For the second four-bar phrase (0:40), Goodman returns to the high register and descends with a similar, but more syncopated phrase that again targets the tonic C. The easy-going quality of Goodman's playing derives in part from the alignment of his phrases with the natural division of the A section into four-bar halves and the closing of his phrases on held-out Cs.

B section—8 bars as 4 + 4

0:45   Goodman begins the B section with a pickup. He brings greater intensity to his solo at this point, in part by emphasizing a concert E, which poignantly colors the change of harmony to A minor with a tinge of the blues. Continuing to emphasize E, Goodman alternates between the middle and high registers of the instrument for a dramatic contrast to his A section. Again, however, his playing divides into two halves that correspond to the four-bar divisions of the section. The phrase beginning in the second four bars (0:50) extends into the final A section.

A section—8 bars as 4 + 4

0:55   The first four bars of the final A section, continuing from the B section, close on a C (as in the first A section). For the second four bars (1:00), Goodman emphasizes a high G toward the top of the clarinet's range. The bluesy E that was such an important note in the B section occurs here as well. Goodman again divides the eight bars of this A section into two equal halves. Moreover, each of Goodman's phrases ends on the same long note, the tonic C, which also ended both phrases of the first A section. Thus, while referencing the blues and elegantly varying his subphrases, Goodman imparts a relaxed and unified feeling to his playing by ending many of his phrases on long notes.

Listen to this music in an animated Active Liste Guide available at the text website.

Goodman's solo in "Down South Camp Meeting" demonstrates several characteristics of his playing:

▶ Frequent **arpeggiation** of the harmonies and use of scale fragments

▶ Basic eighth-note rhythm

▶ Blues effects

A **pickup** is a short melodic idea that ends on the downbeat.

An **arpeggiation**, **arpeggiated figure**, or **arpeggio** is the notes of a chord played in sequence rather than simultaneously. (Listen to Track 2 of the **AP** Audio Primer to hear various arpeggios.)

© iStockphoto.com/fotomy

The clarinet was one of the popular solo instruments of the swing era.

▶ Note choices that emphasize the notes of the chord (**inside playing**)

▶ Fast vibrato on some held notes

▶ Frequent alignment of his improvisation with the natural four- and eight-bar divisions of the form

Coleman Hawkins

During the late teens and early twenties, the front line of clarinet, trombone, and cornet dominated New Orleans– and Chicago-style jazz, relegating the saxophone to use as a novelty vaudeville instrument. As the 1920s wore on and the big-band sound evolved, the saxophone grew more and more popular until it became an important reed voice. By the 1930s Coleman Hawkins, a powerful soloist, had made the saxophone a serious improvisational instrument.

Coleman Hawkins, known as "Bean" or "Hawk," was the player most responsible for elevating the tenor saxophone to prominence as a jazz voice. Born in 1904 in

St. Joseph, Missouri, Hawkins began playing tenor saxophone at age nine. Three years later he was working professionally for school dances. In 1921 he was living in Kansas City and playing in the Twelfth Street Theater orchestra, where vocalist Mamie Smith heard him and invited him to tour with her group, the Jazz Hounds.

Hawkins's first recordings, with Mamie Smith, date from 1922, but he initially attracted national attention during his ten-year association with the Fletcher Henderson Orchestra in New York from 1924 to 1934. His earliest recorded solos with the Henderson orchestra, on such compositions as "Dicty Blues," were sometimes rhythmically square and used such dated novelty devices as **slap-tonguing**, which produces a humorous effect on the instrument. Hawkins's style quickly became more authoritative and more legato under the influence of Louis Armstrong during the latter's residence in the Henderson orchestra. Hawkins's solo in "The Stampede," for example, used call-and-response patterns that may owe a debt to Armstrong.

Hawkins's burgeoning solo style demonstrated a hard propulsive attack, a wide vibrato, and technical virtuosity. Drawing on his skill at the piano, Hawkins developed an improvisational saxophone style rooted in harmonic conception. That is, Hawkins often created solos with arpeggiated figures that often followed the chord progression. In addition, his sophisticated harmonic knowledge made him fluent in chord substitution, which allowed him to replace the given harmonies of a composition for added effect in his improvisations.

After his work in the Henderson band, Hawkins left for Europe, where he worked from March 1934 to July 1939. His five years in Europe were seminal for the development of European jazz as he performed widely with top European players. After arriving in London, Hawkins toured with the Jack Hylton band, where his success convinced him to remain in Europe. By 1935 he was performing throughout the Continent with a Dutch group called the Ramblers, with whom he also recorded. He also freelanced in various cities and assembled his own groups for recording; a particularly famous session in 1937 included both Django Reinhardt and Benny Carter. Hawkins then returned to England before sailing for the United States in July 1939.

Hawkins's eagerly awaited return to the States began dramatically: his October 1939 recording of "Body and Soul" (Listening Guide, Track 25) is an acknowledged masterpiece and one of the most well-known recordings of a jazz ballad. The record solidified Hawkins's standing as the undisputed master of tenor saxophone; for example,

Inside playing is the jazz technique of playing melodic lines that favor the principal notes of the harmonies. (Listen to Track 8 of the 🅿 Audio Primer to hear examples of inside playing.)

Slap-tonguing is a saxophone novelty technique that produces a humorous effect.

Voice leading is a means of making logical melodic and harmonic sequences within an improvised solo. **Step connection**, a key element in voice leading, is the principal means of stringing together the melodic and harmonic elements. The steps are often based on the scale determined by the key of the piece.

A **vertical improvisation** is one based on the chord harmonies (stacked vertically) as opposed to the melodic contour (running horizontally).

in *Down Beat* magazine that year, the general public voted him "Best Tenor Saxophonist."

In "Body and Soul," we glimpse Hawkins's mature style. Many players emulated his techniques as heard in this solo, which include the following:

▶ Sensitive, smoothly articulated melodies

▶ Complex melodic connections based on motivic development and **voice leading**

Saxophonist Coleman Hawkins in the 1940s. A competitive player, always interested in cutting-edge developments, Hawkins performed with many of the younger musicians who were innovating bebop in the early 1940s.

Bettmann/Corbis

▶ Rich, sensuous tone

▶ Loose, free phrasing over the beat, with irregular phrase lengths that remain **vertical**, that is, tied to the prevailing harmony

▶ Emotional expression

▶ Large variety of note values

▶ Use of the entire range of the instrument

▶ Improvisation based on the underlying scale/chord structure (inside playing)

A dominating force in the 1930s, Hawkins influenced practically all other saxophonists. His contemporaries—Ben Webster, Chu Berry, and Herschel Evans—acknowledged allegiance to Hawkins; later tenor players such as John Coltrane rediscovered his works. In his relentless quest for virtuosity on the instrument, Hawkins constantly sought new modes of expression. In an unusual step, he recorded unaccompanied saxophone solos entitled "Hawk Variations" (1945) and "Picasso" (probably 1948). His willingness to absorb and adapt to new styles was evident in his performances with new generations of musicians—Max Roach, Dizzy Gillespie, and Thelonious Monk in the 1940s and Sonny Rollins in the 1960s. Hawkins continued to record and perform prolifically until his death in 1969.

Lester Young

During the 1930s the most significant tenor saxophonist to escape the influence of Hawkins was Lester Willis Young. Billie Holiday claimed to have given him the nickname "Pres" (or "Prez"), short for *president*. Gunther Schuller points out that "Lester could not accept Hawkins's essentially staccato, hard-tongued, vertical, chord-anchored approach to the saxophone. His way of hearing music was the way of the blues—and of telling a story in music."[5]

Young, who in the mid-thirties leaped to prominence as a featured soloist with the Count Basie Band, located his influences in white saxophonists Jimmy Dorsey and Frank Trumbauer. Young cultivated their lighter sound with less vibrato, in contrast to Coleman Hawkins's muscular approach. Reputedly, Young even carried a copy of Trumbauer and Beiderbecke's recording "Singin' the Blues" (Track 13) in his saxophone case. Young was also attracted to Trumbauer's ability to develop an improvisation in a logical and unhurried sequence of events. As Young put it:

> I had to make a decision between Frankie Trumbauer and Jimmy Dorsey—y'dig: I wasn't sure which way I wanted to go, y'dig. . . . The only people that was tellin' stories that I liked to hear were them. . . . Ever hear him [Trumbauer] play "Singin' the Blues?" That tricked me right there, that's where I went.[6]

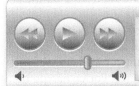

LISTENING GUIDE   Track 25
"Body and Soul"

Coleman Hawkins and His Orchestra: "Body and Soul" (Green-Heyman-Sauer-Eyton). Victor 20-2539. New York, October 11, 1939. Hawkins, tenor saxophone and leader; Tommy Lindsay, Joe Guy, trumpets; Earl Hardy, trombone; Jackie Fields, Eustis Moore, alto saxophones; Gene Rodgers, piano; William Oscar Smith, bass; Arthur Herbert, drums.

The Main Point The mature style of Coleman Hawkins is apparent on "Body and Soul." Its romantic, understated eloquence remains unimpeded throughout, even by the forceful phrases in the last part of the second chorus. In the recording, Hawkins departs frequently from the tune's melody. His "vertical" style of improvisation, based on his ability to outline the chordal harmonies, is in evidence throughout the solo.

Introduction

0:00 The piece begins with a four-bar piano introduction in tempo. Pianist Rodgers plays a chord at the beginning of each measure, followed by a brief melodic idea.

1st chorus—AABA

0:09 Hawkins plays the first A section, both stating the melody and improvising around it. Hawkins's gentle lyricism is enhanced by his use of vibrato at the ends of phrases.

0:30 Hawkins departs further from the melody by including more improvisation during this second A section.

0:50 In the B section, Hawkins starts to use a wider range, using both higher and lower notes than previously.

1:11 The final phrase of the B section carries over into the return of the A section, masking somewhat the sectional division.

2nd chorus—AABA

1:31 Listen for Hawkins's ability to repeat and develop melodic ideas based on rhythm and shape. During the A sections of the second chorus, the horns play a slow-moving background behind Hawkins.

2:11 Return of the B section.

2:32 In the final A section of the second chorus, Hawkins's tone gets increasingly louder and edgier, setting up an effective climax, which he prepares by moving up through E♭ and E-natural to a climactic high F.

That is, Hawkins slowly and artfully builds each chorus but saves the highest point of the solo for the third A section of the second chorus.

2:48 Hawkins plays a short unaccompanied passage before the final chord.

  Listen to this music in an animated Active Listening Guide available at the text website.

Born in 1909 outside New Orleans in Woodville, Mississippi, Young moved with his father to Minneapolis at age eleven. Young's father formed a minstrel-type band with which Young toured the Midwest, playing carnivals in the Dakotas, Kansas, and Nebraska. A versatile musician, Young played the violin, drums, and alto saxophone before making the tenor his primary instrument. While still in his late teens and early twenties, Young toured with several bands, including King Oliver's group and Walter Page's Blue Devils. In 1933 he settled in Kansas City.

The following year Young joined Count Basie's band, but he left briefly to move to New York to replace Coleman Hawkins, who had just left Fletcher Henderson to

A **formula** (more popularly called a **lick**) is a worked-out melodic idea that fits a common chord progression. Most improvisers develop formulas for up-tempo pieces because the rapid tempo does not allow time for total spontaneity.

move to Europe. Young's lighter sound and laid-back lyrical style, however, were radically different from Hawkins's approach and were disliked by Henderson's

Lester's "way of hearing music was the way of the blues—and of telling a story in music."
—Gunther Schuller

band members. As a result, Young left Henderson and New York and eventually returned to Kansas City to

rejoin Basie's band, a move that would have a significant impact on his career.

Young made his earliest recordings in 1936 with Basie. His solos on "Oh, Lady Be Good" and "Shoe Shine Boy" had an immediate and lasting impact. In his discussion of Young's style, jazz historian Lewis Porter has pointed out many of Young's melodic formulas, which reappear in numerous solos.[7] (The use of the word **formula** to describe the melodic patterns developed by jazz musicians is a technical term; it is not pejorative.) In addition, Porter shows Young's ability to logically develop a solo through repeated reference to these formulas—what Young referred to as "tellin' stories." This can be heard in many of Young's solos, but may be less apparent on "Every Tub" (Listening Guide, Track 20) because his solo is only 24 bars long.

Young's "Every Tub" solo shows the following characteristics, all of which influenced the next generation of jazz saxophonists:

▶ Rhythmic variety within eighth-note swing lines occasionally tinged by the blues

▶ Light, airy tone

LISTENING GUIDE
"Every Tub"

Track 20

Count Basie and His Orchestra: "Every Tub" (Durham-Basie). Decca 1728. New York, February 16, 1938. Bill "Count" Basie, piano, leader; Buck Clayton, Ed Lewis, Harry Edison, trumpets; Eddie Durham, Benny Morton, Dan Minor, trombones; Earl Warren, Jack Washington, alto saxophones; Herschel Evans, Lester Young, tenor saxophones; Freddie Green, guitar; Walter Page, bass; Jo Jones, drums; Eddie Durham, arranger.

The Main Point In Chapter 5 we cited "Every Tub" as exemplary of Count Basie's classic swing style in the 1930s. The recording is also a fine example of Lester Young's up-tempo saxophone style and use of melodic formulas. As mentioned in our previous discussion of the piece, Young is featured on the piece's introduction and the first section of the arrangement. His solo follows rhythm changes, but deviates in that it is ABA rather than AABA.

Introduction—8 bars

0:00   The introduction features Young's tenor saxophone solo punctuated by ensemble chords. Young matches the energy of the band with exciting eighth-note lines that thread between the ensemble chords, outline the harmony, and lead into the first section of his solo. He follows the first figure he plays with a second (0:02) that is a close variant—both starting high, then working down. For the third and fourth figures (0:04 and 0:06), Young starts low, then works up to contrast the first two figures. Thus, the four short figures that Young plays through the introduction come across effectively as matched pairs.

A phrase—8 bars

0:07   Over a rhythmic riff in the brass, Young begins with a melodic idea that moves up through the tonic B♭ triad from a B♭ to an F. He begins his second figure by completing the upward arpeggiation to a high B♭, from which an eight-note swing line finishes the phrase.

B phrase—8 bars

0:16   During the bridge, Young plays a long eighth-note phrase that divides the eight bars unevenly into 6 + 2. He begins with an up-and-down scalar eighth-note line that became associated with the local Kansas City jazz scene and may have influenced the work of Charlie Parker, a bebop pioneer whom we examine in Chapter 7. Dividing the eight-bar section as 6 + 2 contrasts the first A section, in which the phrasing was regular and balanced.

A phrase—8 bars

0:24   The phrase begun in the last two bars of the B section concludes on the downbeat of this last A section. Young here reaches a high (concert) B♭, which then proceeds to a high D (0:25), the highest note in his solo. Young then briefly articulates rhythmic B♭s, which echo the brass figures, before concluding his solo with an eighth-note line that returns to the middle register of the instrument. Although brief, the solo is well constructed, with a balance of phrase length and type, all of which are characteristic of his style.

   Listen to this music in an animated Active Listening Guide available at the text website.

▶ Use of space between phrases (though less evident here than in many of Young's solos)

▶ Balance of regular and irregular phrase lengths

▶ Melodic connections based on motivic contrast, voice leading, and use of formula

▶ Concentration on the midrange of the instrument

▶ Cool expression

Lester Young, 1939. Notice the tilt of Young's head and the angle at which he holds his saxophone.

Courtesy Frank Driggs Collection

Like many of the players associated with Kansas City, Young derived much of his repertory from the blues and from compositions written over rhythm changes. One of Young's famous solos is from his composition "Lester Leaps In," based, like "Every Tub," on rhythm changes in B♭ major.

Young remained with Count Basie until 1940. Playing both tenor and clarinet, he also made several recordings with Billie Holiday, a singer with whom he developed a close bond. After leaving Basie, Young put together several groups of his own, none of which was particularly successful, and he rejoined Basie in 1943. The following year Young won first place for tenor saxophonists in the *Down Beat* poll. Unfortunately, Young was also inducted into the army in 1944, an experience that proved hellish for the thirty-five-year-old tenor player. Arrested for marijuana use and court-martialed, he spent much of the following year in detention barracks.

After returning to civilian life, Young was at the peak of his popularity and made several fine recordings, such as "These Foolish Things" in 1945, and continued to win numerous polls. Around 1952, his playing became more inconsistent, although in Leonard Feather's jazz musician poll in 1956, Young won the category of "Greatest Tenor Saxophone Ever." Exacerbated by chronic drinking, Young's health had begun to deteriorate in the late fifties. He died in March 1959, only a few months before the death of his close friend Billie Holiday.

Young's controlled style of playing affected a generation of musicians. He influenced the maturing Charlie Parker, who adapted the flexibility and blues of Young's melodic lines to greater virtuosity (discussed in Chapter 7). Saxophonists who acknowledged a debt to Young included many associated with the later *cool* style of playing, such as Stan Getz, John Haley "Zoot" Sims, Jimmy Giuffre, Al Cohn, Gerry Mulligan, Paul Desmond, and Lee Konitz.

Young's embrace of understated, lyrical improvisation overturned the dominance of such virtuosos as Louis Armstrong and Coleman Hawkins. In the words of Gunther Schuller, Young's legacy was the launching of "a completely new aesthetic of jazz—for all instruments, not just the tenor saxophone. The essence of his heritage is that he proposed a totally new alternative to the language, grammar, and vocabulary of jazz."[8]

Roy Eldridge

Because the trumpet, as part of the big band, was a major voice in jazz during the swing era, it may be misleading to select one soloist as dominating stylistically. For one thing, Louis Armstrong remained the most famous personality in jazz and a major swing-era stylist as well, despite his pioneering work in the 1920s. But if Armstrong's overwhelming presence is set aside, no swing-era player is more significant than Roy Eldridge.

Although Eldridge was hailed as the successor to Armstrong, as well as the predecessor to Dizzy Gillespie, Eldridge mostly evaded Armstrong's influence until he heard the older trumpeter live in 1932. Until then Eldridge had absorbed the playing of trumpeters Rex Stewart and Cladys "Jabbo" Smith, although Armstrong's Hot Five "King of the Zulus" (1926) had some impact on his style. In addition, Eldridge had brought to the trumpet the more harmony-based, vertical improvisation approach of Coleman Hawkins.

After 1932 Armstrong exerted a strong influence on swing-style improvisation, but the younger Eldridge would move beyond him through forward-looking melodic and rhythmic innovations. For example, he fully exploited the three-octave range of the trumpet, and his solos exhibited a fiery vigor and an ability to handle breakneck tempos. His keen awareness of harmony and his instrumental dexterity significantly influenced the pioneers of the subsequent bebop era, especially Dizzy Gillespie.

Born in Pittsburgh in 1911, Eldridge came to New York in 1930. His first recorded solos are from 1935 with the Teddy Hill Band, and he later spent a year with the Fletcher Henderson Orchestra. In the late thirties, he led a small group at the Three Deuces in Chicago in 1937 and larger bands at various clubs in New York in 1939. His recordings from this period—"Florida Stomp," "After You've Gone," and "Heckler's Hop"—show him completely at ease in rapid playing. He had a penchant for highlighting unusual melodic intervals, and his sinuous melodic lines would sometimes encompass two or more octaves within a single phrase.

Eldridge's stature as the leading trumpet soloist of the swing era led to offers from numerous successful white bands, and in 1941 he joined Gene Krupa's band as a featured soloist and, occasionally, as a singer. His vocals, along with those of female vocalist Anita O'Day, were heard on the band's hits "Let Me Off Uptown" and "Knock Me a Kiss." Eldridge played ballads and up-tempo numbers equally well, and his performance on Krupa's recording of "Rockin' Chair" includes one of his most famous solos.

Flamboyant high-note playing, which comprised more crowd-pleasing antics than successful musical statements, characterized some of Eldridge's work from the 1940s. As a trumpet virtuoso, he thrived in the competitive world of the jam session.

In the early forties, Eldridge played in some of the sessions at Minton's Playhouse, the club that would become the birthplace of the bebop movement. His trumpet battles with Dizzy Gillespie were legendary, and Gillespie frankly acknowledged the musical debt he owed to Eldridge. Thus Eldridge indirectly helped spawn the bebop movement, although he never embraced the newer bop concepts.

Eldridge joined Artie Shaw's seventeen-piece band in 1944, but after numerous racial incidents while touring with the white group, he left after a year to front his own ensembles. While touring Europe with the Benny Goodman band in 1950, Eldridge left to spend a year in Paris. Until he suffered a stroke in 1980, Eldridge led his own groups and performed with Benny Carter, Johnny Hodges, Ella Fitzgerald, and Coleman Hawkins. He died in 1989.

Jack Teagarden

Jack Teagarden (1905–1964) seemingly spanned all periods and styles with his warm, friendly, blues-oriented approach to the trombone. Possessed of considerable technical skill, he eschewed the rough technique of the early New Orleans players. Nevertheless, he became prominently associated with the New Orleans revival of the 1940s, performing often with Louis Armstrong and the fine swing-Dixieland trumpeter Bobby Hackett. His singing was always as relaxed and appealing as his playing. Much thirties swing trombone technique can be traced to Teagarden, but he imbued it with a unique personality and a feeling for the blues that even avant-garde players respected.

Earl Hines

Earl Hines established himself as a major talent on piano by performing superbly on the Louis Armstrong and His Hot Five recordings in the late 1920s. As discussed in Chapter 3, Hines was the musician most responsible for developing a linear concept of jazz piano, applying an Armstrong-based "trumpet style" to the keyboard. The dramatic change of style that Hines initiated in the mid-twenties can be appreciated by comparing the earlier Armstrong records, with pianist Lil Hardin, to the later Hot Five selections with Hines. The graceful, easygoing sense of forward movement he contributed to the band anticipated the swing style of the 1930s, even while the other sidemen remained entrenched in the New Orleans sound.

Born in Duquesne, Pennsylvania, in 1903, Hines was raised in a musical family. He studied classical piano and played his first gigs in his hometown, which was near Pittsburgh. In 1923 his musical travels brought him to Chicago, where he played with the Carroll Dickerson

Earl Hines conducting his orchestra during a 1940 session.

band and met Louis Armstrong. He performed with Armstrong for several years but decided to continue with his own groups after Armstrong headed off to New York with the Dickerson group.

With some earlier experience directing bands, Hines now put together his own group for the Grand Terrace Ballroom. The band eventually grew into a twelve-piece group that used arrangers Cecil Irwin and Jimmy Mundy. (Mundy later became an arranger for Benny Goodman.) Hines met with increased celebrity when his band began doing radio broadcasts around 1932.

Hines's solo piano recordings from 1928—"Blues in Thirds," "I Ain't Got Nobody," and "57 Varieties"—show his superb stride-based piano technique as well as his unparalleled rhythmic creativity. He made characteristic use of double-time figures, incorporated occasional left-hand runs, and displayed remarkable independence of the hands. Flights of fancy and liberties with meter and harmony leave the listener wondering if Hines will land on his feet. Moreover, his improvisations in a group setting contributed to the single-line style of soloing, similar to the linear style of horn players. Hines's stunning technique elevated the piano to the level of a lead voice that filled the same role as that of the other solo improvisers.

In 1943 Hines directed a band that contributed to the evolution of bebop style. This historic band included Charlie Parker and Billy Eckstine. In the late 1940s Hines rejoined Louis Armstrong, remained until 1951, and continued to perform as a soloist or as a leader of small groups until his death in 1983. Hines was a phenomenal technician whose ability to provide consistently inventive improvisations never diminished. He was indeed one of the finest jazz pianists of any era.

Teddy Wilson

Teddy Wilson was probably the most imitated of the swing-era pianists. Earl Hines excelled in both solo piano work and group playing, but Wilson, despite many fine solo efforts, was principally a group pianist. Wilson came to national attention as the pianist in Benny Goodman's trio and quartet from 1936 to 1939. His crystalline touch and refined elegance showed an almost classical restraint. Goodman remarked, "My pleasure in playing with Teddy Wilson equaled the pleasure I got out of playing Mozart, and that's saying something."[9]

Born in Austin, Texas, in 1912, Wilson grew up in Alabama, where he studied classical piano and music theory. He learned jazz piano by memorizing works such as Fats

> "... nobody really cared about the money they were getting; they were more interested in the excitement of playing with seven men who were all as good as they were."
> —Teddy Wilson

Waller's "Handful of Keys" note for note. Wilson eventually forged his own style out of the influences of Earl Hines, Fats Waller, and Art Tatum, but his playing avoided the flamboyance of his mentors. In 1930 Wilson replaced Tatum as the pianist for the Milt Senior Band and soon moved to Chicago. He began playing with Louis Armstrong, Erskine Tate, and Jimmie Noone and occasionally subbed for Earl Hines at the Grand Terrace Ballroom. Through the intercession of John Hammond, Wilson joined Benny Carter's band and moved to New York in 1933. Wilson's earliest recording, dating from 1932, is with Carter's group.

Hammond's advocacy of Wilson laid the groundwork for some of Wilson's most significant musical achievements in the 1930s. For instance, Hammond introduced Wilson to Billie Holiday and set up the famous Brunswick recording series that led to Wilson and Holiday's recording numerous sides together. Between 1935 and 1939, Wilson played and wrote these seven-piece arrangements for Holiday and brought together in the recording studio such luminaries as Benny Goodman, Ben Webster, Roy Eldridge, Johnny Hodges, and Lester Young. Much later Wilson remembered those sessions:

> People have often asked me how I ever managed to get together such a collection of star musicians to accompany Billie Holiday on those records. . . . They were all big names and it was natural to think it must have cost a fortune to get them together. . . .

Photo courtesy of the Morgan Collection

Pianist Teddy Wilson on the cover of a piano arrangement of "Goodnight Sweetheart," published in London in 1931. Wilson was probably the most influential swing pianist.

I can only explain the mystery by saying that it was only in those sessions that those artists could only play with a group which was at their own level. In their own bands they were the number one soloist, but at my recording sessions they themselves were one of seven top soloists….

So the Teddy Wilson small group sessions were the only chance these men had to play with their peers instead of being the best in the whole band. The result was that nobody really cared about the money they were getting; they were more interested in the excitement of playing with seven men who were all as good as they were.[10]

Hammond also introduced Wilson to Benny Goodman, who was impressed with Wilson's suave pianism. Along with drummer Gene Krupa, Goodman invited Wilson to form the Benny Goodman Trio, the "band-within-a-band" that was featured alongside the Goodman Orchestra. Later vibraphonist Lionel Hampton joined the small group to create the Benny Goodman Quartet. As noted earlier, Goodman's group became the first important racially mixed band to play and tour publicly.

Because there was no bassist in Goodman's trio and quartet recordings, Wilson contributed significantly to the sound of the group, taking on the equally important roles of accompanist and soloist. Wilson used his left hand in a modified stride style, especially "walking" tenths that provided a linear bass and tenor line on the beat. Wilson also used the *swing-bass*, the stride-derived practice of alternating bass note and midrange chord on every beat.

Although Wilson's right-hand work was rooted in Hines's "trumpet style" of improvisation, Wilson's solos were more restrained and conservative than Hines's flights of fancy. At their best Wilson's small-group recordings with Goodman's trio and quartet had a chamber music quality of improvisation, a balanced conversation among musical peers. This quality can best be heard in Goodman's 1935 landmark recordings of "After You've Gone" and "Body and Soul," as well as on the Goodman Quartet version of "Moonglow," recorded the following year, and "Avalon."

After leaving Goodman in 1939, Wilson briefly led his own band. In his later career, Wilson continued to perform, fronting his own small groups and performing with Goodman on reunion concerts, touring Russia with Goodman in 1962, and appearing with Goodman at Carnegie Hall twenty years later. He taught jazz piano at Juilliard beginning in 1950 and performed well into the 1980s. Acclaimed as one of the world's great jazz pianists, Wilson died in 1986.

Jimmy Blanton

Jimmy Blanton revolutionized bass playing during his brief tenure with the Duke Ellington band. He was born in 1918 to a musical family (his mother was a pianist) and was raised in Chattanooga, Tennessee. Although he attended Tennessee State College briefly, his musical interests and ambitions eventually led him to St. Louis in the late 1930s, where he played in the Jeter-Pillars Orchestra and the Fate Marable riverboat bands. Duke Ellington discovered Blanton in 1939 and hired him for his orchestra. Blanton's performances with the Ellington orchestra were exceptional; one of his best-known showcases was "Jack the Bear." (Recall from Chapter 5 the discussion of Blanton's playing in "Ko-Ko," Track 22.)

Blanton's strength, virtuosity, and ability to carry a solo changed the perceived role of the bass player in the jazz ensemble. He was a strong player, whose ability to swing a band through a walking bass line was exemplary. Moreover, before Blanton it was rare to give a solo to a bass player; after Blanton it became common as bandleaders grew to expect more from their bassists than routine time-keeping. Thus, Blanton helped the bass to become accepted as a solo instrument. Paradoxically, Blanton's playing may have been a source of liberation for the next generation of rhythm players: if a strong bassist kept time, drummers and pianists were freed to provide kicks and accents, factors characteristic of the rhythm section in the bebop era.

In addition to his fine work with the Ellington ensemble and in small-group settings, Blanton can be heard in an interesting set of piano-bass duos recorded with Ellington. Sadly, Blanton was diagnosed with tuberculosis and died in 1942.

Jo Jones

In Chapter 5, we discussed how Jo Jones modernized drumming techniques by transferring the timekeeping role from the bass and snare drums to the cymbals, particularly the hi-hat. His feel for time helped popularize the four-beats-to-the-bar orientation of most of the swing bands; he was also well known for his work with brushes.

Born in Chicago in 1911, Jones grew up in Alabama. He worked as a tap dancer in carnival shows before joining Walter Page's Blue Devils in Oklahoma City in the late 1920s. He eventually made his way to Kansas City, where he joined Count Basie in 1934. After leaving Basie, he toured in 1947 with Jazz at the Philharmonic; in later life he continued to work in swing-style groups. He died in 1985.

Gene Krupa

Originally from Chicago, Gene Krupa (1909–1973) worked with Red McKenzie and Eddie Condon's Chicagoans in the late 1920s. After he performed with numerous bands, his reputation in the New York recording-studio scene led to an opportunity to join Benny Goodman in late 1934. Krupa became one of Goodman's most important sidemen and possibly the most idolized. Inevitably, he broke from Goodman in 1938 to form his own band, which was among the most popular of the early forties. At the height of his popularity, in 1943, Krupa was famously busted for marijuana use, an incident that greatly affected his later life and reputation.

Gene Krupa and His Orchestra (with Roy Eldridge), "Rockin' Chair" (1941)

Later in the decade, Krupa worked with his own groups, performed with Tommy Dorsey, and found time for occasional reunions with Goodman. After breaking up his band in 1951, he performed with the Jazz at the Philharmonic tours. In 1954 he founded a percussion school in New York with drummer William Randolph "Cozy" Cole.

Gene Krupa was probably the best-known drummer of the swing era, though his contributions to technique did not equal those of such pioneers as Jo Jones or Kenny Clarke (see Chapter 7). Although famous for his showmanship, he was just as often criticized for being heavy handed and unswinging, with a tendency toward crowd-pleasing antics. We heard an example of his work, however, on the Goodman recording of "Down South Camp Meeting" (Track 21), in which he drives the band

Drummer Gene Krupa was known for his drive and the high level of excitement he brought to his performances.

tastefully, without unnecessary theatrics. As such, Krupa's legacy remains positive—he was able to generate tremendous excitement as well as work with Goodman to create a band unequaled in its appeal, a band that derived its energy from Krupa's energy and power.

Charlie Christian

Charlie Christian's legendary career was meteoric and brief. John Hammond, hearing of the guitarist from Oklahoma City, arranged an audition for Christian with Benny Goodman in 1939. Goodman hired him immediately. As a member of Goodman's sextet, Christian recorded outstanding solos on "Flying Home," "Seven Come Eleven," "Star Dust," and "Air Mail Special." In 1941 he was taking part in the groundbreaking jam sessions and playing nightly sessions with the future architects of the bebop movement, including Dizzy Gillespie and Thelonious Monk (see Chapter 7). By March 1942 he was dead of tuberculosis at the age of twenty-five.

Born in 1916, Charlie Christian revolutionized jazz guitar playing and had a profound influence on later generations of guitarists. He was also the first major player to feature electric guitar in jazz ensembles. Indeed, Christian played a fundamental role in the shift to the electric

A **trill** is a rapid alternation between a note and a note that is a step higher. The higher note generally embellishes the lower note.

Swing-bass is the stride-derived practice of alternating bass note and midrange chord on every beat.

---

guitar, an instrument available by 1935. (In 1936, when the Gibson company released its arched-top model, its popularity began to grow.) Although the arched-top acoustic guitar—such as the one played earlier in the decade by Eddie Lang—was suitable in the studio, where microphones could be strategically placed, it was frequently drowned out in live performance. In the era of the big band, amplification became necessary.

Christian recorded in the studio, often as part of the Benny Goodman Sextet, and can be heard in many fine performances with both the smaller group and the big band. However, for many musicians of the swing era the more informal jam session was a central activity. There they could improvise at greater length, take chances, and interact more informally with other players. Minton's Playhouse, in Harlem, was an important hub for musicians seeking opportunities to jam. As will be discussed in Chapter 7, the sessions there helped establish the bebop style, which evolved from swing. Some sessions, fortunately, were recorded, including the wonderful performance of "Swing to Bop" (Listening Guide, Track 26) by Charlie Christian, who attended sessions there regularly.

With his swinging eighth-note lines, Christian developed an improvisational style with a fluidity akin to that of a horn player. Christian thus made his mark not as a rhythm guitarist, in the manner of Freddie Green's four-to-the-bar style of propelling the Basie band, but as a complete soloist. Although his recordings span a mere two years, they show him to be one of the most fertile improvisers of the era.

Christian was perfectly poised between swing and bebop. A relaxed sense of swing, perfect voice-leading control, subtle motivic manipulation, variety of phrase length, and imaginative harmonies characterized his style. His solos are remarkably elegant—swing based, but also anticipating upcoming developments in bebop. In light of

---

LISTENING GUIDE   Track 26
"Swing to Bop (Topsy)"

Charlie Christian (jam session): "Swing to Bop (Topsy)" (Durham). *Live Sessions at Minton's*, Everest FS-219. Recorded at Minton's Playhouse, New York, May, 1941. Christian, electric guitar; Kenny Clarke, drums; piano (unknown); bass (unknown).

The Main Point   This recording features a loose, jam-session atmosphere that allows the soloists ample space to improvise. The players are not restricted to the three-minute time limit for issued recordings from this period.

The tune "Topsy" was written by Eddie Durham (who also composed "Every Tub," Track 20) and was recorded, for example, by the Count Basie band in 1937. It became a jam session favorite. When this live recording was issued, the track was called "Swing to Bop," although the piece used the chord progression of "Topsy." The "Swing to Bop" title echoed Minton's role in helping initiate bebop style, hints of which can be detected in Christian's marvellous playing. There is no head here, as the recording begins amid Christian's improvisation. Although we excerpt Christian's solo only, the remainder of the recording does not feature a head melody either, but does include solos by an unknown trumpeter, the pianist, then Christian again, then the trumpeter as the recording fades out.

We should not necessarily read too much into the motivic interplay that will be evident in the solo. Christian was playing in an informal atmosphere, not creating a record as a finished product to be listened to repeatedly. Still, it is uncanny how riff figures return, and, in the middle of the solo (what we have of it, that is) a G-A♭ **trill** begins to figure prominently, leading in fact to the solo's end.

1st (incomplete) chorus—AA'BA 32-bar form

0:00	The recording fades in toward the end of the first A section. An unusual feature of the piece is that it is in the minor mode. Swing tunes (and pre-1950s jazz generally) more commonly featured major keys.
0:03	The beginning of the second A section. The chord structure of this piece is slightly unusual in that the second A harmonically varies the first A by beginning with four bars of subdominant (iv) harmony before returning to the tonic for the last four bars.

0:11 The B section or bridge has more harmonic movement than the A sections, with chord changes coming every two bars. Christian begins with two-bar phrases that follow the harmony, but then shortens his melodic figures as the section closes to prepare for the final A section of the piece.

0:20 The return of the (first) A section. Christian moves from the swing-style lines of the B section to a riff that largely fills this final A of the first chorus. At this point, we can hear that the principal A section has only a bare-bones chord progression (as performed here) and can be construed as eight bars of the tonic harmony. From this perspective, we can understand the function of the second A section as introducing harmonic variation to the changes. The move to (iv) gives a blues flavor to the piece as a whole (because the subdominant is an important chord in the blues). The pianist is playing a **swing-bass**, with bass notes on the first and third beats and chords on two and four. As discussed earlier, this style of accompaniment, heard in stride piano and ragtime, was a mainstay of 1920s and 1930s pianists.

2nd chorus

0:29 The riff played in the final A section of the first chorus leads into Christian's swing-style lines in the second chorus.

0:38 As Christian moves into the second A´ section, he lands squarely on a note (A♭) that signals the change to the F-minor (iv) chord. He then repeats the phrase to further emphasize the A♭. In general, Christian deftly moves between riff-based passages (e.g., the last A of the first chorus) and passages that closely follow the chord changes.

0:47 Christian's B section is especially striking in its virtuoso swing lines, darting through the range of the guitar with unexpected twists and turns. This aspect of his art became influential in the development of bebop.

0:55 Again Christian turns to a riff for his final A section. Here the riff is virtually identical to the riff he played on the last A of the first chorus (0:20), but an octave higher.

3rd chorus

1:04 Again, the riff from the previous A launches the material for the third chorus. Here the riff is transformed into a more definite tune.

1:13 Christian moves to the higher register of the instrument for the second A´ section, then returns to the middle register to end the section.

1:22 The B section, with its greater harmonic activity, includes a more virtuosic line, much as we heard in the B section of the second chorus.

1:31 The energy of the previous B section proceeds into a striking passage with single notes, all off the beat, before Christian winds down the section for the fourth chorus. He ends the chorus pensively on a sustained note (G), which then initiates the improvisation on the fourth chorus.

4th chorus

1:39 As begun at the end of the third chorus, the G sets up a riff repeated through the fourth chorus. Previously, Christian had used riffs for the final A sections of choruses one and two; here he begins with a riff. It is possible that Christian used these riffing sections to think about how he wished to continue the improvisation. Note that the lack of specified solo time available (such as on a studio recording) allows time for such reflection.

1:48 Christian again shows the move to the F minor chord of the second A section by emphasizing the change from G (first A section) to A♭ (here).

1:57 Yet again, Christian turns to more active lines that articulate the chord changes. His last high note of this section (D) is a particular surprise.

2:06 To complete the chorus, Christian remains in the high register, while the line itself recalls the riff he used in previous choruses. The chorus ends with Christian trilling on a G (to A♭) to set up the fifth chorus.

5th chorus

2:15   In this A section, Christian begins by continuing the G-A♭ trill that ended the fourth chorus. He combines this trill with a riff that takes up a considerable portion of the A section.

2:23   In the second A´ section, Christian keeps his lines restrained, so as to set up the B section that follows.

2:32   The B section follows Christian's strategy of contrasting more restrained A sections with more virtuosic lines that range around the guitar and follow the changes carefully. Again, as heard earlier, he ends the bridge with a surprising leap to a high D.

2:41   The final A continues the intensity of the bridge.

6th chorus

2:50   In this A section, Christian relieves the intensity of the previous two A sections by returning to a riff pattern.

2:58   In the second A section, Christian plays a syncopated riff that creates a cross-rhythm with the underlying rhythmic pattern. The riff includes the G-A♭ trill figure that Christian used earlier.

3:07   The B section is introduced without break, as Christian continues his virtuosic lines from the previous section. As usual, Christian's lines use much of the range of the instrument. Again, he ends with the high D.

3:16   For the final A section of the solo, Christian ends meditatively on a figure that includes the G-A♭ trill that had figured earlier in the solo. He continues this figure into the beginning of the trumpet solo that begins the next chorus.

Listen to this music in an animated Active Listening Guide available at the text website.

such recordings as "Swing to Bop," it is interesting to speculate on whether Christian would have developed into one of the distinguished voices of the newer bop idiom. His recorded work shows him confidently bridging the two styles. With his exemplary command, Charlie Christian was one of the greatest guitar players in jazz history.

Christian's influence was so great that most of the electric guitarists who followed him cultivated his phrasing and sound. His guitar timbre was sharp edged, which influenced bebop players such as Barney Kessel (1923–2004) in the later 1940s and early 1950s. In the later 1950s and 1960s, players such as Wes Montgomery and Jim Hall cultivated a more mellow timbre. Vastly different electric guitar sounds emerged in the 1960s when the jazz-rock players restyled the sound with feedback, a much more piercing timbre, and electronic effects. We will examine some of these players in chapters to come.

Benny Carter

Performing, arranging, composing, and even touring until the turn of the twenty-first century, after eight decades in the music business Benny Carter personified the history of jazz. Although an elegant alto saxophone stylist who also recorded impressively on the trumpet and other instruments, Carter was most noted for his superb arrangements. Among the most significant are "Keep a Song in Your Soul," written for Fletcher Henderson in 1930, and

"Lonesome Nights" and "Symphony in Riffs" from 1933, both of which show Carter's fluid writing for saxophones. Given Carter's fine performing ability and arranging prowess, he was so multitalented that he is difficult to categorize.

Born in 1907 and raised in New York, Carter worked with several local teachers but primarily taught himself. He performed with Earl Hines in the mid-twenties and with Fletcher Henderson from 1930 to 1931. After a stint as the music director of McKinney's Cotton Pickers, he started his own band in New York in 1932—a band that influenced the newly emerging swing style. He worked in London as a staff arranger for the British Broadcasting Corporation from 1936 to 1938 and returned to New York to form a new orchestra at the Savoy Ballroom in 1939.

As the swing era began to wane, Carter saw his future in writing and arranging for Hollywood. He moved to Los Angeles in 1942, led some bands, and grew more involved in studio work, which eventually led to uncredited work on the movie *Stormy Weather* (1943). From 1946 on he was associated with the Jazz at the Philharmonic tours. In the 1950s and 1960s, he concentrated on arranging and scoring, and in the seventies he resumed active performing. He died in 2003.

Carter was probably one of the two leading alto saxophone stylists of swing, the other being Johnny Hodges of the Duke Ellington band. As an arranger, Carter helped innovate swing style and was especially well known for his writing for saxophones. Also a songwriter, he composed numerous popular tunes, including the standard "When Lights Are Low."

Billie Holiday

Billie Holiday was the touchstone of jazz singing. From Louis Armstrong's model, Holiday cultivated a free sense of rhythm and phrasing, much like an instrumental soloist, and she had an uncanny ability to inhabit and project the lyric of a composition. Despite an untrained voice, "Lady Day," as Lester Young named her, had an unerring sense of pitch. She was perhaps best known for her performances of slow, poignant ballads, frequently of unrequited love; these songs came to mirror her own complex and tragic life. Her later life was marred by failed romances and, ultimately, drug addiction.

Holiday was born in Philadelphia in 1915, but the details of her early life remain murky. We do know that her mother moved to New York and left the young child with family in Baltimore. There she was abused—raped as a child and compelled to work as a prostitute during her early teens. To be with her mother, she moved to New York in 1928 and began working small clubs as a singer in the early thirties. In 1933 John Hammond heard her sing and arranged for her to record with Benny Goodman.

At the peak of her vocal prowess, in the 1930s and 1940s, Holiday usually performed with small jazz groups. Her studio recordings with Teddy Wilson from 1935 to 1942

for the Brunswick label are treasures of the swing era, featuring such soloists as Chu Berry, Lester Young, Benny Goodman, and Roy Eldridge (see the earlier discussion of Teddy Wilson in this chapter). Of these recordings the 1937 version of "A Sailboat in the Moonlight" shows the extraordinary musical rapport Holiday had with tenor saxophonist Lester Young, who weaves his melodic lines around Holiday's vocals in the same relaxed, behind-the-beat manner as her singing. Holiday is usually faithful to the melody, but she often **back phrases**—that is, she delays her entrances a bit behind

Billie Holiday and Eddie Heywood and His Orchestra, "All of Me" (1941)

the beat to convey a conversational, intimate performance of the tune. Many of the sidemen on "A Sailboat in the Moonlight" were from Basie's band, and Holiday worked with Basie's big band in 1937. Her performances with Artie Shaw in 1938 number among the first instances of a black singer working with a white band.

> "I don't think I'm singing. I feel like I am playing a horn. I try to improvise like Les Young, like Louis Armstrong, or someone else I admire. What comes out is what I feel."
> —Billie Holiday.

Holiday's popular appeal increased. While appearing at New York's Cafe Society in 1939, she recorded "Strange Fruit," a song about lynching in the South. This brave and unusual step for a jazz performer won her critical acclaim as her signature song. (Holiday sometimes claimed to have written the song, but in fact a white male composer, Lewis Allen, wrote it.) She began to focus on dark ballads, exemplified by her own composition "God Bless the Child," as well as "Lover Man," "Gloomy Sunday," and "Don't Explain." Audiences took these works as autobiographical, reflecting her two failed marriages, arrests, incarceration, and drug addiction.

Increasingly, Holiday's arrests and failing health during the 1950s sidelined her career. Although drug abuse ravaged her vocal range and timbre, she could still sing with tortured expression. Her version of the blues song "Fine and Mellow" from the 1957 television show "Sound of Jazz" shows how much she could express with so few notes still available in her range. She died in 1959, only a few months after the death of Lester Young.

Lionel Hampton and Billie Holiday perform together at Esquire's Fourth Annual All-American Jazz Concert held at the Metropolitan Opera House in New York City in 1944.

Bettmann/Corbis

Back phrasing is momentarily delaying the entry of a new phrase, in effect freeing the rhythm of a composition.

LISTENING GUIDE
"Body and Soul"

Track 27

Billie Holiday and Her Orchestra: "Body and Soul" (Green-Heyman-Sauer-Eyton). Vocalion 5481. New York, February 29, 1940. Holiday, vocal and leader; Roy Eldridge, trumpet; Jimmy Powell, Carl Frye, alto saxophones; Kermit Scott, tenor saxophone; Sonny White, piano; Lawrence Lucie, guitar; John Williams, bass; Harold "Doc" West, drums.

The Main Point   Holiday interprets the classic "Body and Soul" beautifully, with graceful phrasing and heartfelt emotion. Since its introduction in 1930, the song itself has become one of the most enduring jazz ballads. A particularly nice feature of this recording is the presence of Roy Eldridge, one of the great trumpeters of the swing era.

Introduction

0:00   The piece begins with a four-bar piano introduction featuring Eldridge. The saxophones hold chords as a cushion behind the trumpet soloist.

1st chorus—AABA

0:11   The A section. The original melody alternates between B♭ and C, but Holiday simplifies the tune by remaining on C after the first B♭. After simplifying the melody in measure 1, she embellishes it in measure 2 by adding a G not found in the original. Finally, in these first two bars, notice how she back phrases, delaying the F in measure 2.

For the subphrase of measures 3 and 4, Holiday again changes the melody. In measure 2 she adds a G but omits the E♭ on beat 4 of the original melody; this E♭ is then changed to B♭ on the "and" of beat 1 in measure 4. Through such embellishments, simplifications, and back phrasing as heard in the first four bars, Holiday personalizes the song throughout, making it her own.

The saxophones continue to hold chords as a background.

0:35   The second A section. The same background texture continues.

0:58   In the B section, we can hear Eldridge, muted, added to the saxophone chords.

1:21   The last A section returns to the background texture of saxophone chords without trumpet.

2nd chorus—ABA

1:45   Roy Eldridge trumpet solo, muted. The repeat of the A section is omitted, probably to fit the performance into three minutes (due to the limitations of recording technology, records could not exceed much more than three minutes). Eldridge begins by quoting the melody but, in contrast to Holiday, does not continue with a literal statement; he instead develops an original solo line. The saxophones continue with chords in the background.

2:08   Holiday returns for the bridge. Again, saxophone chords provide the backup.

2:32   In the final A section, Eldridge joins the saxophone section in providing backup chords for Holiday. The tempo slows at the end of the piece for a more conclusive ending.

Listen to this music in an animated Active Listening Guide available at the text website.

Few jazz singers escaped Holiday's influence and her interpretive style. As she herself described it:

> I don't think I'm singing. I feel like I am playing a horn. I try to improvise like Les Young, like Louis Armstrong, or someone else I admire. What comes out is what I feel. I hate straight singing. I have to change a tune to my own way of doing it. That's all I know.[11]

Summary of the Features of Swing

The following tables summarize features of swing-era music, most of which have been discussed in the past several chapters.

Features of Swing on Piano

RIGHT-HAND TEXTURE

- Single-note improvisation much like swing-style, melodic improvisation on other instruments
- Less syncopated than ragtime with less pivoting around fixed notes
- Looser, greater use of long eighth-note lines
- Brilliant runs between phrases
- Less aggressive interlock of left hand and right hand (as heard in stride style)

LEFT-HAND TEXTURE

- Stride-derived practice of bass as swing-bass, but bass notes often in tenths
- Use of walking tenths and occasional cross-hand textures
- Light, accompanying chords often emphasizing a tenor-voice "thumb line"

HARMONY

- Mostly diatonic (based on the chords of the major scale)
- Sixth and seventh chords predominating in the left hand, with ninth chords occurring from time to time

Features of Swing Improvisation in Ensembles

TIMBRE

- More refined and polished than 1920s jazz
- Less use of vibrato
- Smoother, lighter saxophone tone
- More brilliant trumpet tone
- Less use of specific instrumental effects
- Instrumental ranges extended upward

- Softer attacks and more-legato playing
- Somewhat less use of blue-note effects

PHRASING

- In two-bar or four-bar units, but more varied in later swing styles (ballad playing featured more-irregular phrasing)
- Not much space between phrases

RHYTHM

- More swinging, although less syncopation than in 1920s jazz
- Up-tempo reliance on eighth-note lines
- Ballads that feature a greater variety of rhythmic values

THEMATIC CONTINUITY

- Less reliance on motive and song embellishment in up-tempo solos; more reliance on voice leading
- In ballads, motivic relationships more prominent

CHORD-TO-SCALE RELATIONS

- Inside playing
- In later swing, more experimentation with extended chord tones within melodic lines

LARGE-SCALE COHERENCE

- Voice leading and song paraphrase more often than motivic structure
- Gestural balance

FORM AND STRUCTURE

- Strophic AABA, ABAC, or blues forms
- Tempos ranging from slow to very fast
- Improvisations structured by voice leading and motivic relationships

 MindTap™

Test Yourself on Key Concepts with additional Chapter Quizzes and Listening Activities on the text website.

Exam Review Questions

Use these questions and the materials on the text website to help you understand and pass tests on the content of this chapter.

1. What were some of the important big bands of the swing era besides Ellington, Basie, and Goodman?

2. Can differences of style be detected between the black and white swing-era bands?

3. How did Lester Young's style on tenor saxophone differ from that of Coleman Hawkins?

4. How did swing-era piano style differ from the stride style of the 1920s? Did some pianists retain elements of stride? Who? How did they?

5. Identify women's contributions to jazz during the swing era.

Key Terms

Test your knowledge of this chapter's key terms by defining the following. If you can't remember the meaning of a term, refresh your memory by looking up the boldfaced term in the chapter, turning to the Glossary at the back of the book, or working with the flash-cards at the text website.

arpeggiated figure (arpeggio, arpeggiation) 174

back phrasing 187

formula 178

inside playing 175

lick 178

pickup 174

slap-tonguing 175

soli 169

step connection 176

swing-bass 184

trill 184

vertical improvisation 176

voice leading 176

RAY'S IDEA
by RAY BROWN and "GIL" FULLER

BE-BOP

(THE NEW JAZZ)

DIZZY GILLESPIE

Series of

PIANO

SOLOS

Arranged by FRANK PAPARELLI

Published by J. J. ROBBINS & SONS Inc.
1585 Broadway, Manhattan, New York, U.S.A.

BOSWORTH & CO. LTD.
Regent Street, London, W.I.
British Empire and Europe
Newfoundland and Australasia)
Made in England   Imprimé en Angleterre

PRICE

3/-

The Bebop Era

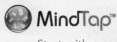

Start with a quick
warm-up activity.

WE THINK OF THE "MODERN JAZZ" ERA AS
beginning with bebop in the mid-forties, but what makes bebop "modern," distinguishing it from the preceding swing era? This chapter explores bebop's most significant characteristics:

▶ General aesthetics grounded in improvisation and solo virtuosity—that is, in individual solos, not in melody, popular song, and arrangement

▶ The emergence of bebop melodies—"heads"—that stylistically complement the improvisations

▶ Smaller groups favored over big bands

▶ Musical performances in jazz clubs rather than large dance halls

▶ De-emphasis on commercial or popular success

▶ De-emphasis on dancing:

  ■ Tempos that are considerably faster or slower than in swing

  ■ Rhythmic pulse that is less obviously articulated than in swing

▶ Rise in black consciousness resulting from a new perception of African Americans' contributions to jazz

Many of these points provided the cultural context of jazz for the remainder of the twentieth century. Besides defining a more modern sensibility, these characteristics helped transform jazz from popular entertainment into an art form in many of its substyles. Before exploring the origins and characteristics of bebop further, we set the scene for this music by reviewing a few of the important events of the 1940s.

1939—Beginnings of bop at Minton's Playhouse and Monroe's Uptown House in Harlem
1941—Ellington records "Take the 'A' Train"
1942—Evolution of bop well under way
—Big bands depleted by draft
—Recording ban imposed by the American Federation of Musicians (AFM)
1943—Earl Hines band formed, including Parker and Gillespie
—Ellington appears at Carnegie Hall
1944—End of recording ban, begin early bop recordings
1945—Dizzy Gillespie's first big band formed
—Gillespie records "Salt Peanuts" (Track 28)
—Parker records "Ko Ko" (Track 29)
1946—Parker-Harris, "Ornithology"; Gillespie records "A Night in Tunisia"
1947—Herman records "Four Brothers"
1948—First long-playing 33 1/3 twelve-inch record
—Gillespie records "Manteca" (Track 30)
1949—Bud Powell records "Tempus Fugit" (Track 31)
—Miles Davis, Gil Evans, and Gerry Mulligan begin collaboration on *Birth of the Cool*
—Herman records "Early Autumn"
1950—Dave Brubeck begins collaboration with Paul Desmond
1951—Thelonious Monk records "Four in One" (Track 32)

Jazz

1940   1950

1939—World War II begins
1941—United States enters war after the bombing of Pearl Harbor
1944—Invasion of Normandy by Allies
—Mechanical calculating machine produced by IBM
1945—Germany surrenders
—First atomic bomb dropped on Hiroshima
—United Nations formed
1947—India gains independence from Britain
—Tennessee Williams, *A Streetcar Named Desire*
—Camus, *The Plague*
1948—Zionists proclaim Israel's independence
—Transistor invented
1949—Mao Zedong organizes revolution in China
—Arthur Miller, *Death of a Salesman*
—George Orwell, *1984*

Historical Events

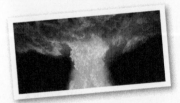

The War Years and the 1940s

The early forties marked a turning point both in jazz and in the United States at large. Just as the United States became a full-fledged major power after World War I, after World War II it emerged as the world's premier economy, with a dominant role in the North Atlantic Treaty Organization (NATO). The year 1945, in particular, witnessed the surrender of Germany and Japan (with the dropping of the atomic bombs in Japan—hence, the beginning of the nuclear age) and the founding of the United Nations. Through the late 1940s and early 1950s, the cold war between NATO and the Soviet Union developed, then continued to increase in intensity. The premier symbol of the cold war was perhaps the Berlin Wall, separating the city into areas controlled by East and West. (Symbolically, its fall in 1989 marked the end of the cold war.)

Technologically, the 1940s witnessed the invention of jet planes (1941) and another achievement, at the time not regarded as especially significant: IBM's first mechanical calculating machine (1944).

Among important works in the other arts were Orson Welles's film *Citizen Kane* (filmed 1941), Aaron Copland's ballet score *Appalachian Spring* (1944), and George Orwell's novel *1984* (1949).

Revolution Versus Evolution

The emergence of **bebop** in the 1940s irrevocably altered the jazz landscape. In contrast to the well-polished big bands of the swing era—many of them incredibly successful—some jazz musicians began gravitating toward smaller groups. Initially, they developed their musical ideas in impromptu jam sessions, especially in such after-hours Harlem clubs as Monroe's Uptown House and Minton's Playhouse. By the end of World War II, these cutting-edge musicians had moved downtown to appear at the nightclubs on West Fifty-second Street. Dozens of clubs—such as the Three Deuces, the Onyx, the Downbeat, the Famous Door, the Spotlite, Kelly's Stables, and the Hickory House—opened their doors on what became known as "The Street." They called the new music *rebop* (eventually to fall into disuse), *bebop*, or just *bop*.

Many of the architects of bebop—such as Charlie "Yardbird" or "Bird" Parker, John Birks "Dizzy" Gillespie, and Kenny Clarke—began their careers playing in big bands, but bebop represented a radical rejection of the musical conventions of the swing era. Instead of elaborate dance halls, bebop players performed in bars and nightclubs, and many seemed indifferent to commercial success as entertainers—they played for listening rather than dancing. Rather than the slick show-business theatrics of the big bands, beboppers aimed to capture the informal spirit of the jam session. Its groups often comprised only five or six musicians—two or three horn players and a rhythm section of piano, bass, and drums. Whereas the big-band arrangers of the swing era carefully inserted improvised solos within longer written arrangements, the smaller bebop bands avoided elaborate charts and emphasized, above all, virtuosic improvisational skill.

Many older musicians were perplexed by these new sounds. Bandleader Cab Calloway is said to have derided trumpeter Dizzy Gillespie's playing as "Chinese music." In

> " … it's really no good and you got no melody to remember and no beat to dance to."
> —Louis Armstrong, on bebop

1948 trumpeter Louis Armstrong dismissed bebop as an annoying novelty performed by overly competitive musicians. He said:

> All they want to do is show you up, and any old way will do as long as it's different from the way you played it before. So you get all them weird chords which don't mean nothing, and first people get curious about it just because it's new, but soon they get tired of it because it's really no good and you got no melody to remember and no beat to dance to.[1]

Drummer Dave Tough, a "Chicagoan" in the 1920s who later became an important drummer during the swing era, reacted with less hostility but was clearly confused by the music. After first hearing Dizzy Gillespie and Oscar Pettiford's band on Fifty-second Street, he noted:

> As we walked in, see, these cats snatched up their horns and blew crazy stuff. One would stop all of a sudden and another would start for no reason at all.

We never could tell when a solo was supposed to begin or end. Then they all quit at once and walked off the stand. It scared us.[2]

Reactions such as these were not uncommon in the music world, but the fans of traditional jazz were the most disappointed: the music they loved was being called passé, old-fashioned, and—the worst insult of all—unhip. While bebop was taking root, many traditionalists bemoaned the demise of classic jazz and argued that bebop abandoned jazz music's most treasured principles. Modernists called these listeners **moldy figs**. Arguments between the two sides enlivened much jazz discourse in the late 1940s.

Bebop began in the early 1940s as "insider's" music—a music for musicians. Despite the efforts of the moldy figs, bebop would become the dominant jazz style by the end of the decade. Among other factors, a wartime tax on dance halls triggered the decline of the big bands. Small jazz clubs, such as the ones found on Fifty-second Street, boomed. Younger players, who had fewer outlets for musical employment than the stars of the big bands, joined small groups and experimented with the new musical language.

Bohemianism added an attractive element to the music. Performers and their **hipster** audiences often took on the affectations and inside slang of beboppers. Some of these affectations—such as Dizzy Gillespie's beret, goatee, and horn-rimmed glasses—were benign; others—such as Charlie Parker's heroin addiction—were not.

With bebop, jazz ceased to be a strongly commercial music. Some musicians, such as Dizzy Gillespie, felt that bebop should try to adapt to dancing. Many of its devotees, however, interpreted the music as a political statement, a rejection of all things conformist and mainstream. This view included a reaction against American racism and segregation. Many players felt that Louis Armstrong and other older musicians conformed to racial stereotypes of black entertainers. Bebop challenged and defied these stereotypes. Indeed, political activism among some black musicians can be traced to the nonconformity of the beboppers. As institutional segregation came under attack

---

Bebop and **bop** are terms that came about in the 1940s to describe the nervous, energetic style of the younger jazz musicians. The terms probably developed from the nonsense syllables used by scat singers to re-create the characteristic melodic phrases of the new style.

Moldy figs was a term used by younger musicians and fans in the 1940s to describe older jazz fans who clung to the music of the 1920s and 1930s and derided the newer bebop style.

The word **hipster** was used to describe a young follower of jazz who affected the dress, speech, and manner of jazz musicians working in the new jazz styles of the late 1940s and early 1950s.

in the 1950s and 1960s, black musicians often used their music as a public statement of their political beliefs. Thus the conventions of bebop laid the foundation for modern jazz, both in musical style and in the convictions of its players.

Despite these dramatic, possibly revolutionary, developments, much of the musical style of bebop evolved naturally from swing style. Players carried over to bebop features of earlier jazz:

▶ Improvisation on the following:

■ Popular songs in 32-bar AABA or ABAC form

■ Rhythm changes (a 32-bar set of changes in AABA form)

■ The 12-bar blues chord progression

In 1943 the "zoot-suit riots"—named for the stylized clothing of young Chicanos—erupted in Los Angeles and continued for a week as whites, including soldiers and sailors on leave, attacked Hispanics. A future recording supervisor of jazz for Mercury Records, Norman Granz, organized a concert at the Philharmonic Auditorium in Los Angeles to benefit Mexican youths, and an enduring concert series began. Here is the 1949 program for Jazz at the Philharmonic, picturing, among others, Ray Brown on bass and Shelly Manne on drums. Notice the integrated seating, part of an antidiscrimination clause Granz wrote into all his contracts.

Photo courtesy of the Morgan Collection

▶ Improvisation based mostly on eighth-note melodic lines

▶ Characteristic instrumentation of rhythm-section plus horns

▶ Overall performance formats of head-solos-head (although bebop emphasized this far more than earlier styles did)

Seen in this light, bebop was a natural next step in the musical development of jazz. This should not be surprising because the musicians who innovated bebop had trained extensively in swing bands. Although many of the revolutionary aspects of bop were more social than musical, jazz musicians and fans at the time were indeed caught up in what they perceived as the radical newness of its language. In the description of bebop style to follow, we emphasize these innovations rather than the older swing elements.

Characteristics of the Bebop Style

The new music that offended or confused older musicians such as Cab Calloway, Louis Armstrong, and Dave Tough differed from earlier jazz in improvisational style, melodic language, and harmonic language. Much of the repertory changed considerably. In typical bebop compositions, the horns played the melody, improvised solos followed, and a reprise of the melody formed the ending. The horns frequently stated the melody in unison or in octaves, creating a starker, leaner sound than the full-voiced chords played by big bands. Bebop groups played at faster tempos than those of swing bands but played their ballads much more slowly.

Bebop also departed from swing because the newer style did not support dancing as well as the older style. As we have seen, musicians created the jazz of the 1920s and 1930s for dancing. The musicians of the era speak fondly of the energizing give-and-take between the dancers and the bands. The beboppers, however, disassociated jazz from the jitterbugging crowds of the 1930s to win respect for their music as an art form. The radical change in tempo also certainly affected dancing. Further, some argue that the swing era had run its course, making the separation of the music from dancing and popular song inevitable. To remain vibrant, jazz needed to evolve. The popular audience, of course, wanted danceable, singable music—a void soon to be filled by rock and roll.

The repertory for the bop-style bands remained dependent on the 12-bar blues and compositions based on the chords of "I Got Rhythm"—both a legacy of the Kansas City style—as well as the 32-bar AABA or ABAC form in standard popular songs. But the bebop players emphasized recomposition of these popular songs into a bebop framework. In recomposition players abandoned the original melody and composed a new one, sometimes called a **contrafact**, over the harmonic structure of the original. Although this practice did occur in earlier jazz—"Tiger Rag," for example, provided the chords to some jazz tunes—the beboppers turned recomposition into a standard practice (See the box "A Contrafact: Dizzy Gillespie's 'Groovin' High.") For the bebop player, such recompositions had two advantages:

Dizzy Gillespie
Ken Burns's Jazz,
"Groovin' High" (1945)

▶ The new melody resembled the bebop improvisations that followed and kept the musical language unified.

▶ Performers and record companies did not have to pay song royalties to the original composers because they did not use the original melodies.

Many of the significant early works of the bebop era were contrafacts:

BEBOP-STYLE TUNE (COMPOSER)	ORIGINAL (COMPOSER)
"Ko Ko" (Charlie Parker)	**"Cherokee"** (Ray Noble)
"Hot House" (Tadd Dameron)	**"What Is This Thing Called Love?"** (Cole Porter)
"Crazeology" (Benny Harris)	**"I Got Rhythm"** (George Gershwin)
"Groovin' High" (Dizzy Gillespie)	**"Whispering"** (Vincent Rose–Richard Coburn–John Schonberger)

Dizzy Gillespie, one of the founders of the new style, acknowledged the obvious differences in bebop from earlier jazz but was keenly aware of how the music evolved logically from swing. When asked to contrast the newer bebop music with the older style, he cited several differences:

> Chords.... And we stressed different accents in the rhythms. But I'm reluctant to say that anything is the difference between our music of the early forties and the music before that, of the thirties. You can get records from the early days and hear guys doing the same things. It just kept changing a little bit more; one guy would play a phrase one way, and another guy would come along and do something else with it.... Charlie Parker was very, very melodic; guys could copy his things quite a bit. [Thelonious] Monk was one of the founders of the movement too, but his playing, my playing, and Charlie Parker's playing were altogether different.[3]

The one characteristic that players most frequently singled out as new was the harmony. As saxophonist Illinois Jacquet pointed out, "The major difference in the new music was the chord changes."[4] The harmonies used by the bebop players sometimes emphasized the upper parts of chords such as ninths, elevenths, and thirteenths. These additions to chords, called **extended chord tones**,

---

A **contrafact** is a new melody composed to fit the harmonic and formal structure of a previously composed popular song.

Extended chord tones, sometimes called **tensions**, are notes added to seventh chords to make the harmony richer and more pungent. These tones are usually ninths, elevenths, and thirteenths. Extended chord tones usually resolve to more-stable pitches, such as roots, thirds, and fifths.

Insider's Guide to...

A Contrafact: Dizzy Gillespie's "Groovin' High"

Dizzy Gillespie's recomposition "Groovin' High" was a contrafact of the original melody of "Whispering," recorded by Paul Whiteman and His Orchestra in 1920.

The "Whispering" melody, which is primarily diatonic, almost masks its harmonic progression. In "Groovin' High" Gillespie writes a new melody mostly in eighth notes and with more notes than in the original composition—typical of the bebop melodic language. Here are some features of Gillespie's recomposed melody:

■ It is much more chromatic.

■ It is jagged and angular.

■ It outlines and highlights the harmonic progression through a repeated motive.

■ It has accents that crop up in unexpected places.

These are the features of bebop that swing fans sometimes found hard to understand. Gillespie's melody, too, has the typical double-eighth-note figure prevalent in bebop melodies and improvisations. This characteristic two-note figure may very well be the source of the word *bebop.*

Reharmonization refers to the bop practice of inserting different chords into the fundamental chord structure of a well-known song to freshen the interpretation and expand harmonic options for the soloist.

Running the changes refers to improvising by maintaining mostly up-tempo eighth-note lines that articulate the chord changes in a virtuoso manner. The practice is particularly associated with bebop, where it became widespread.

Dropping bombs is a technique in which bebop drummers used the bass drum for sharp, irregular accents in the rhythmic accompaniment.

Comping refers to a technique in which a pianist or guitarist plays a chord progression in a rhythmically irregular fashion. The term *comp* is probably derived from a contraction of the word *accompany* or *complement*. Listen to Al Haig's syncopated comping behind Charlie Parker and Dizzy Gillespie on "Salt Peanuts" (Track 28). For an early example of piano comping in a swing-band setting, listen to Count Basie's accompaniment to Lester Young's tenor solo on "Every Tub" (Track 20).

---

or **tensions**, would be contributed not only by the accompanying pianist but also sometimes by the soloist. Hearing the emphasis on these extensions, early critics of the music thought the improvisers were playing "wrong notes."

Reharmonization was another important new aspect of bebop harmony. Bebop players often inserted new chords and chord progressions into a standard composition; this gave soloists more chords to improvise over and made the harmonies more chromatic, often aligning them with the tensions or extended chord tones. Reharmonization was popular at the jam sessions in Harlem in the early 1940s. "We'd do that kind of thing in 1942 around Minton's a lot," Dizzy Gillespie recalled. "We'd been doing that kind of thing, Monk and I, but it was never documented because no records were being made at the time."[5] Historians have frequently cited pianist Art Tatum's influence on bebop reharmonization because of his extensive harmonic reworkings of popular songs. (See Tatum's performance of "Tiger Rag" in Chapter 4.)

Bebop players also became known for **running the changes**: improvising by maintaining mostly up-tempo eighth-note lines that articulate the chord changes in a virtuoso manner. Some swing improvisation can also be seen as running the changes, but the practice is particularly associated with bebop, where it became widespread.

The way rhythm players accompanied soloists also changed. In particular, because of the influence of Kenny Clarke, Max Roach, and others, bebop drummers kept time very differently. Many swing-era drummers marked all four beats of a 4/4 measure with the bass drum, but bebop drummers such as Clarke switched to the ride cymbal to maintain the pulse. They used the bass drum for **dropping bombs**—sharp, irregular accents that were far more disruptive than

the accents of the swing drummers. Bebop drummers used the snare drum to punctuate the musical texture with accents, or "kicks," or to maintain a kind of irregular chattering as an aside to the principal beat on the ride cymbal. (Accents on the bass drum are also called kicks.)

The faster tempos of the bebop players lay behind some of these changes in drumming. Clarke admitted that he was unable to maintain the breakneck speeds and keep his foot playing the bass drum on all four beats, so he switched the timekeeping role to the ride cymbal. Clarke, nicknamed "Klook" or "Klook-mop" (those syllables mimicked the sound of his unpredictable accents), played a fundamental role in developing this new style of drumming.

The faster tempos also brought about changes in piano playing. Bebop pianists abandoned the left-hand striding style that kept steady time. Instead, they broke up the texture with chords, often syncopated, leaving the timekeeping role to the bass and the drummer's ride cymbal. This type of accompanying came to be called **comping**. During their improvisations, the bebop pianists also played with the right-hand lines like those of horn players while the left hand accompanied with short, staccato chords.

With the pianist's left hand and drummer's bass drum no longer projecting the pulse, bands relied on their bassists to keep time, usually by walking the bass on each beat of the measure. Following the influence of Ellington's bassist Jimmy Blanton (see Chapter 6), bebop bassists played in a more linear fashion instead of merely playing the root notes of each chord. Blanton also influenced such bassists as Oscar Pettiford and Ray Brown, who became renowned for their ability to improvise solos as well as accompany and keep time.

The Historical Origins of Bebop

Many factors, both musical and social, contributed to the rise of bebop in the 1940s. In this section we look at the people, places, and political forces that helped create this musical phenomenon. Later we focus on the specific contributions of several key players in bebop's early development.

The Early Forties: Jamming at Minton's and Monroe's

The earliest stirrings of bebop took place in the informal jam sessions in Harlem. In 1940, Minton's Playhouse on West 118th Street hired drummer Kenny Clarke as a bandleader. For the house band, Clarke hired trumpeter Joe Guy, bassist Nick Fenton, and an eccentric pianist named Thelonious Monk. Musicians would stop by Minton's and sit in after they had completed their gigs. The atmosphere was informal, so they could try out ideas, network, and engage in friendly (or not so friendly) competition with the other players. In other words, the jam sessions helped the players make connections, develop new ideas, and establish a rough pecking order of talent. The club, as trumpeter Miles Davis pointed out, was "the music laboratory for bebop."[6]

Guitarist Charlie Christian (see Chapter 6), a member of the Benny Goodman band, was a regular participant at Minton's—he even kept a spare amplifier at the club. Thanks to a jazz fan named Jerry Newman, who had a portable recorder, some of these sessions were captured and eventually released. The recordings reveal a music in transition. The rhythm section plays with a lighter, more buoyant sound than the steady chugging of swing-era rhythm: Kenny Clarke accents offbeats on the bass and snare drums, and Christian supplies supple guitar lines in which the eighth notes are more evenly spaced than the swing eighths of earlier players.

Pianist Thelonious Monk composed regularly for the band at Minton's. While a member of the house band there, he wrote some of his most enduring compositions, including two haunting ballads, "'Round Midnight" and "Ruby My Dear," which showed the unique harmonic sense that characterized Monk's style. Other musicians adopted the Monk tunes heard at Minton's. Trumpeter Cootie Williams used "Epistrophy," which Monk wrote with Kenny Clarke, as his radio theme song in 1942, although he changed the title to "Fly Right." Williams was also the first to record Monk's "'Round Midnight," in 1944. Even when playing standard tunes, Monk often made unusual reharmonizations, especially in introductions. One musician in the audience remembered that Monk "generally started playing strange introductions going off, I thought to outer space, hell knows to where."[7]

Monroe's Uptown House on West 134th Street was another site for jam sessions. Run by pianist Allen Tinney, they normally began at 3 a.m. and lasted until daylight. The house band included Max Roach, a brilliant drummer who eventually became the regular drummer in Charlie Parker's quintet. Many new musical ideas came out of these competitive jam sessions. As one participant at Monroe's remembered, "The musicians used to go there and battle like dogs, every night, you know, and just playing for nothing and having a good time."[8]

Thelonious Monk,
"'Round Midnight"
(1947)

Charlie Parker, in town with the Jay McShann band, was so stunned by the level of musical activity at Monroe's that he left the McShann band and remained in New York:

> At Monroe's I heard sessions with a pianist named Allen Tinney; I'd listen to trumpet men like Lips Page, Roy [Eldridge], Dizzy, and Charlie Shavers outblowing each other all night long. And Don Byas was there, playing everything there was to be played. I heard a trumpet man named Vic Coulson playing things I'd never heard. Vic had the regular band at Monroe's, with George Treadwell also on trumpet, and a tenor man named Pritchett. That was the kind of music that caused me to quit McShann and stay in New York.[9]

Big Bands in the Early 1940s

If the uptown Harlem clubs like Minton's and Monroe's functioned as the "laboratories" for bebop, the more commercial format of the big band also provided opportunities for many of the newer players to develop and test their ideas. Particularly significant in the early part of the 1940s were the big bands of Earl Hines and, shortly thereafter, Billy Eckstine. These bands included both Charlie Parker and Dizzy Gillespie, so they were especially notable.

Unfortunately, much of the music that marked the transition from swing to bebop in the early 1940s was never documented on studio recordings because the American Federation of Musicians (AFM) called a strike in August 1942. Protesting the lack of payment to musicians for records played on the radio, the union insisted on a recording ban—with the exception of V-discs (Victory discs) produced specifically for the armed forces overseas. Decca settled in September 1943, Columbia and Victor held out another year, and eventually the strike ended.

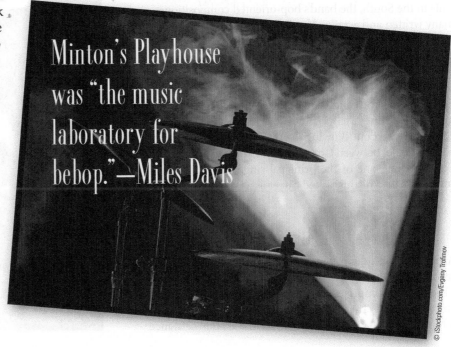

Minton's Playhouse was "the music laboratory for bebop."—Miles Davis

© iStockphoto.com/Evgeny Trofimov

These three record companies held the lion's share of the market before the ban, but several smaller labels sprang up shortly afterward and focused their attention on recording the younger players.

For his big band in 1942, Hines recruited Gillespie on trumpet and Parker on tenor saxophone (there was no opening for an alto saxophone player). Outside of Harlem jam sessions, this was the first time Parker and Gillespie had worked together on the bandstand. Also playing trumpet with the Hines band was another player in step with the latest musical developments: "Little" Benny Harris. Harris's composition "Ornithology," a contrafact of the swing standard "How High the Moon," became a bebop classic. The band also featured two outstanding singers who would develop major careers: Sarah Vaughan and Billy Eckstine.

Sarah Vaughan (1924–1990) became a preeminent jazz singer, possibly the greatest to develop in the bebop era. Her leap to the limelight came during the heyday of bop, when she sang with both the Earl Hines and Billy Eckstine big bands in the early 1940s. There, her associations with Parker and Gillespie established her reputation and refined her ability to sing with the looseness and unexpected vocal twists and turns of the newer style. (We return to Sarah Vaughan in our discussion of jazz singers in Chapter 10.)

Billy Eckstine (1914–1993) was a suave baritone vocalist who also played trumpet and valve trombone. In the early 1940s, he had a hit with the Hines band in the slightly bawdy blues song "Jelly, Jelly." Persuaded to form his own band, Eckstine left Hines and hired Gillespie as musical director. Gillespie convinced many of the most forward looking of Hines's musicians to join Eckstine's band, including Parker, pianist John Malachi, and eventually drummer Art Blakey.

The Eckstine band of 1944 has frequently been called the "first bebop big band," but the group did not achieve significant commercial success. Although they played at dance halls in the South, the band's bop-oriented compositions—many written and arranged by Gillespie—kept most people off the dance floor. Parker soon left the band, never having recorded with Eckstine, and Gillespie remained a short time afterward. In April 1944 Gillespie recorded some blues-oriented compositions with Eckstine, including "I Stay in the Mood for You" and "Good Jelly Blues," both cut in the mold of Eckstine's "Jelly, Jelly" hit. At the end of the year, Gillespie played on "Blowing the Blues Away," a tenor saxophone "battle" between Gene Ammons and Dexter Gordon. Eckstine, long one of the principal singers in jazz, would continue with a distinguished career as a jazz vocalist.

Bebop Moves to Fifty-second Street

Around the middle of the 1940s, the clubs of West Fifty-second Street became the primary venue for bebop bands. "The Street" comprised two blocks between Fifth Avenue and Broadway. The jazz clubs were tiny, crowded, and often poorly lit—far removed from the elaborate dance halls played by the big bands. In fact, most had no dance floors, merely tables for listening and an area where listeners were not required to buy drinks. During the war an immense concentration of jazz players developed in the city. For the cost of the cover charges, a listener could stroll down The Street and stop in to hear Sidney Bechet, Art Tatum, Coleman Hawkins, or Fats Waller anytime between 9 p.m. and 3 a.m. Gradually, the newer bebop bands worked their way into Fifty-second Street.

As Dizzy Gillespie remembered it, the birth of the bebop era came after he left the Eckstine band in 1944. With bassist Oscar Pettiford, Gillespie formed a band to play at the Onyx Club, one of several acts on the bill. Gillespie and Pettiford hired Max Roach on drums and George Wallington on piano; both had been in the house band at Monroe's Uptown House. Gillespie tried to contact Charlie Parker, who had returned to Kansas City after leaving Eckstine, but Parker never received the telegram. When tenor saxophonist Don Byas, an accomplished player with a big sound reminiscent of Coleman Hawkins, began sitting in, they eventually invited him to join the band.

W. 52 ST.

NO PARKING
IN THIS BLOCK
8 A.M TO 6 P.M
MON TO FRI. INCLU
PARKING
LIMIT
OTHER TIMES ONE HOUR
POLICE   DEPT

Around the middle of the 1940s, the clubs of West Fifty-second Street became the primary venue for bebop bands.

With the horns playing in unison, the group's repertory was new and startling:

> In the Onyx Club, we played a lot of original tunes that didn't have titles. We just wrote an introduction and a first chorus. I'd say, "Dee-da-pa-da-n-de-bop…" and we'd go on into it. People, when they'd wanna ask for one of those numbers and didn't know the name, would ask for bebop. And the press picked it up and started calling it bebop. The first time the term *bebop* appeared in print was while we played at the Onyx Club.[10]

The group itself did not record, but much of the band—Gillespie, Pettiford, Roach, and Byas—assembled in the studio in early 1944 under the auspices of Coleman Hawkins for a series of historic recordings. Hawkins, some twenty years into his career, placed himself into the musical vanguard by hiring the more talented young players on the scene. According to many, this attempt resulted in the first bebop recordings. Although half of the six tunes were ballads for Hawkins, the rest were in the newer style: Gillespie's "Woody n' You," Budd Johnson's "Bu-Dee-Daht," and a blues piece called "Disorder at the Border." In these recordings bebop had an embryonic sound: the ponderous big band, the rhythm section, and many of the solos still seemed weighted down by the conventions of swing. Only Gillespie's energetic start-and-stop solos hinted at the music to come—the music fundamentally indebted to the innovations of Gillespie and Parker.

The Architects of Bebop

Numerous musicians contributed to the formation of bebop, but none were more significant than Charlie Parker and Dizzy Gillespie. Kenny Clarke, whose role in modifying drum styles also greatly affected bebop, was discussed earlier. Among pianists, the preeminent contributors included Thelonious Monk and Bud Powell.

Charlie Parker

Charlie Parker was probably the greatest, most brilliant jazz saxophonist of all time. His influence on jazz history rivals that of Louis Armstrong: both generated a major jazz style while radically increasing the level of technical proficiency on their instruments. Parker's improvisations left a mark on almost every subsequent jazz musician.

Born in Kansas City, Kansas, on August 29, 1920, Parker and his family moved across the river to Kansas City, Missouri, seven years later. At first he played baritone and alto horns in his school bands, but in 1933 he turned to the alto saxophone. Within two years he left school to play full time with a local bandleader known as Lawrence "88" Keyes.

Parker's talent was not immediately apparent. Bassist Gene Ramey described Parker as the "saddest thing in the Keyes band."[11] In the cutthroat world of the Kansas City jam session, Parker learned about competition the hard way. In a radio interview, Parker recalled his first jam session:

> I'd learned how to play the first eight bars of "[Up a] Lazy River," and I knew the complete tune to "Honeysuckle Rose." I didn't never stop to think about there was other keys or nothin' like that. [Laughter] So I took my horn out to this joint where the guys—a bunch of guys I had seen around were—and the first thing they started playing was "Body and Soul," long beat [implied double time] you know, like this. [*Demonstrates.*] … So I go to playin' my "Honeysuckle Rose" and [unintelligible], I mean, ain't no form of conglomeration [unintelligible]. They laughed me right off the bandstand.[12]

But Parker was diligent. Known for carrying his horn in a paper bag, the teenager learned a few Lester Young solos note-for-note while studying basic harmony with some of the local guitarists. He joined the band of Buster Smith, a saxophonist who was an early influence on Parker. Then in 1938 he joined the band of Jay McShann, a pianist based in Kansas City but originally from Oklahoma.

In early 1939 Parker moved to New York for the first time, playing sessions at Monroe's Uptown House and washing dishes at Jimmy's Chicken Shack so that he could hear pianist Art Tatum, who often performed there. Undoubtedly, Tatum's sophisticated harmonic sense influenced Parker, and his effortless virtuosity and streams of high-speed runs quite likely helped determine the mature Parker style. In a famous anecdote, Parker credited a guitarist named Biddy Fleet with teaching him more-advanced harmonies: playing "Cherokee," which would become one of his signature tunes, Parker realized that he could emphasize the higher chordal extensions—ninths, elevenths, or thirteenths. These too became a feature of his mature style.

In 1940 Parker returned to Kansas City and the McShann band to become one of its musical directors. An amateur recording, probably from 1940, is the first we have of Parker. This recording preserved a solo practice session on "Honeysuckle Rose" followed by "Body and Soul"—significant choices given the story of Parker's first jam session.

Parker cut his first professional recordings informally at a radio station in Wichita, Kansas, on November 30, 1940, with the McShann band. These tunes, known as the Wichita transcriptions, revealed the group's Kansas City origins: "Moten Swing," "Honeysuckle Rose," and "Oh, Lady Be Good." In 1941 and 1942, still with the McShann band, Parker made his first studio recordings, including "Swingmatism," "Hootie Blues," "Sepian Bounce," and "The Jumpin' Blues." "Hootie Blues" featured Parker's first important solo—one that dramatically announced the arrival of a new saxophone stylist.

Parker and the McShann band returned to New York in late 1941 or early 1942 to play at the Savoy Ballroom.

© iStockphoto.com/sadrak

Parker was diligent. Known for carrying his horn in a paper bag, the teenager learned a few Lester Young solos note-for-note.

At that time he immersed himself in the New York scene, frequently attending the after-hours sessions at Minton's and Monroe's. Parker shared the stand with trumpeters Roy Eldridge, Dizzy Gillespie, and Charlie Shavers, as well as saxophonist Don Byas. Drummer Kenny Clarke, who in 1941 considered himself among the newer innovators, was stunned by Parker's playing:

> Bird was playing stuff we'd never heard before. He was into figures I thought I'd invented for drums. He was twice as fast as Lester Young and into harmony Lester hadn't touched. Bird was running the same way we were, but he was way out ahead of us. I don't think he was aware of the changes he had created. It was his way of playing jazz, part of his own experience.[13]

Surrounded by this high level of musical activity, Parker decided to remain based in New York, playing

> ### "Bird was playing stuff we'd never heard before."
> ### —Kenny Clarke

in the big bands of Earl Hines and Billy Eckstine. Earning awestruck respect from his fellow musicians, he was rapidly becoming an underground hero. Increasingly

during this time, he found himself jamming and sitting in with various groups in the heart of Fifty-second Street.

Parker's performances with the band of guitarist Tiny Grimes became especially significant. On September 15, 1944, Grimes invited Parker to cut four sides with the band, which included Clyde Hart on piano, Harold "Doc" West on drums, and Jimmy Butts on bass. Parker was featured in all four tunes, including his own composition "Red Cross." In the two takes of "Red Cross," we hear Parker's first recorded solos with **rhythm changes**. More generally, as Parker's first small-group records featuring him as soloist, we hear the early crystallization of Parker's bebop playing.

Although the Grimes band was more of a swing than a bop group, Parker plays his solos superbly, presenting several of his trademarks:

- ▶ A lean, edgy tone
- ▶ Use of blues inflections
- ▶ Double-time sixteenth-note runs
- ▶ Bebop-style licks that were to become the mainstay of the new style

After the Grimes recordings of late 1944, Parker began working with small groups as his bebop style matured. His most significant partnership was with Dizzy Gillespie, and their musical relationship flourished. By May 1945 the two were fronting a band at the Three Deuces on Fifty-second Street, where they remained until July. The group recorded several tunes that became mainstays of the bebop era, including "Groovin' High," "Dizzy Atmosphere," "All the Things You Are," and "Salt Peanuts" (SP) (Listening Guide, Track 28).

Rhythm changes are derived from the form and harmony of the 1930 George and Ira Gershwin song "I Got Rhythm." (The final two-bar tag of the original song is omitted so that a symmetrical 32-bar AABA plan results.) The bridge in rhythm changes consists of two-bar harmonies following a circle-of-fifths pattern that returns to the tonic. For example, if rhythm changes are performed in B♭, the harmonies of the eight-bar bridge are D7 (2 bars), G7 (2 bars), C7 (2 bars), and F7 (2 bars). The F7, as the dominant of the tonic B♭, leads back to the A section. Extremely popular since the 1930s, rhythm changes are still commonly used by jazz musicians for improvisation and composition. (Listen to Track 10 of the Audio Primer to hear an example of rhythm changes.)

LISTENING GUIDE

Track 28

"Salt Peanuts"

Dizzy Gillespie and His All Stars: "Salt Peanuts" (Gillespie-Clarke). Guild 1003. New York, May 11, 1945. Gillespie, trumpet and vocal; Charlie Parker, alto saxophone; Al Haig, piano; Curley Russell, bass; Sidney Catlett, drums.

The Main Point "Salt Peanuts" may be the best-known bebop tune, perhaps because its humorous motivic idea is unforgettable. The tune is a crowd pleaser, less often adopted for performance by Parker, who generally refused to play up to his listeners. Yet there are instances of Parker's performing—and singing—"Salt Peanuts" in live versions! This classic recording, an early instance of Parker and Gillespie together on record, has a remarkably complex layout for an early bebop tune. Compare it with the modern version by Steve Coleman (Track 60).

Introduction—16 bars as 8 + 8

0:00 Introduction, part 1. A driving drum solo sets a very bright tempo—typical for a tune in bebop style. Catlett sets the tempo with the first four measures, then states the rhythm of the head (played by the horns at 0:12) for the next four measures.

0:06 The rest of the ensemble enters. Notice the prevalence of **tritones** played by the horns—the first pitches heard are B♭ and E, followed by G♭ and C. The last two bars of the introduction (measures 7 and 8) feature a break for pianist Haig playing the "Salt Peanuts" (SP) octave motive.

1st chorus head—32-bar AABA

0:12 The head consists of two licks, the second of which is the SP motive. Parker and Gillespie divide the SP motive, with Parker on the lower note and Gillespie on the upper.

0:19 Repeat of the A section.

0:26 The bridge features Parker and Gillespie in octaves. There are alterations in the harmonies, which themselves are based on rhythm changes. Some of the melodic leaps include tritones.

0:32 The third A section completes the first chorus.

Interlude A—8 bars

0:39 A composed line for Parker and Gillespie on the A section changes.

2nd chorus head—32-bar AABA

0:45 Parker takes the first lick of the tune himself, while Gillespie sings the SP motive.

0:52 Repeat of the A section.

0:58 Parker solos on the bridge.

1:05 The third A section completes the two-chorus presentation of the head, with Parker on the tune's first lick and Gillespie singing the SP motive.

Interlude—16 bars as 8 + 8

1:11 The rhythm section plays alone for the first eight bars.

1:18 Parker and Gillespie rejoin the band for the second section of the interlude, which features prominent tritones. Haig takes the last two bars as a solo break.

3rd chorus—32-bar AABA piano solo

1:24   Haig solos on a full chorus. Haig's left hand is relatively inactive, while the right hand concentrates on "running the changes," as is typical in up-tempo bebop.

4th chorus—32-bar AABA alto saxophone solo

1:50   Parker's solo is virtuosic and features the edgy tone for which he was well known.

Interlude—10 bars

2:16   An interlude to set up Gillespie's entrance and solo break in the last two bars.

5th chorus—32-bar AABA trumpet solo

2:23   The first two bars of Gillespie's solo continue the break from the interlude. His use of extreme high notes is typical of his style as is the fleet dexterity of the entire improvisation.

Drum solo

2:50   Catlett's drum solo maintains the time, leading into the introduction.

Introduction—As coda

3:09   The second part of the introduction repeats, with the band singing the final SP motive.

 Listen to this music in an animated Active Listening Guide available at the text website.

A **tritone** comprises a diminished fifth or an augmented fourth—a popular interval in bebop melodies; it is sometimes called a flat five by jazz musicians.

From "Salt Peanuts" we can summarize these characteristic features of Parker's up-tempo style:

▶ Disjointed, irregularly accented melodic lines, mostly comprising eighth notes with occasional arpeggiations

▶ Little space between phrases

▶ Melodic connections based on extremely subtle motivic interrelations and voice leading

▶ A commanding, insistent tone quality

▶ Use of melodic chord extensions

▶ Intense, powerful expression

▶ Frequent blues inflections

▶ Concentration on middle and upper range of instrument

▶ Scale-chord relationships generated from the use of altered and extended chord harmonies

Gillespie's style echoes Parker's, and bop melodic playing in general, in its use of the following elements:

▶ Angular melodic lines made up largely of eighth notes

▶ Less rhythmic variety because of the eighth-note emphasis

▶ Phrases of irregular length

▶ Long phrases that may complete a section or more of a chorus

▶ Use of extended and chromatic extended chord tones

▶ A lack of vibrato in up-tempo playing

▶ Emotional though virtuosic playing

▶ Emphasis on the middle and upper range of the instrument

▶ Melodic continuity based on voice leading and large-scale phrasing

▶ De-emphasis of motive structure, at least in up-tempo playing

▶ Few blues inflections in up-tempo playing

▶ Adventurous chord-scale associations

On November 26, 1945, Parker supervised his first session as a leader. These recordings for Savoy Records included some of his most important performances as well as the original compositions "Billie's Bounce," "Ko Ko," "Now's the Time," and "Thriving on a Riff." "Ko Ko," a contrafact of "Cherokee," also featured Dizzy Gillespie on trumpet, but a nervous, nineteen-year-old trumpeter from St. Louis named Miles Davis played the other cuts. The title "Now's the Time" was later said to have prophesied two important trends: the acceptance of bebop and the growing importance of the civil rights movement.

"Ko Ko" became one of Parker's most famous solos—a classic statement of bebop virtuosity. Interestingly, earlier live recordings of Parker performing its source tune, "Cherokee," demonstrate that he was developing the principal ideas for the solo since at least 1942.

The "Ko Ko" recording session has become one of the most famous and most analyzed in jazz history. There are several reasons for this:

▶ It was Parker's first session as a leader.

▶ Many of the pieces recorded, including "Ko Ko," became signature works for Parker.

▶ The session was itself disorganized, so the sequence of events remains unclear, and, indeed, the identity of the pianist on "Ko Ko" remains controversial.

(The most likely scenario is that Gillespie plays trumpet on the piece's introduction, then switches to piano for Parker's solo, then switches back to trumpet for the end of the recording.)

Parker had been performing "Cherokee" since the early 1940s, where it was a featured piece for him as a member of the Jay McShann band. Parker's earlier, informal recordings of the piece show him gradually developing the

> "Ko Ko," a contrafact of "Cherokee," also featured Dizzy Gillespie on trumpet, but a nervous nineteen-year-old trumpeter from St. Louis named Miles Davis played the other cuts.

ideas that coalesce into the classic recording of November 26, 1945. Many of these ideas continue to appear in the live recordings of "Cherokee" and "Ko Ko" that we hear through the remainder of Parker's career.

LISTENING GUIDE   Track 29
"Ko Ko"

Charlie Parker's Reboppers: "Ko Ko," take 2 (Parker). Savoy 597. New York, November 26, 1945. Charlie Parker, alto saxophone and leader; Dizzy Gillespie, trumpet and piano; Argonne Thornton (aka Sadik Hakim), piano (?); Curly Russell, bass; Max Roach, drums.

The Main Point   "Ko Ko" is perhaps the most electrifying recording of Parker's early maturity. The composition is based on the challenging chord changes of "Cherokee," a popular song by Ray Noble that was a major hit in 1939. Indeed, the brief first take at the session includes the beginning of the original melody of "Cherokee." That initial take is quickly cut off, and the second take avoids the original melody entirely.

When are we hearing "Ko Ko" and when are we hearing "Cherokee"? There are two determining factors: the original melody of "Cherokee" and Parker's written introduction to "Ko Ko." When the introduction is present and the original melody of "Cherokee" missing, then we are hearing "Ko Ko"; if the original "Cherokee" tune is present, the piece is "Cherokee." One further note: Noble wrote "Cherokee" with the customary 32-bar AABA form doubled to 64 bars. If you count in "half time"—every other beat—it will still sound like a 32-bar form.

In the composed introduction of "Ko Ko," Parker and Gillespie play either written phrases together or improvised phrases singly, which provide contrast. The introduction follows a conventional four-phrase pattern with each phrase as eight bars, but because there are no chord changes and the drums provide the only accompaniment, the pattern may not be clear. It was music such as this that earned bebop the reputation of being abstract and not based on more conventional melodies and harmonies.

Introduction—32 bars as 8 + 8 + 8 + 8

0:00   Introduction, phrase 1. Over the bright tempo maintained by Max Roach playing with brushes, we hear Parker's written melody played in octaves by Parker and Gillespie. Though a B♭ major chord may be inferred, there is no harmonic support provided, and indeed Parker's melodic line is harmonically ambiguous.

0:06   Introduction, phrase 2. Gillespie improvises the next eight bars.

0:12   Introduction, phrase 3. Parker improvises the next eight bars.

0:19   Introduction, phrase 4. Here Parker and Gillespie return to written-out melodic figures, first in harmony, then back to octaves. The introduction concludes with a tritone C–F♯ "bebop" figure (0:24).

Parker improvisation, 1st chorus—64-bar AABA

0:25   In Parker's first A section, we hear a melodic line in eighth notes that concludes with a B♭–F♯ "bebop" figure (0:27). This melodic line can be conceived as a part of the thematic identity of "Ko Ko," because it later returns in Parker's solo. Parker's second phrase (0:28) has a repeating melodic figure (sometimes called the "Woody Woodpecker lick") that Parker will deploy in his "Ko Ko" solos from time to time.

0:37   The second A section of Parker's solo. Notice that the phrase heard here corresponds closely to the phrase Parker played at the beginning of the first A section (0:25). This repetition lends thematic identity to the phrase.

0:50   Unlike the A section of the piece, which is straightforward, the harmonies of the bridge are difficult. In earlier recordings of the piece (by the bands of Charlie Barnet and Count Basie) soloists avoided improvising on the bridge. Parker's conquering of the bridge's chord changes laid claim to the piece as "his own." The beginning of the bridge features a phrase whose earlier versions can be heard in Parker's previous recordings of the piece, while the phrase played at 0:59, one of his best-known formulas, serves here to introduce the final A section of the first chorus.

1:03   The third A section completes the first chorus. Here, the phrase begun during the bridge at 0:59 does not conclude until the second bar of this A section. Phrases that overlap sectional boundaries are not uncommon with Parker and influenced future improvisers. Surprisingly, Parker ends his first chorus with a poignant sustained F (1:13), which serves both to contrast the brilliancy of his previous phrases and as a brief rest for him to regroup for the second chorus. Notice how Gillespie adroitly picks up this F and accents it in the piano an octave lower (1:15).

Parker improvisation, 2nd chorus—64-bar AABA

1:15   Parker begins his second chorus with a conscious nod to jazz history, referencing in fact Dixieland! The arpeggio-like figure is the beginning of a famous clarinet obbligato from the trio of the march "High Society," a staple of the New Orleans repertory in the earlier part of the century. Interestingly, Parker often quotes it in his future recordings of "Cherokee" or "Ko Ko." (He quotes it at other times, too, always over a B♭ major harmony.)

1:28   Parker's second A section.

1:41   The beginning of the bridge again features a lick whose earlier versions can be sampled in Parker's previous recordings. Here Parker adds a dazzling cross-rhythm, all the more impressive as it involves the harmonic shift at the beginning of the bridge that most musicians of the era found difficult to navigate. At 1:48, the turn to the higher register beautifully contrasts the earlier cross-rhythm with a phrase that prepares us for the well-known Parker lick (1:51; first heard at 0:59) that leads to the final A section.

1:55   Again, Parker begins the third A section with a phrase begun during the bridge. This phrase should be compared to its previous statements in Parker's first chorus (0:25 and 0:37). All three versions of the phrase end with the B♭–F♯ "bebop" motive. Its reappearance here serves thematically to tie the solo together and prepare the ending. After this thematic phrase, Parker summarizes much of what he played previously in bringing his solo to a satisfying conclusion.

Drum solo—32 bars

2:07   Roach's drum solo maintains the 32-bar form (as a half chorus) and develops rhythmic motives.

Introduction as coda—29 bars as 8 + 8 + 8 + 5

2:30   The drum solo allowed Gillespie the opportunity to switch back to trumpet. He and Parker now reprise most of the "Ko Ko" introduction. The written-out phrases are the same, but the improvised ones are varied.

2:36   Gillespie's improvised phrase.

2:42   Parker's improvised phrase.

2:49   Parker and Gillespie come back together for the final phrase of the coda. Note that Parker omits the final three bars of the introduction (compare 0:22), so that the coda only has 29 bars. The harmonic ambiguity of the introduction is maintained to the very end of the recording: nontonic Fs are played first by Gillespie, then by Parker, then by bassist Russell (accented with Roach) as the last note of the piece.

 Listen to this music in an animated Active Listening Guide available at the text website.

After the "Ko Ko" session, in December 1945, Parker traveled to the West Coast with a band led by Gillespie for an engagement in Hollywood. In one sense the trip was an experiment, an attempt to see whether bebop, developed largely on the East Coast, would generate excitement elsewhere. The gig, at a club called Billy Berg's, was not successful. Gillespie and the band returned to New York within a few months, while Parker stayed on. Reputedly, he pawned his plane ticket to support his heroin habit. His addiction, which had developed when he was a teenager, caused Parker increasingly intense physical and emotional problems.

While still in California, Parker continued to record, thanks to the interest of Ross Russell, founder of Dial Records and an ardent admirer. Some of the recordings from early 1946 were brilliant, particularly a session on March 28 that featured "Moose the Mooche" (named after Parker's drug supplier) and "A Night in Tunisia." The latter cut featured one of the most spectacular saxophone breaks ever recorded—Russell even issued it as "Famous Alto Break." But Parker's addiction was growing worse. The breakdown came during a recording session on July 29, in which Parker was virtually unable to play. Back at his hotel, Parker (it was claimed) set fire to his mattress and was seen walking around nude. Arrested by the police, he was eventually sentenced to a term in Camarillo State Hospital, where he remained for six months. Later, much to Parker's anger, Russell issued the recordings from Parker's July 29 session. Parker was ultimately released from Camarillo, and after several performances and recordings he returned to New York in April 1947.

The following four years proved to be the most intensely productive period of Parker's career, in part because he was temporarily free of his heroin dependency and because bebop had, while Parker was on the West Coast, become even more popular back East. Indeed, Parker returned to New York as one of the most famous musicians in jazz. He formed his most long-lived working quintet with trumpeter Miles Davis, pianist Duke Jordan, bassist Tommy Potter, and drummer Max Roach—a group that remained together for a year and a half. It is quite possible that the fame of Parker's group established the model for the future jazz quintet: trumpet, saxophone, piano, bass, and drums. Many groups continued to follow this small-group format during the next couple of decades.

The quintet recorded many Parker compositions that became jazz standards. For example, "Scrapple from the Apple" was a kind of double recomposition: the A section used the harmonies from Fats Waller's "Honeysuckle Rose," and the B section took the chords from "I Got Rhythm." "Confirmation" became one of Parker's best-known bebop heads. It was also one of his few tunes not based on recomposition over preexisting chord changes. The melody for "Confirmation" was itself tricky to negotiate, a repository of bebop melodic devices.

A 1947 recording of "Crazeology" presents Parker in his prime, working with innovative variants to rhythm changes. An unusual chord change to G♭ in the A section forces Parker to rethink how he plays rhythm changes in B♭ because he cannot rely on his established note patterns. As we discussed in Chapter 6, such established patterns are called **formulas** or, more popularly, **licks**. Parker excelled at developing formulas for use in up-tempo improvising.

A **formula** is a worked-out melodic idea that fits a common chord progression. Most improvisers develop formulas, especially for up-tempo improvisation because the rapid tempo does not allow time for total spontaneity. A formula is more popularly known as a **lick**.

A unique item among Parker's formal recordings is a session in which he played tenor saxophone. Recall that Parker played tenor in the Hines band but was never formally recorded at the time. This session, under the direction of Miles Davis on August 14, 1947, shows another side of Parker's artistry, with a tenor style that recalls Don Byas.

As he gained wider public acceptance and acclaim, Parker undertook other new and interesting projects. In November 1948 he signed a contract with Norman Granz of Mercury Records; most of the Parker's recordings for the remainder of his life were under Granz's supervision. In addition, Granz organized several concerts and tours of top-flight jazz performers under the title Jazz at the Philharmonic, a venue that became extremely well known in the late 1940s and 1950s. Parker often participated in these concerts and tours under Granz's direction.

Parker made two European tours, playing Paris in 1949 and Sweden the following year. Thanks to Granz, Parker recorded in many different settings, including sessions with Machito's Afro-Cuban band, a group we discuss later in this chapter. Most significant was the unusual step of recording with string accompaniment, in which Parker fulfilled a long-held ambition. In *Charlie Parker with Strings*, Parker played standards in a subdued mood. His recording of "Just Friends," from the first strings session on November 30, 1949, became a classic; it was not only Parker's best-selling record but reputedly his favorite of his recorded solos. The strings recordings became so popular that Parker took a string quartet (along with an oboe player) on the road for several club dates in 1950 and 1951.

Although Parker recordings, both studio and live, abound, it is disappointing to learn that he was filmed performing only once, on a television broadcast on February 24,

1952. There he appeared with Dizzy Gillespie for a performance of "Hot House." (Pianist Dick Hyman also appeared on the show.) Although the television program was the only instance of Parker performing live on film, he did *appear* in a Gjon Mili film of 1950 (with Coleman Hawkins) for Jazz at the Philharmonic publicity, but the recording was made earlier. In the film, Parker and Hawkins attempt to sync their playing to the previously recorded sound track.

One of Parker's most significant devices, not new to jazz but one that he developed extensively, was his tendency to quote other music in his solos. The quotations ranged from classical themes to well-known pop tunes, jazz heads, and children's songs. For example, in a solo on "Salt Peanuts" performed in Paris in 1949, Parker quoted the beginning of Igor Stravinsky's *The Rite of Spring*, a famous classical work that had premiered in Paris in 1913. At the other extreme, in a solo on "Just Friends" recorded in 1950, Parker quoted "Pop Goes the Weasel." Both of these performances were live; Parker tended to quote more often in live settings than in studio recordings.

Charlie Parker,
"Just Friends" (1949)

Perhaps he chose the live venues because he realized that the humor implied in a quotation would quickly become stale on repeated listening. He also may have needed the informal atmosphere of a live audience to feel comfortable making a joke. Of note is the unequaled ingenuity with which Parker wove his quotations into the flow of his solos. Parker's freewheeling quotations greatly influenced later generations of players.[14]

The original caption for this photo read: "The show at the new Birdland Restaurant, which opened on Broadway, December 15 (1949), offers music to suit just about every taste. Entertaining at their specialties are (left to right), trumpeter Max Kaminsky, Dixieland style; saxophonist Lester Young, swing; (Oran) "Hot Lips" Page, famed for sweet swing; Charlie Parker on the alto sax, representing bop; and pianist Lennie Tristano, exponent of a new style called 'music of the future.' It marked the first time that these noted musicians, representing completely different schools of modern music, were gathered on the same stage."

Bettmann/Corbis

Parker spent his final years in a downward slide, both physically and mentally. He suffered from ulcers, became overweight, and drank heavily. When one of his daughters, Pree, died of pneumonia, Parker became severely depressed. In 1954 he twice attempted suicide and voluntarily committed himself to Bellevue Hospital in New York. Parker last performed at a club named for him, Birdland. The performance was disastrous, a visible airing of his feud with pianist Bud Powell. A week later, on March 12, 1955, he died at the apartment of the Baroness Pannonica de Koenigswarter, a jazz patron who had befriended him. His body was ravaged by years of substance abuse. Although the story is not authenticated, jazz legend has it that the examining doctor listed Parker's age as fifty-three. He was only thirty-four.

Dizzy Gillespie

Along with Charlie Parker, John Birks "Dizzy" Gillespie (1917–1993) played a crucial role in innovating and promoting the new bebop style in the 1940s. "Bird might have been the spirit of the bebop movement," said Miles Davis, "but Dizzy was its 'head and hands,' the one who kept it all together."[15] Despite Gillespie's reputation for clowning around—which earned him the nickname "Dizzy" early on—he was dedicated to his craft as a musician. He made a point of working out experimental harmonies and chord progressions at the piano, often enthusiastically teaching and coaching the other players. Gillespie clearly rejected the stereotype of the untutored, "natural" jazz musician. As he told *Time* magazine in 1949,

> Nowadays we try to work out different rhythms and things that they didn't think about when Louis Armstrong blew. In his day all he did was play strictly from the soul—just strictly from the heart. You got to go forward and progress. We study.[16]

Although his style had originally been influenced by trumpeter Roy Eldridge, Gillespie soon developed an improvisational technique that was much more distinct. With his impressive command of the upper register of

> "Bird might have been the spirit of the bebop movement, but Dizzy was its 'head and hands,' the one who kept it all together."
> —Miles Davis

the trumpet, he punctuated his solos with wild leaps into the "stratosphere." He could play much faster than previous trumpeters, with sinuous chromatic lines in dramatic contrast to the diatonically based solos of swing.

As a composer and an arranger, Gillespie was prolific. Many of his bebop heads became jazz standards in their own right, such as "Groovin' High," "Woody n' You," "Salt Peanuts," and "A Night in Tunisia." Written while Gillespie was a member of the Hines band during the early 1940s and originally titled "Interlude," "A Night in Tunisia" was perhaps his most famous piece. Although unusual in its exoticism, it showed many of the hallmarks of the nascent bebop style. The use of the Latin-tinged rhythm in the opening section reflected Gillespie's interests in Afro-Cuban music.

Gillespie was born in Cheraw, South Carolina, on October 21, 1917. Years later, after receiving a scholarship to the Laurinburg Institute in North Carolina, he moved with his family to Philadelphia and there joined a band led by Frankie Fairfax. In 1937 he left Fairfax to move to New York, where he rapidly made his way into the better-known bands, working as the featured soloist with Teddy Hill and, in 1939, Cab Calloway. He was summarily dismissed from the band in 1941 after Calloway mistakenly accused Gillespie of hurling a spitball at him during a performance.

Like Parker, Gillespie frequently participated in the after-hours sessions at Minton's and had been a member of the big bands of Earl Hines and Billy Eckstine. Gillespie soon achieved success as a composer-arranger, contributing original numbers to the bands of Boyd Raeburn and Woody Herman. After winning the New Star Award in the *Esquire* magazine jazz poll in 1944, Gillespie formed the band with bassist Oscar Pettiford that performed at the Onyx Club on Fifty-second Street. It was the recordings and performances with Charlie Parker, however, that thrust Gillespie squarely into the front line of the bebop movement. The 1945 performances and recordings of the two principal talents of bebop culminated in the disastrous West Coast trip at the end of the year (discussed earlier).

Charlie Parker and His Orchestra (with Dizzy Gillespie), "Bloomdido" (1950)

After his split with Parker, Gillespie returned to the large-group format and led his own big band with increasing commercial success through 1950. On many of their recordings, we hear the successful translation of bebop from small group to big band, including the exciting "Things to Come," a prophetically titled piece written and arranged by Gillespie and Gil Fuller. Gillespie, always attracted to Afro-Cuban elements in jazz, hired conga player Chano Pozo to perform with his band and featured him in a Carnegie Hall concert in 1947. This Afro-Cuban element, which Gillespie felt complemented and expanded the rhythmic resources of jazz, became an important facet of Gillespie's work. We hear it, for example, on the Gillespie-Pozo composition "Manteca" as well as on "Cubana Be/Cubana Bop," written by Gillespie, Pozo, and George Russell. After a discussion of the roots of Latin jazz, we turn to one of the most

Habanera rhythm was probably the most common Latin ingredient in jazz until the 1940s. In the habanera and other Latin rhythms, the beat is divided into two even halves, contrasting with the "swung" eighth notes more typical of swing.

Claves are two thick wooden sticks that, when struck together, produce the characteristic *click* of the Latin percussion sound.

famous cubop recordings of Dizzy Gillespie, "Manteca" (Listening Guide, Track 30).

Compared with Charlie Parker, Gillespie presented a more commercial side to bebop. He insisted that the music be entertaining and lamented its separation from dancing. To the mainstream audience, his stage persona—which included hipster posturing with beret, goatee, and glasses—became at least as well known as his music. His many innovations and tireless championing of the music, however, made Gillespie a significant founder and a fundamental contributor to the development of bebop. He continued to perform bop-based jazz with groups both large and small for decades to come as one of the great personalities and elder statesmen of the jazz scene. He died on January 6, 1993.

Latin Jazz

Latin music has had a continuous influence on jazz throughout the twentieth century. For example, it is quite possible that Latin rhythms helped furnish the characteristic syncopation of New Orleans hot melody in the teens. Moreover, many of the important early New Orleans musicians had Latin roots from a variety of countries.

Latin rhythms also appear in ragtime. As early as 1902, it appears in the ragtime hit, "Under the Bamboo Tree" (Cole-Johnson); moreover, the habanera rhythm can be heard in Scott Joplin's "Solace—A Mexican Serenade" from 1909. The **habanera rhythm** was probably the most common Latin ingredient in jazz until the 1940s. In the habanera and other Latin rhythms, the beat is divided into two even halves, contrasting with the "swung" eighth notes more typical of swing.

The habanera beat appears in what is undoubtedly the most important blues tune of classic jazz: W. C. Handy's "Saint Louis Blues." Handy, in his autobiography *Father of the Blues*, recalls that around 1910 he saw the effect on the dancers of the Latin-tinged tune "Maori" by Will Tyer. At that moment he made the decision to try to incorporate the habanera rhythm into his works. That same beat crops up with one of the more famous techniques associated with Jelly Roll Morton: his so-called Spanish tinge is also based on the habanera beat. This rhythm can be heard on Morton's 1923 recordings of "Mamanita" and "New Orleans Joys"; it also appears in Morton's "The Jelly Roll Blues," which was published in 1915, although Morton claimed to have written it in 1905.

Meanwhile, Latin dances in the United States supplemented the exploding number of ballroom dance fads through the teens, twenties, and thirties. Well-known Latin bandleaders such as Desi Arnaz and Xavier Cugat promoted the tango, the rumba, and other Latin dances, many of which became highly popular with the public. Among the important percussion instruments that set the style and pace for these dances was the **claves**, essentially two thick wooden sticks that, when struck together, produce the characteristic *click* of the Latin percussion sound. The impulse of the clave beat is syncopated over the duple meter of the underlying beat and is one of the characteristic sounds of much Latin rhythm.

Most of the Latin influence in early jazz can be traced to Mexico and South America, although there is a decisive Caribbean influence as well. In the late 1920s, there began a major immigration of Cubans to New York City. Their music, which was distinguished from earlier Latin music, was called Afro-Cuban and was often more aggressive in its rhythmic power, possibly because of its closer connection to African roots. As an addition to the claves among the Latin percussion, the conga drum was popularized by Afro-Cuban musicians. Their music grew in popularity through the 1940s. Among the influential promoters of the Afro-Cuban sound was Machito (born Frank Grillo), a Cuban vocalist who came to New York in 1937 and

Machito, an important innovator in blending Afro-Cuban music with bebop, plays the maracas; the young woman is playing the claves.

teamed up with trumpeter Mario Bauza, who had played with numerous jazz big bands. Machito called his group "the Afro-Cubans" and often worked with well-known jazz performers as soloists.

Since **cubop** of the 1940s, Latin music has sustained a major presence in jazz. For many decades the best-known Latin musician with jazz associations was percussionist and bandleader Tito Puente (1923–2000), a New York native raised in Spanish Harlem. Puente's first big break in the music business—when he was all of thirteen years of age—was becoming Machito's drummer.

Separate contributions came from Brazil, although we note that some commentators classify Brazilian music as distinct from Latin. (Latin music is typically more driving and rhythmically aggressive; moreover, it is normally associated with Spanish-speaking countries, whereas the primary language of Brazil is Portuguese.) The **samba**, a fast, syncopated dance, was introduced in the United States from Brazil in the 1930s and 1940s. During the 1960s a blend of jazz harmonies with softened, sultry melodies and textures, known as **bossa nova**, became extremely popular.

Many Brazilian musicians became well-known in jazz circles through the bossa nova fad as it developed through the 1960s. Jazz musicians such as tenor saxophonist Stan Getz did much to popularize the samba and the bossa nova. The most important composer of bossa nova tunes was Antonio Carlos Jobim (1927–1994), who wrote "Desafinado," "One-Note Samba," and many other hits. On Track 36, we hear tenor saxophonist Stan Getz perform Jobim's perhaps most famous song, "The Girl from Ipanema."

Cubop, the 1940s blending of bebop with Afro-Cuban music, was brought to New York City by an immigration of Cubans in the 1920s.

The **samba** is a fast, syncopated dance introduced in the United States from Brazil in the 1930s and 1940s.

The **bossa nova** is a Latin jazz style that developed from Brazilian music in the late 1950s and early 1960s.

LISTENING GUIDE
"Manteca"
Track 30

Dizzy Gillespie and His Orchestra, with Chano Pozo: "Manteca" (Pozo-Gillespie-Fuller). Victor 20-3023-A. New York, December 30, 1947. Gillespie, trumpet, leader; Dave Burns, Elmon Wright Jr., Benny Bailey, trumpets; William Shepperd, Ted Kelly, trombones; John Brown, Howard Johnson, alto saxophones; Joe Gayles, George "Bick Nick" Nicholas, tenor saxophones; Cecil Payne, baritone saxophone; John Lewis, piano; Al McKibbon, bass; Kenny Clarke, drums; Pozo, conga.

The Main Point   An excellent example of big-band bebop with an Afro-Cuban element, which Gillespie felt complemented and expanded the rhythmic resources of jazz.

Introduction

0:00   In much Afro-Cuban music, the groove, projected by the rhythm section, is an essential part of the composition. In the introduction to "Manteca," we hear a groove that builds through the addition of instruments and leads to a solo statement by Gillespie. After the bass-and-conga beginning, we hear the baritone saxophone entering at 0:08, overlaying another vamp to add to the groove. The rest of the brass enter at 0:16, and finally Gillespie at 0:19. The accumulated forces culminate in chords for the full band at 0:31 with a "fall-off" on the last chord, leaving just the bass, drums, and conga.

Head—40-bar AABA

0:38   The groove, continuing from the introduction, leads into the head. Here there is a pickup figure in the saxophones that is answered by the full brass in a call-and-response pattern. The eight-bar A section builds into its pattern, repeated intensely in measures 7 and 8 (0:46).

0:49   Repeat of the eight-bar A section.

1:00 The bridge is unusual in being 16 bars instead of the customary eight. For the first eight bars, we hear lush saxophone chords that provide a fine contrast to the A section. For the second eight bars (1:11), Gillespie solos over the chordal cushion provided by the saxophones.

1:22 Return of the eight-bar A section.

Interlude

1:34 The groove of the introduction returns and leads to entries of intense brass figures. These figures culminate in a restatement of the basic AABA form of the tune but with the AA as a tenor solo.

Tenor saxophone solo—16-bar AA

1:48 The groove changes to a swing beat as the band provides a background for the first eight bars of "Big Nick" Nicholas's tenor solo.

1:59 The second eight bars of Nicholas's tenor solo use the rhythm section alone as accompaniment.

B section—Bridge, 16 bars

2:10 The bridge returns, scored for full band.

2:21 Gillespie returns to solo with the second half of the bridge. He is accompanied by chords in the saxophones in addition to the rhythm section.

A section—Head, 8 bars

2:33 The call-and-response figure that characterizes the head returns, as does the original Latin groove.

Introduction—As coda

2:44 The groove established in the introduction returns, but now grows quieter until a sudden surge in the drums ends the piece.

Listen to this music in an animated Active Listening Guide, available at the the text website.

Bud Powell

Earl "Bud" Powell (1924–1966), generally considered the finest of the bop pianists, transferred Parker's and Gillespie's bebop techniques to piano. He gained acclaim for playing up-tempo lines at blistering speed and exercised a profound influence on a generation of pianists. He best codified the right-hand bop piano style, in which sparse, sharply articulated chords in the left hand punctuated and rhythmically set off linear improvisations in the right. But he was also an immensely capable player in the more two-handed style derived from Art Tatum and the classic stride masters.

A New Yorker, Powell began gigging around town when he was a teenager. He soon joined the scene at Minton's, where house pianist Thelonious Monk took an early interest in his development. As the pianist with trumpeter Cootie Williams's band in 1944, Powell made his earliest recordings, which demonstrate his style in transition—equally at home in the swing of Earl Hines as well as in the nascent bebop style. He became a mainstay on Fifty-second Street, where he played with Gillespie, John Kirby, Don Byas, Dexter Gordon, and others.

Early on, Powell showed signs of mental instability. "Bud was always—ever since I've known him—he was a little on the border line," recalled tenor saxophonist Dexter Gordon. "Because he'd go off into things—expressions, telltale things that would let you know he was off."[17] During a racial incident with a policeman, Powell took a beating, especially to his head. Afterward his erratic behavior increased, and he was institutionalized five times between 1945 and 1955. Despite his often moody and withdrawn behavior, however, Powell's playing astounded his contemporaries.

Powell's performances are well documented by recordings. In January 1947 Powell made his first recording as a leader, with Curley Russell on bass and Max Roach on drums. Powell later recorded frequently with Roach. Although he did not often record with Charlie

Parker (they supposedly never got along), Powell joined Parker's first studio session when Parker returned to New York from Los Angeles in May 1947. The group recorded "Donna Lee," "Chasin' the Bird," and "Cheryl."

Powell's trio recordings of 1949, with bassist Ray Brown, showed him to be not only a stunning pianist but also a gifted composer. One of Powell's tunes, "Tempus Fugit" (Listening Guide, Track 31), showcased the pianist playing at breakneck speed. Another, a fine solo track called "I'll Keep Loving You," revealed a tender side of his playing and contains references to Art Tatum.

As Charlie Parker set new standards for up-tempo saxophone improvisation, Powell did similarly for pianists.

In fact, one can compare Powell's bebop improvisational lines to Parker's much as in the 1920s we saw a relationship between Earl Hines's lines and Louis Armstrong's. Although Art Tatum was certainly never surpassed by any jazz pianist in keyboard fluency, Powell's virtuosity is different: rather than a full, two-handed, Tatumesque approach to the instrument, Powell streamlined his left hand, letting the rhythm section handle timekeeping and focusing on right-hand brilliancy and invention. He relied primarily on single-line runs in the right hand, with sparse but aggressive left-hand accompaniment. (However, Powell was certainly capable of playing stride piano, as he demonstrates admirably on some of his solo piano recordings.)

LISTENING GUIDE   Track 31
"Tempus Fugit"

Bud Powell Trio: "Tempus Fugit" (Powell). Clef 11045. New York, January–February 1949. Bud Powell, piano and leader; Ray Brown, bass; Max Roach, drums.

The Main Point "Tempus Fugit" is Latin for "time flies," an apt title for the tune, as time is indeed flying. Brilliantly fast, Bud Powell, in a piano trio setting with bass and drums, demonstrates his mastery in a fiery bebop performance.

"Tempus Fugit" recalls Dizzy Gillespie's bebop hit "A Night in Tunisia," because Powell's work is an AABA tune in D minor with references throughout to the signature chord progression of "Tunisia," E♭7–Dm. The marvellous creativity Powell displays in this piece recalls the hectic breathlessness of Parker's "Ko Ko," with constant and inventive reworking of improvised formulas. One particularly interesting feature of the piece is that despite the references throughout to E♭7–Dm, Powell does not articulate chord changes clearly in his improvisation. Rather, Powell's left hand often drones on lower notes, including the aforementioned E♭ and D (sometimes played together with an A). This gives the piece the hypnotic sense of a constant D minor harmony, which foreshadows jazz experiments in the 1950s in which harmonic change was sometimes greatly slowed down.

In "Tempus Fugit" we hear a piano trio, an ensemble mentioned earlier in our discussion of Art Tatum. It became gradually more popular through the 1940s and may have reached an apex of popularity in the 1950s and 1960s with the work of Bill Evans, a pianist we discuss in Chapter 10. Keeping time with brushes on the snare drum is a common practice for drummers in piano trios, because the volume of the drums played with sticks can overwhelm the pianist. Roach's use of brushes on "Tempus Fugit" is tasteful and swinging.

Introduction—1-beat pickup + 8 bars

0:00   A one-beat sixteenth-note pickup sets a very bright tempo with Powell playing the melody in octaves. Notice the syncopated accents with drummer Roach and bassist Brown at 0:04–0:05, then again at 0:05–0:06. The accents of the introduction serve as a foil to the straight ahead eighth-note orientation of the main theme. The piano melody above the insistent chords twice highlights a characteristic bebop interval, the flatted fifth above the bass (0:04 and 0:06).

Head—32-bar AABA

0:07   The rhythm section keeps time, the fast tempo maintained by walking bass and brushes on the snare drum. Each of the melodic phrases ends with a typical bebop gesture of a descending two-note idea. Listen for the way Roach punctuates, playing a bass drum kick directly after the melodic phrases in the piano.

Although the head is in AABA 32-bar form, the chord changes are understated, and in fact sometimes only implied. That is, while the right hand lays out the melody, the left hand does not provide constant harmonic and rhythmic support, as heard in the work of the stride pianists, but rather accompanies freely. During the cadence of this first A section, dyads (groups of two notes) as tritones enter, which imply a harmonic progression establishing the key of D minor. Further, the final two notes of the tune at the cadence (F and D) are the "bebop" rhythmic pattern so often found in tunes and improvisations in this style.

0:14 Repeat of the A section.

0:20 The eight-bar bridge features a chordal texture that contrasts angular linearity of the A section. The right-hand melody avoids the running eighth notes of the A section, with, instead, chords in slower note values. Meanwhile, the left hand plays on-the-beat octaves. The bass duplicates the piano left-hand melody. The syncopated accents at the end of the bridge (0:25) break up the second of the four-bar phrases and recall the introduction. A cymbal roll at the end of the bridge brings back the final A section of the head.

0:27 The third A section completes the presentation of the head with the eighth-note bebop melody played in Powell's right hand.

Interlude—6 bars

0:34 An interlude sets up the first improvised chorus. It begins with a four-bar section of piano chords played with unpredictable accents and duplicated by the rhythm section, a texture that again recalls the introduction. When the rhythm section drops out, Powell's two-bar break at 0:37 leads into the first improvised chorus.

1st improvised chorus—32-bar AABA

0:39 Powell's bebop solo is highly linear: that is, he relies on melodies that might be also be played by a horn player. Note Powell's left hand, which is unusual here: instead of the punctuated midrange chords we usually hear in bebop pianists, Powell adds soft bass notes. These may be single notes or dyads (two notes at once), usually tritones, perfect fifths, or octaves.

0:45 Repeat of the A section.

0:52 The bridge.

0:58 During the final A section of this first chorus listen for the drum kicks that appear on the fourth beat of the first several measures. Powell creates a climactic line in the middle of this A section (1:01), before continuing into its second half.

2nd improvised chorus—32-bar AABA

1:04 At the top of Powell's second chorus, he insistently repeats a fast riff six times before the melodic line then continues. That riff appears every three beats. This is something of a signature sound for Powell. Strong accents at the beginning of the riff create a driving cross-rhythm.

1:11 On the repeat of the A section, we again hear Powell on an insistent three-beat riff. This pattern, different from the first one played, is also heard six times (although Powell begins on a different note for its last appearance).

1:17 For the bridge, Powell relaxes (at least relative to the A sections), because there are no syncopations and an entire bar of silence (the fourth bar of the bridge). Powell then begins a melodic idea that continues into the following A section, effectively masking the return to that section.

1:23 In the third A section, Powell continues and ends the phrase begun in the bridge. He then finishes the chorus with a single four-bar phrase that rises, providing an effective contrast to the descent of the previous phrase.

3rd (final) improvised chorus—32-bar AABA

1:29 As in the previous chorus, Powell repeats a riff six times, again every three beats. This type of repeated gesture was one that later bebop-oriented pianists, such as Oscar Peterson, would adopt. This pattern is similar to the second pattern (beginning on the same note, a high C) and continues into the sixth bar of the chorus before breaking off to end the first A section.

1:35   During the following A section (1:35), against the blistering right-hand lines, Powell plays a melodic idea in his left hand in octaves. At the end of this section, the drummer plays an accent in the bass drum and cymbal (1:41), an example of the bebop practice of "dropping bombs."

1:41   Powell begins the bridge with the same formula that he used to begin the second improvised bridge (1:17). After a bar, however, Powell deviates from what he played earlier.

1:47   In the final A section the drummer continues to play more aggressively, using the brushes to play accents on the snare drum. Powell fills the first six bars with a single phrase before setting up the return of the head in mm. 7–8.

Out chorus—32-bar AABA + 2-bar tag

1:54   A repeat of the head. The second A occurs at 2:00, the bridge at 2:06, and final A at 2:12.

2:18   The performance concludes with a brief tag: the group repeats the final two measures, slowing down the tempo. "Tempus Fugit" ends with a rolled chord in the piano.

Listen to this music in an animated Active Listening Guide, available at the the text website.

Several of Powell's compositions were elaborate. For example, "Un Poco Loco" was a complex Latin-oriented composition in which Powell soloed over a repeated single-chord vamp and made use of exotic pitches and scales. Another complex piece, "Glass Enclosure," written in four sections, was a disturbing evocation of his time spent in mental asylums. A third example, "Parisian Thorough-fare," was recorded twice in 1951, once with a trio and again as a solo piano feature.

Powell displayed his fiery spirit in a famous concert recorded at Massey Hall, Toronto, on May 15, 1953, in which he performed with Charlie Parker, Dizzy Gillespie, Max Roach, and bassist Charles Mingus—a recording justly acclaimed as reuniting Parker and Gillespie in a "summit meeting" of the top talents in bebop. His work after 1953 was less even. He recorded for Blue Note, Verve, and Victor, but his mental problems, often made worse by drinking, interfered with his playing. Powell moved to Paris in 1959 and recorded with another American expatriate, tenor saxophonist Dexter Gordon. Unfortunately, Powell continued to suffer health problems and was diagnosed with tuberculosis in 1963. He died in 1966.

The quintessential bebop pianist, Powell had a direct impact on the piano styles of Barry Harris, Hank Jones, Tommy Flanagan, and Sonny Clark. Indeed, no pianist who followed Powell could escape his influence. His right-hand-dominated style became the prime technique for nearly all jazz pianists and made Powell the father of modern jazz piano.

Thelonious Monk

Thelonious Sphere Monk was an original. Avoiding the virtuosic flamboyance of Art Tatum and the up-tempo facility of Bud Powell, Monk instead created a piano style

The influential pianist Bud Powell. His piano style combined up-tempo bebop lines in the right hand with sparse chordal punctuations in the left hand.

BUD POWELL

GALE AGENCY Inc.
48 West 48th St.
New York   N.Y.

Photo courtesy of the Morgan Collection

Metric displacement is a technique whereby the soloist implies or states a rhythm in the melody line that seems to go against the underlying basic rhythm of the piece. It also can be achieved by placing melodic phrases irregularly against the underlying rhythm.

---

that struck many of his contemporaries as erratic, awkward, or just plain odd. But all of Monk's peers considered him one of the prime movers of bebop. "Monk's contribution to the new style of music was mostly harmonic," Dizzy Gillespie said, "but also spiritual."[18]

Thelonious Monk performing at the Beehive Club, Chicago in 1955.

Frank Malcolm/Frank Driggs Collection

Although Monk's technique was rooted in the Harlem stride tradition, his solos were devoid of the flashy virtuosity of the older school. His playing was lean and spare, making abundant use of silence around the notes. A noted characteristic of his playing used clusters and "crushed notes"—a dissonant group of pitches out of which Monk would release all but one or two notes.

Much of Monk's influence on bebop came from his practice of reharmonizing popular standards, a practice evident early in his career. In his introduction to "Sweet Lorraine," as recorded by Jerry Newman at Minton's in 1941, Monk played the melody of the song with an accompaniment that departs radically from the original. Even in this early recording, he displayed much of the wit and quirkiness that would come to be associated with his style. As Miles Davis put it, "Monk had a great sense of humor, musically speaking. He was a real innovative musician whose music was ahead of his time.... He showed me more about music composition than anyone else on 52nd Street."[19]

Born in 1917 in Rocky Mount, North Carolina, Monk came to New York with his family when he was four. Largely self-taught, he played piano and organ in church. He also acquired some European classical technique in his youth but abandoned it early in favor of his own idiosyncratic jazz style.

As house pianist at Minton's during the early 1940s, Monk was positioned to have his pieces performed frequently by the up-and-coming bebop players. Curiously, however, they rarely asked Monk to record with them. He made his first studio recording with Coleman Hawkins in 1944, but he did not record in earnest for Blue Note Records until 1947. Blue Note's producer, Alfred Lion, was intrigued by Monk's

Technique and Technology

Monk and Metric Displacement

Some of Thelonious Monk's compositions and improvisations rely on the technique of **metric displacement**. In Monk's composition "Straight, No Chaser," the main idea of the melody first begins with a pickup to the downbeat of the measure. Yet when it is restated, it appears one beat earlier in the measure, anticipating the fourth

beat. Because this second statement of X is now displaced in the measure relative to the first statement, it distorts the sense of the underlying 4/4 meter. This happens again in the third and fourth measures. The fifth statement of X appears in yet another metric position by anticipating the third beat of the measure.*

* For further discussion of these techniques of metric displacement in Monk's compositions and improvisations, see Cynthia Folio, "An Analysis of Polyrhythm in Selected Improvised Jazz Solos," an essay contained in *Concert Music, Rock, and Jazz: Essays and Analytical Studies*, ed. Betsy Marvin and Richard Hermann (Rochester: University of Rochester Press, 1995), 111–118.

Thelonious Monk,
"Straight, No Chaser"
(1966-67)

dramatically innovative style, but Lion cautiously insisted on recording fourteen selections before agreeing to release a single 78 rpm record.

Working with both trios and sextets, Monk continued to record for Blue Note for the next five years. These recordings highlight his strengths as a composer. His poignant ballads "'Round Midnight," "Ruby My Dear," and "Monk's Mood" featured a rich harmonic vocabulary. A medium-tempo number, "In Walked Bud," was a tribute to pianist Bud Powell that outlined both the melody and the harmony of Irving Berlin's "Blue Skies" in an effective recomposition.

Some of his melodies, such as those in "Straight, No Chaser" and "Criss Cross," seemed to shift the beat around by using motives repeated in different parts of the measure. (See the box "Monk and Metric Displacement.")

Monk's distinctive approach to jazz dramatically foreshadowed the minimalism and abstract objectivity that were to become fashionable in the West from the 1950s on. Monk's performances draw us into a conscious awareness of each note and ask us to judge it, to place it in its context, and to enjoy its unique occurrence at that particular moment. In his decision to revamp traditional jazz piano values, Monk addressed the problem of how to imbue each pitch—out of the few pitches available—with special significance and still create good music. Hence, Monk did not rely on dazzling the listener with ornate, previously worked-out licks.

LISTENING GUIDE
Track 32
"Four in One"

Thelonious Monk Quintet: "Four in One" (Monk). Blue Note 1589. New York, July 23, 1951. Monk, piano; Sahib Shihab, alto saxophone; Milt Jackson, vibraphone; Al McKibbon, bass; Art Blakey, drums.

The Main Point   "Four in One" is a characteristic Monk composition. This piece also shows off to excellent advantage Monk's idiosyncratic piano playing in a group setting.

Introduction—8 bars

0:00   Piano solo. Blakey taps the hi-hat lightly on the second and fourth beats of each bar. The third and fourth bars contain the syncopated whole-tone runs from the tune's A section.

Head—AABA, first two A sections

0:12   The entire band first plays the melody in unison and then moves quickly to notes occasionally harmonized in seconds and thirds. During the third and fourth bars, listen for syncopated and repeated whole-tone runs in thirds.

0:20   The eight-bar A section ends humorously with a "bebop" figure. In a piano voicing below the alto saxophone melody, Monk adds a lowered major ninth—a "wrong-note" D—a ninth below an E♭ melody note in an E♭ major chord.

0:24   The A section repeats.

Head—AABA, B section (bridge)

0:37   The eight-bar bridge begins with the vibraphone and the alto sax on the melody. The II–V harmonic patterns are conventional for the first two bars, then move up a half step for the third bar and back down for the fourth bar.

The second four-bar group begins as though it were a transposition of the first group; but instead of following the pattern, it turns to Monk-style humorous "wrong-note" chords for measures 6 and 7. The downbeat chord of measure 6 is especially sharp, comprising an E, D, and E♭.

A dominant-seventh harmony at the end of the bridge sets up the return to the A section.

Head—AABA, final A section

0:49   Repeat of the A section.

Monk piano solo—1 chorus (AABA)

1:02   As the solo begins, Monk refers to the head's melodic motives.

1:34   At the downbeat of the sixth bar of the bridge, Monk repeats the sharply dissonant chord from the B section of the head. He ends the bridge with a paraphrase of the head, which continues during the first two bars of the last A section.

1:41   During the whole-tone sequence of measures 3 and 4 of the last A section, however, Monk develops an alternate higher-register whole-tone syncopation. The solo is remarkable in its imaginative references to the head.

Shihab alto solo—First half of chorus (AA)

1:51   Shihab has a Parker-like quality to his tone, lines, and bebop phrasing.

2:04   At the start of the second A section, he refers directly to the melody.

Jackson vibraphone solo—Second half of chorus (BA)

2:15   Entering at the bridge, Jackson continues the pattern of clear melodic references. His final A section is freer.

2:17–2:21   Monk's accompaniment in the B section ranges from single notes in octaves…

2:23–2:29   …to dense chords.

2:30–2:35   He then moves on to parallel tenths in the final A section.

Reprise of the head

2:39   The head repeats almost exactly. As a brief coda, Monk plays a witty "bebop" cutoff in measure 7 of the last A section.

Listen to this music in an animated Active Listening Guide, available at the the text website.

Monk's compositional and pianistic trademarks, heard in such pieces as "Four in One," include the following:

▶ Unusual rhythmic irregularities in the melodic line

▶ Use of the **whole-tone scale**

▶ A conventional large-scale form (AABA with eight-bar sections) that, because of its predictability, sets off the more personal, stylistic elements

▶ From time to time, intriguing harmonies that break the conventional "rules" of jazz harmony

▶ A whimsical effect created by the contrast between Monk's personal idioms and bebop norms

Although Monk would eventually leave a legacy of jazz standards, he was slow to achieve recognition as a performer. During the 1950s he recorded with such musicians as Sonny Rollins and Gigi Gryce, and he continued to innovate rhythmically. His solo from "Bags' Groove" with the Miles Davis All Stars in 1954 was a tour de force of the techniques of metric displacement—Monk

---

A **whole-tone scale** has whole steps only and thus no dominant, making it impossible to form major or minor triads. There are only two whole-tone scales: C–D–E–F♯–G♯–B♭ and D♭–E♭–F–G–A–B. Notice that they share no notes. The scale is often associated with French twentieth-century composers such as Claude Debussy. (Listen to Track 1 of the 🅿 Audio Primer; the whole-tone scale is the fifth scale played.)

deliberately repeats motives in different parts of the measure, in effect "turning the beat around."

In the later fifties, Monk gained visibility and praise from his masterly album *Brilliant Corners* (1956) and his celebrated 1957 engagement at the Five Spot in New York with saxophonist John Coltrane. In 1959 at New York's Town Hall, he appeared in a concert that featured his big-band compositions. By 1964 his visibility and reputation had increased so much that *Time* magazine pictured him on its cover. Interestingly, his solo piano recording from that same year, *Solo Monk*, revealed Monk's indebtedness to the Harlem stride school.

Although Monk continued to perform and record into the mid-seventies, he spent his last years living in seclusion at the home of his patron, Baroness Pannonica de Koenigswarter. He died in 1982.

Slightly outside the mainstream bop tradition, Monk's playing nevertheless enormously influenced several generations of pianists. For example, Herbie Nichols and Elmo Hope both owed a debt to Monk during the 1950s; and Andrew Hill, Randy Weston, and Chick Corea all took something from Monk's style. Some aspects of Monk's style prefigure the **free jazz** that burst on the scene in the late 1950s. Although Monk was relatively neglected during his lifetime, devoted players and groups have kept his music alive. For instance, the jazz group Sphere (taking Monk's middle name) formed in the early 1980s to perform Monk's compositions.

Other Bebop Artists

Apart from Parker, Gillespie, Powell, and Monk, many other players contributed in various ways to bebop. Here we look at three artists who provided stylistic innovations on trombone, trumpet, and tenor saxophone, respectively: J. J. Johnson, Fats Navarro, and Dexter Gordon.

J.J. Johnson

Although common enough in all types of jazz ensembles, the trombone has never enjoyed the popularity of the other horns. The up-tempo single-note lines pervasive in jazz wind styles are difficult to execute on the trombone because of the slide mechanism. Because this is especially true for the low register, agile trombone playing usually occurs in the upper register.

J. J. Johnson (1924–2001) shook up jazz trombone playing in the late 1940s, although his technical developments followed logically from the work of the swing players. Johnson emphasized the high register and astonished everyone with boplike lines—at the time thought to be impossible on the trombone—that were reminiscent of Parker and Gillespie.

After working with big bands in the 1940s, Johnson made a series of significant records with smaller groups in the late 1940s and early 1950s. He eventually teamed up with fellow trombonist Kai Winding (1922–1983) to jointly lead a two-trombone quintet in 1954. With a distinguished career that continued into the 1990s, Johnson became well established as both a trombonist and a composer.

Fats Navarro

In addition to Dizzy Gillespie, a notable trumpeter of the bebop era was Theodore "Fats" Navarro (1923–1950), who in 1945 replaced Gillespie in Billy Eckstine's band. Over the next five years, he recorded frequently as a sideman, playing with Kenny Clarke, Coleman Hawkins, Illinois Jacquet, Dexter Gordon, and Bud Powell. He also performed with the band of composer-arranger Tadd Dameron, playing an impressive solo on Dameron's "Good Bait," based on rhythm changes. Navarro transferred Charlie Parker's bebop language to trumpet, playing chromatic melodic lines that were dexterous and cleanly executed. Navarro set the standard for a future generation of trumpeters that included Clifford Brown (see Chapter 8). Like many bebop players, Navarro succumbed to the ravages of heroin addiction, leading to ill health and death from tuberculosis in 1950 at the age of twenty-six.

Bud Powell (with Fats Navarro and Sonny Rollins), "52nd Street Theme" (1949)

Dexter Gordon

Despite Charlie Parker's overwhelming influence on alto saxophone, significant bebop tenor players emerged during the 1940s. Chief among them was Dexter Gordon, whose career lasted into the 1980s. Gordon's bebop playing was confident and extroverted, offering a rich, muscular, and warm sound on the tenor. He also often played with humor, picking up Charlie Parker's habit of quoting melodies from other pieces within his improvisations. Initially influenced by such Basie regulars as Herschel Evans, Gordon's relaxed, behind-the-beat phrasing owed a special debt to Lester Young.

Free jazz refers to the 1960s jazz sub style that overturned many of the traditional elements of the music. It's also known as avant-garde and the New Thing.

© iStockphoto.com/Chris Schmidt

Johnson astonished everyone with boplike lines—at the time thought to be impossible on the trombone—that were reminiscent of Parker and Gillespie.

Gordon was born in Los Angeles in 1923. While still a teenager, he became a member of Lionel Hampton's group and shared the bandstand with saxophonist Illinois Jacquet, an early role model for Gordon. In 1944 Gordon joined the Billy Eckstine band, which was staffed with many of the fiery young bebop players of the day. Shortly after, Gordon was featured in a saxophone "duel" with Gene Ammons on Eckstine's "Blowin' the Blues Away." This was the first of many saxophone "duels" for Gordon; his 1947 recording "The Chase" pitted him against another important bebop tenor player, Wardell Gray (1921–1955).

Like so many others of the bebop era, Gordon was plagued by heroin abuse; but despite incarceration and parole in the 1950s, he continued to evolve as a player. Gordon influenced two upcoming tenor players—John

Coltrane and Sonny Rollins, but the impact was reciprocal: Coltrane's hard-edged sound attracted Gordon, and in the late 1970s he took up soprano saxophone, which was largely popularized by Coltrane. Gordon also displayed a talent for theater: he provided the music for, played for, and acted in the 1960 Jack Gelber play *The Connection*.

Prior to moving to Europe in 1962, Gordon recorded for Blue Note, issuing *Go, Doin' Alright*, and *A Swingin' Affair*. He lived in Copenhagen, played frequently at the Jazzhus Montmartre, and toured, recorded, and taught. When he returned to the United States in 1977, the *Down Beat* readers' poll pronounced him "Musician of the Year." He also received that title in 1980. Gordon starred in the 1986 movie *'Round Midnight*, in which he played an expatriate jazz musician living in Paris, and was nominated for an Academy Award. Gordon died in 1990.

Bop-Style Big Bands of the Late 1940s

As we have seen, the bebop revolution emphasized the small ensemble. Further, the late 1940s witnessed the demise of many celebrated big bands. Despite all this, bebop proved attractive to some of the large bands. Dizzy Gillespie's big band was probably the first to commit completely to the new music. Other large ensembles soon followed and built much of their repertory along bebop lines. Some bands achieved even more popularity than Gillespie's band.

The big bands that made it through the end of the 1940s all seemed to jump on the bebop bandwagon. Swing drummer Gene Krupa and his band redid "Lemon Drop," written by bebop pianist George Wallington and popularized by Woody Herman in 1948. In Krupa's 1949 version, "Lemon Drop" trombonist Frank Rosolino supplied a bebop scat vocal in the style of Dizzy Gillespie. Krupa's staff arranger, Gerry Mulligan, created a hit for Krupa with his bop-oriented "Disc Jockey Jump." The more-commercial bebop recordings of Herman and Krupa did much to popularize the music among white audiences. As we saw in Chapter 5, even Benny Goodman briefly tried his hand at leading a bop-style group in the late 1940s.

Woody Herman

Woody Herman (1913–1987), a clarinetist from Milwaukee, brought the bebop sounds to a wider audience and probably achieved the greatest commercial success in this style. Primetime radio shows, sponsored by Old Gold cigarettes and Wild Root hair tonic, broadcast Herman and his band. These broadcasts—largely unavailable to the black bands, whose mass media exposure was severely limited—made Herman's band the first bebop-oriented music that many people in the U.S. heard.

Herman started with a swing group in the mid-thirties, and in 1945 Herman's Herd earned a jukebox hit with "Caldonia." This novelty tune made deliberate and humorous use of the hip vernacular that was emerging from the clubs on Fifty-second Street. Largely a head arrangement, "Caldonia" featured a celebrated five-trumpet unison passage, written by trumpeter Neal Hefti, which had obviously originated in the solo lines of Gillespie. The band's rhythm section—Ralph Burns on piano, Greig "Chubby" Jackson on bass, Billy Bauer on guitar, and Dave Tough on drums—created a furious drive on

the up-tempo arrangements of "Northwest Passage" and "Apple Honey."

Herman reformed his band in 1947 into a group known as the Second Herd. The band boasted several rising stars, including tenor saxophonists Stan Getz and Zoot Sims, both of whom based their distinctive sounds on that of Lester Young. In contrast to the normal saxophone section of two altos, two tenors, and one baritone, Herman's band featured the three tenors and one baritone. Known as the Four Brothers after a Jimmy Giuffre composition of the same name, the section was renowned for its clean, swinging ensemble sound.

Claude Thornhill

Less successful commercially but largely committed to the new bebop music was the band of pianist Claude Thornhill (1909–1965). Like Woody Herman and Gene Krupa, Thornhill's career began during the swing era of the mid-thirties (he even recorded with Billie Holiday in

Bandleader and clarinetist Woody Herman on the cover of "Early Autumn." This number featured saxophonist Stan Getz.

1938), but he devoted some recordings of 1947–1948 to big-band arrangements of bebop compositions by Charlie Parker and others. The arrangements were unusual and original. Thornhill's arranger, Canadian Gil Evans (1912–1988), was influenced by the French Impressionist composers as well as by jazz, and he experimented with coloristic sounds and instruments not often heard in a big band: French horn, tuba, and bass clarinet. The absence of vibrato in the horns gave the band a stark, moody sound. For Thornhill, Evans arranged Parker's compositions "Yardbird Suite," "Anthropology," and "Donna Lee." (The authorship of "Donna Lee" was credited to Charlie Parker, although it was probably composed by Miles Davis.)

Despite the use of bebop compositions, some listeners still found the spirit of Thornhill's band at odds with the small groups of Fifty-second Street. Miles Davis, who would collaborate with Gil Evans in the following years, noted, "I didn't really like what Thornhill did with Gil's arrangement of 'Donna Lee,' though. It was too slow and mannered for my taste. But I could hear the possibilities in Gil's arranging and writing on other things."[20]

Miles Davis and many of Thornhill's players—Gil Evans, baritone saxophonist and arranger Gerry Mulligan, and alto saxophonist Lee Konitz—eventually retreated from the prevailing bebop style. The result was known in the following decade as *cool jazz*, which we explore in Chapter 8.

See the following table for a summary of bebop characteristics.

Bebop-era Melodic Features

TIMBRE

- Tougher, edgier sound than swing; often raspy
- Little use of vibrato except on ballads
- Little use of instrumental effects
- Strong attacks combined with legato lines
- Little use of blue-note effects on up-tempo pieces
- Instrumental ranges extended upward, especially for brass

PHRASING

- Highly irregular, perhaps to off set symmetrical AABA forms
- Little space between phrases

RHYTHM

- Great reliance on eighth-note lines in up-tempo pieces
- Ballads featuring more rhythmic variety

THEMATIC CONTINUITY

- Voice leading almost exclusively in up-tempo pieces
- Motivic relationships less obvious, except on ballads

CHORD-SCALE RELATIONS

- Inside, but based on more-complex scales that include extended chord tones

LARGE-SCALE COHERENCE

- Voice leading
- Occasional reliance on use of climax followed by relaxation
- Balance of gesture

Exam Review Questions

Use these questions and the materials on the text website to help you understand and pass tests on the content of this chapter.

1. What are some of the differences between swing and bebop? What are some of the similarities? In what ways are the differences revolutionary or evolutionary?

2. How was Charlie Parker the consummate bebop musician? Refer to aspects of his life and music.

3. How did the lives of Dizzy Gillespie and Thelonious Monk differ from that of Charlie Parker? Refer to big bands, compositions, attitudes toward music, and personal history.

4. How did the repertory of bebop change from that of swing? What aspects of the repertory stayed the same?

5. Is it appropriate to regard bebop as the beginning of "modern jazz"? Cite both musical and sociological factors in arguing your case.

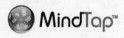 MindTap™

Test Yourself on Key Concepts with additional Chapter Quizzes and Listening Activities on the text website.

Key Terms

Test your knowledge of this chapter's key terms by defining the following. If you can't remember the meaning of a term, refresh your memory by looking up the boldfaced term in the chapter, turning to the Glossary at the back of the book, or working with the flash-cards at the text website.

bebop/bop **192**

bossa nova **209**

claves **208**

comping **196**

contrafact **195**

cubop **209**

dropping bombs **196**

extended chord tones **195**

formula **205**

free jazz **217**

habanera rhythm **208**

hipster **193**

lick **205**

metric displacement **214**

moldy figs **193**

reharmonization **196**

rhythm changes **200**

running the changes **196**

samba **209**

tensions **196**

tritone **201**

whole-tone scale **216**

only *2* simple controls

TURN IT ON — SELECT STATION — *that's all!*

BRAND-NEW and BEAUTIFUL CONSOLE gives life-size pictures at lower cost!

BILT-IN-TENNA
No outside antenna in good signal areas.

16" BROADVIEW SCREEN
Life-size pictures of startling new clarity.

Want your TV BIG? Want it BRIGHTER and CLEARER than ever before? Want it in a BEAUTIFUL mahogany or limed oak cabinet? Then ask your dealer for a demonstration of the new Motorola 16K2. It's one of a *brand new* line of magnificent Motorola's—more handsome—better performing and yes, LOWER PRICED—8½ to 19½ inch screen sizes—to fit every home and budget. *See them soon!*

See your classified directory for your nearest Motorola dealer.

Motorola TELEVISION

Encouraged by advertisements like one featuring Hopalong Cassidy on a 1950 Motorola television, mainstream America grew entranced with the new medium.

WILLIAM BOYD as HOPALONG CASSIDY America's favorite Television Cowboy

The 1950s and New Jazz Substyles

8

THE DECADE OF THE 1950s WAS A TRANSITIONAL TIME for America and American culture. The years following World War II brought about the cold war, the period of mutual mistrust and hostility between the Communist Soviet Union and the West. The early years of the decade saw the commitment of American troops to the Korean conflict (usually referred to as the Korean War). The cold war also created for a time an intense climate of fear in the United States, culminating in the McCarthy hearings (1953–1954), in which Senator Joseph McCarthy of Wisconsin accused politicians, actors, artists, and others of being affiliated with the Communist Party.

Yet for some the years of the Eisenhower presidency (1952–1960) coincided with a period of prosperity and optimism. The decade witnessed the rise of the suburbs, which provided housing communities away from urban centers. Children born during this time were part of the postwar baby boom (the term *baby boomers* refers to those born between 1946 and 1964). At the same time writers and artists—particularly those associated with the Beat movement—rebelled against what they perceived as the sterile buttoned-down conformity of the Eisenhower years. Novelist John Clellon Holmes's *Go* (1951), poet Allen Ginsberg's *Howl* (1956), and novelist Jack Kerouac's *On the Road* (1957) challenged prevailing social values and championed themes of alienation and nonconformity.

Among jazz musicians, rebellion often took a more sinister turn. Perhaps taking their cue from Charlie Parker, a staggering number of jazz musicians became addicted to heroin. The allure of the drug seemed to seduce jazz musicians, whether white or black, living on the East Coast or West, or playing hard bop or cool. Several ended up doing time in prison as a result of drug-related charges, including singer Billie Holiday, baritone saxophonist Gerry Mulligan, tenor saxophonist Sonny Rollins, and trumpeter Chet Baker, who served time in an Italian prison. Tenor saxophonist Stan Getz was arrested several times, once in 1954 after attempting to hold up a Seattle pharmacy in

Jazz

1949–1950—Davis recordings made, later retitled *Birth of the Cool*, including "Jeru" (Track 33)
1951—Dave Brubeck Quartet formed
1952—Modern Jazz Quartet's first recordings
1953—Massey Hall jazz concert with Parker, Gillespie, Bud Powell, Charles Mingus, and Max Roach
1954—Davis records "Walkin"
—First Newport Jazz Festival
—Joe Williams joins Count Basie
1955—Death of Charlie Parker
—Coltrane joins Miles Davis Quintet
—Charles Mingus forms workshop
1956—Goodman tours Far East
—Davis records "'Round About Midnight"
—MJQ records "Versailles" (Track 34)
1957—Thelonious Monk and John Coltrane record "Ruby, My Dear"
1958—Miles Davis and Gil Evans collaborate on *Porgy and Bess*
—Davis records *Milestones*
1959—Ornette Coleman records *The Shape of Jazz to Come*
—Davis records *Kind of Blue*, including "So What" (Track 40)
—Brubeck records "Take Five" and "Blue Rondo à la Turk" (Track 35)
1963—Getz and Gilberto record "The Girl from Ipanema" (Track 36)

1950   **1955**   **1960**

Historical Events

1949—NATO formed
1950—Korean War begins
1952—Hydrogen bomb tested
—Ralph Ellison publishes *Invisible Man*
1953—Eisenhower inaugurated
—Korean War ended
—Death of Stalin
1954—French defeated in Vietnam
—Supreme Court, *Brown v. Board of Education of Topeka* against racial segregation in public schools
1955—Polio vaccine, invented by Jonas Salk, declared effective
1956—Neutrino discovered
1957—Soviet Union launches Sputnik
—Jack Kerouac publishes *On the Road*
1959—Fidel Castro leads Communist revolution in Cuba
1960—Civil Rights Act
—Laser invented

order to obtain drugs. Alto saxophonist Art Pepper provided chilling details of his own incarceration in the San Quentin federal penitentiary in a frank autobiography entitled *Straight Life*. Some jazz musicians, such as Miles Davis and John Coltrane, found their best and most innovative musical work after they beat their heroin addiction.

Jazz and the New Substyles

Both changes in America and the controversies surrounding bebop in the 1940s led to a profoundly different jazz environment in the 1950s. No longer was it possible to speak of "jazz" and expect everyone to understand the meaning. It became necessary to indicate the *kind* of jazz, for the music now included a variety of substyles, the most important being *hard bop* and *cool*. Hard bop developed directly from bebop, whereas cool developed both from bebop and

as a reaction against it. In addition, Dixieland continued to flourish everywhere, thanks to a revival in the early 1940s. Finally, popular performers such as Ella Fitzgerald and Frank Sinatra who had roots in the swing bands of the 1930s or early 1940s retained many of the elements of swing from the big-band era while at the same time accommodating themselves to musical developments in the new decade.

It is difficult to track general trends in such a complex jazz world, but there was one point of view that musicians in the vanguard shared at the time: *modernism*. According to this view, jazz must develop, even progress. This was not an entirely new idea. As far back as the 1930s, jazz musicians thought of themselves as technically and artistically more advanced than the "rough" and "naïve" early players. But in the 1950s, many musicians, propelled by the changes of the late 1940s, came to consider jazz one of the fine arts, a category that embraced the principle of progressive development and mandated change. If jazz was to remain *art*, the artist and the music had to move forward in a constant, conscious evolution. Thus the advancing of jazz, as we shall see, became an important goal for many of its players and writers.

The decade of the 1950s witnessed a flowering of jazz styles as the music branched off in several directions. We examine two general trends: cool jazz and hard bop (and one prominent aspect of hard bop, known as funky jazz or soul jazz). In addition, we highlight some more specific trends that take place in the 1950s: third-stream music and modal jazz.

General trends:

▶ Cool jazz

▶ Hard bop

　■ Funky or soul jazz

Other trends:

▶ Third-stream music

▶ Modal jazz

These labels are generally useful but should not be taken as absolute categories. Moreover, some performers were associated with more than one trend: for example, Miles Davis's 1949–1950 recordings, later released as *Birth of the Cool*, set the standard for cool jazz of the 1950s, but many of Davis's recordings in the fifties are more closely associated with hard bop. Generally, jazz critics and record executives, rather than the musicians themselves, coined these labels.

Record companies starting using the term *cool* around 1953. That year Capitol released a 10-inch record entitled *Classics in Jazz: Cool and Quiet*, and over the next several years the word appeared on the title of numerous records: Dave Brubeck's *Jazz: Red, Hot, and Cool* (1955); *Stan Getz and the Cool Sounds* (1956); and Lee Konitz's *Very Cool* (1957).

The **cool jazz** style, which was associated with the West Coast, rejected some of the significant features of bebop and pursued different aesthetic principles. Miles Davis, Gerry Mulligan, Chet Baker, Dave Brubeck, the Modern Jazz Quartet (MJQ), and others emphasized the following characteristics:

▶ Restraint

▶ Lyricism

▶ Musical space

▶ **Counterpoint**

▶ Quieter dynamic range, including subdued accompaniment by drummers

▶ Sometimes extensive arrangements, including written introductions and composed passages between improvisations

▶ Influence of classical music on choice of instruments

In contrast to the breathtaking pace of some of the bebop players, many of the cool players concentrated on relaxed tempos. Tenor saxophonists such as Stan Getz, Zoot Sims, Jimmy Giuffre, and Al Cohn—all members of Woody Herman's Four Brothers saxophone section during the late 1940s—emulated Lester Young's light sound along with his relaxation, control, and wit. Composers Charles Mingus, George Russell, Gunther Schuller, J. J. Johnson, and Pete Rugolo frequently focused on larger, ambitious works, such as suites and multimovement compositions. Cool jazz groups took different sizes, although after Miles Davis's nine-piece group made its highly influential recordings for Capitol Records in 1949, several eight- to ten-piece groups arose. Note that the players did not always embrace the term *cool jazz*, because it implied a lack of passion and emotional depth.

Although cool jazz provided some players with an alternative to bebop, many other musicians during the 1950s were committed to perpetuating it. These players

… many the cool players concentrated on relaxed tempos.

© iStockphoto.com/Jeff deVries

Cool jazz was in part a reaction to bebop. It embraced the values of increased compositional complexity, slower tempos, and at times less overt emotional involvement.

Counterpoint is the use of simultaneously sounding musical lines. Music that has counterpoint is often called **polyphonic**.

Hard bop drew on the speed, intensity, and power of bebop and sometimes married bop to gospel and blues-influenced music in a substyle known as funky or soul jazz.

Funky jazz, or **soul jazz** is a style that combines elements of gospel music and R&B with jazz. It began to emerge in the 1950s as an outgrowth of hard bop and became quite popular in the 1960s.

Overdubbing, or multitracking, is a recording-studio technique that was generally available by the 1950s. Recording tape has several parallel "tracks" that enable musicians to record additional performance parts at later times. The added part is called an overdub. By wearing headphones, the players follow and "play to" the previously recorded tracks. In current recording studios, computer-controlled equipment and digital technology permit virtually unlimited overdubbing and editing of recorded parts.

An **LP** is a long playing-record that typically plays at 33⅓ rpm (revolutions per minute). LPs first became commercially available in 1948. LPs were made with polyvinyl chloride (hence the nickname "vinyl" for records) and allowed up to about twenty-five minutes of music per side.

---

forged a style that came to be known as **hard bop**. Interestingly, many of them came to New York from the urban centers of Detroit and Philadelphia. The hard bop groups

varied in size, but their instrumentation often kept the standard bebop quintet of a rhythm section (piano, bass, and drums) and two horns (typically a tenor saxophone and a trumpet). Many of these groups favored 32-bar compositions and straight-ahead improvisation full of intensity, speed, and volume.

In addition, the repertoire of hard bop groups often included music that wedded the traditions of bebop to simpler, earthier blues, creating a style sometimes known as **funky jazz**, **gospel jazz**, or, in the 1960s, **soul jazz**. Strongly influenced by currents in black music, funky/soul jazz took much of its inspiration from gospel music, blues, and rhythm and blues, as in the music of gospel singer Mahalia Jackson and blues singer–pianist Ray Charles. Leaning toward the popular-music side of jazz, funky/soul jazz used a bluesy harmonic style; catchy, earthy melodies; and, often, the call-and-response formulas of the black churches.

New jazz venues—concerts especially—arose during the 1950s. Annual jazz festivals sprang up and allowed the music to reach large audiences. The first international jazz festival opened in Nice, France, in 1948; in the United States, the famous Newport Jazz Festival, directed by George Wein, began in Newport, Rhode Island, in 1954. These festivals had enormous power to help or revive performers' careers. One legendary jazz story tells how Duke Ellington's 1956 performance at Newport jump started his flagging career. In addition to jazz festivals, students on

Technique and Technology

Technological Advances in the 1950s

The decade of the 1950s profited from two technological advances in recording. By the end of the 1940s, magnetic-tape recording had replaced the more limited and cumbersome metal discs. Tape recording offered several advantages:

▶ Performance editing (splicing together different parts to create a performance with fewer errors)

▶ Overdubbing (adding new parts to a previously recorded performance)

▶ Longer performance times, which encouraged the creation of longer compositions specifically for listening

▶ More-convenient live recording, when tape machines became more portable

Recording tape has several parallel tracks that enable musicians to record additional performance parts at later times. The added part is called an *overdub*. By wearing headphones, the players follow and play along with the previously recorded tracks.

© iStockphoto.com/FotografiaBasica

In current recording studios, computer-controlled equipment and digital technology permit virtually unlimited overdubbing and editing of recorded parts.

Along with tape recording, the **LP** (long-playing disc) contributed greatly to the evolution of jazz. LPs first became commercially available when Columbia released its 33⅓ rpm recordings in 1948. LPs were made with polyvinyl chloride (hence the nickname *vinyl* for records), which allowed more than twice the number of grooves on each side of the record than the 78 rpm did. The new "microgroove" records thus allowed more playing time per side—up to twenty-five minutes (versus the previous three or four). LPs and magnetic tape freed musicians to record in longer segments and to approximate live performances more closely than ever before.

college campuses in the 1950s sponsored jazz concerts that helped such groups as the Dave Brubeck Quartet and the MJQ gain visibility and popularity. Finally, jazz received a boost from the new recording technology, which allowed artists to record at length. (See the box "Technological Advances in the 1950s.")

Cool Stylists

Many artists contributed to the cool jazz style. One of the most influential was Miles Davis, with his groundbreaking pieces later collected as the album *Birth of the Cool*. Other artists and groups who played major roles include Gerry Mulligan, Chet Baker, the MJQ, Dave Brubeck, and Stan Getz.

Miles Davis and *Birth of the Cool*

A series of influential recordings for Capitol Records in 1949 and 1950, later released as *Birth of the Cool*, helped set the tone of jazz for the decade to come. Through three studio sessions, trumpeter Miles Davis led a nine-piece group in startling compositions that represented a drastic shift for Davis. Since coming to New York in 1944, he had been recording and performing consistently with bebop players, particularly Charlie Parker. In contrast to the freewheeling, loose, intense improvisations of Parker's quintet, the *Birth of the Cool* sessions exhibited careful arranging, musical restraint, and lyricism.

Davis capitalized on the cool elements of his style, which had begun to emerge in his earlier recordings: he focused his trumpet in the middle register, played without virtuosic bravura, and used more *space*, or rests between phrases. Given his natural inclination toward the cool, Davis admired the arrangements Gil Evans had created for the Claude Thornhill band. He decided to emulate Thornhill's sound with fewer instruments yet with more energy than was usually projected by the larger band. The result was his nonet, which had three rhythm players (on piano, bass, and drums) and six winds. The winds were grouped in pairs of high and low ranges: trumpet/trombone, French horn/tuba, and alto saxophone/baritone saxophone. Significantly, there was no tenor saxophone, an unusual omission for a medium-sized band. Even more striking was the use of French horn and tuba, instruments more common to the European classical tradition than to modern jazz, but part of Evans's earlier arrangements for Thornhill.

In 1948 Davis's nonet was booked for a two-week performance at New York's Royal Roost, where they alternated sets with Count Basie. With their unusual instrumentation, the nonet played to lukewarm reviews and was no longer working when the group entered the studio in 1949. Over fifteen months they recorded twelve sides. Many were initially released on 78s. In 1954 eight of the twelve compositions appeared on a 10-inch LP. Only in

The young Miles Davis signed this Fontana publicity postcard for a fan in Belgium.

1957 were the majority of the recordings released under the title *Birth of the Cool*.

Gil Evans was not the only arranger for the group. Baritone saxophonist Gerry Mulligan, pianist John Lewis, and trumpeter Johnny Carisi all contributed charts and compositions. Many of the arrangements, such as Carisi's "Israel," featured the horns in counterpoint, creating a web of parts moving independently. Others, such as "Budo" (a slightly revised version of Bud Powell's "Hallucinations"), paid tribute to bop, but the nonet version purged the music of its demonic energy. The harmonies were lush, the writing often dense. Gil Evans's arrangement of "Moon Dreams"

Miles Davis,
Birth of the Cool,
"Budo" (1949)

was a slow, dreamy work, with virtually no improvisation. In some works, arrangers abandoned the nearly universal jazz practice of playing compositions in eight-bar sections; for example, the first A section in Mulligan's arrangement of "Godchild" is eight and a half bars.

LISTENING GUIDE
"Jeru"

Track 33

Miles Davis and His Orchestra: "Jeru" (Mulligan), from *Birth of the Cool*. Capitol T762. New York, January 21, 1949. Davis, trumpet and leader; Kai Winding, trombone; Junior Collins, French horn; Bill Barber, tuba; Lee Konitz, alto saxophone; Gerry Mulligan, baritone saxophone, composer-arranger; Al Haig, piano; Joe Schulman, bass; Max Roach, drums.

The Main Point   Gerry Mulligan's "Jeru" (the title was Mulligan's nickname) is a fine example of the *Birth of the Cool* recordings. The piece features a complex formal structure that in many ways anticipates third-stream practice.

AA section—Head, 16 bars

0:00   No introduction; the head is in AABA form. The whole band plays and repeats the eight-bar A section.

B section—Head, 12 bars with meter changes

0:21   The bridge is irregular: twelve bars with various meter changes in measures 2 through 8, then back to 4/4 for measures 9 through 12.

0:30   The baritone saxophone has a solo for the last four bars of the bridge.

A section—Head, 9 bars

0:36   The return of the A section features a one-bar extension of the form leading to the Davis trumpet solo.

Davis trumpet solo—32 bars (AABA)

0:48   Davis's solo consists of a regular 8 + 8 + 8 + 8 grouping, dropping the irregular groupings heard previously in the head.

AA section—18 bars as 9 + 9, band alternates with Mulligan baritone solo

1:31   When the band re-enters, the arrangement features a section that is in stop time. Here the meter changes to 3/4 for four bars, then to 2/4 for one bar before the regular 4/4 time returns in measure 6.

1:35   Mulligan solos through measures 6 through 9 in 4/4.

1:41   The format repeats for the second A.

BA section—16 bars, last part of Mulligan solo

1:51   For the bridge and final A section of Mulligan's solo, the form is straightforward: two 8-bar sections.

AABA out-chorus—Irregular as 8 + 8 + 12, final A extended with coda

2:13   The two A sections from the head are dramatically recomposed for the climactic out-chorus.

2:35   The 12-bar B section is similar to its earlier presentation: various meter changes in measures 2 through 8, then back to 4/4 for measures 9 through 12.

2:50   The final A section uses the out-chorus theme but is extended with a coda. The final chord uses a dissonant voicing, with the baritone saxophone on the major seventh of the E♭ maj7 chord.

Listen to this music in an animated Active Listening Guide available at the text website.

Davis's *Birth of the Cool* recordings were extremely influential for the cool jazz players of the 1950s for the following reasons:

▶ Nine-piece ensemble featuring balance between written and improvised sections

▶ Quiet dynamics and unhurried pace

▶ Smooth blend of the horns, which include instruments more characteristic of European classical music (such as French horn)

▶ Complex formal structure that anticipates third-stream practice

Many of the players on *Birth of the Cool* were strongly associated with cool jazz throughout the 1950s. Alto saxophonist Lee Konitz, a student of pianist Lennie Tristano, brought a light, airy, vibratoless sound to the horn. He went on to record as a leader. Baritone saxophonist Gerry Mulligan gained increasing fame during the decade for his pianoless quartet with Chet Baker (discussed in the next section). Pianist John Lewis, a veteran of Dizzy Gillespie's band, gained prominence with the MJQ. In the late 1950s, Gil Evans collaborated again with Miles Davis on the significant Columbia recordings *Miles Ahead*, *Porgy and Bess*, and *Sketches of Spain*.

The *Birth of the Cool* recordings had an enormous influence. Their emphasis on subtlety and their balance of composition and improvisation provided an alternative model to bebop. Jazz critic Nat Hentoff described the influence of *Birth of the Cool* as follows:

> These records were comparable in their impact on a new generation of jazz musicians to the Louis Armstrong Hot Five and Hot Seven records of the 1920s, some of the Duke Ellington and Basie records of the Thirties, and the records made by Parker and his associates in the early and middle Forties.[1]

Gerry Mulligan and Chet Baker

Mulligan's role in creating the *Birth of the Cool* sessions has sometimes been undervalued. Not only did he play baritone saxophone and compose "Jeru," "Venus de Milo," and "Rocker," but he also arranged "Darn That Dream" and "Godchild." After completing the *Birth of the Cool* recordings, Mulligan hitchhiked to California and began playing and arranging on the West Coast. Although born in New York in 1927, from the time he arrived in California, Mulligan was associated with West Coast jazz.

After leading a ten-piece group in a recording modeled on the *Birth of the Cool* instrumentation, Mulligan formed his most famous group while performing on Monday nights at a Los Angeles club called The Haig. The quartet featured Mulligan on baritone saxophone, Chet Baker on trumpet, Bob Whitlock on bass, and Chico Hamilton on drums. Instrumentation that lacked

Gerry Mulligan in a publicity photograph.

Photo courtesy of the Morgan Collection

an instrument that played chords, such as a piano, was unusual. The group developed an airy, open sound based on ingenious counterpoint of the baritone saxophone and the trumpet—a technique that allowed the horn players to weave spontaneous lines and create call-and-response patterns. Without piano the group exhibited a spareness that operated at low volume.

The quartet quickly found success. They recorded their first hit, "My Funny Valentine," in 1952. In this piece listeners could hear the plaintive and fragile trumpet style of Chet Baker (1929–1988). Baker, who hailed from Oklahoma, was only twenty-two years old at the time of the recording and earlier that year had performed on a tour of southern California with Charlie Parker. Tall and photogenic (producers considered him for movie roles before his heroin habit proved too consuming), Baker played quietly, with a fragile and delicate lyricism, and was also well regarded as a vocalist. Listeners and critics compared Baker's trumpet playing to that of Miles Davis, although Baker played with a softer tone. Baker's singing style closely resembled that of his trumpet: quiet, relaxed, and with a shade of vibrato at the end of a phrase.

With the band's success and his newly won recognition in the polls of *Down Beat* and *Metronome*, Baker left the group over a financial disagreement with Mulligan. He continued to perform throughout the 1950s and recorded frequently, often with West Coast pianist Russ Freeman. After spending four months on drug-related charges at Riker's Island prison in New York City, Baker moved to

Chet Baker,
Chet Baker Sings,
"My Funny
Valentine" (1952)

Tall and photogenic, Chet Baker was considered for movie roles before his heroin habit proved too consuming.

Europe in 1959. His heroin addiction continued to plague him, however, and he was arrested repeatedly in Europe. He achieved something of a comeback in the 1970s and 1980s but died tragically in Amsterdam after falling from a window.

When Baker left the group in 1954, Mulligan continued to lead his own bands, a sextet as well as newer versions of his quartet. His performance at the Salle Pleyel in Paris featured trombonist Bob Brookmeyer; a later version of the sextet included saxophonist Zoot Sims. After leading the thirteen-piece Concert Jazz Band in the late 1950s and early 1960s, Mulligan continued to work as both a leader and a sideman, playing with Dave Brubeck from 1968 to 1972. He also composed several film scores. In his later years, Mulligan became one of the most popular artists on the jazz concert scene. He died in 1996.

Along with Duke Ellington's baritone saxophonist Harry Carney, Mulligan was probably the most well-known and celebrated baritone saxophonist in jazz. He took the baritone out

of the big band and placed it in a small-group setting. During the 1950s only Serge Chaloff and Pepper Adams rivaled Mulligan as improvisers on the instrument.

The Modern Jazz Quartet

Ironically, the group known as one of the leading exponents of cool jazz started out by playing bebop with Dizzy Gillespie. The original members of the Modern Jazz Quartet (MJQ)—pianist John Lewis, drummer Kenny Clarke, bassist Ray Brown, and vibraphonist Milt Jackson—came together in Gillespie's big band in 1946. Five years later they began recording as the Milt Jackson Quartet. After Percy Heath (1923–2005) replaced Ray Brown on the bass, they issued their first records as the MJQ on the Prestige label. Connie Kay (1923–1994) became the drummer after Kenny Clarke left the group in 1955.

The MJQ became celebrated for their polished, refined performances. Like many jazz groups of the 1950s, the MJQ attempted to avoid the stigma of the disreputable jazz musician and to bring greater respectability to jazz performances. In formal tuxedos they performed with the serious demeanor of the classical musician—and they filled concert halls.

Milt Jackson (1923–1999) and John Lewis (1920–2001) were the fire and ice of the band. Jackson, the primary soloist, played an exuberant, swinging, blues-based vibraphone above the subtle accompaniments and

The Modern Jazz Quartet in the mid-fifties. *Left to right*: Percy Heath, Connie Kay, John Lewis, and Milt Jackson.

countermelodies of pianist Lewis. In a style that often featured single-line counterpoint rather than the chordal punctuation typical of bebop pianists, Lewis's simplicity and restraint on the piano contrasted well with Jackson's ebullience.

The band was known not only for improvisation but also for sophisticated arrangements and compositions. John Lewis was the primary architect. He often sought to merge elements of jazz with those inspired by European classical techniques—as the title of their album *Blues on Bach* suggests. For example, counterpoint figured in Lewis's accompaniments, and he based some of his compositions, such as "Vendome," "Concorde," "Versailles," and "Three Windows," on the Baroque technique of the **fugue**.

Lewis consciously attempted to develop extended compositions and forms—to move away from the 32-bar frameworks that were the mainstay of jazz. As he noted in an address in 1958:

> The audience for jazz can be widened if we strengthen our work with structure. If there is more of a reason for what's going on, there'll be more overall sense, and therefore, more interest for the listener. I do not

think, however, that the sections in this "structured jazz"—both the improvised and written sections—should take on too much complexity. The total effect must be within the mind's ability to appreciate through the ear.[2]

One of the best examples of Lewis's interest in this "structured jazz" can be heard in his "Versailles" (Listening Guide, Track 34), a jazz composition that uses techniques of the fugue.

A **fugue** is a Baroque form characterized by continuous counterpoint based on a principal melodic idea called the **subject**. At the beginning of a typical fugue, in a section known as the exposition, each voice (or part) in the texture enters by stating the subject.

Third-stream music blends jazz with European concert music. In many instances third-stream composers create concert works that allow for improvisation within larger-scale structures influenced by both jazz and concert music.

LISTENING GUIDE   Track 34
"Versailles (Porte de Versailles)"

The Modern Jazz Quartet: "Versailles" (John Lewis), from *Fontessa*. Atlantic 1231. Hackensack, New Jersey, January 22, 1956. Milt Jackson, vibraphone; John Lewis, piano; Percy Heath, bass; Connie Kay, drums.

The Main Point "Versailles" illustrates how jazz players sought to merge principles of improvised jazz with classical music, a direction that Gunther Schuller dubbed **third-stream music**. "Versailles" is a jazz version of the fugue, a compositional procedure most closely associated with composer Johann Sebastian Bach (1685–1750). The fugue begins with an individual melody (the **subject**), which then appears consecutively in different melodic voices. In "Versailles" the vibraphone initially states the subject before the piano, then bass, immediately imitate that melodic idea. The result is anything but academic, and the performance exhibits the sparkling swing for which the quartet was celebrated.

The improvisational sections are in AABA form and adopt rhythm changes (the chord progression from George Gershwin's "I Got Rhythm") for the A sections. The B sections depart from rhythm changes, however; such adaptations of rhythm changes are common in jazz practice. Notice that pianist John Lewis does not accompany the solos with characteristic comping—rather than play syncopated chords, he accompanies with individual melodic lines. This contributes further to the sense of polyphony (simultaneous musical lines) characteristic of the fugue. The work is highly structured, and later statements of the subject alternate with the improvisations. Although the dynamics are restrained, a frequent characteristic of cool jazz, vibraphonist Milt Jackson plays with energy and drive.

Statement of fugal subject—C major, 24 bars

0:00   The vibraphone begins alone, stating the four-bar subject. The drummer begins halfway through the subject, playing beats 2 and 4 on the triangle. The subject is then answered by the piano (0:04), which plays the same melodic idea (transposed up a fourth), while the vibes continue to play. The bassist follows (0:09) with the subject as both vibes and piano continue to play.

0:14   The process repeats with vibes (0:14), piano (0:18), and finally vibes and bass together (0:23) each playing versions of the subject while the other instruments continue.

Piano solo—C major, 32 bars as AABA

0:28   The piano solo begins as the drums and bass move to traditional jazz roles, with walking bass and timekeeping on the cymbal (rather than the triangle). Notice that vibraphonist Milt Jackson accompanies by playing melodic riffs that are derived from the subject. The two 8-bar sections use rhythm changes.

0:46   In contrast to the rhythm changes of the A section, the 8-bar B section uses a chord progression that consistently moves down a fifth. This creates a stylized harmonic progression, probably intended to invoke an eighteenth-century atmosphere, one that recalls Bach's fugues. Note that there is no harmonic comping, but the melodic ideas imply the descending fifth harmonic progression.

0:55   The final A section returns to rhythm changes, again with vibraphonist Jackson accompanying Lewis's piano improvisation.

Transitional section and return of subject (in G)

1:04   A four-bar transitional section uses the stylized harmonic progression heard in the previous B section of Lewis's solo. It creates a move to a new key center of G major.

1:09   Like a Bach fugue, later statements of the subject often occur in a new key. Here the subject statement appears in G (rather than in C, where it originally appeared), initially played by vibes, piano (transposed up a fourth), bass, and vibes. Notice that the drummer returns here to playing accompaniment on triangle.

Bass solo—G major, 32 bars as AABA

1:27   The bass solo begins, structured similarly to the piano solo, but now in G major. This key shift to the dominant mimics the motion that frequently takes place within fugues. Notice that in addition to the bass solo, both piano and vibes play separate 2-bar accompanimental riffs. Those three players create three layers of melodic activity, enhancing the sense of polyphony.

1:45   The B section again uses the stylized descending fifth chord progression.

1:54   The A section again returns to rhythm changes, as the piano and vibes accompany the bassist with melodic riffs.

Transitional section and return of subject (in F)

2:03   Again, a descending fifth stylized harmonic progression brings about a move to a new key, this time to F.

2:08   All the players improvise for four bars.

2:12   The subject returns, stated first in vibes, then piano, and finally bass. The subject is in the key of F major, the subdominant of the opening key of C major. This transposition to F again mimics the typical harmonic motion that might be heard in a fugue.

Vibes solo—F major, 32 bars as AABA

2:26   As the vibraphone solo begins, the bassist returns to walking bass and the drummer to keeping time on the cymbal (rather than the triangle). Jackson's solo is exuberant and swinging. Lewis accompanies on piano with individual melodic lines.

2:37   Jackson plays a blues-based idea with repeated notes, a trademark sound of his.

2:44   The 8-bar B section uses the stylized descending fifth progression. The group returns to the final A section (2:52) as Jackson negotiates a tricky melodic figure on the vibraphone, providing a climax for the performance before the return to the subject statements.

Transitional section and final statements of subject—C major

3:01 A four-bar transitional section uses the descending fifth progression to return to the original key of C major. This tonal move is in keeping with the formal plan of a fugue, which returns to the original key at the end.

3:05 Many fugues end directly following a "pedal point," a climactic section that places the dominant of the key in the bass. Here, in a clever nod to that tradition, the piano and bass repeat the dominant pitch in a low register.

3:14 The final ingenious homage to fugal tradition comes at the very end, in which each of the instruments (piano, vibes, and bass) enter in overlapping statements of the subject, a technique known as **stretto**.

 Listen to this music in an animated Active Listening Guide available at the text website.

The MJQ performance of "Versailles" exhibits the following:

▶ A jazz fugue—a combination of jazz and classical music principles representative of third-stream practice.

▶ A highly structured and arranged composition with moves to different keys, reflecting fugal practice.

▶ The use of melodic rather than chordal accompanimental textures in the piano and vibes, creating polyphony (simultaneous melodic lines) typical of fugues.

▶ A use of restrained dynamics typical of cool jazz, but with a sparkling sense of swing.

▶ Improvisational sections with harmonic progressions that combine standard jazz practice of "rhythm changes" (A sections) with stylized harmonic progressions that evoke the eighteenth century (B sections).

▶ Use of vibraphone by one of its preeminent practitioners, Milt Jackson.

Even more ambitious were collaborations with Gunther Schuller, the composer who had coined the term *third stream*. The MJQ made a recording entitled *Third Stream Music* with the Beaux Arts String Quartet and performed Schuller's *Concertino for Jazz Quartet and Orchestra* with the Stuttgart Symphony.

The MJQ broke up in 1974 because Milt Jackson wanted to pursue a solo career, but it reunited in 1981 to seek concert bookings. They continued to perform together for different tours through the 1990s.

Dave Brubeck

One of the most commercially successful jazz musicians of the 1950s and 1960s was pianist and composer Dave Brubeck (1920–2012). Brubeck's quartet, with alto saxophonist Paul Desmond, came together in 1951 and gained visibility through concerts on college campuses. Brubeck in turn brought academic respectability to jazz by performing and recording at such schools as Oberlin College, Ohio University, and the University of Michigan during a time when the music was considered inappropriate for campus concerts—jazz had long been performed on campus, but usually only at parties. Brubeck's success led to his appearance on the cover of *Time* magazine in 1954. Moreover, he consistently won the *Down Beat* popularity polls throughout the fifties and sixties. Critics admired Brubeck's writing (and Desmond's improvising), but they sometimes vilified his piano style as heavy handed and unswinging.

Brubeck grew up listening to Fats Waller and swing, but while a student at Mills College during the midforties, he studied composition with French composer Darius Milhaud, famous as a member of Les Six, a group of French composers. Some of Milhaud's compositions from the 1920s made use of jazz elements. Under this influence Brubeck embraced a style of composition and improvisation that drew on the European preoccupation with form. Many of Brubeck's compositions resonated with the contrapuntal techniques learned from his teacher.

In 1946 Brubeck organized an octet with like-minded students to create jazz works with a European sensibility;

Stretto refers to a series of instruments or parts entering with overlapping statements of a fugue subject

The cover of the Dave Brubeck classic. *Left to right*: Paul Desmond, composer, on saxophone; Joe Morello on drums; Eugene Wright on bass; and Dave Brubeck on piano. Based in California, far from New York's Fifty-second Street, Brubeck was especially popular on college campuses.

the titles included "Rondo," "Prelude," and "Fugue on Bop Themes." Brubeck's arrangement of "Just the Way You Look Tonight" wove together the main theme and the bridge of the composition, a contrapuntal experiment rarely heard in jazz arranging. Although the Brubeck octet was far less influential than Miles Davis's nonet from *Birth of the Cool*, the two groups had some interesting features in common: the groups were similarly sized, and their arrangements juxtaposed written and improvised sections with considerable counterpoint.

The quartet with Paul Desmond was the group that made Brubeck famous. Originally from San Francisco, Desmond (1924–1977) played alto saxophone with a liquid, creamy sound. Consistently inventive and lyrical, he rarely played a wasted note. In 1959 Desmond penned the group's most famous composition, "Take Five," a catchy, bluesy melody in 5/4, a meter rarely explored in jazz. (Drummer Max Roach was one of the few jazz musicians to have used 5/4 prior to Brubeck's band.)

By the time "Take Five" was recorded on Brubeck's 1959 album, *Time Out*, Brubeck's famous quartet had taken shape: Brubeck on piano, Desmond on alto, Joe Morello (b. 1928) on drums, and Eugene Wright (b. 1923) on bass. The group was celebrated for its exploration of unusual meters. Brubeck wrote "Blue Rondo à la Turk" (Listening Guide, Track 35) in a 9/8 meter that he subdivided into groupings 2 + 2 + 2 + 3.

Dave Brubeck
Time Out "Take Five"
(1959)

LISTENING GUIDE
"Blue Rondo à la Turk"

Track 35

Dave Brubeck Quartet: "Blue Rondo à la Turk" (Brubeck), from *Time Out*. Columbia CL 1397. New York, New York, August 8, 1959. Dave Brubeck, piano; Paul Desmond, alto saxophone; Eugene Wright, bass; Joe Morello, drums.

The Main Point   Like the MJQ's "Versailles," the Dave Brubeck Quartet's performance of "Blue Rondo à la Turk" melds principles of jazz with classical music. As a result, it provides another example of third-stream music. Its clever organization juxtaposes the head statements—featuring unusual metric groupings—with the improvisations, based on the 12-bar blues.

The unusual metric organization in the head statements of "Blue Rondo" use groupings of 9 beats. They appear primarily in irregular groupings of 2 + 2 + 2 + 3, occasionally alternating with the more conventional triple groupings of 3 + 3 + 3. Brubeck claimed that the music he heard in Turkey inspired his use of the irregular groupings. Following this opening material, the group moves to the improvisations that feature the 12-bar blues, walking bass, and 4/4 meter, but not before a transitional chorus directly alternates the blues improvisation with the irregular metric groupings.

The form of the head statements reveals Brubeck's keen interest in European music and ideas of form. He takes as his point of departure the "rondo," a European classical form that alternates a recurring section (the "refrain") with other sections (the "episodes"). As a result, the opening head statement is highly structured, as the refrain (or A section) alternates with four other sections, creating an ABACADAE form. There is an effective climax in the E section, just before the alto saxophone improvisation begins. Brubeck abbreviates the form during the final head statement following the improvisations.

The title, then, calls attention in a pithy way to the disparate elements that make up the piece: blues, rondo, and Turkish rhythms. It is an effective performance that combines Brubeck's compositional ambitions with Desmond's cool and sparkling sound.

Head statement—Rondo as ABACADAE

0:00   The piano states the A section (the refrain) in F major. Listen for the irregular groupings, stating 2 + 2 + 2 + 3 beats three times, before followed by a grouping of 3 + 3 + 3. This creates the overall pattern heard throughout the entire head. The piano begins unaccompanied. The bass and drums appear midway through this section.

0:11   The alto saxophone plays the melody to the B section, now in A minor.

0:22   The piano returns with the melody to the A section refrain.

0:34   The piano also plays the melody to the new material heard at the C section.

0:45   Saxophonist Paul Desmond now plays a harmonization of the original tune of the A section refrain.

0:56   The piano alone has the D theme.

1:07   Alto saxophone again plays a harmonization of the A section refrain.

1:19   The E section is the longest section, and the melody moves upwards to the climax at 1:38, with Brubeck playing full chordal voicings. At the climax, the beats become organized regularly in groups of 3. This provides the pulse for the following 4/4 section. The section ends in A major.

Transitional section and alto saxophone improvisation

1:52   The ingenious transitional section moves to walking bass in 4/4 meter, as Paul Desmond begins his alto saxophone improvisation over the 12-bar blues. However, after two bars, the group returns to segments from the rondo refrain, with Brubeck playing the melody. This alternation continues twice more, creating an unusual and direct juxtaposition of the blues with the irregular metric groupings of the rondo.

2:13   Desmond's improvisation now moves to the 12-bar blues in 4/4, and the group leaves behind the irregular metric groupings of the rondo. The solo demonstrates some of Desmond's finest attributes as a quintessential cool jazz improviser: his unhurried pacing, clear sound without much vibrato, and elegant use of space. Brubeck does not provide accompaniment during the saxophone solo, enhancing the sense of space and the relaxed feel.

2:37   At the beginning of Desmond's second 12-bar blues chorus, he plays a slide up to a blue note.

3:02   Again, Desmond plays a blues-based idea. Although his playing exhibits significant space, he occasionally moves into faster sixteenth-note phrases, here and in his final chorus (beginning at 3:26). The excerpt fades at the end of his solo.

Transitional section and return to head—Rondo as AE (Times in parentheses apply to complete recording of "Blue Rondo à la Turk" rather than to excerpt)

3:53
(5:32)   This section follows the piano solo (not included in excerpt). The group returns to the transitional section heard earlier at 1:52, an alternation of two bar ideas (with alto saxophone improvisation) and a segment from the A section rondo refrain.

4:12 (5:51)	The rondo refrain returns in its entirety, providing one last return of the A section. The piano plays the melody, then joined by alto saxophone harmonizing the melody.
4:23 (6:02)	Rather than repeating the entire ABACADAE form heard at the beginning of the performance, the group moves immediately to the final E section that includes the climax. The piece ends in A major with a drum roll on the tom-toms.

 Listen to this music in an animated Active Listening Guide available at the text website.

Overall, "Blue Rondo à la Turk" demonstrates the following:

▶ A third-stream example that juxtaposes the blues, the rondo, and irregular rhythms

▶ Jazz improvisation by Paul Desmond with a light, airy tone and cool ambience

▶ Use of 12-bar blues in the improvisation

▶ Structured compositional design of the head indebted to classical musical principles

Although Brubeck became well known as a jazz pianist, his principal interest was composition. Not surprisingly, he disbanded his group in 1967 to devote more time to composing. He has since written ballets, an oratorio, cantatas, and other music for jazz groups and orchestras, while occasionally performing and recording with jazz groups. In the late 1990s, he intensified his touring schedule and recorded with his sons, keyboardist Darius Brubeck, trombonist–electric bassist Chris Brubeck, and drummer Danny Brubeck.

Stan Getz

Like Paul Desmond, many of the cool saxophonists avoided the influence of Charlie Parker. Instead, they looked back to tenor saxophonist Lester "Pres" (or "Prez") Young for a lighter, airier sound and a more relaxed approach. As tenor saxophonist Stan Getz noted by his aptly named composition, they sought "Prezervation."

Stan Getz
Getz/Gilberto,
"Desafinado" (1963)

The young Stan Getz on the cover of a jazz samba collection.

Earlier, we mentioned that many prominent disciples of Lester Young were white players who formed the saxophone section known as the Four Brothers from Woody Herman's Herd of the late 1940s. They included tenor saxophonists Stan Getz, Zoot Sims, Al Cohn, and Jimmy Giuffre. Of these Getz won the most praise. Born in Philadelphia in 1927, Getz came to Herman's band in 1947 after making his first recording at age sixteen with Jack Teagarden and having played with both Stan Kenton and Benny Goodman.

Getz was certainly capable of playing virtuosic bebop—his 1949 recording of "Crazy Chords" traveled through the blues in all twelve keys at a hair-raising tempo—but he also had a distinctive tone that shone beautifully in ballads. His sound was breathy and relaxed, with evident vibrato, yet surprisingly strong and centered. Getz's solo feature in Woody Herman's 1948 version of "Early Autumn" established him as a formidable lyrical improviser. Soon after, Getz left Herman to lead small groups. Although problems with drug addiction led him to live in Scandinavia for much of the late 1950s, he returned to the United States in 1961.

Once back in the States, Getz embarked on several projects. His 1961 album, *Focus*, featured daring string arrangements by Eddie Sauter that overtly merged jazz with elements of classical music. Several of his recordings combined Brazilian rhythms with jazz in a fusion known as **bossa nova**. The most famous of these was "The Girl from Ipanema" (Listening Guide, Track 36), sung by Brazilian vocalist Astrud Gilberto. In 1964 this tune became a hit that brought Getz much commercial popularity.

His landmark record, *Jazz Samba* (1962), contributed significantly to the bossa nova craze and catapulted his name into public consciousness. Rarely did another post-fifties mainstream jazz musician, with the possible exception of Julian "Cannonball" Adderley, achieve Getz's commercial success.

When the popularity of bossa nova began to ebb in the late 1960s, Getz continued to perform widely, often with many of the best-known names in jazz, including Chick Corea and Bill Evans. Other notable collaborations toward the end of his career included work with pianists Joanne Brackeen, Kenny Barron, and Andy LaVerne. Getz died in 1991.

The **bossa nova** is a Latin jazz style that developed from Brazilian music in the late 1950s and early 1960s. Stan Getz was prominent among jazz players with bossa nova hits.

LISTENING GUIDE
"The Girl from Ipanema"
Track 36

Stan Getz and João Gilberto: "The Girl from Ipanema" (Jobim, deMoraes, Gimbel), from *Getz/Gilberto*. Verve 810 048-2. New York, March 18–19, 1963. Stan Getz, tenor saxophone; Antonio Carlos Jobim, piano; João Gilberto, guitar and vocals; Astrud Gilberto, vocals; Tommy Williams, bass; Milton Banana, drums.

The Main Point   The most famous of Getz's bossa nova releases was "The Girl from Ipanema," which included vocals by Brazilian vocalist Astrud Gilberto. It became a 1964 popular hit, moving to number five on the *Billboard* top singles chart that July and bringing Getz significant commercial popularity. The song combined the cool, unruffled ambience of the Brazilian bossa nova with Getz's unmistakably rich lyrical sound. (It may be useful to compare Getz's tenor saxophone sound with that of John Coltrane, who maintained an edgier and more urgent tone. Listen to Track 42.) The entire album, entitled *Getz/Gilberto*, included six songs by Brazilian composer Antonio Carlos Jobim, who wrote many popular bossa nova and samba compositions; he played piano on this track.

Introduction and first chorus—32 bars as AABA

0:00   The recording begins with the sound of acoustic guitar and wordless vocals by João Gilberto. The quiet introduction is placid, with subtle syncopations in the guitar comping as well as in the wordless vocals.

0:07   The opening A section begins, and throughout this initial chorus, Gilberto sings in Portuguese. The vocal style is intimate and conversational, and never rushed or frenzied. There is a sense of naïve innocence to the vocals, contributing to the sense of space and moody seductiveness of the performance. At the second A section (0:22), the bass and drums enter quietly, with the drum accompaniment focused on the hi-hat. During the bridge (B section), the piano begins playing simple fills, usually added when the vocalist is not singing. Throughout here and the final A section of this chorus (1:06), listen for the guitarist's soft and syncopated comping.

Second chorus—AABA

1:21   At the second chorus, singer Astrud Gilberto (João's wife at that time) sings the lyrics in English. Her vocal sound is even, cool, and restrained. At the bridge (1:50), she imparts a hint of seductive innocence by occasionally singing a little below pitch.

Third chorus—Saxophone solo, AABA

2:34   Getz begins his solo by paraphrasing the melody. His playing is serene and spare, and every note exhibits his intensely personalized sound: light, airy, and coloristic. During the second A section (2:49), he again refers to the melody, but now weaves improvised lines around it. At the bridge (3:03), his tone becomes a little edgier, and his last A section (3:33) now syncopates the opening three notes of the melody. Notice how he often follows short melodic ideas with longer ones, as if making up for lost time.

Fourth chorus—Piano solo (AA) and final vocal (BA)

3:47   Perhaps inspired by Getz's syncopation of the melody at the end of his solo, pianist Jobim also syncopates the melody, playing it in a chordal texture, avoiding the single-line textures that might be expected in a piano solo. Like the saxophone solo, the solo uses a significant degree of space.

4:17   The vocals return at the bridge, as Getz plays fills around Astrud Gilberto's vocal line. During the final A section (4:49), that dialogue continues, with Getz playing subtle syncopated pitches. The song closes with a "tag," that is, the group and singer repeat the final line of the song ("She just doesn't see"), and the song ends with a studio-created fade.

Listen to this music in an animated Active Listening Guide available at the text website.

Lennie Tristano

Although he never reached the level of popularity and commercial success that some of the other cool jazz players did, pianist Lennie Tristano earned widespread acclaim from many jazz critics and musicians. Tristano (1919–1978), a blind pianist born in Chicago, founded an informal school of musicians. Among his students were saxophonists Lee Konitz and Warne Marsh and guitarist Billy Bauer. Konitz and Marsh recorded more frequently and received more visibility than Tristano himself did.

Tristano's playing exhibited virtuosic cool precision. He sounded relaxed even at breakneck tempos, tossing off long, even streams of eighth notes with surprising syncopations and **cross-rhythms**. Many of his improvisations also made use of the **locked-hands style** of Milt Buckner (a style also used during the 1950s by George Shearing). (See Music Example 8-1 on page 242 and listen to Track 9 of the 🅟 Audio Primer to hear an example of locked-hands style.) Although some performers found Tristano's playing overly intellectual and precise, he nevertheless fashioned a viable alternative to bebop ensemble playing and improvisation.

In contrast to the fiery bebop drumming of Max Roach or Roy Haynes, Tristano sometimes insisted that his drummer use brushes to accompany the soloists quietly. (Listen to Track 35 of the 🅟 Audio Primer to hear an example of brushes.) Often making use of the eighth-note musical language of bebop, Tristano managed to avoid many of bebop's clichés. He preferred instead to explore contrapuntal textures and fiendishly difficult unison figures.

Upon moving to New York in 1946, Tristano quickly gained critical recognition when *Metronome* magazine

named him its "Musician of the Year" for 1947. Tristano's 1949 sextet recordings—with his students Konitz, Marsh, and Bauer, along with bassist Arnold Fishkin and various drummers—showed Tristano's distinctly modern outlook. For example, while opening with a standard chord progression, "Tautology" unfolded in surprising harmonic twists. Tristano wrote the melody in a rigorous contrapuntal style that encompassed all twelve notes of the chromatic scale.

Some of Tristano's compositions were even more exploratory. Anticipating the *free jazz* movement by a decade, his 1949 recordings of "Intuition" and "Digression" were collective improvisations without preset melodies, meters, or harmonic progressions. In the mid-fifties Tristano investigated the possibilities of overdubbing. His "Turkish Mambo" boasted three separate piano tracks in which he created left-hand patterns of five, six, or seven beats—all conflicting with each other and all beneath a right-hand improvisation.

Cross-rhythms refer to the performance of simultaneous and contrasting rhythms, such as patterns with duple and triple groupings. Superimposing one rhythmic pattern on another creates a cross-rhythm. Cross-rhythms are sometimes called **polyrhythms**.

Locked-hands style is a mode of performance in which the pianist plays a four-note chord in the right hand and doubles the top note with the left hand an octave below. The hands move together in a "locked" rhythmic pattern as they follow the same rhythm. This style is also called **block-chord or full-chord style**. (Listen to Track 9 of the 🅟 Audio Primer for an example of locked-hands style.)

Tristano's influence as a teacher was legendary. His protégés studied and learned the classic solos of such jazz masters as Louis Armstrong, Earl Hines, Lester Young, Charlie Parker, and Bud Powell. An admirer of the contrapuntal organization of J. S. Bach, Tristano had his students performed arrangements of Bach's *Inventions*.

Alto saxophonist Lee Konitz (b. 1927) became the best-known player of the Tristano circle. Konitz cultivated a light, airy tone on the alto, using almost no vibrato. Like many other cool saxophonists, his sound and his style rejected the intimidating speed and edgy timbre of Charlie Parker. Instead, he offered an alternative approach to the alto saxophone by bringing to the instrument the dry timbre of Lester Young's tenor sound and by avoiding many of Parker's bebop licks. In addition to playing with Tristano, Konitz performed with the Claude Thornhill band and joined several Thornhill alumni in Miles Davis's *Birth of the Cool* recordings. He also won the *Metronome* poll for 1954 (as did Tristano and Tristano's student Billy Bauer), and he performed with the Metronome All-Star Band of poll winners the following year.

The 1950 version of the Metronome All-Star band included—along with Konitz, Tristano, and Bauer—trumpeter Dizzy Gillespie, drummer Max Roach, clarinetist Buddy DeFranco, trombonist Kai Winding, tenor saxophonist Stan Getz, and baritone saxophonist Serge Chaloff. Their recording of Tristano's "No Figs," a complex and difficult work, was particularly successful. Tristano wrote this recomposition of "Indiana" (a tune from 1917) in triplets and sixteenth notes, creating a dense harmonic web for the horns, guitar, and piano. Konitz's solo, with his characteristic legato, smooth, and light tone, remained in the upper register of the horn. Tristano's blisteringly fast solo, in quadruple time, was all the more astonishing for his harmonizations in a block-chord style.

Konitz redefined his approach in the mid-fifties, offering a simpler, more concentrated style. Despite his cool label, he also played down-home blues, as in "Cork 'n' Bib" from his 1956 *Inside Hi-Fi* record. As late as 1975, he rejoined fellow Tristano student Warne Marsh for a recording entitled *Jazz Exchange*. His subsequent bands, particularly his nonet modeled on *Birth of the Cool* instrumentation, have perpetuated the cool jazz tradition, although he has experimented with other approaches.

Jazz on the West Coast

The musical aesthetic of cool jazz, in part an alternative to bebop, became a touchstone for many bands and performers of the 1950s. This was particularly true for players on the West Coast. Shelly Manne, a highly visible drummer at the time, acknowledged the importance of Miles Davis and described some of the fundamental characteristics of the West Coast music scene during the 1950s:

> I think the main influence on West Coast Jazz, if one record could be an influence, was the album Miles

Davis made called *Birth of the Cool*. That kind of writing and playing was closer to what we were trying to do, closer to the way a lot of us felt, out on the west coast. . . . It had a lot to do not only with just improvisation and swing. It was the main character of the music we liked—the chance for the composer to be challenged too. To write some new kind of material for jazz musicians where the solos and the improvisation became part of the whole and you couldn't tell where the writing ended and the improvisation began.[3]

The term **West Coast jazz** has often been used interchangeably with *cool jazz*, although they are not synonymous. Not all cool jazz players lived in California, and not all West Coast musicians played cool jazz. Nevertheless, several jazz players in and around Los Angeles were considered significant figures. Many of them had been affiliated with the postwar bands of Woody Herman and of Stan Kenton and had settled in California. They earned their livings performing in the studio music industry and at jazz clubs such as the Lighthouse and The Haig.

The big band of pianist Stan Kenton (1911–1979) was, for some, "the starting point for West Coast jazz."[4] Kenton's band earned immense popularity during the late 1940s as well as intense condemnation from critics who

> "Let's face it," shrilled one critic of Kenton's band, "this is the loudest band ever."

considered it unswinging, bombastic, and pretentious. "Let's face it," shrilled one critic, "this is the loudest band ever."[5] In trying to avoid any of the old associations of jazz with dance music, Kenton championed what he called "progressive jazz," named after his 1949 twenty-piece band. Kenton envisioned concert works, and he and staff arrangers Pete Rugolo, Bill Holman, and Bill Russo wrote arrangements with such titles as "Artistry in Rhythm," "Artistry in Bolero," "Fantasy," and "Opus in Pastels."

Although Kenton's arrangements often emphasized improvisations less than written compositional structures, his band included significant soloists strongly associated with jazz on the West Coast, such as Lee Konitz, Art Pepper, Stan Getz, Zoot Sims, and Bud Shank. (All these saxophonists were strongly indebted to Lester Young's playing.) Art Pepper (1925–1982) was the leading saxophone soloist of the Kenton band between 1946 and 1951. One of the "hotter" players of the cool West Coast style,

---

West Coast jazz was a jazz style from the 1950s that embodied many of the principles of cool jazz as performed by a group of players centered in California.

he played with an intense, fiery passion. Pepper's career suffered from his drug addiction and incarceration, which he chronicled in painful detail in his autobiography *Straight Life*.

The West Coast cool players and bands that emerged during the decade emphasized written arrangements, compositional structures, restrained dynamics, and unusual instrumentation. Miles Davis's *Birth of the Cool* nonet—with a single representative of each instrument rather than big-band sections—became the model for many octets, nonets, and tentets that arose in California during the decade. Composer, arranger, and trumpeter Shorty Rogers (born Milton Rajonsky in 1924) adopted this instrumental technique for recordings with his group Shorty and His Giants. Rogers, who had played and written for Woody Herman and Stan Kenton, devised intricate, contrapuntal orchestrations for his music, heard on "Pirouette" and "Popo," a 12-bar blues that became his theme song.

Much of West Coast cool jazz emphasized subdued dynamics, with the drummer providing an understated accompaniment. Shelly Manne (1920–1984), a drummer working with his own groups and in a trio with pianist André Previn, was known for his elegant and supportive brushwork. In his 1953 recording "Mallets," we can hear Manne using mallets on the drums in a dialogue with the horns. Instead of aggressively driving the band, drums for Manne played a different role, one that made them an equal melodic partner with the horns:

> I have always felt that the drums have great melodic potential. . . . If a drummer must play an extended solo, he should think more about melodic lines than rudiment lines. . . . On some of my records, the writers have written definitive "melodic" lines for the drums to play, and if these lines were left out, it would be like one of the horns dropping out.[6]

Another West Coast drummer with an even more subdued approach was Foreststorn "Chico" Hamilton (1921–1913), who played quietly not only when accompanying soloists but also when performing his delicate and subtle drum solos. Hamilton's group exhibited another trait of several groups on the West Coast: the use of unusual combinations of instruments. Hamilton's quintet included a guitarist, a bassist, a drummer, a cellist, and a saxophonist who doubled on flute and clarinet. At the time cello and flute were rarely encountered in jazz. In the 1960s Hamilton changed his style and became a more driving player.

Perhaps the most unusual instrumental combinations were recorded by saxophonist Jimmy Giuffre (1921–2008), who had replaced Zoot Sims in the Woody Herman Four Brothers saxophone section. Giuffre began his career as a cool tenor saxophonist in the Lester Young tradition, but he was a restless experimenter. As noted earlier, Giuffre had written Herman's hit "Four Brothers" with its unusual saxophone choir of three tenors plus baritone. On his 1956 album, *The Jimmy Giuffre Clarinet*, he featured a work for

solo clarinet; a work for clarinet and celesta; a work for flute, alto flute, bass flute, clarinet, and drums (with Shelly Manne playing drums with his fingers); and an arrangement of the well-known standard "My Funny Valentine" for clarinet, oboe, bassoon, English horn, and bass.

The most radical recording of the West Coast cool players may have been Giuffre's 1955 *Tangents in Jazz*. On it he sought to free the bass and the drums from their traditional timekeeping roles by composing individual, contrapuntal parts for them. This vision represented a strong experimental stance, particularly to those who considered a swinging pulse—as provided by bass and drums—to be one of the most fundamental aspects of jazz. In answer to the question, What is this music? the liner notes replied:

> Jazz, with a nonpulsating beat. The beat is implicit but not explicit; in other words, acknowledged but unsounded. The two horns are the dominant but not domineering voices. The bass usually functions somewhat like a baritone sax. The drums play an important but nonconflicting role.[7]

Third-Stream Music

Many of the features associated with West Coast jazz were not confined to California. Other musicians were similarly intrigued by the emphasis on compositional structures and counterpoint, the understated role of the rhythm section, and the inclusion of instruments more typical of European classical music than jazz (such as the French horn or the cello). To composer and jazz historian Gunther Schuller (b. 1925), these elements were part of an aesthetic that suggested a new synthesis. For Schuller, who had himself played French horn on the *Birth of the Cool* sessions, this fusion seemed part of an inevitable trend. In a 1957 lecture at Brandeis University, Schuller labeled this trend *third-stream music*, representing the merging of the two streams of jazz and classical music into a unique third stream.

Certainly, the blend of jazz and the concert tradition was not new, as can be seen in works ranging from Scott Joplin's ragtime opera *Treemonisha*, to George Gershwin's *Rhapsody in Blue*, to Duke Ellington's *Black, Brown and Beige*. But Schuller's term *third stream* captured a renewed interest in the synthesis that the changing artistic consciousness of the musicians themselves had sparked during the decade. Thus, as pointed out earlier, many jazz composers in the 1950s—Dave Brubeck in his "Blue Rondo à la Turk" and John Lewis in his "Versailles"—borrowed the compositional forms and procedures of European classical music. Other jazz composers moved even more decisively toward synthesizing classical and

Stan Kenton,
City of Glass,
"Thermopylae" (1947)

jazz ideas, such as Jimmy Giuffre's 1953 "Fugue" and Robert Graettinger's ambitious four-movement work *City of Glass* (written for Stan Kenton). These two works also explored *atonality*, a twentieth-century classical technique that abandons tonal centers.

Schuller also composed third-stream works that united complex compositions and improvisation. One of his most notable was *Concertino for Jazz Quartet and Orchestra*, which was performed by the MJQ. Schuller's "Transformation" explored both the classical and the jazz elements. This work, like others of Schuller's, merged **twelve-tone composition** (pioneered by Viennese composer Arnold Schoenberg) and rhythmic asymmetry (found in the music of Russian composer Igor Stravinsky) with jazz improvisation.

George Russell,
The Jazz Workshop
"Concerto for Billy
the Kid" (1956)

The soloist on "Transformation" was pianist Bill Evans, who also recorded some memorable works with composer George Russell (1923–2009). Russell featured Evans on Concerto for Billy the Kid, inspired by the classical concerto, which normally pits the soloist against the ensemble. In this work Russell used the harmonic progression from the jazz standard "I'll Remember April." As early as 1949, Russell had explored the combination of jazz and classical music with his "A Bird in Igor's Yard," the title wittily acknowledging both Charlie "Yardbird" Parker and Igor Stravinsky.

Besides embracing rhythmic and formal experimentation, atonality, and serialism, the third-stream idea inspired an important music theory that would affect jazz composition and performance. In the 1950s George Russell devised what he called the "Lydian Chromatic Concept of Tonal Organization." Afterwards he based many of his works on the theory, which came to apply to improvisation as well. As Russell conceived it, the Lydian Concept supplies objective musical laws; once they are understood, the artist creates within those laws:

> I approach music like an architect. First with an idea in mind. The overall idea is manifested into a blueprint. The architect uses bricks and I use notes, rhythms, and different modes of music. By modes I don't mean modes in a simplistic musical sense but modes of behavior, tonal behavior, rhythmic behavior, psychological behavior, timbre behavior. I translate them and build my house. The orchestration is like the paint, the decorative factor.[8]

Third-stream music has never provided a full-blown direction for jazz artists, and some have argued that it is tangential to jazz. Nevertheless, the works of the 1950s reflect an earnest desire to investigate different and extended forms. From its genesis in ragtime and the blues, jazz had evolved rapidly, particularly in the sphere of instrumental technique, harmony, and rhythm. Yet jazz forms had remained relatively static. Much of early jazz was limited to the 16-bar strains of ragtime (derived from the march) and the 12-bar blues; later, players often confined themselves to 12-bar blues and 32-bar song forms. Those composers writing third-stream music offered jazz challenging new ideas in the one realm—the formal—that had so far remained unchanged.

Piano Stylists

In Chapter 7 we explored pianist Bud Powell's astounding single-line improvisations and sparse left-hand accompaniments, which greatly influenced the bebop pianists of the day. Other pianists, however, developed alternative styles. The quintet of blind pianist George Shearing was known for its distinctive sound resulting from Shearing's locked-hands, or block-chord, style (see Music Example 8-1 on page 242). Earlier, Milt Buckner, the pianist for Lionel Hampton, had used this method of rendering melodies. In Shearing's quintet the vibraphone doubled the upper note of the piano while the guitar doubled the pianist's lower note, providing an elegant and sophisticated sound. With its five notes contained within the octave, locked-hands style emulated big-band writing for saxophone sections.

Shearing's somewhat commercial ensemble sound was immensely popular. His most famous composition was the hit "Lullaby of Birdland," written in 1952 and titled after the New York jazz club named after Charlie Parker.

Shearing (1919–2011) was born in London, where he trained as a classical pianist. He developed an extensive repertory, learning to read music through Braille notation and picking up jazz from the recordings of Earl Hines, Fats Waller, Teddy Wilson, and Art Tatum. After immigrating to the United States in 1947, he came under the influence of some of the bebop players, especially Bud Powell and Hank Jones; yet throughout his career, Shearing never lost touch with his roots in traditional jazz piano.

Pianist Erroll Garner (1921–1977), on the other hand, had no formal musical education, was completely self-taught, and did not read music. Although he was a mainstay on Fifty-second Street in the mid-forties and even recorded with Charlie Parker on the West Coast in

---

In **twelve-tone composition**, as it was originally conceived, all twelve pitches of the chromatic scale are arranged into ordered sets. A set is also called a tone row or a series. Twelve-tone composition was pioneered by Viennese composer Arnold Schoenberg in the 1920s.

Music Example 8-1

1947, Garner stood apart from the mainstream bebop tradition.

Originally from Pittsburgh, Garner cultivated a highly distinctive solo piano style in which the left hand kept a quarter-note pulse, playing four chords to the bar.

Digital Vision/Jupiter Images

His insistent style often pushed or anticipated a bar's downbeat with the preceding upbeat. Against the left hand, Garner's right hand often played full chords that dragged behind the beat. He often led off compositions by playing an extended, involved, and often witty introduction. In ballads, such as his famous "Misty" (also recorded by singer Johnny Mathis), he made use of full, thick chords, creating a dense, orchestral texture. Garner's 1955 trio recording *Concert by the Sea* became one of the best-selling jazz records of the 1950s.

Pianist Oscar Peterson's prodigious technique made him particularly suited to inherit the mantle of virtuoso Art Tatum. Encouraged and mentored by

> Against the left hand, Garner's right hand often played full chords that dragged behind the beat. He often led off compositions by playing an extended, involved, and often witty introduction.

Tatum himself, Peterson concentrated on fast boplike lines and blues lines in an energetic style. Frequently in his solos, Peterson would burst into right-hand glissandos, a chorus in locked-hands style, left-hand stride piano, or walking tenths. He recorded with countless players throughout his career—Ben Webster, Lester Young, Dizzy Gillespie, Stan Getz, Ella Fitzgerald, and Milt Jackson—and his own piano trio has been extremely successful since the 1950s.

Peterson (1925–2007) grew up in Montreal, where jazz concert promoter Norman Granz heard him play and brought him to the United States. After a pivotal appearance in 1949 at Carnegie Hall, Peterson toured with Granz's Jazz at the Philharmonic series. He then formed his first American trio with piano, bass, and guitar, an instrumentation popularized by Art Tatum and Nat "King" Cole. With bassist Ray Brown and guitarist Herb Ellis, Peterson wowed audiences and critics, playing blues and sophisticated, complex arrangements of standards such as "Love for Sale" and "Swinging on a Star." In 1959 drummer Ed Thigpen replaced guitarist Ellis and remained in the group for six years.

In his later years, Peterson's playing was sometimes more dazzling than creative, although some of his solo piano recordings, such as *Tracks*, showed Peterson at his most harmonically advanced and exploratory. Despite the loss of some dexterity after suffering a stroke in 1993, Peterson was able to regain some use of his left hand.

One of the most popular jazz musicians of our time, Peterson continued to perform and record until his death in 2007.

Hard Bop and Funky/Soul Jazz

For some players and listeners, cool jazz was overly cerebral and devoid of energy and emotion. The complexity of Lennie Tristano's piano playing, the airy counterpoint of Gerry Mulligan and the Chet Baker Quartet, the smoky atmosphere of Sinatra with strings, the compositional experiments of the Dave Brubeck Quartet, and the concert hall settings of the tuxedo-clad MJQ—all seemed to renounce the elemental fire and passionate core of the jazz tradition. The compositional sophistication of many of the West Coast players and third-stream composers too frequently seemed an attempt to align with the European classical tradition—a pretentious striving for the cachet of "high art."

In contrast, the hard bop players continued to extend the bebop tradition with its emphasis on improvisation, 32-bar formal structures, 12-bar blues, and straight-ahead swinging. In the 1950s the bands of Art Blakey and the Jazz Messengers, Horace Silver, the Clifford Brown–Max Roach Quintet, and Miles Davis were representative of the driving hard bop bands. Further, some of the compositions of these bands made use of the simpler, earthier style known as funky (or soul) jazz.

Art Blakey and the Jazz Messengers

Drummer Art Blakey, born in Pittsburgh in 1919, recorded the 1956 album *Hard Bop*, which gave its name to the 1950s resurgence of forceful, swinging jazz. Blakey became one of the leading exponents of the hard bop tradition. Never cool, Blakey's drumming was aggressive, strong, and loud. His group, the Jazz Messengers, remained active from the 1950s until Blakey's death in 1990.

Blakey began his career with pianist Mary Lou Williams and Fletcher Henderson, but in the mid-forties he played drums for the Billy Eckstine band, from where he quickly moved to the center of the growing bebop

> Dizzy Gillespie called Blakey "the fire" of jazz drumming.

movement. He played with Eckstine from 1944 to 1947, sharing the stage with Charlie Parker, Dizzy Gillespie, Dexter Gordon, and Miles Davis. Blakey organized his first group in 1947, a rehearsal band called the Seventeen Messengers, and later that year recorded with an octet called the Jazz Messengers.

Art Blakey performing with characteristic energy in a publicity shot from the 1970s.

In 1955 he formed another group with pianist–musical director Horace Silver that kept the name Jazz Messengers; this was the group that helped propel Blakey to fame. The quintet—with tenor saxophonist Hank Mobley, trumpeter Kenny Dorham, and bassist Doug Watkins—recorded three albums before Silver left the group. Blakey continued to lead the Messengers. With its classic small-band instrumentation (even after the group added a trombone in the early sixties to become a sextet) and its emphasis on aggressive soloing accompanied by Blakey's powerful drumming, it was the quintessential hard bop group. The band's personnel shifted over time, and Blakey staffed the group with young players, many of whom—such as trumpeters Donald Byrd, Freddie Hubbard, Lee Morgan, and Chuck Mangione; saxophonists Johnny Griffin, Jackie McLean, and Wayne Shorter; and pianists Cedar Walton, Bobby Timmons, and Keith Jarrett—would go on to develop successful careers on their own.

Blakey gave ample room to his players as both soloists and composers. Some of them contributed jazz compositions that would become standards of the jazz repertory. In the late 1950s, Blakey's pianist, Bobby Timmons, composed several tunes representative of funky/soul jazz. His "Moanin'" (Listening Guide, Track 37) made use of call-and-response formulas and the "Amen" harmonic church cadence (technically called a **plagal cadence**). Other Timmons compositions were similarly earthy, especially

---

A **plagal cadence**, sometimes called a **church cadence** or an **Amen cadence**, contains the harmonic progression IV–I (instead of the more common progression V–I). It is often used at the ends of hymns with the concluding "Amen." Plagal cadences were featured frequently in funky/soul jazz.

A **shuffle** is the 4/4 rhythmic pattern shown here. Each beat is represented by the drummer playing a dotted-eighth and a sixteenth note, usually on the ride cymbal.

the second and fourth beats of the measure, the tom-tom roll, and Blakey's **shuffle** pattern, sometimes even called the "Blakey Shuffle." Blakey was also one of the first drummers to use polyrhythms extensively, playing even eighth notes against triplets on the cymbal.

Between 1954 and 1964, the personnel of the Jazz Messengers changed several times. Freddie Hubbard replaced the impassioned trumpeter Lee Morgan in 1961. Morgan and Hubbard, both born in 1938, were strongly influenced by hard bop trumpeter Clifford Brown. Tenor saxophonist Wayne Shorter replaced Blakey's earlier players, Benny Golson and Hank Mobley. Shorter joined the group in 1959 and remained for five years, becoming its musical director and altering the group's sound somewhat to accommodate his innovative compositions, such as "Ping Pong." With Hubbard and Shorter, Blakey added trombonist Curtis Fuller and pianist Cedar Walton, enlarging his group from a quintet to a sextet. They played from 1961 to 1964. Until his death Blakey continued to tour, often with his classic small-band instrumentation, while keeping alive the hard bop tradition. (See Chapter 12 for a discussion of the Jazz Messengers in the 1980s.)

his "Dis Here" and "Dat Dere." Tenor saxophonist Benny Golson contributed "Whisper Not," a minor-key work that employed stop time. Golson's "I Remember Clifford" was a plaintive and posthumous tribute to trumpeter Clifford Brown, who played with Blakey in 1954.

Dizzy Gillespie called Blakey "the fire" of jazz drumming. Blakey, who had visited Africa in the late 1940s, derived some of his techniques from African drumming—altering the pitch of the tom-tom by using an elbow, or playing on the side of the drum. His impact on jazz drumming was tremendous, and many of his techniques came to identify his style: the precise clicking of the hi-hat on

---

LISTENING GUIDE   Track 37
"Moanin'" (excerpt)

Art Blakey and the Jazz Messengers: "Moanin'" (Timmons), from *Moanin'*. Blue Note Reissue CDP 7 46516 2. New York, October 30, 1958. Lee Morgan, trumpet; Benny Golson, tenor saxophone; Bobby Timmons, composer, piano; Jymie Merritt, bass; Blakey, drums.

The Main Point   "Moanin'" is a fine example of funky/soul jazz. The melody features a written-out call-and-response that can be heard as an "Amen" or "Yes, Lord." (In a vocal arrangement recorded by Lambert, Hendricks, and Ross, the "Yes, Lord" was sung.) In funky/soul jazz we can sometimes interpret bluesy pieces such as "Moanin'" as major or minor. For example, the first time through the bridge, Timmons plays a clear F minor harmony at measure 4 (0:37); other times the chord played sounds closer to F major. Note also the "Amen" (or plagal) cadence from measures 3 and 4 of the bridge, which echoes the A section and further helps infuse the tune with a gospel and blues feel. With its expressive blues inflections and considerable passion, Lee Morgan's solo is especially memorable. The listening guide concludes after Golson's tenor saxophone solo.

1st A section—Head, 8 bars after 3-beat pickup

0:00   Pianist Timmons states the head with no introduction. The band answers with the two-note "Amen" (or "Yes, Lord") motive.

2nd A section—Head, 8 bars

0:15   For this second time through the A section, the trumpet and the tenor saxophone state the call. The piano, drums, and bass take over the response.

Bridge—Head, 8 bars

0:31 The bridge goes into straight time with the trumpet and the tenor saxophone on the melody—a perfect example of a *release*, an older term for the B section. The elegant chromatic chord progression of the bridge unleashes the tension built up in the repetitive A section. The plagal cadence of measures 3 and 4 echoes the A section.

Final A section—Head, 8 bars

0:44 The pianist returns with the call, while the rest of the band, led by the trumpet and the tenor saxophone, take the response.

Morgan trumpet solo—2 choruses

1:00 Morgan's solo begins with half-valve inflections and catchy funky riffs. The half-valve inflections are the almost squeaky, "bent" sounds. Blakey's drumming keeps a constant backbeat, emphasizing beats 2 and 4.

1:15 In the second A section of the first chorus, Morgan incorporates *double-tonguing*, a technique that allows him to repeat the same note rapidly. The double-tonguing idea returns twice.

2:55 Double-tonguing wraps up the solo.

Golson tenor saxophone solo—2 choruses

3:04 Golson picks up the end of Morgan's solo to launch his own and begins simply with variants of phrases strung together logically.

4:03 The beginning of his second chorus displays a move to the higher register that signals greater activity to come. The solo in fact becomes quite modernist in its second chorus: the bluesy runs and the use of the high register sometimes seem to run outside the chord changes in ways that sound like the work of John Coltrane.

 Listen to this music in an animated Active Listening Guide available at the text website.

Horace Silver

Pianist Horace Silver (1928–2014) left the Jazz Messengers in 1956 to lead his own quintet. Among the most imaginative of the major funky jazz players of the 1950s, Silver became one of its most notable and prolific composers as well. Although Silver was born in Norwalk, Connecticut, his family was from the former Portuguese colony of Cape Verde, off the coast of northern Africa. As a child he was exposed to Cape Verdean folk music by his father, who encouraged him to adopt the idiom to jazz. Although bebop pianist Bud Powell influenced him early on, Silver's piano playing by comparison became less technical, simpler, more tuneful, and bluesier. In reacting against the bop players, Silver learned to play with fewer notes, emphasizing instead a few funky figures and favoring tremolos and crushed notes separated by generous space.

Many of Silver's compositions were infectious and catchy, such as his "Song for My Father," a Latin-tinged work dominated by a simple tonic-and-fifth bass motive. Silver wrote numerous blues compositions, some with written sections ingeniously added to the 12-bar blues form: his "Opus de Funk" and "Señor Blues" were recorded by dozens of other artists. In typical hard bop fashion, the trumpet and the tenor saxophone generally stated the melody in Silver's compositions, although his works often involved more than just a string of solos following the head. Many made extensive use of fixed introductions, written shout choruses, connecting passages, and mixed rhythmic forms. In "Nica's Dream" (written for the Baroness Pannonica de Koenigswarter), for example, Silver changed the accompaniment pattern within the song itself, providing a Latin-oriented backup to the A section and a swinging walking bass for the B section. Some of Silver's compositions were even more complex:

toured Europe with Lionel Hampton's band, making several records there.

Brown's most outstanding legacy is his participation in the Clifford Brown–Max Roach Quintet with drummer Max Roach. Roach and Brown formed their cooperative quintet in 1954. The hard bop band, along with Brown on trumpet and Roach on drums, included bassist George Morrow, pianist Richie Powell (the brother of bebop pianist Bud Powell), and saxophonist Harold Land. (Sonny Rollins replaced Land in 1955.) The group was one of the most brilliant in jazz, lasting until Brown's death in 1956 in an automobile accident that also killed Richie Powell.

Along with jazz standards, the group recorded many of Brown's originals, some of which showed his effortless ability to negotiate difficult chord progressions. For example, "Joy Spring"—one of his most famous compositions—was a 32-bar AABA composition with a twist: the second A section modulated a half step from F to G♭. After a modulating bridge, the final A section returned to F. Other fine Brown originals include "Sweet Clifford," "Daahoud," and "Sandu."

"The Outlaw," from a 1958 recording entitled *Further Explorations*, used a 54-bar theme made up of four sections of 13 + 13 + 10 + 18 measures.

During the 1960s and 1970s, Silver continued to hire outstanding sideman, such as tenor saxophonist Michael Brecker, who brought to Silver's music a more aggressive and chromatic approach to improvisation. Silver's substantial output is aptly described by the title to his 1993 recording, *It's Gotta Be Funky*. In summary, Silver helped solidify the hard bop and funky tradition, codifying its instrumentation and providing some of its most memorable compositions.

Clifford Brown–Max Roach Quintet

Many of the trumpeters of the 1950s followed Miles Davis and Chet Baker by cultivating a lyrical, restrained style in the medium range of the instrument. Others kept alive the bebop tradition of Dizzy Gillespie and Fats Navarro. Clifford Brown was perhaps the finest trumpet player of the 1950s, perpetuating the running eighth-note style of Gillespie but with a personal, intimate sound that was arguably warmer than the older player's style. Brown's playing emphasized clean technique, a vast variety of articulations, and a satisfying, logical progression to his solos that usually avoided the gratuitous, showy high notes of Gillespie. Brown had a slightly percussive attack and negotiated impossibly fast tempos with ease.

Brown won the *Down Beat* "New Star" award in 1954. His career ended two years later in an accident, however—one of the great tragedies in jazz. As a result, Brown's recorded output is relatively small although immense, given the number of years he worked professionally. His recordings, by any measure, establish him as one of the finest of jazz trumpet players. Originally from Wilmington, Delaware, where he was born in 1930, Brown worked mostly around Philadelphia and New York. In 1953 he

Max Roach (1924–2007) had become one of the leading innovative drummers of the bebop generation, performing and recording with Dizzy Gillespie and Charlie Parker in the 1940s. He became a member of Parker's longest-lived quintet and was also heard on eight tracks of Miles Davis's *Birth of the Cool*. With other bebop drummers such as Kenny Clarke, Roach was instrumental in transferring the pulse from the bass drum and the hi-hat to the ride cymbal. He developed a conversational style of accompanying improvisers, creating a dialogue with the soloists and accenting with the bass and snare drums.

Roach's technique provided a foundation for modern jazz drumming. By giving separate roles to each hand and foot, Roach's style helped establish what came to be called "coordinated independence."

Sonny Rollins

A star with the Brown–Roach quintet, Theodore "Sonny" Rollins has been one of the leading tenor saxophonists in jazz since the 1950s. Rollins's playing boasted rhythmic imagination, harmonic ingenuity, and a strong, muscular sound.

LISTENING GUIDE   Track 38
"Powell's Prances"

Clifford Brown–Max Roach Quintet: "Powell's Prances" (Powell), from *At Basin Street*. EmArcy 36070. New York, January 4, 1956. Brown, trumpet; Sonny Rollins, tenor saxophone; Richie Powell, piano, composer-arranger; George Morrow, bass; Roach, drums.

The Main Point   "Powell's Prances" is a fine example of the Brown-Roach quintet. This up-tempo, swinging number with an unusual structure typifies the sound of the band. The bluesy quality of the piece derives from its shift to the subdominant harmony during the B section of the ABA form. It is a minor mode composition in the tradition of earlier bop works such as Bud Powell's "Tempus Fugit" (heard on Track 31).

Head—24-bar ABA

0:00   After a short drum-fill introduction, the head begins. It is in C minor with an up-tempo, driving sound. The trumpet and the tenor saxophone play the melody in octaves. The unusual form of the head is ABA, with each section having eight bars. The middle eight bars are in stop time and feature a harmonic shift to the subdominant, F minor.

Brown trumpet solo—2 choruses

0:22   Listen for Brown's variety of articulations and for his warm sound. The clarity of each note derives from his ability to tongue at a rapid tempo. The solo uses running eighth-note lines and bebop figures, such as the two-note bebop idea that ends the phrase at 0:27.

0:41   Brown begins his second chorus by emphasizing and repeating the sixth of the C minor harmony, A.

Rollins tenor saxophone solo—2 choruses

1:00   Rollins contrasts his solo with Brown's by including passages of longer note values. Listen to how he develops a motivic idea in the second chorus, bridging the end of the first A section and the beginning of the B section. His solo closes with a blues-based idea, using ♭5–4 (G♭–F).

Powell piano solo—2 choruses

1:38   Powell's solo concentrates on developing simple blueslike riffs in the piano's midrange. It moves out of the range only briefly for a short contrast.

Roach drum solo—2 choruses

2:15   Roach begins his solo by echoing and developing the rhythm at the end of Powell's final riff. Roach maintains the energy and the drive of the preceding solos. Notice that he avoids playing the cymbals during his solo, concentrating instead on the snare drum, bass drum, and tom-toms.

Reprise of the head—24-bar ABC

2:48   After the solos the head returns but is not literally restated. A new section (C) replaces the final A section, with the piano and the horns playing a passage in unison that arpeggiates numerous chords and sounds like an exercise.

Coda

3:08   The C section of the head has introduced a coda consisting of a dramatic series of out-of-time chords prolonged over drum fills. These chords are unusually dissonant, beginning with a C major triad with a D♭ in the bass.

Listen to this music in an animated Active Listening Guide available at the text website.

He achieved his big, dramatic tone by infusing the traditional, full-throated eloquence of Coleman Hawkins with the edgy raspiness sometimes heard in Charlie Parker.

Rollins was born in 1930 in New York and raised in the same neighborhood that produced Coleman Hawkins, Bud Powell, and Thelonious Monk. Rollins was a teenager while bebop was taking hold as the dominant jazz style. In fact, he made one of his first recordings in 1949 with bebop pianist Bud Powell. This recording displays Rollins's sound and inventiveness and makes clear his ties to the New York bebop world.

During the 1950s Rollins recorded and performed with many significant players and groups, including J. J. Johnson, Art Blakey, Thelonious Monk, and the MJQ. He formed an association with Miles Davis that continued throughout the decade and brought Rollins to the forefront not only as an exceptional improviser but also as a composer. To a Davis recording session for Prestige in 1954, Rollins contributed three compositions that were to become jazz standards: "Oleo," based on rhythm changes; "Doxy," and "Airegin," a minor key romp whose title was a thinly disguised reference to Nigeria. Rollins's sense of humor resonated throughout his playing and his occasionally idiosyncratic choice of repertory, such as his 1957 album *Way out West*, which boasted "I'm an Old Cowhand" and "Wagon Wheels" in a pianoless trio of saxophone, bass, and drums.

Rollins was passionately committed to his musical progress. He even traveled to Chicago in 1950 to study percussion and enhance his rhythmic flexibility. Highly self-critical, he took three extended sabbaticals during which he stopped performing in public. The first of these, which began in November 1954, ended a year later when he joined the Clifford Brown–Max Roach Quintet, where he remained until 1957. During his tenure with the hard bop group, Rollins earned prestige for his technical proficiency and the fertility of his musical ideas.

Evident in such songs as "I'll Remember April" and "Powell's Prances," Rollins's style includes the following characteristics:

▶ A wide variety of melodies, from bop lines to floating phrases slightly reminiscent of cool jazz

▶ Melodic connections based on voice leading and motivic development, some of which are quite subtle

▶ Varied melodic rhythms

▶ Highly irregular phrase lengths, from single notes to long bop phrases

▶ Rich tone with occasional raspiness

▶ Use of space between phrases

▶ Use of entire range of the instrument

▶ Full range of emotional expression

▶ Variety of articulations

▶ Mostly inside playing, with chord-scale relationships based on the bop practice of using extended chords and altered scales

During the latter half of the 1950s, Rollins continued to record as a leader. His tune "Valse Hot" was one of the first hard bop compositions in 3/4 meter. In 1956 he recorded *Saxophone Colossus*—a quartet recording hailed by critics as a milestone. It included the sunny calypso tune "St. Thomas," the first of several Rollins compositions in that vein. His performance of "You Don't Know What Love Is," earlier recorded by Billie Holiday, was elegiac and profound.

Rollins's ability to thread motives through his solos was especially memorable on his performance of "Blue Seven." This cut, from *Saxophone Colossus*, exemplified logical development in improvisation. In a well-known article entitled "Sonny Rollins and the Challenge of Thematic Improvisation," Gunther Schuller singled out this solo—a mysterious 12-bar blues based on the interval of a tritone—as representing a breakthrough in improvisational technique.[9] For Schuller this solo contained an unprecedented display of interrelated themes and motives, making the solo a unified and coherent whole. Not all critics agreed: in a response to Schuller, jazz historian Lawrence Gushee suggested that Schuller's analysis was an oversimplification of Rollins's style, one that ignored many other disparate aspects of Rollins's improvisational approach. Still, Rollins's penchant for motivic improvisation is such that he often preferred tunes with strong, simple melodies that he could easily allude to, for example, his recording of "Surrey with the Fringe on Top" or his own "St. Thomas."

Perhaps in reaction to Schuller's laudatory article, the ever self-critical Rollins took another sabbatical between 1959 and 1961. During his self-imposed retirement, his late-night practice sessions on the Williamsburg Bridge over the East River became legendary. When he returned to performing, he made reference to his nocturnal habit in an album titled *The Bridge*, which included guitarist Jim Hall.

In the early 1960s Rollins continued to expand musically with projects that encompassed both the old and the new. For the latter he attempted to come to grips with the free jazz movement of Ornette Coleman. He collaborated with several musicians who had been associated with Coleman, including trumpeter Don Cherry, drummer Billy Higgins, and pianist Paul Bley. Yet he also recorded with his idol Coleman Hawkins in an album entitled *Sonny Meets Hawk*. Picking up on a practice Hawkins had embraced in the 1940s, Rollins experimented with performing unaccompanied saxophone solos.

Several years after providing the soundtrack to the 1965 Michael Caine movie *Alfie*, Rollins took yet another sabbatical, this time from 1969–1972; upon his return he concentrated on playing in a slightly more commercial vein. Influenced by jazz trends in the late 1960s and early 1970s, he brought the electric piano and the electric bass into his groups, began emphasizing rock and funk rhythms, and often doubled on soprano saxophone. Currently, Rollins remains one of the most honored players in jazz, appearing in prestigious venues throughout the world, both as a guest and with his own groups.

Charles Mingus

Bassist and composer Charles Mingus attained legendary status for both his uncompromising view of the jazz tradition and his innovative approach to the art form. As a bassist he developed a flawless technique, extending the accomplishments of Duke Ellington's bassist, Jimmy Blanton. As a composer Mingus became increasingly visible and influential throughout the 1950s and 1960s. He wrote works that encompassed numerous influences, especially the music of Ellington and the soulful expressiveness of the black church.

The scope of Mingus's music was enormous, embracing the whole of jazz—from historical references to the New Orleans tradition to a forward-looking use of collective improvisation that provided a significant precedent for free jazz. Much of Mingus's work paid homage to the blues and gospel music, but it also included inventive instrumentation, tempo changes, and stop time. Although he began by composing and arranging conventionally—writing a careful score with worked-out parts—his later technique of dictating from the keyboard recalled the head-arrangement procedures of early jazz and its spirit of collective improvisation.

Born in Arizona in 1922, Mingus was raised in the Watts section of Los Angeles, where he paid his dues as a bass player and a sideman with both swing and bop groups, working with Louis Armstrong, clarinetist Barney Bigard, and vibraphonist Lionel Hampton. As a member of vibraphonist Red Norvo's trio, along with guitarist Talmage "Tal" Farlow, Mingus became nationally known. The group, which had no drummer, was celebrated for its ability to play fiendishly rapid tempos. The sole black player in the trio, Mingus left Norvo's group when he was excluded from a television performance because of his race. After moving to New York, he took part in the Jazz Composers' Workshop, contributing written compositions along with Teo Macero and Teddy Charles.

Bassist Charles Mingus in a publicity still from the 1960s.

Mingus founded his own workshop in 1955, putting together a group to feature his compositions. The group numbered from four to eleven players. Dissatisfied with printed musical notation, Mingus dictated from the piano the parts and lines he wanted his sidemen to play. Considering his "workshop" to be just that, he sometimes shouted instructions to his players on the bandstand or interrupted compositions in midstream to correct one of his musicians or castigate the audience for being noisy. He made reference to New Orleans pianist Jelly Roll Morton in "Jelly Roll Soul" and to gospel music in "Wednesday Night Prayer Meeting" and "Better Git It in Your Soul"; he paid tribute to Charlie Parker in "Bird Calls" and to Lester Young in "Goodbye Pork Pie Hat." "Nostalgia in Times Square" was an altered 12-bar blues, originally written for the John Cassavetes film *Shadows*.

Some of Mingus's compositions were quite complex. "Fables of Faubus"—a denunciation of Arkansas Governor Orval Faubus, who attempted to defy desegregation—had a 71-bar theme written in four sections that incorporated tempo changes within the solos. Arguably, Mingus's most ambitious composition was "The Black Saint and the Sinner Lady," a complicated four-movement work recorded in 1963. It evoked Ellington with Jaki Byard's piano introduction to the second movement, and the plunger trombone work of Quentin Jackson recalled Ellington's "jungle sound" from the Cotton Club. "Black Saint" was also highly experimental, interweaving sections with changing tempos or without tempo. Mingus also used overdubbing on the recording.

Mingus wrote about his career in a highly creative and sometimes fanciful autobiography, *Beneath the Underdog* (1971). He rarely performed between 1966 and 1969 but was granted a Guggenheim Fellowship in 1971. During his final years, he suffered from Lou Gehrig's disease and was confined to a wheelchair. In the mid-seventies he

---

LISTENING GUIDE
"Hora Decubitus"

Track 39

Charles Mingus and His Orchestra: "Hora Decubitus" (Mingus), from *Mingus, Mingus, Mingus, Mingus, Mingus*. Impulse AS-9234-2. New York, September 20, 1963. Mingus, bass, director; Eddie Preston, Richard Williams, trumpets; Britt Woodman, trombone; Don Butterfield, tuba; Eric Dolphy, Dick Haffer, Booker Ervin, Jerome Richardson, woodwinds; Jaki Byard, piano; Walter Perkins, drums.

The Main Point   "Hora Decubitus" is a hybrid work. Although based on the 12-bar blues, it also suggests some elements of free jazz. (In discussing its form here, we anticipate some of the stylistic attributes of free jazz described more fully in Chapter 9.) Throughout the performance Mingus maintains control of the ensemble through forceful, interesting bass lines.

The following analysis shows that the fundamental idea of the piece is a mixture of various lines in counterpoint. These are introduced gradually, slowly building a complex group sound.

Introduction—Mingus bass solo, 12 bars

0:00   Alternating octaves here reveal Mingus's strength and sense of forward momentum. Mingus sets the tempo, harmony, and mood for the blues choruses that follow.

Head—1st chorus

0:12   A rifflike blues tune in E♭ is played on the baritone saxophone. The first four measures use the notes of the E♭ blues scale, but the next two measures transpose the riff up a fourth. The use of C♭ in measures 5 and 6 takes the riff out of the E♭ blues scale. Although the rhythmic and melodic character of the tune is traditional, the sonorities created by the gradually entering instruments begin to imply atonality.

Head—2nd chorus

0:24   The baritone saxophone continues to play the theme, joined now by the other saxophones, sometimes playing in unison but occasionally splitting into different parts.

Head—3rd chorus

0:37   A trombone is added, playing a counter-riff that often seems to clash with the saxophones, which meanwhile repeat their second chorus.

Head—4th chorus

0:50   An alto saxophone separates from the reed section to add still another part, while the trombone and the remaining saxophones repeat what they had played in the preceding chorus.

Head—5th chorus, final chorus of head

1:02   A trumpet player joins the others with still another riff in counterpoint with the ongoing parts. This set of contrasting and competing lines remains traditional in its blues-riff orientation as well as in the marvelous cacophony of everyone playing together.

Ervin tenor saxophone solo—4 choruses

1:15   At first reminiscent of gospel jazz, Ervin's solo finishes with the fleet, atonal runs that are somewhat more typical of free jazz. As accompaniment, the orchestra enters from time to time with background figures derived from the opening riffs of the head.

1:51   On Ervin's last chorus, Mingus pushes the beat so forcefully that he seems almost ahead of the pulse.

Dolphy alto saxophone solo—4 choruses

2:03   After beginning with the more "outside" melodic lines of free jazz, Dolphy returns to a more typical blues line, though many of his pitches still purposely avoid the chord changes.

2:40   Mingus briefly quotes his opening introductory statement in the middle of Dolphy's solo as if trying to forge together the disparate sections of the work. The other instruments freely enter with riffs and sharp punctuations as if to comment on Dolphy's solo.

Williams trumpet solo—4 choruses

2:56   A few bebop licks can still be heard from time to time. The passionate cries Williams injects into the solo are both expressive and appropriate.

Reprise of the head—3 choruses

3:40   Some of the opening riffs are heard but are exchanged here, that is, played by different groups of instruments. The alto saxophones "lay out" (don't play) during the second chorus. During the third chorus, the ensemble plays the main riff tune in unison, which lends a feeling of finality to the performance.

Tag

4:16   Here are two chords that may be heard as echoing the IV–I "Amen" cadence heard in church music. On the first of these chords, the instruments freely interpolate runs and fills in the manner of a cadenza. The second chord is not so heavily scored, and as it dies out Mingus plays the last few notes himself, thus recalling his solo introduction.

 Listen to this music in an animated Active Listening Guide available at the text website.

collaborated with pop singer Joni Mitchell for her album *Mingus*, a tribute to the bassist. After his death in 1979, his family found portions of a score for a two-hour work entitled *Epitaph*. Gunther Schuller completed the partial score and recorded it in 1989.

Charles Mingus was one of the very few artists in jazz to contribute directly to the formation of a jazz substyle and a new way of thinking about music. Today the Mingus Big Band is a renowned large jazz ensemble, and the Mingus Dynasty is a repertory group consisting of six to seven players. Under the direction of his widow, Sue, these groups continue to explore the dimensions of Mingus's original and challenging music.

Miles Davis in the 1950s

Earlier in this chapter, we explored Miles Davis's seminal contributions to cool jazz. But there was much more to his career; in fact, Davis was to become one of the most profoundly influential figures in the history of jazz. Lasting over four decades, his career was marked by an uncanny ability to explore and develop new styles. Davis was consistently on the cutting edge of musical developments:

▶ Bebop in the mid- to late 1940s

▶ Cool jazz in the late 1940s and the early 1950s

▶ Hard bop in the mid-1950s

▶ Modal jazz in the late 1950s and the early 1960s

▶ Jazz-rock fusion in the 1970s

▶ MIDI sequencing and sampling in the 1980s

Never content with relying on earlier successful formulas, Davis hired the best young players, who continued to challenge him. As one of his former sidemen noted, Davis was a "star maker": many of the most important jazz performers in the later twentieth century at one time had played in his band.

Though nurtured on bebop, Davis did not follow Dizzy Gillespie in developing fireworks in the trumpet's higher register. His playing was usually lyrical and spare, impassioned and centered in the middle range of the instrument. He cited trumpeter Freddie Webster as an early influence; Webster played in an unfussy style without much vibrato.

Davis was born in Alton, Illinois (near St. Louis), on May 26, 1926,[10] and began playing professionally as a teenager. A pivotal event occurred when he was eighteen: the Billy Eckstine band, with Charlie Parker, Dizzy Gillespie, and Sarah Vaughan, came to town, and Davis was asked to fill in. In his autobiography, Davis wrote, "[Hearing the band] changed my life. I decided right then and there that I had to leave St. Louis and live in New York City where all these bad musicians were."[11] For the remainder of his life, Davis claimed that he was always attempting to recapture the awesome musical experience of that St. Louis performance.

Davis arrived in New York in fall 1944, ostensibly to study at the Juilliard School of Music, but he was more interested in pursuing bebop opportunities with Charlie Parker. The following year, at age nineteen, Davis achieved his first remarkable success: he recorded for Savoy as part of Parker's first session as a leader. That session,

"I had to leave St. Louis and live in New York City where all these bad musicians were."
—Miles Davis

Joseph/Dreamstime.com

on November 26, 1945, was in fact Davis's second recording session; though brilliant for Parker, this recording was not entirely successful for the young trumpeter. Davis's playing on "Billie's Bounce" and "Now's the Time" revealed him to be almost out of his depth with the group. Because Davis was unable to perform the virtuosic "Ko Ko" with Parker, Dizzy Gillespie played the cut.

As Davis continued to improve and develop his own voice, critics began speaking of him as representing a new generation of trumpeters with a warmer, softer, mellower sound than Gillespie's. Davis performed with Parker through December 1948, becoming a member of his working quintet. He contributed such compositions as "Donna Lee" (though the tune is attributed to Parker) and hired Parker to play tenor saxophone for his own Savoy session with the originals "Milestones," "Little Willie Leaps," "Sippin' at Bells," and "Half Nelson." Davis's compositions were in the bebop tradition, and they offered slightly more complexity: for example, "Sippin' at Bells" was a 12-bar blues with eighteen chord changes.

Despite Davis's long association with Parker, the alto saxophonist was unpredictable and often difficult to work with. On December 23, 1948, Davis's irritation with what he considered Parker's lack of professionalism came to a head. Davis stormed off the bandstand of the Royal Roost, later claiming, "Bird makes you feel about one foot high."[12] No longer part of the Davis quintet, Parker struck out on his own.

While working on the *Birth of the Cool* sessions, Davis traveled to Paris to perform at the Festival de Jazz in 1949, which earned him increased visibility and critical attention. When he returned to the States, Davis, like many other jazz players of his generation, succumbed to heroin addiction. Although he won the *Metronome* critics poll each year between 1951 and 1953, some of his performances for Prestige suffered from technical problems that can probably be traced to his addiction. Some writers even began to consider Davis's best work behind him.

Fortunately, Davis overcame his addiction in 1954 and in the same year recorded several brilliant performances. His recording for Prestige with J. J. Johnson on trombone, Lucky Thompson on tenor saxophone, Horace Silver on piano, Percy Heath on bass, and Kenny Clarke on drums included "Blue 'n' Boogie" (a Dizzy Gillespie composition) and Richard Carpenter's "Walkin'." Both were blues compositions firmly rooted in the bebop tradition. Hailed for his early involvement in cool jazz on the *Birth of the Cool* sessions, Davis now returned to his bebop roots, providing some of the finest hard bop music of the decade. Davis discussed the difference:

> *Birth of the Cool* had . . . mainly come out of what Duke Ellington and Billy Strayhorn had already done; it just made the music "whiter," so that white people could digest it better. And then the

other records I made, like "Walkin'" and "Blue 'n' Boogie"—which the critics called hard bop—had only gone back to the blues and some of the things that Bird and Dizzy had done. It was great music, well played and everything, but the musical ideas and concepts had mostly been already done; it just had a little more space in it.[13]

Davis continued to record other jazz classics that year. Two months after the "Walkin'" session, in June 1954, he took the same rhythm section, added Sonny Rollins on tenor saxophone, and recorded three Rollins originals: "Airegin," "Doxy," and "Oleo." The A section of "Oleo" included Rollins's start-and-stop melody based on a three-note motive, and it was played in unison by the horns without piano. On Christmas Eve, Davis assembled pianist Thelonious Monk and vibraphonist Milt Jackson and recorded six sides, including two takes each of Jackson's "Bags' Groove" and Gershwin's "The Man I Love." The session was notorious: Monk was reputedly furious over Davis's request that Monk not plays behind Davis's solos. Davis's playing showed a mastery of timing and a depth in his economical style.

The 1954 recordings helped revive Davis's career, as did his performance on Thelonious Monk's "'Round Midnight" at the Newport Jazz Festival the following year. In this piece he enraptured the audience with a wistful solo. Davis was becoming a hot commodity. Signing with Columbia Records, he put together a hard bop quintet that featured some rising stars: tenor saxophonist John Coltrane, pianist Red Garland, bassist Paul Chambers, and drummer Joseph Rudolph "Philly Joe" Jones. The group combined poignant ballads, often performed with Davis on muted trumpet (using a **harmon mute**), along with fiercely intense swing. Ever interested in the use of space and openness in his music, Davis asked pianist Garland to listen and learn from Chicago pianist Ahmad Jamal, whose strategic use of silence Davis admired.

In addition to his rise in popularity, Davis found notoriety. Critics and audiences noted his prickly personality, his unwillingness to announce compositions, and his disappearance from the bandstand when other soloists were playing. Yet this almost surly behavior helped Davis become a cult figure, noted for his mystique. He was also laconic and temperamental. In a flash of anger in 1956, he raised his voice too soon after a throat operation, thereby permanently reducing his voice to a whisper.

A **harmon mute** is a hollow metal mute that, when placed in the bell of the trumpet, gives the sound a distant, brooding quality. Miles Davis's use of the harmon mute from 1954 onward helped popularize its use. (Listen to Track 14 of the 🎧 Audio Primer to hear an example of a harmon mute.)

Miles Davis,
Milestones,
"Milestones" (1958)

In 1958 alto saxophonist Cannonball Adderley joined the band, making it a sextet. The two saxophonists, Coltrane and Adderley, had markedly different styles: Coltrane's playing was rigorous, technical, and exploratory; Adderley's was traditional, rooted in the blues and bebop. The sextet's recording *Milestones* showed a new musical direction for Davis, particularly on the title tune. Coltrane commented:

I found Miles in the midst of another stage of his musical development. There was one time in his past that he devoted to multichorded structures. He was interested in chords for their own sake. But now it seemed that he was moving in the opposite direction to the use of fewer and fewer chord changes in songs.[14]

Coltrane was referring to a move to *modal jazz.* (See the box "What Is Modal Jazz?") Instead of the complex chord progressions of bebop and hard bop, Davis's compositions incorporated fewer chords. Significantly, the improvisations over each of these chords were often based on a single scale. The decisive shift toward modal jazz was evident in Davis's 1959 recording *Kind of Blue,* an album universally acclaimed as one of the most significant in the history of jazz. All the elements of Davis's mature style—his deep lyricism, economy, and searching—crystallized on this record. The introspective nature of much of the record was inspired by Davis's pianist, Bill Evans—a lyrical player who brought an impressionistic transparency to the music. Evans wrote the liner notes to the album: "Miles conceived these settings only hours before the recording dates and arrived with sketches that indicated to the group what was to be played."[15]

Three of the other tunes on *Kind of Blue,* "Flamenco Sketches," "Blue in Green," and "All Blues," have become

---

Modal jazz is a body of music that makes use of one or more of the following characteristics: modal scales for improvising, slow harmonic rhythm, pedal points, and the absence or suppression of functional harmonic relationships. Significant early examples of modal jazz come from Miles Davis's recording *Kind of Blue* (1959) and the recordings of John Coltrane's classic quartet (1960–1964).

Insider's Guide to...

What Is Modal Jazz?

Modal jazz loosely describes a body of music that originated in the late 1950s and 1960s. Jazz historians typically refer to Miles Davis's recordings on *Kind of Blue* (and Davis's earlier 1958 composition "Milestones"), as well as the music of John Coltrane's classic quartet (1960–1964), as important points of departure for modal jazz.

Modal jazz gets its name from the idea that modes (particular scales) provide improvisers with the appropriate pitches to use in their solos over individual chords. In the liner notes to Kind of Blue, pianist Bill Evans indicates that each chord is associated with a particular scale. These scales are the modes, including the Ionian, Dorian, Phrygian, Lydian, Mixolydian, Aeolian, and Locrian.

The term modal jazz often leads to confusion, however, because many of the qualities attributed to modal jazz do not necessarily have to do with the use of modes. In fact, as critics of the term point out, improvisers do not always restrict themselves to the pitches of the mode in their solos.* In addition, the term often refers to a composition or an accompaniment that makes use of one or more of the following techniques:

- Slow-moving harmonic rhythm, in which a single chord may last for four, eight, sixteen, or more measures

- Use of pedal points (static bass pitches over which the harmonies may shift)

- Absence or suppression of standard functional harmonic patterns, such as V–I or ii–V–I

- Chords or melodies that make use of the interval of a perfect fourth

As this list suggests, many of the features associated with modal jazz concern composition and accompaniment rather than improvisation. Accounts of modal jazz, however, often do not distinguish among these three related yet distinct ideas. After Miles Davis and John Coltrane, such performers as Herbie Hancock, Wayne Shorter, and McCoy Tyner were considered important exponents of modal jazz.

---

*See Barry Kernfeld, "Adderley, Coltrane, and Davis at the Twilight of Bebop: The Search for Melodic Coherence" (Ph.D. diss., Cornell University, 1981).

LISTENING GUIDE
Track 40
"So What" (excerpt)

Miles Davis Sextet: "So What" (Davis), from Kind of Blue, Columbia CS 1355. New York, March 2, 1959. Davis, trumpet, leader; John Coltrane, tenor saxophone; Julian "Cannonball" Adderley, alto saxophone; Bill Evans, piano; Paul Chambers, bass; Jimmy Cobb, drums.

The Main Point   Arguably, Miles Davis reached the apex of his improvisational ability in the 1950s and 1960s with a stream of brilliant albums and solos. Among his many fine small groups, a classic sextet was established in the 1950s with John Coltrane, alto saxophone player Cannonball Adderley, and pianist Bill Evans. Kind of Blue, which contains the classic recording of "So What," is one of this sextet's finest albums and has remained consistently popular. Miles Davis's trumpet solo on "So What" is masterly, combining elements of cool jazz with the emerging modal style.

Although "So What" is a normal 32-bar AABA composition, each of the eight-bar A sections is based on a single chord and scale (or mode); the eight-bar B section transposes the original chord and scale up a half step. The slow-moving harmony (one chord per eight measures) and the use of a single scale over that chord are important characteristics of modal jazz. The listening guide here describes a portion of the performance, including the opening Miles Davis trumpet solo and the following John Coltrane tenor saxophone solo.

Introduction

0:00	"So What" begins out of tempo, with the bass and the piano laying down a moody introduction. The left hand of the piano doubles the melodic line played by the bassist.

Head—AABA

0:32	For the first A section, the bass plays the melody and the piano answers with the two-chord ("So what") figure. The two instruments establish a call-and-response idea, with the drums playing softly on the cymbals.
0:47	At the return of the A section, the alto and tenor saxophones and the trumpet join the piano on the two-chord answering figure, while the drummer continues keeping time on the cymbal.
1:02	The B section repeats the A section, but now it is played a half step higher. Again the bass plays the melody for the call, and the piano and the horns provide the response.
1:16	Return of the A section.

Davis solo—2 choruses (AABA)

1:31	A cymbal crash announces the change to a walking bass and the two-chorus trumpet solo. Davis's solo begins with his characteristically lyrical and wistful sound that relies on the use of space between phrases.
1:46	At the second A section, Evans's comping creates a dialogue with the trumpet solo.
2:00	During the B section, Evans's comping uses dense chords beneath the trumpet solo.
2:14	Again, Davis uses a significant amount of space between his melodic ideas in this final A section of his first chorus.
2:28	Second chorus. During this first A section of Davis's second chorus, bassist Chambers continues to keep time but plays only a few different notes. This gives a static quality to the pulse of this section that contrasts with the following A section.
2:43	Chambers now returns to a walking bass beneath the solo, effectively setting up a feeling of release during this second A section. Davis uses bent notes in this section, an effect achieved by pushing the trumpet valves only halfway down.

2:56	B section.
3:10	Davis concludes his solo with some lyrical ideas focused in the midrange of the horn.

Coltrane solo—2 choruses (AABA)

3:25	In contrast with the restrained lyricism of Davis's solo, the tenor saxophone solo maintains an urgent tone.
3:39	In this second A section, Coltrane starts relying on faster notes that display his celebrated technical ability on the instrument. Here Evans's comping is unusual: he plays quick, short notes in the right hand while playing longer-held chords in the left hand.
3:52	In the B section, Coltrane uses faster notes and the upper register of the instrument more frequently.
4:06	In the final A section of this second chorus, Coltrane repeats and develops a single melodic idea.
4:20	Second chorus. Coltrane continues to develop single melodic ideas in each section. As in Davis's solo, Chambers uses only a few different bass notes, setting up a feeling of stasis that will be released in the following section.
4:34	Chambers returns to a walking bass in this second A section.
5:01	Listen for Coltrane's combination of faster notes combined with the use of longer-held tones at the ends of phrases in this final A section of his solo.

Listen to this music in an animated Active Listening Guide available at the text website.

jazz standards. The album is one of the best-selling jazz records of all time and was strongly influential on a generation of musicians.

Although Davis underwent various style changes throughout his career, the following list summarizes his cool/early modern playing:

▶ Sensitive melodic lines with frequent blues inflections

▶ Irregular phrase lengths

▶ Wide range of note values

▶ Use of space between phrases

▶ Concentration on midrange of trumpet

▶ Full but reticent tone (especially obvious in his playing with a harmon mute)

▶ Melodic connections based on motives and large-scale gestures

▶ Sensitive and cool expression

▶ Little reliance on previously composed licks

▶ Inside playing, using conservative chord-scale associations

During the late 1950s, Davis revived his collaboration with arranger Gil Evans, with whom he had worked in the *Birth of the Cool* sessions a decade earlier. The pair turned out four recordings, noted for their lush instrumentation beneath Davis's distinctive sound. Davis also began to use flugelhorn, which is like a trumpet but has a larger bore and a much mellower timbre. The first of these collaborations, the album *Miles Ahead*, featured Davis as soloist with a nineteen-piece orchestra. More remarkable was their 1958 recording of *Porgy and Bess*, in which Davis put his stamp on Gershwin's compositions, such as "Summertime." The concerto ideal—soloist with accompanying orchestra—reached its culmination in *Sketches of Spain*, which actually featured an arrangement of a guitar concerto, the *Concierto de Aranjuez* by Joaquín Rodrigo. The fourth collaboration was *Quiet Nights*, an album less successful than the other three.

By the end of the 1950s, Davis had established himself as one of the leading figures in jazz, exploring new directions for improvised ensemble music. We return to his seminal quintet of 1964–1967 in our discussion of the music of the 1960s in Chapter 10.

Cool and Hard Bop Melodic Styles

QUALITY	COOL	HARD BOP
Timbre	■ Softer, smoother, more relaxed ■ Midrange of instruments emphasized ■ Almost no use of blue-note effects ■ Soft attacks and legato	■ Beboplike, hard-edged, brittle, insistent ■ Use of upper registers ■ Blue-note effects, blues riffs ■ Wide variety of attacks and articulations
Phrasing	■ Irregular, like bebop phrasing ■ Much use of space between phrases	■ Slightly more regular than bebop phrasing ■ Return to two-and four-bar units in funky/soul jazz
Rhythm	■ Much greater variety than bop in up-tempo and medium tempo pieces	■ More syncopated ■ Trend toward simpler blues patterns ■ More variety than bebop
Thematic continuity	■ Balanced between motivic and voice leading	■ Motives sometimes emphasized over voice leading
Chord-scale relations	■ Inside, often with the extended chord tones heard in bop	■ Inside, often based on blues scale
Large-scale coherence	■ Motivic structure and voice leading ■ Balance of gesture	■ Motivic, especially in funky/soul jazz, use of climax/release, and gestural balance

Exam Review Questions

Use these questions and the materials on the text website to help you understand and pass tests on the content of this chapter.

1. What new jazz substyles developed in the 1950s? Which performers were associated with which substyle?

2. How was cool jazz distinguished from bebop? Was the separation always distinct?

3. Why is cool jazz sometimes called West Coast jazz?

4. What aspects of the jazz tradition were modified or experimented on by third-stream musicians? Who were some of the notable third-stream musicians?

5. Who were the principal hard bop musicians? How did their music differ from cool jazz and third-stream music?

6. How did Miles Davis transcend some of the standard 1950s substyle boundaries?

 MindTap™

Test Yourself on Key Concepts with additional Chapter Quizzes and Listening Activities on the text website.

Key Terms

Test your knowledge of this chapter's key terms by defining the following. If you can't remember the meaning of a term, refresh your memory by looking up the boldfaced term in the chapter, turning to the Glossary at the back of the book, or working with the flash-cards at the text website.

Amen cadence **243**

block-chord style **238**

bossa nova **237**

church cadence **243**

cool jazz **225**

counterpoint **225**

cross-rhythms **238**

fugue **231**

full-chord style **238**

funky jazz **226**

gospel jazz **226**

hard bop **226**

harmon mute **253**

locked-hands style **238**

LP **226**

modal jazz **254**

overdubbing **226**

plagal cadence **243**

polyphonic **225**

polyrhythms **238**

shuffle **244**

soul jazz **226**

stretto **233**

subject **231**

third-stream music **231**

twelve-tone composition **241**

West Coast jazz **239**

The 1960s Avant-Garde

9

Start with a quick
warm-up activity.

THE STYLISTIC INNOVATIONS IN JAZZ DURING THE 1950s led directly to the formation of a controversial avant-garde in the 1960s. Heated debates arose, recalling the vitriolic exchanges between the beboppers and the moldy figs during the 1940s. The principal issue in the 1960s (as in the 1940s) was disagreement between innovators and populists: innovators felt that the music must progress, while populists thought that the music should attract and please a mass audience. Even today these controversies remain far from settled. In many respects they mirror the general tension in the West between popular and fine art. What ultimately validates an art form? Acceptance by a large audience (the popular) or the originality resulting from cutting-edge experimentation (the avant-garde)?

Given that this issue had been around a while, what made the 1960s free jazz or the avant-garde so controversial? The principal reason was that the avant-gardists radically rejected aspects of the jazz tradition that many players and listeners considered fundamental. Improvisation still remained, but other elements were drastically altered—changes that made the music seem incoherent to some. These changes included the following:

▶ *Absence of a steady pulse or meter.* The 4/4 swing feel, often considered essential to the jazz tradition, was frequently abandoned.

▶ *Absence of a predetermined harmonic structure.* For the avant-garde soloists, improvisations did not have to be bound by an underlying harmonic progression. Horn soloists sometimes resorted to a **nontempered intonation** that could conflict with a pianist or guitarist comping the changes. Many groups did away with the instruments that normally provided harmonic support, such as piano or guitar.

Jazz

1960—Ornette Coleman records *Free Jazz*
1962—Classic Coltrane quartet formed with Elvin Jones, Jimmy Garrison, and McCoy Tyner
—Bill Dixon–Archie Shepp Quartet
1964—Coltrane quartet records A *Love Supreme,* including "Acknowledgement" (Track 42)
—Albert Ayler records "Ghosts" (Track 43)
—Death of Eric Dolphy in Berlin
1965—Association for the Advancement of Creative Musicians (AACM) founded
—Coltrane records *Ascension*
1966—Cecil Taylor, *Unit Structures*
1967—Death of John Coltrane
1968—Anthony Braxton, For Alto (solo saxophone)
1970—Death of Albert Ayler

1960   **1965**   **1970**

Historical Events

1960—Civil Rights Act
1961—Yuri Gagarin, first manned space flight
—Berlin wall erected
—Peace Corps established
1963—Assassination of President Kennedy
—Pop Art movement begins
1964—Passage of Civil Rights Act
1965—Martin Luther King Jr. leads civil rights march in Selma, Alabama
—Mariner 4 flies by Mars
1967—First heart transplant
—Six Day War between Arabs and Israelis
—Marquez, *One Hundred Years of Solitude*
1968—Martin Luther King Jr. and Robert
F. Kennedy assassinated
1969—U.S. astronauts walk on the moon

Nontempered intonation is the use of pitches unrestricted by the "equal-tempered," twelve-note chromatic scale. For example, a nontempered pitch might be a note between D and E♭. Pitches between the tempered notes of the chromatic scale are sometimes called **microtones**.

Free jazz, the **avant-garde**, and the **New Thing** are terms used to describe the 1960s jazz substyle that overturned many of the traditional elements of jazz.

▶ *Altered role for rhythm-section instruments.* Avant-garde bassists and drummers often no longer performed their typical timekeeping roles but instead participated in collective improvisation.

▶ *Freer formal structures.* Before the 1960s, musical structures were based on smaller groupings of four, eight, and sixteen measures, helping listeners orient themselves within the form.

Many avant-garde players eschewed this regularity in composing and improvising.

▶ *Use of extended or unusual instrumental sounds.* The avant-garde soloists cultivated new timbres and sounds. Percussion became more prominent; saxophonists and trumpeters explored the highest registers and incorporated shrieks and wailing, often imitating the human voice.

Not all these features are in evidence on all free jazz performances. Some free jazz players made use of many of these features; others, only a few. Free jazz therefore offered a wide range of possibilities in the areas of meter, harmony, form, and instrumental technique. How they were adopted varied from performance to performance and—sometimes—within a single performance.

This chapter considers the key figures of the avant-garde of the 1960s along with some of the larger social and cultural upheavals taking place during the decade.

> What ultimately validates an art form?
> Acceptance by a large audience (the popular)
> or the originality resulting from cutting-edge
> experimentation (the avant-garde)?

Ornette Coleman and Free Jazz

With the arrival of alto saxophonist Ornette Coleman on the New York scene in 1959, **avant-garde** jazz—also called **free jazz** or the **New Thing**—received its strongest initial boost. In fact, free jazz received its label from the 1960 Coleman album of the same name. A cover painting by abstract expressionist Jackson Pollock reinforced its avant-garde statement. Coleman, who initially played a plastic alto saxophone, polarized the jazz community in New York in the late 1950s: some hailed him as a genius, while others denounced him as a charlatan.

Coleman's music was controversial. His quartet—with trumpeter Don Cherry, bassist Charlie Haden, and drummer Billy Higgins (replaced by Ed Blackwell in 1960)—had no chordal instruments such as the piano. Some listeners dismissed his music as a radical rejection of the jazz tradition, but those who praised him considered his music an extension of historical practice. Among Coleman's earliest champions was pianist John Lewis of the Modern Jazz Quartet, who had heard Coleman's group in California:

> I've never heard anything like Ornette Coleman and Don Cherry before. Ornette is, in a sense, an extension of Charlie Parker—the first I've heard. This is the real need . . . to extend the basic ideas of Bird until they're not playing an imitation but actually something new.[1]

As his album titles *Change of the Century* and *The Shape of Jazz to Come* suggested, Coleman's music was new. The improvised solos were not necessarily tied to traditional harmonic progressions but instead were based on loose and shifting tonal centers. Without any harmonic accompaniment, the soloists could move freely to different harmonic areas, although Haden's bass lines sometimes retained the pieces' original forms.

Coleman was an astonishingly prolific composer whose tuneful, sometimes cheerful compositions were written to be interpreted freely. Coleman noted:

> I don't tell the members of the group what to do. I want them to play what they hear in the piece themselves. I let everyone express himself just as he wants to. The musicians have complete freedom, and so, of course, our final results depend entirely on the musicianship, emotional make-up, and taste of the individual members.[2]

Unlike traditional jazz improvisation, in which the soloist and the accompaniment often follow a repeating 32-bar structure, Coleman's work sometimes abandoned this form. Most of his compositions, however, retained the large-scale organization of head-solos-head associated with more-conventional jazz.

Coleman was born in Fort Worth, Texas, in 1930. After beginning his career performing in rhythm-and-blues (R&B) bands in the mid-forties, he briefly moved to New Orleans in 1948, working mostly in nonmusical jobs, then returned to Fort Worth. Joining the R&B band of Pee Wee Crayton, Coleman traveled to Los Angeles, where he settled in 1954 after being fired by Crayton. He worked for a while as an elevator operator—a job that allowed him to read and study music theory while parked on the tenth floor. Participating in Los Angeles jam sessions, he occasionally encountered scorn from other musicians, but he also found like-minded players interested in his music and in his freer approach to improvisation.

In 1958 Coleman signed with Contemporary Records and recorded two albums for the label. His first, *Something Else!!!! The Music of Ornette Coleman*, was cut in 1958 and featured a conventional rhythm section with drummer Billy Higgins and pianist Walter Norris; the second, *Tomorrow Is the Question*, was recorded the following year and abandoned the use of piano.

The forms for Coleman's early compositions were frequently conventional, following the structure of the 12-bar blues and the 32-bar AABA song form. Of his irregular pieces, "Mind and Time" used a 10-bar form, and "Giggin'" was a 13-bar blues. Coleman's unique contribution, however, was his ability to veer into different tonal directions, dissociating himself from a fixed harmonic scheme in his solos. Although his albums for Contemporary were less radical than his work to come, they show how his music was evolving toward complete freedom from syntactic constraints.

> "I've never heard anything like Ornette Coleman . . . before. Ornette is, in a sense, an extension of Charlie Parker." —John Lewis

Photo Courtesy of the Morgan Collection

After signing with Atlantic Records in 1959, Coleman recorded *The Shape of Jazz to Come* and *Change of the Century* with his own quartet, comprising Cherry, Haden, and Higgins. Coleman's approach to the alto saxophone

Coleman shaped large-scale form by establishing loose, shifting tonal centers and through musical gestures such as dynamic climax, melodic contour, and sectionalization. All in all, Coleman succeeded in allying passionate expres-

Coleman worked for a while as an elevator operator—a job that allowed him to read and study music theory while parked on the tenth floor.

was unique: he emulated the human voice, using bent pitches and unusual intonation. "There are some intervals," he stated, "that carry that human quality if you play them in the right pitch. You can reach into the human sound of a voice on your horn if you're actually hearing and trying to express the warmth of a human voice."[3] Coleman's unusual intonation and motivic playing was often embedded in a relatively simple rhythmic language, creating, as one writer put it, "a touch of folksong naiveté."[4]

These features summarize Coleman's style:

> ## "You can reach into the human sound of a voice on your horn if you're actually hearing and trying to express the warmth of a human voice."
> ## —Ornette Coleman

sion to rigorous linear structure; his playing was emotional, powerful, and thoroughly individual.

John Lewis arranged for Coleman and Don Cherry to attend the Lenox School of Jazz in Massachusetts in the summer of 1959. That November, Coleman and his group came to New York for their legendary gig at the Five Spot. Despite the acclaim of Lewis and other famous musical figures such

- Fragmented, angular melodies instead of the long, spun-out eighth-note phrases of bebop

- Melodic connections based on motivic structure and large-scale gestures and more-abstract relations among sets of pitches

- Little if any use of conventional harmony and voice leading, but solos often establish loose, shifting tonal centers

- Variety of melodic rhythm but avoidance of even-note phrases

- Nasal, insistent tone

- Rhythm at times loosely connected to background pulse

- Concentration on middle and upper range of instrument

- Passionate expression

- Deviations from standard intonation

As tightly controlled as Coleman's playing was, his pitch structure and his rhythmic fluidity created an impression of freewheeling spontaneity. He combined a sensuous, linear approach to the instrument with a strikingly original sound, created in part by his unique, well-controlled intonation. Although harmony in the conventional sense of chord changes did not often factor into Coleman's music, harmony in the larger sense of related intervals and control always appeared. Without conventional harmony,

as Gunther Schuller and Leonard Bernstein, the group experienced derision by some of the older established players. For example, trumpeter Roy Eldridge claimed, "He's putting everybody on. They start with a nice lead-off figure, but then they go off into outer space. They disregard the chords and they play odd numbers of bars. I can't follow them."[5]

In December 1960 Coleman took the unprecedented step of bringing together eight players (two quartets) in a composition entitled *Free Jazz*. Coleman had expanded his quartet—Cherry, Haden, and Blackwell—with Higgins, bassist Scott LaFaro, and bass clarinetist Eric Dolphy. The group recorded two takes (one of them lasted thirty-six minutes): they combined solo improvisation, collective improvisation, and prearranged ensemble passages.

To many listeners *Free Jazz* was daunting: it seemed formless and chaotic, a radical rejection of all jazz conventions. Careful listeners, however, heard within its collective freedom a musical conversation in which motives and ideas were stated, then drawn out, reinterpreted, and developed by other players. The role of the rhythm-section players seemed predetermined as well: Haden and Blackwell maintained the fundamental rhythmic pulse, while LaFaro and Higgins played against the time.[6] Coleman's written ensemble passages were used as transitions between the improvised sections.

Free Jazz profoundly influenced the emerging jazz avant-garde. It suggested new sets of relationships among improvisers and allowed the rhythm section to jettison routine timekeeping. Both the use of collective improvisation based on freely improvised motives and the abandonment of cycling harmonic-metric forms redefined the possibilities of group interaction. Other players, such as pianist Cecil Taylor, may also have been experimenting with freely improvised music, but Coleman's greater visibility forced many players to reevaluate their own approaches to the inherited practices of the jazz tradition.

Coleman revealed his interest in contemporary concert music and the third stream by his appearance on Gunther Schuller's 1960 album *Jazz Abstractions;* Coleman was the alto saxophone soloist on "Abstractions," a serial work by Schuller for alto, string quartet, two double basses, guitar, and percussion. Continuing in a third-stream vein, Coleman premiered in England his chamber music work, *Sounds and Forms for Wind Quintet,* performing trumpet interludes between all ten movements. It showed his ability to create extended compositional structures. This work helped Coleman win the prestigious Guggenheim award for composition; he was the first jazz composer to be so honored.

By 1962 Coleman had temporarily withdrawn from public performance; he returned in 1965, playing not only saxophone but also trumpet and violin in a trio with drummer Charles Moffett and bassist David Izenzon. An even more radical player than Haden, Izenzon contradicted the pulse at times, provided melodic commentary, and often used the bow. Coleman brought an intensely percussive, furious, driving approach to the violin, while he centered his trumpet playing in the instrument's higher register, alternating rapid runs with smeared notes and strong accents. Approaching new instruments in an unorthodox manner, Coleman continued to generate controversy among musicians and listeners, although his European tour in 1965 had a significant impact on the avant-garde overseas. On his recording from Stockholm, *Live at the Golden Circle,* Coleman's alto saxophone solos remained highly organized motivically, as can be heard in his compositions "Dee Dee" and "European Echoes."

Coleman's work in the 1970s and 1980s has been influenced by what he calls *harmolodic theory,* a term first discussed in the liner notes to *Skies of America.* Coleman noted that **harmolodics** presented "melody, harmony, and the instrumentation of the movement of forms." He later wrote that they "had to do with using the melody, the harmony, and the rhythm all equal."[7] Gunther Schuller suggested that harmolodics relates to the use of similar melodic material in different clefs and keys, producing a texture of predominantly parallel motion, although Schuller freely admitted that it was unclear how this idea related directly to Coleman's own compositional technique. The term is characteristic, Schuller noted, of Coleman's obscure and often contradictory yet often poetic pronouncements on music.[8] Despite Coleman's own writing on the subject, the theory remains vague.

During the early 1970s, Coleman worked sporadically, sometimes insisting on compensation for recordings and appearances that was too large for a jazz musician of his celebrity and audience appeal. He preferred to remain underemployed and underrecorded rather than sacrifice his artistic principles.

Coleman regained the jazz limelight during the mid-seventies, combining his free style with funk rhythms and reemerging as a notable and innovative player. Coleman formed the group Prime Time to incorporate these changes in his style and in his interests. As with his earlier music, much of the improvisational material was not governed by conventional harmonic structure. This time, however, Coleman used electric instruments.

Prime Time began as a quintet, with two electric guitarists and an electric bassist; it was later expanded to a sextet, with the addition of a second drummer. The group featured an interesting amalgam of rhythm and blues, free jazz, and other influences, including Moroccan music. Against an unusual combination of rock and funk **backbeats** (heavy emphases on beats 2 and 4) alongside rhythm-and-blues vamps, Coleman improvised atonally, often using microtonal pitches. Clearly, he was attempting to broaden his status as an avant-garde figure and reconnect with his R&B origins.

Coleman achieved a wider degree of recognition after touring and recording with fusion guitarist Pat Metheny between 1985 and 1986. He recorded with Metheny on the 1985 album *Song X.* In 1987 Coleman recorded *In All Languages,* in which his original 1959 quartet including Don Cherry, Charlie Haden, and Billy Higgins was juxtaposed with his Prime Time electric ensemble. This album, now considered a Coleman classic, was reissued on CD by Verve/Harmolodic in 1997. It provides a remarkable summary of Coleman's distinguished career.

In 1997 Lincoln Center presented an entire evening dedicated to Coleman—*Civilization: A Harmolodic Celebration*—that featured performances of his group, Prime Time, and reunited Coleman with Charlie Haden and Billy Higgins. Among the other guests were Lou Reed and Laurie Anderson. There the New York Philharmonic Orchestra performed Coleman's large-scale work for orchestra (written in 1971) entitled *Skies of America,* with movements that included "Foreigner in a Free Land" and "The Men Who Live in the White House."

By the 1990s Coleman was accepted as one of the elder representatives of the jazz avant-garde. He was inducted into the French Order of Arts and Letters in 1997 and was elected to the prestigious American Academy of Arts and Letters the same year. In 2007 Coleman's

---

Harmolodics is a theory of music devised by Ornette Coleman. Although its meaning is unclear, harmolodics has provided the theoretical motivation behind Coleman's work since the 1970s.

Backbeats are heavy emphases on beats 2 and 4, as played by the drummer (usually) on the snare drum. (Other drums or the hi-hat can be used for quieter backbeats.) They can be added to a 4/4 swing rhythm as well. Backbeats increase dance ability by clarifying the rhythm and adding to the excitement of the music.

LISTENING GUIDE

"Street Woman"

Track 41

Ornette Coleman: "Street Woman" (Coleman), from *Science Fiction*. Original issue Columbia KC31061. Reissued on Sony SRCS 9372. New York, September 9–13, 1971. Don Cherry, pocket trumpet; Coleman, alto saxophone; Charlie Haden, bass; Billy Higgins, drums.

The Main Point "Street Woman" shows the joyful, up-tempo sound of Coleman's best-known quartet. Like so many of Coleman's pieces, "Street Woman" projects a basic tonal center (in this case, G), although it avoids standard chord progressions.

The motivic tightness of the melody is remarkable: after the opening three figures present their abrupt flourishes, the remainder of the melody releases the built-up tension with descending three-note ideas. These three-note descents are either two steps or a step and a third.

Head—1st time through

0:00 The melodic basis of "Street Woman" lies in a series of melodic figures.

Haden's bass accompaniment consists largely of rapid alternations between single-pitch octaves. He follows the horns through the figures of the melody, while his bass line imparts a sense of harmonic movement to the head without detailing specific chords.

Head—2nd time through

0:14 The principal melody is repeated in virtually the same manner.

Coleman alto saxophone solo

0:31 This solo begins with a flourish up to G that recalls one of the melodic figures from the head. He works largely with pitches from the G major scale, then deviates, then returns to the basic G pitch center, which he articulates in numerous ways.

1:28 and 1:56 Coleman returns to the high G in a passionate statement several times toward the end of his solo. The reiteration of the high G helps unite the work, giving it a focus on an emotional high point. At the same time, the G is the overall tonality of the composition and performance.

Haden gradually assumes a walking bass as accompaniment, although he will return to octaves from time to time.

Haden bass solo

2:07 Haden works with the idea of keeping one pitch constant and moving the other.

2:46 Later he moves into a freer statement that ushers in Cherry's pocket trumpet solo.

Cherry trumpet solo

3:11 Cherry presents ideas that recall strongly the figures of the head, particularly melodic figure 1. His solo begins energetically with a flurry of notes. Haden returns to the octave idea of the head.

3:35 Cherry's lines become more lyrical and tonal, emphasizing G minor.

4:02 Cherry ends his solo with an almost classical F♯–G (leading tone-to-tonic) phrase.

Head—Reprise

4:07 The head is played twice, as it was heard at the beginning of the performance.

Coda

4:41 The opening melodic figure is repeated three times with a follow-up high G. Haden closes the bass line on E♭, avoiding the traditional cadence to the tonic G.

The excerpt is representative of Coleman's quartet output in the following ways:

▶ Head-solos-head format, but without harmonic instrument (such as guitar or piano)

▶ Lack of standard harmonic progression, and freer improvisational style

 Listen to this music in an animated Active Listening Guide available at the text website.

album *Sound Grammar* won the prestigious Pulitzer Prize for music, the first such award granted to a recording, and the first granted to purely improvised music.

John Coltrane

In the twelve years from 1955, when he joined Miles Davis's quintet, to his death in 1967, John Coltrane, initially an obscure and often criticized tenor player, became the leading saxophonist of his generation and one of the most important jazz artists of all time. His influence was profound. He was consistently devoted to his craft, to technical proficiency, to musical exploration, and to endless practicing and studying. His album titles, such as *A Love Supreme* and *Om*, revealed the connection of his music to his religious beliefs and spiritual quest. Fans and listeners heard his extended solos as reaching for the ineffable. Particularly with his quartet of 1960–1965, Coltrane became the symbol of the improvising musician as exploratory seeker. Even in his later, successful years, Coltrane remained uncompromising in his musical ideals and overall goals.

Overview of Coltrane's Career

Although Coltrane underwent many changes and transformations in his sound and his style, his career encompasses three general periods:

▶ 1955–1960: Hard bop and "sheets of sound"

▶ 1960–1965: Classic quartet and modal compositions

▶ 1965–1967: Avant-garde

In the first period, Coltrane and Sonny Rollins competed to be the premier tenor saxophonist in jazz. At that time Coltrane was often described as a hard bop player with an edgy sound. Jazz critic Ira Gitler coined the phrase **sheets of sound** to describe Coltrane's rapid-fire

execution, irregular groupings of notes, unusual phrasing, and technique of inserting several harmonies over a single chord. Coltrane's 1959 composition "Giant Steps"

The career of John Coltrane was marked by a restless search for musical growth and the transcendental.

Photo Courtesy of the Morgan Collection

Sheets of sound, an expression coined by jazz critic Ira Gitler, describes a method of playing that features extremely fast notes with irregular phrase groupings. Sometimes unusual harmonies are introduced over the given chord.

was a tour de force of improvisation over rapid and unusual harmonic shifts, which showed off his dazzling ability to execute eighth-note lines over a difficult sequence of chord changes.

Coltrane launched his second period by bringing together his well-known and long-lived quartet, which included McCoy Tyner on piano, Jimmy Garrison on bass, and Elvin Jones on drums. The repertory of the quartet emphasized modal composition, often with particular attention to minor modes such as the Dorian. (See the box "What Is Modal Jazz?" in Chapter 8.) The group's extended improvisations, such as in their performance of "My Favorite Things," featured fewer and slower-moving harmonies. The quartet's modal approach reached its zenith in the December 10, 1964, recording *A Love Supreme*, a four-movement suite. (Listen to Track 42 to hear one of these movements.)

Coltrane's third and final period spanned the last two years of his life, when he became increasingly involved in the jazz avant-garde. His album *Ascension*, which used several young, radical musicians, provided a significant document of the free jazz movement.

Early Years

Born in Hamlet, North Carolina, on September 23, 1926, and raised in High Point, North Carolina, Coltrane played, at age thirteen, alto horn, clarinet, and then alto saxophone. Initially influenced by Johnny Hodges, who played in Ellington's group, he eventually came under the inescapable spell of Charlie Parker. After moving to Philadelphia in 1943, Coltrane studied at several local music schools; he then joined the U.S. Navy band and was stationed in Hawaii between 1945 and 1946. The following year while on tour in California with the King Kolax band, Coltrane met Parker, recently released from Camarillo State Hospital. Coltrane attended Parker's February 19 recording session for Dial—which included pianist Erroll Garner—and later took part in a jam session with the altoist.

In 1948 Coltrane joined the band of Eddie "Cleanhead" Vinson. It was at that time that Coltrane took up the tenor saxophone, which opened up a range of possibilities:

When I bought a tenor to go with Eddie Vinson's band, a wider area of listening opened up for me. I found I was able to be more varied in my musical interests. On alto, Bird had been my whole influence, but on tenor I found there was no one man whose ideas were so dominant as Charlie's were on alto. Therefore, I drew from all the men I heard during this period, beginning with Lester [Young], and believe me, I've picked up something from them all, including several who have never recorded. The reason I like Lester so was that I could feel that line, that simplicity...There were a lot of things that [Coleman] Hawkins was doing that I knew I'd have to learn somewhere along the line. I felt the same way about Ben Webster...The first time I heard Hawk, I was

fascinated by his arpeggios and the way he played. I got a copy of his "Body and Soul" and listened real hard to what he was doing.[9]

This quotation reveals Coltrane's ability to absorb a huge array of influences. Throughout his career he remained profoundly interested in the musical developments of his colleagues and was extremely supportive of many of the younger musicians. In addition to his appetite for music, however, Coltrane displayed an inclination toward substance abuse. He began using heroin in the late 1940s, and he frequently drank and ate obsessively. He remained addicted to heroin for nearly ten years.

In 1949 Coltrane joined Dizzy Gillespie's band, with which he made his first commercial recording. During this time Coltrane continued to study and absorb the styles of other tenor saxophonists, particularly bebop pioneers Dexter Gordon and Wardell Gray, as well as Sonny Stitt, a bop altoist who also doubled on tenor.

Taking on a staggering variety of gigs as a sideman, Coltrane appeared in the R&B bands of Earl Bostic, as well as Gay Crosse and His Good Humor Six. In 1954 he joined the band of one of his earliest idols, alto saxophonist Johnny Hodges. Coltrane appreciated Hodges's musical sincerity and confidence and noted that "I liked every tune in the book."[10] Unfortunately, Coltrane's problems with drugs and alcohol caused him to leave the band and return to Philadelphia to recuperate. Although he had already accumulated numerous professional experiences, his most significant ones were yet to come.

Hard Bop with Miles Davis

Flush with success from his 1955 appearance at the Newport Jazz Festival, Miles Davis formed a working quintet that year, hiring Coltrane on tenor. Although Davis had been using tenor saxophonist Sonny Rollins, Rollins had moved to Chicago, taking the first of his extended sabbaticals from performing. Davis's drummer, Philly Joe Jones, and pianist Red Garland—both Philadelphians—persuaded Davis to hire Coltrane, who was then working with organist Jimmy Smith. In September 1955, in the same week that he married his fiancée, Naima Grubbs, Coltrane played his first performance with Davis.

"When Coltrane joined Miles Davis's quintet in 1955," writes Thomas Owens, "he formed a musical alliance that would have a great impact on the evolution of jazz."[11] Coltrane's years with Davis were indeed formative. Although some critics were initially hostile to Coltrane's aggressive technique and steely tone, his virtuosity was dazzling. Phrases frequently began with an upward glissando, moving to a longer-held vibratoless pitch.

Despite his technical advances, Coltrane's drug habit, along with that of Philly Joe Jones, was causing problems on the bandstand. Miles Davis's biographer, Jack Chambers, recounts the story of Coltrane's falling asleep onstage during an entire set. Present was a record executive

Saxophonist Sonny Rollins was working and recording with the Miles Davis Quintet before Coltrane. Jazz writers and analysts singled out Rollins's musically inventive and thematically coherent solos.

intent on signing him to a major record label; after seeing his condition, he left without talking to Coltrane.[12]

The year 1957 was pivotal in Coltrane's career. Exasperated by his behavior, Davis fired him. Shaken, Coltrane managed to get off heroin and quit drinking alcohol. During the spring and summer, he worked with pianist Thelonious Monk; later that fall the two teamed up for a famous engagement at New York's Five Spot. Monk gave Coltrane further freedom to experiment, with extended solos often backed by only bass and drums. In Coltrane's words, Monk was "a musical architect of the highest order ... I felt I learned from him in every way—through the senses, theoretically, technically."[13] Coltrane

also claimed that Monk was the first to show him how to produce two or three notes simultaneously on the tenor saxophone.

Around this time Coltrane also recorded his first album as a leader. On the LP *Coltrane*, his version of "Violets for Your Furs"—a song earlier recorded by singer Frank Sinatra (and later by Billie Holiday)—showed the depth of tone and emotion that Coltrane could summon on ballads. For these slower, more sensitive solos, he frequently balanced melodic paraphrase with florid runs.

Other Coltrane improvisations showed a turn to the long, sixteenth-note phrases and patterns that were to become a distinctive part of his style. Some of Coltrane's hard bop compositions, such as "Moment's Notice" from his 1957 recording *Blue Train*, contained unusual and quick-moving harmonic twists.

As his technique and approach to the instrument continued to evolve, Coltrane rejoined Davis in 1958. Gitler's term *sheets of sound* was an apt description for Coltrane's torrid scalar passages. In addition, Coltrane made conscious use of unusual and irregular phrasing:

> I found there were a certain number of chord progressions to play in a given time, and sometimes what I played didn't work out in eighth notes, sixteenth notes, or triplets. I had to put the notes in uneven groups like fives and sevens in order to get them all in.[14]

Similarly, Coltrane was candid about harmonic experimentation, sometimes superimposing extra chords on the tunes' basic changes. His solo in "Straight, No Chaser" (from Miles Davis's *Milestones*) contained unusual harmonic substitutions. Referring to Davis's music, Coltrane said, "Due to the direct and free-flowing lines in his music, I found it easy to apply the harmonic ideas that I had. I could stack up chords—say, on a C7, I sometimes superimposed an E♭7, up to an F♭7, down to an F. That way I could play three chords on one."[15]

Davis's modal music supplied the ideal repertory for Coltrane's experiments in **harmonic superimposition**. On his solo on Davis's "So What," from *Kind of Blue* (Track 40), Coltrane "stacked" harmonies over the given D Dorian and E♭ Dorian modalities. In the spring of 1959, the same time he recorded *Kind of Blue* with Davis, Coltrane took his own group into the studio and recorded one

"When Coltrane joined Miles Davis's quintet in 1955, he formed a musical alliance that would have a great impact on the evolution of jazz."

—Thomas Owens

of his most famous works, "Giant Steps." This imaginative composition used the harmonic patterns of hard bop

Harmonic superimposition is the technique of adding chords on top of the harmonies already present in a song. It creates further harmonic complexity.

A **pentatonic scale**, or **pentatonic set**, is a five-note set that avoids the interval of a tritone and can be arranged as a series of perfect fourths or perfect fifths. The black notes of the keyboard form one such scale.

---

but reworked them into a large-scale format with fast key changes linked by major thirds. Its fast-moving harmonies differed drastically from the slow-moving harmonic progressions of modal jazz. In this tour de force, Coltrane showed his mastery of bebop harmonies and unusual progressions in a driving, up-tempo format.

Coltrane's Classic Quartet

In 1960 Coltrane took the decisive step of leaving the Davis sextet and forming his own quartet, which opened at the Jazz Gallery in May. At first, the personnel were unstable. Coltrane initially tried pianist Steve Kuhn, bassist Steve Davis, and drummer Pete LaRoca, but he quickly replaced Kuhn with Philadelphian McCoy Tyner, a hard-driving, percussive pianist who had been a member of the Art Farmer–Benny Golson Jazztet.

In McCoy Tyner (b. 1938) Coltrane found a pianist in sympathy with his own modal interests. Tyner's harmonic sound was based on chords built in fourths. In backing up Coltrane, he frequently intoned a bass-register open fifth in his left hand, operating as a kind of drone that created a tonal center. This open-fifth drone focused the

---

Pianist McCoy Tyner's powerful playing is based on modal harmonies built in fourths.

Photo Courtesy of the Morgan Collection

tonality, leaving Coltrane free to depart from and return to the tonal center within his improvisations. Tyner's own solos projected an extremely forceful and clipped staccato touch on improvised lines, which sometimes culminated in thunderous tremolos. On his earliest recordings—including his own *Inception* and *Reaching Fourth*—Tyner played his staccato and even eighth-note lines in a hard bop idiom, skillfully negotiating each harmony. During his five years with Coltrane, however, he interpreted the harmonies more freely, ranging both inside and outside the tonal centers, often through **pentatonic scales**.

Renowned for his powerful touch and almost demonic energy, Tyner has remained one of the most popular pianists in jazz. He continues to work with his own groups, including a big band, and has appeared as a special guest both live and on recordings with other major artists.

Like Tyner, Coltrane's drummer, Elvin Jones, was also a fiery, intense player. Born in Pontiac, Michigan, Jones (1927–2004) came from a musical family that included his equally renowned brothers, trumpeter Thad Jones (1923–1986) and pianist Hank Jones (1918–2010). Before joining Coltrane, Elvin Jones had recorded with Miles Davis, Art Farmer, J. J. Johnson, and Sonny Rollins. Jones's years with Coltrane brought him fame not only for his complex polyrhythms but also for sheer physical endurance. In the context of the band's extended improvisations, Jones generated unbelievable energy and drive as both a powerful timekeeper and a complementary voice to Coltrane's own style. Their performances often included extended duets without piano or bass accompaniment. The level of energy generated by Jones's playing brought about an increased participation for the drummer relative to the bassist and the pianist. Jones was aware of this role. In discussing his playing with Coltrane, he said:

> I always realize I'm not the soloist, that John is, and I'm merely the support for him. It may sound like a duet or duel at times, but it's still a support I'm lending him, a complementary thing. . . . It's being done in the same context of the earlier style, only this is just another step forward in the relationship between the rhythm section and the soloist. It's much freer—John realizes he has this close support, and, therefore, he can move further ahead; he can venture out as far as he wants without worrying about getting away from everybody and having the feeling he's out in the middle of a lake by himself.[16]

Coltrane's classic quartet was rounded out by bassist Jimmy Garrison (1934–1976), who joined at the end of 1961. Like its other members, Garrison had played and recorded with numerous hard bop musicians in the late fifties. Garrison had even performed with Ornette Coleman on *Ornette on Tenor* and was a regular member of Coleman's band just before joining Coltrane. Less technically oriented than Tyner and Jones, Garrison was a thoroughly solid player who often relied on drones and fixed patterns in addition to the more customary walking lines when he was accompanying soloists. In his own solos, Garrison featured unusual bass techniques, sometimes strumming the bass with three-note chords in a quasi-flamenco style.

The quartet became one of the premier groups in jazz; at the same time, Coltrane continued to expand his musical interests and influences by studying the music and the scales of Africa and India. He also took up the soprano saxophone, which provided further inspiration and new paths to explore. Coltrane featured the soprano on some of his best-known performances, including "My Favorite Things," recorded in 1960.

The Coltrane quartet built much of its repertory on a modal foundation. Instead of negotiating a set of changes, modal jazz players often piled up chords, sometimes in fourths, freely chosen from the modal scale. The relationship of their melodies to the chords could also be quite free, often extending chromatically beyond that modal scale. In Coltrane's performance of "My Favorite Things," for example, the song's original harmonic progression was simplified to single modal areas during the solos, which the Coltrane quartet then stretched to the breaking point. The length of each modal area was not predetermined but emerged spontaneously during performance. (Miles Davis used a similar strategy in his recording of "Flamenco Sketches" from *Kind of Blue*.)

Another important tune in the quartet's repertory was Coltrane's "Impressions," which bore an interesting resemblance to Miles Davis's "So What." The pieces had identical 32-bar AABA forms and modal areas: D Dorian for the A sections and E♭ Dorian for the B section. The E♭ Dorian bridge was largely a transposition of the A section—again, resembling "So What."

As Coltrane continued to explore the outer limits of modality, he also incorporated a shift in his improvisational language. In place of the hard bop formulas carefully integrated into his earlier solos (such as "Giant Steps"), Coltrane more and more worked from short motivic ideas, which he would explore through repetition with extensive, sometimes obsessive variation. As Coltrane worked through the variants of these **motivic cells**, the effect on the listener was hypnotic, often recalling the incantational atmosphere created by some Eastern musical styles. In part this effect derived from Coltrane's deep interest in the music of Asia and the Near East.

John Coltrane,
*The Complete 1961
Village Vanguard
Recordings,*
"India" (1961)

During 1961 and 1962, Coltrane's quartet was frequently expanded to a quintet, incorporating Eric Dolphy on flute and bass clarinet. (Dolphy also arranged and conducted the big band on Coltrane's 1961 *Africa/Brass*.) Dolphy's influence on Coltrane's group was liberating: his extended improvisations on such compositions as "India," based on the

G Mixolydian mode, triggered hostility from music critics. Some of them attacked what they perceived as Coltrane's move toward free jazz, and they criticized Dolphy's use of speechlike cries in his playing. *Down Beat* editor John Tynan dismissed the music as "anti-jazz":

> At Hollywood's Renaissance club recently, I listened to a horrifying demonstration of what appears to be a growing anti-jazz trend exemplified by these foremost proponents [Coltrane and Dolphy] of what is termed avant-garde music. I heard a good rhythm section . . . go to waste behind the nihilistic exercises of the two horns . . . Coltrane and Dolphy seem intent on deliberately destroying [swing] . . . They seem bent on pursuing an anarchistic course in their music that can but be termed anti-jazz.[17]

Nevertheless, Coltrane's 1964 recording *A Love Supreme* was enormously successful and was hailed as a masterpiece. *A Love Supreme* represented the crystallization of the musical ideas Coltrane had developed since he had formed his quartet: modal improvisation, extended pedal points, and the motivic cell approach to solos. Coltrane also made ingenious use of a four-note **ostinato** keyed to the lyric "a love supreme." Moved by Coltrane's fervor and intensity, audiences received the recording as a profound, courageous statement of a man seeking musical and spiritual truth. *A Love Supreme* is a suite in four movements: "Acknowledgement" (Listening Guide, Track 42), "Resolution," "Pursuance," and "Psalm."

Each part of the suite is equally compelling. (See the Listening Guide for more on "Acknowledgement.") As the next movement, "Resolution," begins, the bass continues to solo in E♭ Dorian. Thus the shift to E♭ Dorian provides a connecting link between the two movements and underscores Coltrane's conception of the album as an extended work rather than a collection of separate pieces. "Resolution" proceeds with an eight-measure theme over a single harmony.

John Coltrane,
A Love Supreme,
"Pursuance" (1964)

Tyner's piano solo is a powerful statement that demonstrates his ability to create a sense of harmonic evolution over a single modal center. The third movement, "Pursuance," is a 12-bar blues in B♭ minor, played over a blisteringly fast tempo. "Psalm" returns to the out-of-tempo playing of the opening, with Jones doubling on timpani. Coltrane biographer Lewis Porter has shown that the saxophone melody is in fact a wordless recitation to Coltrane's poem included in the liner notes to the album.[18]

Motivic cells, also called **thematic cells**, are short melodic ideas subject to variation and development.

An **ostinato** is a repeated melodic or harmonic idea that forms the basis for a section or an entire composition.

John Coltrane: "Acknowledgement," from *A Love Supreme* (Coltrane), from the album of the same name. Impulse A-77. Englewood Cliffs, New Jersey, December 9, 1964. Coltrane, tenor saxophone; McCoy Tyner, piano; Jimmy Garrison, bass; Elvin Jones, drums.

The Main Point The following schema illustrates the sections of "Acknowledgement":

Intro	I	II	III	IV	V
Cadenza	Add bass	Tenor solo	Transposed	Vocal	Drop vocals
	Add drums		motives		Drop piano
	Add piano				Drop drums
					Bass solo ending

Introduction

0:00 The piece begins with a sparsely accompanied, out-of-tempo cadenza.

I—Layered background texture

0:32 Garrison on bass begins a four-note ostinato that establishes the tempo, beat, and modal center F Dorian on the motive, F–A♭–F–B♭. This ostinato provides the thematic material, that is, its motivic cell.

Jones on drums joins the bass, playing a relatively simple beat that grows more complex and insistent as the piece intensifies.

Tyner on piano follows with chords that reinforce the modal center. The rhythmic backdrop is complete.

II—Coltrane tenor saxophone solo

1:04 This solo is an immediate improvisation rather than a head statement. It centers on a few notes in F Dorian but begins to veer off the mode, which is perceived as a point of harmonic stability to which Coltrane returns.

1:44 The solo gradually becomes more elaborate and intense as he varies and explores the numerous rhythms and patterns he can make with the first few notes.

3:52 Here the solo achieves its greatest intensity, highlighting Coltrane's preference for the high notes of the tenor, as if he were reaching for unplayable notes to express the ineffable.

II continued—Piano and bass

4:14 Coltrane develops a three-note idea here. Tyner and Garrison sometimes follow Coltrane's harmonic excursions but just as often react freely to them, as if to illuminate rather than track his musical path.

III—Transposed motives

4:56 Coltrane transposes the motive to all twelve keys before returning to state it in unison with the bass.

IV—Vocal

6:07 Coltrane chants "a love supreme" along with the bass motive in a reprise of the four-note ostinato with added lyric. (According to a research by Lewis Porter, the added voice you hear is Coltrane overdubbing himself.) The transposing-motives section followed by the vocal provides a recapitulation of this minimal but cogent thematic material.

V—Instruments drop out; motive transposed to E♭

6:37   In the midst of the vocal section, the motive and the general modal center abruptly drops down a whole step to E♭. One by one the vocals, the piano, and the drums drop out, disassembling the background texture erected at the beginning of the piece, to leave the bass to finish alone.

 Listen to this music in an animated Active Listening Guide available at the text website.

The following points summarize Coltrane's mature modal jazz style:

► Free melody, usually not formed into square phrases

► Melodic connections based on development of motivic cells rather than voice leading, which was more prominent in his bop-oriented work

► Widely varying melodic rhythm, from long emotion-charged pitches to fast sheets of sound

► Concentration on upper range and extreme upper range of instrument

► Passionate expression

► Full, rich tone with raspy edge

► **Outside playing**, often featuring free chord-scale relationships

A Love Supreme, possibly Coltrane's most popular record, exemplifies his deeply felt spiritual commitment and confirms his intense religious faith.

Coltrane and the Avant-Garde

Despite his musical advances and the great success of *A Love Supreme*, Coltrane was still interested in exploring new worlds. He had been supportive of the avant-garde players and took a strong interest in their expansion of musical resources. One of Coltrane's influences was tenor saxophonist Albert Ayler; another was Sun Ra's saxophonist John Gilmore, who provided a model for Coltrane's use of motivic cells. Among Coltrane's newly developing musical gestures were sounds that imitated human cries, an increased use of **multiphonics**, and an ability to create a "dialogue" within his solos by alternating different registers of the horn.

Coltrane's 1965 album *Ascension* unveiled a strong move to the jazz avant-garde. This was not completely surprising: the loose modal improvisation in *A Love Supreme* and other albums had foreshadowed Coltrane's evolution into free jazz. Although Ornette Coleman had been advocating jazz without tonal centers since the late 1950s,

Coltrane had not rushed to embrace the controversial new style but had instead progressed naturally to it.

In addition to his regular quartet, Coltrane's group on *Ascension* was augmented by a second bassist (Art Davis, who during this time was working frequently with Coltrane's quartet), two trumpeters (Dewey Johnson and Freddie Hubbard), two alto saxophonists (Marion Brown and John Tchicai), and two other tenor saxophonists (Farrell "Pharoah" Sanders and Archie Shepp). The group recorded two takes of the composition "Ascension." In its use of collective group improvisation, it bore a superficial resemblance to Ornette Coleman's 1960 double quartet recording *Free Jazz*, but *Ascension* was much denser and more dissonant. For example, the relative transparency of Coleman's *Free Jazz* arose from a looser exchange of motivic ideas passed around among the soloists, whereas Coltrane's *Ascension* often relied on dense blocks of sound created by the seven horn players, generating what writer Ekkehard Jost called **sound fields**.[19]

Ascension used both group improvisation and individual solos. Despite its freedom and spontaneity, it contained some predetermined material, which helped provide overall direction. Throughout the eight collective improvisational sections, the group loosely invoked different modes. Additionally, the melodic idea in the first

---

The more players depart from the notes of the harmonies, the more they are said to be playing **outside**. The terms *inside* and *outside* are most commonly associated with modern jazz. (Listen to Track 8 of the 🄰 Audio Primer to hear examples of inside and outside playing.)

Multiphonics is a technique of producing more than one note at a time on a wind instrument. Using nonstandard fingering and appropriate embouchure, the player splits the air stream into two or more parts, thus producing a multinote "chordal" effect. The technique is difficult to control, may be strident, and is generally associated with avant-garde playing.

Sound fields result when coinciding melodic lines fuse into an indistinguishable web or mass of sound with irregular accentuation within each line.

collective improvisation section—stated by Coltrane—was a motive comprising the same intervals as the motivic cell of "Acknowledgement" had.

Coltrane continued to align himself with the avant-garde. Saxophonist Pharoah Sanders joined the group in the fall of 1965, as did a second drummer, Rashied Ali. Coltrane's 1965 recordings *Om* and *Kulu se Mama* moved closer to totally free improvisation and away from the modal improvisations of previous years. Unhappy with the group's new directions, both Jones and Tyner left the band by the end of 1965. Coltrane's wife, harpist and pianist Alice Coltrane, replaced Tyner. Among Coltrane's final recordings were *Interstellar Space* (a duet with drummer Rashied Ali) and *Expression*. Coltrane died of liver cancer on July 17, 1967, at the age of forty.

Since 1950 only Miles Davis has exerted a more powerful influence on jazz than John Coltrane has. Coltrane's intensity, technical skill, spirituality, and continual search for new sounds remain an inspiration to all jazz musicians. His legendary status was enhanced by his unfortunate early death, probably brought on by the effects of his heroin addiction and excessive drinking. Uniting non-Western musical models and modal jazz with his original mastery of bebop, John Coltrane created some of the most personal, powerful, and exciting jazz of the 1950s and 1960s.

Eric Dolphy

Perhaps no saxophonist has managed the borderline between hard bop and free jazz as convincingly as Eric Dolphy has. In parlance that was new at the time, Dolphy was equally convincing at playing both inside and outside; that is, he could move outside the harmonic progressions—with pitches not part of the given chord or mode—then deftly return inside to take up the harmonies. Dolphy's album titles *Outward Bound* and *Out to Lunch* punned on the notion of outside playing.

Born in Los Angeles, Eric Dolphy (1928–1964) performed on alto saxophone, flute, and bass clarinet. On alto he developed an original sound, characterized by wide intervallic leaps, unusual phrasing that often floated untethered from the beat, and the use of glissandi, smears, and nontempered intonation. In contrast to more-conventional players, Dolphy's rhythmic conception tended to be freer, that is, less tied to the beat. His influences ranged from Ornette Coleman to African and Indian music. He even attempted, he said, to imitate the music of birds.[20] His flute playing was more traditional; Dolphy often turned to the more pastoral instrument for jazz standards, as he did in his recording of "You Don't Know What Love Is" from *Last Date* (1964).

As his work with John Coltrane on "India" (from *Impressions*) and with Ornette Coleman on *Free Jazz* revealed, Dolphy was an outstanding virtuoso on bass clarinet, helping generate interest in an instrument fairly new to jazz settings. In addition to these recordings and his own, Dolphy appeared on several other significant albums with bassist Charles Mingus, trumpeter Booker Little, and arranger Oliver Nelson.

Dolphy made his first important musical alliance when he joined the quartet of Chico Hamilton in 1958. He recorded *Gongs East* with Hamilton, a West Coast drummer (discussed in Chapter 8), whose ensemble was notable for including a cellist. After moving to New York in 1959, Dolphy began to work with Charles Mingus, an association that lasted until Dolphy's untimely death in 1964. Together Dolphy and Mingus recorded an astounding duet, "What Love," in which the two players floated in and out of tempo, creating a conversation between Mingus's bass and Dolphy's bass clarinet that mimicked human speech. Dolphy's alto solo on Mingus's "Hora Decubitus" bordered on free jazz (see Chapter 8 and Track 39): the solo at times ignored and at other times projected the harmonic progression of the 12-bar blues.

Dolphy's album *Far Cry* featured Booker Little, a trumpeter who maintained a close musical relationship with Dolphy until Little's tragic death in 1961 at the age of twenty-three. A hard bop player from Memphis, Little began his career as a devotee of Clifford Brown. He recorded his first albums with the Max Roach Quintet before he was twenty years old. Roach even recorded some of Little's compositions with a pianoless quintet that included Ray Draper on tuba. Little's "Larry LaRue," from Roach's *Words, Not Deeds*, was harmonically complex, with the melody—scored for trumpet, tenor saxophone, and tuba—frequently moving in parallel motion, a compositional technique that Little often brought to his writing. Little's playing was technically polished, lyrical, and creative.

Dolphy took part in Little's own recording for Candid Records, *Out Front*. The two also collaborated on a gig at the Five Spot, which was recorded and released in a series of albums that included Mal Waldron on piano, Richard Davis on bass, and Ed Blackwell on drums. On the Five Spot recordings, Dolphy's influence on Little is clear, as Little often adopted Dolphy's flurry-of-notes approach. Little's compositions employed complex and unusual forms.

Dolphy's work on Ornette Coleman's trailblazing *Free Jazz* solidified his reputation as a major presence in the jazz avant-garde; even so he never abandoned more-traditional settings. Amazingly, on the same day that he recorded *Free Jazz*—December 21, 1960—Dolphy also recorded his own album *Far Cry*, with a standard rhythm section consisting of Ron Carter on bass, Jaki Byard on piano, and Roy Haynes on drums. Several of the compositions paid tribute to Parker, such as Byard's "Ode to Charlie Parker" and the 12-bar blues "Mrs. Parker of K.C." On "Mrs. Parker" the rhythm section experimented with breaking up the time for the first chorus of each solo, creating rhythmic and harmonic conflicts before moving into a 4/4 swing. Dolphy's unaccompanied alto solo on the popular standard "Tenderly" showed his ability to underscore and outline the harmonies of the tune.

An invitation to Dolphy to join the John Coltrane Quartet between 1961 and 1962 led to controversy, eliciting the negative label of "anti-jazz" from critics who thought the solos too long, anarchistic, and unswinging. Of course, Coltrane had a more positive view: he insisted that Dolphy's inclusion in the group "had a broadening effect on us. There are a lot of things we try now that we never tried before. We're playing things that are freer than before."[21] Dolphy recorded *Live at the Village Vanguard* and *Impressions* with Coltrane and toured Europe with the group at the end of 1961.

Dolphy was also involved in third-stream and twentieth-century concert music; for example, he performed on Gunther Schuller's 1960 recording *Abstractions*. His interest in the European avant-garde led to a performance of Edgard Varèse's *Density 21.5* for unaccompanied flute at the Ojai Music Festival in California. After touring Europe with Mingus in 1964, Dolphy elected to remain abroad rather than return to the United States. Shortly after, he died in Berlin from a heart attack brought on by diabetes.

Although critics often focused on the radical elements in Dolphy's playing, Dolphy's musical collaborators considered his breadth enormous and maintained that he was in complete control of all the musical elements. Pianist Jaki Byard remembered:

> Eric's freedom in playing and writing is never chaos. He always makes sense, and those critics who call him disorganized should first have the chords and the overall forms of his tunes written out for them before they make that kind of accusation. Eric is very well organized, but it's not the kind of organization that is immediately apparent to people who are accustomed to more conventional ideas of form.[22]

Avant-Garde Jazz and Black Activism

As the avant-garde jazz movement expanded during the 1960s, it became intimately connected to and nurtured by black nationalism and militant protest (see the box "Voices of Discontent"). As pointed out earlier, an increase in black ethnic pride has paralleled the history of jazz. This increase was rooted in the Harlem Renaissance and, before that, in the writings of W. E. B. Du Bois and others. Du Bois's concept of the "talented tenth"—the elite of the black population, whose achievements could inspire and "uplift" blacks as a whole—helped spur the growth of a black intelligentsia. The Harlem Renaissance was an early realization of Du Bois's vision (see Chapter 4). Later the bebop musicians of the 1940s upheld the importance of black achievement when they worked to separate themselves from what they perceived as the subservience of older black entertainers to the white mainstream.

In the 1950s growing activism among blacks, including the brilliant legal tactics of Thurgood Marshall, led to pivotal court victories in which societal barriers to equality were overturned. For example, the Supreme Court decision in *Brown v. Board of Education* struck a major blow against segregation in the South. Further protests against segregation, including the "freedom" demonstrations of the early 1960s, eventually led to the passage of the Civil Rights Act of 1964, which officially outlawed discrimination. Leaders such as Martin Luther King Jr. were instrumental in these efforts. Unfortunately, the legal end to segregation and discrimination did not lead to immediate acceptance of blacks into the dominant society.

The fight for civil rights was the hallmark of the 1950s and 1960s. Dr. Martin Luther King Jr. (1929–1968) was at the forefront of nonviolent protest against segregation. This poster advertises his last speech, given at a rally in support of striking garbage collectors; later that evening James Earl Ray shot and killed King as he stood on his motel balcony.

Black militancy in the 1960s was a direct result of these developments.

This revolution in black activism anticipated a wider rebellion within middle-class society as well. Inspired by the Beat movement of the 1950s, many young people in the subsequent decade rebelled against what they considered unthinking conformity and social duty. This rebellion took particular aim at the war in Vietnam, which many people, young and old, considered pointless and unwinnable. The smaller but more visible group called "flower children" embraced the hippie lifestyle and derided their parents' sexual timidity as "uptight." "Do your own thing" became a catchphrase.

The 1960s have rightly been considered pivotal in the history of U.S. society and of the West as a whole. The civil rights movement and racial rebellion formed only one part of a general cultural upheaval. The decade witnessed increasing activism among feminists, whose roots reached back to the women's suffrage movement in the nineteenth century but whose demands now included equal access to jobs and careers and equal pay for equal work. The so-called sexual revolution together with the birth control pill challenged conventional sexual mores, leading to growing sexual activity among unmarried adults and increasingly graphic depictions of sex in novels, movies, and television.

This was paralleled by a dramatic upturn in violence and explicit language in virtually all media. The Stonewall Rebellion—the rioting incited by a 1969 police raid on a gay bar in New York—galvanized political activism for gay rights and led to a growing acceptance of what were called "alternative lifestyles." The increasing popularity of rock music and political activism by leading rock stars provided a focal point for social protest and the antiwar movement. This era of unprecedented social rebellion was reflected in jazz, in particular, by musical substyles that were as uncompromising as the attitudes of its foremost musicians.

Archie Shepp

Archie Shepp (b. 1937) was one of the most vocal and articulate of the avant-garde musicians championing the cause of blacks. His album, *Fire Music* (1965), featured the piece "Malcolm, Malcolm, *Semper* Malcolm," a tribute to black leader Malcolm X. Shepp studied dramatic literature at Goddard College, where he earned his bachelor of arts degree in 1959. Originally an alto player, he switched to tenor through the inspiration of John Coltrane, with

Issues of Race

Voices of Discontent

In part as a result of blacks' frustrations in their attempt to gain equality with whites, much social and racial turbulence erupted in the 1960s. Black separatism became a significant force in the African American community as many intellectuals sought to distance themselves from what they considered to be the unyielding white power structure. These efforts were often accompanied by conscious attempts to incorporate Afrocentrism into art and everyday life: African names and clothing as well as Afro hairstyles became more common.

Despite the Supreme Court rulings of the 1950s and the 1964 Civil Rights Act, the 1960s did not see the expected improvement in the relationship between the races. In fact the separation of whites and blacks increased through the creation of the black ghettos in U.S. inner cities during this time. The ghettos were created largely by "white flight" to the suburbs, which left blacks in decaying city centers

without jobs or opportunity. Long frustrated at the ingrained racism of white society, black people grew angry at the crime, housing conditions, poverty, and lack of opportunity in the inner city. This anger fueled greater militancy on the part of many. The phrase "Black power" was coined by activist Stokely Carmichael in response to the intransigence of white society. At the same time, the Black Panther Party was formed to promote a

> volatile mix of race, sex, and Maoist revolution [that] coalesced in a new violent cultural figure—a photogenic caricature of black masculinity, which the New Left loved for its seditious outrageousness and "authenticity" and which would haunt the public's understanding of young black males for the next 30 years.[23]

Given such tension, small events could trigger major explosions. Eventually, rioting erupted in such urban centers as Newark, the Watts section of Los Angeles, and Detroit.

Musicians aroused by political concerns also became involved in the general turbulence of the black population. Early on, in the 1940s and 1950s, jazz musicians had focused on the importance of black contributions to music. In the 1960s LeRoi Jones—who later changed his name to Amiri Baraka—made an influential contribution to American social history by writing *Blues People* (1963). In this book he claimed that jazz and American popular music in general were essentially black. Baraka argued that the blues defined blacks as Americans—that is, it made them American Negroes rather than displaced Africans working in a new land. The blues, once matured, later defined jazz:

> When Negroes began to master more and more "European" instruments and began to think musically in terms of their timbres, as opposed to or in conjunction with the voice, blues began to change, and the era of jazz was at hand.[24]

whom he eventually performed. He also worked with Cecil Taylor, Bill Dixon, Roswell Rudd, and others.

Shepp thought that free jazz ought to be a political medium. His calls for justice for blacks have not wavered through the years. In 1999 he pointed out that Jewish survivors of the Holocaust were seeking monetary compensation: "What if our people asked for compensation for all the years of slave labour?"[28]

Archie Shepp,
Fire Music,
"Malcolm, Malcolm,
Semper Malcolm"
(1965)

Shepp performed on Coltrane's free jazz album, *Ascension* (1965). In addition to *Fire Music,* Shepp recorded several other important albums in the 1960s, including *Four for Trane* (1964). Eloquent in his defense of black nationalist principles, Shepp became an educator, teaching at the State University of New York at Buffalo and the University of Massachusetts at Amherst.

Albert Ayler

Another notable contributor to the scene, Albert Ayler (1936–1970), brought a fiercely independent style and an abundance of avant-garde techniques to the tenor saxophone. Like Shepp, Ayler worked with Cecil Taylor. *Ghosts* and *Spiritual Unity* (both 1964) were two of his most outstanding albums. His works encompassed shrieks, cries, wails, multiphonics, and other techniques that can be summed up as a "sound"-oriented approach to the instrument rather than anything one could notate easily. Unfortunately, the jazz world would lose this innovator all too soon. In 1970 Ayler disappeared for almost three weeks before his body was found in New York's East River. He most likely committed suicide, but the official verdict was death by drowning.

Albert Ayler,
Spiritual Unity,
"Ghosts: Second
Variation" (1964)

Ayler's "Ghosts" had followed the first wave of the avant-garde jazz recordings by artists Ornette Coleman and Cecil Taylor. Many of the avant-garde tenor saxophonists of the 1960s, such as Ayler, Archie Shepp, and Pharoah Sanders, drew much of their initial inspiration from John Coltrane. For his part Coltrane keenly supported these players, even helping Ayler, Shepp, and Sanders obtain record contracts from Impulse Records.

Bettmann/Corbis

The original New York City newspaper caption read: "Noted jazz trumpeter Miles Davis (left) is led into court for arraignment here, August 26th [1959]. Davis, thirty-two, was arrested for felonious assault and disorderly conduct after allegedly grappling with a policeman outside the Birdland Jazz Emporium on Broadway [where Davis was performing]. Police said that Davis suffered a head laceration when a detective hit him with a blackjack. The trouble reportedly happened when patrolman Gerald Kilduff ordered the trumpeter to clear the sidewalk. Police said that Davis refused to move and that the jazz musician wrested a nightstick from the patrolman when Kilduff took Davis by the arm to lead him to the police station."

In the 1960s the onset of black militancy and separatism espoused by Malcolm X and the Black Panthers was paralleled by angry claims that, although jazz was a form of black music, its economic rewards flowed to whites, its imitators. These views were forcefully argued in 1970 by Frank Kofsky in *Black Nationalism and the Revolution in Music,* in which he stated:

Whites can learn to play jazz … but for most whites … this new accomplishment will ordinarily come later in life than if they had been raised in the traditions of the ethnic group that they now seek to emulate; and in most cases the "second language" thus acquired will always be a touch more stiff and stilted for the "outsider" than for the "insider."[25]

Kofsky also claimed:

The number of white musicians who have made a permanent contribution to the tradition of jazz … is astonishingly small. More than likely, one could count them on one's fingers. … It is probably safe to state that there have been more black innovators of consequence on any two instruments we might choose at random—trumpet and trombone, say—than there have been whites on all instruments put together.[26]

Kofsky also proclaimed his view of the essential economic injustice of jazz. He quoted tenor saxophonist Archie Shepp at length, including Shepp's succinct summary of their views: "You own the music and we make it."[27]

"Ghosts" is from Ayler's most productive period: he recorded four albums in 1964. Ayler uses the entire range of the tenor saxophone during his solo. Gary Peacock is on bass, Sunny Murray is on drums, and there is no piano, which is typical of many free jazz recordings of the 1960s.

The excerpt (Listening Guide, Track 43) characterizes Ayler's playing, and free jazz in general, in the following ways:

▶ Use of extended saxophone sounds, including non-tempered intonation and multiphonics

▶ Free collective improvisation: bass and drums do not fulfill typical timekeeping roles

▶ Absence of steady pulse and meter, absence of predetermined harmonic structure, and absence of harmonic instrument (such as piano or guitar)

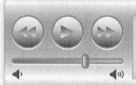

LISTENING GUIDE
"Ghosts: First Variation" (excerpt)
Track 43

Albert Ayler Trio: "Ghosts: First Variation" (Ayler), from *Spiritual Unity*. ESP 1002. New York, July 10, 1964. Ayler, tenor saxophone; Gary Peacock, bass; Sunny Murray, drums.

The Main Point   Like many of the avant-garde recordings, the improvisation to "Ghosts" makes listening particularly challenging. What is unusual, however, is the simplicity of its melody.

Drawn to this simplicity, Ayler recorded at least five different versions of "Ghosts." "I'd like to play something—like the beginning of 'Ghosts'—that people can hum," he acknowledged. "And I want to play songs that I used to sing when I was real small. Folk melodies that all people would understand."[29]

The group follows the traditional melody-solos-melody format; but following the statement of the melody, members engage in free collective improvisation. The players abandon a regular pulse, an underlying tonal center or harmonic progression, and a predetermined formal structure.

Ayler plays extremely freely, developing a repertory of extended tenor saxophone techniques, overblowing notes and distorting pitches. Peacock's solo displays his clean technique; his sound and facility on the instrument are reminiscent of bassist Scott LaFaro (heard with Bill Evans on "Autumn Leaves," Track 49). Murray's earlier work with Cecil Taylor contributes to the "arhythmic" approach to the drums heard here. Murray often played with a stripped-down drum set, using only cymbal, snare drum, and bass drum.

Introduction—8 bars

0:00   Ayler plays an introductory melody alone, using both fixed and indeterminate pitches.

Melody—Three 8-bar phrases

0:10   Bass and drums enter, accompanying Ayler beneath the melody. The melody is based on the pentatonic scale (in this case F pentatonic, consisting of F–G–A–C–D–F), a scale often used in folksongs. Note Ayler's use of slides up to pitches, as well as distorted or overblown pitches. The hummable melody is similar to Sonny Rollins's lyrical calypso melody "St. Thomas."

0:21   Two folklike eight-bar ideas closely related to the melody appear, setting up a clear tonal center.

Ayler tenor saxophone solo

0:44   In the first minute of the solo, Ayler vaguely recalls the melody: the pitches are often indeterminate, but the phrasing seems to echo the starting and stopping places of the melody. Careful listening reveals the use of some of the motives from the melody.

Listen to this music in an animated Active Listening Guide available at the text website.

Black Activism and the Avant-Garde Today

The struggle for equality and recognition of black achievement continues today, as it probably will for some time. Among the younger generation of musicians who have sought greater recognition and advocated multiculturalism is clarinetist Don Byron (b. 1958). Byron has gained a reputation for combining jazz with Jewish klezmer music in addition to other crossover experimentation. Recently, he confronted racial stereotypes with his album *Nu Blaxploitation* (1998). Byron leads a band called Existential Dred, a name that neatly evokes contemporary angst, the *Dred Scott* Supreme Court decision of 1857, and Byron's own dreadlocks hairstyle. His album *Music for Six Musicians* (1995) featured a piece called "Shelby Steele Would Be Mowing Your Lawn." (Steele is a black scholar who has written against affirmative action programs.)

Although social statement remains an important mission of the black avant-garde, its message seems less urgent forty years later, particularly after the 2008 election of the nation's first black president, Barack Obama. Nonetheless, the black nationalist movement continues to focus attention on the essential black contribution to jazz. In addition, the growth of scholarship in African American studies further highlights these substantial cultural contributions. Some feel, however, that this focus has gone too far, that a kind of reverse racism has resulted, with white contributions to the music undervalued and fine white players overlooked. For example, the argument of the essential blackness of jazz has been countered recently by Gene Lee's *Cats of Any Color* (1995) and Richard Sudhalter's *Lost Chords: White Musicians and Their Contributions to Jazz, 1915–1945* (1999). These books argue that jazz is an American music whose innovators have been largely black but to which whites have contributed significantly, and that without whites and their input, jazz would not be the rich music it is.

In any case, the jazz avant-garde of the 1960s pioneered forceful political statements that heightened awareness of and emphasis on the African heritage of jazz. The general atmosphere of the 1960s, in both the black community and society in general, provided a sympathetic backdrop for musical revolution.

Cecil Taylor

Because much of the free jazz of the 1960s—such as Ornette Coleman's seminal quartet and the music of Albert Ayler—did not include piano, it is interesting that one of the foremost proponents of free jazz, Cecil Taylor, is a pianist. Taylor's piano style is dissonant and athletic. His power, energy, and unlimited drive produce a fascinating and sometimes foreboding wall of dense sound blocks. Taylor's study of timpani as a youth may have influenced his rhythmic conception because his keyboard concept is as much rhythmic as melodic, with rapid-fire clusters of hands, fists, forearms, and elbows. Throughout his career Taylor has remained a controversial and fiercely uncompromising figure.

Taylor drew his wide-ranging musical ideas from both jazz and the European concert tradition. Among jazz pianists, he was initially attracted to the dense harmonies of Dave Brubeck and the linear clarity of Lennie Tristano before turning to Duke Ellington, Thelonious Monk, and Horace Silver. He was also inspired by European composers Igor Stravinsky and Béla Bartók. Thus much of Taylor's music invoked the aesthetic of the European avant-garde alongside that of traditional jazz.

Born in 1929, Taylor was raised in the Corona section of Queens, New York, and began studying piano at age five. In 1952 he moved to Boston to attend the New England Conservatory of Music, where he studied piano, popular music, and music theory. At the conservatory Taylor studied the music of European composers while exploring Ellington, Monk, Silver, and other jazz and popular stylists.

Only gradually did Taylor reject convention and arrive at his mature style: his recordings prior to 1960 are

Cecil Taylor's dissonant, athletic pianism was and remains fiercely uncompromising.

Photo Courtesy of the Morgan Collection

considerably closer to the jazz mainstream than his later ones are. His first album as a leader was *Jazz Advance*, a trio and quartet recording from December 1955, with Steve Lacy on soprano saxophone, Buell Niedlinger on bass, and Dennis Charles on drums. The quartet still adhered to chorus structures; for example, Duke Ellington's "Azure" was given a fairly conventional reading, although both Taylor and Niedlinger occasionally wandered outside the harmonic structure. In other pre-1960 recordings, Taylor's harmonic language was often dissonant, but he continued to explore standards—Cole Porter's "Love for Sale" and "I Love Paris," for example. As a pianist he maintained the usual technique of right-hand melody accompanied by left-hand chords.

In 1957 Taylor's engagement at the Five Spot and appearance at the Newport Jazz Festival enhanced his visibility. Unfortunately, commercial success was slow in coming, so Taylor had to work as a cook and a dishwasher to support himself.

On his two Candid albums from 1960 and 1961, *The World of Cecil Taylor* and *New York R&B* (later rereleased), Taylor's performances became decidedly less traditional. He clearly was redefining his overall approach and innovating a new conception of jazz piano. Joined by Shepp, Niedlinger, and Charles, Taylor performed passages in dynamic free rhythm. In part because of *The World of Cecil Taylor*, Taylor won the *Down Beat* "New Star" award for pianists. Ironically, at the time he was unemployed.

Because Taylor's evolving stylistic direction began to conflict with the traditional role of the drummer as time-keeper, Taylor replaced Dennis Charles with Sunny Murray (b. 1937). Murray, who remained with Taylor until 1964, tended to avoid steady meter, instead projecting a fluid and kinetic style that matched Taylor's free approach to the keyboard.

In 1966 Taylor recorded two albums for Blue Note, *Unit Structures* and *Conquistador*, with two bassists—Henry Grimes and Alan Silva—and drummer Andrew Cyrille, who worked with Taylor from 1965 to 1975. Like his predecessor Sunny Murray, Cyrille conformed readily to full-group improvisation while downplaying pulse and meter.

The title track from *Unit Structures* was sectional and highly organized; it showed Taylor's independence from the jazz mainstream. The work was conceived in five large sections, entitled "Anacrusis," "Plain 1," "Area 1," "Plain 2," and "Area 2." Following "Anacrusis," which lasted less than a minute, "Plain 1" comprised fifteen differentiated "units"—brief sections lasting anywhere from five to forty seconds. Some of the material in these units was composed, with the instruments introduced in varying combinations. At times the horns played in a loose unison; at other times the instruments interacted polyphonically, with fluctuating tempos. Included in the work were primary and subsidiary themes that were later reprised.

The complex organization of *Unit Structures* showed Taylor rejecting not only the traditional harmonic and rhythmic principles of the jazz mainstream but also its usual methods for generating form. It was a repudiation of both the repeating chorus structure of traditional jazz and the head-solos-head organization that long dominated the music. In place of traditional methods of determining form, in *Unit Structures* we find the following:

Cecil Taylor,
Unit Structures,
"Unit Structure/As of a Now/Section"
(1966)

▶ Various "unit sections" providing an overall large-scale shape

▶ Predetermined motivic or textural ideas replacing conventional harmonic progressions

▶ A separation and independence of sections, which undermined traditional progression and development

Along with saxophonist Jimmy Lyons, who successfully translated some of Charlie Parker's bebop rhetoric into a free jazz context, *Unit Structures* also featured Ken McIntyre on bass clarinet and oboe. The inclusion of instruments not associated with the jazz mainstream was also typical of Taylor's approach.

Taylor won increased recognition during the 1970s. He taught at the University of Wisconsin–Madison and at Antioch College in Ohio, where he recorded his solo piano album *Indent*. During the decade he was awarded a Guggenheim Fellowship and an honorary doctorate from his old school, the New England Conservatory of Music. Taylor also performed for Jimmy Carter's 1979 White House Jazz Day. His solo piano recording, *Silent Tongues*, won the 1974 *Down Beat* "Jazz Album of the Year" award in its international critics poll. In discussing his composition "Abyss" from *Silent Tongues*, Taylor pointed out the plan at work in his conception of the different registers of the piano:

> Just in the keyboard element I can, if I want to, have four or five bodies of sound existing in a duality of dimension. In other words, I might decide to have three or four different voices or choirs existing and moving with different weight propelling their ongoing motion ... so that one can have—say that two or three octaves below middle C is the area of the abyss, and the middle range is the surface of the earth, the astral being the upper range—you have three constituted bodies also outlined by a specific range, a specific function of how the innards of these groups relate to themselves and then to each other. You have, therefore, what starts out as a linear voice becoming within itself like horizontal because of the plurality of exchange between the voices.[30]

Taylor has continued to record and perform with his ensemble, the Cecil Taylor Unit, whose membership has remained somewhat fluid. Alto saxophonist Jimmy Lyons, who began playing with Taylor in 1960, was still with the group in 1978 for their recording *Idut*, which also included trumpeter Raphé Malik, violinist Ramsey Ameen, bassist Sirone (born Norris Jones), and drummer Ronald Shannon Jackson.

Over the decades some audiences have found Taylor's music difficult or impenetrable. As one writer observed, an initial unprepared encounter with Taylor's music usually causes complete confusion.[31] Nevertheless, even the unprepared respond to the music's intensity and energy.

Sun Ra

A unique jazz personality, Sun Ra led a legendary big band called the Myth-Science Solar Arkestra—one among several of its varied but similar names. Established in the mid-fifties, the Arkestra played "intergalactic music" that painted "pictures of infinity." It also contained numerous musicians loyal to Sun Ra, the music, and its uniquely mystical ambience. With the players and audiences chanting "Space is the place," the band's performances were transcendental. As his reputation continued to grow, Sun Ra emerged as one of the most colorful and discussed pioneers of the avant-garde.

Sun Ra made wide-ranging contributions to the avant-garde. He was among the first jazz performers to use electric keyboards and synthesizers and was one of the few big-band leaders to encourage extensive free improvisation. The group was especially creative with percussion, exploring a large palette of sound colors with timpani, celesta, bells, chimes, and other instruments less often heard in jazz. The emphasis on unusual timbre extended to nonpercussive instruments as well: Sun Ra's saxophonists doubled on such instruments as piccolo, oboe, bassoon, and bass clarinet. As alto saxophonist Marion Brown noted, "Sun Ra plays the piano, but his real instrument is the orchestra."[32] A number of writers have suggested that, with his idiosyncratic arranging techniques and the long-term tenure of many of his players, Sun Ra was something of an avant-garde Duke Ellington.

Sun Ra, however, remained an underground phenomenon, never achieving the mainstream success that Ellington had. He was born Herman Blount in Birmingham, Alabama, in 1914 and moved to Chicago in the mid-forties, working as the arranger-pianist Le Sony'r Ra in a variety theater. Between 1946 and 1947, he played piano for bandleader Fletcher Henderson. He then formed his own band; among his musicians were tenor saxophonist John Gilmore, who became a long-standing associate and who would later influence John Coltrane. His first recordings from the mid-fifties with the Myth-Science Solar Arkestra (*Sun Song* and *Sound*

"Sun Ra in typical regalia and headdress."

Photo Courtesy of the Morgan Collection

of Joy) merged Ellington-like ensemble colors with an idiosyncratic hard bop orientation. They featured unusual sounds, such as the timpani solos in "A Street from Hell." The band also included timpani on "A Call for All Demons," which hilariously combined atonal improvising with a mambo beat.

The Arkestra relocated from Chicago to New York in 1960. Once settled, the group continued to rehearse prodigiously, with all of the band members becoming multi-instrumentalists, especially on percussion. As the band moved decisively toward free jazz, the players collectively improvised, often over a background of dense percussion. Indeed some compositions focused primarily on percussion.

In general, improvised solos in the Arkestra often used modal or tonal centers rather than standard harmonic progressions. On some of the recordings from the 1960s, such as *The Heliocentric Worlds of Sun Ra*, there seemed to be no prewritten music; only the general formal outline was predetermined, invoked by cues from Sun Ra.

Sun Ra,
Heliocentric Worlds,
Vol. 1,
"The Cosmos" (1965)

In the 1970s the Arkestra relocated again—this time to Philadelphia—and began using the city as a base for concert performance. Their 1976 television appearance on *Saturday Night Live* increased the band's exposure. Around this time the group began performing works of Duke Ellington, Fletcher Henderson, and Thelonious Monk.

The use of microtonal melodies and electronic effects enhanced the space-age aura of Sun Ra's music, as did his flowing robes and headdresses. Sun Ra's live performances recalled the "happenings" of the 1960s, complete with the psychedelic paraphernalia. Sun Ra died in 1993.

Chicago: AACM, the Art Ensemble of Chicago, and Anthony Braxton

By the later 1920s, the so-called "Second City" of Chicago was eclipsed by New York as the country's jazz center. Nevertheless, Chicago's jazz scene has remained active and was especially influential during the 1950s. Tenor saxophonist Sonny Rollins took the first of his extended sabbaticals there in 1955. Saxophonist Johnny Griffin, pianist Ahmad Jamal, and Sun Ra's band were based in the city. Additionally, several young Memphis jazz players came to Chicago in the 1950s to study, including pianist Harold Mabern, saxophonist George Coleman, trumpeter Booker Little, and alto saxophonist Frank Strozier. Drummer Walter Perkins's group, MJT + 3, employed at different times many Chicago-based players, including pianist Muhal Richard Abrams. Abrams became instrumental in creating the Association for the Advancement of Creative Musicians (AACM), a school and cooperative on the South Side that became the center of Chicago's avant-garde jazz scene.

Although Abrams began as a hard bop pianist, he gradually turned his attention toward free jazz, forming the Experimental Band in 1961, a rehearsal group that met weekly. By 1965 the band evolved into the AACM, an organization that sponsored concerts and performances, and—most important—fostered self-determination for musicians. In allowing musicians to be independent of commercial promoters and agents, it promoted artistic and creative goals. Later the group also produced radio shows and brought jazz education to inner-city schools.

The liner notes to alto saxophonist Joseph Jarman's recording *As If It Were the Seasons* (1968) described the aims of the organization:

> The Association for the Advancement of Creative Musicians, a nonprofit organization chartered by the State of Illinois, was formed … when a group of Musicians and Composers in the Chicago area saw an emergent need to expose and showcase original Music

which, under the existing establishment (promoters, agents, etc.) was not receiving its just due. A prime direction of our Association has been to provide an atmosphere conducive to serious Music and the performance of new, unrecorded compositions. The Music presented by the various groups in our Association is jazz-oriented.[33]

The music was indeed jazz oriented. It was particularly indebted to the free jazz movement, as Jarman's tribute "Ornette" suggested, but it was also new in other ways. Jarman's own background in drama inspired him to add extramusical, theatrical elements to the performances. On Jarman's "Non-cognitive Aspects to the City" (from his recording *Song For*), he recited his own spoken poetry following a prelude consisting of fragmented melodic ideas and a drum solo.

Along with poetry and social statement, much of the music of the AACM explored timbre, tone color, nontempered intonation, collective improvisation, and the use of unusual instruments. It also relied on humor and surprise. Trumpeter Lester Bowie's earliest experiences were with R&B bands and the tent shows of an itinerant carnival troupe, experiences he brought to bear on his work with the AACM. His album *Numbers 1 and 2* used gongs, police sirens, and nonsense syllables sung in falsetto. In it, after someone yells "Ring the bell, man," a cowbell is played furiously. In search of freedom, the AACM players were clearly seeking a release from the conventions of traditional jazz. As Bowie noted in the liner notes to *Numbers 1 and 2*:

> Jazz, at first apart from this struggle for renewal in the western world, has come to face these "freedoms." But there is only one true freedom for us, and that is what this music seeks. The signs of the revolution permeate most of jazz today, and in Chicago there are young musicians who, desiring freedom, are beginning to know how it is created.[34]

Bowie's *Numbers 1 and 2* was made with saxophonists Jarman and Roscoe Mitchell and bassist Malachi Favors, who together became the four founders of the Art Ensemble of Chicago. Pursuing the path begun by the early AACM recordings, the Art Ensemble of Chicago relied heavily not only on free, collective improvisation but also on theater: they incorporated into their performances dramatic sketches, poetry, costumes and makeup, dance, pantomime, comedy, and parody. The group moved to Paris in 1969, recording albums for the French label BYG, including several film scores.

"Ring the bell, man!"

Rejecting specialists' roles as performers, the members of the Art Ensemble of Chicago each played several instruments. When the group moved to Europe, they took about 500 instruments with them. On recordings such as *A Jackson in Your House*, the group mixed comical pastiche—mock Dixieland and swing—with sound explorations and free improvisations that were in part a rejection of the showy virtuosity of bebop. The recordings the group made during their eighteen months overseas revealed the varied instruments, many of them percussion, handled by the performers. A list of their instruments compiled by Ekkehard Jost shows this breadth:

▶ Lester Bowie: flugelhorn, trumpet, cow horn, and bass drum

▶ Roscoe Mitchell: soprano, alto, and bass saxophone; clarinet; flute; cymbals; gongs; conga drums; steel drum; logs; bells; siren; and whistles

▶ Joseph Jarman: soprano, alto, and tenor saxophones; clarinet; oboe; bassoon; flutes; marimba; vibraphone; guitar; conga drums; bells; gongs; whistles; and sirens

▶ Malachi Favors: double bass, Fender bass, banjo, zither, log drum, and other percussion instruments[35]

The group added drummer Don Moye, whose first recording with the band was on the soundtrack to *Les Stances à Sophie*. Moye increased the huge arsenal of percussion instruments and joined the others in wearing African hats, costumes, and makeup. The group continued to record after resettling in the United States in 1971, although the players also concentrated on their own projects. Their recordings for ECM Records included *Nice Guys* and *Urban Bushman*, the latter a double-LP live recording that showed the dramatic breadth of the group. The members of the Art Ensemble of Chicago continued to collaborate—involved in tours and projects that took them throughout the world—and stayed together for more than thirty years.

Whereas the Art Ensemble of Chicago celebrated African elements in its music and theater, the music of another Chicagoan tilted toward European formal organization. Alto saxophonist Anthony Braxton (b. 1945) joined the AACM in 1966. Braxton's earliest influences were cool jazz altoists Paul Desmond and Lee Konitz, but after joining the AACM he began studying Ornette Coleman and John Coltrane, seeking in part to translate Coltrane's raw expressiveness to the alto. He also studied the techniques of avant-garde concert-music composers such as John Cage and Karlheinz Stockhausen.

Along with Leroy Jenkins and Leo Smith, Braxton formed the Creative Construction Company in 1967. The group explored free improvisational methods on Braxton's *Three Compositions*, recorded the following year. In 1968 Braxton made *For Alto*, his first unaccompanied alto saxophone recording. It was the first solo jazz saxophone album. Following in the footsteps of the Art Ensemble

of Chicago, the Creative Construction Company traveled to Paris in 1969. The group was not particularly well received—in part, thought Braxton, because they lacked a rhythm section.

Braxton later teamed up with the stellar rhythm section of pianist Chick Corea, bassist Dave Holland, and drummer Barry Altschul. The new group, Circle, recorded a concert in Paris for ECM in February 1971. Braxton's improvisations were masterpieces of free interaction, weaving together multiphonics, unusual sonic and timbral resources, and pointillism. When Corea disbanded Circle in 1971, Braxton formed his own group, combining the bassist and the drummer of Circle with Kenny Wheeler on trumpet. Braxton's later recordings for Arista Records in the 1970s—*New York Fall 1974*, *Five Pieces 1975*, and *For Trio*—incorporated echoes of bebop, combined notated and improvised music, and brought together free collective improvisation, individual solos, and written ensemble passages.

As a result of his many activities, Braxton became one of the leading figures of the avant-garde. In addition to his jazz work, Braxton has written for band and large orchestra, sometimes with elements of theatricality that recall the early work of the AACM. His compositions often avoid conventional titles and use instead geometric designs, arrangements of numbers and letters, and human and animal figures. Braxton has served as a member of the faculty of Wesleyan University in Middletown, Connecticut, for many years.

Black Artists Group and the World Saxophone Quartet

Inspired by artistic independence, self-sufficiency, and many of the ideals of black nationalism—the same goals that helped launch the AACM—other cities formed creative arts organizations that embraced the avant-garde. A particularly successful group of free jazz players in St. Louis formed a cooperative organization in 1968, the Black Artists Group (BAG). Like the AACM, the BAG tutored young musicians, sponsored musical and multimedia performances, and received support from government and state grants. Although the BAG folded in 1972, three of its former members—alto saxophonists Oliver Lake and Julius Hemphill and baritone saxophonist Hamiet Bluiett—formed the World Saxophone Quartet (WSQ) in 1976. The fourth member was a Californian, tenor saxophonist David Murray.

The WSQ was unique—a versatile ensemble that turned the absence of a rhythm section to their advantage. Although the players were influenced by the free jazz of Ornette Coleman and Albert Ayler, they also relied heavily on both composed music and traditional styles of improvisation. The four saxophonists produced a remarkable cross section of twentieth-century music, incorporating elements of bebop, swing, and collective improvisation into an eclectic mix that ranged from the sound of the Ellington saxophone section to that of Stravinsky-style ballet. Their album *Live in Zurich* demonstrated their diversity, combining swing and mambo in "Hattie Wall," bebop in "Funny Paper," and French classical saxophone quartet music in "Touchic." For improvisational sections, one or two saxophones would create an ostinato figure over which another improvised.

Bluiett's muscular, sometimes raucous baritone provided the underpinning for the group. Of the two alto saxophonists, Lake was initially influenced by bebop altoist Jackie McLean, but he later rejected the predictability of the style. Hemphill maintained a cleaner, purer alto sound. Murray was strongly eclectic, able to draw upon the entire history of tenor saxophone playing.

A long-lived group, the World Saxophone Quartet has continued to perform in recent years. They are highly effective in concert, with marked variety of programming and a lighthearted, engaging stage manner. Recent projects of the WSQ have included other musicians, especially drummers and African percussionists.

The jazz avant-garde of the 1960s, like the jazz styles of earlier eras, has inspired numerous artists and innovative approaches in our own day. After consideration of the more mainstream musical currents of the 1960s in Chapter 10 and the pop-fusion jazz of the late 1960s and 1970s in Chapter 11, we return to the avant-garde in Chapter 12 to examine its legacy.

Free Jazz Styles

TIMBRE
- Emphasis often on hard-edged sound
- Use of entire range of instrument, but upper range more prominent
- Wide variety of attacks and articulations
- Use of vocal sounds—cries, shrieks, etc.—played by instruments
- Extended techniques such as multiphonics on individual instruments emphasized

PHRASING
- Extremely irregular

RHYTHM
- Free use of extreme rhythms, from held notes to "sheets of sound" effects
- Syncopations
- Often lack of steady pulse

THEMATIC CONTINUITY
- Usually motivic

CHORD-SCALE RELATIONS
- Outside playing, if a tonal center exists at all

LARGE-SCALE COHERENCE
- Gestural, motivic, sometimes based on set-theoretical principles

Exam Review Questions

Use these questions and the materials on the text website to help you understand and pass tests on the content of this chapter.

1. How did the 1960s avant-garde overturn traditional practices in jazz? Cite factors that include instruments, repertory, melody, harmony, and rhythm.

2. Who were the principal musicians of the jazz avant-garde? How did these musicians differ in terms of their level of political involvement? Was this evident in their music?

3. What were John Coltrane's three stylistic periods? In a brief biographical outline, show how his musical evolution paralleled his spiritual and professional life.

4. How did the social movements that called for integration and the greater acceptance of blacks into mainstream society affect avant-garde jazz works? Can the word *freedom* be applied to both musical and political relationships? How?

5. How did free jazz resemble the New Orleans and Chicago Dixieland jazz of the 1920s?

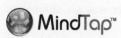 MindTap™

Test Yourself on Key Concepts with additional Chapter Quizzes and Listening Activities on the text website.

Key Terms

Test your knowledge of this chapter's key terms by defining the following. If you can't remember the meaning of a term, refresh your memory by looking up the boldfaced term in the chapter, turning to the Glossary at the back of the book, or working with the flashcards at the text website.

avant-garde **261**

backbeat **263**

free jazz **261**

harmolodics **263**

harmonic superimposition **267**

microtones **260**

motivic cells **269**

multiphonics **271**

New Thing **261**

nontempered intonation **259**

ostinato **269**

outside playing **271**

pentatonic scale (pentatonic set) **268**

sheets of sound **265**

sound fields **271**

thematic cells **269**

Mainstream Jazz: Into the 1960s

10

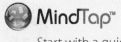
In THIS CHAPTER WE FOLLOW THE EVOLUTION OF relatively mainstream jazz styles from the 1950s into the 1960s. The previous chapter described how avant-garde jazz artists in the 1960s offered distinctly different paths. But at the same time, many players continued to follow mainstream traditions. We begin this chapter by surveying some of the significant mainstream jazz vocalists (especially Ella Fitzgerald and Sarah Vaughan) and examining the legacy of big bands, with particular focus on the bands of Count Basie and Duke Ellington. We then turn to trumpeter Miles Davis and several significant jazz pianists. Finally, we consider the impact of funky (soul) jazz and hard bop in the 1960s.

Vocalists in the 1950s and 1960s

The 1950s and 1960s were an important time for vocalists as well as instrumentalists. With its intrinsic focus on melody, singing provided a respite from the hectic instrumental pyrotechnics of bebop. During the 1940s many popular singers established themselves with solo careers as heirs to the big bands. These singers' careers flourished into the 1950s and 1960s.

In general, five main characteristics identify jazz singing:

▶ Loose phrasing, often becoming back phrasing

▶ Use of blue notes and occasional blues inflections

▶ Free melodic embellishment

▶ A repertory of songs preferred by jazz musicians

▶ Use of instrumental jazz musicians as accompanists

Jazz

1952 Count Basie forms "New Testament" band (Track 46)
    1956—Ella Fitzgerald begins recording "songbooks" for Verve (Track 44)
      —Ellington comeback at Newport Jazz Festival
    1959—Ellington records *The Queen's Suite*, including "Sunset and the Mockingbird" (Track 47)
      —Davis records *Kind of Blue*
    1960—Ornette Coleman records *Free Jazz*
      1962—Classic Coltrane quartet formed with Elvin Jones, Jimmy Garrison, and McCoy Tyner
      1963—Ron Carter, Tony Williams, and Herbie Hancock join the Miles Davis Quintet
      —Davis records *Seven Steps to Heaven*
        1965—Davis records *E.S.P.* (Track 48)
        —Association for the Advancement of Creative Musicians (AACM) founded
        1966—Adderley records "Mercy, Mercy, Mercy" (Track 51)
        1967—Death of John Coltrane
        —Davis records *Nefertiti*
        1968—Davis records *Miles in the Sky*
        1969—Davis records *In a Silent Way, Bitches Brew*
        1970—Davis records *At Fillmore*
        —Death of Albert Ayler

| 1950 | 1955 | 1960 | 1965 | 1970 |

Historical Events

1960—Civil Rights Act
    1961—Yuri Gagarin, first manned space flight
    —Berlin wall erected
    —Peace Corps established
1963—Assassination of President Kennedy
    —Pop Art movement begins
1964—Passage of Civil Rights Act
    1965—Martin Luther King Jr. leads civil rights march in Selma, Alabama
    —Mariner 4 flies by Mars
    1967—First heart transplant
    —Six Day War between Arabs and Israelis
    1968—Martin Luther King Jr. and Robert F. Kennedy assassinated
    1969—U.S. astronauts walk on the moon

Of the five main characteristics of jazz singing, the first is by far the most important. Back phrasing has influenced the performance of all American popular music, including rock. Although many jazz singers are talented at scat singing, this technique does not necessarily occur in the best jazz singing. For example, Billie Holiday—the standard against whom much jazz singing is measured—was not a scat singer.

Ella Fitzgerald

The career of Ella Fitzgerald spanned six decades. Her supreme vocal dexterity, extensive pitch range, dramatic dynamic contrasts, use of melodic ornaments, and—above all—scat singing made her name synonymous with jazz singing. From the time of her earliest recordings with Chick Webb in the 1930s, her ability to straddle jazz and popular styles made her one of the most beloved performers in jazz.

Fitzgerald was born in Virginia in 1917, but in early childhood she moved to New York. As a teenager she overcame her basically shy nature by entering local talent contests, with dreams of becoming a dancer. It soon became clear that dancing was not her strength, but she had tremendous talent as a singer. Chick Webb hired her to work in his band soon after she appeared in a singing contest at the Apollo Theater in 1934. Their recordings of such songs as "A-tisket, A-tasket" and "Undecided" catapulted Fitzgerald to fame.

Fitzgerald led Webb's band for several years following his death in 1939, but later she pursued a solo career.

A publicity shot of the young Ella Fitzgerald ca. 1940. Fitzgerald was as admired for her ability to deliver a song as for her talent for scat singing. With a career that stretched from the mid-thirties to the early nineties, she was one of the most influential of jazz singers.

Photo Courtesy of the Morgan Collection

She preferred the backing of a small group, often a quartet or a trio, which for four years included her onetime husband, bassist Ray Brown.

Some critics find her strongest work to be the "songbooks" recorded for Verve between 1956 and 1964, each interpreting the repertory of a particular American popular-song composer or songwriting team, including Cole Porter, Richard Rodgers and Lorenz Hart, Duke Ellington, George and Ira Gershwin, and Harold Arlen. These recordings helped introduce Fitzgerald to a wider audience. The 1957 songbook album devoted to Ellington's music included Duke Ellington's big band (Listening Guide, Track 44).

As "Take the A Train" aptly demonstrates, Fitzgerald's improvisational skill was unparalleled. Her scat singing, influenced somewhat by Dizzy Gillespie's bebop lines (Gillespie himself plays on this performance of "Take the A Train"), showed an improvisational ability equaling that of the best instrumental soloists and an affinity with bebop style. Her ballad singing has sometimes been criticized for a lack of gravity, but her technique and inventiveness have made her a jazz virtuoso.

Blessed with a long career, Fitzgerald worked through the latter part of the twentieth century. Her health compromised by diabetes, she began to have difficulty with her eyesight in the 1970s. She had heart surgery in 1986 but did not stop performing until the early 1990s. She died in 1996.

Sarah Vaughan

A number of singers who began their careers with big bands gained even greater popularity as solo artists in the 1950s and 1960s. Along with Ella Fitzgerald, Sarah Vaughan was perhaps the most impressive jazz performer. Vaughan (mentioned in Chapter 7 for her work with the bebop big

---

LISTENING GUIDE   Track 44
"Take the A Train" (excerpt)

Ella Fitzgerald and Duke Ellington: "Take the A Train" (Strayhorn), from *Ella and Duke*. Verve MGV4008-2. New York, June 24, 1957. Clark Terry, Cat Anderson, Willie Cook, Harold "Shorty" Baker, Ray Nance, Dizzy Gillespie, trumpets; Quentin Jackson, Britt Woodman, John Sanders, trombones; Jimmy Hamilton, clarinet and tenor saxophone; Johnny Hodges, alto saxophone; Russell Procope, alto saxophone and clarinet; Paul Gonsalves, tenor saxophone; Harry Carney, baritone saxophone, clarinet, bass clarinet; Duke Ellington, piano; Jimmy Woode, bass; Sam Woodyard, drums; Ella Fitzgerald, vocals.

The Main Point   The performance teams jazz singer Ella Fitzgerald with Duke Ellington's big band in a performance of Ellington's theme song, "Take the A Train," written by Billy Strayhorn. The recording is from one of many "songbooks" that Fitzgerald recorded during the 1950s and 1960s. Each of Fitzgerald's songbooks were single or double albums devoted to a single songwriter, reflecting the golden era of American popular song, which reached its apex in the music of Ellington, Irving Berlin, Jerome Kern, George Gershwin, Cole Porter, and Richard Rodgers. Even today, jazz and cabaret singers continue to explore these songs. Additionally, pop and country singers as diverse as Rod Stewart, Willie Nelson, and Linda Ronstadt have crossed over to make entire recordings devoted to this repertory. Unlike Fitzgerald's other songbooks, there are several performances on the Ellington songbook during which she scat sings, including "Take the A Train." The title and the lyrics refer to the New York subway line that goes uptown to Harlem.

Introduction

0:00   "Take the A Train" opens with its signature piano introduction, played by Ellington.

0:05   Trombones play a repeated note. The reeds and trumpets create a "train" effect, which alternates with Fitzgerald's improvised scat singing. The musical depiction of a train was a common technique used by Ellington and other arrangers. (Compare with Wynton Marsalis's "Express Crossing," Track 56)

0:20   An interlude in the lower horns and the bass then return to the trombones, reed train effects, and Fitzgerald's improvised scat singing (0:25).

First chorus—AABA

0:44   Fitzgerald begins singing the lyrics, as the bassist begins walking in 4/4 and the reeds provide a subtle accompaniment. Listen for the use of Fitzgerald's understated vibrato at the ends of phrases. The lyrics develop one of Ellington's (and Strayhorn's) ongoing themes, the role and significance of New York's African American community, Harlem.

1:05   At the bridge section, the horns play a quiet riff behind Fitzgerald. Listen for her slides up to particular pitches, such as the first syllable to the word "coming." During the return to the A section, Fitzgerald takes further liberties with the melody, syncopating the phrase "get on the A Train."

Second chorus—AABA, improvised scat singing

1:26   The chorus provides an excellent example of Fitzgerald's celebrated scat singing. Here it begins above written accompaniment provided by the trombones and the reeds. Her improvisation makes use of a variety of melodic ideas, similar to the ideas that might be played by a jazz instrumentalist.

1:37   During the second A section, her improvisation makes frequent use of repeated notes.

1:47   The scat singing continues during the bridge. Listen for the broad vocal range heard at 1:52, moving gradually from low pitches to high.

1:58   The melodic ideas of the bridge continue into the final A section, as Fitzgerald repeats and develops a single motivic idea, before culminating in an impressive vocal display at 2:03, moving into a high vocal register.

Third chorus—AABA, trumpets trade 4 bars

2:08   Following Fitzgerald's improvised chorus, the individual members of the trumpet section each trade four-bar ideas. It is interesting to compare the different styles of Clark Terry (2:08), Shorty Baker (2:13), Willie Cook (2:18), Cat Anderson (2:23), Dizzy Gillespie (2:28), and Ray Nance (2:34). During the opening A sections, the first four players improvise in a style indebted to that of the swing era. In contrast, trumpeter Dizzy Gillespie at the bridge (2:28) displays his trademark bebop orientation. The Listening Guide concludes with this chorus.

Listen to this music in an animated Active Listening Guide available at the text website.

band of Billy Eckstine) had a wide vocal range, near-perfect intonation, and an astounding variety of vocal colors that she called on to embellish the melody to the song, although she engaged in scat singing less than Fitzgerald did. In 1945

Vaughan recorded a version of "Lover Man" with Charlie Parker and Dizzy Gillespie (in the same recording session that produced "Salt Peanuts"; Track 28), and in the ensuing years she gained wider popularity with her recordings of

Sarah Vaughan,
Embraceable You,
"Sassy's Blues" (1967)

"Tenderly," "It's Magic," "Mean to Me," "Lullaby of Birdland" (Listening Guide, Track 45), and "Sassy" (Vaughan's nickname). Like many of the singers of the 1950s, Vaughan recorded both in jazz and in more commercial venues with studio orchestras. During the next several decades, Vaughan often toured with a piano trio (and sometimes with a symphony orchestra), and her performances usually included a version of her most popular hit, Errol Garner's "Misty." In 1987, three years before her death, she recorded an impressive album of Brazilian music, *Brazilian Romance*.

Cool Singing in the 1950s: The Big Band Legacy

In addition to Ella Fitzgerald and Sarah Vaughan, other jazz singers formed solo careers in the 1950s after singing with big bands. Anita O'Day (1919–2006) launched her career in the 1940s, singing with the big bands of Gene Krupa and Stan Kenton before recording a series of solo albums in the 1950s for Verve, including *Pick Yourself Up* and *Cool Heat* (with Jimmy Giuffre). O'Day's dusky voice and free rhythmic phrasing were influential on other singers, such as June Christy (1925–1990) and Chris Connor (1927–2009). Less of an improvising jazz singer than O'Day, Christy replaced O'Day in Stan Kenton's band, and she helped define the cool singing style of the 1950s with such solo albums as *Something Cool* (1954) and *That Misty Miss Christy* (1955–1956). Chris Connor likewise sang with the Stan Kenton band (she joined it in 1953), and her ensuing solo recordings revealed a dark, husky voice used to great advantage in haunting ballads.

Finally, another singer who characterized the 1950s cool vocal style was Peggy Lee (1920–2002). Lee was the singer with Benny Goodman's big band in the 1940s, but as a solo singer she achieved even greater popular success, culminating in her 1958 hit "Fever." Typical of singers in the 1950s, Lee recorded both jazz-influenced compositions and popular and novelty numbers. Like June Christy and Chris Connor, Peggy Lee rarely experimented with scat singing; also like Christy and Connor, her vocal style was smoky, restrained, and sensuous.

Joe Williams

Virtually no other singer has so successfully bridged jazz and blues as Joe Williams (1918–1999), who first achieved major success in the 1950s. After working with Coleman Hawkins and others, Williams attracted attention as a replacement for Jimmy Rushing in the Count Basie band of the 1950s. He left Basie in 1961 to pursue a solo career, at the same time enlarging and enriching his style.

Sarah Vaughan had a wide vocal range, near-perfect intonation, and an astounding variety of vocal colors.

His big, rich, smooth tone established a virtual genre of its own in jazz singing. Williams's lengthy solo career led to a Grammy award in 1984 for best jazz vocalist, and his recording career continued up to 1995 with his final album, *Feel the Spirit*.

Vocalese: Eddie Jefferson and Lambert, Hendricks, and Ross

Eddie Jefferson (1918–1979) was a unique jazz vocalist, an original artist who established an alternative singing style dissociated from the Billie Holiday–Ella Fitzgerald mainstream. Jefferson was interested not only in improvising vocally but also in composing lyrics to fit existing instrumental solos, a technique called **vocalese**. To provide a change of pace from these carefully worked-out settings, Jefferson also mixed scat singing into his performances.

Vocalese is the technique of setting lyrics to existing jazz solos. Eddie Jefferson was probably the most notable pioneer of this technique, although the practice can be traced to the late 1920s.

LISTENING GUIDE
"Lullaby of Birdland"

Track 45

"Lullaby of Birdland" (Shearing-Foster), from *Sarah Vaughan with Clifford Brown*. EmArcy EP1-6099. December 16, 1954 (master take). Vaughan, vocal; Brown, trumpet; Herbie Mann, flute; Paul Quinichette, tenor saxophone; Jimmy Jones, piano; Joe Benjamin, bass; Roy Haynes, drums; Ernie Wilkins, arranger-conductor.

The Main Point   "Lullaby of Birdland," recorded in 1954, shows many of the best features of Sarah Vaughan's singing: scat singing, masterful improvisation, virtuosic command of her entire vocal range, and use of different vocal colors. Compare her scat singing with that of Ella Fitzgerald (Track 44).

"Lullaby of Birdland" was composed by British pianist George Shearing (discussed in Chapter 8), and its title was a tribute to the famous jazz club Birdland (named in honor of Charlie Parker). As Shearing's most famous composition, "Lullaby of Birdland" was chosen as the title to Shearing's 2005 autobiography. Many jazz artists recorded the song during the 1950s.

Not only does Vaughan sing the lyrics to the 32-bar composition, she also "trades fours." That is, she alternates four-bar vocal improvisations (using scat singing) with the instrumentalists, including saxophonist Paul Quinichette, trumpeter Clifford Brown, and flutist Herbie Mann. The use of the flute as a jazz instrument became increasingly common during the 1950s and 1960s. Herbie Mann (1930–2003) later became a popular jazz flutist. Drummer Roy Haynes (b. 1925) worked extensively with Charlie Parker and has become one of the most celebrated jazz drummers.

Introduction (4 bars) and head (32 bars as AABA)

0:00   During the four-bar introduction, Vaughan sings wordless vocals, using the same melodic idea as the flute, trumpet, and saxophone (the three instruments voiced in chords). This introduction is arranger Ernie Wilkins's principal contribution to the chart, and it returns as a coda to conclude the performance. In this section Vaughan sings with straight tone (with no vibrato).

0:08   During the head statement, Vaughan sings the lyrics to the composition. She is accompanied by the rhythm section, with drummer Roy Haynes playing brushes (rather than sticks) and bassist Joe Benjamin playing "in two"—playing every two beats (rather than walking the bass by playing every beat). Vaughan's subtle vocal inflections are in evidence throughout. She subtly elaborates the last syllable of the word "Lullaby," and she uses vibrato when singing longer notes at the ends of the phrases ("... land," "I," "hear," and "sigh"). During the second A section (0:24), she elaborates the melody similarly.

0:40   During the B section, listen for the bass drum accents coordinated to occur with the first syllable of each line: "and," "he," "that's," "if." By the third line, pianist Jimmy Jones uses block chords, phrasing them with Vaughan.

0:57   In the final A section of this first chorus, Vaughan changes her vocal color as she leaps down to lower pitches, at "high," "sky," "(a)bove," and "love."

Second chorus (32 bars as AABA)—piano, bass, and drum improvisation

1:13   The piano improvisation lasts for the first two A sections. Jones plays primarily in block-chord (or "locked hands") style, undoubtedly an acknowledgment of George Shearing, who composed "Lullaby of Birdland" and who made the block-chord style a primary feature of his style. Notice that here the bassist moves to walking bass, playing every beat.

1:45   Bassist Benjamin improvises during the B section, playing bebop-oriented melodic lines. The pianist plays quiet chords in the upper register of the piano, in order to provide harmonic support but not interfere with the bass solo.

1:59   For his unaccompanied solo, drummer Roy Haynes uses brushes. He keeps the underlying eight-bar form of the final A section of the solo. There is a progression to his solo, consisting of a series of two-bar ideas.

His first two-bar idea is spacious, and Haynes uses snare drum (played with brushes) and bass drum (played by a foot pedal). The second two-bar idea (2:03) becomes more active, played merely on the snare drum. The third two-bar idea (2:07) becomes more syncopated, returning to both snare and bass drum; and the final two-bar idea eventually moves to an underlying triplet idea, which helps usher in the vocal improvisation.

Third chorus (32 bars as AABA)—Vaughan trades fours with the instrumentalists

2:14   The chorus consists of four-bar alternations between Vaughan's improvised scat singing and improvisations by the flute, tenor saxophone, and trumpet. She begins by scat singing a long uninterrupted vocal line in eighth notes. Listen for her extensive vocal range, moving from low to high (2:20–2:21). Flutist Herbie Mann begins simply, then moves to playing faster pitches at the end of his four bars.

2:29   In response to Mann's faster line, Vaughan begins by improvising a faster melody in sixteenth notes, then decelerates into eighth notes. Again, listen for her extensive range: she moves to a high note (2:33) before ending her phrase with an extended low note that overlaps with Quinichette's saxophone solo. The tenor saxophone solo is unhurried, indebted to the cool style of 1950s saxophone playing.

2:45   Vaughan's scat singing is exuberant during the B section, and her phrases explore the low end of her vocal range (2:49–2:51). Trumpeter Clifford Brown (discussed in Chapter 8) begins in understated fashion with his horn muted, before moving to a more active line.

3:00   Vaughan sings the entire final A section of this chorus. Her bebop-oriented improvisation shows her the equal of the best instrumental improvisers, and her creative melodic ideas are sung with unerring pitch both in chest voice (lower range) and in head voice (higher range).

Return to lyrics—final chorus (BA as 16 bars) + 4-bar coda

3:16   Vaughan's previous improvised line overlaps with her return to the lyrics. The group omits the opening two A sections and moves directly to the B section here, a common strategy employed by singers following the improvisations. The bass continues to walk.

3:31   During the final A section, the bass stops walking, and plays "in two," articulating every other beat. The flute, trumpet, and saxophone play together a riff beneath Vaughan's lyrics.

3:47   Following the final A section, the group returns to the four-bar introduction, now played as a coda. The recording ends as Vaughan swoops up to a high note.

 Listen to this music in an animated Active Listening Guide available at the text website.

Jefferson's performance strength lay in his tremendous vocal agility. His flexible range, which included a deft use of falsetto, never seemed to strain or bury the lyric. Unlike the regular four-bar phrases usually found in popular songs, the jazz solos he set usually featured complex phrasing. Despite the difficulty of setting lyrics to freely wandering instrumental lines, Jefferson often found felicitous solutions that incorporated intriguing rhyme schemes.

Vocal ensembles were certainly not new: after all, the Rhythm Boys (including Bing Crosby) were a principal feature of the Paul Whiteman Orchestra in the 1920s. Featured groups, such as the popular Boswell Sisters and the Andrews Sisters, who sang in harmony with band backups, continued through the swing era. But the 1950s witnessed a different kind of vocal ensemble, one allied more with the jazz tradition than with rendering popular songs in close harmony. In the latter half of the decade, a pioneering vocal group broke onto the scene. This trio—Jon Hendricks, Dave Lambert, and Annie Ross—mixed three distinct styles:

▶ Imitation of big-band textures and arrangements

▶ Vocalese

▶ Traditional scat

Hendricks provided many of the vocalese lyrics for this extremely inventive group, who provided much inspiration for such contemporary singing ensembles as the Manhattan Transfer and the New York Voices.

Frank Sinatra

No survey of vocalists in the 1950s and 1960s can ignore the overwhelming importance of Frank Sinatra (1915–1998), whose active career lasted well into the 1990s. Although a popular icon, he has rightfully been included in the ranks of the jazz singers for his exceptionally free phrasing, his swinging big-band recordings, his identification with outstanding songs, and his ability to convey the meaning and the emotional content of a lyric. Given these attributes, his domination of the pop-vocal market for five decades, and the respect many jazz musicians have given him, Sinatra's significance remains indisputable. Like the other singers discussed in this chapter, he established many of the essential attributes of his persona during the 1950s and 1960s.

In some ways Sinatra belied the image of the cool 1950s. He projected a macho persona—the girl-chasing, booze-loving tough guy who hobnobbed not only with the elite Kennedy family but also with gangsters. Nonetheless, much of Sinatra's work from the 1950s and 1960s captured the essence of jazz singing: loose phrasing, direct expression, and the ability to make a song his own. Among Sinatra's best

recordings were those on the Capitol label with arrangers Nelson Riddle and Billy May, as well as his collaborations with Count Basie. Along with most of the singers discussed in this section, Sinatra first recorded in the big-band era. In the 1940s he achieved teen idol status, bringing screaming fans to their feet much in the way that Elvis Presley would in the 1950s and the Beatles in the 1960s.

The Big Bands Persevere

The association of big bands with the swing era of the 1940s is unavoidable. Yet big bands continued well past the midpoint of the twentieth century. Many popular big bands did break up shortly after the end of the Second World War, but several persevered. Both Count Basie and Duke Ellington, whom we examined as central figures of the Swing Era, continued to lead exceptional big bands, playing arrangements that were exciting and innovative. The mainstream tradition of the big band continued to flourish in the 1950s and 1960s.

Sinatra projected a macho persona—the girl-chasing, booze-loving tough guy who hobnobbed not only with the elite Kennedy family but also with gangsters.

Count Basie and The New Testament Band

Basie's big band of the 1930s and 1940s was remarkable for its ability to create a loose small-group improvisational

Count Basie,
April in Paris,
"April in Paris"
(1965)

atmosphere with sparkling and swinging arrangements. In 1952 Basie formed a new band, updating his personnel. This new group became known as the "New Testament" band (and the 1930s–1940s one the "Old Testament"). The band's subsequent arrangements were penned by many of the best arrangers in the business, such as Neal Hefti—known for "Li'l Darlin'" and "Girl Talk"—as well as Thad Jones, Benny Carter, and Quincy Jones. Many of these arrangements featured driving swing, dynamic contrasts (soft and loud), and shout choruses to enhance the excitement of the performances. Basie's version of "April in Paris" became a popular hit for the group, renowned for its thunderous two repeated shout choruses, led off by Basie calling out "one more time," and—finally—"one more once." That performance was the title track from Basie's 1955 *April in Paris* recording: it also included "Corner Pocket" (Listening Guide, Track 46) in a quintessential performance by Basie's New Testament band.

For the remainder of his career, Basie continued to record and tour with his group—including visits to Europe and Japan. One highly acclaimed performance is his live recording with Frank Sinatra at the Sands hotel in Las Vegas, in which Basie gives many of Sinatra's most familiar songs a hard-edged, brilliant swing without commercial compromises. Basie's health began to deteriorate in the 1970s when he suffered a heart attack, but he continued to perform.

LISTENING GUIDE
"Corner Pocket"

Track 46

Count Basie Orchestra: "Corner Pocket" (Freddie Green), from *April in Paris*. Verve MGV8012. New York, July 26, 1955. Wendell Culley, Reunald Jones, Joe Newman, Thad Jones, trumpets; Henry Coker, Bill Hughes, Benny Powell, trombones; Marshal Royal, clarinet and alto saxophone; Bill Graham, alto saxophone; Frank Wess, tenor saxophone and flute; Frank Foster, tenor saxophone; Charlie Fowlkes, baritone saxophone and bass clarinet; Count Basie, piano and leader; Freddie Green, guitar; Eddie Jones, bass; Sonny Payne, drums.

The Main Point   "Corner Pocket" offers a glimpse into Count Basie's New Testament band. It reveals how the big-band tradition continued well past its heyday in the swing era, and shows why the Count Basie Orchestra remained one of the primary exponents of infectious and uncluttered swing. The group made unparalleled use of dynamics to create exciting performances, moving from a roar to a whisper. A comparison with the earlier 1938 Basie performance of "Every Tub" (Track 20) shows how the juxtaposition of loud and soft playing remained a mainstay of the group's performances. In fact, "Corner Pocket" has an understated piano solo during the bridge of the shout chorus, creating an "eye of the hurricane" effect, one similar to that heard during the fourth chorus of "Every Tub," recorded some two decades before "Corner Pocket."

Guitarist Freddie Green wrote "Corner Pocket"; listen for Green's swinging guitar comping that states chords every beat. Notice too how drummer Sonny Payne plays significantly louder during the shout chorus, often playing the same rhythmic figures as the horns. Interesting as well is the stylistic attitude of the soloists, and the bebop-oriented trumpet solos contrast markedly with the older swing-style improvisation of the tenor saxophone. Cementing together the entire performance is pianist Basie, whose playing is characteristically understated and tasteful.

Introduction—14 bars

0:00   The performance begins with Basie's signature sound of upper-range chords, here accompanied by the drummer keeping time on the hi-hat. Basie's chords are punctuated by his left-hand bass, doubled by the bassist. The introduction ends with a rising melody in the bass (0:20). Like many of Basie's big-band arrangements, "Corner Pocket" begins merely with the rhythm section, setting up a small-group atmosphere prior to the entrance of the horns.

Head—32 bars as AABA

0:23 The saxophones play the melody to the head statement. Listen for Green's guitar comping on all four beats, propelling the music forward. The brass (trumpets and trombones) enter for a short phrase at the end of the A section (0:35).

0:37 Repeat of A section. Again the saxophones state the melody, answered by the brass (0:48).

0:51 During the B section, the saxophones again state the melody, with a brief interjection by the trumpets (0:56). Notice that although the saxophones played the A section in unison (all playing the same pitches), here the saxophone parts are given a fuller voicing.

1:05 The A-section melody returns, now played by muted trumpets in unison. The section ends with a clear break (1:16), setting up the beginning of the trumpet solo.

Trumpet solos—32 bars as AABA

1:18 Trumpeter Thad Jones begins his break by quoting the melody from the popular 1955 hit song "Cherry Pink and Apple Blossom White." That melody, with its long drop-off on the fourth note, became something of a well-worn cliché for soloists of that time. Jones's bebop orientation is especially clear in the end of his phrase at 1:27, which uses a rising triplet followed by a two-note bebop figure.

1:32 During the second A section, the saxophones provide a driving accompaniment figure, and the trumpet relies on longer held notes.

1:47 The second trumpet soloist, Joe Newman, takes over here. He begins his solo by echoing the previous phrase played by Jones. In this B section the trombones provide the accompanimental figure.

2:00 During the last A section of this chorus, this second trumpet soloist moves to the upper register. The melody played here will become the melody ultimately heard during the shout chorus. The saxophones return to playing their driving accompaniment, and the section ends with the entire band playing a punchy figure (2:11) that sets up the tenor saxophone solo.

Tenor saxophone solo—32 bars as AABA

2:15 The tenor saxophonist (credited as Frank Wess in the original liner notes) begins his tenor saxophone solo sparely. Notice that he uses a significant degree of space. The tenor saxophone sound, indebted more to swing style more than to bebop, uses considerable vibrato.

2:28 Wess begins his second A section by stating an initial melodic idea of seven notes, then repeating and varying it somewhat. This section ends with a blues-based idea (2:36).

2:42 During this B section, listen for Basie's tasteful piano comping, with upper-range chords that nicely complement the solo.

2:56 The solo coolly develops a single idea. Listen for how the bass drum accents work in support of the main notes of the saxophone melody (2:59 and 3:02).

Band plays AABA—32 bars

3:10 Here the entire band returns, with all the horn players playing the same rhythm. Notice how Basie's well-placed note (3:11) sounds like a chime and fills the gaps within the ensemble passage. Here too the band operates like a well-oiled machine, beginning relatively softly, sliding up to a louder chord (3:16), coming in with a roar at 3:18, before finally returning to a quieter volume (3:22). Notice the ways in which the drummer duplicates the rhythm of the horns on his snare drum during the loudest portion at 3:17, adding to the excitement.

3:23 The band repeats the previous eight bars, with the same move to a higher volume followed by a quick dynamic dropoff. A short drum fill (3:35) helps set up the B section.

3:39 The saxophones play a unison melody during the B section. The melody decorates a single note for the first four bars, and a note a step higher for the second four bars.

3:52   Again the exciting dynamic contrasts of the A sections of 3:09 and 3:23 reappear. At the end of this section, the drummer plays an extended fill on the snare drum (4:03), setting up the move to the shout chorus.

Shout chorus—32 bars as AABA + tag

4:06   The term *shout chorus* is appropriate here, as the horns provide the climactic final chorus to the performance. While the horns play the melody together, listen for the ways in which the drummer enhances the excitement, through bass drum kicks with the horns, as well as through fills between the melodic statements.

4:19   The band repeats the previous eight-bar section, maintaining the energy level.

4:34   During the B section, the bottom drops out: only the rhythm section plays, keeping time beneath Basie's sparse quiet chords, the upper register harmonies exemplifying Basie's signature piano style. Basie's understated chords allow the composer, guitarist Freddy Green, to shine through. This section provides an extreme dynamic contrast with the previous section, and sets the following A section into further relief. Note too the dramatic drum fill that brings about the return to the next section.

4:48   Again, the return to the A section shout chorus is accompanied by explosive drumming. During the second half of this section (4:54), the saxophones return to the original melody heard at the beginning of the performance. Basie frequently used the sequence of three crisp piano chords (4:59) to end his big-band performances. Here they precede the tag and the drum fill that sets off the final two chords of the performance.

This "Corner Pocket" performance exemplifies the following aspects of Basie's New Testament band: (1) an infectious sense of swing supported by the rhythm section players, including Freddie Green's guitar comping every beat, Basie's clean and spare chords, and drummer Payne's use of kicks and fills; (2) a dramatic arrangement beginning quietly and moving inexorably to the climactic shout chorus; (3) extreme dynamic contrasts between loud and soft, enhancing the excitement of the performance, particularly during the shout chorus; and (4) stylistically diverse solos, frequently accompanied by riff figures in the horns.

Listen to this music in an animated Active Listening Guide available at the text website.

In the early 1980s he began working with Albert Murray on his autobiography, *Good Morning Blues*, which was published in 1985. After Basie's death, his band continued to tour and perform under various leaders, including Frank Foster.

Basie's legacy is undiminished. Ironically, his piano style is so familiar that other pianists cannot appropriate

> "The main thing for me is the music. That's what excites me. That's what keeps me going."
> —Count Basie

it without sounding clichéd. For example, Basie-style performances sometimes include a signature ending in which the band breaks for three light chords in the upper register of the piano, a trademark not unlike the piano vamps that opened his arrangements in the 1930s.

Fans will always revere Basie's music for its joy, its swing, and its exemplary balance between freewheeling

improvisation and classic arranging. As Basie himself put it at eighty years old, "The main thing for me is the music. That's what excites me. That's what keeps me going. The music and people having a good time listening to it. People dancing or just patting their feet."[1]

Duke Ellington After 1950

By mid-century Ellington's celebrated Cotton Club performances and radio broadcasts were a distant memory. Moreover, he was having difficulty maintaining some of his personnel as the popularity of swing music diminished.

> "I was born in 1956 at the Newport Festival."
> —Duke Ellington

In 1951 his mainstays—Johnny Hodges, Sonny Greer, and Lawrence Brown—all left the band, but Ellington attracted strong replacements. Louie Bellson replaced Greer, and

Ellington added a fine young player in the bebop mold, Clark Terry, on trumpet. The departure of his star soloist, Johnny Hodges, was short-lived; Hodges returned to Ellington in 1955.

In July 1956 the fortunes of the band miraculously reversed themselves. Onstage at the Newport Jazz Festival, during a performance of "Diminuendo and Crescendo in Blue," tenor saxophonist Paul Gonsalves stood up and played twenty-seven electrifying choruses. The response of the crowd was overwhelming: listeners danced in the aisles, stood on chairs, and cheered. Ellington was in vogue again. With characteristic irony he noted, "I was born in 1956 at the Newport Festival."[2]

The band continued to perform widely, undertaking a State Department–sponsored tour of India and the Middle East. At the end of the decade, Ellington wrote the score for the 1959 Otto Preminger film *Anatomy of a*

Murder; the soundtrack won three Grammy awards. He and composer-arranger Billy Strayhorn (their long-standing collaboration is discussed in Chapter 5) continued to turn out larger musical suites, notably *Such Sweet Thunder*, inspired by Shakespeare and written for the Shakespeare Festival in Stratford, Canada, and *The Queen's Suite*, in honor of Queen Elizabeth II. John Steinbeck's novel *Sweet Thursday* inspired the collaboration with Strayhorn on *Suite Thursday*, which they wrote for the 1960 Monterey Jazz Festival. The interval of a descending minor sixth musically dominates the work. Another significant collaboration with Strayhorn was *The Far East Suite*, which resulted in adding four movements to the previous five-movement *Impressions of the Far East*. *A Drum Is a Woman* was a somewhat whimsical history of jazz, narrated by Ellington, in which "Madame Zajj" goes from the Caribbean, to New Orleans, Harlem, and the moon.

LISTENING GUIDE   Track 47
"Sunset and the Mockingbird"

Duke Ellington: "Sunset and the Mockingbird" (Duke Ellington), released on *Ellington Suites*. Pablo 2310-762. New York, April 1, 1959. Clark Terry, Harold "Shorty" Baker, Ray Nance, trumpets; Quentin Jackson, Britt Woodman, John Sanders, trombones; Jimmy Hamilton, clarinet and tenor saxophone; Russell Procope, clarinet and alto saxophone; Johnny Hodges, alto saxophone; Paul Gonsalves, tenor saxophone; Harry Carney, baritone saxophone; Duke Ellington, piano; Jimmy Woode, bass; Jimmy Johnson, drums.

The Main Point "Sunset and the Mockingbird" is a movement from the Ellington–Strayhorn collaboration *The Queen's Suite*, written in honor of Queen Elizabeth II, whom Ellington met while in England in the late 1950s. Although recorded in 1959, merely one copy of the recording was pressed, which Ellington sent as a special gift to the queen. Only in 1976, following Ellington's death, was *The Queen's Suite* released to the public. It is one of a number of suites (a series of short compositions linked by an overall idea) that Ellington wrote, usually in collaboration with Billy Strayhorn.

In contrast to many of Ellington's works that celebrate urban life, particularly Harlem, "Sunset and the Mockingbird" evokes nature and the outdoors. Rather than a melody and a series of solos, the work is comprised primarily of restatements of the eight-bar melody, played by different solo instruments (piano, clarinet, and tenor/alto saxophone) and accompanied by the band.

Introduction and first statement of melody

0:00   A short delicate piano introduction begins the work, accompanied by bass and triangle (played by the drummer). Ellington plays the two chords in an unusual way. He strikes a group of notes and releases immediately all but one of the notes, which is held. He repeats the pair of chords.

0:11   The piano plays the melody, still accompanied by bass and triangle. The repeated pitches of the melody create a warbling effect, likely intended to convey the sound of a mockingbird. The harmony and eight-bar melody show how Ellington made use of the sound of the blues, without writing a 12-bar blues. The first two chords move from I to IV7, the same progression as the opening to a blues progression. Just before the band enters at 0:31, Ellington uses an interesting harmonic color that leads back to the tonic, a major seventh harmony a half step above the tonic. This chord substitutes for the dominant chord.

0:31   The band plays a short section that sets up a slow, relaxed tempo. The drummer ceases playing triangle and begins playing on the drum set, using sticks. The trombones alternate a pair of chords, as the reeds play individual pitches in the background, and Ellington plays splashy chords in the upper register. Above this, the clarinetist improvises.

Melody statements by piano and clarinet

0:44   The piano plays the eight-bar melody again, as the bass begins walking in a slow 4/4 meter. The reeds accompany the piano with syncopated chords, played on the "and" of the first beat of each measure. With the held chords in the reeds, listen for the vibrato in the top voice, the lead alto saxophone.

1:10   The clarinet now takes the melody and elaborates it subtly. The brass and reeds accompany, each section playing its own melodic idea. Listen for the slide to the brass chord at 1:24. The melody ends on the ninth (B♭) of the tonic A♭ harmony.

Interlude and piano melody

1:38   The eight-bar interlude provides a contrast to the previous melody statements. The piano plays the melody to this section in octaves, duplicating the melody in both hands. The reeds accompany. However, at 1:55, listen for the ingenious accompanying orchestration that alternates brass, reeds, brass, reeds, before both sections play together (2:02).

2:04   The piano returns to the main melody for this climactic section. Again, Ellington plays the melody in octaves, as the horns begin accompanying at a louder volume. These accompanimental chords appear on beat 2, and notice that the drummer plays a "kick" (accent) on that same beat, supporting the horns. Above this, the clarinetist plays improvisatory fills.

Melody statements by saxophone and piano

2:30   Following a lead-in ascending melodic line, alto saxophonist Johnny Hodges states the eight-bar melody. Listen for his use of slides up to melodic pitches, as well as his vibrato. The accompaniment again uses brass (single pitches) and reeds (chords) in an interesting alternation, beginning with brass, then reeds (first measure), and reeds, then brass (second measure). The same alternation continues throughout the section.

2:58   The final statement of the melody occurs in the piano. The reeds accompany by playing chords on the "and" of beat 1.

Final coda

3:19   The performance ends with a return of the section that appeared at 0:31. The trombones alternate two held chords, the reeds play individual pitches, and the piano plays the chords in the upper register. Above this, the clarinet improvises.

     "Sunset and the Mockingbird" includes features of Ellington's mature compositional style, including the sound of the blues without using the 12-bar blues form; structured composition, here consisting primarily of an eight-bar melody passed around different instruments, rather than a series of improvised solos; rich harmonic language; and ingenious use of reeds and brass to accompany the melodic statements.

Listen to this music in an animated Active Listening Guide available at the text website.

Though usually modest about his own piano-playing abilities, Ellington showcased his playing in several small-group recordings in the early 1960s. He cut an album with John Coltrane and recorded *Money Jungle* with Charles Mingus and Max Roach in 1962. Much of Ellington's final work involved religious compositions. For example, San Francisco's Grace Cathedral commissioned him to write a liturgical work. The resulting *Concert of Sacred Music*, which

Unlike the vast majority of popular music, a **standard** outlasts its contemporaries and enjoys a long-lasting place in current repertories. "I Got Rhythm," for example, is a standard written by George and Ira Gershwin in 1930.

incorporated segments of some of his earlier pieces such as *Black, Brown and Beige* and *New World a-Comin'*, premiered in 1965. Ellington performed his *Second Sacred Concert* two years later and performed the third and most introspective of his sacred concerts in 1973, the year before his death.

Ellington's influence and legacy continue to be profound. He had the administrative ability to run a large band for decades. As a pianist he recorded solos, worked with his large band, and found time to record small-group works. Dozens of his compositions have kept their status as **standards** of jazz literature, and their melodic and harmonic structures still attract jazz musicians. As an orchestrator, Ellington created instrumental effects that were dazzling, hypnotic, and masterly. As a composer of larger works, he elevated the perception of jazz to a music worthy of the concert stage. Some consider him the greatest American composer in any category.

Thad Jones–Mel Lewis Big Band

Despite shifts in personnel, Basie's and Ellington's big bands lasted decades, staffed with road-tested veterans crisscrossing the country and the world. Other big bands continued to tour, record, and perform mainstream jazz during and after the 1960s, including those of Woody Herman and Stan Kenton. A notable big band that formed during the 1960s was the Thad Jones–Mel Lewis Big Band. The eighteen-piece group began playing together in 1966 under the leadership of trumpeter, cornetist, and arranger Thad Jones (brother of pianist Hank Jones and drummer Elvin Jones) and drummer Mel Lewis. Formed with some of New York's finest jazz musicians, the band began a long-standing tenure playing Monday nights at the Village Vanguard. The group was known as a "rehearsal band," that is, the players met once a week at the club to play Jones's arrangements and did not maintain an ongoing consistent touring schedule.

Previously, Thad Jones arranged for and played with the Basie New Testament band (his solo on "Corner Pocket" is heard on Track 46). His compositions and arrangements for the Jones–Lewis band showed off the group's top-flight soloists. Several of his compositions ("Little Pixie II" and "Fingers") offered extraordinarily difficult ensemble passages based on rhythm changes, all propelled by the swinging and effortless timekeeping of drummer Mel Lewis. Lewis took over the leadership of the group after Jones left the band in 1979, and the group began performing arrangements of trombonist Bob Brookmeyer and pianist Jim McNeely. After Lewis's death in 1990, the group became the Vanguard Jazz Orchestra; it still performs weekly.

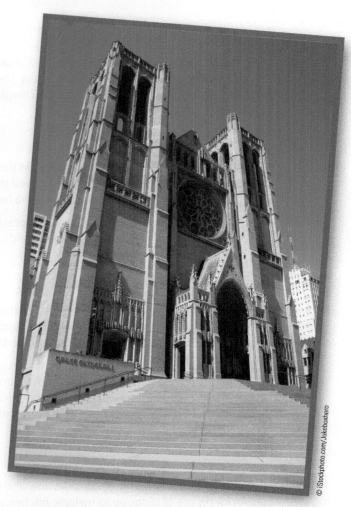
© iStockphoto.com/Jukeboxhero

In 1965 San Francisco's Grace Cathedral commissioned Duke Ellington to create a liturgical work: the *Concert of Sacred Music*. The concert's showpiece was the fifteen-minute-long "In the Beginning God," featuring singer Jon Hendricks, Harry Carney, Paul Gonsalves, "Cat" Anderson, and Louie Bellson, supported by the choirs and the rest of the band.

Miles Davis in the 1960s

Davis flowed into the sixties on a flood tide of activity, garnering immense critical success as his band evolved into one of the most notable groups in jazz. As we saw in Chapter 8, his hard bop quintet and sextet in the late 1950s featured the dynamic saxophonists John Coltrane and Cannonball Adderley. On the collaborations *Porgy and Bess* and *Sketches of Spain*, Davis's spare lyricism acted as a foil to arranger Gil Evans's lush orchestrations and dense harmonies. Finally, Davis's 1959 recording *Kind of Blue*, spurred by the poetic pianism of Bill Evans, set the standard for modal improvisation.

For the next several years, Davis's group underwent several changes of personnel. Coltrane's departure in 1960 was an enormous loss for Davis. After trying saxophonist Sonny Stitt (born Edward Boatner Jr.), whose alto style was closely derived from Charlie Parker's, and tenor player Jimmy Heath, Davis eventually hired Hank Mobley on tenor. With Art Blakey and Horace Silver, Mobley (1930–1986) had helped found the Jazz Messengers. He performed with Davis from 1961 to 1962, then continued his distinguished career through the sixties and beyond. On Davis's recording *Someday My Prince Will Come*, Mobley displayed a more conventional rhythmic and harmonic sensibility than his predecessor had, avoiding Coltrane's searching intensity and sheets of sound technique.

Along with Mobley, Davis used Jamaican-born pianist Wynton Kelly (1931–1971). Kelly's improvisations displayed a sparkling sense of swing, heard especially on 12-bar blues compositions such as "No Blues," from *Miles Davis at Carnegie Hall* (1961). Although his harmonies were typically less lush and dense than those of Bill Evans, in ballads such as "Old Folks" from *Someday My Prince Will Come* some Evans-style voicings could be heard beneath Davis's poignant, muted trumpet. These two sides to Kelly—his exuberant, joyful swing and his sophisticated harmonic sense—earned him high praise from Davis, who described his work as "a combination of Red Garland and Bill Evans."[3] Davis also praised Kelly's accompanying ability: his rhythmically subtle and creative comping anticipated and complemented the soloist.

In the early 1960s, Davis was only in his mid-thirties, but he found himself in the odd position of seeming

> In the early 1960s, Davis was only in his mid-thirties, but he found himself in the odd position of seeming old-fashioned.

old-fashioned. Ornette Coleman, Cecil Taylor, and Eric Dolphy were stirring up the jazz world with their challenging and controversial innovations. At the same time that Coleman was launching his radical *Free Jazz*, Davis's repertory remained rooted in 32-bar standards, 12-bar blues, and ballads. Davis's rhythm section of Wynton Kelly on piano, Jimmy Cobb on drums, and Paul Chambers on bass was a fine, swinging unit, but the group projected a conventional hard bop approach.

This soon changed. In 1963 Davis formed the nucleus of a group that would stay together for the next five years. His most dramatic move was to revitalize his rhythm section by taking on younger players. On piano he hired

A Ron Carter publicity shot from CTI Records.

twenty-three-year-old Herbie Hancock, who had been working with trumpeter Donald Byrd and recording under his own name as a leader for Blue Note. Ron Carter, an accomplished classical and jazz bassist, left trumpeter Art Farmer to join Davis. Davis's most astonishing choice was an incredibly young drummer from Boston named Tony Williams, who joined the group at age seventeen. Despite his youth Williams already showed flawless technique, consistent creativity, and fierce drive. Even on their earliest recordings, the new Davis rhythm section was stunning. Hancock, Carter, and Williams interacted at nearly telepathic levels, bringing fresh, free interpretations to Davis's traditional repertory.

The group's unparalleled polish and technical aplomb often disguised their high level of creativity. On one of their earliest recordings—Victor Feldman's "Joshua," from *Seven Steps to Heaven*—the rhythm section shifted seamlessly between the 4/4 meter of the A section and the 3/4 meter of the B section. When playing jazz standards during their live performances from 1963 to 1964, the rhythm section experimented further, often superimposing different meters on a standard composition. On ballad performances, such as "My Funny Valentine" and "Stella by Starlight," the three players rapidly shifted moods and tempos, freely interpreting the harmonic structure to create what sounded like a multimovement suite. Drummer Tony Williams would lay out (stop playing) for stretches

Comping refers to a technique in which a pianist or guitarist plays a chord progression in a rhythmically irregular fashion. The term *comp* is probably derived from a contraction of the word *accompany* or *complement*.

---

at a time, return playing the tempo, then move effortlessly into double time. The group negotiated blistering tempos, propelled by Williams's intense drumming.

Williams's interest in the jazz avant-garde had a major impact on the group, as Hancock later acknowledged:

> Tony Williams turned me on to different rhythms, overlapping this and that. Tony was really into Paul Bley, Gary Peacock... Ornette [Coleman]—like I never paid that much attention to Ornette when he first came out, but Tony got me interested in Ornette and got me to the point where I could get into it.[4]

Although the rhythm section was in place, Davis was unable to settle quickly on a tenor saxophone player. The recordings from 1963 and 1964 featured George Coleman, a strong, assertive player from Memphis who ultimately proved too conservative for the group. On Williams's recommendation Davis replaced Coleman with Sam Rivers, whom Williams had known in Boston. Rivers remained for a short time, appearing on the recording *Miles in Tokyo*. Finally, in the fall of 1964, Davis hired the saxophonist he had been after for several years, Wayne Shorter. With this final addition, Davis's group was set. "Getting Wayne made me feel real good," said Davis, "because with him I just knew some great music was going to happen. And it did; it happened real soon."[5]

Davis had been trying to lure Shorter into his band since 1960, but Shorter was reluctant to leave Art Blakey and the Jazz Messengers. When he finally joined Davis, Shorter contributed numerous compositions, significantly altering the group's sound and approach. On tenor he owed his tone quality and musical ideas in part to Coltrane, although Shorter's melodies were more oblique and spacious.

With Davis, Shorter, Hancock, Carter, and Williams on board, the group was now stabilized. They tended to emphasize popular standards in live performance and Shorter's compositions in the studio. An outstanding example of their live work is *The Complete Live at the Plugged Nickel*, which, although recorded in December 1965, was not released in its entirety in the United States until the 1990s. On it we can hear the Davis quintet pushing the envelope on the performance of well-known jazz and popular standards. For example, on "Stella by Starlight," recorded in the first set of December 23, Davis's solo maintains the form of the tune but just barely. Hancock deviates radically from the changes of the song, and Williams goes into double, then quadruple time. On the song's C section, a consistency of motivic reference establishes that the band is in fact following the form. Shorter's solo, which follows Davis's, is even more abstract.

Shorter's compositions were also unusual. Avoiding the standard harmonic clichés of the hard bop idiom, he instead explored unusual voicings and progressions. The melodic lines of his compositions lay sometimes outside the bop tradition, too; for example, "E.S.P." (from the album of the same name; Listening Guide, Track 48) and "Masqualero" (from *Nefertiti*) emphasized the ambiguous interval of a perfect fourth. Shorter's composition "Nefertiti" was made even more radical by its reversal of the roles of horn soloists and rhythm section: the trumpet and the saxophone merely restate the slow-moving 16-bar melody throughout, providing a static *obbligato*, while the "accompanying instruments"—the piano, bass, and drums—improvise beneath, providing the active role. "Footprints," a well-known tune from *Miles Smiles*, was a minor blues composition in 6/8.

Miles Davis,
Nefertiti,
"Nefertiti" (1967)

Although Shorter wrote the majority of compositions for the quintet, all of the members contributed tunes. Most of them maintained a conventional role for the rhythm section, keeping a 4/4 swing feel with walking bass. But often Hancock would stop backing the trumpet or saxophone solos for long stretches of time, which rendered the harmony ambiguous and brought about the group's distinctive open sound. Without Hancock's **comping**, in compositions such as "Orbits" and "Dolores," the accompanying bass and drums abandoned the underlying form, merely retaining the 4/4 swing feel. In his own solos, Hancock often omitted the punctuating chords in his left hand entirely, playing only long right-hand melodic lines.

Hancock must have been surprised when, at a Davis recording session toward the end of 1967, he was confronted with an unknown instrument:

> I walked into the studio and I didn't see any acoustic piano. I saw this little box sitting there, this little toy, so I said, "Miles, where's the piano?" He said... "I want you to play this." ... So I tested it and I heard this sound—this big mellow sound coming out.... I liked it right away.[6]

The instrument was a Fender Rhodes electric piano. Davis had been intrigued by the electric piano ever since hearing Josef Zawinul play a Wurlitzer electric piano in the Cannonball Adderley band. Davis's first recording with the Fender Rhodes was the 1968 release *Miles in the Sky*, and his continued use of the instrument signaled the onset of an inexorable trend. Thereafter Davis continued to bring about a gradual shift in jazz to rhythms influenced by rock, pop, and soul music. For Davis fans finally acclimated to the innovations of the 1963–1968 quintet, this newer rock-influenced music was difficult to swallow, but for Davis it was only the beginning.

LISTENING GUIDE   Track 48
"E.S.P."

Miles Davis Quintet: "E.S.P." (Shorter), from *E.S.P.* Columbia CS 9150. Los Angeles, January 20, 1965. Miles Davis, trumpet; Wayne Shorter, tenor saxophone; Herbie Hancock, piano; Ron Carter, bass; Tony Williams, drums.

The Main Point   "E.S.P." has a straightforward, 32-bar, ABAC form, although it is difficult to follow during the solos by Shorter, Davis, and Hancock because the chord changes are opaque and the quintet avoids articulating the form clearly. As such, it is a concentrated example of the sound of Davis's 1960s quintet, with its open, freewheeling character. Yet, in contrast to the free jazz discussed in Chapter 9, the piece does indeed follow a given set of changes, which are constantly elaborated.

Head—32 bars, 1 chorus, in ABAC

0:00   Davis and Shorter state the up-tempo head in unison. The basic identity of the tune is the perfect fourth, as shown by the pitch sequence of the head's opening phrase: C–G–D–G–C–G–D–C–G. (Use of the perfect fourth is also common in modal compositions.) The B and C sections of the head are quite similar melodically, with an alteration at the end of the C section for the cadence. The tune also ends with two fourths: a downward E♭–B♭ followed by an upward A–D.

Shorter tenor solo—2 choruses

0:29   Shorter's fine tenor solo begins obliquely, putting space in unusual places. Tony Williams keeps time on the ride cymbal while playing inventive fills that complement Shorter's ideas.

1:03   The second chorus, measures 9–11, alludes to the head, with an arpeggiation that spans the range of the tenor from high to low.

Davis trumpet solo—6 choruses + 4 bars

1:23   This is an extremely dexterous solo by Davis, who sometimes has been accused of lacking technical facility. With great agility, he builds to several climaxes. Williams and Hancock accompany him brilliantly, rarely articulating the formal boundaries of the tune but always remaining in step with Davis's emotional story. Davis builds to several satisfying climaxes as the group stretches the form to the breaking point.

Hancock piano solo—2 choruses (beginning in the 4th bar)

4:04   Hancock's solo is typically excellent. In the left hand, he often uses three-note chords that are voiced in fourths, or a three-note chord built with a tritone between the lower two notes and perfect fourth between the upper two.

4:40–4:45   Listen for the interplay between Hancock and bassist Ron Carter; Hancock plays a bass note in answer to Carter's emphasized low note.

Reprise of the ABAC head—1 chorus

4:54   The tune is stated as in the opening, with a prolonged final chord.

Listen to this music in an animated Active Listening Guide available at the text website.

Joe Zawinul was an early promoter of the electric piano in jazz.

Silver, as suggested by Evans's early recordings, which were considerably more centered in the bebop mainstream than his later recordings were. The refined harmonic language of George Shearing also contributed to Evans's stylistic heritage.

Born in 1929, Evans was from Plainfield, New Jersey. As a teenager he listened to swing and bop, and he occasionally played piano in local bands. Following high school, Evans attended Southeastern Louisiana University with a scholarship for classical piano—an interesting choice of school for a future jazz musician from the Northeast. After Southeastern Louisiana, Evans was drafted, served in the army, then moved to New York in 1956. He attended the Mannes College of Music for a semester and recorded his own albums *New Jazz Conceptions* (1956) and *Everybody Digs Bill Evans* (1958).

Evans also played on several recordings with jazz composer George Russell in the 1950s. Working with Russell allowed Evans to show off the various facets of his approach to improvisation. For example, on Russell's tribute to Evans, *Concerto for Billy the Kid*, Evans played long, chromatic lines over the chord progression to "I'll Remember April." Occasionally, Evans verged on atonality, as on Russell's "New York, New York."

Evans joined Miles Davis's sextet in 1958, performing on Davis's *Jazz at the Plaza* and the profoundly influential

With this move to rock and funk came a shift to electric instruments. These became increasingly more common on Davis's records, although he continued to use acoustic bass on both *Miles in the Sky* and the following *Filles de Kilimanjaro*. The latter album also included pianist Chick Corea on electric keyboard. We return to Davis's significant landmarks on the road to jazz-rock fusion (beginning with his recordings *In a Silent Way* and *Bitches Brew*) in Chapter 11.

Pianist Bill Evans was a lyrical, poetic player whose improvisations elasticized the underlying meter.

Pianists

As we have seen, several keyboard artists made their mark in the jazz world of the 1960s. Here we look at Bill Evans and three significant pianists whom he influenced: Herbie Hancock, Chick Corea, and Keith Jarrett.

Bill Evans

When Miles Davis's *Kind of Blue* was released in 1959, his listeners were introduced to a young, recently established pianist whose identity at the keyboard was in its own way as individual as Thelonious Monk's. Bill Evans's pianism—his dense, impressionistic voicings; his dreamy, introspective moodiness; his singing lyricism—appeared fresh and original. Despite its apparent uniqueness, Evans's style was rooted in the work of Lennie Tristano, Bud Powell, and Horace

Kind of Blue. As with so many other sidemen, Evans found that his stint with Davis incisively enhanced his visibility and his reputation; he was to remain at the forefront of jazz piano for the remainder of his career.

Evans drastically redefined postbop piano. He was praised for the poetic beauty of his playing, which was enhanced by his sensitivity to dynamic shadings. His ballad performances exhibited a rich harmonic vocabulary, often whispered at remarkably soft dynamic levels. On solo piano recordings such as "I Loves You Porgy" and "People," Evans brought to the fore sophisticated **voice-leading** techniques, creating a contrapuntal texture by moving the inner voices of chords. On ballads as well, Evans frequently reharmonized the chord progressions with compelling originality. Even Evans's posture at the piano—hunched over the keyboard, listening intently to each and every note—seemed to symbolize his elusive quest for musical transcendence.

Evans generally avoided working with larger groups, preferring the trio format of piano, bass, and drums. Sophisticated listeners heard an unprecedented level of interaction among the members of the group, particularly because of Evans's uncanny ability to develop long, even phrases that stretched across bar lines and created an **elastic meter** effect by avoiding strongly emphasized downbeats. To superficial listeners Evans's style was merely pretty, but beneath the elegant veneer were a sensibility and a formal control that number among the very best in jazz.

Evans preferred sidemen who could interact with him rather than merely provide accompaniment. His bassists were usually virtuoso soloists in their own right, who often played in the upper registers of the instrument. They frequently emerged from a subsidiary role to musically comment on and converse with Evans's solo lines. Evans's drummers often did the same thing, preferring to complement and punctuate the phrasing of the piano and the bass rather than merely keep time.

Evans's landmark trio was formed in 1959. It consisted of an unusually sensitive and coloristic drummer, Paul Motian, and a superb twenty-three-year-old bassist, Scott LaFaro, who, despite his youth, had already performed with Chet Baker, Sonny Rollins, Barney Kessel, and Benny Goodman. This trio set the standard for Evans's future groups. Its performance of "Autumn Leaves" (Listening Guide, Track 49), from the Riverside album *Portrait in Jazz*, showed off the group's most characteristic features. During the introduction the trio projected a meter at odds with the 4/4 rhythm to follow. Evans's solo lines moved between eighth notes and triplets, with phrasing that was often irregular. These phrases were sometimes separated by dramatic pauses that were themselves punctuated by Motian's drumming and LaFaro's countermelodies. With all the members contributing to the musical conversation, the trio frequently broke up the sense of regular metric flow.

Evans particularly sought to explore sophisticated aspects of **metric displacement** in his playing. He expressed this concern in an interview with pianist Marian McPartland for her radio show *Piano Jazz*:

> As far as the jazz playing goes, I think the rhythmic construction of the thing has evolved quite a bit. Now, I don't know how obvious that would be to the listener, but the displacement of phrases and…the way phrases follow one another and their placement against the meter … is something that I've worked on rather hard and it's something I believe in.[7]

Like many other jazz musicians, Evans wrote numerous compositions, many of which have become jazz standards. He was particularly fond of waltz time (3/4), which was not often heard in traditional jazz performances, and he composed many jazz waltzes, including the popular "Waltz for Debby." When not performing originals, Evans tended to draw his repertory from the golden age of American popular song, roughly 1920 to 1950.

Evans suffered a severe musical and personal blow when Scott LaFaro died in a car accident in July 1961. Although only twenty-five at the time, LaFaro had revolutionized the role of the bass within the context of the jazz trio. (He had also taken part in the groundbreaking *Free Jazz* sessions with Ornette Coleman.) LaFaro's immediate replacement was Chuck Israels. Later bassists included Eddie Gomez, an imposing virtuoso who appeared on Evans's 1968 *Live in Montreux* album, which won a Grammy award.

Evans also made recordings without his trio. His unique 1963 recording *Conversations with Myself* included solo piano tracks on which Evans overdubbed himself, often in three layers consisting of a bass line, midrange accompanying chords, and upper solo and melodic lines. On his version of "'Round Midnight" from that album, Evans used colorful arpeggios, making clear his debt to classical music, particularly the French composers Claude

Voice leading is a means of making logical melodic and harmonic sequences within an improvised solo. **Step connection**, a key element in voice leading, is the principal means of stringing together the melodic and harmonic elements. The steps are often based on the scale determined by the key of the piece.

An **elastic meter** is a rhythmic effect created when the soloist or rhythm section masks the strong metric downbeats so that the meter seems to be stretched beyond its normal parameters. This illusion is often created by playing unusually long phrases that move the melodic emphasis off the expected downbeats that occur at the beginning of each measure.

Metric displacement is a technique whereby the soloist implies or states a rhythm in the melody line that seems to go against the underlying basic rhythm of the piece. It also can be achieved by placing melodic phrases irregularly against the underlying rhythm.

LISTENING GUIDE

Track 49

"Autumn Leaves" (excerpt)

Bill Evans Trio: "Autumn Leaves" (Prevert-Mercer-Kosma), from *Portrait in Jazz*. Riverside RLP-1162. New York, December 28, 1959. Evans, piano; Scott LaFaro, bass; Paul Motian, drums.

The Main Point   "Autumn Leaves" provides an excellent example of Bill Evans's groundbreaking trio. Whereas conventional piano trios of the 1950s and 1960s often relegated the bass and the drums to accompanimental roles, Evans's trio featured a high degree of interaction among all three members. This resulted in a conversational approach among pianist, bassist, and drummer—particularly during LaFaro's bass solo, during which the meter is implied but not overtly stated.

"Autumn Leaves" is a 32-bar composition. The form is AAB, with the A sections comprising two 8-measure sections, and the B section consisting of sixteen measures.

Introduction and head—AAB

0:00   The performance begins with an eight-measure introduction. During the first four measures, Evans plays a five-note motive that moves down by step each measure, while the bass and drums, along with chords played in Evans's left hand, punctuate the offbeats. During the second four measures, Evans reuses the five-note motive, but now the five notes are stated evenly across each bar. This almost suggests a meter of 5/4 during these four measures. The bass and the drums punctuate the second and fourth note of each five-note grouping.

0:08   Evans states the melody of the first two A sections. Throughout this section Evans plays a single-line melody with chordal accompaniment. Note that LaFaro avoids playing on the downbeats of most of the measures of both A sections, thus avoiding the standard timekeeping role. Drummer Motian plays brushes.

0:28   In the B section, the bass begins to walk, playing each beat. Evans initially begins this section with a single-line melody with left-hand accompaniment, before moving to two-handed dense chords, then suggesting a locked-hands effect. He returns to a single-line melody with accompaniment in the last four bars, setting up a break for the bass solo.

LaFaro bass solo—2 choruses

0:45   LaFaro begins his solo unaccompanied for the first eight-measure A section. In the second half of the section, he repeats a riff four times.

0:56   For the second A section, Evans begins by playing along with the bass solo. Note that Evans plays a melody line in the right hand, which is doubled an octave below in the left hand. The two players create an improvisational conversation by trading short melodic ideas that are punctuated by rests. While the two players maintain the underlying meter, the melodic ideas and their rhythmic placement create a sense of implied (or even ambiguous) meter because neither maintains a customary timekeeping role. Throughout, Evans projects a sense of elasticized meter, often by delaying the sense of motion to a new chord.

1:06   Motian joins Evans and LaFaro in this B section. Rather than keeping time, he participates in the conversational interaction, sometimes echoing the rhythm of Evans's melodic lines. Again the 4/4 meter is maintained by the players, but the time is not overtly stated (Motian and LaFaro avoid the usual techniques of walking bass or steady ride cymbal pulse).

1:25   LaFaro continues to solo during the A sections of this second chorus. Evans begins on the third beat of the chorus, again playing in octaves.

1:44   B section. Toward the end of the B section (1:54), Evans switches to playing chordal accompaniment. This sets up his piano solo.

Evans piano solo—1st 2 choruses

2:02   During Evans's piano solo, LaFaro walks the bass, clearly establishing the 4/4 meter. Evans begins to develop longer ideas, several of which reach or exceed four bars. His sense of metric elasticity comes to the fore between the two A sections (at 2:12). There the last note of the phrase is stated an eighth note before the downbeat of the second A section, then held over into the next section. This syncopation effectively camouflages the sectional division.

2:21   During the B section of Evans's first chorus, most of his ideas are based on D♭ (a blue note in the key of G minor) and C.

2:39   During the A sections of this second chorus, notice that Evans's long lines often end on the fourth beat of the measure—a typical signature of Evans's style.

2:58   For the B section of the second chorus, Evans continues to repeat and develop individual ideas.

"Autumn Leaves" characterizes Bill Evans's landmark trio through the following: (1) conversational style of improvisation, in which during the bass solo the piano also improvises melodic lines, thus implying rather than overtly stating the meter; (2) LaFaro's fleet virtuosic improvisation; and (3) Evans's use of long melodic lines, some of which elasticize the underlying meter.

Listen to this music in an animated Active Listening Guide available at the text website.

Debussy and Maurice Ravel. Evans's interest in European concert music was even more evident on the record *Bill Evans Trio with Symphony Orchestra* (1965), on which he performed jazz arrangements of classical works by Gabriel Fauré, Alexander Scriabin, Sergei Rachmaninoff, and others. Evans also recorded with larger jazz groups. The album *Crosscurrents* (1977), for example, included Lee Konitz on alto saxophone and Warne Marsh on tenor.

Evans's solo piano albums—such as *Alone* (1968) and *Alone (Again)* (1975)—usually emphasized American popular standards. Evans preferred slow, dreamy ballads, though occasional faster tempos provided variety. In these solo piano improvisations, he developed a distinctive piano texture of right-hand melodic lines above a thin—often three-note—texture in his left hand. The left-hand voicings often consisted of a bass pitch along with the third and seventh of the harmony. This kind of voicing in his solo style contrasted with his chordal approach when performing with bass players: in the latter circumstances Evans usually allowed the bassist to take the chordal roots, while adding ambiguous three-note voicings in the midrange.

Evans recorded two duo albums with a remarkably compatible guitarist, Jim Hall (1930–2012), entitled *Undercurrent* (1959) and *Intermodulation* (1966). Hall, who achieved recognition through working with both Evans and Sonny Rollins, became one

Bill Evans, *Alone,* "Midnight Mood" (1968)

of the premier guitar stylists of the 1960s. Earlier he had worked with Jimmy Giuffre in Los Angeles. The wonderful sensitivity of his playing closely echoed Evans's style, making Hall the pianist's alter ego on guitar. Hall maintained a distinguished and active career. In his later years he also experimented with writing for orchestra.

Evans's work in his later trios, with bassist Eddie Gomez and drummer Marty Morrell, or in his final trio, with bassist Marc Johnson and drummer Joe LaBarbera, maintained the same high standard, although the pianist sought to refine his approach and take more chances. Evans also wrote new material while exploring previously untapped veins in the jazz repertory. For example, he recorded Herbie Hancock's "Dolphin Dance" as well as "Morning Glory," by country singer Bobbie Gentry, the latter being a particularly imaginative choice for a jazz reading. Evans remained committed to some compositions for decades: he first recorded "Some Other Time" in a 1958 session; the same composition appeared on his 1975 duet album with singer Tony Bennett.

Bill Evans and Jim Hall, *Intermodulation,* "I've Got You Under My Skin" (1966)

Evans died in 1980 at age fifty-one, succumbing to years of drug and alcohol abuse. Regardless of his early death, Evans was arguably the most influential postbop pianist of the 1960s.

Rhythmically and harmonically, Evans profoundly affected the major pianists of the 1960s. The sixties witnessed the coming of age of three of the most important jazz pianists of the latter half of the twentieth century: Herbie Hancock, Chick Corea, and Keith Jarrett. These three pianists, who also worked as sidemen for Miles Davis, appropriated some of Evans's characteristic harmonic voicings, such as a three-note chord voiced as a major third atop a minor second. Evans's "So What" voicing used on *Kind of Blue* was also imitated. (This voicing consists of open fourths with the two top notes separated by a major third.) These harmonies had an ambiguous, open sound, appropriate for modal playing.

Additionally, from Evans they learned his sophisticated techniques of metric elasticity. During the 1960s many of the compositions played by Hancock, Corea, and Jarrett relied on 32-bar forms with underlying four-bar phrases, but a key component of their improvisations relied on their ability to mask the underlying four-bar divisions. Their improvised lines frequently disguised these usual arrival points of the form.

Although traces of Bill Evans's approach to the keyboard can be heard in the works of Hancock, Corea, and Jarrett, each is also a remarkably innovative player in his own right, with a distinct style as well as varying musical interests.

Herbie Hancock

From 1963 to 1968, Herbie Hancock formed part of Miles Davis's legendary quintet. With performances that were consistently creative, fresh, and versatile, Hancock remained one of the most sought-after pianists for studio recordings throughout the 1960s.

Born in 1940 in Chicago, Hancock was a child prodigy. At age eleven he performed the first movement of a Mozart piano concerto with the Chicago Symphony Orchestra in a young people's concert. An early jazz influence was pianist Oscar Peterson.

After graduating from Grinnell College, Hancock found himself in demand as a pianist in Chicago. Joining the quintet of trumpeter Donald Byrd, Hancock moved to New York in the early sixties. On his Blue Note recordings with Byrd, he assimilated a vast array of styles, from the blues-based approach of funky jazz to the harmonic sophistication and refined lyricism of Bill Evans. He even experimented with classically based compositional principles, which he learned while studying music composition at Grinnell.

Hancock recorded his first album as a leader for Blue Note in 1962: *Takin' Off*. He wrote all the compositions for the session, which included veteran tenor saxophonist Dexter Gordon and trumpeter Freddie Hubbard, whose own experiences ranged from Art Blakey and the Jazz Messengers to Ornette Coleman's *Free Jazz*. With its characteristic two horns and rhythm section, *Takin' Off* was a typical hard bop LP, but Hancock's catchy, bluesy

A signed Herbie Hancock publicity photograph. Hancock's own Blue Note recordings and his work with the Miles Davis Quintet left many listeners unprepared for his phenomenal success in jazz-rock fusion in the 1970s.

composition "Watermelon Man" became a popular hit, making it to the Top 100 of the popular-music charts. The composition became even more popular when recorded by Mongo Santamaria in the mid-sixties; it was recorded yet again by the big bands of Woody Herman and Maynard Ferguson. Between 1962 and 1963, Hancock also appeared with saxophonist Eric Dolphy, who induced Hancock to play more freely.

As a member of the Miles Davis Quintet, Hancock joined drummer Tony Williams and bassist Ron Carter to create the most influential and innovative rhythm section of the 1960s. When Hancock improvised, the uncanny sense of communication among the three players enhanced the inventiveness of his solos.

Although part of the Davis quintet, Hancock continued to record as a leader for Blue Note. By embracing more open-ended improvisations, fewer chord changes, and subtle metric displacements, Hancock moved away from the standard hard bop feel of his first recordings. On *Empyrean Isles*, for example,

Herbie Hancock,
Maiden Voyage,
"The Eye of the
Hurricane" (1965)

"One Finger Snap" was an unusually structured, twenty-measure composition (rather than the typical 32-bar format). Its opening four bars used all twelve pitches of the **chromatic scale**. The most radical composition, "The Egg," incorporated passages of free improvisation.

Hancock's "Dolphin Dance" from *Maiden Voyage* became well known. Its melody grew out of the opening four-note motive, while the complex harmonic progression featured shifting chords over pedal points in the bass. Ballads such as "Dolphin Dance" most fully revealed the connection to Bill Evans in Hancock's style. Yet Hancock's projection of Evans's harmonic palette was enhanced by his more ambitious textural and tonal sense. Evans responded to his trio but tended to think like a soloist, whereas Hancock seemed to listen to and anticipate his accompaniment more perceptively than Evans did. Evans worked with a sense of absolute stylistic command, whereas Hancock always seemed to be reaching, trying to stretch his harmonic concept to the very limit.

This continuous searching perhaps led to Hancock's eventual disillusionment with the modern modal style, which he thought had become too abstract and not responsive enough to the audience. In the early 1970s, he found a release in the repetition, heavy beat, and electronic orientation of jazz-rock funk.

Before his plunge into fusion, however, and before departing from Davis's touring band, Hancock recorded several notable acoustic albums during the 1960s. On both *Speak Like a Child* and *The Prisoner*, the size of the group was augmented to include bass trombone, alto flute, and trumpet. The coloristic writing for the horns evoked the work of arranger Gil Evans. With *Fat Albert Rotunda*, originally written for the animated Bill Cosby television show *The Fat Albert Animated Special*, a pronounced shift took

Chick Corea

Like Hancock, Chick Corea is a significant composer as well as a pianist. Less subtle than Hancock as a player, Corea developed a steely, percussive touch, particularly on his early recordings, where the influence of John Coltrane's pianist, McCoy Tyner, strongly appeared.

Corea was born in 1941 in Chelsea, Massachusetts. Raised in a musical atmosphere—his father was a gigging musician—Corea as a teenager transcribed solos by bop pianists Bud Powell and Horace Silver. He received early professional experience in the Afro-Cuban bands of Willie Bobo and Mongo Santamaria; not surprisingly, much of his later work reflected Latin and Afro-Cuban music. Corea's first recording as a leader came in 1966, when he made *Tones for Joan's Bones*, named after a composition that Corea had recorded earlier with trumpeter Richard "Blue" Mitchell.

Corea could be sensitive and lush, as his playing on Stan Getz's *Sweet Rain* made clear, but his hard-driving, staccato style was especially influential. Like McCoy Tyner, Corea favored pentatonic scales and harmonies based on open fourths. These stylistic attributes came to infuse both his improvisations and his compositions.

On his second recording, *Now He Sings, Now He Sobs*, Corea appeared with a trio that included Czech bassist Miroslav Vitous and drummer Roy Haynes. The trio was energetic, overtly dramatic, and highly interactive, a distinctly different sensibility from the quiet

Chick Corea,
Now He Sings,
Now He Sobs,
"Matrix" (1968)

> "I saw this little box sitting there, this little toy, so I said,
> 'Miles, where's the piano?'"
> —Herbie Hancock, on first encountering a Fender
> Rhodes electric piano

place: Hancock performed on a Fender Rhodes electric piano. Most significantly, several of the compositions, such as "Wiggle Waggle," were simple, funky, riff-based tunes.

Hancock turned exclusively to electric keyboards with his sextet of 1971–1973, playing synthesizer and even featuring a second synthesist, Patrick Gleason, along with bassist Buster Williams, drummer Billy Hart, reed player Bennie Maupin, and trombonist Julian Priester. With its electronic sounds, the group seemed to evoke the "space music" of Sun Ra in extended improvisations such as "Ostinato," a riff in 15/8 meter from the album *Mwandishi*. Hancock's phenomenal commercial success coincided with his 1973 fusion album *Headhunters* (see Chapter 11).

introspection of the Bill Evans Trio. Corea composed all the tunes for the album. Both "Matrix" and "Steps" were 12-bar blues. Like Evans and Hancock, Corea developed strategies for elasticizing the meter and masking the usual four-bar divisions of his compositions.[8]

In 1968 Corea replaced Herbie Hancock in Miles Davis's group, where he was quickly swept into the

---

A **chromatic scale** has all twelve notes of the Western musical system; for example, all the adjacent notes on the piano. There are twelve notes in an octave, which create a chromatic scale.

jazz-rock experiments of the late 1960s. Despite his initial reluctance to play anything other than acoustic piano, Corea often performed on the Fender Rhodes electric piano. "At first, Miles kind of pushed the Fender piano in front of me against my will," Corea admitted, "and I resisted. But then I started liking it, especially being able to turn up the volume and combat the drummer."[9]

Corea left Davis two years later, along with bassist Dave Holland, and returned for a while to acoustic piano. The album *Song of Singing* featured an acoustic trio that strongly reflected the jazz avant-garde. With bassist Holland and drummer Barry Altschul, the trio experimented with free improvisations that frequently avoided predetermined chordal structures. The music reflected the influence of both pianist Paul Bley's work and that of Ornette Coleman.

A driving pianist and inventive composer, Chick Corea gradually moved toward electric keyboards during his work with Miles Davis in the late 1960s. His group Return to Forever was one of the celebrated fusion groups of the 1970s.

Photo Courtesy of the Morgan Collection

In 1971 Corea augmented his group with the alto/soprano saxophonist Anthony Braxton. As mentioned in Chapter 9, the quartet, called Circle, recorded a concert in Paris (issued by ECM Records) that was largely given over to free improvisation. Nonetheless, their ties to the tradition appeared in their performance of "There Is No Greater Love," which shifted in and out of free playing, at times moving into a traditional 4/4 swing feel with walking bass. A détente between traditional and free playing also surfaced in Corea's two solo piano albums recorded in the early 1970s, *Piano Improvisations*, Volumes 1 and 2. The first side of each recording reflects a marked lyrical simplicity, while the second side incorporates free atonal playing.

Corea returned to electric keyboards in the early 1970s and soon became one of the key figures in the jazz-fusion movement. We resume his story in Chapter 11.

Keith Jarrett and ECM Records

Like Herbie Hancock and Chick Corea, Keith Jarrett is a significant and innovative pianist whose career began in the 1960s. Although Jarrett made some recordings on electric piano—particularly during his tenure with Miles Davis between 1969 and 1971—he has dedicated himself almost exclusively to the acoustic instrument as the vehicle for his widely heralded, virtuosic performances. Jarrett's playing is eclectic, bringing to the piano not only elements of traditional jazz but also free jazz and traces of classical, folk, and gospel music. Like Hancock and Corea, Jarrett was inspired by the lyricism of Bill Evans. He also owed a strong debt to the freer, open-ended playing of pianist Paul Bley, as well as to John Coates, a pianist Jarrett heard while growing up in Pennsylvania, whose jazz style similarly blended gospel and folk elements. Moreover, Jarrett cultivated a legato, classically based touch on the piano, a technique that has served him well in widely publicized performances and recordings of works in the European concert tradition.

Born in Allentown, Pennsylvania in 1945, Jarrett began playing at age three; by seven he was already composing and improvising. He moved to Boston after receiving a scholarship from the Berklee College of Music in 1962. Although he attended Berklee for only a year, he remained in Boston, playing gigs with Roland Kirk and Tony Scott. After moving to New York in 1965, Jarrett and his wife were nearly penniless until Art Blakey heard him at a jam session. Jarrett joined Blakey's band and in 1966 recorded the album *Buttercorn Lady* with the group, which included trumpeter Chuck Mangione. In this traditional hard bop ensemble, Jarrett exhibited his virtuosic technique and even experimented with avant-garde concepts, such as playing inside the piano—strumming the strings—during Mangione's ballad "Recuerdo."

As a member of the Charles Lloyd Quartet between 1966 and 1969, Jarrett received full rein to explore his experimental tendencies and eclectic musical interests.

Lloyd (b. 1938) was a West Coast tenor saxophonist and flutist who had performed with Chico Hamilton and Cannonball Adderley in the early 1960s. Lloyd's quartet, which included Jarrett, drummer Jack DeJohnette, and bassist Cecil McBee (later replaced by Ron McClure), was astonishingly successful. At the height of the 1960s "flower power" era, Lloyd's followers consisted of not only jazz fans but also teenagers who thronged to hear the group at rock-music venues such as the Fillmore auditorium in San Francisco. Lloyd was something of a guru to the flower

"I play love vibrations."
—Charles Lloyd

children. "I play love vibrations," he insisted in the liner notes to the aptly titled record *Love-In*. "Love, totality—like bringing everyone together in a joyous dance."[10]

John Coltrane's quartet strongly influenced Lloyd and his band. For instance, on the band's first recording, *Dream Weaver*, "Autumn Sequence" (which served as an introduction to "Autumn Leaves") incorporated an extended modal vamp. But Lloyd's group was also wildly eclectic, merging elements of traditional jazz, free jazz, gospel, and R&B. Lloyd's Latin-tinged "Forest Flower" became his best-known composition.

Jarrett's performances with Lloyd's quartet dazzled audiences and critics. Even on jazz standards such as "East of the Sun," from *Forest Flower*, Jarrett's solo moved the band from traditional 4/4 swing into completely free improvisation—with sections using piano clusters reminiscent of avant-garde pianist Cecil Taylor—before returning to a subdued ending. Elsewhere, Jarrett's gospel- and rock-oriented approach set the tone in simple blues compositions, such as "Island Blues" from *The Flowering*. Jarrett's solo on "Autumn Leaves" (from Lloyd's *Dream Weaver*) owed no small debt to Bill Evans's 1959 version (Track 49), but Jarrett's techniques for elasticizing the meter during his solo seem also to draw from the jazz avant-garde. In his third chorus of the solo, he plays an idea that superimposes a 6/4 meter above the underlying 4/4 meter while at the same time using pitches outside the harmonic structure.

After leaving Lloyd, Jarrett played electric piano and organ during his eighteen months with Miles Davis. Jarrett rarely performed on electric instruments after that. One exception was his inspired electric piano work on Freddie Hubbard's recording *Sky Dive*.

Ignoring the jazz-rock electric fusion trends of the 1970s, Jarrett recorded more than a dozen albums between 1971 and 1976 with a quartet consisting of tenor saxophonist Dewey Redman, bassist Charlie Haden, and drummer Paul Motian. The choice of sidemen itself revealed much about Jarrett's interest in the free jazz of Ornette Coleman

---

LISTENING GUIDE   Track 50
"The Windup" (excerpt)

Keith Jarrett: "The Windup" (Jarrett), from *Belonging*. Oslo, Norway, April 24–25, 1974. ECM 829 115-2. Keith Jarrett, piano; Jan Garbarek, soprano saxophone; Palle Danielsson, bass; Jon Christensen, drums.

The Main Point   "The Windup" exhibits Keith Jarrett's eclecticism. Recorded in Norway, it combines Jarrett with three European musicians with whom Jarrett recorded extensively. It begins with a gospel piano feel. The head statements sound catchy and easy, but use complex mixed meter. The piano solo begins with single line melodic ideas, without rhythm section accompaniment. When the drums and bass enter, the players engage in interactive free jazz textures reminiscent of the Ornette Coleman Quartet (compare to "Street Woman" by the Ornette Coleman Quartet, Track 41). Further, the conversational approach between bass and piano resembles that heard in the Bill Evans Trio (compare to "Autumn Leaves," Bill Evans Trio, Track 49).

Introduction and Head

0:00   Jarrett begins the introduction by himself. He sets up the tempo and the tonal center by playing a left-hand vamp that elaborates three notes (C, A, and G) against gospel-tinged chord progressions in the right hand. The bass and drums enter; the bass doubles Jarrett's left-hand vamp, and the drums play a rock-based, straight eighth-note feel.

0:39   The head begins with the soprano saxophone playing the exuberant freewheeling melody. The melody consists of four brief melodic ideas (Phrases 1–4). The first two each begin with a short exclamatory pitch, followed by a longer line of 6–7 notes. Phrases 3 and 4 (0:42) rely on a new melodic idea, with the fourth appearing a step below the third and ending with two declarative pitches. The meter during the third and fourth phrases is complex—you can count it as three measures of 5 + 6 + 6 beats.

0:47 Phrases 1–4 repeat. A linking section, with melody played by both saxophone and piano (0:54), brings back a return to the opening melody (1:00), but this time omitting the first phrase and consisting only of Phrases 2–4. The first head statement concludes with a tag (1:05), played in mixed meter (5 + 6 + 5 and 5 + 6 + 4).

1:13 The group returns to the opening vamp, begun again with solo piano before the drums and bass enter. They play the entire head again (1:20).

1:47 The tag, heard earlier at 1:05, returns to set up the piano solo.

Piano Solo

1:54 The bass and drums cease playing, and the piano solo begins unaccompanied. Listen for how Jarrett maintains the pulse even while only playing right-hand melodic lines without left-hand chords. Jarrett's piano technique is legato: that is, he plays the melodic lines in a connected and even fashion, rather than clipped and detached. He mixes longer and shorter melodic ideas, set off by space. The melodic lines move inside and outside of the prevailing tonality. His vocalizing is audible on the recording.

2:29 The drums and bass enter, setting up a texture that departs from the gospel feel of the head. Because Jarrett does not play left-hand chords, the melodic piano lines operate almost like horn lines, and the resultant open sound is indebted to that of the Ornette Coleman Quartet. There is a loose sense of pulse, and bassist Danielsson plays freely and interactively. Jarrett's melodic ideas develop brief ideas and tonal centers.

2:47 Jarrett plays a rhythmic idea that encourages more interaction from the drums; at 2:55 he develops a stop-and-start idea. The drums and bass provide the pulse more definitively at 2:57.

3:03 Jarrett moves to a bluesy melodic idea.

3:17 The bassist alternates a walking texture with more interactive playing.

3:31 Jarrett begins playing lightning-fast runs.

3:36 Here Jarrett begins developing a single idea almost obsessively, before moving to a series of faster pitches.

3:44 A repeated pitch in the piano gives way to a jagged descending melody. Jarrett's enthusiastic vocal interjection is audible between his phrases (3:52).

3:53 Jarrett's improvisation focuses on a group of repeated pitches. As the piano lines become faster, listen for how the drummer responds by playing more interactively and freely (3:56).

4:09 The piano lines move in a seesaw motion, alternating up and down melodic ideas as the bassist relies on playing a series of repeated pitches.

4:24 Jarrett now uses his left hand to play a downward set of descending pitches that appear between his right-hand phrases.

4:33 The improvisation now moves back to the opening key, and Jarrett refers to some melodic ideas from the head, helping bring back the return of a head statement.

Restatement of Head

4:40 Here Jarrett returns to the opening vamp, relying on the three-note left-hand bass figure heard at the opening of the performance. The saxophonist plays Phrases 2–4 in the same manner heard initially at 1:00.

4:47 The tag returns here. The Listening Guide" concludes with the break that follows this tag, just prior to the saxophone solo.

Listen to this music in an animated Active Listening Guide available at the text website.

as well as the lyricism of Bill Evans; both Redman and Haden had played with Coleman, and Motian had been Evans's drummer in the early 1960s. Much of the quartet's work seemed inspired by Ornette Coleman, although it was sometimes rooted in a more definite harmonic structure. These influences of Bill Evans and Ornette Coleman are also apparent in Jarrett's collaborations with European jazz musicians such as Jan Garbarek, a Norwegian saxophonist with whom Jarrett recorded extensively.

As "The Windup" shows, the eclecticism of Jarrett's work grew especially pronounced in the 1970s. Throughout the quartet recordings, Jarrett drew on the whole tradition of piano improvisation, including traditional jazz. For example, a ragtime-inspired solo piano composition entitled "Pardon My Rags" appeared on *El Juicio*. Jarrett's 1972 recording *Expectations* included free improvisations and gospel-tinged works along with pieces for string orchestra and piano. The sound of the quartet owed much to the rich tenor saxophone sound of Dewey Redman. Interestingly, Jarrett also played soprano saxophone on the recordings, as well as organ and percussion.

In contrast to most contemporary jazz pianists, Jarrett explored solo piano performance extensively. His first such album, *Facing You*, was a studio recording; with eight different original compositions, the album exhibited Jarrett's fine technique and legato touch. By 1973 Jarrett began performing live solo concerts, which generally comprised extended, freely improvised works. Many of these lasted an entire side (or longer) of an LP and often began rhapsodically, out of tempo, before launching into an extended ostinato over which Jarrett would improvise.

An important label that issued Keith Jarrett's recordings and became one of the most prominent exponents of nonfusion music during the 1970s and 1980s was ECM Records. Founded in Cologne, Germany, in 1969 by Manfred Eicher, ECM released albums by such other U.S. jazz artists as pianist Chick Corea, vibraphonist Gary Burton, and guitarist Pat Metheny. The label also sponsored European jazz players such as Norwegian saxophonist Jan Garbarek and bassist Eberhard Weber.

Some jazz critics and jazz musicians dismissed ECM's music as atmospheric "Euro-jazz"—sterile, moody, cerebral, introspective, and overly refined—a precursor to the New Age music that arose in the 1980s on labels such as Windham Hill. Nevertheless, ECM maintained consistently high standards of musicianship in recordings admired for their engineering and high technical quality. Many of the ECM artists were distinguished by a pronounced allegiance to European classical music and aesthetics. For example, "Mirrors," from Jarrett's recording *Arbour Zena*, incorporated a string ensemble, using the orchestra for accompaniment beneath the improvisations of Jarrett on piano and Garbarek on saxophone.

The ECM label also released recordings best characterized as free jazz. One of the most significant was bassist Dave Holland's 1972 recording *Conference of the Birds*, which featured saxophonists Sam Rivers and Anthony Braxton, who were largely associated with the jazz avant-garde. Far from having a single distinctive sound, ECM has represented a wide array of jazz performers and styles. Among its most successful records were Keith Jarrett's recordings of live solo piano recitals.

Solo Concerts and *The Köln Concert*, both recorded for ECM, included some of Jarrett's most acclaimed improvisations, which ranged from rock, gospel, and folk to atonal free playing. Jarrett's approach to the keyboard was nearly orgasmic; at times he would stand, grimace, and writhe, and he sometimes sang along with his melodies or moaned between phrases. Jarrett has been taken to task for both his emotional extravagance and his lack of editing. For example, his recording *Sun Bear Concerts* is a ten-record set assembled from five different concerts in Japan.

Some of Jarrett's work in the 1970s was tangential to the jazz mainstream. For example, his album *In the Light* included compositions for string orchestra, brass quintet, and string quartet; *The Celestial Hawk* was a three-movement work for piano and orchestra, recorded at Carnegie Hall in 1980, in which Jarrett performed with the Syracuse Symphony Orchestra. Jarrett has also recorded the music of European composers as diverse as J. S. Bach and Dmitri Shostakovich.

Since the 1980s Jarrett has largely returned to comparatively straight-ahead jazz. His trio with bassist Gary Peacock and drummer Jack DeJohnette has been devoted to recording the standard jazz repertory with chorus structures, chord changes, and regular meter. Within this traditional format, Jarrett's debt to Bill Evans is even more apparent than in his earlier work, both in his performances of harmonically lush ballads and through the techniques of metric displacement pioneered by Evans in the fifties and sixties. Though partially incapacitated with chronic fatigue syndrome in the late 1990s, Jarrett has since recovered and continues as a major force in jazz piano.

Funky/Soul Jazz

The **funky jazz** tunes recorded in the 1950s by such groups as Art Blakey and the Jazz Messengers and the Horace Silver Quintet were infectious blues-based works steeped in the gospel tradition. As noted in Chapter 8, the gospel singing of Mahalia Jackson and the blues-based and gospel music of Ray Charles provided two significant influences for funky jazz. Ray Charles (1930–2004) was a blind singer-pianist who injected heartfelt, soulful singing into rhythm and blues. Charles also recorded with jazz artists such as vibraphonist Milt Jackson, and he earned commercial success with hits that included "What'd I Say" and "Georgia on My Mind."

Funky jazz, or **soul jazz**, is a style that combines elements of gospel music and R&B with jazz. It began to emerge in the 1950s as an outgrowth of hard bop and became quite popular in the 1960s.

Singer-pianist Ray Charles. Charles's earthy, blues-based music influenced many of the funky/soul jazz players.

During the 1960s funky jazz continued to attract musicians who preferred more-direct communication with audiences than either cool jazz or free jazz could provide. The term **soul jazz** came about after 1960; it was initially used by Riverside Records to promote the Cannonball Adderley Quintet.

Cannonball Adderley

Julian "Cannonball" Adderley (1928–1975) was a superb alto saxophonist from Tampa, Florida. After moving to New York and appearing at various venues, his growing prominence led to an invitation in 1957 to join Miles Davis's group, where he remained until 1959. Adderley was a major factor in the success of Davis's *Milestones* and *Kind of Blue* albums, in which he helped balance the lyricism of Davis and the emotional intensity of Coltrane. After leaving Davis, Adderley formed his own group with his younger brother, cornetist Nat Adderley (1931–2000).

The Adderley group specialized in both hard bop and funky/soul jazz. The latter included such well-known tunes as Nat Adderley's "Work Song," which featured call-and-response between the rhythm section and the horns in imitation of a chain gang. Once the melody was stated, however, the rhythm section reverted to a 4/4 swing with walking bass. Adderley's popular 1966 hit "Mercy, Mercy, Mercy" (Listening Guide, Track 51), written by Austrian

pianist Josef Zawinul, incorporated a funky rock beat throughout. In his work with Adderley's group, Zawinul was one of the earliest jazz players to feature the electric piano (partly inspiring Miles Davis's later use of the instrument). Zawinul's other compositions recorded with Adderley, such as "Country Preacher," typified the gospel themes of funky/soul jazz.

The Blues In Funky/Soul Jazz

In stark contrast to the avant-garde wing of jazz, some of the funky/soul jazz of the 1960s was commercially quite successful. After his 1963 hit "Watermelon Man," which reached the Top 100 of the popular-music charts, Herbie Hancock later recalled that on his subsequent albums he tried to include at least one tune with the even eighth notes of funky/soul jazz.[11] Also in 1963 hard bop trumpeter Lee Morgan recorded a hit with "The Sidewinder," a catchy, instrumental blues with a funky/soul jazz feel.

The 12-bar blues was the mainstay of much funky/soul jazz, particularly the music played by the jazz organists who sprang up during the late 1950s. Although Fats Waller recorded wonderful jazz solos on the pipe organ in the late twenties, musicians generally thought that the organ was not well suited to jazz because the attack of the notes was extremely smooth and lacked the bite usually heard in jazz phrasing. Beginning in 1935 the Hammond company manufactured an electronic organ, which was portable and lighter than the traditional pipe organ (usually only found in churches because of its huge size and weight). The electronic organ was soon adopted by jazz musicians Glenn Hardman and Milt Buckner, although the instrument remained relatively uncommon in jazz settings until the mid-fifties. Meanwhile, by the fifties the electronic organ had become a mainstay in black churches and the backbone of modern gospel music. As a result of its practicality and popularity, the electronic organ soon found its way into black neighborhood clubs, where it was often heard in a trio setting with saxophone and drums. Instead of having a bass player, the organist could play bass lines with either the feet or the left hand.

Jimmy Smith and Jazz Organists

One of the most influential jazz organists to emerge in the late 1950s was Jimmy Smith (1925–2005), who was born in Norristown, Pennsylvania. Although he began his career as a pianist, Smith formed his first organ trio in 1955.

LISTENING GUIDE

Track 51

"Mercy, Mercy, Mercy"

Cannonball Adderley Quintet: "Mercy, Mercy, Mercy" (Zawinul), from *Mercy, Mercy, Mercy: Live at the Club*. Capitol [S]T2663. Hollywood, California, October 20, 1966. Nat Adderley, cornet; Cannonball Adderley, alto saxophone; Joe Zawinul, Wurlitzer electric piano; Victor Gaskin, bass; Roy McCurdy, drums.

The Main Point "Mercy, Mercy, Mercy," recorded live, became a popular hit for Adderley's group. Such compositions seemed to offer specific possibilities for blending jazz, rock, and R&B, and inspired a number of jazz-rock (or jazz-funk) fusion artists of the late 1960s and 1970s, a trend examined in Chapter 11. Yet much of the later jazz-rock fusion of the 1970s, in contrast to "Mercy, Mercy, Mercy," featured more involved textures, interlocking rhythms, studio production techniques, virtuosic funk drumming and electric bass playing, and flashy improvisation.

The melody of "Mercy, Mercy, Mercy" makes use of rhythm-and-blues based ideas, and the keyboard improvisation emphasizes the catchy underlying groove feel. "Mercy, Mercy, Mercy" decidedly avoids walking bass, a swinging orientation, and a series of bop-oriented solos. In addition to Adderley's hit version heard here, "Mercy, Mercy, Mercy," with added lyrics, became a 1967 pop radio hit for The Buckinghams.

On the recording, composer Zawinul plays the Wurlitzer electric piano; shortly after this recording he switched to the Fender Rhodes electric piano, a keyboard that became virtually mandatory for fusion keyboardists of the 1970s. (Zawinul himself would go on to become one of the founding members of the fusion band Weather Report.)

You will hear how the informal setting of the live performance elicits spirited participation from the audience. This formula of recording and releasing live soul jazz performances was one used throughout the 1960s: for example, pianist Ramsey Lewis's hit "The In Crowd," recorded in 1965 in Washington, DC, similarly exhibits an exuberant party atmosphere. Although the recording's original liner notes described Adderley's performance of "Mercy, Mercy, Mercy" as taking place in Chicago in an 800-seat venue called The Club, the reissue producer later revealed that the performance actually took place before an invited audience at the Capitol Records studio in Hollywood, with free drinks provided to the invited guests. Likely the open bar helped fuel the crowd enthusiasm.

Introduction

0:00 The performance begins with Adderley announcing the composition. The rhythm section plays the harmonic progression to the head beneath his commentary. Clearly, Adderley relished speaking to his audiences while providing them with some background of the music to be heard.

Head statement—20 bars as 8 + 8 + 4

1:04 The two horns, alto saxophone and cornet, provide the melody to the head. The first eight bars consist of a two-bar funky figure repeated four times. The electric piano also plays the melody and plays chords between each statement.

1:26 The following eight bars move to a new melodic idea. During the first four bars, the melody uses a common R&B figure that heightens the energy level. The alto saxophone has the melody. The cornet plays the same rhythm as the alto but remains on a single repeated pitch. The following four bars provide a climactic outburst, and the harmonic progression of this section makes use of the IV–I "Amen" (plagal) progression frequently heard in gospel jazz. (Compare this with the discussion of "Moanin'," by Art Blakey and the Jazz Messengers, Track 37.)

1:49 The final four bar section initially moves to a quieter dynamic level, before ending again more loudly. A slight break in the rhythm (1:58), set off by a cymbal accent and roll on the snare drum, sets up the beginning of the piano solo.

Piano solo—2 choruses

2:01   Zawinul's piano solo uses short funky ideas surrounded by ample space. Like much soul jazz, the intent is on musical expression that directly connects with an audience. Throughout the solo, the audience responds energetically, not unlike the congregation participation in evangelical religious services. In many ways, the audience participation is an integral part of the music, creating its own form of call-and-response.

2:23   During the second eight-bar section, Zawinul plays the melody from the head. Notice that throughout the solo he relies largely on chordal textures rather than on the fleet running eighth-note lines more characteristic of bebop pianists. The rhythm of the drums and Zawinul's left hand uses straight eighth notes typical of R&B.

2:45   As in the head, the dynamic level drops to a quiet level during the final four bar section of this chorus.

2:57   During Zawinul's second chorus, he similarly relies on chordal textures and funky figures set off by space. Notice how Gaskin's bass playing becomes more active, particularly during the third and fourth beats of each measure.

3:19   Again, Zawinul states the melody to the second eight-bar section, intensifying the energy level of the music and of the audience. Again, the dynamic level drops considerably during the final four-bar section (3:41).

Final head statement

3:53   The horns return to state the head.

4:15   The second eight-bar section again increases the musical intensity.

4:37   The group slows the tempo for the final four bar section, making clear its role in ending the performance. Adderley once again announces the name of the composition over the audience applause.

 Listen to this music in an animated Active Listening Guide available at the text website.

A **swell** is the rapid change in volume that can be created by pushing down or releasing the volume pedal on an electronic or conventional organ.

His New York debut was at the Cafe Bohemia the following year, but his international career lifted off in 1957 after a performance at the Newport Jazz Festival. Even the titles of Smith's albums, such as *The Sermon* and *Prayer Meetin'*, emphasized the gospel origins of his music.

Jimmy Smith,
Prayer Meetin',
"Prayer Meetin'"
(1960)

Smith's approach to the organ set the standard for the instrument. Although he used bebop tunes on his earliest albums, he gravitated toward the blues, combining blistering right-hand runs against bass lines played by his left hand and feet. He made abundant use of idiomatic organ sounds, working the volume pedal to create swells in the style of the gospel church organists or sustaining a single high note above rapid-fire, sixteenth-note lines.

Smith influenced virtually all subsequent jazz organists. Many, such as "Brother" Jack McDuff, Richard "Groove" Holmes, and Jimmy McGriff, maintained Smith's strutting approach to the blues. Don Patterson, who had recorded and performed with altoist Sonny Stitt, switched from piano to organ after hearing Smith play, but he remained more tied to the bebop tradition than Smith did.

Many jazz organists favored the muscular tenor players, some of whom began their careers playing in R&B bands. Tenor saxophonist Stanley Turrentine (1934–2000) played with Ray Charles before recording with Jimmy Smith and Turrentine's wife, organist Shirley Scott. Houston Person, another full-throated tenor player, recorded with organists Groove Holmes and Charles Earland.

Jimmy Smith, organist, in a smooth publicity pose.

Photo Courtesy of the Morgan Collection

Guitarists

Organists also showcased their guitarists, many of whom were strongly rooted in the blues. Kenny Burrell had a mellow guitar sound; although he played fluently, he often preferred simple, singable lines, as heard on Jimmy Smith's recording, *Midnight Special*.

Of the guitarists who emerged in the late 1950s and 1960s, Wes Montgomery (1923–1968) was perhaps the most influential. (His collaboration with organist Jimmy Smith appears on Track 52.) His extremely personal sound on the instrument was a result of using his thumb rather than a pick. In addition to playing single lines, his solos often built intensity by shifting to playing octaves and chords. Although he performed with organ trios, he worked principally with mainstream jazz groups. Montgomery became known in the fifties from several albums recorded for Riverside. His recordings with the Wynton Kelly Trio, especially the live recording *Smokin' at the Half Note*, are among many guitarists' most listened-to and studied recordings. He later played with John Coltrane. During the mid-sixties Montgomery became more commercially successful with hit pop-jazz records, such as *Goin' Out of My Head* (1965) and *A Day in the Life* (1967).

LISTENING GUIDE   Track 52
"James and Wes" (excerpt)

Jimmy Smith and Wes Montgomery: "James and Wes" (Smith), from *Jimmy & Wes: The Dynamic Duo*. Verve V6 8766. Englewood Cliffs, New Jersey, September 28, 1966. Jimmy Smith, organ; Wes Montgomery, guitar; Grady Tate, drums.

The Main Point   The recording of "James and Wes" pairs two of the most distinctive mainstream players of the 1960s. It shows how improvisation in a 12-bar blues form creates an infectious groove that at times can be thoughtful and serene, or strutting and virtuosic, all drenched in the tradition of the blues. In their solos, guitarist Wes Montgomery and organist Jimmy Smith make dramatic use of blue notes, short repeated riffs, and the earthy blues-based figures of funky/soul jazz. It captures the essence of the organ trio sound. Note that there is no bassist on the recording: instead Smith plays the walking bass on the organ. (Smith at times played bass lines on the organ with the instrument's foot pedals, and at other times with his left hand.) You can hear Montgomery's signature technique of soloing initially with single pitch lines before then improvising with octaves, creating more intensity as the guitar solo proceeds. Smith displays his command of the Hammond B-3 organ with fiery runs.

Head statements—2 choruses as 12-bar blues

0:00   The organ plays the head in two consecutive choruses. It is based on a simple two-bar groove riff. Listen for how the accompanying instruments enhance the groove: Montgomery plays chords on beat 1 and the "and" of 2, and drummer Grady Tate accents beat 4 of every measure by playing a rimshot on the snare drum.

Guitar solo—8 choruses

0:37   The guitar solo opens with Montgomery playing blues-based figures. Montgomery's distinctive mellow sound comes about, in part, from using the side of his thumb rather than a pick. Nevertheless, listen for the range of articulation in his opening chorus, from short detached notes at the outset, to more forceful playing (0:46), followed by more connected pitches. Within Montgomery's second chorus (0:55), he turns to developing a single rhythmic idea. At the end of both choruses, he phrases his melodic ideas to end in the second to last measure of the 12-bar form.

1:13   Smith plays a sustained chord on the organ at the outset of Montgomery's third chorus, and the guitarist responds by playing octaves, sliding up to the upper pitch of the organ chord. This launches a call-and-response idea in the guitar, alternating the octave slides with more standard runs. At the end of Montgomery's fourth chorus (1:43), he brings in chordal textures, before moving to octaves at the top of the fifth chorus (1:48). Montgomery shifts now to playing his improvised lines in octaves, creating more intensity. He begins with another call-and-response idea, alternating a slide to the blue note A♭ with a melodic figure. Notice how Montgomery uses space (rests between melodic ideas) to set his improvised melodies into relief.

2:05   For the remainder of Montgomery's solo, he plays his melodies in octaves. With each chorus he moves to a new melodic idea that he continues to develop throughout the chorus. His commitment to improvising repeated memorable motives indicates why Montgomery is considered a lyrical improviser. He plays a figure that makes use of repeated notes in his sixth chorus (2:05), a descending motive in the seventh chorus (2:22), and an ascending blues idea in the eighth (2:38). The motives in the seventh and eighth chorus create a subtle metrical conflict since they repeat every three beats, and you can hear how the drum accompaniment in the eighth chorus responds to the three-beat pattern with cymbal accents. The drum accompaniment and Jimmy Smith's organ comping become more assertive and energetic in Montgomery's final chorus (2:55), all heightening the dramatic intensity.

Organ solo—8 choruses

3:11   Smith begins his solo with a sustained chord in the organ for four bars, before moving to single lines. His second chorus (3:28) uses a two-bar call and response figure that he repeats, a standard groove figure that would become part of the arsenal of any number of jazz organists. At the beginning of Smith's third chorus (3:45), he begins with a quotation from the popular song "Frankie and Johnny." Montgomery's comping is subtle but amazingly varied—throughout Smith's third chorus, he repeats a two-bar riff.

4:01   Smith moves to blisteringly fast sixteenth-note runs at the top of his fourth chorus, a swaggering display of his command of the instrument, as the drums respond with more aggressive accompaniment. During the following chorus (4:18), you can also hear how Montgomery's comping becomes more assertive, and he repeats a four-bar accompanimental idea beneath Smith's two-bar riffs. Smith returns to fast sixteenth-note runs during his sixth chorus (4:34). Smith's penultimate chorus (4:50) trades in standard blues figures idiomatic to the keyboard, and his final chorus (5:07) almost obsessively repeats a fast blues-scale figure.

5:23   We fade our excerpt as Smith returns to a varied restatement of the head to "James and Wes."

Listen to this music in an animated Active Listening Guide available at the text website.

Montgomery influenced legions of guitarists, including George Benson. Benson created a major impact with his 1976 album *Breezin'*, which became quite popular thanks to the hit recording of "This Masquerade." Benson had begun his career with organist Jack McDuff, whose bluesy orientation strongly influenced the guitarist:

> That was a value I learned in Jack McDuff's band, the value of playing everything with a little blues touch. You know, adding a bended note here and there, a little cry over there, a little glissando here. It really helped to give me a concept, something to build on.

Benson also acknowledged how jazz organists helped highlight guitarists:

> I think that's what really helped the guitar to come to the front...as far as jazz music is concerned, because there was never any real, dynamic guitar playing, except for exceptional guys like Wes Montgomery, and even he came by way of the organ at first. And Kenny Burrell and just a couple of others, but I think the organ gave the guitar a form... It featured the guitar so much. Guys could really test themselves, and night after night they had to come with some interesting solos, so it was a good format for guitar players.[12]

The Hard Bop Legacy in the 1960s

During the 1960s many jazz artists continued the tradition of hard bop. Here we look at some of these key players. Many mainstream jazz musicians recorded with Blue Note Records, which had built a reputation since the 1930s for promoting fine jazz.

Blue Note Records

Two of the leading hard bop groups of the 1950s, the Horace Silver Quintet and Art Blakey and the Jazz Messengers, recorded primarily for Blue Note Records. Blue Note was established in 1939, and it developed a reputation for interest not only in newer music but also in recording fine jazz players who had not gained popular appeal. For example, during the 1940s its catalog included jazz elder statesmen James P. Johnson and Sidney Bechet as well as bebop pioneer Thelonious Monk. In the 1950s Blue Note earned a reputation for its high standards in recording the finest hard bop players and bands. Much of the label's success was due to the vision of its founder, Alfred Lion, as well as recording engineer Rudy Van Gelder, who supervised many of the sessions.

Blue Note continued as a major force in jazz recording during the sixties; as in the fifties, the groups that recorded on the label helped keep alive the mainstream legacy. In the midst of the free jazz upheaval, the Blue Note bands—usually standard quartets, quintets, and sextets—maintained the hard bop tradition and sometimes adapted to newer musical developments, such as modal improvisation.

Lee Morgan and Freddie Hubbard

Many of the artists who recorded on Blue Note in the 1960s began their careers with the Art Blakey and Horace Silver bands. Trumpeter Lee Morgan, born in Philadelphia in 1938, played with Blakey's Jazz Messengers between 1958 and 1961 and returned briefly in 1964 and 1965. He also participated in John Coltrane's 1957 *Blue Train* recording. Morgan was heavily influenced by Clifford Brown, with a swaggering and virtuosic style, confidently in control of all registers of the horn.

Morgan recorded his funky jazz hit "The Sidewinder" in 1963. He wrote other notable compositions as well. His album *Cornbread*, which included Hank Mobley on tenor saxophone and Jackie McLean on alto, contained a beautiful Latin-based composition, "Ceora." The 12-bar blues "Our Man Higgins," also from *Cornbread* and dedicated to drummer Billy Higgins, contained an unusual twist: the opening choruses of each solo used the whole-tone scale before returning to the standard 12-bar blues chord changes. Morgan experimented with other tangents in modern jazz, as well. For example, the title track from his *Search for the New Land*, with guitarist Grant Green, explored modal improvisation. Morgan died in 1972, murdered at a gig by his common-law wife.

Morgan was replaced in the Jazz Messengers by trumpeter Freddie Hubbard. Like Morgan, Hubbard was born in 1938 (he died in 2008), and he was an equally fiery player, although his tone was slightly mellower. Interestingly, Hubbard participated in several significant free jazz recordings, including Ornette Coleman's *Free Jazz*, John Coltrane's *Ascension*, and recordings with Eric Dolphy between 1960 and 1964. Nonetheless, Hubbard's own Blue Note albums made during the early 1960s, *Goin' Up* and *Hub Tones*, showed him to be a fundamentally more traditional player than the avant-garde musicians. *Hub Cap*, recorded in 1961, kept the same instrumentation as Blakey's Jazz Messengers, combining

Lee Morgan,
Cornbread,
"Our Man Higgins"
(1965)

Photo Courtesy of the Morgan Collection

Trumpeter Lee Morgan was one of the many significant players to work with Art Blakey and the Jazz Messengers. On his recordings for Blue Note Records, his own compositions touched on hard bop, funky/soul jazz, and modal jazz.

three horns (trumpet, trombone, and tenor saxophone) with a rhythm section of piano, bass, and drums.

Hubbard's work as a sideman on two of Herbie Hancock's Blue Note recordings, *Maiden Voyage* and *Empyrean Isles*, contained some of his finest work. After 1970 Hubbard turned to more commercially promising music, recording jazz-rock fusion and funk.

Wayne Shorter

Hubbard's band mate in Blakey's Jazz Messengers was tenor saxophonist Wayne Shorter. Shorter was born in 1933 in Newark, New Jersey. After earning a bachelor's degree in music education from New York University in 1956, Shorter worked with Horace Silver and Maynard Ferguson. Beginning in 1959

Wayne Shorter,
Speak No Evil,
"Witch Hunt"
(1965)

Shorter served as music director for the Jazz Messengers until his defection to Miles Davis in 1964.

Shorter's early Blue Note recordings were in the hard bop mainstream, but as both tenor player and composer he was attracted to the exploratory and the experimental. On his composition "Witch Hunt" from his 1964 album *Speak No Evil*, the melody emphasized the interval of a perfect fourth over slow-moving modal harmonies in the A section. In addition to modal compositions, Shorter experimented with a funky/soul jazz rhythmic feel on the title track of his quartet recording *Adam's Apple*, and he moved decisively toward free jazz playing on *The All Seeing Eye*. In recent years Shorter has been writing for orchestra, often with pieces that feature himself as soloist. His work with the fusion group Weather Report is discussed in Chapter 11.

Joe Henderson

Another significant tenor saxophonist to emerge in the sixties was Joe Henderson (1937–2001), born in Lima, Ohio. Henderson was a member of the Horace Silver Quintet between 1964 and 1966, appearing on Silver's best-known tune, "Song for My Father." On tenor Henderson combined Coltrane's intensity with Sonny Rollins's motivic approach to improvisation. His highly individual approach to the tenor saxophone also reflects some of the sound-based ideas from the jazz avant-garde.

In 1963 Henderson made his first recording for Blue Note, *Page One*, which included bebop trumpeter Kenny Dorham. The album featured Dorham's "Blue Bossa," which became a jazz standard, as well as Henderson's own Latin-based "Recorda Me."

Henderson's subsequent recordings for Blue Note blended traditional hard bop instrumentation with modally based compositions, such as his 1966 *Mode for Joe*. This album included Blakey alumni Curtis Fuller on trombone and Lee Morgan on trumpet, along with Joe Chambers, one of the finest yet most underrated drummers of

the decade. Henderson produced some of his most creative pieces working as a sideman; for example, he played open-ended modal improvisations on McCoy Tyner's *The Real McCoy* and on Herbie Hancock's *The Prisoner*.

During the last decade of his life, Henderson went on to achieve greater national visibility and acclaim. He won Grammy awards for a series of songbooks recorded during the nineties, including *Lush Life* (1991), dedicated to the music of Billy Strayhorn; *So Near, So Far (Musings for Miles)* (1992); and *Double Rainbow: The Music of Antonio Carlos Jobim* (1994). Henderson died in 2001 due to complications from emphysema.

Other Blue Note Artists

Under the influence of John Coltrane's and Miles Davis's groups, many other Blue Note artists in the 1960s moved into modal composition and improvisation. Organist Larry Young (1940–1978) abandoned the funky/soul jazz orientation of the organ; his *Unity*, with Joe Henderson and trumpeter Woody Shaw (1944–1989), responded strongly to Coltrane's modal innovations. The recordings of vibraphonist Bobby Hutcherson (b. 1941) featured some of Davis's and Coltrane's sidemen—pianists McCoy Tyner and Herbie Hancock and bassist Ron Carter—with the latter two on Hutcherson's *Components*. Pianist Andrew Hill (b. 1937), a devotee of Thelonious Monk, recorded modal jazz and free jazz on his *Point of Departure*, made with Eric Dolphy and Joe Henderson; Henderson also performed on Hill's *Black Fire*.

Thus the Blue Note label not only kept alive the hard bop tradition but also adapted to the innovations of the decade. In addition, the label recorded many of the most important exponents of funky/soul jazz, including guitarist Grant Green and organist Jimmy Smith. Although the bulk of its recordings represented the jazz mainstream, Blue Note was not totally averse to controversy: the label also issued some of the freest jazz of the decade, Cecil Taylor's *Unit Structures*.

Exam Review Questions

Use these questions and the materials on the text website to help you understand and pass tests on the content of this chapter.

1. What were the major innovations of mainstream singers and big bands during the late 1950s and 1960s?

2. What was Miles Davis's response to the free jazz revolution of the 1960s?

3. Which principal jazz pianists matured in the 1960s? Compare and contrast their styles.

4. What factors led to the rise of funky/soul jazz? Discuss the importance and history of the Hammond electronic organ.

5. How did the bebop style of the 1940s continue to develop through the 1950s and the 1960s? What was this continuation called, and who were the principal musicians involved?

 MindTap™

Test Yourself on Key Concepts with additional Chapter Quizzes and Listening Activities on the text website.

Key Terms

Test your knowledge of this chapter's key terms by defining the following. If you can't remember the meaning of a term, refresh your memory by looking up the boldfaced term in the chapter, turning to the Glossary at the back of the book, or working with the flashcards at the text website.

chromatic scale **307**

comping **300**

elastic meter **303**

funky jazz **311**

metric displacement **303**

soul jazz **312**

standard **298**

step connection **303**

swell **314**

vocalese **289**

voice leading **303**

Jazz-Rock, Jazz-Funk Fusion

11

MindTap

Start with a quick warm-up activity.

THE DEVELOPMENT OF **JAZZ-ROCK** AND **JAZZ-FUNK FUSION** during the 1970s remains controversial. **Fusion** involved the incorporation of rock, soul, and funk elements into jazz, and it drastically altered the musical directions taken in the postbop era.

Elements of Jazz-Rock and Jazz-Funk Fusion

The key elements of jazz-rock and jazz-funk include the following:

▶ Replacement of the 4/4 swing feel with rock or funk rhythms

▶ Harmonies and progressions that were usually simpler and often characterized by a slow harmonic change or use of long vamps

▶ Electric and electronic instruments as the norm; specifically:

   ▪ Replacement of the acoustic bass with the electric bass

   ▪ Replacement of the acoustic piano with electric piano and synthesizers (so pianists became "keyboardists")

   ▪ Rise to prominence of the electric guitar as a characteristic instrument of the fusion ensemble

▶ Intense amplification and use of electronic effects

1969—Miles Davis records "In a Silent Way/It's About That Time" (released in 1970; Track 53)
—Davis records *Bitches Brew*
1971—Death of Louis Armstrong
1972—John McLaughlin records *Inner Mounting Flame*
—Chick Corea records *Light as a Feather*
1973—Herbie Hancock records "Chameleon"
—Chick Corea and Return to Forever record *Hymn of the Seventh Galaxy*
1974—Death of Duke Ellington
1976—George Benson records *Breezin'*
—Hancock records *V.S.O.P.*
1977—Weather Report records *Heavy Weather*, including "Birdland" (Track 55)

Jazz

1970 **1975** **1980**

Historical Events

1971–1974—U.S. space probes to Mars, Mercury, and Jupiter
1972—Nixon visit to China
—DDT banned
1973—Beginning of Watergate
—U.S. vacates Saigon, end of Vietnam War
1974—Nixon resigns presidency
1975—Communists control South Vietnam and Cambodia
—U.S.–Soviet joint mission in space
1976—Viking landing on Mars
—Jimmy Carter first president from Deep South in 125 years
1977—Apple II computer is released
1978—Pope John Paul II becomes first non-Italian pope since 1523
—United States and China establish full diplomatic relations
1979—Iranian revolution

Jazz-rock, **jazz-funk**, or **fusion** is a form of jazz that combines elements of rock (or R&B funk) and jazz.

The **synthesizer** was originally developed for musical use in the early 1950s. Unlike acoustic instruments, the synthesizer produced sound electronically: in analog synthesizers an oscillator supplies a voltage to an amplifier, from which it is routed to a speaker.

The Synthesizer

An important element in fusion was the addition of the **synthesizer** to the ensemble. As synthesizers underwent development in the seventies and became less expensive and more convenient to play (smaller and more portable), the typical fusion ensemble became more likely to adopt them.

Synthesizers were originally developed for musical use in the early 1950s. Unlike acoustic instruments, the synthesizer produced sound electronically: in analog synthesizers an oscillator supplies a voltage to an amplifier, from which it is routed to a speaker. The earliest models pioneered by RCA, Bell Laboratories, and European companies were cumbersome: they did not have attached keyboards and were unsuitable for live performance.

In the sixties manufacturers produced the first synthesizers that allowed keyboardists to conveniently control and manipulate the sound during live performances. During the

An early, more compact RCA Mark II synthesizer

Peter FORREST/Susurreal/Lebrecht Music & Arts

seventies synthesizers became cheaper and more compact, leading to the familiar sight of the rock-band multikeyboardist surrounded by stacks of electric pianos, synthesizers, mixers, and other gear. The Minimoog was perhaps the first widely used synthesizer, a standard keyboard accessory in rock bands and fusion groups in the early seventies.

The mid-seventies witnessed the dual breakthroughs of polyphonic and digital synthesizers. *Polyphonic* models enabled the keyboardist to play chords. *Digital* synthesizers were even more flexible: their numerical translations of complex sound waves allowed for the creation of a greater number of timbres, or sound qualities, for each note.

In addition to synthesizers, **samplers** were gradually developed: when acoustic instrumental sounds (or in fact any kinds of sounds) are recorded and reproduced for musical use, the practice is known as **sampling**. **Sound modules** are electronic devices that play back recorded samples, which can be digitally stored on a computer for playback.

Curiously, even early jazz synthesizer solos reflected the instrument's potential. The synthesizer was then at the forefront of the developing jazz-rock and jazz-funk styles. Musicians were intrigued by the expressive qualities of the new instrument, and many imaginative solos were created.

The Role of the Electric Guitar

In addition to adopting the new timbre of the synthesizer, jazz musicians began modifying the role of the electric guitar. The traditional mellow timbre of the hollow-body electric guitar had been defined by such players as Charlie Christian in the late 1930s and maintained in jazz through the 1960s. In fusion this sound was superseded by the steely, cutting timbre; the sustained notes; and often the distortion obtained from the solid-body electric guitar. (Listen to Tracks 39 and 40 of the 🅟 Audio Primer to compare these sounds.) A common form of distortion was created by intentional **feedback**. Musicians such as Jimi Hendrix in the rock world showed how feedback could be controlled and used as a musical quality.

The radical changes of instrumental timbre associated with fusion were accompanied by changes in the roles of the players themselves. In particular, the concept of solo accompaniment was radically modified: instead of the improvised comping of the pianist or guitarist, the group often relied on repeated vamps or ostinato figures.

The Character of Seventies Fusion

For the most part, seventies jazz fusion can be broken down into either *jazz-rock* or *jazz-funk*. The latter term, though less common, was often more accurate because the music incorporated elements of R&B and funk more often than rock.

In a very general sense, differences between rock and funk are perhaps best understood by their rhythmic underpinning. Music Example 11-1 compares a rock drum pattern with a funk drum pattern.

The funk drum pattern is more complex because it is based on a sixteenth-note subdivision and incorporates more syncopation; the rock rhythm is based on an eighth-note subdivision. Hence funk music is more likely to be syncopated and rhythmically complex; rock music is generally less syncopated and often characterized by the use of "straight" or "even" eighth notes. Both drum patterns incorporate a heavy use of **backbeats**, almost always played on the snare drum.

Music Example 11-1

A rock drum pattern and a funk drum pattern.

Samplers are electronic devices used to both sample and play back sounds. **Sampling** is the practice of digitally recording sounds for musical use in playback. Any kind of sound can be sampled, from a note on an acoustic instrument, to natural sounds, to a passage of music already recorded. For playback the sound is usually activated by computer or by pressing a key on a keyboard.

Sound modules are electronic devices that play back recorded samples, which can be digitally stored on a computer for playback.

Feedback is a distorted effect created when the sound coming from a speaker is picked up by the electronic sensing device of an instrument (or a microphone) and routed back to the speaker. As this process multiplies, harsh electronic wails are created. Feedback commonly (and annoyingly) occurs in PA (public address) systems when the microphones pick up the sound coming from the speakers.

Backbeats are heavy emphases on beats 2 and 4, as played by the drummer (usually) on the snare drum. (Other drums or the hi-hat can be used for quieter backbeats.) They can be added to a 4/4 swing rhythm as well. Backbeats increase dance ability by clarifying the rhythm and adding to the excitement of the music.

Smooth jazz is a popular form of fusion jazz that is common today. It combines rock or funk grooves with an electronic ambience to create an "easy listening" feel. Although improvisation may be present, the pleasant quality of the groove and the melody are its dominant features.

The first experiments in fusion took place in the late sixties. Much of the impetus for and early development of the style came from Miles Davis and his sidemen. Davis's watershed albums *In a Silent Way* and *Bitches Brew*, both from 1969, helped introduce both electric keyboards and rock/R&B rhythms and harmonies to the jazz audience.

The first wave of popular jazz-rock groups in the early seventies—Mahavishnu Orchestra, Weather Report, Return to Forever, and Herbie Hancock's Headhunters—were formed by former Davis sidemen. These groups earned extensive critical and popular acclaim. Using electronic instruments and the rhythmic grooves of rock and funk, these new groups displayed first-rate improvisational skills and strongly defined compositional structures.

> "I really wanted to become the fastest guitarist in the world."
> —Al Di Meola, fusion guitarist

Recordings by these groups sold well too, surpassing many of the musicians' expectations for commercial success. For the first time since the swing era, a form of jazz had become popular again.

Despite the potential of these early fusion groups, two trends occurred that helped, as musician/critic Bill Laswell described, "assassinate the promise of fusion"[1] during the second half of the seventies. The first negative trend, according to some critics, was an overreliance on flashy but largely empty technique. Some of the fusion players relied on faster and faster playing in their improvisations. As guitarist Al Di Meola candidly admitted, "I really wanted to become the fastest guitarist in the world. Just like the track stars want to become the fastest runner in the world."[2]

The second negative trend in fusion's evolution was its commercialization. Whereas a typical jazz record might sell 10,000–20,000 copies, some of the most popular fusion records (such as Herbie Hancock's *Headhunters*) sold more than a million. To tap into this market, record companies put subtle—and sometimes not so subtle—pressure on musicians to simplify their music. The more commercially oriented fusion products gravitated toward slickly packaged, danceable, ingratiating music, with catchy melodic hooks replacing the substance of an improvisational or compositional core.

Because of these commercial trends, fusion musicians soon sustained withering critical scorn for "selling out." For

example, in a telling interview with keyboardist George Duke in 1977, *Down Beat* interviewer Lee Underwood soundly reprimanded Duke for his commercial leanings: "There are some artists who shoot for immortality," Underwood pontificated, "not just for a heated swimming pool and a house in the Hollywood hills."[3]

Although some fusion artists continue to break new ground, one of the legacies of fusion—**smooth jazz**—is unabashedly oriented toward extensive radio airplay (see Chapter 12). Although one can argue that smooth jazz is simply satisfying popular demand—much like the cookie-cutter swing tunes of the late 1930s—one can also contend that latter-day fusion has not fulfilled its earlier artistic promise. Its detractors disdainfully refer to the music as "lite jazz," "hot-tub jazz," or "fuzak" (a combination of *fusion* and *Muzak*).

The Appeal of Rock and Funk

Many jazz musicians developed a fascination with rock and soul music as these styles developed during the 1960s. These types of music were popular with youth to an unprecedented degree and largely embodied the rebellion of the sixties against the mores and values of the previous generation. The new generation of jazz musicians—often naturally rebellious—grew up listening to rock and funk; it was natural for them to incorporate these elements into their experimentation with jazz.

Soul and, later, funk developed out of rhythm and blues, which itself was the offspring of the so-called race

> Eventually, many of the jazz stalwarts gave in to pressure from the record companies and other musicians to incorporate rock tunes into their recordings and performances.

records of prewar African American music. The rhythm and blues of the 1940s embraced a danceable style with a heavy beat and often syncopated rhythms. As the sounds of the swing-era big bands faded away and bebop proved to be uncommercial, rhythm and blues filled the demand for popular music among black audiences.

The soul and funk groups of the sixties and the early seventies strongly influenced the development of fusion. The band of singer James Brown, the self-proclaimed "hardest working man in show business," featured horns, electric guitar, electric bass, and drums. Brown's hits such as "Papa's Got a Brand New Bag" and "I Feel Good" made prominent use of harmonies heard in jazz, such as ninth chords. Brown's music was also rhythmically complex, with strong backbeats and highly syncopated, rhythmically interlocking parts for the bass, guitar, and drums. The dense interplay of the rhythm-section instruments in funk suggested a way for upcoming jazz-fusion players to integrate their jazz-oriented harmonies with syncopated rhythms.

Herbie Hancock made explicit the connection between Brown's funk rhythms and the new jazz fusions:

> In the popular forms like funk, which I've been trying to get into, the attention is on the interplay of rhythm between the different instruments. The part the Clavinet plays has to fit with the part the drums play and the line that the bass plays and the line that the guitar plays. It's almost like African drummers where seven drummers play different parts. They all play together and it sounds like one part. To sustain that is really hard.[4]

Another influential soul band, particularly admired by Miles Davis and Herbie Hancock, was Sly and the Family Stone, whose hits in the late sixties and the early seventies included "There's a Riot Going On," "I Want to Take You Higher," and "Everyday People." The group's electric bassist was Larry Graham, who developed a technique of thumping the low strings while plucking the higher strings, creating a percussive funky sound. This **slap bass** style was picked up by other funk players and by fusion electric bassists such as Stanley Clarke, Alphonso Johnson, Marcus Miller, and Jaco Pastorius, who made the "slapping and popping" sound an important component of their playing.

In addition to soul and funk, rock also made an impact on the development of fusion. Rock, which came of age in the 1950s, developed out of a complicated mix of 1940s R&B, country and folk music, and Delta and electric blues, among other elements. With the so-called British invasion of the mid-sixties, groups such as Cream and the Rolling Stones earned phenomenal popularity by covering compositions by African American blues and R&B artists such as Chuck Berry, Muddy Waters, and Robert Johnson.

After first performing in the United States in 1964, the Beatles became cultural icons impossible to ignore. In 1966 jazz drummer Art Taylor conducted a series of interviews for his book *Notes and Tones*, asking jazz musicians what they thought of the Beatles.[5] Intense opinions about them, pro and con, also arose in George Simon's interviews with big-band leaders Count Basie, Woody Herman, Stan Kenton, and Artie Shaw in Simon's book *The Big Bands*.[6] Eventually, many of the jazz stalwarts gave in to pressure from the record companies and other musicians to incorporate rock tunes into their recordings and performances. On the recording *Ellington '66*, Duke Ellington recorded versions of the Beatles' compositions "All My Loving" and "I Want to Hold Your Hand." Count Basie recorded *Basie's Beatle Bag*, consisting entirely of Beatles compositions. Jazz guitarist Wes Montgomery's albums *Michelle* and

A Day in the Life were titled after the Beatles compositions included on each record. Woody Herman's late-sixties group played the Fillmore auditoriums and recorded rock songs such as the Doors' "Light My Fire."

Despite such experimentation, covering popular rock tunes in a jazz setting proved to be relatively infertile. As fusion developed, the music retained the rhythms, harmonic concepts, and electric ambience of rock music but used these elements to support improvisation and original composition. Covering hit tunes became far less common.

Early fusion artists expressed admiration for the solos of rock guitarist Jimi Hendrix. Hendrix (born Johnny Allen Hendrix) was a self-taught guitar virtuoso who used feedback, distortion, and electronic devices in his extended and flamboyant solos. His hit "Purple Haze" (the title based on a nickname for the hallucinogenic drug LSD) prominently featured a sharp ninth chord, a harmony frequently found in jazz settings. Hendrix took part in two of the most famous rock festivals of the late sixties: the Monterey Pop Festival and Woodstock. His psychedelic performance of "The Star-Spangled Banner" at Woodstock is one of the most compelling and famous moments in the film of the concert. He also had an interest in jazz. For example, he recorded with fusion guitarist John McLaughlin and organist Larry Young late in his career, and he had several discussions with Miles Davis about recording an album, which sadly never materialized. Hendrix died of a drug overdose in 1970 at the age of twenty-seven.

Other rock-oriented bands of the late sixties and the early seventies managed to fuse jazz with rock while appealing to a wider public. Blood, Sweat & Tears thrived on a formula of horns and jazz-based solos to augment their

> # Jimi Hendrix had several discussions with Miles Davis about recording an album, which sadly never materialized.

rock compositions, which featured the soul-based singing of David Clayton-Thomas. The group penned a string of Top 40 hits, as did the band Chicago, which used similar instrumentation. Some experimental rock groups, such as the British bands Soft Machine and King Crimson, featured even more extended improvisation. Jazz artists Chick Corea

---

Slap bass is a technique in which the bass player percussively hits the low strings of the instrument while picking melodies on the higher ones. This "slapping and popping" style was created by Larry Graham and subsequently imitated by jazz, funk, and pop bass players.

and Gary Burton both acknowledged the influence of King Crimson on their work.

The Fusion Music of Miles Davis

In a remarkable jazz life in which he was always at or near the center of the action, Miles Davis managed to pioneer jazz development yet again with his groundbreaking work in fusion. Davis was increasingly drawn to the popular rock and soul music of James Brown, Jimi Hendrix, and Sly and the Family Stone, as well as Cannonball Adderley's soul-jazz hit, "Mercy, Mercy, Mercy." (Listen to Track 51.) Davis began experimenting with rock rhythms and electric instruments (such as the Fender Rhodes electric piano) on *Miles in the Sky* and *Filles de Kilimanjaro* (see Chapter 10).

But Davis's *In a Silent Way* was even more radical, presenting music that was both harmonically and rhythmically far simpler than his previous work. The riff-oriented album featured three electric keyboardists— Herbie Hancock, Chick Corea, and Josef Zawinul—as well as British electric guitarist John McLaughlin. In place of the usual recorded performances of individual compositions, *In a Silent Way* was assembled by producer Teo Macero, who edited the studio sessions to create two compositions, each of which took up the entire side of an LP. "In a Silent Way/It's About That Time" (Listening Guide, Track 53) was a medley, with the opening drumless section providing a four-minute introduction that was spliced in again at the end to provide a frame for the entire work.

Davis's next studio recording, *Bitches Brew*, was pivotal. From here on, his music centered on rock-based rhythms and completely abandoned the 4/4 swing feel that had defined it for twenty-five years. The compositions amalgamated rock and soul influences; a steady, insistent

LISTENING GUIDE   Track 53
"It's About That Time/In a Silent Way" (excerpt)

Miles Davis: "It's About That Time" (Davis)/"In a Silent Way" (Zawinul), from *In a Silent Way*. Sony C3K 65362. New York, February 1969. Davis, trumpet and leader; Wayne Shorter, soprano saxophone; Chick Corea, electric piano; Herbie Hancock, electric piano; Josef Zawinul, organ; John McLaughlin, electric guitar; Dave Holland, acoustic bass; Tony Williams, drums.

The Main Point   The original album side consisted of a medley, beginning with "In a Silent Way" (lasting about four minutes), followed by "It's About That Time" (eleven minutes), and concluding with the four-minute "In a Silent Way," spliced in again to create an overall ABA structure. The excerpt here, beginning about five minutes into "It's About That Time," consists of the soprano saxophone solo and the trumpet solo and concludes with the first statement of the melody to "In a Silent Way."

"It's About That Time" includes two repeated sections for the improvisations. The first (Part I) is a repeated three-note bass riff around E♭; the second (Part II) is a two-bar groove riff.

"It's About That Time"—Soprano saxophone solo (Timings in parentheses indicate location in complete track.)

0:00 (9:09)	For Part I the bass riff repeats every bar. Above it the electric piano repeats a six-chord pattern, setting up three-bar phrases. Drummer Williams plays in a subdued manner, keeping time by playing a rock beat that articulates all four beats of the measure. Although the use of rock rhythms in a jazz context was fairly new, a single repeated bass riff beneath shifting harmonies in the piano had already been used in modal jazz, and it is instructive to compare this excerpt with John Coltrane's "Acknowledgement" from *A Love Supreme* (Track 42).
0:22 (9:31)	Shorter begins his solo with simple rifflike ideas that emphasize the pitches C and F. Notice that each of his melodic ideas seems to build on and develop the previous idea. Just before Part II he begins to spin out longer melodic lines.
1:19 (10:28)	The band begins Part II with the groove riff heard in the bass. Playing over the riff, Shorter relies on fairly short, simple blues riffs. Around 2:02 he begins to play longer, more jazz-inflected lines. He winds up his solo after the band returns to part I, by echoing the three-note bass riff.

"It's About That Time"—Trumpet solo

2:42 (11:51) In Part I Davis begins his solo by referring to the melody played by the keyboardists in their six-chord vamp. Note that this induces the keyboardists to move away from that original vamp and begin comping in a more rhythmic manner. Many of their comping figures now echo the three-note bass riff.

3:32 (12:41) Over the groove riff of Part II, Davis uses a generous amount of space between his phrases. Most of his phrases stay concentrated in the middle register, and they seem often to return to the pitch F, the underlying key center.

4:01 (13:09) Still in Part II, Williams begins playing in a high-energy rock style, drumming loudly and energetically. Despite the intensity, Davis still plays with characteristic restraint, although in his first phrase he briefly moves to the higher register.

4:40 (13:49) The band returns to Part I. Davis often uses short, clipped phrases. Although many of Davis's lines stay within the overall tonal center of F, he once responds to the keyboardists' comping when they move outside the tonal center: at 5:22 he plays and holds a G♭, a dissonant note a half step above the tonal center. Organist Zawinul's comping on organ frequently echoes the three-note bass motive.

5:31 (14:40) While the band plays Part II, Davis often plays longer and more-chromatic lines. His solo winds down, and he stops playing while the band continues the groove riff.

"In a Silent Way"—Melody played by guitar

6:29 (15:38) Here the recording is spliced to merge with "In a Silent Way," a haunting, dreamy composition written by Zawinul. (Zawinul described the composition as a "tone poem" that recalled his boyhood in Austria.) Guitarist McLaughlin plays the melody, accompanied by bowed bass and keyboards. Although Zawinul's original version of the composition was faster and had far more harmonic changes, the musicians played this version out of tempo and adhered to a single harmonic center.

 Listen to this music in an animated Active Listening Guide available at the text website.

rock or funk beat underscored the freewheeling improvisations by Davis or bass clarinetist Bennie Maupin. Davis also augmented the group's personnel, often including three drummers and a percussionist to create a densely textured and layered rhythmic foundation. For many of the compositions, Davis provided only a general sketch consisting of melodic ideas and a tonal center. The recording sold well, although most of the tracks were long and uncompromising.

In A Silent Way (and *Bitches Brew*) were influential for fusion of the 1970s for the following reasons:

▶ Rock-based rhythms and simpler harmonic structures based on ostinato figures

▶ Electric keyboards and electric guitar

▶ Musicians (Chick Corea, Herbie Hancock, John McLaughlin, Wayne Shorter, Tony Williams, and Josef Zawinul) who were to become the significant fusion artists during the 1970s

▶ Dense percussion textures and Davis's use of electric effects

Davis virtually never turned back. After his fusion experiments in the late sixties, he continued to explore creative, improvised music within rock, funk, and computer-controlled synthesizer frameworks. By doing this he gained an even higher degree of popularity and commercial success. After releasing *Bitches Brew*, Davis began playing at rock music venues, such as the Fillmore East in New York and the Fillmore West in San Francisco. In this astute professional move, Davis tapped into a wider audience by opening for rock acts such as the Grateful Dead; the Band; Santana; and Crosby, Stills, and Nash.

With his move to fusion and accompanying popularity, jazz traditionalists such as singer Betty Carter accused Davis of selling out by cashing in on a popular trend: "It's all about money… They [Davis, Herbie Hancock, and Donald Byrd] have a 'reasonable' excuse for the why of what they're doing, but the only excuse is money."[7]

Miles Davis,
A Tribute to Jack Johnson
"Right Off" (1970)

A **wah-wah pedal** is a pitch-frequency filter, operated by the foot, that is usually used by guitarists or electric keyboardists. When the pedal is pressed, the note or chord being held makes a *wah* sound. (An acoustic *wah* sound can be achieved by brass players' using their left hands or mutes over the bells of their instruments.) The up-and-down movement of the pedal creates the repeated *wah-wah* effect. (Listen to Track 41 on the Audio Primer to hear jazz-rock guitar with wah-wah pedal.)

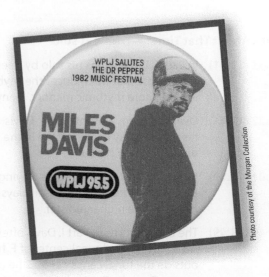

Photo courtesy of the Morgan Collection

Nevertheless, a review of Davis's early 1970s recordings shows just how uncompromising and uncommercial much of his music actually was. In contrast to the well-rehearsed, high-octane precision of fusion groups like the Mahavishnu Orchestra and Return to Forever or to the dance-floor grooves of Herbie Hancock, Davis's groups often performed dissonant, atmospheric, seemingly free-form medleys stitched together loosely by a rock or funk beat. With a band consisting of keyboardists Chick Corea and Keith Jarrett, drummer Jack DeJohnette, bassist Dave Holland, and saxophonist Steve Grossman, Davis gave his musicians plenty of improvising space. As a result, many of the pieces seemed to rewrite themselves each night: "Friday Miles" (named for the night the group performed), from his 1970 recording *At Fillmore*, combined versions of "Sanctuary," "Bitches Brew," "Miles Runs the Voodoo Down," "I Fall in Love Too Easily," and "The Theme." The record-side length of each composition on the double album was created by splicing together chosen segments of longer, live performances.

In the live performances themselves, Davis developed a musical system to signal the group to segue into another piece, as Enrico Merlin shows here:

> I have discovered three types of what I call "coded phrases" corresponding to particular characteristics of the relative piece:
>
> 1. The first notes of the tune
> 2. The bass vamp
> 3. The voicings of the harmonic progressions
>
> For example, in the case of "It's About That Time" the coded phrase is taken from the voicings of the descending chord progressions played by the electric piano.[8]

Merlin's observations have been corroborated by musicians who played with Davis during this period. Interestingly, Merlin notes that Davis developed the medley concept before he turned to fusion. For example, with his acoustic bands of the mid-sixties Davis would often begin the next piece while the previous piece was ending.

Captivated by the guitar playing of Jimi Hendrix, in the seventies Davis began incorporating guitar into his ensembles, at times recording with two and sometimes even three guitarists. He soon dispensed with acoustic

bass by hiring Michael Henderson, an electric bassist who had played R&B and soul in the Motown studios with songwriter-vocalist Stevie Wonder. Henderson provided the anchor for Davis's group, establishing the tonal center and two- or four-bar ostinato riffs over which the soloists would improvise. Al Foster was often the drummer called on to set the groove with Henderson.

In contrast to the funk-based rhythm sections, Davis's horn lineup was more in keeping with his bands of the past. For his saxophonist Davis often used a player strongly influenced by John Coltrane, such as Dave Liebman, Gary Bartz, or Sonny Fortune. Usually, these players played soprano saxophone. Davis himself played both trumpet and organ. Like the rock guitarists and keyboardists of the era, he often used a **wah-wah pedal** on trumpet. During live performances Davis would stalk the stage, often directing the musicians from the organ with cues that were sometimes overt and sometimes imperceptible to the audience.

Davis stopped performing between 1975 and 1981 because of declining health. He had developed problems from cocaine addiction and had an arthritic hip and stomach ulcers exacerbated by alcoholism. He returned from seclusion with the 1981 album *The Man with the Horn*, which included saxophonist (not pianist) Bill Evans, bassist Marcus Miller, drummer Al Foster, and guitarist Mike Stern, whose heavy-metal, Hendrix-like solos jazz critics loved to hate. Davis again showed his flair for hiring rising young stars of jazz by picking up guitarist John Scofield in 1982. Scofield inspired Davis to return to his blues roots: the trumpeter featured a 12-bar blues on "It Gets Better" from *Star People*.

As in the past, these newer sidemen continued with prominent careers after their association with Davis. Guitarists Stern and Scofield are among the outstanding guitarists of today; Miller flourished with an accomplished career as a bassist, synthesist, and producer. Saxophonist Bill Evans recorded a number of albums after leaving Davis.

Although Davis continued to tour and perform, he turned more often to the studio for his albums rather than recording live as he had in the early seventies. For example,

Davis created a landmark album in 1985—*Tutu*—which was named after Archbishop Desmond Tutu, winner of the Nobel Peace Prize for his work in ending apartheid in South Africa. *Tutu* made extensive use of studio technology; the tracks were arranged and the synthesizers were programmed by Davis's former bass player Marcus Miller, with the help of Jason Miles. The album was constructed by introducing layers of synthesized drum tracks, percussion, and keyboards. The funk grooves and the catchy melodic ideas provided a foundation over which Davis later added his trumpet solos. In some ways Miller was something of a fusion-era Gil Evans, providing lush dense backdrops for Davis. (See Chapter 8 for Gil Evans's collaborations with Davis.)

Despite the elaborate studio technology used on *Tutu*, Davis's playing was unmistakable. Over the funky vamp on "Splatch," for example, Davis displayed his trademark **harmon-muted** trumpet—the same subtlety of phrasing and the same start-and-stop ideas that had characterized his playing for four decades. Despite the sometimes radical change of musical circumstances, his style was remarkably consistent throughout his career. Trombonist and composer J. J. Johnson sums up this point neatly:

> Miles is doing his natural thing. He's just putting in today's setting, on his own terms. If you put Miles and his new group in the studio and record them on separate mikes and then you cut the band track and you just played the trumpet track, you know what you'd have? The same old Miles. What's new is the frame of reference.[9]

On his final albums, Davis continued to experiment with studio technology. His work from the late eighties featured sampled, electronically derived soundscapes—much like Miller's work on *Tutu*—over which Davis added trumpet improvisations. Davis died of a stroke on September 28, 1991, at the age of sixty-five. Shortly before his death, he returned to playing in a more traditional format, performing at the Montreux Jazz Festival in a retrospective of his collaborations with Gil Evans. His last recording, *doo bop*, was released posthumously and incorporated hip-hop grooves and rap. Davis had been an integral part of the jazz scene for more than four decades, always moving and changing. Interestingly, nearly half of his career was dedicated to fusion music after he helped spark the trend in the late sixties.

Regarding Davis's role in incorporating aspects of R&B, rock, and funk music into the jazz idiom, pianist Ramsey Lewis noted:

> It was not until the late sixties when Miles Davis gave his stamp of approval by incorporating some of these ideas into his albums that musicians accepted the fact that rock rhythms and influences other than the traditional ones could be integrated with jazz. . . . Davis extended the harmonic concept, employed polyrhythmic patterns, added electronic instruments and devices to his trumpet along with his highly unique and creative ability, and set the pace for what has come to be known as fusion music.[10]

Other Fusion Pioneers

Miles Davis was not the only prominent jazz musician responding to rock and funk in the sixties. Jazz guitarist Larry Coryell (b. 1943) was one of the earliest musicians to incorporate rock, blues, and even country elements into his jazz playing. Like some of the other young players in the mid-sixties, Coryell took a wildly eclectic approach. He later remembered, "We were saying, We love Wes [Montgomery], but we also love Bob Dylan. We love Coltrane but we also love the Beatles. We love Miles but we also love the Rolling Stones."[11]

"We love Wes, but we also love Bob Dylan. We love Coltrane but we also love the Beatles. We love Miles but we also love the Rolling Stones."
—Larry Coryell

Photo courtesy of the Morgan Collection

A **harmon mute** is a hollow metal mute that, when placed in the bell of the trumpet, gives the sound a distant, brooding quality. Miles Davis's use of the harmon mute from 1954 onward helped popularize its use. (Listen to Track 14 of the 🎧 Audio Primer to hear an example of a harmon mute.)

A **bent pitch** is a small glissando or slide from one frequency to (usually) a slightly higher one. On guitar it is achieved by pushing against the string on the fret board, thus "bending" it.

In 1966 Coryell was part of the Free Spirits, one of the very earliest jazz-rock groups; the following year he joined the Gary Burton Quartet, recording with Burton the albums *Duster* and *Lofty Fake Anagram*. Most of Coryell's solo from "Walter L." (from *Gary Burton in Concert*) could have come from a late-sixties rock band. Coryell used blues-based licks, playing with sustain and distortion that approached feedback in one spot. Coryell's performance with guitarist John McLaughlin on Coryell's 1970 recording *Spaces* provided one of the high points of early fusion guitar. In the seventies Coryell formed the group Eleventh House, but his playing was eclipsed by emerging fusion guitarists such as McLaughlin.

Another early form of jazz-rock fusion was played by the Fourth Way, a San Francisco–based band led by New Zealand pianist Mike Nock (b. 1940). Nock was one of the first players to make extensive use of electric keyboards, playing synthesizers and a Fender Rhodes electric piano and using devices such as the wah-wah pedal on the three albums the group recorded between 1968 and 1971.

The late sixties also witnessed the formation of an influential band called Dreams. Among its players were many of the up-and-coming stars of the fusion movement, including drummer Billy Cobham (b. 1944); tenor saxophonist Mike Brecker (1949–2007); Mike's brother, trumpeter Randy Brecker (b. 1945); and guitarist John Abercrombie (b. 1944). Abercrombie's use of feedback and distortion on "Try Me," from the 1970 recording *Dreams*, showed the attraction of high-energy rock guitar playing.

Lifetime

One of the most important early fusion bands was Lifetime, a dynamic trio formed by Tony Williams, the drummer who had earned tremendous acclaim with Miles Davis in the sixties. Originally from Boston, Williams had been a drumming prodigy, playing regularly around the city by age fifteen. In 1963, at age seventeen, Williams recorded for Blue Note in New York with saxophonist Jackie McLean and was soon asked to join Miles Davis's quintet. Williams's style changed along with Davis's: for example, on Davis's 1969 album *In a Silent Way*, Williams kept up a steady, regular rhythm, abandoning the explosive, unpredictable playing that had previously been his trademark with the Davis quintet. (Listen to Track 53.)

In a Silent Way included an astounding British guitarist who had arrived in the United States only two weeks before: John McLaughlin. Born in Yorkshire in 1942, McLaughlin had played in British rock and jazz groups during the fifties and sixties and had participated in studio sessions with pop singers Tom Jones, Petula Clark, and David Bowie. McLaughlin's 1969 album *Extrapolation*, recorded while he was still living in England, demonstrated his remarkably fast execution in an acoustic jazz format. Instead of the syncopated phrasing of traditional jazz guitarists, McLaughlin's playing was even, hard, and cutting. He occasionally used **bent pitches** in the manner of rock guitarists.

Invited by Williams, McLaughlin left Britain to come to the States and join Lifetime. The group began as a trio; along with Williams on drums and McLaughlin on guitar was organist Larry Young. Lifetime not only was indebted to the jazz tradition but also drew inspiration from jam-oriented rock bands such as Cream and the Jimi Hendrix Experience. On the title track from the Lifetime recording *Emergency!* the group alternated a repeated four-bar figure with a half-tempo improvisation by McLaughlin. "Spectrum" probably best showcased the group's hybrid approach: it moved from a Hendrix-like rock vamp to improvisational sections with a 4/4 swing feel, with walking bass played by Young on the organ. The rapid unison line of "Spectrum," played by guitar and organ, foreshadowed McLaughlin's later work with the Mahavishnu Orchestra.

Blending jazz and rock rhythms and held together by Williams's high-energy style of drumming, Lifetime never achieved a wide popularity. The group's raucous energy, propelled by the distortion and the sheer volume of the guitar and the organ, was too extreme for mainstream jazz fans, and its often dissonant and extended improvisations proved too esoteric for mainstream rock fans. Lifetime's second album, *Turn It Over*, was even more explicitly rock based: it included bassist Jack Bruce of Cream on three of the tracks.

Tony Williams's work with Miles Davis and Lifetime earned him almost legendary status among jazz drummers of the eighties and nineties. He continued with a variety of projects involving both jazz and rock, including reunions with the Miles Davis rhythm section of Herbie Hancock and Ron Carter in a group known as V.S.O.P. ("Very Special One-time Performance"). He also performed with some up-and-coming younger players such as Mulgrew Miller and Donald Harrison. The jazz world was greatly saddened in 1997 by Williams's early death from heart failure at age fifty-one. His final albums, *Wilderness* and *Young at Heart*, are interestingly varied: the former includes experiments with merging the classical and jazz worlds, and the latter is a piano trio record featuring Mulgrew Miller and bassist Ira Coleman. In 1997 Williams was elected to the *Down Beat* Hall of Fame.

Mahavishnu Orchestra

Lifetime was short lived—the group broke up in 1971—but the hard-driving energy of the music was something fresh. John McLaughlin was emerging as one of the paramount guitarists on the jazz scene. McLaughlin and Larry Coryell were perhaps the two musicians most responsible for bringing the sound of rock guitar into the jazz idiom.

McLaughlin's concept of jazz-rock guitar included elements of non-Western musical traditions, especially classical Indian styles, along with the blues licks typical of fifties and sixties R&B guitar playing. During this time McLaughlin adopted as his guru Sri Chimnoy; accordingly, the titles of McLaughlin's solo albums *Devotion* and *My Goal's Beyond* reflected his newly formed spiritual interests. On *Devotion* McLaughlin hired two of Jimi Hendrix's sidemen, drummer Buddy Miles and bassist Billy Cox; *My Goal's Beyond* used two Indian musicians, Badal Roy and Mahalakshmi, along with such jazz players as saxophonist Dave Liebman, bassist Charlie Haden, and drummer-percussionist Airto Moreira. One side of *My Goal's Beyond* was merely solo acoustic guitar.

After Lifetime broke up, McLaughlin assembled one of the first—and most significant—fusion bands of the seventies. The Mahavishnu Orchestra was named by McLaughlin's guru. McLaughlin hired drummer Billy Cobham, who had played with Horace Silver and the band Dreams; Czech keyboardist Jan Hammer, who had been a member of Sarah Vaughan's trio; Irish bassist Rick Laird; and violinist Jerry Goodman, who had been a member of the rock group The Flock.

The success of the Mahavishnu Orchestra was phenomenal. Their 1971 recording *The Inner Mounting Flame* reached number 89 on the *Billboard* chart; the following year their second album, *Birds of Fire*, reached an astounding 15 on *Billboard*. (The *Billboard* chart records the Top 200–selling albums on a weekly basis; jazz albums have rarely shown up even at the bottom of the chart.) Like that of Miles Davis, the Mahavishnu Orchestra's popularity enabled them to play concerts and tour on the rock music circuit.

In contrast to the loose, often ethereal jazz-rock improvisations of Miles Davis, however, the Mahavishnu Orchestra was tightly rehearsed. The group played dazzling unison figures, complex meters (such as 7/8 or 5/16), ostinato figures—sometimes indebted to Indian music—and rock rhythms pounded out at a ferocious velocity by drummer Billy Cobham, who used a drum set with double bass drums, one played by each foot. On **double-necked guitar**, using a wah-wah pedal and other electronic devices, McLaughlin tore through rapid-fire sixteenth-note solo passages, bending notes and using distortion at deafening volume.

The Mahavishnu Orchestra did not rely exclusively on high-octane, blisteringly fast playing. For example, "A Lotus on Irish Streams," from *The Inner Mounting*

Mahavishnu Orchestra,
The Inner Mounting Flame,
"The Dance of Maya"
(1971)

Flame, and "Open Country Joy," from *Birds of Fire,* are pastoral, acoustic reveries. Much of the band's impact derived from the dramatic juxtaposition of acoustic works such as these with high-energy electric compositions.

All in all, as one writer has observed, the Mahavishnu Orchestra's recordings "remain benchmarks for ensemble cohesion and inspired jazz-rock improvisation."[12] The group seemed to awaken new possibilities at a time when many jazz musicians were excited by the potential of jazz-rock. Keyboardist George Duke recalled:

> When fusion was first happening, it was the most interesting music I had heard in my life. It reached its peak with the Mahavishnu Orchestra.... But it seemed like after that everybody was copying each other and getting too technically oriented, playing so many notes and scales that the feeling was going out of the music.[13]

The group disbanded in 1973. McLaughlin formed a second Mahavishnu Orchestra in 1974. The short-lived, eleven-piece group included Jean-Luc Ponty, a highly talented French violinist who went on to create his own fusion recordings during the seventies and eighties, including the albums *Imaginary Voyage* and *Enigmatic Ocean.* After the Mahavishnu Orchestra broke up, much of McLaughlin's work abandoned the fusion directions he had helped chart. He concentrated on acoustic guitar, playing with the Indian-based group Shakti and later in an acoustic guitar trio with Paco de Lucia and Al Di Meola.

Nevertheless, McLaughlin's recordings of the 1970s make abundantly clear his contributions to the first wave of jazz-rock fusion. His brash, energetic playing is on full display in his 1978 recording "Phenomenon: Compulsion." (Listen to Track 54.)

Herbie Hancock and *Headhunters*

With his work as a member of the breakthrough Miles Davis Quintet between 1963 and 1968 and with his own Blue Note recordings, Herbie Hancock distinguished himself as one of the most outstanding jazz pianists and composers of the sixties. Hancock was Davis's first sideman to use the Fender Rhodes electric piano, on the album *Miles in the Sky.* After leaving Davis's band, Hancock continued to use electric piano on his recordings *Crossings, Mwandishi,* and *Sextant.* Hancock's group for these recordings—usually a sextet—was booked into rock music venues such as the Fillmore, but their spacey, open-ended improvisations proved unsuccessful, and Hancock was forced to disband the group in 1973. Before abandoning the rock circuit, however, Hancock had the significant experience of opening for the R&B pop group the Pointer Sisters at the Troubadour club in Los Angeles. Hancock was impressed by the direct audience appeal of the Pointer Sisters. He started thinking about taking his music in a

---

A **double-necked guitar** has two necks. Sometimes the second neck has twelve strings rather than the usual six.

LISTENING GUIDE
"Phenomenon: Compulsion"

Track 54

John McLaughlin: "Phenomenon: Compulsion" (McLaughlin), from *Electric Guitarist*. Columbia JC 35326. North Hollywood, January 16–20, January 26–February 2, 1978. John McLaughlin, guitar; Billy Cobham, drums.

The Main Point "Phenomenon: Compulsion" reunites two members of the Mahavishnu Orchestra, guitarist John McLaughlin and drummer Billy Cobham. The duo performance maintains the flashy virtuosity and high energy that characterized many of the Mahavishnu Orchestra recordings (as well as McLaughlin's earlier work with Miles Davis and with Lifetime). It shows how 1970s jazz musicians were profoundly influenced by rock music. For McLaughlin, the use of cutting guitar textures, distortion, and guitar effects, as well as ultimate dexterity, show the appeal of rock guitar in general, and Jimi Hendrix, in particular. Like those guitarists, McLaughlin relies on electronic devices—often activated by a foot switch—to help create those sounds. Even the tonal center (the key of E) is one that is more typically used by rock than by jazz musicians. A comparison with guitarist Wes Montgomery (Track 52) shows just how far fusion guitarists departed from earlier sound ideals of jazz guitar. Cobham, one of the most widely imitated fusion drummers, maintains a driving rock rhythm throughout, and close listening reveals his use of two bass drums, each played by a pedal, with either foot. There is a loose jam session attitude to the performance, although the complex stop-and-go melody played by the guitar is duplicated rhythmically by the drums.

Introduction

0:00 Following McLaughlin's two-note lead-in, the drums enter with a rock beat. The drum accompaniment subdivides each beat into triplets, maintaining a driving feel. McLaughlin begins with single lines, before moving to chordal textures that echo Cobham's triplet subdivisions (0:07). McLaughlin continues the chordal textures with a syncopated rhythm (0:16) as Cobham begins playing with a backbeat, emphasizing beats 2 and 4.

Melody

0:26 The melody consists of a series of six short riffs. Each of the first three riffs state a single pitch five times, each using the same rhythmic profile. The final three riffs consist of rapid lines: the first two descend, and the last ascends. The players state that overall melody three times. Notice how Cobham duplicates the rhythms on the drums. The first time the overall melody is stated, he plays only snare drums and tom-toms; during the second melody statement he uses the cymbal once, and during the third melody statement he plays the cymbal consistently (0:36). The use of fast lines played in unison was a frequent characteristic of fusion performances, one that added to the visceral excitement of the music.

Improvisation

0:40 Following the three melody statements, the players move to an improvised section. Rather than consisting of a harmonic progression, there is a single tonal center maintained. There is no bassist on the recording, but you can hear a lower held drone pitch that maintains the underlying tonality, operating as a pedal point, and activated by a guitar synthesizer. McLaughlin's improvised lines are fast and precise—often moving in sixteenth notes—and Cobham's accompaniment focuses on the snare drum, maintaining the same sixteenth-note orientation.

1:01 Cobham's playing becomes much more active.

1:09 McLaughlin plays a blisteringly fast repeated melodic idea.

1:16 The players return to a segment of the original melody.

1:20 McLaughlin plays a chordal passage that moves in and out of the tonality. Cobham's playing is remarkably assertive, consisting of rolls and cymbal crashes.

1:40   The players return to play again a segment of the original melody.

1:43   McLaughlin begins a series of rapid-fire runs. Such playing provided a point of departure for any number of fusion guitarists, but it also became a lightning rod for fusion critics that decried flashy indulgent virtuosity too far removed from the jazz mainstream tradition.

Return to melody

2:07   The players return to the original melody, again stated three times.

2:22   McLaughlin plays a series of chords, during which you can hear Cobham using the double bass drums with both feet at 2:26.

2:31   McLaughlin uses nontraditional guitar effects. With his left hand he mutes but does not hold down the guitar strings, and he rakes his pick across the strings with his right hand. Cobham plays more freely. With McLaughlin's sound-based improvisation and Cobham's freer time, both players indulge in some elements characteristic of free jazz.

2:59   The players refer to the rhythm of the melody to signal the end of the performance. The performance closes with McLaughlin using a vibrato bar (a bar attached to the guitar body that—when pressed—causes the pitch gradually to descend; guitarists sometimes refer to this as a "whammy" bar). The use of effects such as these was much more central to the rock than the jazz tradition.

Listen to this music in an animated Active Listening Guide available at the text website.

direction that had more popular appeal, one rooted in the funk and R&B styles of James Brown, Stevie Wonder, and especially Sly and the Family Stone. Introduced to Nichiren Shoshu Buddhism by his bassist, Buster Williams, Hancock experienced a revelation while chanting:

> My mind wandered to an old desire I had to be on one of Sly Stone's records. It was actually a secret desire of mine for years—I wanted to know how he got that funky sound. Then a completely new thought entered my mind: Why not Sly Stone on one of my records? My immediate response was: "Oh, no, I can't do that." So I asked myself why not. The answer came to me: pure jazz snobbism.[14]

Although Hancock never recorded with Stone, he did achieve a breakthrough into popular culture with his phenomenally successful album *Headhunters*. The album reached number 13 on the *Billboard* chart, then eventually went platinum (sold a million copies). With the exception of reed player Bennie Maupin, who was with his earlier group, all the members of Hancock's new quintet had been steeped in funk music. His intent, Hancock claimed, was to hire not jazz musicians who could play funk, but funk musicians who could play jazz. *Headhunters* made extensive use of overdubs and studio technology, including tape loops. In addition to playing the Fender Rhodes electric piano, Hancock also played **Arp synthesizers**, the **Mellotron**, and other electronic keyboards.

Hancock's solo on "Chameleon" established him as one of the finest live performers on synthesizer. Much of the success of the *Headhunters* album was due in fact to "Chameleon," which became a hit largely because of its syncopated, danceable two-measure bass riff and catchy melody.

Herbie Hancock,
Headhunters,
"Chameleon" (1973)

On *Headhunters* Hancock revived his earlier hit "Watermelon Man," a composition recorded on his first album more than ten years earlier. On the updated version, percussionist Bill Summers plays an African-like rhythm by blowing on a beer bottle. Although Hancock was later criticized for "selling out," not all of the compositions on *Headhunters* were overtly commercial. "Sly," a homage to Sly Stone, included several

---

Arp synthesizers were among the first synthesizers made specifically for live performance.

The **Mellotron** is an electronic instrument that was used for string-ensemble effects in the 1970s. An early, analog sound module, the Mellotron produces notes by activating short tape recordings of a string ensemble playing each note of the scale. When a key is pressed, the tape recording of the chosen note plays.

drastic tempo changes and featured daring improvisations by both Hancock and saxophonist Bennie Maupin.

Compositional subtlety and extended improvisation gradually faded from Hancock's later recordings. The group's next project, *Thrust*, used repetitive funk and dance rhythms, although Hancock's composition "Butterfly" was haunting and evocative, reminiscent of some of his earlier impressionistic recordings for Blue Note in the sixties. Hancock's subsequent recordings were marketed squarely as commercial products, placing strong dance grooves in the forefront. Hancock's *Manchild* was aimed at the burgeoning seventies disco market; nevertheless he found space for an impressive acoustic piano solo on "Hang Up Your Hangups."

In response to the sometimes hostile comments from jazz critics, Hancock insisted that his dance music recorded in the seventies and eighties was not jazz:

> Jazz fusion is another idiom. It uses elements of jazz and elements of popular forms, but it established its own idiom. I'm not concerned with changing that idiom, or changing disco. I want to play the music I'm playing and still have it be dance music. Making some music that is fun to dance to and really nice to listen to, some music that has emotion in it. . . . It's funny because many of the elements are simpler than before. For example, a lot of the music happening today has simpler chord structures and simpler harmonies than in the past. The complexity is now in the textures and in keeping the groove going.[15]

Hancock's biggest success came with "Rockit," from the 1983 album *Future Shock*, which stayed on the pop-music charts for more than a year and became a classic MTV video. The album went platinum and won a Grammy for best R&B instrumental. Musically and commercially successful, Hancock's work within fusion and funk-based styles numbers among the most important of any jazz artist in the seventies and eighties.

Despite success in the pop-funk market, Hancock frequently returned to an acoustic jazz format, playing in a hard bop idiom with the V.S.O.P. Quintet. The group reunited Hancock with his former band mates from the Miles Davis Quintet—bassist Ron Carter, drummer Tony

> ## "I want to play the music I'm playing and still have it be dance music."
> ### —Herbie Hancock

Williams, and saxophonist Wayne Shorter—and included trumpeter Freddie Hubbard. The group performed a number of compositions recorded earlier with the 1963–1968 Davis quintet. Hancock also returned to the hard bop

and modal idiom in recordings with trumpeters Wynton Marsalis and Wallace Roney. On his 1996 album, *The New Standard*, Hancock performed jazz arrangements of pop hits by the Beatles and others, succeeding where many earlier attempts to cover such tunes failed.

On the 1998 album *Gershwin's World*, Hancock teamed up with an impressive array of players from the jazz, popular, and classical fields, such as jazz pianist Chick Corea, classical soprano Kathleen Battle, the Orpheus Chamber Ensemble, and pop musicians Stevie Wonder and Joni Mitchell. Hancock's 2001 album *FUTURE2FUTURE* finds the keyboardist continuing to explore new fusions with performances that link jazz players with hip-hop, turntable, and techno artists. We return to Hancock and his 2007 recording *River: The Joni Letters* in Chapter 12 in order to examine its crossover appeal and its hints at possible directions for jazz in the twenty-first century.

Chick Corea and Return to Forever

Herbie Hancock's replacement in the Miles Davis Quintet was Chick Corea, who joined Davis in the fall of 1968. In summer 1970 Corea gave notice to Davis to pursue his own projects and an interest in what he called musical "abstraction." His recordings *Song of Singing* and *Circle: The Paris Concert* made extensive use of free improvisation. The next year, however, Corea became interested in communicating with a wider audience, as Hancock had. His two solo piano albums, *Piano Improvisations*, Volumes 1 and 2, showed Corea in a transitional stage: the first side of each contained songs marked by relatively simple forms, structures, and lyrical melodies; the second side of both albums were free atonal improvisations.

With his group Return to Forever, Corea abandoned free playing, moving decisively toward airy, Brazilian-influenced music. He hired bassist Stanley Clarke, saxophonist-flutist Joe Farrell, drummer Airto Moreira (who often went by his first name only), and Airto's wife, singer Flora Purim. The group made two recordings, *Return to Forever* and *Light as a Feather*, which highlighted Corea's sophisticated compositions. Some of these—such as "Spain" and "La Fiesta"—were playful references to Spanish music. "Spain," in fact, opened with a solo piano introduction that borrowed material from composer Joaquín Rodrigo's *Concierto de Aranjuez*—a melody that was used earlier on the Miles Davis/Gil Evans collaboration *Sketches of Spain*. Both Airto and Purim were Brazilian, and the group played Brazilian sambas and Latin-influenced rhythms with astonishing clarity and freedom. Corea's tunes caught on. "It seemed like after we made that record," said saxophonist Joe Farrell about *Light as a Feather*,

Chick Corea,
Light as a Feather,
"Spain" (1972)

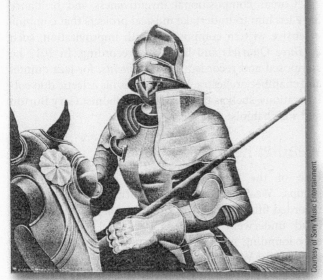

Return to Forever: The Masters.

Chick Corea, Stanley Clarke, Lenny White and Al DiMeola have created a music that presents staggering technical demands, emphasizes interplay between musicians, and insists on constant originality.

They've developed a style which is increasingly imitated. But there's no doubt who the masters are. Return to Forever. "Romantic Warrior." A radically original album on Columbia Records.

The members of Return to Forever were Chick Corea, Stanley Clarke, Lenny White, and Al Di Meola; an ad for their 1976 album *Romantic Warrior* for Columbia Records.

"everybody and their brother started playing sambas and songs with melodies. It became very popular."[16]

The title *Light as a Feather* characterizes the album as a whole. The lightness is achieved by the relative lack of bass drum in the rhythm section. Instead the bass—itself never too heavy—dominates the lower frequencies. The amplified acoustic bass here offers a delicate sound, more akin to an unamplified bass than the heavier electric bass usually heard in jazz-rock. The prominent Latin rhythms and the lively character of the performances imbue the work with a feeling of joy and exhilaration throughout.

Corea reorganized Return to Forever in 1973, converting the group into an electric quartet. Only Stanley Clarke remained from the earlier band, but he switched from amplified acoustic bass to electric bass. Lenny White, who had performed on Miles Davis's *Bitches Brew*,

was the drummer. The electric guitarist on *Hymn of the Seventh Galaxy*, the first album of the revamped Return to Forever, was Bill Connors, but he was soon replaced by Al Di Meola. As for the repertory and the overall style of the group, Corea drew on his own experiences playing with Miles Davis, but he was equally inspired by John McLaughlin's Mahavishnu Orchestra. "John's band, more than my experience with Miles," Corea admitted, "led me to want to turn the volume up and write music that was more dramatic and made your hair move."[17]

Like the Mahavishnu Orchestra, Return to Forever excelled in playing exciting, impressive unison lines at breathtaking speed. Corea performed not only on electric piano but also on Moog and Arp synthesizers, clavinet, and organ. As heard on "Vulcan Worlds" from the album *Where Have I Known You Before*, Clarke was one of the fastest and most facile electric bassists around. Adept at both improvising and accompanying, he made effective use of the slap-and-pop techniques of funk bass. *Where Have I Known You Before* also contained occasional solo interludes on acoustic piano, with the free-flowing harmonies of the title cut sounding like an homage to Bill Evans's "Peace Piece." At its best, Return to Forever's music was compositionally sophisticated: the group effectively blended complex forms, meter and tempo changes, and well-written ensemble passages with dynamic and virtuosic improvisation.

The group's follow-up recordings, *No Mystery* and *Romantic Warrior*, pursued the path begun with the earlier albums, although some of the compositions were shorter and contained less improvisation. It is possible that the group and its record company were aiming for selections suitable for commercial radio airplay. On these recordings the group experimented with numerous subgenres of jazz-rock, rock, and funk; there were funk grooves ("Sophistifunk" and "Jungle Waterfall"), "art-rock" orchestral effects ("Romantic Warrior"), and even heavy metal ("Excerpt from the First Movement to Heavy Metal").

Corea broke up the electric group in 1975. Bassist Stanley Clarke (b. 1951) worked sporadically with Corea during the remainder of the decade but also issued a series of commercially oriented recordings under his own name. Among them "School Days" was a successful hit; even more popular was "Sweet Baby," a collaboration between Clarke and keyboardist George Duke that made the Top 20 in 1981.

Like Clarke, guitarist Al Di Meola (b. 1954) continued as one of the most successful names in fusion. He released a series of albums in the Return to Forever mold, most notably *Elegant Gypsy* and *Casino*. These emphasized Di Meola's brilliant though flashy technique and were testaments to his desire to become "the fastest guitarist in the world." Among later projects, Di Meola played in an acoustic guitar trio with John McLaughlin and Paco de Lucia and experimented with synthesizer textures as accompaniment to the acoustic guitar.

Photo courtesy of the Morgan Collection

Stanley Clarke in an early promotional photograph. Clarke made the switch to electric bass as a member of Return to Forever when Corea turned the group electric.

Corea went on to create a larger, more orchestral version of the Return to Forever concept by making use of strings and horns. A series of "thematic" albums followed in the second half of the seventies. *Mad Hatter*, with its Alice in Wonderland motif, included lesser efforts such as the "The Trial," distinguished by the repeated phrase "Who stole the tarts, was it the Queen of Hearts?" On one cut, however, Corea returned to a postbop, acoustic jazz format, playing in a straight-ahead swinging quartet context on "Humpty-Dumpty" with drummer Steve Gadd, saxophonist Joe Farrell, and bassist Eddie Gomez. Similarly, *MusicMagic* featured dazzling solos as well as stunning, complicated written ensemble passages for horns side-by-side with simpler pop-style tunes sung by Corea's wife, Gayle Moran, and bassist Stanley Clarke. One of

Corea's most dramatic and sparkling improvisations was played over a Latin-based rhythm on "Armando's Rhumba" (from *My Spanish Heart*), played with Clarke and violinist Jean-Luc Ponty.

Like Hancock, Corea's subsequent career in the 1980s and 1990s included work in both electric and acoustic formats. His group, Chick Corea's Elektric Band, with bassist John Pattitucci and drummer Dave Weckl, was a significant fusion band of the eighties, playing dynamic and well-rehearsed music that recalled the electric Return to Forever group of the 1970s. Corea also returned to the acoustic trio format on two recordings: *Trio Music* (featuring the compositions of Thelonious Monk) and *Live in Europe*. The trio reunited Corea with bassist Miroslav Vitous and drummer Roy Haynes, who had performed on Corea's 1968 *Now He Sings, Now He Sobs*.

Corea's compositional inventiveness and brilliance have led him to undertake musical projects that combine extensive written composition with improvisation, such as *Three Quartets* and his *Sextet* recording. In 2012 he composed and recorded *The Continents*, for jazz quintet and chamber orchestra. He continues his eclectic duo collaborations, such as those with vibraphonist Gary Burton and with banjoist Béla Fleck.

Weather Report

One of the longest-lasting and best-known fusion groups, Weather Report, first formed in 1970. They recorded fifteen albums in their fifteen-year history. The band underwent numerous personnel changes, with only founding members keyboardist Josef Zawinul and saxophonist Wayne Shorter—both of whom worked with Miles Davis in the sixties—remaining through the band's tenure. In addition to personnel turnover, Weather Report also undertook several changes in musical direction. They began as an acoustic group, using collective improvisation that was sometimes metrically free. By their third album, 1973's *Sweetnighter*, however, keyboardist and composer Zawinul was moving the group toward more strongly defined compositional structures and more rock- and funk-based rhythms and grooves. They reached the apex of their popularity when electric bassist Jaco Pastorius joined the band and they recorded their hit composition "Birdland," from the album *Heavy Weather*.

Born in Austria in 1932, Zawinul was raised in Vienna and studied at the Vienna Conservatory. Arriving in the United States in 1959, he worked early on with bandleader Maynard Ferguson and singer Dinah Washington. But it was his ten-year stint, from 1961 to 1970, with alto saxophonist Cannonball Adderley that gave Zawinul national exposure. Foreshadowing his later interest in synthesizers and fusion, Zawinul played electric piano with Adderley during the late sixties. His use of the instrument helped bring its sound into the jazz idiom. (Zawinul was not first to promote the electric piano in jazz, however: Ray Charles and Sun Ra had performed on electric keyboards

By *Sweetnighter* the group had moved toward danceable grooves underlying the solos. In "Boogie Woogie Waltz," for example, the band maintained a consistent 3/4 rock beat beneath Shorter's oblique saxophone lines and Zawinul's Fender Rhodes parts, colored by the sound of the wah-wah pedal. The composition also showed new directions that the group would continue to explore: the use of electric bass (on the piece, both electric and acoustic bass are heard) and a short, catchy four-measure melody that is repeated. The latter highlighted Zawinul's ability to write brief melodic ideas as song hooks.

Sweetnighter was the first of Weather Report's recordings on which Zawinul also played synthesizer. He would soon become one of the premier synthesists in fusion, mining the vast compositional and coloristic possibilities of the instrument. By the group's next album, *Mysterious Traveller*, Zawinul was behind a stack of Moog and Arp synthesizers as well as electric piano augmented by wah-wah pedal, **phase shifter**, and **Echoplex**. With electric bassist Alphonso Johnson replacing Miroslav Vitous, the group also took a decisive turn toward funk rhythms and grooves. Johnson, who played fretless electric bass, laid down a syncopated, funky, repeated figure on "Cucumber Slumber"; as on Hancock's "Chameleon," the bass figure dominated the groove.

A 1979 publicity photo of Weather Report: Joe Zawinul, Wayne Shorter, Pter Erskine, and Jaco Pastorius

Weather Report,
Sweetnighter,
"Boogie Woogie Waltz" (1973)

in the late fifties, and Earl Hines had both performed and recorded on a Storytone electric piano as early as 1940.)

Showing a natural talent for pop-jazz crossover, Zawinul wrote the Adderley band's prominent soul-jazz hit, "Mercy, Mercy, Mercy." (Listen to Track 51.) On this cut Zawinul played the Wurlitzer electric piano; on the group's other big hit, "Country Preacher," he played a Fender Rhodes. In the latter performance, he altered the tone bars to give the instrument a more percussive sound. In 1969 Miles Davis paid the distinct compliment of recording Zawinul's composition "In a Silent Way" (Track 53) while hiring him to play keyboards alongside Chick Corea and Herbie Hancock. Zawinul rerecorded the composition on his own album, *Concerto Retitled*, the following year.

In 1970 Zawinul and Wayne Shorter formed Weather Report with Czech bassist Miroslav Vitous. The quintet was initially filled out by drummer Alphonse Mouzon and percussionist Airto Moreira (who did not tour with the group but who overdubbed the percussion parts). With Zawinul on electric piano and Shorter primarily on soprano saxophone, Weather Report's first two albums, *Weather Report* and *I Sing the Body Electric*, emphasized mood, color, and collective improvisation.

Beginning with the 1976 album *Black Market*, electric bassist Jaco Pastorius joined the band. Pastorius redefined electric bass playing with ripping, staccato funk accompaniments; fast, clean solos; interjections of surprising harmonics and entire chords; and a liquid sound that often incorporated *vibrato* at the ends of phrases.

A **phase shifter** is an electronic device that alters the sound of an instrument by altering the sound wave's shape. The resulting sound has a bubbling or slightly hard-edged quality.

The **Echoplex** is a commercial electronic device that adds echo to a sound. The rate of speed of the echo can be altered to make the delay effect slight or more pronounced. This device was popular in the late 1960s and the 1970s.

Born in Morristown, Pennsylvania, in 1951, Pastorius began his career playing in local soul and jazz bands. He made the trio recording *Bright Size Life* with guitarist Pat Metheny, but it was his own 1975 recording *Jaco Pastorius* that showcased his remarkable abilities. On "Donna Lee," accompanied only by percussion, Pastorius glided effortlessly through the melody of the bebop classic, then followed with an astounding solo; on "Come On, Come Over," with vocals by soul singers Sam [Moore] and Dave [Prater], Pastorius's percussive accompaniment revealed new and exciting approaches to funk bass playing.

With Weather Report, Pastorius's outgoing exuberance brought more and more fans to the band's live performances, which generally showcased the bassist in a solo feature that might combine Jimi Hendrix's "Purple Haze" and "Third Stone from the Sun" with "Donna Lee" and the Beatles tune "Blackbird." Pastorius was "an electrifying performer and a great musician," noted Zawinul. "Before Jaco came along, we were perceived as a kind of esoteric jazz group . . . but after Jaco joined the band we started selling out concert halls everywhere."[18]

Pastorius was a talented composer too, writing "Teen Town" and "Havona" for Weather Report's best-selling album, *Heavy Weather*. Largely on the popularity of Zawinul's composition "Birdland," *Heavy Weather* reached 30 on the *Billboard* chart and became a gold record, selling more than 500,000 copies. The tune was later recorded by bandleader Maynard Ferguson and, with added vocals,

LISTENING GUIDE   Track 55
"Birdland"

Weather Report: "Birdland" (Zawinul), from *Heavy Weather*. Columbia PC 34418. North Hollywood, California, 1977. Josef Zawinul, keyboards; Wayne Shorter, soprano and tenor saxophone; Jaco Pastorius, bass, mandocello, vocals; Alejandro Acuna, drums; Manalo Badrena, tambourine.

The Main Point   As do many of Zawinul's fusion compositions, "Birdland" comprises tightly connected sections of brief, singable melodies. The piece is a marvel of ingenuity, with its varied sections uniting in an imaginative and well-crafted whole.

As the following shows, the piece exhibits a complex structure with numerous sections of unpredictable length, rather than the usual eight-bar units of AABA formats.

Introduction—12 measures

0:00   A four-bar synthesizer bass line is heard three times.

Part I—AAB, 24 measures

0:18   A four-bar main thematic idea (A), played by bassist Jaco Pastorius, is added to the four-bar vamp. The idea is played four times: twice in a lower register, then twice in a higher register; an eight-bar B section idea completes Part I, with a saxophone added.

G Pedal—4 measures

0:55   A transition pedal point that reaffirms the G tonality.

Part II—20 measures

1:02   The piano introduces a new four-bar vamp idea. At the end of the third statement of the vamp, a new bass line enters that recalls the earlier bass line, but in augmentation (longer note values).

Part III—9 measures

1:32   A saxophone melody is joined to the next section to create this unusual nine-bar unit.

Transition—9 measures

1:46   The saxophone melody deconstructs into call-and-response funky figures among various timbres.

Part IV—24 measures

1:59   A new four-bar vamp idea appears that implies a III–VI–II–V–I "turnaround" chord pattern.

Transition—8 measures

2:36   Recalling the earlier G pedal, this transition emphasizes G. During the second four bars of the eight-bar section, a backbeat (in part syncopated) is added in the snare and continues into the next section.

Synthesizer solo—12 measures

2:49   The synthesizer solo grows out of the bass line almost imperceptibly. The harmonic focus continues to be on a G pedal.

Saxophone solo—14 measures

3:07   The static G of the last two sections beautifully sets up the background for the saxophone solo: the synthesizers create a two-bar vamp of chords moving down in half-step chromatic motion. This is the climax of the performance. Shorter's saxophone solo shows the group's ability to interweave written and improvised sections seamlessly.

Transition—4 measures

3:29   The texture is again radically simplified for contrast with the preceding section: the G pedal returns.

Reprise of Part I—24 measures

3:35   Over the simplified texture of the preceding section, the melody from Part I returns. As it proceeds, the original bass line is added; then the B section returns with heightened energy.

Reprise of Part II—8 measures, modified

4:11   The four-bar vamp from Part II returns in a modified form.

Reprise of Part IV—Fade-out

4:23   The material from Part IV returns with a long fade-out combining added texture and improvisation.

5:00–5:56   Sparsely at first, Zawinul adds a synthesizer solo to the texture, which gradually becomes more active. A handclap is added as a backbeat, increasing the energy and adding a jam-session aura during the fade.

Listen to this music in an animated Active Listening Guide available at the text website.

by Manhattan Transfer. "A Remark You Made," also from *Heavy Weather*, was a hauntingly evocative ballad featuring Wayne Shorter on tenor saxophone.

On some subsequent Weather Report albums of the late seventies—as with other promising fusion bands, such as the Brecker Brothers—the group turned to formulaic disco rhythms. Their 1978 album *Mr. Gone*, with Peter Erskine on drums, received negative reviews. *Mr. Gone* earned only a one-star "poor" rating in *Down Beat;* according to the critic, Weather Report had abandoned its creative moorings:

It seems that the general Weather Report idea is to fill each composition with a mechanical bass ostinato, dense synthesized chording, and funky, cluttered drumming. . . . Where earlier Weather Report albums possessed a sense of adventure, *Mr. Gone* is coated with the sterility of a too completely pre-conceived project.[19]

The review generated enormous controversy, and the group angrily responded to the criticisms in a *Down Beat* interview the following month.

Chorus reverberation is an electronic effect that guitarists use to "fatten," or fill out, sounds. The sound signal is enriched through the addition of reverb (echo) and a chorus effect (that is, added frequencies complement the sound, giving the effect of several voices or tones sounding at once).

Digital delay is an electronic effect that creates an echo or secondary sound so that a guitarist can, in effect, play several parts at once.

Nevertheless, the group remained enormously popular. In 1980 Weather Report won the reader's poll category in *Down Beat* for the ninth year in a row. Pastorius left the group in 1982, forming his own group, Word of Mouth, which recorded two albums. Unfortunately, alcohol and cocaine addiction brought about severe personal problems for Pastorius, who died after a barroom fight in 1987.

After Pastorius left, Weather Report persisted, releasing several albums—*Procession* (1983), *Domino Theory* (1984), *Sportin' Life* (1985), and their final recording, *This Is This* (1986). After the group broke up in 1986, Zawinul formed Weather Update, a short-lived group that played Weather Report compositions; in 1988 he put together the Zawinul Syndicate with guitarist Scott Henderson.

The Zawinul Syndicate continued to explore musical styles that blend different cultures. For example, Zawinul's album *Stories of the Danube* (1996) unites orchestral music and jazz in a tapestry linked thematically by the Danube and the cultures influenced by the river. In 1998 the band toured the world and released a two-CD set called *World Tour*. Zawinul also was involved in staging multicultural festivals throughout the world, before his death in 2007.

As mentioned in Chapter 10, Wayne Shorter has also pursued a variety of projects. For example, he recorded an interesting duo album with Herbie Hancock in 1997, *1 + 1*. Other projects include large-scale orchestral works that sometimes feature Shorter on saxophone.

Weather Report remains Shorter and Zawinul's legacy from the seventies and eighties. During the fifteen years they kept the band together, Weather Report explored a remarkable abundance of compositional styles and approaches. As Stuart Nicholson summarizes:

> Despite being routinely described as a "jazz-rock" band, their stylistic outlook was extremely broad, perhaps the most inclusive in jazz. Their range extended from classical influences such as the French Impressionists to free jazz, from World music to bebop, from big-band music to chamber music, from collective improvisation to tightly

written formal structures, from modal vamps to elaborately conceived harmonic forms, from structures with no apparent meter to straight-ahead swing. . . . Both Zawinul and Shorter created a large body of work that, outside of Duke Ellington, numbers among the most diverse and imaginative in jazz.[20]

Pat Metheny

Guitarist Pat Metheny was one of the most original and popular fusion artists to emerge in the mid-seventies. Much of his work avoided the cutting, hard-rock sound favored by other fusion guitarists such as John McLaughlin. Metheny preferred bright, lyrical, and often gentle timbres.

Metheny's distinctive sound was created by his use of electronic devices, such as **chorus reverberation**, **digital delay**, and phase shifters. He used them not for distortion and power effects, but rather to give his instrument

> "Even today I think of what I'm playing as sort of a Kansas City style, evolved or modernized. It's that melodic, lyrical thing."
> —Pat Metheny

a fatter, richer sound. In addition, Metheny shunned the pyrotechnics of other fusion guitarists, such as John McLaughlin and Al Di Meola. "I'm not," he made clear, "drawn to the athletic approach to the music." Rather, he saw his lyricism as part of the midwestern melodic tradition of Lester Young and Kansas City: "Even today I think

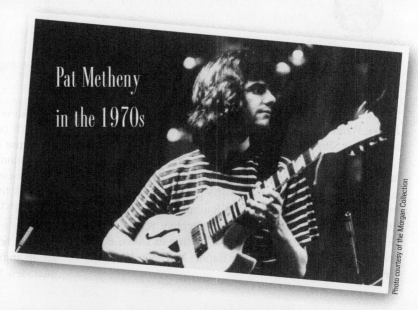

Pat Metheny in the 1970s

Photo courtesy of the Morgan Collection

of what I'm playing as sort of a Kansas City style, evolved or modernized. It's that melodic, lyrical thing."[21]

Metheny was born in Lee's Summit, Missouri, in 1954. A musical prodigy, he taught guitar at the University of Miami at age eighteen. Two years later he was invited by vibraphonist Gary Burton to join the faculty at the Berklee College of Music in Boston. Metheny continued his association with Burton by recording and performing in the vibraphonist's quartet.

Metheny's first album, *Bright Size Life*, was released in 1976. Created with bassist Jaco Pastorius and drummer Bob Moses, it showed Metheny's penchant for clear melodic lines with an occasional country twang. "Unity Village" was a quiet solo guitar piece on which Metheny overdubbed himself. Elsewhere he displayed his affinity for the music of Ornette Coleman—whom Metheny called "one of the most melodic musicians ever"[22]—by recording two of Coleman's compositions in a medley, "Round Trip/Broadway Blues."

After *Bright Size Life*, Metheny put together a quartet for touring, consisting of drummer Danny Gottlieb, electric bassist Mark Egan, and keyboardist Lyle Mays. The group built a national reputation by playing one-nighters throughout the country. *Watercolors*, his next album, was followed by the lyrical *The Pat Metheny Group* in 1978. The moody, gentle "Phase Dance" from the latter album featured simple, spacious, diatonic harmonies, with pianist Lyle Mays capturing the folksy quality sometimes heard in Keith Jarrett's playing.

Metheny's next several albums explored a variety of genres. For example, in contrast to his earlier work, *American Garage* was more rock oriented and was dedicated to the garage bands across the country. "Heartland"—one of his many compositions recalling his midwestern roots—had a decidedly country flavor. Metheny brought Brazilian percussionist Nana Vasconcelos into his group for *As Falls Wichita, So Falls Wichita Falls*, but the dreamy ostinatos featured on many of that album's compositions caused some to dismiss the recording as musically thin—a cross between Muzak and New Age. For his album *Offramp*, Metheny made use of what was then the most sophisticated synthesizer, the Synclavier.

Metheny also performed superbly in acoustic jazz settings. His recording *80/81* included Ornette Coleman's former bassist Charlie Haden along with drummer Jack DeJohnette and saxophonists Michael Brecker and Dewey Redman. The group engaged in open-ended improvisation on Ornette Coleman's "Turnaround." On *Rejoicing*—recorded with Charlie Haden and another Coleman alumnus, drummer Billy Higgins—Metheny featured three of Coleman's compositions. On *Song X* Metheny finally recorded with Ornette Coleman himself. The record was an uncompromising enterprise that both enhanced Metheny's status in the jazz world and brought Coleman to a larger listening public.

On subsequent recordings Metheny merged his neoromantic streak with Brazilian elements, as on the 1987

Still Life Talking, which won a Grammy award, and on *Letter from Home* (1989), which brought to the fore another aspect of Metheny's music: the use of wordless vocals. Metheny's albums have enjoyed both popular and critical success. *Still Life Talking, Letter from Home*, and *Secret Story* all went on to become gold records.

More recently, Metheny—by now an eminent and respected elder statesman of fusion—was involved in several related projects that built on his previous work and reputation and that sometimes involved nonfusion concepts as well. In 1999, for example, he released albums with his longtime hero, guitarist Jim Hall, and saxophonist Dave Liebman.

The Pat Metheny Group, after recording and touring for more than twenty-five years, went on hiatus in 2005. It owed some of its ongoing commercial success to receiving airplay on smooth-jazz radio stations (see Chapter 12 for a discussion of smooth jazz); however, the group's recordings—such as "The Gathering Sky" on the 2002 CD *Speaking of Now*—continue to offer inspired lyrical improvisations and sophisticated compositional structures. Since 2012 he has been recording and touring with his Unity Band (with saxophonist Chris Potter). In a recent article, Metheny summed up his beliefs:

> I made a commitment to focus on and bring into sound the ideas I heard in my head that might not have existed until my time, to try to represent in music the things that were particular to the spiritual, cultural and technological potentials that seemed to be actively available to me in the shaping of my own personal esthetic values.[23]

This statement may serve as a general credo for the ideals of jazz-rock fusion. At its best it is a happy marriage of rock, funk, technology, and jazz. Despite reactions against fusion on the part of some musicians (see Chapter 12), its basic philosophy has provided an important direction for jazz in the twenty-first century.

Other Fusion Bands: The Brecker Brothers and Steps

Following the first wave of popular fusion groups in the early 1970s (Mahavishnu Orchestra, Headhunters, Return to Forever, and Weather Report), other fusion bands were quick to emerge. The Brecker Brothers, named for trumpeter Randy Brecker and tenor saxophonist Michael Brecker, released their first album in 1975. *The Brecker Brothers* featured funky R&B grooves, energetic improvising, and exciting ensemble passages. "Some Skunk Funk" contained a rapid-fire melody that moved inside and outside the harmony, and it became something of a test case for aspiring fusion horn players. On later albums the group responded to pressure from record executives by channeling the formulaic disco rhythms that were becoming omnipresent in the late seventies. Still, their

1981 recording *Straphangin'* showed Randy and Michael Brecker to be formidable improvisers and composers. Both were comfortable in a number of settings, including mainstream jazz, fusion, and studio pop work.

Michael Brecker also played with the group Steps (later renamed Steps Ahead). Started in 1979 by vibraphonist Mike Mainieri, the group began with players known for their mainstream jazz work, such as bassist Eddie Gomez (an acoustic bassist who played with the Bill Evans Trio). The band changed personnel several times: their first American-released recording, *Steps Ahead*, featured Brazilian pianist Eliane Elias. Owing in part to the use of vibraphone, acoustic bass, and acoustic piano, the group successfully negotiated a détente between fusion and more-mainstream jazz.

By the mid-eighties the group changed personnel and moved more decisively toward electronic instruments and commercially oriented fusion. Mike Mainieri and Michael Brecker remained in the group, and several of the group's newer players were known for their fusion work, especially guitarist Mike Stern, who had toured and recorded extensively with Miles Davis. With changing personnel Steps Ahead continued to record and perform through the 1990s.

Michael Brecker became one of the most widely imitated and influential tenor saxophonists of the past several decades. His playing boasted a virtuoso technique that combined some of the improvisational approaches of John Coltrane with the earthiness of R&B saxophonists such as Junior Walker. In addition to tenor saxophone, he performed on the EWI (electronic wind instrument), which allows different timbres and looping effects. He returned to more-acoustic jazz formats in later years, as both a leader and a sideman. Brecker's final recording,

Pilgrimage, made with such jazz stalwarts as Herbie Hancock, Pat Metheny, and Jack DeJohnette, was released shortly after his untimely death in 2007 due to leukemia.

Jazz-Rock, Jazz-Funk Styles

TIMBRE

- Electronic; either
  - → Very hard-edged, raucous
  - → Smooth, vague
- Upper instrumental ranges emphasized
- Use of blue note effects, particularly in funky substyles
- Ambience of rock with many electric and electronic instruments in addition to more-traditional instruments
- High volume in many forms

PHRASING

- Highly irregular in improvisation, but thematic heads often composed in two- and four-bar units

RHYTHM

- Wide variety of rhythmic values, but eighth notes emphasized in up-tempo improvising
- Highly energetic
- Very relaxed; sometimes out of tempo

THEMATIC CONTINUITY

- Motivic

CHORD-TO-SCALE RELATIONS

- Inside, although can become outside in high-energy modal rock performances
- Blues scale usages in funky styles

LARGE-SCALE COHERENCE

- Motivic

Exam Review Questions

Use these questions and the materials on the text website to help you understand and pass tests on the content of this chapter.

1. What are the principal differences between rock and funk?

2. What changes in rhythm and instrumentation did fusion bring to jazz? Describe the new instrument that the fusion bands of the 1970s began to use.

3. How did the performance and sound of the electric guitar change in the fusion bands compared with electric guitar in earlier jazz groups?

4. How does the keyboardist's accompaniment in a fusion band generally differ from that of a pianist in an acoustic jazz group?

5. How can Miles Davis's career be seen as a virtual history of jazz from the late 1940s to the 1970s?

6. What were some of the most significant fusion bands? Who were their key musicians?

 MindTap™

Test Yourself on Key Concepts with additional Chapter Quizzes and Listening Activities on the text website.

Key Terms

Test your knowledge of this chapter's key terms by defining the following. If you can't remember the meaning of a term, refresh your memory by looking up the boldfaced term in the chapter, turning to the Glossary at the back of the book, or working with the flash-cards at the text website.

Arp synthesizer **333**

backbeat **323**

bent pitch **330**

chorus reverberation **340**

digital delay **340**

double-necked guitar **331**

Echoplex **337**

feedback **323**

fusion **321**

harmon mute **329**

jazz-funk **321**

jazz-rock **321**

Mellotron **333**

phase shifter **337**

sampler **323**

sampling **323**

slap bass **325**

smooth jazz **324**

sound module **323**

synthesizer **322**

wah-wah pedal **328**

Jazz Since the 1980s

12

Start with a quick
warm-up activity.

ALTHOUGH THE SEVENTIES WERE THE DECADE
of fusion, numerous nonfusion artists and substyles prospered then: Dixieland and traditional jazz (Doc Cheatham, Preservation Hall), swing-based styles (Count Basie, Benny Carter), bebop (Johnny Griffin, Phil Woods, Art Blakey), big bands (Toshiko Akiyoshi and Thad Jones/Mel Lewis), and free jazz (Ornette Coleman, Lester Bowie). Fusion gained the most attention, however, by attracting many of the younger players and by generating the most controversy among the media and jazz fans.

The proliferation of nonfusion jazz styles in the seventies is no surprise: musical styles launched in the course of jazz history almost never disappear. As a result, the history of jazz should be seen not as a linear progression from style to style—with each new style displacing the previous one—but as a profusion, with styles added as younger musicians tinker with, build on, or modify the work of more-established artists. Jazz history is a rich overlapping of improvisational approaches—a general succession from artist to artist, not from style to style.

Still, because fusion was the big story of the seventies, the eighties have rightly been seen as a return to jazz traditionalism: a revival of the acoustic formats and postbop approaches that were forged in the late fifties and the sixties. For many of the younger players of the eighties, this return to traditionalism meant a reconnection to the roots of jazz, roots sometimes neglected by the fusion players of the seventies. For some, such as Wynton Marsalis, this traditional stance became ideological: Marsalis has positioned himself as a forceful, influential, and articulate spokesperson in support of the traditional aesthetic. Traditional values remain extremely popular in the twenty-first century.

As with other jazz styles since the eighties, fusion has not dropped from the scene; indeed smooth jazz, fusion's commercial legacy, remains quite popular, with such well-known artists as Kenny G generating interest and impressive record sales. Further, many commercial radio stations are devoted entirely to the smooth-jazz format. In the case of seventies fusion, there have been three spin-offs: the popular-music connection, the recent

1980—Digital CD begins to replace analog LP as the commercial record format
1984—Grover Sales publishes *Jazz: America's Classical Music*
—Wynton Marsalis becomes the first musician to win Grammy awards in both classical and jazz categories
1986—Jazz at Lincoln Center is started
—Death of Benny Goodman
1988—Maria Schneider starts her first band (Track 57)
1990s—Jon Faddis (b. 1953) directs the now-discontinued Carnegie Hall Jazz Band
1990—Smithsonian Jazz Masterworks Orchestra is founded
1991—Death of Miles Davis
1993—Death of Dizzy Gillespie
1994—Us3's "Cantaloop (Flip Fantasia)" reaches the Top 20 on the pop charts
—Steve Coleman and Five Elements record "Salt Peanuts" (Track 60)
1996—Death of Gerry Mulligan
—Death of Ella Fitzgerald
1997—Wynton Marsalis's *Blood on the Fields* becomes first jazz composition to win Pulitzer Prize for music
1998—Brian Setzer Orchestra, *The Dirty Boogie*, sells in quadruple-platinum figures (4 million CDs)
2000—Ken Burns multiepisode documentary *Jazz*
2007—Ornette Coleman is second jazz artist to be awarded competitive Pulitzer Prize
2010—UNESCO designates April 30 as "International Jazz Day"
2011—Esperanza Spalding becomes first jazz artist to win Grammy Award for Best New Artist
2014—Jazz at Lincoln Center receives $20 Million private donation for jazz advocacy

Jazz

| 1980 | 1985 | 1990 | 1995 | 2000 | 2005 | 2010 | 201 |

Historical Events

1980—Emergence of Solidarity in Poland
1981—Reagan oldest president to enter office
1985—Gorbachev comes to power in Soviet Union
1989—Collapse of Communism in Eastern Europe and Soviet Union
1990—Iraqi invasion of Kuwait
—Reunification of Germany
—Release of African National Congress leader Nelson Mandela from prison
1991—Persian Gulf War
—Dissolution of the Soviet Union
1992—United States sends troops to Somalia
—Treaty on European Union
1994—Mandela becomes president of South Africa
1995—End of the Bosnian War
1997—Hong Kong returned to China
1999—War in Kosovo
2001—Terrorist attack on World Trade Center
—War against terrorism in Afghanistan
—Apple launches iPod
2003—U.S.-led invasion of Iraq
2004—Social media site Facebook is launched
2005—Hurricane Katrina devastates U.S. Gulf Coast
2006—Israel's invasion of south Lebanon
2007—Expansion of European Union
2008—Barack Obama elected first African-American U.S. president
2010—Apple releases iPad
—Arab Spring begins as series of demonstrations in the Arab world
2011—Japanese tsunami causes extensive damage to Fukushima nuclear power plant
2012—Barack Obama reelected
2013—Nelson Mandela dies

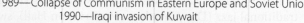

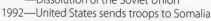

jazz avant-garde, and world music(s). Similarly, the sixties avant-garde can also be seen as having three legacies: a continuation of an acoustic avant-garde scene, an electronic avant-garde scene (intersecting with a legacy of fusion), and a world-music connection. These legacies are in many cases called **crossover music** because they combine jazz (or jazz values) with the styles and music of other cultures.

To summarize, we can think of contemporary jazz as

▶ Traditionalist or mainstream

▶ A legacy of seventies fusion:

 ■ Popular-music connections, electronic or smooth jazz

 ■ Electronic avant-garde

 ■ Crossover to world music in popular formats

▶ A legacy of sixties avant-garde:

 ■ Acoustic avant-garde

 ■ Electronic avant-garde

 ■ Crossover to world-music cultures

The rest of this chapter discusses these three trends in further detail, beginning with an overview of the traditionalists and their return to jazz "classicism."

Classicism and the Jazz Repertory Movement

Jazz since the eighties has witnessed an exploding interest in its history. This mini-renaissance has had two key results:

▶ Increases in the re-creation and live performance of the older jazz music

▶ Complete works of older jazz artists reissued on digital compact discs (CDs) or made available for downloading

The live performance of earlier jazz—usually in concert hall settings—is called the **jazz repertory movement**.

To introduce the repertory movement and its widespread implications for jazz in the twenty-first century, we examine the notable appearance of complete-works jazz recordings on CD, a movement parallel to and thematically linked with the repertory movement.

Complete Jazz-Recording Reissues

After the LP was introduced in the late 1940s, record companies realized that profiting from the highlights of their **back catalog** was simpler and cheaper than developing and promoting unknown artists. Many of the major labels, however, such as Columbia and RCA, initially failed to capitalize on this idea. Instead, smaller independents—such as Riverside and Original Jazz Library (OJL)—reissued this material, often by drawing on collectors who had meticulously preserved the original 78 recordings. When the major labels discovered the profits that could be made by issuing this material, they compiled their own reissue series, beginning in the late fifties and the early sixties and continuing through today.

The digital CD replaced the analog LP as the commercial record format of the 1980s and 1990s. Record companies realized that they could sell the same albums they had issued in the fifties, sixties, and seventies to a new generation of listeners (and in many cases to the same audience who had purchased the LPs originally and now wanted the same material on CD). Also, the development of digital sound **remastering** enabled companies to reissue with superior sound quality much of the material originally released on 78s.

Hence the 1980s and 1990s witnessed an explosion of CD reissues. *Down Beat*, for example, began a column devoted entirely to reissues. What used to be a difficult collector's task—tracking down every recording made by a particular artist—has become much simpler. Current CD reissues comprise not only studio recordings but also live works.

Complete reissues in jazz arguably began with Charlie Parker, whose collected Savoy studio recordings appeared on LP in 1978. The company decided to include every scrap of recorded material, no matter how insignificant. Sometimes excerpts were only a few seconds long, with the recording cut off by Parker, the recording engineer, or the producer following a **false start**, a technical

---

Crossover music combines jazz or jazz values with other styles and music of other cultures.

The **jazz repertory movement** refers to a movement since the 1980s in which ensembles devoted themselves to the re-creation and performance of the works of historically significant jazz artists. Just as classical music has an accepted repertory of great works, the jazz repertory movement is trying to establish an official canon for jazz.

A **back catalog** includes the complete recordings that a company holds in its vaults or claims the rights to by having purchased other record labels. Many of these recordings are out of print or were never issued in their original form.

Remastering is the digital enhancement of an original recording's sound quality; it includes such techniques as filtering out extraneous noise and boosting certain frequencies.

A **complete reissue** duplicates an artist's or a group's entire available body of recorded material—including errors, outtakes, and technical problems.

A **false start** is an incorrect start of a performance: a musician begins playing a measure or two, and then, realizing a mistake, stops abruptly.

Jazz pedagogy is the discipline that comprises the methods and the philosophies of teaching students how to perform jazz.

problem, or other blatant error. No matter—every flub was issued, available for scrutiny. This completist philosophy was subsequently extended to Parker's other two record companies, Dial and Verve, as well as to his live performances, often captured on amateur equipment in informal settings.

The completist philosophy also has implications for the general direction of jazz. This practice marks a phase of jazz in which the past has overtaken the present in importance. As such it marks a turning point for jazz by promoting an art form that is less alive, less immediate, and more self-conscious than jazz has ever been before. Historically, European concert music reached a similar point around the end of the nineteenth century and the beginning of the twentieth century, when listeners and many professional performers de-emphasized contemporary music and made earlier compositions the focus of their repertory. Some have argued that this point marked a downturn in the immediacy and vitality of European concert music. Interestingly, this turn to the past in classical music may have created the opportunity for the success of jazz: the West was ready for something new, a spontaneous art form that could mirror the increased rhythmic pace and speed of industrialization and communication in the new century.

A refocusing of interest on the jazz past is evident not only in the huge number of CD reissues but also in the repertory movement itself. These practices are mutually related: CD reissues stimulate interest in an artist and lead to more concert performances, while the repertory ensembles stimulate more reissues. Much attention in jazz is focused on what has been accomplished, not on what is happening now. It remains to be seen how this preoccupation will affect the second century of jazz.

Jazz Pedagogy

The growth of **jazz pedagogy**—the teaching of jazz and jazz improvisation—over the past three decades has been astonishing. Jazz education has become firmly established as an important part of the musical curriculum in higher education. The College Music Society currently lists about 1,400 colleges and universities that offer studies in jazz and indicates thirty-three schools with graduate degrees in jazz studies.

The Berklee College of Music, the University of North Texas, Indiana University, and the University of Miami were among the first institutions to offer degrees in jazz performance. Music conservatories, such as the Eastman School of Music and the New England Conservatory, also became training grounds for aspiring jazz musicians. Conservatories in Europe, such as the Amsterdam Conservatory, offer jazz programs.

More than 70 percent of the nation's 30,000 junior and senior high schools offered at least one big-band or jazz ensemble by 1980.

Since the 1970s, educators such as Jerry Coker, David Baker, and Jamie Aebersold have established clinics and summer camps and published a wide array of books and practice methods for up-and-coming players. The International Association for Jazz Education (IAJE, formerly the National Association of Jazz Educators) was founded in 1968 and flourished for four decades before the organization declared bankruptcy in 2008. Stepping into the shoes of the IAJE is the Jazz Education Network (JEN), whose first conference took place in 2010. According to its mission statement, the group is dedicated to "building the jazz arts community by advancing education, promoting performance and developing new audiences." The proliferation of jazz websites over the past several decades further contributes to the enterprise of jazz pedagogy.

Jazz Repertory

The appearance of a book in 1984 by Grover Sales called *Jazz: America's Classical Music* speaks of the impetus of the jazz repertory movement. The idea of jazz as American classical music is not new. Indeed, U.S. violinist Misha Elman claimed as far back as 1922 that in Europe jazz had "become known as the American classical music."[1] But the difference between current times and the 1920s is that older jazz has now become the preoccupation of major performance organizations, whereas before it was not.

Interestingly, stride pianist and composer James P. Johnson predicted this practice in 1947 when he wrote that "jazz musicians of the future will have to be able to play all different kinds of jazz—in all its treatments—just like the classical musician who, in one concert, might range from Bach to Copland."[2]

The idea that jazz should be appreciated and studied alongside the history of Western concert music has generated controversy. Some have argued that such a practice demeans jazz—that by calling it "classical" we are somehow evaluating it through aesthetic and formal criteria developed for European music. Others have countered by claiming that jazz must be appreciated on the same level as European music but not judged by the same aesthetic criteria.

These concerns have helped spark the jazz repertory movement, which is devoted to re-creating older jazz styles and the masterpieces of earlier eras. For example, the Lincoln Center Jazz Orchestra in New York has performed much of the music of major jazz figures at its Jazz at Lincoln Center concerts. Composer and conductor Gunther Schuller has also played a pivotal role in transcribing, performing, and promoting the music of Scott Joplin, Jelly Roll Morton, Duke Ellington, and others. By publishing transcriptions and edited editions of important

jazz artists, recent jazz scholarship also supports this historical focus.

Of the nation's repertory jazz ensembles, the two most influential are the Lincoln Center Jazz Orchestra (associated with Jazz at Lincoln Center) and the Smithsonian Jazz Masterworks Orchestra in Washington, DC. During the 1990s Jon Faddis (b. 1953) also directed the now-discontinued Carnegie Hall Jazz Band, which was a third important group. Although the Carnegie Hall Jazz Band was technically a repertory orchestra, the group premiered numerous new works. Nor did Faddis want to perform older music exactly as it was played previously; as he pointed out, "One of our goals is to try and do the classical jazz repertoire in our own way."[3]

The Smithsonian Jazz Masterworks Orchestra was founded by Gunther Schuller and David Baker, a jazz trombonist who has taught at Indiana University for many years. It is associated with the National Museum of American History and was established in 1990 by an act of Congress in recognition of jazz in American culture. Baker generally uses a twenty-year benchmark in choosing works for programming—that is, any music played should be at least twenty years old so that its historical significance and musical value are reasonably clear.

The best-known repertory organization by far is Jazz at Lincoln Center, which appears often on national radio and television. The director, Wynton Marsalis, is undoubtedly the most visible jazz artist today. The program has enjoyed astounding success: beginning with three concerts in 1987, the program soon became a department at Lincoln Center, and then in 1996 it became a full-fledged member of the arts consortium, equal in stature to the New York Philharmonic and the Metropolitan Opera. In 1998 Jazz at Lincoln Center announced the creation of a new concert space that would include a 1,100-seat auditorium and other performance spaces, as well as office suites and rehearsal rooms. This space opened in 2004 to critical acclaim.

Jazz at Lincoln Center has benefited immensely from the work of its former executive director, Rob Gibson, and writers Stanley Crouch and Albert Murray, but no one has contributed more to its success than Marsalis, who has sought to identify and promote a canon of jazz masterpieces. In making Jazz at Lincoln Center an expression of his musical personality and interests, Marsalis is perhaps the primary spokesperson for the traditionalist point of view.

Wynton Marsalis

Wynton Marsalis embodies many of the jazz traditionalist values of the eighties and nineties. Many jazz musicians have cited him as a primary catalyst responsible for the resurgence of jazz since the eighties. Born in New Orleans in 1961, at an early age Marsalis showed extraordinary talent as a trumpeter, in both the European classical tradition and jazz. His father, Ellis Marsalis, is a professional jazz pianist and a prominent educator, and his older brother Branford is a well-known saxophonist.

Wynton Marsalis's talent became clear at an early age. He attended the Juilliard School of Music briefly but dropped out in 1980 to join Art Blakey's Jazz Messengers. He subsequently toured with Miles Davis's brilliant 1960s rhythm section of Herbie Hancock, Ron Carter, and Tony Williams. This association led to his first album as a leader, *Wynton Marsalis* (1981). In 1984 Marsalis became the first musician to win Grammy awards in both classical and jazz categories.

In 1991 Marsalis was named artistic director of Jazz at Lincoln Center. He has filled this position capably, fostering a greater appreciation of the music. He was featured prominently in the Ken Burns multiepisode documentary *Jazz*, which was first broadcast on PBS in January 2001. Not everyone has agreed with Marsalis's protraditionalist point of view, yet there is no denying the positive effect he is having on the appreciation of jazz.

Lincoln Center Jazz Orchestra with Wynton Marsalis, *Blood on the Fields,* "Work Song (Blood on the Fields)" (1994)

Despite his rise to prominence as a trumpet player, Marsalis is focusing more and more on composition. His earliest pieces followed a postbop and modal style, but he moved away from this direction as his interests turned to earlier jazz. For example, in 1987 he wrote a song called "In the Afterglow," which appeared on the album *Marsalis Standard Time*, volume 1. About this composition Marsalis comments:

That was the first time I wrote something with a certain type of traditional [chord] progression. Before that, I would write stuff that was modal, with no chords on it. But "In the Afterglow" got me to try to break out of writing the typical type of New York–scene tune and trying to experiment with form, with modulations, with developing themes in different keys, with different grooves…. That's when my [composed] music really started to evolve.[4]

After this point Marsalis began incorporating earlier jazz traditions, as his 1989 album *The Majesty of the Blues* testified. His jazz-roots evolution continued with such albums as *Soul Gestures in Southern Blue* (1991), *Blue Interlude* (1992), and *In This House, On This Morning* (1994), the last a large-scale work based on a traditional Baptist church service.

Marsalis's extended oratorio, *Blood on the Fields*, was his first composition for large ensemble and included a libretto by Marsalis. It premiered in 1994 and in 1997 became the first jazz composition to win the Pulitzer Prize for music. The work examines American slavery and

its aftermath. As a result of Marsalis's award, the Pulitzer Prize in music is now offered for large-scale works of any musical genre, whereas the Pulitzer had previously been restricted to concert music. (In 2007 Ornette Coleman was the second jazz artist to be awarded the competitive Pulitzer Prize.)

Above all, *Blood on the Fields* reveals Marsalis's ambitions to create large-scale pieces in the Duke Ellington tradition. Indeed, Marsalis credits Ellington's *Black, Brown and Beige* as a precedent for his composition and has frequently cited Ellington as his primary compositional inspiration.

A 1989 photograph of Wynton Marsalis. Despite his Grammy awards for jazz and classical music, as well as his Pulitzer Prize, Marsalis may be most widely known for his work promoting music education, his commentary on the Ken Burns Jazz series on PBS, and his work promoting the rebirth of music in post-Katrina New Orleans.

Ken Frankling/Bettmann/Corbis

LISTENING GUIDE
"Express Crossing"

Track 56

Wynton Marsalis Ensemble: "Express Crossing" (Marsalis), from *Jazz: Six Syncopated Movements* (1993), *They Came to Swing*. Columbia CK 66379. New York, January 14, 1993. Wynton Marsalis, leader and trumpet; Marcus Printup, trumpet; Wycliffe Gordon, Ronald Westray, trombones; Todd Williams, tenor saxophone; Wes Anderson, alto saxophone; Kent Jordan, piccolo and flute; Victor Goines, baritone saxophone; Eric Reed, piano; Reginald Veal, bass; Herlin Riley, drums; Robert Sadin, conductor.

The Main Point   "Express Crossing" is from the larger dance work *Jazz: Six Syncopated Movements*, written for the New York City Ballet. The live performance analyzed here is highly spirited and reveals a composer with a fertile imagination that blends influences ranging from early jazz, to Ellington, to contemporary modernism. The piece can be compared, for example, with Ellington's "Daybreak Express" (1933), a well-known jazz depiction of a train. Though Marsalis is at heart a traditionalist, this piece can be called postmodern in its blending of disparate styles.

Section I—AA, irregular 8 bars repeated, at tempo I

0:00   After three dissonant chords serving to "start the train," the rhythm begins in a complex first section in F major. For the first two bars, the trombones play on-the-beat quarter notes, but an eighth rest at the top of the third bar pushes the quarter notes off the beat. The fourth bar is in 9/8, which serves to bring the quarter notes back on the beat. (Compare Robert Sadin's comment in the main discussion.)

             For the last part of the first A, the alto and tenor saxophones trade rapid quintuplets followed by a "train whistle" honk in the tenor to end the part. Despite the rhythmic irregularities, the basic feel of part A is that of an eight-bar thematic statement.

0:15   Part A is then repeated.

Section II—B, irregular 9 bars, at tempo I

0:27   The B part maintains the up-tempo drive of section I. Its nine bars are punctuated by a 7/8 fourth bar and a 7/8 ninth bar. Again, the odd bars serve to turn the beat around.

Section III—C, 4 bars in 4/4, at tempo II

0:40   The tempo changes abruptly for four bars. Amid train whistles and honks, the piccolo occasionally interjects the chromatic idea heard in the A section. There is also a new syncopated motive played in lower-register trumpets and alto and baritone saxophones.

Section IV—D, 32 bars in 4/4 as 16 + 16, at tempo I

0:48   A return to the hectic tempo of sections I and II. The sixteenth-note idea is developed in the piccolo, alto, and tenor into a perpetual motion of sixteenth notes. The bass walks in double time. The brass punctuate with sharp chords and occasionally sustain longer chords with glissandi and falloffs. The last two bars of the first half feature a break with wah-wah chords in the brass.

1:10   The wah-wah chords continue into the second sixteen bars as the sixteenth notes in the winds return. The harmonies of the D section are based on the Dixieland classic "Tiger Rag."

Section V—D, 32 bars in 4/4, at tempo I; Marsalis trumpet solo

1:33   Using the "Tiger Rag" chord progression of part D, Marsalis offers a virtuosic muted trumpet solo. Interestingly, the solo is based on bebop-style chromatic lines. The ensemble backs Marsalis with punctuated chords.

1:52–1:54   Bars 15 and 16 are a break for Marsalis.

2:14–2:16   Bars 31 and 32 are also a break for the ensemble to introduce the next section.

Section VI—D, 32 bars in 4/4, at tempo I

2:17   The ensemble returns for a written-out piccolo solo that alternates in turn with Marsalis's (now open) trumpet, honks, brass punctuation and wah-wah chords, and a short bass solo. The final two bars again serve as a break for the ensemble to introduce the next section.

Interlude—3 bars in 2/4 and 1 bar in 4/4, at tempo I

3:01   The piano repeats the quintuplet runs first heard in the alto and the tenor at the end of section I. The D bass note at the end of the interlude signals the new key.

Section VII—E, 22 bars in 4/4 + 1 extra beat, at tempo I

3:04   This new section changes key from F major to D major and is largely a duet featuring counterpoint between Marsalis's muted trumpet and the flute. The rhythm continues, and the ensemble punctuates with chords. The last two bars (plus one beat) are a break for the ensemble that combines hints of D major and the original key of F major.

Section VIII—A, 4 bars in 4/4, at tempo I

3:35   This section recalls the opening A material, combined with the running sixteen-note idea in the flutes. The trombones, alternating notes, speed up the rhythm of the alternation. The alto and the tenor alternate the quintuplets at the end of the section. This section is in G, however, rather than F of the original part A.

Section IX—F, 32 bars in 4/4 at tempo III; 2 beats clipped from the last bar

3:46   The mood completely changes as this section features new material in a slower 4/4 swing tempo. The key of G remains from the preceding section. The "Tiger Rag" layout remains roughly as the thirty-two bars divided into a 16 + 16, although the chords are modified.

Section X—A, irregular 8 bars

4:45   In a reprise of section I, A returns. The last couple of beats are clipped from the alto-tenor quintuplet alteration. The piece ends abruptly.

Listen to this music in an animated Active Listening Guide available at the text website.

Marsalis goes beyond traditionalism, however, in works such as "Express Crossing." This piece represents quintessential **postmodernism**, an imaginative collage of elements that spans twentieth-century jazz and concert music. These elements include the following:

▶ Modernist dissonance

▶ Modernist irregular time signatures

▶ Modernist tempo changes

▶ Dixieland harmonic progressions

▶ Train simulations that recall early jazz and boogie-woogie blues

▶ Bebop-style improvisation

Postmodernism is an attitude toward art and culture that has become common since the 1970s. It disavows some of the cerebral, audience-distancing tenets of modernism and replaces them with a freewheeling conception of culture. Some postmodernist practices do the following:

▶ Blend styles and cultures

▶ Forgo structural unity as a necessity for art

▶ Incorporate older styles and genres

▶ Project an ironic, even cynical conception of art and expression

▶ Break down barriers between popular and fine art

Robert Sadin, who conducted the piece, compares it to composer Igor Stravinsky's *Pulcinella*, a work that similarly weaves in earlier musical elements. Sadin summarizes the impact of "Express Crossing":

> Conducting "Express Crossing" for me was an experience very similar in feeling to conducting Stravinsky's *Pulcinella*. Although Wynton's borrowings are less literal than Stravinsky's, there is a kindred sense of respecting and at the same time revisiting and even refreshing the past.
>
> The blending of elements of Ellington's train music, of Kansas City shuffle, with a sense of the unexpected rhythmic flavor is very characteristic of Wynton (the irregular meters at the beginning, which have the effect of turning the beat around). All of this makes for a very exhilarating musical experience.
>
> Characteristic of Marsalis is that although with the exception of a few solos (and the rhythm section, of course), the music is entirely written out, and yet the players are expected to bring a great deal of personal color and imagination to their parts while also executing the not inconsiderable technical difficulties.[5]

Marsalis's expectation that individual musicians will contribute "personal color and imagination to their parts" recalls the bandleading techniques of Duke Ellington. Clearly, Ellington has provided Marsalis with a potent role model. In a *New York Times* article celebrating the Duke Ellington centennial in 1999, Marsalis described what he admires most about how Ellington handled his own career:

> After his [Ellington's] initial fame, he could easily have escaped into the art world of the "serious composer" and created some very interesting and tongue-twisting theories about harmony and what-not. He could have retreated to the university to rail bitterly against the establishment while creating a distinguished body of work that ran people out of the concert hall. Or he could have become a tired imitator of pop trends, which have proved to be the creative graveyard for so many jazz musicians. He didn't.[6]

The description seems to apply to Marsalis as well. He seems to be patterning both his jazz career and his musical values after Ellington. With the international platform provided by Jazz at Lincoln Center and its ties to public television and other prominent forums, it is likely that Wynton Marsalis—as both a bandleader and a spokesperson—will remain among the most significant jazz artists in the decades to come.

The Blakey Alumni

In addition to the repertory movement, there has been a significant resurgence of tradition-minded players since the fusion developments of the 1970s. The traditionalists have in many ways rejected fusion in either its commercial or its avant-garde legacies. Some traditionalists, such as Marsalis, have returned to classic jazz for their inspiration. Most of the others look back to the bebop or the hard bop of the 1950s. Marsalis first gained national recognition as a member of the Art Blakey Quintet; many keepers of the hard bop flame since 1980 also include those who first gained attention playing with Blakey.

Even in the 1950s, drummer Art Blakey showed a knack for hiring musicians who would go on to form significant groups of their own and establish a major presence in jazz. The finest players from Blakey's early bands included Horace Silver, Kenny Dorham, Wayne Shorter, Benny Golson, Hank Mobley, Lee Morgan, Freddie Hubbard, and Cedar Walton. Retaining his traditional hard bop orientation and instrumentation through the 1980s, Blakey was something of a university for up-and-coming jazz players, providing them with a rich environment for musical growth. Membership in Blakey's band constantly shifted, but it allowed his later sidemen to trace their lineage back to the hard bop roots of the fifties and sixties. Blakey's sidemen—in particular, "Blakey's class of 1980–89"[7]—played a significant role in the hard bop renaissance of the 1980s and 1990s.

During his stint with Blakey from 1980 to 1982, Wynton Marsalis and his brother Branford helped elevate the group's visibility. After they departed, they were replaced by nineteen-year-old trumpeter Terence Blanchard and saxophonist Donald Harrison.

Also working as a team through the 1980s, Blanchard and Harrison recorded five albums as coleaders. Blanchard has also maintained an active career as a film composer: his score for *Mo' Better Blues* was nominated for a Grammy in 1990. Harrison, on the other hand, has lately been working with merging mainstream jazz with funk, which he calls "nouveau swing."

Blanchard was replaced in Blakey's band by Wallace Roney, whose often spare and thoughtful playing contrasted with many of the busier hard bop trumpeters. Roney's visibility was enhanced considerably after he was chosen to perform with Miles Davis at a tribute sponsored by the Montreux Jazz Festival in July 1991.

Alto saxophonist Bobby Watson (b. 1953) served as music director for Blakey from 1977 to 1981. Watson earned a music degree from the University of Miami and then went to New York in 1976. In the past two decades, Watson has recorded more than a dozen albums as a leader.

Watson and Harrison are not alone among the fine altoists who have worked with Blakey. For instance, Kenny Garrett is one of the most accomplished players on the scene. In addition to Blakey, Garrett has also performed with the Mercer Ellington Orchestra, Freddie Hubbard, and Miles Davis. Born in 1961, Garrett worked with Davis through the late eighties for some five years and served as Davis's personal assistant.

Other Traditionalists

Tradition-minded musicians abound. Although it is impossible to compare and contrast all of today's most important artists, the following table surveys some of the most notable ones currently working.

SAXOPHONISTS		
NAME	*INFLUENCES*	*LIFE AND WORK*
Joe Lovano (b. 1952) Tenor saxophone	John Coltrane	■ 2013 recording *Cross Culture* with his quintet Us Five includes bassist Esperanza Spalding. ■ Collaborated with Gunther Schuller on *Rush Hour* (1995), an album featuring elements of third-stream music.
Joshua Redman (b. 1969) Tenor saxophone	Son of saxophonist Dewey Redman	■ Successful records have led to some criticism for playing "accessible" music. ■ 2013 recording *Walking Shadows* includes orchestral ensemble and pianist Brad Mehldau.
James Carter (b. 1969) All saxophones and bass clarinet	Mixes both traditional and free jazz elements	■ Mixes inside and outside playing in a popular blend. ■ Anything-goes approach shows influence of postmodernism.
Phil Woods (b. 1931) Alto saxophone	Charlie Parker	■ Since 1974 has worked in a quartet that included bassist Steve Gilmore and drummer Bill Goodwin.
Charles McPherson (b. 1939) Alto saxophone	Charlie Parker	■ First worked with Charles Mingus. ■ *A Tribute to Charlie Parker* (2001) includes compositions associated with Parker.

TRUMPETERS		
NAME	*INFLUENCES*	*LIFE AND WORK*
Tom Harrell (b. 1946)	Bebop with more-modern harmonies	■ Worked with Stan Kenton, Woody Herman, and Horace Silver through the 1970s before moving to New York. ■ *Play of Light* (1982) established him as a significant composer-arranger-leader.
Nicolas Payton (b. 1973)	Fats Navarro, Clifford Brown	■ Won Grammy award for his collaboration with trumpeter Doc Cheatham (nearly seven decades his senior) in 1998. ■ Regular soloist at Jazz at Lincoln Center. ■ 2004 CD *Sonic Trance* incorporates hip-hop grooves.
Roy Hargrove (b. 1969)	Clifford Jordan, Jackie McLean, Slide Hampton, Jon Faddis, Freddie Hubbard	■ First championed by Wynton Marsalis. ■ Traditionalist, with an interest in world music and funk.
Ryan Kisor (b. 1973)	Bebop	■ Won Monk Competition in 1990. ■ Worked with various bands including the Lincoln Center Jazz Orchestra and the Mingus Big Band.

PIANISTS		
NAME	*INFLUENCES*	*LIFE AND WORK*
Kenny Barron (b. 1943)	Thelonious Monk, McCoy Tyner	■ Performed with various groups as a sideman from the 1960s through the 1980s. ■ Founder and member of the group Sphere, honoring Thelonious Monk and his music. ■ Jazz educator at Rutgers University since 1973.

Marcus Roberts (b. 1963)	Early jazz pianists from Jelly Roll Morton through stride and bop stylists	■ Championed by Wynton Marsalis, with whom he recorded and performed from 1985 to 1991. ■ Has developed jazz interpretations of Scott Joplin's ragtime works, Gershwin's *Rhapsody in Blue*, and James P. Johnson's *Yamekraw*. ■ Teaches at Florida State University
Cyrus Chestnut (b. 1963)	Gospel	■ Noted for blending jazz improvisation with gospel stylings and rhythms.
Fred Hersch (b. 1955)	Bill Evans, Keith Jarrett, European classical traditions	■ Works in trio formats and has recorded a number of solo jazz piano albums.
Jacky Terrasson (b. 1965)	Bill Evans	■ Worked as accompanist for Betty Carter. ■ Likes to work in trio format pioneered by Bill Evans
Brad Mehldau (b. 1970)	Kenny Werner, European classical traditions	■ *Art of the Trio* recordings draw on harmonies and arrangements in Bill Evans's style.
Eliane Elias (b. 1960)	Brazilian jazz	■ Mixes Brazilian rhythms and harmonies with traditional jazz repertory.

OTHER INSTRUMENTS

NAME	INFLUENCES	LIFE AND WORK
Joey DeFrancesco (b. 1971) Organ	Jimmy Smith, Groove Holmes, Jimmy McGriff	■ Discovered at age sixteen by Miles Davis, with whom he toured and recorded. ■ Plays in hard bop and funky jazz style.
Steve Turre (b. 1948) Trombone and conch shells	Eclectic	■ Originally with rock band Santana in 1970. ■ Has recorded with many leading jazz musicians and bands.
Mark Whitfield (b. 1967) Guitar	George Benson	■ Worked with a variety of bands and styles, from pop-fusion to traditional postbop.

VOCALISTS

NAME	INFLUENCES	LIFE AND WORK
Betty Carter (1929–1998)	Bebop	■ Major vocal stylist since the 1940s. ■ Mentor to dozens of young musicians.
Bobby McFerrin (b. 1950)	Jazz, opera, pop, rock	■ Widely versatile, able to produce many vocal sounds. ■ Multitracks elaborate arrangements of standards and his own compositions.
Cassandra Wilson (b. 1955)	Sixties rock, postbop jazz, Betty Carter, Delta blues	■ Popular singer who has recorded works not normally associated with jazz, including songs by country legend Hank Williams and by the pop group the Monkees.
Diana Krall (b. 1965)	Nat Cole	■ Canadian-born singer in straight-ahead repertory from American popular song.
Kevin Mahogany (b. 1958)	Blues	■ Worked on a number of film soundtracks for Clint Eastwood.

VOCALISTS		
NAME	*INFLUENCES*	*LIFE AND WORK*
Kurt Elling (b. 1967)	Mark Murphy, Tony Bennett, pop-jazz standards	■ Applies vocalese to solos by Coltrane and others.
Norah Jones (b. 1979)	Etta James, Sade, Nick Drake, soul, American popular song	■ Straight-ahead repertory from country and pop-folk.
Diane Reeves (b. 1950)	Sarah Vaughan, Billie Holiday, Carmen McRae	■ Sarah Vaughan tribute recording *The Calling* won Grammy award in 2001.

Ghost bands are groups whose founding leaders have died but who continue to travel and work under new direction.

Many fine pianists have also been associated with Blakey. Among the most distinguished is James Williams (1951–2004), who, like Bobby Watson, was with Blakey from 1977 to 1981, and Mulgrew Miller (1955–2013), from Greenwood, Mississippi.

Big Bands

Many of the big bands today are known as **ghost bands**—groups that tour and sometimes record even though the founders who established the bands are no longer alive. There is a long tradition of ghost bands. The most important early ghost band was the one associated with Glenn Miller (discussed in Chapter 6), which continued for many years under such leaders as Ray McKinley.

Of the current ghost bands, perhaps the most important is the Count Basie Orchestra, which has been led by such fine talents as Thad Jones, Frank Foster, and more recently Grover Mitchell. Some of the surviving players who worked with Basie himself are members. Another notable ghost band featuring the works of Duke Ellington was led by Ellington's son, Mercer Ellington, until his death in 1996.

A fascinating big band that unites a creative modern unit, a traditional ghost band, and a repertory ensemble is the Mingus Big Band, which continues the legacy of the bassist and composer. Because Mingus never led a big band, the players often contribute arrangements. Andy McKee, the band's bassist and one of its musical directors, points out:

> [Mingus] expected musicians to find their own paths through his work. That spirit of improvisation and freedom is entirely characteristic of Mingus's method. This often will determine who will work out well in the band and who won't. A player may be a tremendous musician but needs more structure to frame his work. This band needs musicians who know how to frame themselves. That's my understanding of how Mingus's original groups worked.[8]

The Mingus Big Band and a smaller ensemble, the Mingus Dynasty, were organized by Sue Mingus, the bass player's widow.

Toshiko Akiyoshi has been one of the most successful big-band composers in jazz for many years. She was born in China in 1929 and began studying jazz in Japan in 1947. Encouraged by Oscar Peterson, she studied at Boston's Berklee College of Music during the late 1950s and worked briefly with bassist Charles Mingus. In 1973 she and reed player Lew Tabackin started a big band in Los Angeles, which became one of the most successful groups

A young Toshiko Akiyoshi. Born in Dairen, Manchuria, Akiyoshi began studying jazz in Japan in 1947.

of the seventies and early eighties. Her writing style can be traced to Gil Evans and Thad Jones; it incorporates considerable modernism and occasional influences of Japanese music. After leading a big band for thirty years, she retired it in October 2003 with a Carnegie Hall performance of her work "Hiroshima: Rising from the Abyss," a tone poem that dealt with the aftermath of the atomic bomb that was dropped on Hiroshima in 1945. The composition reflected her experiences as a daughter of Japanese parents living in Manchuria.

Whereas Akiyoshi has been associated with a post-bebop musical vocabulary, composer-arranger Carla Bley (b. 1938) has ventured memorably into the avant-garde. She has written for George Russell, Jimmy Giuffre, and Charlie Haden's Liberation Music Orchestra. She is perhaps best known for *Escalator over the Hill*, a jazz opera completed in 1971.

One of the most visible of the current big bands is led by composer-arranger Maria Schneider. Born in 1960 in Windom, Minnesota, Schneider studied at the University of Minnesota and the Eastman School of Music, and is one of the distinctive recent voices in jazz composition. She led the Maria Schneider Jazz Orchestra at New York's Visiones Jazz Club during the 1990s. After graduating from Eastman, Schneider studied with composer and trombonist Bob Brookmeyer. In 1985 she became Gil Evans's assistant and in 1988 started her first band.

Schneider's first album, *Evanescence* (1994), established her reputation as innovative yet steeped in the tradition of Gil Evans and other arranger-composers such as Brookmeyer. Schneider's second album, *Coming About* (1996), was even more successful; her third album, *Allégresse*, was released in 2000. Schneider brings to her work a sophisticated compositional palette derived from jazz and Western concert music, and she creates an excellent balance between composition and improvisation.

Photo by Lourdes Delgado; Courtesy of Maria Schneider

Steeped in the tradition of composer-arranger Gil Evans, bandleader Maria Schneider is renowned for her subtle and sophisticated compositions.

More recently Schneider began marketing her own recordings and provided for limited release her CDs *Concert in the Garden* (2004) and *Sky Blue* (2007).

LISTENING GUIDE
"Hang Gliding" (excerpt)

Track 57

Maria Schneider Orchestra: "Hang Gliding" (Schneider), from *Allégresse*. Enja ENJ-9393 2. New York, January 2000. Schneider, leader and conductor; Tim Ries, soprano saxophone, flute; Charles Pillow, alto and soprano saxophones, flute; Rich Perry, tenor saxophone; Rick Margitza, tenor saxophone; Scott Robinson, baritone saxophone; Tony Kadleck, trumpet and flugelhorn; Greg Gisbert, trumpet and flugelhorn; Laurie Frink, trumpet and flugelhorn; Ingrid Jensen, trumpet and flugelhorn; Dave Ballou, trumpet and flugelhorn; Keith O'Quinn, trombone; Rock Ciccarone, trombone; Larry Farrell, trombone; George Flynn, bass trombone; Ben Monder, acoustic guitar; Frank Kimbrough, piano; Tony Scherr, bass; Tim Horner, drums; Jeff Ballard, percussion.

The Main Point   About the work, Schneider wrote in the liner notes, "'Hang Gliding' is entirely about movement, an impression of my experience of hang gliding in Rio de Janeiro: the suspension, grace, lift and acceleration accompanied by the rush of apprehension and exhilaration." The composition richly conveys that sense of floating and flying, through the use of mixed meter, a rich array of instrumental combinations, dynamic pacing, and a colorful harmonic language. Rather than based upon a chorus structure, the form consistently evolves while making use of earlier melodic ideas, and avoids consistent four- and eight-bar divisions. (The sectional divisions in the following discussion correspond generally to Schneider's placement of measure numbers in her notated score.)

The excerpt here starts softly and sparsely and builds to a gentle climax, before moving to an eerily still and spare flugelhorn solo. In contrast to the Basie and Ellington big bands discussed in Chapter 10, which maintain a swinging 4/4 ambience, Schneider's work uses an unusual meter. It is probably easiest to count the meter as an alternation of groupings of six and five beats. (Schneider's score indicates the measures as 3 + 3 + 3 + 2 beats.) The irregular meter recalls that heard in Dave Brubeck's "Blue Rondo à la Turk" (Track 35). Such irregular meters suggest a modernist orientation, one that seeks alternatives to the more conventional 4/4 meter. The complete performance of "Hang Gliding" lasts over thirteen minutes.

Introduction

0:00   The rhythm section provides the four-bar introduction (playing twice the 6 + 5 grouping). The piano and guitar play a syncopated figure. Rather than keeping strict time, the drummer plays cymbal rolls, perhaps an evocation of a sense of weightless floating. The piece begins in the modality of A♭ Lydian—of all the diatonic modes the Lydian contains the highest number of raised pitches, contributing to the sense of upward lift.

Section 1—14 bars as 5 + 5 + 4

0:08   The soprano saxophone begins quietly with a spacious melody, initially consisting of individual pitches or pairs of pitches, accompanied by the trombones.

Section 2—14 bars as 5 + 5 + 4

0:38   The melody becomes more active. Toward the end of the first five-bar subsection, the saxophones play an ascending melody that leads to a high sustained pitch, enhancing the sense of upward motion. The drummer begins to keep time at the end of Section 2 (1:05).

Section 3—12 bars as 7 + 5

1:10   The drums maintain the time here, as the instruments become more active. Toward the end of the seven-bar section, listen as the horns again play an upward moving melody that leads to a high sustained pitch: here this pitch holds as the harmony shifts underneath at the beginning of the next five-bar section (1:25), creating a dazzling change of harmonic color.

Section 4—16 bars as 8 + 8

1:35   The passage becomes even more driving as the trumpets and reeds create a dialogue. During the second eight-bar passage (1:52), the horn writing becomes more syncopated and involved. Both the harmonic progression and the overall shape of the melody ascend, leading to the climactic section.

Section 5—21 bars as 5 + 5 + 6

2:09   The climactic section begins with the horns begin playing together in a dense harmony. The melody during the first five-bar subsection recalls that heard at the outset of Section 2. During the final six-bar subsection, the meter regularizes to consistent groupings of six beats. Here the horns begin echoing the syncopated figure stated by the piano and guitar.

Flugelhorn solo

2:44   The flugelhorn solo, played by Greg Gisbert, begins quietly, as the drummer returns to playing cymbal rolls and the band provides sparse accompaniment. The piano refers to the syncopated figure it played throughout the earlier sections. At 3:10 listen for the colorful chordal splashes supplied by the horns, which include muted trumpets. Following a mysterious accompaniment in dialogue with the flugelhorn (3:25), the horns drop out, leaving the rhythm section to accompany the soloist, creating a remarkable effect of solitary tranquility. The excerpt fades here.

Listen to this music in an animated Active Listening Guide available at the text website.

The Popular Connection

Another side to jazz is the development of several popular forms stemming from advances in digital technology. Since the 1980s, smooth jazz and acid jazz have carried on the legacy of fusion. Meanwhile other popular interests have arisen as well, such as the retro fad neo-swing, which reflects an interest in a largely acoustic sound.

Digital Technology

In the early 1980s, the jazz-fusion music of the 1970s began adopting new technology. In particular, synthesizers became largely digital, and analog instruments took on a vintage status. Synthesizers were combined with the increasingly popular personal computer. The convenience of storing data on a computer increased the variety, complexity, and interaction of digitally synthesized sounds. Computer memory also enabled the mixing of multiple tracks of digitally produced sound, simulating a multitrack tape recorder. The technology that enabled computers to communicate with synthesizers became known as **MIDI**, for **Musical Instrument Digital Interface**.

MIDI technology is a fundamental part of the work of pop-jazz and avant-garde artists. In general, the widespread use of electronics and MIDI often distinguishes these artists from the traditionalists discussed earlier in this chapter, who tend to rely on acoustic instruments. For example, MIDI-controlled synthesizers and samplers may wholly or in part provide a background texture for the principal voices or instruments in an ensemble; or percussionists or other players may enhance the MIDI textures by interacting with preprogrammed synthesizer textures. This kind of work may take place in both live and recorded performances but is obviously easier to control in the recording studio. Smooth jazz has made extensive use of MIDI technology. More recently, computer technologies include composition and notation programs as well as sound sample libraries, allowing musicians to work directly with their computers and bypass MIDI technologies.

Smooth Jazz

Smooth jazz has been called "the jazz of the '90s"[9] by its advocates, while its detractors describe it as "smooth like a lobotomy flattens out the ridges on a brain."[10] None can deny its popularity. Radio stations that broadcast the format are among the most listened to in a given metropolitan area. In this sense smooth jazz can be compared with the wildly popular swing music of the late 1930s and the

> Detractors of smooth jazz describe it as "smooth like a lobotomy flattens out the ridges on a brain."

early 1940s: for perhaps the second time in its history, a jazz style can be looked on as a type of mainstream U.S. popular music.

Many artists have provided consistently interesting performances of popular-jazz fusion. For example, some of the recent work of guitarist George Benson (b. 1943) has been receiving smooth-jazz airplay. Benson began his career playing funky/soul jazz in organ trios (see Chapter 10), and he recorded with Miles Davis in the sixties. His playing always combined a blues-based approach with agile bebop phrasing, even after he released more-commercial recordings, such as his 1976 *Breezin'* and his 1980 *Give Me the Night*. His 2004 CD *Irreplaceable* has been featured prominently on national smooth-jazz playlists.

The most commercially successful smooth-jazz artist is Kenny G. His commercial recordings have generated controversy among jazz aficionados and led to a heated

---

MIDI is an acronym for **Musical Instrument Digital Interface**. This standard language allows computers to control synthesizers or samplers.

LISTENING GUIDE

"Softly, As in a Morning Sunrise"

Track 58

George Benson: "Softly, As in a Morning Sunrise" (Romberg-Hammerstein), from *Irreplaceable*. GRP B0000599-02. Sherman Oaks, California; Phoenix, Arizona; and New York, 2004. Benson, guitar; Herman Jackson, keyboards; Roberto Vally, bass; Paulinho Da Costa, percussion; Paul Brown, drum programming.

The Main Point   "Softly, As in a Morning Sunrise" shows a smooth-jazz treatment of a 32-bar jazz standard. Benson adheres to jazz tradition by playing the melody, improvising, and returning to the melody. The accompaniment is not driving and is relatively understated. Critics of smooth jazz might argue that because the drums are programmed, the accompaniment is predictable and lacks spontaneous musical interaction between the soloist and the rhythm section. Nevertheless, the recording shows to fine advantage Benson's superb playing. His use of octaves, chordal textures, and dazzling runs reveals the influence of jazz guitarist Wes Montgomery (compare with Track 52).

Introduction and head (AABA)

0:00   During the introduction the bass drum, percussion, and keyboards set the tempo and establish the groove.

0:08   The bass enters, and Benson plays the melody of the first two A sections in octaves on the guitar.

0:37   Benson continues to play octaves over the B section. His statement of the melody here incorporates some improvisation. He returns to the final A section at 0:52.

Benson guitar solo—1 chorus (AAB)

1:07   Beginning his first solo chorus, Benson moves from playing octaves into improvisation on chordal textures. In the second A section (1:22), he proceeds to bluesier ideas.

1:37   In the B section, Benson plays single lines. He begins with two related ideas over the first two chords: note in the second statement his subtle slide up to the fourth note. He follows this by improvising with eighth-note triplets, and in the bridge's two-bar extension he plays a dazzling sixteenth-note run (1:54).

Reprise of melody (AA)

1:56   Benson returns to the melody, playing the A section twice in octaves. At 2:24 he plays a tag, repeating two bars from the final melodic phrase.

Benson solo over extended coda

2:30   Benson solos over repeated statements of a two-bar chord progression. He begins soloing in octaves, then returns to chordal textures. At 2:57 he begins playing single lines. Characteristic of Benson's playing, his single line ideas alternate between bluesy figures (2:57) and bebop figures (3:08), and his agility on the guitar is evident during his sixteenth-note runs. The selection fades following a call-and-response idea (3:40) that alternates a brief blues lick with a sharp chord.

 Listen to this music in an animated Active Listening Guide available at the text website.

Other Pop-Jazz Musicians

The following table summarizes the careers of popular fusion stars other than the ones already discussed in the text.

NAME	FAME	LIFE AND WORK
Chuck Mangione (b. 1940)	Trumpet	▪ "Feels So Good" (1978) was his major hit, featuring a pleasant pop-fusion groove.
Bill Frisell (b. 1951)	Guitar	▪ Use of electronic effects. ▪ Eclectic style, as shown by his country music crossover in his album *Nashville* (1997), which won the *Down Beat* "Jazz Critic's Jazz Album of the Year" award in 1998.
The Yellowjackets	Fusion band	▪ Popular, long-lived fusion band, together since the early 1980s. ▪ Plays in both electronic and acoustic styles.
Medeski Martin & Wood	Fusion band	▪ Popular funk-fusion group, particularly on college campuses. ▪ Exhibits an eclectic blend of styles, often based on funky grooves.
John Scofield (b. 1951)	Guitar	▪ Worked with Miles Davis in the eighties. ▪ Innovative guitarist whose work combines fusion and postbop jazz approaches.
Phish	Rock band	▪ Heavily into improvisation, in the tradition of the Grateful Dead.
Kenny G (b. 1956)	Saxophone	▪ The most popular of all the pop-jazz artists.
David Sanborn (b. 1945)	Saxophone	▪ Has worked with Stevie Wonder.

exchange with guitarist Pat Metheny, who severely criticized Kenny G for overdubbing himself on Louis Armstrong's earlier-recorded composition "It's a Wonderful World." Other smooth-jazz artists include Grover Washington, Charlie Hunter, Earl Klugh, Bob James, and David Sanborn. Trumpeter Chris Botti has attained significant commercial and crossover success through his recordings and performances with pop artists such as Sting and John Mayer. Along with those collaborations, Botti also regularly performs jazz standard compositions in an acoustic format.

Grover Washington, *Strawberry Moon,* "Summer Nights" (1987)

Acid Jazz and Hip Hop

A style that had a major impact on the jazz world in the 1990s is known as **acid jazz**, a fusion of jazz and hip-hop. Groups with hits include Buckshot LeFonque (featuring Branford Marsalis—the group's name comes from a pseudonym for Cannonball Adderley), Incognito, Digable

Planets, and Us3. Nurtured on the rap and hip-hop of the 1980s, the young musicians in these bands were inspired to sample jazz tracks and vamps to form the basis of their new sound. The Digable Planets won a Grammy for their 1993 single "Rebirth of Slick (Cool Like Dat)," and the music video to the single became one of the most popular MTV videos of the early 1990s.

One of the biggest acid jazz hits to date was Us3's "Cantaloop (Flip Fantasia)," from the album *Hand on the Torch*. This single consisted of a rap over samples from Herbie Hancock's "Cantaloupe Island"; it reached the Top 20 pop charts in 1994. For the remainder of the album, raps and electronic effects were introduced over samples from classic jazz recordings in an

Digable Planets, *Reachin' (A New Refutation of Time & Space),* "Rebirth of Slick (Cool Like Dat)" (1993)

Acid jazz is a fusion style that incorporates sampling of older jazz recordings, rap, and hip-hop grooves and techniques.

intriguing collage. "It's Like That," for example, included the riff of Charlie Parker's "Cool Blues" alternating with the theme of the movie *Alfie*, by Sonny Rollins. Substantial portions of the tracks included improvisation. Despite this success and others like it, by the late 1990s the future of acid jazz was unclear, with many of the earlier groups no longer producing records.

Nevertheless, some jazz musicians remain intrigued by the developments of rap and hip-hop. Players such as Herbie Hancock, Dave Douglas, and Wallace Roney have recorded and toured with turntablists, who create rhythms by scratching records with the stylus of a turntable. (Hancock's 1983 hit "Rockit" made early use of these sounds.)

Since the mid-1990s, **nu jazz** is one term that has emerged to refer to jazz-influenced music that makes use of hip-hop grooves, trance grooves, electronica, and house music. Many of these players come from Europe, including trumpeter Nils Petter Molvaer, keyboardist Bugge Wesseltoft (both from Norway), and French trumpeter Erik Truffaz.

The Mass Market: Radio and the Internet

The various types of pop-jazz share an important goal: attracting a mass market. Hence, pop-jazz must generate extensive radio airplay to boost record sales and draw in listeners for live performance. Not surprisingly, to better understand what the public wants to hear, some radio stations interested in jazz conduct in-depth studies of their listeners' preferences. In this process the program director of Seattle's KPLU, Joey Cohn, made an unsettling discovery, as Charles Levin notes here:

> Cohn's research breaks down jazz into six modes: lyrical, instrumental, driving improvisation, contemporary rhythms, vintage, swinging singers and blues. On the ratings scale, "driving improvisation was at the bottom of the list," [KXJZ Music Director Gary] Vercelli says. " 'Driving improvisation' was driving a lot of our audience away."[11]

Cohn's classifications have little to do with jazz history or stylistic congruity: they depend entirely on split-second reactions from listeners with little or no knowledge of jazz. With some radio stations testing market reactions to jazz so carefully, it seems likely that radio play for jazz will continue to feature smooth jazz and the most popular crossover styles. Radio play for a larger spectrum of jazz styles may continue to decline, although satellite radio and digital cable now offer commercial-free jazz.

Another potentially significant development in the realm of electronics has been the use of the Internet for selling music and for live broadcasts. The MP3 digital music format allows recorded music to be transferred and stored for reuse, although controversies have arisen regarding appropriate compensation for artists and record companies. Jazz clubs such as the Blue Note and the Knitting Factory in New York are also broadcasting shows from their websites. The practice of archival broadcasts has arisen as well: a venue can create a video of a performance for later broadcast over the Internet. The long-established Montreux Jazz Festival in Switzerland, for example, has been experimenting with this practice.

Neo-Swing

In a remarkable development of the later 1990s, the big-band swing sound has returned. The music has become quite popular, especially among teenagers and young people in their twenties, who have become enthusiastic about the jitterbug and the older ballroom dances. Their enthusiasm stems in part from nostalgia for the glamour of the 1930s and 1940s; for example, retro clothing styles play a big part in the revival. The music of such groups as Big Bad Voodoo Daddy and the Jet Set Six is reminiscent of forties jump-style swing, which itself was a precursor to rock and roll, rather than the more sedate, smoother sounds of many of the 1930s big bands.

Although the relationship of **neo-swing** to jazz remains controversial, the music offers a distinctive change of pace from the ubiquitous electronic ambience of popular music. Its largely acoustic sound is modernized through amplification, older swing tunes are revived in the process, and, according to journalists' reports, interest in traditional 1930s jazz recordings has been whetted among much of the audience.

A particularly successful neo-swing artist is guitarist Brian Setzer. In the late 1990s, the Brian Setzer Orchestra, a big band with standard instrumentation, was enormously popular; one of its CDs, *The Dirty Boogie* (1998), sold in quadruple-platinum figures (4 million CDs). Their live performances have attracted as many as 4,000 people.

The Avant-Garde, World Music, Crossover, and Jazz to Come

Although it seems safe to say that the principal styles of jazz—from Dixieland to swing to hard bop to fusion—will always have their fans and proponents, jazz will itself continue to evolve in the years to come. It seems likely that future developments will see change regarding such issues as the following:

▶ Greater participation of women

▶ Greater participation of artists from countries other than the United States

---

Nu jazz refers to jazz-influenced music since the mid-nineties that makes use of hip-hop grooves, trance grooves, electronica, and house music.

Neo-swing was a popular movement in the 1990s that re-created the style of the 1930s and 1940s big bands.

► The blend of jazz with music from non-Western cultures

► Crossover with other musical styles and cultures, including

　■ Popular music (such as neo-swing)

　■ Concert music (third-stream experimentation)

We conclude this chapter by looking at where these trends might go. We also mention some of the most significant artists in each area.

Jazz and Feminism

A glance back through this book shows that jazz has been a music dominated by men. Apart from vocalists (such as Ella Fitzgerald and Sarah Vaughan) or pianists and composer-arrangers (such as Lil Hardin and Mary Lou Williams), women are often absent from jazz histories. One consequence of feminism in the 1960s and 1970s has been a remarkable increase in the number of women with jazz careers. Among the important artists of our time, we have discussed composer-arrangers Toshiko Akiyoshi and Maria Schneider. Among others are violinist Regina Carter; drummers Terri Lyne Carrington, Susie Ibarra, and Cindy Blackman; pianists Geri Allen, Eliane Elias, and Renee Rosnes; saxophonist Virginia Mayhew; and trumpeter Ingrid Jensen. The Kennedy Center in Washington, DC, sponsors a Women in Jazz festival in honor of Mary Lou Williams to showcase the many fine women artists at work today.

One of the performers in the 2011 Women in Jazz Festival was bassist, vocalist, and composer Esperanza Spalding (b. 1984), who burst onto the national scene after winning the 2011 Grammy Award for Best New Artist. (She was the first jazz artist to win that award.) Originally from Portland Oregon, Spalding joined the faculty at Berklee College of Music in 2005 at the age of 20, and her recordings blend jazz, Brazilian music, and elements of hip-hop. Her 2012 album *Radio Music Society* features original compositions as well as covers of compositions by Wayne Shorter and the Beach Boys. She has recorded with diverse artists and groups such as Us Five, drummer Jack DeJohnette, and pop artist Bruno Mars. In 2013 she toured as part of an all-female jazz trio with drummer Terri Lynne Carrington and pianist Geri Allen.

Betty Carter,
Look What I Got,
"The Good Life"
(1988)

Pianist Geri Allen (b. 1957) is comfortable in both traditional and avant-garde settings and in both traditional piano trios and larger ensembles. She has also worked extensively with synthesizers and electronic media. Allen has taught jazz piano at the New England Conservatory and has recorded and performed extensively, playing with bassist Charlie Haden, drummer Paul Motian, saxophonist Ornette Coleman, and vocalist Betty Carter; she teaches in the improvisation program at the University of Michigan.

Pioneer Jane Ira Bloom (b. 1955) has been one of the first women to forge a major jazz career on an instrument other than the piano. As a soprano saxophonist, she has worked in numerous venues, most recently in a quartet. As a composer she has worked on projects with NASA and the innovative dance company Pilobolus, and she is on the faculty at the New School in New York.

The big band Diva (with the slogan "No Man's Band") contains all women. Formed in 1992, it includes drummer-lead Sherrie Maricle. The group has been getting much attention and many gigs.

Jazz Abroad

Superb non-Americans have been involved in jazz virtually since its beginnings. Earlier we discussed European enthusiasm for ragtime and how European performers such as Stéphane Grappelli and Django Reinhardt established first-rate jazz credentials as early as the late 1920s (Chapter 2). In addition, a number of U.S. jazz musicians spent extended periods living in Europe, drawn to England and the Continent by the enhanced prestige accorded jazz and jazz musicians there. African American jazz artists also noted a less blatantly racist atmosphere in Europe. Benny Carter worked in England in the 1930s, and Coleman Hawkins spent five years in Europe in the 1930s, even recording with guitarist Django Reinhardt. Saxophonist Dexter Gordon spent much of the 1960s and 1970s based in Copenhagen. Other American artists, such as Stan Getz, Chet Baker, and Steve Lacy, resided for a time in Europe.

European jazz artists left Europe, as well, making their careers in the United States by playing with established jazz musicians. For example, guitarist John McLaughlin and bassist Dave Holland both left England and began playing with Miles Davis in the late 1960s. Austrian pianist Josef Zawinul gained national attention working with Cannonball Adderley, Miles Davis, and Weather Report.

It is important to acknowledge that many European jazz artists remained in their native countries and did not move to the United States. Swiss drummer Daniel Humair performed with the European Rhythm Machine, recording with saxophonist Phil Woods in the late 1960s. Beginning in the 1960s, European participation in free jazz flourished, featuring performers such as German trombonist Albert Mangelsdorff. Free jazz has remained a potent force in European jazz over the past several decades, even as jazz in America returned to more-traditional aesthetics after the 1980s.

Contemporary Jazz Musicians from Other Countries

The following table highlights just a few of the outstanding jazz musicians from outside the United States who have claimed considerable attention and reputation since the 1980s.

SAXOPHONISTS

- **Jan Garbarek** (Norway)
- **Evan Parker** (England)

TRUMPETERS

- **Hugh Masekela** (South Africa)
- **Valery Ponomarev** (Russia)
- **Arturo Sandoval** (Cuba)
- **Tomasz Stanko** (Poland)
- **Erik Truffaz** (France)

PIANISTS

- **Eliane Elias** (Brazil)
- **Abdullah Ibrahim, a.k.a. Dollar Brand** (South Africa)
- **Adam Makowicz** (Poland)
- **Danilo Pérez** (Panama)
- **Gonzalo Rubalcaba** (Cuba)
- **Aziza Mustafa Zadeh** (Azerbaijan)

GUITARISTS

- **John McLaughlin** (England)

BASSISTS

- **Dave Holland** (England)
- **George Mraz** (Czechoslovakia)
- **Miroslav Vitous** (Czechoslovakia)

DRUMMERS/PERCUSSIONISTS

- **Trilok Gurtu** (India)
- **Manu Katché** (France)
- **Airto Moreira** (Brazil)

SINGER-SONGWRITERS

- **Gilberto Gil** (Brazil)
- **Milton Nascimento** (Brazil)
- **Flora Purim** (Brazil)

Jazz musicians hail from all corners of the globe: Canada (Oscar Peterson, Kenny Wheeler, Gil Evans, Paul Bley), Brazil (Airto, Flora Purim, Eliane Elias), South Africa (Abdullah Ibrahim), Japan (Sadao Watanabe), Cuba (Gonzalo Rubalcaba), and Norway (Jan Garbarek, Nils Petter Molvaer). Jazz remains an international phenomenon, and jazz clubs in such cities as London, Paris, Amsterdam, Prague, and Moscow provide venues for local musicians playing traditional jazz (Dixieland), bebop, and avant-garde jazz. Although most jazz histories tend to stress the music as an American phenomenon, the innovations of non-American players and composers have made and continue to make a major impact on the direction of the music.

Latin Jazz: The Afro-Cuban Tradition, The Caribbean, and Salsa

Chapter 7 discussed the relationship of Latin (Afro-Cuban) music to jazz: its rhythms appeared in ragtime and early jazz. Dizzy Gillespie's "Manteca" (Track 30) combined features of Afro-Cuban music and bebop into a hybrid sometimes called "cubop." Further, figures such as Machito (and his band the Afro-Cubans), Mario Bauza, and Tito Puente provided exciting and energizing music for dance fads such as the tango, mambo, cha-cha-cha, and rhumba.

We return to the topic here in order to explore the continuing symbiosis between Latin music and jazz. Cuban musicians such as Arturo Sandoval and Paquito D'Rivera (Track 59) emigrated to the United States and established significant careers in Latin-oriented jazz. D'Rivera, who plays alto and soprano saxophones as well as clarinet, defected from Cuba in 1981. He described his life in Cuba, his problems with the Castro regime there, and his subsequent move to the United States in a colorful autobiography entitled *My Sax Life*.

In addition to the Cuban influence, the role of other Caribbean nations is significant. In particular, a number of New York musicians of Puerto Rican ancestry, such as pianist Eddie Palmieri, contributed significantly to the development of the music in the second half of the twentieth century.

By the 1970s, Latin music came to be known under the general term of *salsa* (Spanish for "sauce"). Salsa remains wedded to its origins as dance music, and much of its excitement comes from the layers of rhythmic activity provided by the rhythm section, particularly the percussion players. The use of timbales, maracas, bongos, congas, and claves help establish the underlying groove feel of the music. The pianist often uses an accompaniment figure known as *montuno*, a two-bar (eight-beat) repeated figure with a strong rhythmic definition. The bassist often plays a particular rhythmic pattern that avoids the downbeat, and instead appears on the "and" of beat two and beat four. This pattern is known as the *tumbao*. All this provides a series of interlocking rhythmic layers that contribute to the excitement of the music. Many of these features are in evidence in Paquito D'Rivera's performance of "Guataca City (To David Amram)," recorded in 1986.

LISTENING GUIDE

Track 59

"Guataca City (To David Amram)"

Paquito D'Rivera: "Guataca City (To David Amram)" (D'Rivera), from *Manhattan Burn*. Columbia FC 40583. New York, September 30, October 1, 1986. D'Rivera, alto saxophone; Claudio Roditi, trumpet; Farreed Haque, guitar; Daniel Freiberg, keyboards; Paul Socolow, electric bass; Ignacio Berroa, drums; Daniel Ponce, tumbadoras (congas); Sammy Figueroa, percussion.

The Main Point While many of the earlier Afro-Cuban bands of the 1950s and 1960s were big bands, jazz musicians also explored using Latin textures in small group settings that highlighted improvisation. Cuban saxophonist Paquito D'Rivera's version of "Guataca City" showcases most of the members of the group in a series of exciting solos. It illustrates the fiery, energetic, and rhythmic quality of salsa in the hands of jazz improvisers.

David Amram (b. 1930), to whom the piece is dedicated, is a leading American concert music composer. Because his work spans classical music, jazz, and various folk traditions, its dedication here is appropriate, for "Guataca City" combines salsa with a twelve-bar blues form.

Head statement—2 choruses as 10 bars + 12 bars

0:00 Short drum introduction sets up the opening head statement. The active syncopated melody is played by D'Rivera on alto saxophone and doubled by the guitarist. During the performance, the form relies on a twelve-bar blues form in a minor key. (The first head statement is abbreviated and lasts only ten bars.) Beneath the melody, the piano accompanies with a two-bar montuno figure. Listen, too, for how the bassist often plays a tumbao figure, playing on the "and" of beat two and on beat four, frequently avoiding the downbeat. The short lead-in to the second head statement, a chromatic line in triplets, helps maintain the driving excitement of the performance (0:09). For the second head statement, a synthesizer is added to the texture, and the rhythm section further participates in playing punchy syncopated rhythms with the horns (0:14).

Trumpet solo—2 choruses

0:20 The band breaks (stops playing) for two bars as Brazilian trumpeter Claudio Roditi begins his solo. His solo balances shorter melodic ideas with longer, bop-oriented eighth-note lines (such as at 0:26). Among the percussion instruments audible beneath the solo are the congas. While the bassist plays primarily the tumbao rhythm, the pianist ceases playing the montuno, and his comping becomes freer.

Restatement of head (1 chorus) and guitar solo (2 choruses)

0:45 The group plays a restatement of the head.

0:55 As with the trumpet solo, the band breaks in order to launch the guitar solo. Guitarist Haque plays aggressive eighth-note melodic lines. At the beginning of his second chorus, he intensifies the energy level by playing a melodic idea that rises chromatically, moving to a longer held bent note (1:08). He ends his solo by repeating a riff three times (1:16).

Restatement of head (1 chorus) and piano solo (2 choruses)

1:19 The group restates the head.

1:30 The piano begins during the band break. The rhythm section beneath the piano solo is quieter, with the drummer playing a rhythmic pattern on the rim of the drums. Listen for the explosive cymbal crash at 1:35. The quieter drum accompaniment allows the maracas and congas to be heard more clearly beneath the piano solo. Pianist Freiburg begins his second chorus by alluding to a montuno figure (1:43).

Restatement of head (1 chorus) and bass solo (2 choruses)

1:53   The group restates the head.

2:04   Following the break, the rhythm section again plays quietly behind the electric bass solo, allowing the congas and maracas to be heard. The bass soloist plays a series of impressive eighth-note lines during his second chorus (2:19). Despite the quiet volume, listen to the intricate interlocking rhythmic patterns created by the percussionists and the pianist.

Restatement of head (1 chorus) and alto saxophone solo (9 choruses)

2:27   The group restates the head.

2:38   D'Rivera's alto saxophone sound is energetic and brash. Compare it to the more placid alto saxophone sound of Paul Desmond (Track 35). He begins his second chorus (2:51) by playing triplet rhythms and briefly moves to the upper register of the saxophone at 3:04.

3:13   He restates a single riff at the beginning of this fourth chorus.

3:35   During the sixth chorus, the pianist returns to using a montuno figure to accompany the solo. D'Rivera moves to the upper register of the alto saxophone (3:38). Listen to how he creates excitement by moving up chromatically at 3:54 to introduce the eighth chorus.

3:57   At the beginning of his eighth chorus, the pianist states a montuno figure, and D'Rivera echoes the principal notes of it in his solo.

4:07   In his ninth and final chorus, D'Rivera plays an energetic idea that rhythmically develops a single note and a blues inflection of it.

Final statement of the head (2 choruses)

4:18   As at the opening, the group plays the head twice, playing again the first statement as an abbreviated ten-bar form. Following the second head statement, the piece ends abruptly.

 Listen to this music in an animated Active Listening Guide available at the text website.

Crossover, Postmodernism, and World Music

Both the neo-swing and fusion movements can be likened to **crossover**, or the blending of one music style with another to attract listeners of the other style. Because jazz combined aspects of the European and African traditions, one could argue that the original jazz crossover was jazz itself. Forms of jazz have almost always maintained crossover connections to popular music, a connection most commonly forged through vocal and dance music. As jazz splintered into numerous substyles in the late 1940s and 1950s, some substyles such as funky/soul jazz retained a tie to instrumental popular music. Much of today's vocal jazz maintains crossover connections to popular music.

Beyond the vocal connection, numerous jazz artists are experimenting with the song repertory of the early 1960s and later as a means of expanding the traditional jazz focus on the great popular standards of 1920–1950. Artists are experimenting with tunes by numerous rock groups, including the Beatles; the Grateful Dead; Bjork; Nirvana; Radiohead; Sly and the Family Stone; Crosby, Stills, Nash & Young; and the Doors. Both John Zorn (discussed later in this chapter) and McCoy Tyner have featured the music of pop songwriter Burt Bacharach. Herbie Hancock issued a record called *The New Standard*.

Crossover is the practice of mixing musical styles and cultures. As first seen in the concert jazz of the 1920s and the third-stream practices of the 1950s, crossover can mix different styles within a given culture—for example, bluegrass and classical music—or it can mix entirely different cultures, such as traditional Japanese music and bebop.

Crossover linkages will likely continue to affect jazz in the near future. Even mainstream artists such as Wayne Shorter and guitarist Jim Hall have experimented with writing for orchestra. The development of jazz depends on its capacity for absorbing and integrating new music.

Crossover that ambitiously attempts to link disparate styles and cultures can be likened to postmodernism, which John Zorn virtually personifies in his musical approach. Zorn has emerged as one of the most intriguing figures of the downtown New York scene. Probably more important as a composer and a conceptual artist than as an altoist, this prolific musician has worked in numerous media, from his quartet Masada, which shows a blending of Ornette Coleman and klezmer music, to commissions for the New York Philharmonic.

The Knitting Factory in New York was for many years Zorn's home base. As Zorn's reputation spread, he became involved in numerous ventures. Although it is difficult to pin down his style, an important quality is its postmodern sensibility of stylistic juxtaposition. Segments of medieval Gregorian chant might segue into a distorted heavy-metal timbre, then into a more conventional jazz like swing within minutes. In a surprising 1997 project, for example, Zorn produced an evening devoted to the music of popular songwriter Burt Bacharach. Zorn's eclecticism virtually defines postmodernism in jazz. In 2013, his sixtieth birthday was celebrated in New York with a marathon four-and-a-half hour concert of his works by thirteen ensembles and soloists.

Dave Douglas (b. 1963), who has worked extensively with Zorn, is one of the most interesting crossover trumpet players today. Always involved in a large number of projects, he has participated in more than one hundred CDs, either as leader or sideman. His numerous projects have included experiments with electronics, Romanian folk music and other eastern European traditions, the twentieth-century styles of Webern and Stravinsky, and Lebanese music. Truly difficult to categorize, Douglas is one of the most adventurous players on the scene. Celebrating his 50th birthday in 2013, he launched the "50 States Project," involving concerts in all fifty states, many in outdoor locales, as a way of helping develop jazz audiences.

Douglas's sextet has released a number of recordings that pay tribute to earlier jazz artists. Their 2000 recording *Soul on Soul* paid homage to Mary Lou Williams and won *Down Beat*'s "Album of the Year." More recently, Douglas's *Freak In* (2003) combines jazz with electronic textures and hip-hop turntablists. *Strange Liberation* (2004), with guitarist Bill Frisell and saxophonist Chris Potter, is a fascinating amalgam of 4/4 swing grooves and rock-based electric textures reminiscent of Miles Davis's electric music of the late 1960s.

Dave Douglas, *Strange Liberation,* "Rock of Billy" (2004)

Strange Liberation also included pianist Uri Caine on Fender Rhodes electric piano. Caine has received international critical attention for his innovative recordings that expand on the music of classical composers such as Gustav Mahler, Robert Schumann, and Johann Sebastian Bach. Caine's recordings use the earlier classical works in innovative and unusual ways, and they may combine jazz textures with, for example, klezmer music, tango, bossa nova, digital recording effects, and electronic samples provided by DJs. The result might be considered a postmodern collage of disparate elements. Caine also records in more-traditional formats, and his 2004 *Live at the Village Vanguard* features an acoustic piano trio performing standards by Jimmy Van Heusen and Irving Berlin, along with Caine's original compositions.

Saxophonist Steve Coleman (b. 1956) is experimenting with combining jazz with rap, funk, and rock grooves. He has been interested in such crossovers at least since the early eighties, when he organized his Five Elements band. Coleman underscores his commitment to crossover when he says, "I'd like to have all those elements in the music, something for people who want to dance, something for people who are intellectual and want to find some abstract

John Zorn at a performance in London, England, in 1989.

Peter Williams/CORBIS

Greg Osby,
St. Louis Shoes,
"East St. Louis
Toodle-Oo" (2003)

Courtesy Steve Coleman /Sonya Arts

meaning, and something for people who just want to forget their troubles."[12]

Coleman has been closely associated with what he calls the M-Base concept, which stands for *Macro-Basic Array of Structured Extemporization.* According to Coleman, M-Base should not be considered a stylistic label; it is a "way of thinking about creating music, not the music itself."[13] Coleman has been deeply influenced by non-Western music, particularly African music and meter. Coleman's ideas have taken hold on a loose-knit community of jazz musicians; among those affiliated with the M-Base concept are saxophonists Greg Osby and Gary Thomas; trombonist Robin Eubanks; vocalist Cassandra Wilson, and keyboardists Geri Allen, Renee Rosnes, and Jason Moran. Moran's own recordings, such as *Ten* (2010) and his 2011 live performances entitled "Fats Waller Dance Party" freely combine stride piano, blues, hip hop, and free jazz. In 2011 Moran was named the Artistic Advisor for Jazz at the Kennedy Center in Washington DC.

Much of Coleman's crossover conception is similarly rooted in jazz tradition. For example, in addition to original compositions, he performs jazz standards of the bebop period, such as "Salt Peanuts" (SP) (Listening Guide, Track 60).

> "I'd like to have all those elements in the music, something for people who want to dance, something for people who are intellectual and want to find some abstract meaning, and something for people who just want to forget their troubles."
> —Steve Coleman

LISTENING GUIDE
"Salt Peanuts"   Track 60

Steve Coleman and Five Elements: "Salt Peanuts" (Dizzy Gillespie–Kenny Clarke), from *Def Trance Beat (Modalities of Rhythm).* RCA-BMG 63181-2. Brooklyn, 1994. Coleman, alto saxophone, leader; Andy Milne, piano; Reggie Washington, electric bass; Gene Lake, drums and percussion.

The Main Point   A prime example of Coleman's crossover approach is his version of "Salt Peanuts," recorded in 1994. Coleman's reinterpretation of the classic Gillespie tune pays homage to the bebop tradition. Yet a comparison with the Gillespie–Parker version (Track 28) reveals startling differences, particularly in rhythm. Coleman's 1994 version imbues the composition with driving rock rhythms played by the drums; the use of electric bass further removes it from the bebop tradition.

Most notably, Coleman alters the meter of the composition, pushing the overall metric feel somewhat off-kilter. In Gillespie's version "Salt Peanuts" comprises thirty-two bars of 4/4 rhythm changes. In contrast, Coleman's version truncates the final measure of each four-bar group, shortening it to 2/4 meter. Following the brief introduction played by Coleman alone, the band comes in at a tempo in which the half note equals about 170 beats per minute. This pulse can be understood as follows: each four-bar section of the tune can be counted as four half notes, followed by three half notes, as illustrated here:

By counting more quickly in quarter notes, you can hear how the band creates the grouping of 8 + 6 quarter notes. This metric reinterpretation poses significant challenges for the improvisers. The group sounds tightly rehearsed, with predetermined ensemble passages as well as improvised sections. Both the original AABA form and the F tonal center are retained throughout.

Introduction

| 0:00 | Coleman plays the introductory riff on saxophone. |

Melody—AABA

| 0:06 | The group plays the melody of the entire AABA form. Note the driving rhythms on the drums and the electric bass. |
| 0:17 | The B section begins. |

Written ensemble + 8-bar drum solo

| 0:27 | Coleman plays the written-ensemble passage of the tune. Lake's drum solo alters the 8 + 6 quarter note orientation described above, and he now groups the quarter notes into 7 + 7 for each four-bar section. The drum solo lasts eight bars. |

Stop time melody

| 0:38 | Two bars of the melody are followed by two bars of silence. The ensemble maintains the 7 + 7 quarter note grouping heard during Lake's drum solo. The group does not play the "Salt Peanuts" (SP) motive. |

Coleman solo, then "mop-mop" figure

| 0:59 | A brief improvisation by Coleman leads to the repeated-note "mop-mop" figure (from the original arrangement as played by Parker and Gillespie), first by Coleman, then by Lake. |

Milne piano solo

| 1:09 | Milne's piano solo develops motives over two choruses, alternating between short rhythmic ideas and longer linear runs. |
| 1:28–1:30 | Drum break takes place between the first and second choruses. |

Coleman solo

| 1:48 | The beginning of Coleman's aggressive and energetic solo overlaps the end of the piano solo. Although Lake plays very actively with Coleman, during much of the solo he keeps the half-note beat audible on the cymbal. |

Coleman's 2nd chorus into B

| 2:28 | During the end of Coleman's second chorus, he begins a repeated figure (from the original arrangement) as if to announce the end of his solo. He plays the figure five times, follows with the B section of the composition, then plays the figure two more times. |

Reprise of AABA

| 2:51 | The group returns to the melody of "Salt Peanuts." This time the band stops while Coleman plays the SP motive. |

Coda

| 3:11 | The group plays the brief coda to the tune, again taken from the original arrangement. |

Listen to this music in an animated Active Listening Guide available at the text website.

Directions for Crossover Jazz

We close this overview of recent crossover developments in jazz with a brief discussion of two fascinating records that appeared in 2007 and 2011 that presage possible directions for the twenty-first century. The first is by an almost legendary older artist, pianist Herbie Hancock. The second is by pianist Vijay Iyer, some of whose music explores links between jazz and South Asian (Indian) music. Both are eclectic, and both are crossover ventures. The Hancock recording uses traditional acoustic instruments in an album largely dedicated to the music of an important folk singer/songwriter. The Iyer recording reimagines the piano trio in a context with tabla (a South Asian percussion instrument) and electric guitar.

Herbie Hancock's 2007 recording *River: The Joni Letters* exhibits Hancock's eclectic tendencies and his willingness to blur stylistic boundaries. It is a tribute album, dedicated primarily to the music of folk artist and songwriter Joni Mitchell. In addition to covers of Mitchell's compositions, the CD also includes a trio performance of Duke Ellington's "Solitude" (Track 62) as well as a remake of Wayne Shorter's "Nefertiti," a composition that Hancock recorded earlier with Miles Davis in 1967. The album won the Grammy for the 2007 Album of the Year, the first time a jazz recording earned that particular award since the *Getz/Gilberto* recording of 1963. ("Girl from Ipanema," from the *Getz/Gilberto* recording, appears on Track 36.)

As a series of remakes of compositions by other musicians, Hancock's *River: The Joni Letters* engages the question of what constitutes a jazz standard. The very idea of jazz standards constitutes a form of historicism described earlier in the chapter: standards enshrine older compositions, composers, or jazz styles. As we have seen throughout this book, different jazz musicians have explored many of the same compositions. Multiple performances of "Maple Leaf Rag," "Tiger Rag," "Down South Camp Meeting," and "Salt Peanuts" provide examples of such standards, with newer versions often made literally decades after earlier ones. They allow players a chance to reflect on earlier versions. At the same time, standards arise because they offer players a richness that permits multiple reworkings, alternate reinterpretations that cut across the grain of earlier performances. They allow jazz musicians to alter and reshape older versions.

Naturally, answers to the question of what constitutes a jazz standard differ, subject to any number of factors such as different jazz communities, musical taste, presence of multiple recordings or performances of compositions, etc. In Hancock's case, it would seem that *River: The Joni Letters* offers an eclectic and inclusive view of jazz standards, one that celebrates the work of non-jazz musicians such as Joni Mitchell, side-by-side with central figures of the jazz tradition such as Duke Ellington.

Hancock was named the Creative Chair for Jazz of the Los Angeles Philharmonic (2010–2014). Such positions, linking jazz artists and established orchestras, highlight further possibilities for crossover endeavors. As Hancock indicated, "Anything I can do to be a force to encourage multiculturalism is what I want to do."[14] It is clear that—even after four decades as a significant jazz figure—Hancock's

LISTENING GUIDE
"Solitude"   Track 62

Herbie Hancock: "Solitude" (DeLange, Ellington, Mills), from *River: The Joni Letters*. Verve B0010063 02. New York and Hollywood, California, 2007. Herbie Hancock, piano; Dave Holland, bass; Vinnie Colaiuta, drums.

The Main Point   The performance of "Solitude" from Hancock's recording River: *The Joni Letters* shows a master performance from one of jazz's current elder statesmen. Hancock has remained a central, innovative, and versatile performer. He has drawn critical acclaim for his acoustic work, particularly for his 1960s recordings with Miles Davis's second classic quintet, and has attracted both acclaim and criticism for his electric fusion performances in the 1970s and later. "Solitude," written by Duke Ellington, was later recorded by many other jazz musicians—perhaps most famously by Billie Holiday—and it still remains a jazz standard. Hancock's piano trio version remains in many ways true to the earlier versions, but it also refigures details of those versions in intriguing ways. For example, these players reharmonize the composition: that is, they change the original harmonic progression. In addition, they keep the AABA form but alter the original 32-bar structure: here the first A section lasts consistently nine (rather than eight) bars, and the second A section lasts eight and a half bars. As a result of these harmonic and formal alterations, the performers paint an abstract version of "Solitude."

The piano improvisation focuses on mood and color rather than on flashy soloing. Throughout, there is a sense of dramatic openness to the performance, brought about by its slow tempo and use of space by the players, as well as in deference to the song's lyrics, which call attention to lost love and loneliness.

Introduction and head—AABA

0:00   The performance begins with a bass riff played by bassist Dave Holland and pianist Hancock, a six-note figure followed by a piano chord. They play the riff twice.

0:14   The players state the opening A section. The drummer plays brushes, usually on the snare drum, and the bassist plays sparingly. Hancock plays the melody in the right hand, accompanied by rich colorful harmonies. The A section lasts nine bars, an alteration from the original version of "Solitude," which features a more traditional eight-bar phrase.

0:52   The A section repeats, now with a different underlying harmonic progression. The upward stepwise motion in the bass at the beginning of this section more closely resembles the original harmonic progression to "Solitude." This A section lasts eight and a half measures, again an alteration to the original's eight-bar phrase. At 1:06, Hancock plays a melodic idea in his left hand, beginning in the middle of the measure—this addition makes the additional half bar more seamless.

1:28   The B section retains the eight-bar orientation from the original performance. Hancock's use of right-hand octaves at 1:43 dramatically punctuates the section. Listen to for the very subtle interplay between piano and drums: an active melodic figure in the piano (1:52–1:53) becomes picked up by the drummer (1:54–1:55).

2:02   The return to the A section lasts six bars, before the performers return to a version of the opening bass riff.

2:27   The players play the opening six-note bass figure twice. This section ends with an open pause that follows a dissonant harmony (consisting of a C major triad above a D♭ bass).

Piano solo—Inserted section and AAB

2:40   Rather than return immediately to the AABA form for the piano solo, the players insert a repeated two-chord progression. The drummer switches from brushes to sticks, and plays more regularly on the cymbal than the snare drum. The piano texture consists largely of right-hand melodic lines surrounded by dense harmonies. All the players use a significant degree of space.

3:09   The group subtly returns to the AABA form here. Hancock's right-hand lines become more active. Again, this first A section lasts nine bars.

3:46   The second A section begins as Hancock refers to the melody. The drummer keeps time primarily on the cymbals, although he plays the tom-toms at 4:05. As in the opening head, this A section lasts eight and a half bars.

4:22   The B section.

Final A section and bass riff

4:56   Hancock returns to the melody for the final A section. The section lasts six bars.

5:21   The group twice plays the six-note bass riff. The performance ends with the dissonant harmony, consisting of a C major triad with Db in the bass. This ending chord suppresses the harmonic and melodic resolution that might be expected, perhaps symbolic of the lyrics' theme of unrequited love.

Listen to this music in an animated Active Listening Guide available at the text website.

future work will maintain a similar eclectic combination of musical styles and cultures as well as incorporate both electronic and acoustic media, all continuing to reflect his ongoing interest in musical crossovers.

Pianist Vijay Iyer is an American-born pianist whose parents emigrated from India, and his music draws from African, Asian, and European musical ideas. In 2012 he won the *Downbeat* International Critics Poll as Jazz Artist of the Year and Pianist of the Year; the following year he was the recipient of a MacArthur Fellowship (informally known as the "genius" grant). His trio recording *Tirtha* was recorded in 2008 and released in 2011. Iyer has collaborated with other instrumentalists of similar backgrounds, such as Rudresh Mahanthappa, an American of Indian heritage who won the 2011 *Down Beat* Critic's Poll for alto saxophone. *Tirtha* notably blends jazz and the music of India; Iyer formed the group when asked to perform a concert in recognition of sixty years of Indian independence. The recording shows the capacity of jazz to absorb and respond to other world musics. In addition to Iyer on piano, the performance of "Falsehood" includes South Indian guitarist Prasanna and Nitin Mitta on tabla. The tabla is a percussion instrument, a hand drum used in North Indian music.

The recording of *Tirtha* by Iyer, Prasanna, and Mittal presents a decidedly alternative vision for jazz in its second century. The blend of jazz with world music—in this case the music of South Asia—corresponds to ideals of American culture as a melting pot, a central meeting place where disparate cultures blend. "What jazz brings to the table is collective improvisation and tolerance, respect and freedom, and when you mix that up with every world musical style, you are creating a cultural passport," says Panamanian pianist Danilo Pérez. "I really believe that what jazz has given to the world is a window, a paradigm of how countries should be interacting with each other."[15] Pérez's comments come in the wake of increasing trends toward the globalization of jazz. In 2012, UNESCO (United Nations Educational, Scientific and Cultural Organization) designated each April 30 to be "International Jazz Day," recognizing jazz as a "universal music of freedom and creativity."[16]

River: The Joni Letters and *Tirtha* present alternative visions for jazz in its second century. *River: The Joni Letters* is delicate, beautifully crafted, and imaginative. It is a *tribute* record—a genre that has become more and more common in jazz. And *Tirtha* seeks to find commonalities between jazz and world musics.

From its inception, jazz music has celebrated cultural blends, from its roots in African and European traditions, its Caribbean influences, its dual position as both music for art and for entertainment, as well as its links to social and cultural movements such as the Harlem Renaissance in the 1920s and the Civil Rights movement of the 1960s. The exciting musical directions and points of view heard in *River: The Joni Letters* and *Tirtha* certainly differ from most of the jazz produced in the twentieth century. They may anticipate directions for the music in its second century, while the older, long-established jazz styles will likely continue to attract audiences.

Vijay Iyer (piano), Prasanna (guitar), and Nitin Mitta (tabla) combine elements of jazz with Indian music in compositions such as "Falsehood."

LISTENING GUIDE
Track 63

"Falsehood"

Vijay Iyer with Prasanna and Nitin Mitta: "Falsehood" (Prasanna), from *Tirtha*. ACT 9503-2 - LC 07644 Brooklyn, August 11–12, 2008. Iyer, piano; Prasanna; guitar, Mitta, tabla.

The Main Point   The blend of jazz with Indian music is evident in the instrumentation, particularly the use of the tabla, the mixed meter (the meter alternates groupings of 7 and 8 beats), and guitarist Prasanna's technique, which owes much to Carnatic music of South India. Its relation to jazz is evident in its harmonies and head-solo-head format. The performance is unusual for the absence of bass, but the piano, guitar, and tabla provide the lower frequencies in the texture. The form alternates two general sections heard throughout head statements and the solos. The piece concludes with a tabla solo. Listen for guitarist Prasanna's technique of sliding between notes, a type of ornamentation indebted to the South Indian vina, a fretted stringed instrument. Throughout the performance, the piano and tabla keep the time and maintain the dreamy feel.

Introduction and Head (AABABA)

0:00	The performance begins with the piano vamping in a complex grouping of 7 + 8 beats. The tabla enters during the second statement of this vamp. The hypnotic feel of the track comes from the repeating vamp and the ensuing guitar melody.
0:10	The A section begins as the guitar states the melody. The A section repeats (0:21).
0:32	The chords of this B section depart from the harmonies established in the A section, contrasting with it through a sense of harmonic motion.
0:43	The A section returns, followed by B (0:53) and A (1:04).

Guitar and Piano Solos

1:16	The guitar solo begins. The sound of the guitar is full and sensuous, owing to the electronic chorus effect.
2:19	The guitar runs become faster and more deliberate.
2:39	The piano solo begins with two-note oscillations in the right hand. The guitar comping helps provide the harmonic accompaniment.
3:00	Iyer moves to chordal textures. The right-hand improvised lines that follow reflect a postbop jazz tradition rather than that of Indian music.

Head and Tabla Solo

4:03	The players return to a head statement.
4:40	The tabla solo begins sparsely, but soon moves to faster rhythmic patterns. Throughout the tabla solo, the piano and guitar accompaniment becomes sparser. The performance ends by leaving the listener with a sense of restful fulfillment.

Listen to this music in an animated Active Listening Guide available at the text website.

The Future of Jazz

A comparison of the first fifty years of jazz with the second reveals an intriguing difference, one that may have implications for the future of the music. Without question, the first fifty years featured three artists of indisputable greatness and incomparable influence on the development of the music: Louis Armstrong, Duke Ellington, and Charlie Parker. In addition to these three, the first fifty years of jazz included such legendary jazz giants as James P. Johnson, Jelly Roll Morton, Bix Beiderbecke, Earl Hines, Sidney Bechet, Lester Young, Coleman Hawkins, Benny Goodman, Thelonious Monk, Dizzy Gillespie, and Clifford Brown.

What about the second fifty years—and beyond? John Coltrane and Miles Davis have certainly influenced jazz in long-lasting and far-reaching ways. Some might claim that since 1970 no artists comparable to Coltrane and Davis have emerged, with the possible exception of Wynton Marsalis. Others counter that current jazz artists such as Wayne Shorter, Steve Coleman, Dave Douglas, Kenny Garrett, Herbie Hancock, Dave Holland, Keith Jarrett, Joshua Redman, and John Scofield (to name just a few) provide evidence that jazz is healthy, developing, and progressing. Still others might argue that the practice of identifying greatly influential individuals is no longer a useful way to understand the recent and future directions of jazz.

Examining the jazz offerings of websites reveals a dizzying array of jazz styles and artists. It also suggests an imbalance of major artists between the first and second halves of the century. The number of available CDs by players no longer living dwarfs the work of contemporary artists. In this respect, jazz resembles classical music. Many, if not most, of the major younger jazz artists receiving attention today are traditionalists of some sort. The end of the first century of jazz may be the first time in its history that middle-aged and older players epitomize the avant-garde, while younger players disavow the new and attempt to refurbish the old. And certainly the venues for performance are in constant flux: rarely is it still possible for jazz players to earn a living solely by performing in jazz clubs. Given this state of affairs, can it be possible that jazz is dying?

The other side can be argued as well: the dearth of decisively influential new artists may be part of a larger historical process. When measured by record sales, attendance at festivals and clubs, interest among scholars, the creation of repertory ensembles, and the growth of jazz pedagogy, jazz is thriving. With music in general, and with jazz, in particular, a splintering of the market seems an almost necessary by-product of the information age. We also should acknowledge that tendencies to blend jazz with other genres—crossovers—have always been an important part of the jazz tradition and might lead to developments currently unimaginable.

A paradox, which has become a cliché of our times, is that as the information age homogenizes culture throughout the world, numerous subcultures have sprung into healthy and even aggressive existence as if in retaliation. Jazz is no exception. Its many competing substyles reveal the urgency of its message and its ability to reach audiences throughout the world.

As jazz begins its second century, its vital signs are mostly positive. Activity throughout the jazz community remains vigorous as it draws from its own historical tradition, non-Western cultures, electronics, the high-culture avant-garde, and the many formats of popular music. With the easy-listening grooves of Kenny G, the postmodern eclecticism of John Zorn, the popular and blues infusions by Stevie Wonder, the neo-traditionalism of Wynton Marsalis, and the straight-ahead swinging of Nicholas Payton, jazz remains vibrant in its stylistic multiplicity and continuing world-class appeal. If the history of the music in the last half-century is any indication, jazz will continue the same complex and paradoxical course begun one hundred years ago. At the same time that new substyles continue to spin off from the center of jazz, reissues of classic jazz will consolidate a greater appreciation of its history and a deeper understanding of its evolution. The outlook is indeed exciting on all fronts.

Exam Review Questions

Use these questions and the materials on the text website to help you understand and pass tests on the content of this chapter.

1. Why is it important not to think of the history of jazz as one style succeeding or supplanting another? Cite contemporary artists mentioned throughout the chapter to argue the point that the history of jazz is not rigidly linear.

2. How can 1980s jazz be described as a reaction against fusion?

3. How has the jazz repertory movement changed the large-scale cultural perspective on jazz?

4. What approach to jazz does Wynton Marsalis personify? How does he do so? Refer to his life, his role in the jazz repertory movement, and, in particular, his work as a composer.

5. What traditional prejudices have restricted the role of women in jazz? How have some of these prejudices been overcome in the past two or three decades?

6. Is jazz a worldwide phenomenon? Cite artists from the 1920s to the present to make your case.

7. Is jazz, most broadly conceived, increasing or declining in either importance or popularity? Cite cultural trends to support your view. Part of your answer may depend on what you consider to be jazz. Another important consideration may be record sales: they measure popularity, but do they measure musical significance?

8. How do Herbie Hancock's *River: The Joni Letters* and Vijay Iyer's *Tirtha* suggest possibilities for the future of jazz? Which possibility do you prefer? Can you think of any possibilities not discussed in the text?

 MindTap™

Test Yourself on Key Concepts with additional Chapter Quizzes and Listening Activities on the text website.

Key Terms

Test your knowledge of this chapter's key terms by defining the following. If you can't remember the meaning of a term, refresh your memory by looking up the boldfaced term in the chapter, turning to the Glossary at the back of the book, or working with the flash-cards at the text website.

acid jazz **361**

back catalog **347**

complete reissue **347**

crossover **366**

crossover music **347**

false start **347**

ghost band **356**

jazz pedagogy **348**

jazz repertory movement **347**

MIDI (Musical Instrument Digital Interface) **359**

neo-swing **362**

nu jazz **362**

postmodernism **352**

remastering **347**

Notes

Chapter 1

1. Richard Alan Waterman, "African Influence on the Music of the Americas," in *Acculturation in the Americas: Proceedings and Selected Papers of the XXIXth International Congress of Americanists,* ed. Sol Tax (University of Chicago Press, 1952), pp. 207–218. Reprinted New York: Cooper Square Publishers, 1967.

2. Olly Wilson, "The Significance of the Relationship Between Afro-American Music and West African Music," *Black Perspective in Music* 2, no. 1 (Spring 1974), p. 16.

3. William Francis Allen, Charles Pickard Ware, and Lucy McKim Garrison, *Slave Songs of the United States* (New York: Peter Smith, 1951; reprint, Mineola, NY: Dover, 1995), p. vi.

4. Quoted in Eileen Southern, *Music of Black Americans,* 2nd ed. (New York: Norton, 1971), p. 192.

5. Jeanette Robinson Murphy's 1899 article, "The Survival of African Music in America," reprinted in *The Negro and His Folk-Lore,* ed. Bruce Jackson (Austin: University of Texas Press, 1967).

6. *Ibid.*

7. Robert Farris Thompson, "Kongo Influences on African-American Artistic Culture," in *Africanisms in American Culture,* ed. Joseph E Holloway (Bloomington: Indiana University Press, 1990), pp. 149–150.

8. Quoted in Robert L. Hall, "African Religious Retentions in Florida," in *Africanisms in American Culture,* ed. Joseph E Holloway (Bloomington: Indiana University Press, 1990), p. 108.

9. See Sterling Stuckey, *Slave Culture: Nationalist Theory and the Foundations of Black America* (New York: Oxford University Press, 1987).

10. Marshall Stearns, *The Story of Jazz* (New York: Oxford University Press, 1958), p. 19.

11. William Francis Allen, Charles Pickard Ware, and Lucy McKim Garrison, *Slave Songs of the United States* (New York: Peter Smith, 1951; orig. pub., New York: A. Simpson, 1867; reprint, New York: Dover, 1997), p. vi.

12. M. Jones, "Blue Notes and Hot Rhythm," *African Music Society Newsletter* 1 (June 1951), p. 10. See also Jones's "African Rhythm," *Africa* 24, no. 1 (January 1954), p. 39; and *Studies in African Music* (New York: Oxford University Press, 1959).

13. Allan P. Merriam, "African Music," in *Continuity and Change in African Cultures,* ed. William R Bascom and Melville Herskovits (Chicago: University of Chicago Press, 1959), pp. 76–80; Paul Oliver, *Savannah Syncopators: African Retentions in the Blues* (New York: Stein and Day, 1970), p. 60.

14. Bruno Nettl, *Folk and Traditional Music of the Western Continents* (Englewood Cliffs, NJ, 1973), p. 185.

15. R. Nathaniel Dett, introduction to *In the Bottoms: Characteristic Suite* (Chicago: Clayton F. Summy, 1913).

16. Thomas L. Riis, *Just Before Jazz: Black Musical Theater in New York, 1890–1915* (Washington, DC: Smithsonian Institution Press, 1989), pp. 5–6.

17. Frederick James Smith, "Irving Berlin and Modern Ragtime," *New York Dramatic Mirror,* January 14, 1914, p. 38.

18. Edward A. Berlin, *Ragtime: A Musical and Cultural History* (Berkeley: University of California Press, 1980), p. 12.

19. Edward A. Berlin, *King of Ragtime: Scott Joplin and His Era* (New York: Oxford University Press, 1994), p. 7.

20. See Berlin, *Ragtime*, esp. pp. 147–170.

21. Blues lyrics quoted in Paul Oliver, *Aspects of the Blues Tradition* (New York: Oak Publications, 1970), p. 18.

22. W. C. Handy and Arna Bontemps, *Father of the Blues* (New York: Macmillan, 1941; reprint, New York: Collier Books, 1970), p. 13.

23. *Ibid.*, p. 56.

Chapter 2

1. Gunther Schuller, *Early Jazz: Its Roots and Musical Development* (New York: Oxford University Press, 1968), pp. 359–372.

2. Walter Kingsley, *New York Sun*, August 5, 1917.

3. Kathy J. Ogren, *The Jazz Revolution: Twenties America and the Meaning of Jazz* (New York: Oxford University Press, 1989), p. 102.

4. Lawrence Gushee, "How the Creole Band Came to Be," *Black Music Research Journal* 8, no. 1 (1988), p. 85.

5. Lawrence Gushee, liner notes to *Steppin' on the Gas: Rags to Jazz 1913–1927*, New World Records 269.

6. Alan Lomax, *Mister Jelly Roll: The Fortunes of Jelly Roll Morton, New Orleans Creole and "Inventor" of Jazz* (New York: Pantheon Books, 1950), p. 109. See also 2nd ed. (Berkeley: University of California Press, 1973).

7. Pops Foster, as told to Tom Stoddard, *Pops Foster: The Autobiography of a New Orleans Jazzman* (Berkeley: University of California Press, 1971), pp. 18–19.

8. Nat Shapiro and Nat Hentoff, eds., *Hear Me Talkin' to Ya: The Story of Jazz as Told by the Men Who Made It* (New York: Rinehart, 1955; reprint, Dover, 1966), p. 22.

9. See William J. Schafer, with Richard B. Allen, *Brass Bands and New Orleans Jazz* (Baton Rouge: Louisiana State University Press, 1977), p. 8. Lewis Porter discusses the relationship of the brass band instrumentation to frontline Dixieland instrumentation in Lewis Porter, Michael Ullman, and Edward Hazell, *Jazz: From Its Origins to the Present* (Englewood Cliffs, NJ: Prentice-Hall, 1993), p. 18.

10. Baby Dodds, as told to Larry Gara, *The Baby Dodds Story* (Baton Rouge: Louisiana State University Press, 1992), pp. 17–18.

11. Lomax, *Mister Jelly Roll*, 2nd ed., p. 62.

12. Christopher Washburne, "The Clave of Jazz: A Caribbean Contribution to the Rhythmic Foundation of an African-American Music," *Black Music Research Journal* 17, no. 1 (1997), p. 75.

13. Dodds, *Baby Dodds Story*, p. 106.

14. Quoted in Donald M. Marquis, *In Search of Buddy Bolden* (Baton Rouge: Louisiana State University Press, 1978), p. 105.

15. Martin Williams, *Jazz Masters of New Orleans* (New York: Macmillan, 1967), p. 1.

16. Lomax, *Mr. Jelly Roll* (original ed.), p. 93.

17. *Ibid.*, p. 109.

18. Lomax, *Mr. Jelly Roll*, 2nd ed., p. 63.

19. Shapiro and Hentoff, *Hear Me Talkin' to Ya*, p. 49.

20. *Ibid.*, p. 45.

21. Sally Placksin, *American Women in Jazz: 1900 to the Present: Their Words, Lives, and Music* (New York: Seaview Books, 1982), pp. 60–61.

22. William Howland Kenney, *Chicago Jazz: A Cultural History, 1904–1930* (New York: Oxford University Press), 1993), p. 12.

23. *Ibid.*, p. 9.

24. *Ibid.*, p. 45.

25. Frederick Ramsey, Jr., and Charles Edward Smith, eds., *Jazzmen* (New York: Harcourt, Brace, 1939), p. 51.

26. Kenney, *Chicago Jazz*, p. 42.

27. Lawrence Gushee, liner notes to *King Oliver, King Oliver's Jazz Band—1923*, Columbia P2 12744.

28. Kenney, *Chicago Jazz*, p. 104.

29. Edmond Souchon, "King Oliver: A Very Personal Memoir," in *Jazz Panorama*, ed. Martin Williams (New York: Collier Books, 1964), pp. 27–29.

30. Martin Williams, *The Jazz Tradition*, 2nd ed. (New York: Oxford University Press, 1983), p. 55. See also original ed., 1970.

Chapter 3

1. Jelly Roll Morton, Library of Congress Recordings, Riverside 9001-12.

2. Ernest Ansermet, *Revue Romande*, October 19, 1919; reprinted in John Chilton, *Sidney Bechet: The Wizard of Jazz* (New York: Oxford University Press, 1987), p. 40. Also in Robert Walser, *Keeping Time: Readings in Jazz History* (New York: Oxford University Press, 1999), p. 11.

3. Richard Hadlock, *Jazz Masters of the Twenties* (New York: Collier Books, 1974), p. 15.

4. Max Kaminsky, with V. E. Hughes, *My Life in Jazz* (New York: Harper & Row, 1963), pp. 39–41.

5. Nat Shapiro and Nat Hentoff, eds., *Hear Me Talkin' to Ya: The Story of Jazz as Told by the Men Who Made It* (New York: Rinehart, 1955; reprint, Dover, 1966), p. 120.

6. Hadlock, *Jazz Masters*, pp. 80–81.

Chapter 4

1. Gunnard Askland, "Interpretations in Jazz: A Conference with Duke Ellington," *Etude* (March 1947), p. 134.

2. Many of the ideas in this section are influenced by Samuel A. Floyd, Jr., "Music in the Harlem Renaissance: An Overview," in *Black Music in the*

Harlem Renaissance, ed. Samuel A Floyd, Jr. (New York; Westport, CT: Greenwood Press, 1990), pp. 1–27.

3. Nathan Irvin Huggins, *Harlem Renaissance* (New York: Oxford University Press, 1971), p. 5.

4. See Nathan Irvin Huggins, "Interview with Eubie Blake," in *Voices from the Harlem Renaissance,* ed.Nathan Huggins (New York: Oxford University Press, 1976), pp. 339–340.

5. Robert Bartlett Haas, ed., *William Grant Still and the Fusion of Cultures in American Music* (Los Angeles: Black Sparrow Press, 1975), p. 134.

6. Floyd, "Music in the Harlem Renaissance," p. 21.

7. Willie "The Lion" Smith, with George Hoefer, *Music on My Mind: The Memoirs of an American Pianist* (New York: Burdge & Co., 1954; reprint, New York: Da Capo Press, 1984), pp. 66–67. *Authors' note:* "The Charleston" in the quotation is correct, but the preferred title is "Charleston."

8. Henry Martin, "Balancing Composition and Improvisation in James P. Johnson's 'Carolina Shout.'" *Journal of Music Theory* 49/2 (Fall, 2005), pp. 277–299.

9. Tom Davin, "Conversations with James P. Johnson," *Jazz Review* 2, no. 6 (July 1959), p. 12.

10. Richard Hadlock, *Jazz Masters of the Twenties* (New York: Collier Books, 1974), p. 153.

11. John Howland, *Ellington Uptown: Duke Ellington, James P. Johnson, and the Birth of Concert Jazz* (Ann Arbor: University of Michigan Press, 2009).

12. James T. Maher and Jeffrey Sultanof, "Pre–Swing Era Big Bands and Jazz Composing and Arranging," in *The Oxford Companion to Jazz,* ed. Bill Kirchner (Oxford: Oxford University Press, 2000), p. 264.

13. Hadlock, *Jazz Masters,* p. 212.

14. Duke Ellington, *Music Is My Mistress* (New York: Da Capo Press, 1976), p. 419.

15. Nat Shapiro and Nat Hentoff, eds., *Hear Me Talkin' to Ya: The Story of Jazz as Told by the Men Who Made It* (New York: Rinehart, 1955; reprint, Dover, 1966), p. 231.

16. Mark Tucker, Ellington: *The Early Years* (Urbana, IL: University of Illinois Press, 1991), p. 148.

17. *Ibid.,* p. 201.

18. Gunther Schuller, *The Swing Era: The Development of Jazz 1930–1945* (New York: Oxford University Press, 1989), p. 48.

19. Tucker, *Ellington,* 201.

20. John Edward Hasse, *Beyond Category: The Life and Genius of Duke Ellington* (New York: Simon & Schuster, 1993), p. 92.

21. Joshua Berrett, personal communication, October 9, 2007.

22. Alyn Shipton, *A New History of Jazz* (New York: Continuum, 2002), p. 360.

23. Ted Heath, *Listen to My Music* (London: Frederick Muller, 1957), p. 31.

24. Shipton, *New History of Jazz,* p. 363.

25. Garvin Bushell, as told to Mark Tucker, *Jazz from the Beginning* (Ann Arbor: University of Michigan Press, 1990), p. 55.

26. Frederick S. Starr, *Red and Hot: The Fate of Jazz in the Soviet Union* (New York: Oxford University Press, 1983), p. 54. Much of our information on jazz in the Soviet Union was provided by Starr's study.

27. *Ibid.,* p. 66.

28. James Lincoln Collier, *The Making of Jazz: A Comprehensive History* (Boston: Houghton Mifflin, 1978), p. 321.

Chapter 5

1. James Lincoln Collier, *Benny Goodman and the Swing Era* (New York: Oxford University Press, 1989), p. 5.

2. "Who Started Swing?" *Metronome* (August 1936), p. 11.

3. George T. Simon, *The Big Bands,* rev. ed. (New York: Macmillan, 1974), p. 4.

4. Ross Russell, *Jazz Style in Kansas City and the Southwest* (Berkeley: University of California Press, 1971), p. 72.

5. Nathan W. Pearson, Jr., *Goin' to Kansas City* (Urbana: University of Illinois Press, 1987), p. 67.

6. Pearson, *Goin' to Kansas City,* p. 119.

7. John Hammond, "Count Basie Marks 20th Anniversary," *Down Beat,* November 2, 1955, p. 11.

8. Teddy Wilson, with Arie Ligthart and Humphrey van Loo, *Teddy Wilson Talks Jazz* (London: Cassell, 1996), pp. 33, 82.

9. *Ibid.,* p. 46

10. Benjamin G. Rader, *Baseball: A History of America's Game,* 2nd ed. (Urbana and Chicago: University of Illinois Press, 2002), p. 156.

11. Benny Goodman and Irving Kolodin, *The Kingdom of Swing* (New York: Frederick Ungar, 1961), p. 140.

12. Goodman and Kolodin, *Kingdom of Swing,* pp. 198–199.

13. John Edward Hasse, *Beyond Category: The Life and Genius of Duke Ellington* (New York: Simon & Schuster, 1993).

14. *Ibid.,* p. 215

15. James Lincoln Collier, *Duke Ellington* (New York: Oxford University Press, 1987), p. 130.

16. Gary Giddins, "Notes on the Music," in the liner notes for *Giants of Jazz: Johnny Hodges,* Time-Life Records TL-J19, 1981, p. 47.

17. Walter van de Leur, *Something to Live For: The Music of Billy Strayhorn* (New York: Oxford, 2002), pp. 59–60.

18. Billy Strayhorn, "The Ellington Effect," *Down Beat,* November 5, 1952, p. 4.

19. For a transcription of this passage, see Gunther Schuller from "Ellington in the Pantheon," first published in *High Fidelity* (1974) and available in Mark Tucker, ed., *The Duke Ellington Reader* (New York: Oxford University Press, 1993), p. 416.

Chapter 6

1. Cab Calloway and Bryant Rollins, *Of Minnie the Moocher and Me* (New York: Crowell, 1976), p. 112.

2. George T. Simon, *The Big Bands,* 4th ed. (New York: Schirmer Books, 1982), pp. 331–332.

3. Whitney Balliett, *Super Drummer: A Profile of Buddy Rich* (Indianapolis: Bobbs-Merrill, 1968), p. 83.

4. Durham, NC: Duke University Press, 2000.

5. Gunther Schuller, *The Swing Era: The Development of Jazz 1930–1945* (New York: Oxford University Press, 1989), p. 548.

6. Nat Hentoff, "Pres," *Down Beat,* March 7, 1956, p. 9.

7. See Lewis Porter's study in *Lester Young* (Boston: Twayne, 1985), especially Chapter 4 (pp. 56–88). Also pp. 175–180.

8. Schuller, *Swing Era,* p. 547.

9. Teddy Wilson, with Arie Ligthart and Humphrey van Loo, foreword to *Teddy Wilson Talks Jazz* (London: Cassell, 1996), p. ix.

10. Wilson, *Teddy Wilson Talks Jazz,* pp. 23–24.

11. Nat Shapiro and Nat Hentoff, eds., *Hear Me Talkin' to Ya: The Story of Jazz as Told by the Men Who Made It* (New York: Rinehart, 1955; reprint, Dover, 1966), p. 201.

Chapter 7

1. "Bop Will Kill Business Unless It Kills Itself First'— Louis Armstrong," *Down Beat,* April 7, 1948, p. 2.

2. Marshall Stearns, *The Story of Jazz* (New York: Oxford University Press, 1958), p. 159.

3. Ira Gitler, *Jazz Masters of the Forties* (New York: Da Capo Press, 1983), pp. 26–27.

4. Dizzy Gillespie with Al Fraser, *To Be or Not … to Bop* (Garden City, NY: Doubleday, 1979), p. 146.

5. *Ibid.,* p. 135.

6. Miles Davis, with Quincy Troupe, *Miles: The Autobiography* (New York: Simon & Schuster, 1989), p. 54.

7. Danny Barker, *A Life in Jazz* (New York: Oxford University Press, 1986), pp. 171–172.

8. Budd Johnson, quoted in Gillespie, *To Be,* p. 218.

9. Gitler, *Jazz Masters,* p. 22.

10. Gillespie, *To Be,* p. 208.

11. "My Memories of Bird Parker," *Melody Maker,* May 28, 1955. Reprinted in Carl Woideck, *The Charlie Parker Companion* (Schirmer Books, 1998), p. 136. Quotation transcribed by Carl Woideck.

12. "Interview: Charlie Parker, Marshall Stearns, Jim Maher, and Chan Parker," in Woideck, *Charlie Parker Companion,* p. 93.

13. Ross Russell, *Bird Lives: The High Life and Hard Times of Charlie (Yardbird) Parker* (New York: Charterhouse,

1973; reprint, New York: Da Capo Press, 1996), p. 138. For more on Parker's solos, see Henry Martin, *Charlie Parker and Thematic Improvisation* (Lanham, MD: Scarecrow Press, 1996).

14. For a detailed discussion of Parker's use of quotations, see Carl Woideck, *Charlie Parker: His Music and Life* (Ann Arbor: The University of Michigan Press, 1996), pp. 161–163.

15. Davis, *Miles,* p. 64.

16. "Louie the First," *Time* 53 (February 21, 1949), p. 52.

17. Gitler, *Jazz Masters,* p. 120.

18. Gillespie, *To Be,* p. 137.

19. Davis, *Miles,* pp. 80–81.

20. Davis, *Miles,* p. 104.

Chapter 8

1. Jack Chambers, *Milestones 1: The Music and Times of Miles Davis to 1960* (Toronto: University of Toronto Press, 1983), p. 129.

2. John Lewis, *The World of Music* (Information Bulletin No. 4, International Music Council, UNESCO House, Paris, May 1958).

3. Chambers, *Milestones 1,* p. 131.

4. Ted Gioia, *West Coast Jazz* (New York: Oxford University Press, 1992), p. 143.

5. "What's Wrong with Kenton?" *Metronome* 64, no. 2 (February 1948), p. 32.

6. Shelly Manne, "Shelly Manne Offers His Concept of Jazz Drums," *Down Beat,* December 14, 1955, p. 9.

7. Liner notes to Jimmy Guiffre, *Tangents in Jazz,* Capitol T634.

8. As quoted in Gil Goldstein, *Jazz Composers Companion* (New York: Consolidated Music Publishers, 1981), p. 128.

9. Gunther Schuller, "Sonny Rollins and the Challenge of Thematic Improvisation," *The Jazz Review* (November 1958), pp. 6–11; reprinted in Schuller's *Musings: The Musical Worlds of Gunther Schuller* (New York and Oxford: Oxford University Press, 1986), pp. 86–97.

10. May 26 appears as the birthdate in Miles Davis, with Quincy Troupe, *Miles: The Autobiography* (New York: Simon & Schuster, 1989), p. 12. This date also appears in John Szwed, *So What: The Life of Miles Davis* (New York: Simon & Schuster, 2002), p. 5. Previous sources list May 25.

11. Davis, *Miles,* p. 9.

12. Ross Russell, *Bird Lives: The High Life and Hard Times of Charlie (Yardbird) Parker* (New York: Charterhouse, 1973; reprint, New York: Da Capo Press, 1996), p. 267.

13. Davis, *Miles,* p. 219.

14. John Coltrane, in collaboration with Don DeMicheal, "Coltrane on Coltrane," *Down Beat,* September 29, 1960, p. 27.

15. Liner notes to Miles Davis, *Kind of Blue,* Columbia CK 64935.

Chapter 9

1. Nat Hentoff, *The Jazz Life* (New York: Dial Press, 1961), p. 238.

2. Ornette Coleman, liner notes to Ornette Coleman, *Change of the Century*, Atlantic 1327.

3. Hentoff, *Jazz Life*, p. 241.

4. Ekkehard Jost, *Free Jazz* (New York: Da Capo Press, 1981), p. 54.

5. Hentoff, *Jazz Life*, p. 228.

6. Jost, *Free Jazz*, p. 59.

7. John Litweiler, *The Freedom Principle: Jazz After 1958* (New York: Morrow, 1984), p. 55.

8. Gunther Schuller, "Coleman, Ornette," in the *New Grove Dictionary of Jazz*, ed. Barry Kernfeld (New York: St. Martin's Press, 1994), p. 230. For example, see Coleman's explanation of harmolodics in *Down Beat*, July 1983, pp. 54–55.

9. John Coltrane, in collaboration with Don DeMicheal, "Coltrane on Coltrane," *Down Beat*, September 29, 1960, p. 26.

10. *Ibid.*

11. Thomas Owens, *Bebop: The Music and the Players* (New York: Oxford University Press, 1995), p. 94.

12. Jack Chambers, *Milestones 1: The Music and Times of Miles Davis to 1960* (Toronto: University of Toronto Press, 1983), p. 249.

13. Coltrane, "Coltrane on Coltrane," p. 27.

14. *Ibid.*

15. *Ibid.*

16. Joe Hunt, *52nd Street Beat: Modern Jazz Drummers 1945–1965* (New Albany, IN: Jamey Aeborsold Jazz, n.d.), p. 44.

17. Quoted in Don DeMicheal, "John Coltrane and Eric Dolphy Answer the Jazz Critics," *Down Beat*, April 12, 1962, p. 20. Originally published in a *Down Beat* review of November 23, 1961.

18. Lewis Porter, "John Coltrane's A Love Supreme: Jazz Improvisation as Composition," *Journal of the American Musicological Association* 38, no. 3 (1983), pp. 593–621.

19. Jost, *Free Jazz*, p. 89.

20. DeMicheal, "John Coltrane and Eric Dolphy," p. 21.

21. *Ibid.*, pp. 21–22.

22. Liner notes to Eric Dolphy, *Far Cry* with Booker Little, Prestige 7747.

23. Charles Johnson, "A Soul's Jagged Arc," *New York Times Magazine*, January 3, 1999, p. 16.

24. LeRoi Jones, *Blues People* (New York: William Morrow, 1963), p. 70.

25. Frank Kofsky, *Black Nationalism and the Revolution in Music* (New York: Pathfinder Press, 1970), p. 17.

26. *Ibid.*, p. 19.

27. *Ibid.*, p. 26.

28. Jerry D'Souza, "Richard Davis—Philosophy of the Spiritual," *Coda Magazine* 285 (May–June 1999), p. 11.

29. Jost, *Free Jazz*, p. 127.

30. J. B. Figi, "Cecil Taylor: African Code, Black Methodology," *Down Beat*, April 10, 1975, pp. 14, 31.

31. Quoted in Jost, *Free Jazz*, p. 83.

32. *Ibid.*, p. 19.

33. Liner notes to Joseph Jarman, *As If It Were the Seasons*, Delmark 410.

34. Liner notes to Lester Bowie, *Numbers 1 and 2*, Nessa N-1.

35. Jost, *Free Jazz*, p. 177.

Chapter 10

1. Count Basie, as told to Albert Murray, *Good Morning Blues: The Autobiography of Count Basie* (New York: Random House, 1985), p. 382.

2. Derek Jewell, *Duke: A Portrait of Duke Ellington* (New York: Norton, 1977), p. 110.

3. Miles Davis, with Quincy Troupe, *Miles: The Autobiography* (New York: Simon & Schuster, 1989), p. 241.

4. R. Townley, "Hancock Plugs In," *Down Beat*, October 24, 1974, p. 15.

5. Davis, *Miles*, p. 270.

6. Townley, "Hancock Plugs In," p. 14.

7. On Track 2, at 1:02, of Marian McPartland, *Piano Jazz*, with guest Bill Evans, The Jazz Alliance TJA-12004.

8. Mark Gridley discusses Corea's solo on "Matrix" in *Jazz Styles: History and Analysis*, 5th ed. (Englewood Cliffs, NJ: Prentice-Hall, 1994), p. 321.

9. Conrad Silvert, "Chick Corea's Changes: A Return to Forever Is Not Forever," *Rolling Stone*, July 15, 1976, p. 24.

10. Liner notes to Charles Lloyd, *Charles Lloyd: Love-In*, Atlantic SC 1481.

11. Ben Sidran, *Talking Jazz: An Oral History*, expanded ed. (New York: Da Capo Press, 1995), p. 268.

12. *Ibid.*, pp. 324–327.

Chapter 11

1. Bill Laswell, foreword to *Jazz-Rock: A History*, by Stuart Nicholson (New York: Schirmer Books, 1998), p. x.

2. Bill Milkowski, liner notes to Al Di Meola, *Electric Rendezvous*, Sony/Columbia 468216-2.

3. Lee Underwood, "George Duke: Plugged-In Prankster," *Down Beat*, March 10, 1977, p. 34.

4. Bret Primack, "Herbie Hancock: Chameleon in His Disco Phase," *Down Beat*, May 17, 1979, p. 42.

5. Art Taylor, *Notes and Tones: Musician-to-Musician Interviews* (Liège, Belgium: Taylor, 1977; reprint, New York: Da Capo Press, 1993).

6. George T. Simon, *The Big Bands*, 4th ed. (New York: Macmillan, 1981).

7. Linda Prince, "Betty Carter: Bebopper Breathes Fire," *Down Beat*, May 3, 1979, p. 14.

8. Enrico Merlin, "Code MD: Coded Phrases in the First 'Electric Period.'" Talk given at "Miles Davis and American Culture II," May 10–11, 1996, Washington University, St. Louis. Available at www.plosin.com/milesAhead/codeMD.html.

9. Liner notes to *Miles Davis at Fillmore*, Columbia CG 30038.

10. Julie Coryell and Laura Friedman, preface to *Jazz-Rock Fusion: The People, The Music* (New York: Delacorte Press, 1978), p. x.

11. Bill Milkowski, "Larry Coryell: Back to the Roots," *Down Beat*, May 1984, p. 16.

12. Mark Gridley, *Jazz Styles: History and Analysis*, 5th ed. (Englewood Cliffs, NJ: Prentice-Hall, 1994), p. 337.

13. Scott Yanow, "George Duke: Dukin' out the Hits," *Down Beat*, November 1984, p. 17.

14. Len Lyons, *The Great Jazz Pianists: Speaking of Their Lives and Their Music* (New York: Da Capo, 1989), p. 276.

15. Primack, "Herbie Hancock," p. 42.

16. Coryell and Friedman, *Jazz-Rock Fusion*, p. 239.

17. Josef Woodward, "Chick Corea: Piano Dreams Come True," *Down Beat*, September 1988, p. 19.

18. Bill Milkowski, *Jaco: The Extraordinary and Tragic Life of Jaco Pastorius, "The World's Greatest Bass Player"* (San Francisco: Miller Freeman Books, 1995), p. 73.

19. Review of *Mr. Gone*, *Down Beat*, January 11, 1979, p. 22.

20. Stuart Nicholson, *Jazz-Rock: A History* (New York: Schirmer Books, 1998), p. 181.

21. Fred Borque, "Pat Metheny: Musings on Neo-Fusion," *Down Beat*, March 22, 1979, pp. 13–15.

22. Nicholson, *Jazz-Rock*, p. 240.

23. Pat Metheny, "In Search of Sound," *Down Beat*, February 1998, p. 19.

Chapter 12

1. Ann Douglas, *Terrible Honesty: Mongrel Manhattan in the 1920s* (New York: Farrar, Straus, Giroux, 1995), p. 352.

2. James P. Johnson, "I Like Anything That's Good," *The Jazz Record* (April 1947), p. 14.

3. Dave Hellend, "Repertory Big Bands," *Down Beat*, January 1997, p. 35.

4. Howard Reich, "Wynton Marsalis," *Down Beat*, December 1997, p. 34.

5. Robert Sadin, personal communication, May 20, 1999.

6. Wynton Marsalis, "Ellington at 100: Reveling in Life's Majesty," *New York Times*, January 17, 1999, Arts and Leisure section.

7. Stuart Nicholson, *Jazz: The 1980s Resurgence* (New York: Da Capo Press, 1990), p. 227.

8. John McDonough, "Doin' 'em Proud," *Down Beat*, January 1997, p. 20.

9. Radio emcee Don Burns of smooth-jazz station KTWV of Los Angeles, as quoted in Eliot Tiegel, "Smooth Moves on the Air," *Down Beat*, December 1996, p. 10.

10. Record producer Michael Cuscuna, as quoted in Eliot Tiegel, "Smooth Moves on the Air," *Down Beat*, December 1996, p. 10.

11. Charles Levin, "Reconfiguring the Public Radio Puzzle," *Down Beat*, April 1999, p. 44.

12. Nicholson, *Jazz Resurgence*, p. 258.

13. Steve Coleman; www.m-base.com/mbase.html [Internet home page].

14. David Hadju, "Rhapsody in Black and White: Herbie Hancock Finds a Soul Mate in George Gershwin," *New York Times Magazine*, October 28, 1998, p. 52.

15. Larry Rohter, "Where Nations Debate, Harmony of a Jazz Kind," *New York Times* (April 29, 2012), *http://www.nytimes.com/2012/04/30/arts/music/united-nations-tunes-up-for-first-international-jazz-day.html?nl=todaysheadlines&emc=tha28_201204301*.

16. *Ibid.*

Glossary

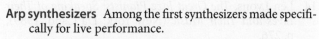

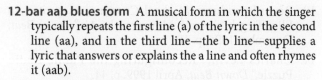

12-bar aab blues form A musical form in which the singer typically repeats the first line (a) of the lyric in the second line (aa), and in the third line—the b line—supplies a lyric that answers or explains the a line and often rhymes it (aab).

32-bar AABA song form A musical form that presents the melody in four sections labeled A, A, B, and A, each section eight bars long for a total of 32 bars. The eight-bar theme (A) plays twice; a contrasting melody (B) follows, also usually eight bars long; and the A theme returns. Quite often the second and third A sections will vary slightly.

AABA song form See *32-bar AABA song form*.

ABAC song form A musical form in which each section is usually eight bars. Musicians often speak of the "first half" of the tune (AB) and the "second half" (AC).

Acid jazz A fusion style that incorporates sampling of older jazz recordings, rap, and hip-hop grooves and techniques.

Amen cadence See *plagal cadence*.

Amplitude modulation Sound modulation in which the amplitude (the range of loud and soft) of the wave is modified by another wave, producing a sound vastly different from the original. See also *modulation* and *frequency modulation*.

Antiphony The trading of melodic figures between two different sections of the band; the formal musical term for *call-and-response*. Listen to Track 47 of the Audio Primer: the trumpet and the saxophone, by trading twos, engage in a form of antiphony.

Arpeggiated figure (arpeggio) The notes of a chord played in sequence rather than simultaneously. Listen to Track 2 of the Audio Primer to hear various arpeggios.

Arp synthesizers Among the first synthesizers made specifically for live performance.

Arrangement A plan of the form of a band's performance often including notation for the parts played by different instruments. The person who creates the plan is the *arranger*. See also *head arrangement* and *stock arrangement*.

Arranger The person who plans the form of a band's performance and often notates the parts for the different instruments. See also *head arrangement*.

Articulation Refers to the manner in which notes are played, as in *legato*, a smooth movement through a series of notes, or *staccato*, short notes with distinct spaces between them.

Atonality A description of music that avoids the standard chords, scales, harmonies, and keys of tonality. It is sometimes associated with free jazz, which flourished in the 1960s.

Avant-garde See *free jazz*.

Backbeat (change-step) A stride piano technique in which the performer breaks up the regular striding left hand with its normal alternation of bass note and mid-register chord—that is, 1–2–1–2 ("1" refers to a bass note and "2" refers to a chord). Instead, the left hand plays a more complex pattern such as 1–1–2–1/1–2–1-2 or 1–2–2–1/2-2–1–2/1–2–1-2, which is called a backbeat. It should not be confused with a drummer's backbeats, which are accents on beats 2 and 4 of a bar (see below). Listen to Track 5 of the Audio Primer to hear a backbeat.

Backbeats Heavy emphases on beats 2 and 4, as played by the drummer (usually) on the snare drum. (Other drums or the hi-hat can be used for quieter backbeats.) Backbeats can be added to a 4/4 swing rhythm as well. They increase danceability by clarifying the rhythm and adding to the excitement of the music.

Back catalog The complete recordings that a company holds in its vaults or claims the rights to by having purchased other record labels. Many of these recordings are out of print or were never issued in their original form.

Back phrasing A musical technique in which the singer momentarily delays the entry of a new phrase, in effect freeing the rhythm of a composition. Occurring most often in ballads, it generally conveys a loose feeling, as though the singer were delivering the song spontaneously.

Balance The ability of a section to blend. In a well-balanced section, none of the players will be too soft or too loud relative to the others.

Banjo A stringed, strummed instrument that often provided the chords in New Orleans and Chicago-style (Dixieland) jazz.

Bar or measure A music segment that represents each instance of the meter.

Bass A low-pitched stringed instrument and one of the members of the rhythm section in a jazz band. Listen to Track 43 of the Audio Primer to hear an acoustic bass.

Beat A steady pulse, such as a heartbeat, and an instance of *rhythm*, the experience of music through time.

Bebop A nervous, energetic style of jazz that developed in the 1940s. The term probably developed from the nonsense syllables used by scat singers to recreate the characteristic melodic phrases of the new style. Also called *bop*.

Bent pitch A small glissando or slide from one frequency to (usually) a slightly higher one. On guitar it is achieved by pushing against the string on the fret board, thus "bending" it.

Big band A large jazz ensemble typically including three to four trumpets, three to four trombones, four to five reeds (saxophones and doublings), and rhythm (typically piano, guitar, bass, and drums).

Block-chord style See *locked-hands style*.

Blue note A bent, slurred, or "worried" note. Most often occurs on the third of the scale, but any note can be made "blue" by varying its intonation in a blues or jazz performance.

Blues An African American folk music that appeared around 1900 and exerted influence on jazz and various forms of U.S. popular music.

Blues form A basic 12-bar chord progression that may be varied depending on the blues or jazz style. The basic progression is shown in Music Example I-5. Its fundamental harmonies are I (4 bars), IV (2 bars), I (2 bars), V (1 bar), IV (1 bar), I (2 bars). Listen to Track 11 of the Audio Primer to hear a modern version of blues form. See *12-bar aab blues form* for how the lyric fits the 12 bars.

Blues harmony A standard set of chord changes. See *blues form*.

Blues scale A form of scale that incorporates the principal notes used in the blues. Most often, 1–♭3–4–♯4–5–♭7

Listen to the second scale played on Track 1 of the Audio Primer. See Example I-6 for a classic blues scale in music notation.

Boogie-woogie A form of blues piano playing in which the performer maintains a driving eighth-note rhythm in the left hand while improvising blues figures in the right hand.

Book See *library*.

Bop See *bebop*.

Bossa nova A Latin jazz style that developed from Brazilian music in the late 1950s and early 1960s. Stan Getz was prominent among jazz players with bossa nova hits.

Brasses A family of the *wind instruments*; a player buzzes the lips into a cup-shaped mouthpiece to create sound.

Break A short pause in a band's playing—usually one or two bars—to feature a soloist. Often a band will play in *stop time* while the soloist improvises breaks between the band's chords.

Bridge The term that describes the B section of a song; *head* describes the A section.

Cadence The closing strain of a phrase, section, or movement. Also refers to a common closing chord progression.

Cakewalk A dance involving an exaggerated walking step. In exhibitions of cakewalking, the most talented couple won a cake at the end of the evening. The cakewalk may have been an imitation of the way members of white "high society" comported themselves.

Call-and-response A musical procedure in which a single voice or instrument states a melodic phrase—the *call*—and a group of voices or instruments follows with a responding or completing phrase—the *response*.

Chair Each member of a section, as in first trumpet chair, first trombone chair, and so on.

Change-step See *backbeat*.

Chart A common term for a jazz band arrangement.

Chicago jazz A type of New Orleans–style jazz created by Chicago musicians in the 1920s.

Chord A group of three or more notes played simultaneously; acts as the basic unit of *harmony*.

Chord progression A sequence of chords, usually within a composition.

Chorus Each time the performers execute or work through the form of a song, it is called a chorus—for example, once through a 12-bar blues or once through a 32-bar song.

Chorus reverberation An electronic effect that guitarists use to "fatten," or fill out, sounds. The sound signal is enriched through the addition of reverb (echo) and a chorus effect (that is, added frequencies complement the sound, giving the effect of several voices or tones sounding at once).

Chromatic scale A scale with all twelve notes of the Western musical system, for example, all the adjacent notes on the piano. There are twelve notes in an octave, which create a chromatic scale.

Church cadence See *plagal cadence*.

Clarinet A single-reed woodwind instrument. Listen to Tracks 20 and 21 of the ⓟ Audio Primer to hear examples of the clarinet.

Claves Two thick wooden sticks that, when struck together, produce the characteristic *click* of the Latin percussion sound.

Collective improvisation The term often applied to the simultaneous improvising of the New Orleans (Dixieland) jazz ensemble. The term may also be used to describe free jazz performances that include simultaneous improvisation.

Comping A technique in which a pianist or guitarist plays a chord progression in a rhythmically irregular fashion. The term *comp* is probably derived from a contraction of the word *accompany* or *complement*. Listen to Al Haig's syncopated comping behind Charlie Parker and Dizzy Gillespie on "Salt Peanuts" (Track 28). For an early example of piano comping in a swing-band setting, listen to Count Basie's accompaniment to Lester Young's tenor solo on "Every Tub" (Track 20).

Complete reissue The duplication of an artist's or a group's entire available body of recorded material—including errors, outtakes, and technical problems.

Concerto A concert composition featuring a soloist accompanied by an orchestra or a larger ensemble.

Contrafact A new melody to fit the harmonic and formal structure of a previously composed popular song.

Cool jazz In part a reaction to bebop, it embraced the values of increased compositional complexity, slower tempos, and at times less overt emotional involvement.

Cornet A medium-range *brass* instrument much like a trumpet but with a larger bore and hence a mellower sound. Heard mostly in New Orleans and Chicago jazz in the 1920s where, like the trumpet, it was a lead instrument.

Countermelody A separate line that runs in counterpoint to the main melody. Like an obbligato, a countermelody is a secondary melody that accompanies the main melody. A countermelody, however, is generally heard on the trombone or in a lower voice, has fewer notes than the *obbligato*, and is often improvised. Another word for countermelody is *counterline*. Listen to Track 7 of the ⓟ Audio Primer; the piano enters in the middle register with a countermelody.

Counterpoint The use of simultaneously sounding musical lines. See also *polyphony*.

Creoles of Color People of mixed black and white ancestry, often from New Orleans. Until the late nineteenth century, they enjoyed more freedom and were better educated than the general black population. Musicians from this group generally had classical training and could read musical scores.

Crossover The practice of mixing musical styles and cultures. As first seen in the concert jazz of the 1920s and the third-stream practices of the 1950s, crossover can mix different styles within a given culture—for example, bluegrass and classical music—or it can mix entirely different cultures, such as traditional Japanese music and bebop.

Crossover music Music that combines jazz or jazz values with other styles and music of other cultures.

Cross-rhythms The performance of simultaneous and contrasting rhythms, such as patterns with duple and triple groupings. Superimposing one rhythmic pattern on another causes a cross-rhythm to develop. Cross-rhythms are sometimes called *polyrhythms*.

Cubop The 1940s blending of bebop with Afro-Cuban music, brought to New York City by an immigration of Cubans in the 1920s.

Digital delay An electronic effect that creates an echo or a secondary sound so that a guitarist can, in effect, play several parts at once.

Dixieland A popular term for the jazz style that originated in New Orleans and flourished in the late 1910s and 1920s. The Dixieland jazz band often had a front line (of trumpet or cornet, trombone, and clarinet) accompanied by a rhythm section (of piano, guitar or banjo, bass, and drums). Also called *New Orleans jazz*.

Double-necked guitar A guitar that has two necks. Sometimes the second neck has twelve strings rather than the usual six.

Dropping bombs A technique in which bebop drummers used the bass drum to make sharp, irregular accents in the rhythmic accompaniment.

Drums The backbone of the jazz rhythm section. Usually a drum kit consists of snare drum, bass drum, several tom-toms, and various cymbals. Listen to Tracks 26–35 of the ⓟ Audio Primer to hear a range of drum sounds.

Duple meter Music alternating between two pulses—one strong and one weak (ONE-two, ONE-two).

Dynamics The volume of sound, from very soft to very loud.

Echoplex A commercial electronic device that adds echo to a sound. The rate of speed of the echo can be altered to make the delay effect slight or more pronounced. This device was popular in the late 1960s and the 1970s.

Elastic meter A rhythmic effect created when the soloist or rhythm section masks the strong metric downbeats so that the meter seems to be stretched beyond its normal parameters. This illusion is often created when musicians play unusually long phrases that move the melodic emphasis off the expected downbeats that occur at the beginning of each measure.

Ethnomusicology The study of music in a cultural context.

Extended chord tones Notes added to seventh chords to make the harmony richer and more pungent. These tones are usually ninths, elevenths, and thirteenths. Extended chord tones will usually resolve to more-stable pitches, such as roots, thirds, and fifths. Also called *tensions*.

False start An incorrect start of a performance—a musician begins playing a measure or two, and then, realizing the mistake, stops abruptly.

Feedback A distorted effect created when the sound coming from a speaker is picked up by an electronic sensing device such as a microphone and routed again back to the speaker. As this process multiplies, harsh electronic wails are created.

Flat The symbol ♭ that lowers the pitch of a given note by one-half step.

Flat five See *tritone*.

Form The organization of music in time by dividing a work into individual units called sections. Each *section* contains a set of measures and divides further into sets of measures called *phrases*. We label a section with a capital letter of the alphabet (A, B, C, and so on) and label a phrase with a lowercase letter (a, b, c)—a system that allows us to describe a work's musical form in abbreviated fashion.

Formula A worked-out melodic idea that fits a common chord progression. Most improvisers develop formulas, especially for up-tempo improvisation because the rapid tempo does not allow time for total spontaneity. A formula is more popularly known as a *lick*.

Free jazz The 1960s jazz substyle that overturned many of the traditional elements of the music. Also called *avant-garde* and the *New Thing*.

Frequency modulation Sound modulation in which the frequency (the range of high and low) of the wave is modified by another wave, producing a sound vastly different from the original. See also *amplitude modulation* and *modulation*.

Front line The lead (melody) instruments in a jazz ensemble, usually melodic (playing one note at a time) and often featured at the front of the stage. The front line usually included trumpet (or cornet), trombone, and clarinet. (Common use of saxophone was a later development.)

Fugue A musical form, prominent in the Baroque era, characterized by continuous counterpoint based on a principal melodic idea called the *subject*. At the beginning of a typical fugue, in a section known as the *exposition*, each voice (or part) enters by stating the subject.

Full-chord style See *locked-hands style*.

Funky jazz A style that combines elements of gospel music and R&B with jazz. It began to emerge in the 1950s as an outgrowth of hard bop and became quite popular in the 1960s. Also called *soul jazz*.

Fusion See *jazz-rock*.

Ghost bands Groups whose founding leaders have died but who continue to travel and work under new direction.

Glissando A technique whereby notes are slurred directly from one to another, producing a continuous rise or fall in pitch.

Guitar A string instrument played as either a lead instrument (through picking) or a rhythm instrument (through chord strumming). It can be acoustic or amplified. Listen to Tracks 36–42 of the ⓟ Audio Primer to hear examples of acoustic and electric guitars in different settings.

Habanera rhythm Probably the most common Latin ingredient in jazz until the 1940s. In the habanera and other Latin rhythms, the beat is divided into two even halves, contrasting with the "swung" eighth notes more typical of swing.

Hard bop A jazz movement of the 1950s that drew on the speed, intensity, and power of bebop and sometimes married bop to gospel and blues-influenced music in a substyle known as funky or soul jazz.

Harlem Renaissance A period—roughly 1921 to 1929—of outstanding artistic activity among African Americans. The movement was centered in Harlem in New York City.

Harmolodics A theory of music devised by Ornette Coleman. Although its meaning is unclear, harmolodics has provided the theoretical motivation behind Coleman's work since the 1970s.

Harmon mute A hollow metal mute that, when placed in the bell of the trumpet, gives its sound a distant, brooding quality. Miles Davis's use of the harmon mute from 1954 onward helped popularize its use. Listen to Track 14 of the ⓟ Audio Primer to hear an example of a harmon mute.

Harmonic substitution The alteration of the original chord progression by the use of new chords that function similarly to the original chords. Listen to Track 6 of the ⓟ Audio Primer to hear examples of harmonic substitution.

Harmonic superimposition The technique of adding chords on top of the harmonies already present in a song, thereby creating further harmonic complexity.

Harmony Defines a *chord*, generally a group of three or four notes played simultaneously.

Head The A section or principal melody of a song; *bridge* describes the B section.

Head arrangement A musical plan and form worked up verbally by the players in rehearsal or on the bandstand.

Hipster A young follower of jazz who affected the dress, speech, and manner of jazz musicians working in the new jazz styles of the late 1940s and early 1950s.

Hot bands Jazz bands that featured fast tempos and dramatic solo and group performances, usually with more improvisation than sweet bands had. See also *sweet bands*.

Improvisation The essence of jazz—refers to a performance technique in which the improviser or soloist spontaneously creates a melody that fits the form and harmony of the piece. Also called an *improvised solo*.

Inside playing The jazz technique of playing melodic lines that favor the principal notes of the harmonies. See also *outside playing*. Listen to Track 8 of the ⓟ Audio Primer to hear examples of inside and outside playing.

Instrumental Music that lacks vocals.

Interval The distance between any two notes.

Intonation The ability of a musician to reproduce a given pitch. Musicians with good intonation are said to be playing "in tune." That is, the players know how to make small adjustments in the pitch of their instruments as they play so that they match the pitches of the other players in the section.

Introduction The section that occurs at the beginning of a piece and sets up the entrance of the melody and first section.

Jazz chair A player hired especially for improvisational fluency; spoken of as the jazz chair of a given section. For example, Bix Beiderbecke occupied the jazz trumpet chair in the Paul Whiteman band, as did Bubber Miley in the Ellington band.

Jazz-funk See *jazz-rock*.

Jazz pedagogy The discipline that comprises the methods and the philosophies of teaching students how to perform jazz.

Jazz repertory movement A movement since the 1980s in which ensembles devoted themselves to the re-creation and performance of the works of historically significant jazz artists. Just as classical music has an accepted repertory of great works, the jazz repertory movement is trying to establish an official canon for jazz.

Jazz-rock A form of jazz that combines elements of rock (or R&B funk) and jazz. Also called *jazz-funk* or *fusion*.

Key Refers to the *tonality* of a piece of music as determined by the scales and chords that the piece uses. If for example, a work uses the C scale (a scale that starts on the note C), the work is said to be in the key of C. A key may take a *major* or *minor* form, as indicated by its scale.

Lead instruments See *front line*.

Lead player The player in a section who usually takes the melody or top part and occupies the first chair of the section. The lead player usually plays slightly more loudly than the other players in the section.

Lead trumpet The lead chair or first trumpet player of the trumpet section. This player needs to be dominating and capable of precision, power, and control of the high register. A big band is particularly dependent on the lead trumpet.

Legato The technique of playing notes smoothly in a connected manner. The opposite of legato is *staccato*.

Library A band's collection of arrangements or pieces. These are usually songs but may also include larger-scale works. A library is necessary for big bands, but smaller groups may have one. Also called a *book*.

Lick See *formula*.

Locked-hands style A mode of performance in which the pianist plays a four-note chord in the right hand and doubles the top note with the left hand an octave below. The hands move together in a "locked" rhythmic pattern as they follow the same rhythm. This style is also called *block-chord* or *full-chord style*. Listen to Track 9 of the 🅟 Audio Primer to hear an example of locked-hands style.

LP A long-playing record that typically plays at 33 ⅓ rpm (revolutions per minute). LPs first became commercially available in 1948. LPs were made with polyvinyl chloride (hence the nickname "vinyl" for records) and allowed up to about twenty-five minutes of music per side.

Measure See *bar*.

Mellotron An electronic instrument used for string-ensemble effects in the 1970s. An early, analog sound module, the Mellotron produces notes by activating short tape recordings of a string ensemble playing each note of the scale. When a key is pressed, the tape recording of the chosen note plays.

Melody The sequential arrangement of the notes of the scale into a coherent pattern.

Meter A rhythmic pattern arising from regular groupings of two or three beats. These define, respectively, duple or triple meter. Most music with a steady pulse has meter. See *duple meter* and *triple meter*.

Metric displacement A technique whereby the soloist implies or states in the melody a rhythm that seems to go against the underlying basic meter of the piece. It also can be achieved by placing melodic phrases irregularly against the underlying rhythm.

Metronomic sense A steady rhythmic pulse, often associated with drums and with music from Africa.

Microtones Pitches between the tempered notes of the chromatic scale. See also *nontempered intonation*.

MIDI An acronym for *Musical Instrument Digital Interface*. This standard language allows computers to control synthesizers or samplers.

Minstrelsy A form of U.S. musical theater and variety show that flourished in the nineteenth century. Traveling troupes performed songs, dances, and skits based on caricatures of African Americans. Performed by both blacks and whites in blackface, minstrelsy is often considered the first distinctively U.S. musical genre.

Modal jazz A body of music that makes use of one or more of the following characteristics: modal scales for improvising, slow harmonic rhythm, pedal points, and the absence or suppression of functional harmonic relationships. Significant early examples of modal jazz come from Miles Davis's recording *Kind of Blue* (1959) and the recordings of John Coltrane's classic quartet (1960–1964).

Modulation Changing a sound by feeding one sound wave through another. See also *amplitude modulation* and *frequency modulation*.

Moldy figs A term used by younger musicians and fans in the 1940s to describe older jazz fans who clung to the music of the 1920s and 1930s and derided the newer bebop style.

Motivic cells Short melodic ideas subject to variation and development. Also called *thematic cells*.

Multiphonics A technique of producing more than one note at a time on a wind instrument. Using nonstandard fingering and appropriate embouchure, the player splits the air stream into two or more parts, thus producing a multinote "chordal" effect. The technique is difficult to control, may be strident, and is generally associated with avant-garde playing.

Multitracking See *overdubbing*.

Mute A device played in or over the bells of brass instruments to alter their tone. Different mutes create different kinds of effects, but a muted brass tone will usually be less brilliant than the "open" horn. Listen to Tracks 13–15, 23, and 24 of the 🅟 Audio Primer to hear examples of muted brass sounds.

Neo-swing A popular movement in the 1990s that recreated the style of the 1930s and 1940s big bands.

New Orleans jazz See *Dixieland*.

New Thing See *free jazz*.

Nontempered intonation The use of pitches unrestricted by the "equal-tempered," twelve-note chromatic scale. For example, a nontempered pitch might be a note between D and E♭. Pitches between the tempered notes of the chromatic scale are sometimes called *microtones*.

Nu jazz Jazz-influenced music since the mid-nineties that makes use of hip-hop grooves, trance grooves, electronica, and house music.

Obbligato A term borrowed from classical music to describe a complementary melodic part played along with the main melody as a necessary, or expected, addition. In early jazz, obbligato parts were often florid, usually played by the clarinet, and sometimes improvised. (Listen to Track 21 of the 🅟 Audio Primer to hear an obbligato-like clarinet melody.)

Octave An interval of eight notes, in which the notes sound exactly the same but are higher or lower than each other, as in the first two notes of "Take Me Out to the Ball Game."

Ostinato A repeated melodic or harmonic idea that forms the basis for a section or an entire composition.

Out-chorus The final chorus of a jazz performance. When exuberant, it may also be called a *shout chorus*.

Outside playing The jazz technique of playing notes that depart from (or are "outside" of) the chords of a given piece. See also *inside playing*. Listen to Track 8 of the 🅟 Audio Primer to hear examples of inside and outside playing.

Overdubbing A recording-studio technique that was generally available by the 1950s. The recording tape has several parallel tracks that enable musicians to record additional performance parts at later times. The added part is called an *overdub*. By wearing headphones, the players follow and "play to" the previously recorded tracks. In current recording studios, computer-controlled equipment and digital technology permit virtually unlimited overdubbing and editing of recorded parts. Also called *multitracking*.

Partial A series of higher notes that occurs when a note is sounded and that contributes to the timbre of the original pitch. These higher notes are based on mathematical relationships to the original note, known as the *fundamental*. *Partial* is also known as *overtone*.

Pedal point A sustained or repeated bass note or drone played to accompany a melody; it is also called a *pedal tone*.

Pedal tone See *pedal point*.

Pentatonic scale A five-note set that avoids the interval of a tritone and can be arranged as a series of perfect fourths or perfect fifths. The black notes of the keyboard form one such scale. Also called *pentatonic set*.

Pentatonic set See *pentatonic scale*.

Percussion instruments Instruments struck with either the hand or a stick or mallet.

Phase shifter An electronic device that alters the sound of an instrument by altering the sound wave's shape. The resulting sound has a bubbling or slightly hard-edged quality.

Phrase A set of measures in a *section*. We label a phrase with a lowercase letter (a, b, c)—part of the system that allows us to describe a work's musical form in abbreviated fashion.

Piano The principal Western keyboard instrument. In jazz it functions as a solo instrument and as part of the rhythm section (usually with bass and drums and sometimes added guitar or banjo). The piano trio (with bass and drums or bass and guitar) is a common small jazz ensemble that features the piano.

Piano rolls Cylinders of rolled paper punched with holes. When fed through a properly equipped player piano, the holes activate hammers that play the piano automatically.

Piano trio A performance group made up of piano, bass, and drums. Another form of the piano trio features piano, bass, and guitar.

Pickup A short melodic idea that ends on the downbeat.

Pitch A note's sound relative to its place higher or lower on the music scale.

Plagal cadence A type of cadence that contains the harmonic progression IV–I (instead of the more common progression V–I). It is often used at the ends of hymns with the concluding "Amen." Plagal cadences were featured frequently in funky/soul jazz. Sometimes called *church cadence* or *Amen cadence*.

Player piano A piano equipped with a mechanism that allows it to play piano rolls.

Plunger A type of mute derived from a plumber's sink plunger. The rubber cup of the plunger is held against the bell of the instrument and manipulated with the left hand to alter the horn's tone quality.

Polyphony Describes music with at least two distinct, simultaneous melodic lines. Another name for a polyphonic texture is *counterpoint*.

Polyrhythms See *cross-rhythms*.

Portamento A smooth, uninterrupted slide from one tone to another, especially with the voice or a bowed stringed instrument.

Postmodernism An attitude toward art and culture that has become common since the 1970s. It disavows some of the cerebral, audience-distancing tenets of modernism and replaces them with a freewheeling conception of culture. Some postmodernist practices blend styles and cultures; forgo structural unity as a necessity for art; incorporate older styles and genres; project an ironic, even cynical conception of art and expression; and break down barriers between popular and fine art.

Prime The symbol ' that when added to a section letter indicates that a section repeats but in modified form.

Race record An early recording, usually of jazz or blues and typically performed by and marketed to African Americans.

Ragtime An African American musical genre that flourished from the late 1890s through the mid-1910s and is based on constant syncopation in the right hand often accompanied by a steady march bass in the left hand. Associated now primarily with piano music, ragtime was originally a method of performance that included syncopated songs, music for various ensembles, and arrangements of nonragtime music. Scott Joplin was ragtime's most famous composer.

Ragtime form Borrowed from the European march form, ragtime form contains three or four sections, called strains, of 16 bars each.

Reeds A family of the *wind instruments*; the player blows through or across a reed, which is attached to the mouthpiece, to create the sound.

Reharmonization The bop practice of inserting different chords into the fundamental chord structure of a well-known song to freshen the interpretation and expand harmonic options for the soloist.

Remastering The digital enhancement of an original recording's sound quality; it includes such techniques as filtering out extraneous noise and boosting certain frequencies.

Rent party An informal gathering in the 1920s, held to help raise money to pay the rent or buy groceries. At such parties musicians would often gather and perform, sometimes in competition with one another.

Rhythm The experience of music through time.

Rhythm changes A term derived from the form and harmony (or chord changes) of the 1930 George and Ira Gershwin song "I Got Rhythm." (The final two-bar tag of the original song is omitted so that a symmetrical 32-bar AABA plan results.) The bridge in rhythm changes consists of two-bar harmonies following a circle-of-fifths pattern that returns to the tonic. For example, if rhythm changes are performed in B♭, the harmonies of the eight-bar bridge are D7 (2 bars), G7 (2 bars), C7 (2 bars), and F7 (2 bars). The F7, as the dominant of the tonic B♭, leads back to the A section. Extremely popular since the 1930s, rhythm changes are still commonly used by jazz musicians for improvisation and composition. Listen to Track 10 of the Audio Primer to hear an example of rhythm changes.

Rhythm section A part of a jazz band that provides the rhythmic pulse, harmonies, and bass line. It may include any of the following: piano, guitar, bass, or drums. Early jazz bands sometimes included banjo and tuba in place of the guitar and bass. Listen to Tracks 44 and 45 of the Audio Primer to hear a modern rhythm section; Track 44 has bass and drums; Track 45 adds the piano.

Riff A short melodic idea, usually one to two bars long, that is repeated as the core idea of a musical passage. Sometimes different band sections trade riffs in a call-and-response format, often over changing harmonies. Usually rhythmic and simple, the riff also can provide an effective background for an improvising soloist. Listen to Track 49 of the Audio Primer to hear a trumpet playing a background riff in a small-group context to back up the tenor soloist.

Ring shout A rhythmic dance performed in a circle, originally derived from African religious practice. Worshipers moved in a counterclockwise direction while singing spirituals and accompanying themselves by clapping and stamping. Some historians describe the ring shout as contributing the essence of African song, dance, and spirit to African American music.

Rubato The technique in which performers take liberties with a steady pulse by speeding up or slowing down the musical flow.

Running the changes Improvising by maintaining mostly up-tempo eighth-note lines that articulate the chord changes in a virtuoso manner. The practice is particularly associated with bebop, where it became widespread.

Samba A fast, syncopated dance introduced in the United States from Brazil in the 1930s and 1940s.

Samplers Electronic devices used both to sample and to play back sounds.

Sampling The practice of digitally recording sounds for musical use in playback. Any kind of sound can be sampled, from a note on an acoustic instrument, to natural sounds, to a passage of music already recorded. For playback the sound is usually activated by computer or by pressing a key on a keyboard. See also *samplers* and *sound modules*.

Saxophone A single-reed instrument made of brass that is common in all jazz styles except New Orleans (Dixieland). The saxophone comes in many sizes and ranges. Listen to Tracks 16–19 of the Audio Primer to hear the four most common saxophones.

Scale Derived from the Italian word for ladder, it arranges notes into a series of octaves, the individual notes of which are labeled A, B, C, D, E, F, G, and repeat in ascending or descending order.

Scat singing A jazz vocal style in which the soloist improvises using made-up or "nonsense" syllables.

Section (of band) A group of related instruments in a big band; three trumpets and three trombones might form the brass section.

Section (of form) A contained set of measures in a work that divides further into *phrases*. We label a section with a capital letter of the alphabet (A, B, C, and so on)—part of a system that allows us to describe a work's *musical form* in abbreviated fashion. See also *form*.

Sharp The symbol ♯ that raises the pitch of a given note by one half-step.

Sheets of sound An expression coined by jazz critic Ira Gitler to describe John Coltrane's method of playing that features extremely fast notes with irregular phrase groupings. Sometimes unusual harmonies are introduced over the given chord changes.

Shout chorus The climactic chorus of a jazz performance; it often occurs at the end of a piece, in which case it might also be called an *out-chorus*.

Shuffle A 4/4 rhythmic pattern in which each beat is represented by the drummer playing a dotted-eighth and a sixteenth note, usually on the ride cymbal.

Sideman A player who is neither a lead player nor a featured soloist.

Slap bass A technique in which the bass player percussively hits the low strings of the electric bass while picking melodies on the higher ones. This "slapping and popping" style was created by Larry Graham and subsequently imitated by jazz, funk, and pop bass players.

Slap-tonguing A saxophone novelty technique that produces a humorous effect.

Slash notation A method of showing the harmonies (or "chord changes") in jazz and popular music. Each slash in a measure denotes a beat. The arranger places chords over the slashes to show the beats on which the harmonies change. (See Music Examples I-4 and I-5, for example.)

Smooth jazz A popular form of fusion jazz that combines rock or funk grooves with an electronic ambience to create an "easy listening" feel. Although improvisation may be present, the pleasant quality of the groove and the melody are its dominant features.

Soli In big-band charts, it often designates a part of the piece written to feature an instrumental section in harmony.

Solo break See *break*.

Song plugger In the 1920s someone who performed a song, usually at a music store, to encourage people to buy the sheet music.

Soul jazz See *funky jazz*.

Sound fields A musical effect created when coinciding melodic lines fuse into an indistinguishable web or mass of sound with irregular accentuation within each line.

Sound modules Electronic devices that play back prerecorded samples, which can be digitally stored on a computer for playback. See also *sampling*.

Speakeasy A Prohibition-era nightclub in which liquor was sold illegally.

Spirituals African American songs that arose in the nineteenth century and consisted of religious lyrics with folk melodies. They were often harmonized for vocal choir.

Staccato The technique of playing short notes with distinct spaces between them. The opposite of staccato is *legato*.

Standard A song that, unlike the vast majority of popular music, outlasts its contemporaries and enjoys a long-lasting place in current repertories. "I Got Rhythm," for example, is a standard written by George and Ira Gershwin in 1930.

Step connection The principal means of stringing together the melodic and harmonic elements. The steps are often based on the scale determined by the key of the piece. This is a key element in *voice leading*.

Stock arrangement (stock) An arrangement created and sold by a publishing company to bandleaders. Bands played stock arrangements to keep up with the latest hit songs.

Stop time A performance technique in which the rhythm section punctuates distinct beats, often to accommodate a soloist's improvisation between the band's chords. Listen to Tracks 46 and 48 of the Audio Primer to hear breaks and stop time.

Stretto A series of instruments or parts entering with overlapping statements of a fugue subject.

Stride piano A school of jazz piano performance based on a moving left-hand accompaniment alternating bass notes and chords with an appropriate right-hand figuration pulling or tugging at the left hand.

String instruments Instruments that produce sound from a player plucking, strumming, or striking strings drawn over a voice box.

Strophic A term used to describe a musical work that has repeated choruses.

Subject The principal melodic idea of a piece, such as a fugue.

Suite A European classical musical work that has several sections, each with distinctive melodies and moods. The sections may be related thematically. Often composers will extract the most popular or most effective sections from extended works, such as operas and ballets, to create a suite for concert performance.

Sweet bands Bands that played relatively less-syncopated, slower pieces, such as ballads and popular songs. See also *hot bands*.

Swell The rapid change in volume that can be created by pushing down on or releasing the volume pedal on an electronic or conventional organ.

Swing Generic term for the jazz and much popular music of the mid-thirties through the mid-forties.

Swing-bass The stride-derived practice of alternating bass note and midrange chord on every beat.

Syncopation The disruption of regular meter that occurs when the weaker notes of the designated meter receive unexpectedly stronger accents, as in the second and fourth beats in 4/4 meter receiving stronger accents. See Music Example 1-2, third measure (page 35), and listen to Track 4 of the Audio Primer. The Joplin phrase is played first as it was written (with syncopation), then without.

Synthesizer Originally developed for musical use in the early 1950s. Unlike acoustic instruments, the synthesizer produced sound electronically: in analog synthesizers an oscillator supplies a voltage to an amplifier, from which it is routed to a speaker.

Tag A short, coda-like section added to the end of a composition to give it closure.

Tailgate trombone The New Orleans style of playing trombone with chromatic glissandos. The trombonist would play in the back—on the tailgate—of the New Orleans advertising wagons when the bands traveled during the day to advertise their upcoming dances. Listen to Track 25 of the Audio Primer to hear an example of tailgate trombone.

Tempo The speed of the music's beat, ordinarily ranging from forty to two hundred beats per minute.

Tensions See *extended chord tones*.

Terminal vibrato A vibrato added to the end of a sustained note.

Territory band In the swing era, a band that played and toured a region around a major city that served as a home base.

Texture The density of musical sound, as determined by the instruments (or voices) heard, the number of instruments, and the number of notes or sounds being played by them. Textures are often described as thick (many notes heard) or thin (few notes).

Thematic cells See *motivic cells*.

Third-stream music A blend of jazz and European concert music. In many instances, third-stream composers create concert works that allow for improvisation within larger-scale structures influenced by both jazz and concert music.

Timbre The specific quality of a given instrument or voice.

Time signature A symbol that appears on a music staff. It consists of two numbers, one on top of the other, which together indicate the music's meter.

Tin Pan Alley The collective name applied to the major New York City sheet music publishers. Tin Pan Alley flourished from the late 1800s until the mid-twentieth century.

Tonality A Western musical system in which pieces are organized according to harmony within some key or with respect to some central pitch.

Tonic The first note of a given scale, it forms the "center of gravity" to which all the other notes in the scale relate.

Trading solos, or trading twos, trading fours, or trading eights Improvisational jazz formats common since the swing era. In trading fours, for example, each soloist improvises for four bars before the next soloist takes over for four bars. Any number of soloists may participate, but most typically two to four do. Trading solos is often used to create climactic moments in performances. Listen to Track 47 of the Audio Primer to hear an example of trading twos.

Transcribe To write in standard, European music notation what the listener, or transcriber, hears. See also *transcription.*

Transcription The notated version of a piece of music. Transcriptions of the same piece of music can vary widely, depending on the quality of the original sound source, the skill of the transcriber, and what the transcriber chooses to include in the notation.

Triad A three-note chord, the most basic chord.

Trill A rapid alternation between a note and a note that is a step higher. The higher note generally embellishes the lower note.

Triple meter Music where two weak pulses separate single strong pulses (ONE-two-three, ONE-two-three).

Tritone A diminished fifth or an augmented fourth—a popular interval in bebop melodies; it is sometimes called a *flat five* by jazz musicians.

Trombone A lower brass instrument that changes pitch by means of a slide. (There is also a less common valve trombone that works largely like a lower-pitched trumpet.) In New Orleans jazz, it typically provides countermelodies to the trumpet lead. Big bands often feature sections of three or four trombones. It is also an important jazz solo instrument. Listen to Tracks 22–25 of the Audio Primer to hear examples of trombone playing.

Tuba A low brass instrument that sometimes provided the bass part in New Orleans and Chicago-style (*Dixieland*) jazz. Uncommon in later jazz styles.

Twelve-tone composition A twentieth-century procedure pioneered by Viennese composer Arnold Schoenberg in the 1920s. In twelve-tone composition, as it was originally conceived, all twelve pitches of the chromatic scale are arranged into an ordered *set*, also called a *tone row* or *series.*

Vamp A repeated melodic or harmonic idea. In jazz, its predictability makes it easier for the performer to devise variations or improvise new ideas.

Vertical improvisation An improvisation based on the chord harmonies (stacked vertically) as opposed to the melodic contour (running horizontally).

Vibrato A method of varying the pitch frequency of a note, producing a wavering sound. A vibrato brings a note to life. Heard mostly on wind instruments, strings, and vocals.

Vocalese The technique of setting lyrics to existing jazz solos. Eddie Jefferson was probably the most notable pioneer of this technique, although the practice can be traced to the late 1920s.

Voice leading A means of making logical melodic and harmonic sequences within an improvised solo. *Step connection*, a key element in voice leading, is the principal means of stringing together the melodic and harmonic elements. The steps are often based on the scale determined by the key of the piece.

Wah-wah pedal A pitch-frequency filter, operated by the foot, that is usually used by guitarists or electric keyboardists. When the pedal is pressed, the note or chord being held makes a *wah* sound. (An acoustic *wah* sound can be achieved by brass players' using their left hands or mutes over the bells of their instruments.) The up-and-down movement of the pedal creates the repeated *wah-wah* effect. (Listen to Track 41 of the Audio Primer to hear jazz-rock guitar with wah-wah pedal.)

Walking bass A musical technique in which the bass player articulates all four beats in a 4/4 bar. The bass lines often follow scale patterns, avoiding too many disruptive leaps between notes. The walking bass is quite common in jazz, heard in all styles since becoming firmly established during the swing era. Listen to Track 43 of the Audio Primer to hear a walking bass.

West Coast jazz A jazz style from the 1950s that embodied many of the principles of cool jazz as performed by a group of players centered in California.

Whole-tone scale A scale with whole steps only and thus no dominant, making it impossible to form major or minor triads. There are only two whole-tone scales: C–D–E–F♯–G♯–B♭ and D♭–E♭–F–G–A–B. Notice that they share no notes. The scale is often associated with French twentieth-century composers such as Claude Debussy. Listen to Track 1 of the Audio Primer; the whole-tone scale is the fifth scale played.

Wind instruments Instruments that produce sound from players' breaths; they divide into two families: *brasses* and *reeds.*

Selected Readings

Allen, William Francis, Charles Pickard Ware, and Lucy McKim Garrison. *Slave Songs of the United States*. New York: Peter Smith, 1951. Orig. pub. New York: A. Simpson, 1867. Reprint, New York: Dover, 1997.

Armstrong, Louis. *In His Own Words: Selected Writings*. Edited and with an Introduction by Thomas Brothers. New York: Oxford University Press, 1999.

_____. *Satchmo: My Life in New Orleans*. New York: Prentice-Hall, 1954. Reprint, New York: Da Capo Press, 1986.

_____. *Swing That Music*. New York: Longmans, Green, 1936.

Balliett, Whitney. *Jelly Roll, Jabbo, and Fats: Nineteen Portraits in Jazz*. New York: Oxford University Press, 1983.

Barker, Danny. *A Life in Jazz*. New York: Oxford University Press, 1986.

Basie, Count, as told to Albert Murray. *Good Morning Blues: The Autobiography of Count Basie*. New York: Random House, 1985.

Bechet, Sidney. *Treat It Gentle: An Autobiography*. New York: Hill and Wang, 1960. Reprint, New York: Da Capo Press, 1978.

Berlin, Edward A. *Ragtime: A Musical and Cultural History*. Berkeley: University of California Press, 1980.

Berliner, Paul F. *Thinking in Jazz: The Infinite Art of Improvisation*. Chicago and London: University of Chicago Press, 1994.

Bethell, Tom. *George Lewis: A Jazzman from New Orleans*. Berkeley: University of California Press, 1977.

Borque, Fred. "Pat Metheny: Musings on Neo-Fusion." *Down Beat*, March 22, 1979, pp. 13 ff.

Brown, Theodore Dennis. "A History and Analysis of Jazz Drumming to 1942." Ph.D. dissertation, University of Michigan, 1976.

Bushell, Garvin, as told to Mark Tucker. *Jazz from the Beginning*. Ann Arbor: University of Michigan Press, 1990.

Calloway, Cab and Bryant Rollins. *Of Minnie the Moocher and Me*. New York: Crowell, 1976.

Carr, Ian. *Miles Davis: A Biography*. New York: Morrow, 1982.

Carver, Reginald and Lenny Bernstein. *Jazz Profiles: The Spirit of the Nineties*. New York: Billboard Books, 1998.

Chambers, Jack. *Milestones 1: The Music and Times of Miles Davis to 1960*. Toronto: University of Toronto Press, 1983.

_____. *Milestones 2: The Music and Times of Miles Davis Since 1960*. Toronto: University of Toronto Press, 1985.

Charters, Samuel and Leonard Kunstadt. *Jazz: A History of the New York Scene*. Garden City, NY: Doubleday, 1962. Reprint, New York: Da Capo Press, 1981.

Chase, Gilbert. *America's Music: From the Pilgrims to the Present*. 3rd ed. rev. Urbana: University of Illinois Press, 1987.

Chilton, John. *Sidney Bechet: The Wizard of Jazz*. New York: Oxford University Press, 1987.

_____. *Who's Who of Jazz: Storyville to Swing Street*. 4th ed. New York: Da Capo Press, 1985.

Collier, James Lincoln. *Benny Goodman and the Swing Era*. New York: Oxford University Press, 1989.

_____. *Duke Ellington*. New York: Oxford University Press, 1987.

_____. *Louis Armstrong: An American Genius*. New York: Oxford University Press, 1983.

Coltrane, John, in collaboration with Don DeMicheal. "Coltrane on Coltrane." *Down Beat,* September 29, 1960, pp. 26–27.

Coryell, Julie and Laura Friedman. *Jazz-Rock Fusion: The People, The Music.* New York: Delacorte Press, 1978.

Crouch, Stanley. *Kansas City Lightning: The Rise and Times of Charlie Parker.* New York: HarperCollins, 2013.

Dance, Stanley. *The World of Earl Hines.* New York: Scribner, 1977. Reprint, New York: Da Capo Press, 1979.

———. *The World of Swing.* New York: Scribner, 1974. Reprint, New York: Da Capo Press, 1979.

Davis, Miles and Quincy Troupe. *Miles: The Autobiography.* New York: Simon & Schuster, 1989.

Deffaa, Chip. *Voices of the Jazz Age: Profiles of Eight Vintage Jazzmen.* Urbana and Chicago: University of Illinois Press, 1992.

DeMicheal, Don. "John Coltrane and Eric Dolphy Answer the Jazz Critics." *Down Beat,* April 12, 1962, pp. 20 ff.

DeVeaux, Scott. *The Birth of Bebop: A Social and Musical History.* Berkeley: University of California Press, 1997.

Dodds, Baby, as told to Larry Gara. *The Baby Dodds Story.* Rev. ed. Baton Rouge: Louisiana State University Press, 1992.

Douglas, Ann. *Terrible Honesty: Mongrel Manhattan in the 1920s.* New York: Farrar, Straus, Giroux, 1995.

Ellington, Duke. *Music Is My Mistress.* Garden City, NY: Doubleday, 1973. Reprint, New York: Da Capo Press, 1976.

Floyd, Samuel A., Jr., "Music in the Harlem Renaissance: An Overview." In *Black Music in the Harlem Renaissance,* ed. Samuel A. Floyd, Jr., New York: Greenwood Press, 1990.

Foster, Pops, as told to Tom Stoddard. *Pops Foster: The Autobiography of a New Orleans Jazzman.* Berkeley: University of California Press, 1971.

Gillespie, Dizzy, with Al Fraser. *To Be or Not … to Bop.* Garden City, NY: Doubleday, 1979. Reprint, New York: Da Capo Press, 1985.

Gioia, Ted. *The Birth (and Death) of the Cool.* Golden, Colorado: Speck Press, 2009.

———. *West Coast Jazz.* New York: Oxford University Press, 1992.

Gitler, Ira. *Jazz Masters of the Forties.* New York: Macmillan, 1966. Reprint, New York: Da Capo Press, 1983.

———. *Swing to Bop: An Oral History of the Transition in Jazz in the 1940s.* New York: Oxford University Press, 1985.

Givan, Benjamin. *The Music of Django Reinhardt.* Ann Arbor: University of Michigan Press, 2010.

Goodman, Benny and Irving Kolodin. *The Kingdom of Swing.* New York: Stackpole, 1939. Reprint, New York: Frederick Ungar, 1961.

Gridley, Mark. *Jazz Styles: History and Analysis.* 5th ed. Englewood Cliffs, NJ: Prentice-Hall, 1994.

Gushee, Lawrence. *Pioneers of Jazz: The Story of the Creole Band.* New York: Oxford University Press, 2005.

———. "Lester Young's 'Shoe Shine Boy.'" In *A Lester Young Reader,* ed. Lewis Porter, pp. 224–254. Washington, DC: Smithsonian Institution Press, 1991. Originally published as International Musicological Society, *Report of the Twelfth Congress, Berkeley, 1977,* ed. Daniel Heartz and Bonnie Wade. Kassel, Germany: Barenreiter, 1981.

———. Liner notes to King Oliver, *King Oliver's Jazz Band—1923.* Columbia P2 12744.

———. Liner notes to *Steppin' on the Gas: Rags to Jazz 1913–1927.* New World Records 269.

Hadlock, Richard. *Jazz Masters of the Twenties.* New York: Macmillan, 1965. Reprint, New York: Collier Books, 1974. Reprint, New York: Da Capo Press, 1988.

Hall, Robert L. "African Religious Retentions in Florida." In *Africanisms in American Culture,* ed. Joseph E. Holloway. Bloomington: Indiana University Press, 1990.

Handy, W. C. and Arna Bontemps. *Father of the Blues.* New York: Macmillan, 1941. Reprint, New York: Da Capo Press, 1991.

Harker, Brian. *Louis Armstrong's Hot Five and Hot Seven Recordings.* New York: Oxford University Press, 2011.

Hasse, John. *Beyond Category: The Life and Genius of Duke Ellington.* New York: Simon & Schuster, 1993.

———, ed. *Ragtime: Its History, Composers, and Music.* New York: Schirmer Books, 1985.

Hentoff, Nat. *The Jazz Life.* New York: Dial Press, 1961.

Hodeir, André. *Jazz: Its Evolution and Essence.* New York: Grove, 1956. Reprint, New York: Da Capo Press, 1976.

Howland, John. *Ellington Uptown: Duke Ellington, James P. Johnson, and the Birth of Concert Jazz.* Ann Arbor: University of Michigan Press, 2009.

Howlett, Felicity. "An Introduction to Art Tatum's Performance Approaches: Composition, Improvisation, and Melodic Variation." Ph.D. dissertation, Cornell University, 1983.

Huggins, Nathan Irvin. *Harlem Renaissance.* New York: Oxford University Press, 1971.

———. "Interview with Eubie Blake." In *Voices from the Harlem Renaissance,* ed. Nathan Huggins. New York: Oxford University Press, 1976.

Hunt, Joe. *52nd Street Beat: Modern Jazz Drummers 1945–1965.* New Albany, IN: Jamey Aeborsold Jazz, n.d.

Jones, A. M. "African Rhythm." *Africa* 24, no. 1 (January 1954), p. 39.

———. "Blue Notes and Hot Rhythm." *African Music Society Newsletter* 1 (June 1951), p. 10.

———. *Studies in African Music.* New York: Oxford University Press, 1959.

Jones, LeRoi. *Blues People.* New York: Morrow, 1963.

———. "The Jazz Avant Garde." *Metronome* 78, no. 9 (September 1961), pp. 9 ff.

Jost, Ekkehard. *Free Jazz.* Graz, Austria: Universal Edition, 1974. Reprint, New York: Da Capo Press, 1981.

Kahn, Ashley. *Kind of Blue: The Making of a Miles Davis Masterpiece.* New York: Da Capo Press, 2000.

———. *A Love Supreme: The Story of John Coltrane's Signature Album.* New York: Viking, 2002.

Kaminsky, Max, with V. E. Hughes. *My Life in Jazz.* New York: Harper & Row, 1963.

Kennedy, Rick. *Jelly Roll, Bix, and Hoagy: Gennett Studios and the Birth of Recorded Jazz.* Bloomington and Indianapolis: Indiana University Press, 1994.

Kenney, William Howland. *Chicago Jazz: A Cultural History, 1904–1930.* New York: Oxford University Press, 1993.

Kirchner, Bill, ed. *The Oxford Companion to Jazz.* New York: Oxford University Press, 2000.

Koch, Lawrence O. *Yardbird Suite: A Compendium of the Music and Life of Charlie Parker.* 2nd ed. Boston: Northeastern University Press, 1999.

Kofsky, Frank. *Black Nationalism and the Revolution in Music.* New York: Pathfinder Press, 1970.

Larson, Steve. *Analyzing Jazz: A Schenkerian Approach.* Hillsdale, NY: Pendragon Press, 2009.

Levine, Lawrence. *Black Culture and Black Consciousness: Afro-American Folk Thought from Slavery to Freedom.* New York: Oxford University Press, 1977.

Lewis, John. *The World of Music.* Information Bulletin No. 4 of the International Music Council, Unesco House, Paris, May 1958.

Litweiler, John. *The Freedom Principle: Jazz After 1958.* New York: Morrow, 1984.

Lomax, Alan. *Mister Jelly Roll: The Fortunes of Jelly Roll Morton, New Orleans Creole and "Inventor" of Jazz.* 2nd ed. Berkeley: University of California Press, 1973. Reprint, Berkeley: University of California Press, 1993, 2001: updated with a new afterword by Lawrence Gushee.

Lyons, Len. *The Great Jazz Pianists: Speaking of Their Lives and Their Music.* New York: Da Capo Press, 1989.

Magee, Jeffrey. *The Uncrowned King of Swing: Fletcher Henderson and Big Band Jazz.* New York: Oxford University Press, 2005.

Marquis, Donald M. *In Search of Buddy Bolden, First Man of Jazz.* Baton Rouge: Louisiana State University Press, 1978.

Martin, Henry. *Charlie Parker and Thematic Improvisation.* Lanham, MD: Scarecrow Press, 1996.

_____. *Enjoying Jazz.* New York: Schirmer Books, 1986.

Merriam, Allan P. "African Music." In *Continuity and Change in African Cultures,* ed. William R. Bascom and Melville Herskovits. Chicago: University of Chicago Press, 1959.

Milkowski, Bill. *Jaco: The Extraordinary and Tragic Life of Jaco Pastorius, "The World's Greatest Bass Player."* San Francisco: Miller Freeman Books, 1995.

Monson, Ingrid. *Freedom Sounds: Civil Rights Call Out to Jazz and Africa.* New York: Oxford University Press, 2007.

_____. *Saying Something: Jazz Improvisation and Interaction.* Chicago and London: University of Chicago Press, 1996.

Murphy, Jeanette Robinson. "The Survival of African Music in America." In *The Negro and His Folk-Lore,* ed. Bruce Jackson. Austin: University of Texas Press, 1967.

Nettl, Bruno. *Folk and Traditional Music of the Western Continents.* 3rd ed. Englewood Cliffs, NJ: Prentice-Hall, 1990.

Nicholson, Stuart. *Jazz-Rock: A History.* New York: Schirmer Books, 1998.

Nicholson, Stuart. *Jazz: The 1980s Resurgence.* New York: Da Capo Press, 1990.

Ogren, Kathy J. *The Jazz Revolution: Twenties America and the Meaning of Jazz.* New York: Oxford University Press, 1989.

Oliver, Paul. *Blues Fell This Morning: The Meaning of the Blues.* 2nd ed. New York: Cambridge University Press, 1990.

Owens, Thomas. *Bebop: The Music and the Players.* New York: Oxford University Press, 1995.

Pearson, Nathan W., Jr., *Goin' to Kansas City.* Urbana: University of Illinois Press, 1987.

Placksin, Sally. *American Women in Jazz, 1900 to the Present: Their Words, Lives, and Music.* New York: Seaview Books, 1982.

Porter, Lewis. *John Coltrane: His Life and Music.* Ann Arbor: University of Michigan Press, 1998.

_____. *Lester Young.* Boston: Twayne, 1985. Reprint, Ann Arbor: University of Michigan Press, 2005.

Porter, Lewis, with Michael Ullman and Edward Hazell. *Jazz: From Its Origins to the Present.* Englewood Cliffs, NJ: Prentice-Hall, 1993.

Ramsey, Frederick, Jr., and Charles Edward Smith, eds. *Jazzmen.* New York: Harcourt, Brace, 1939. Reprint, 1977.

Riis, Thomas L. *Just Before Jazz: Black Musical Theater in New York, 1890–1915.* Washington, DC: Smithsonian Institution Press, 1989.

Roberts, John Storm. *Latin Jazz: The First of the Fusions, 1880s to Today.* New York: Schirmer Books, 1999.

Rondón, César Miguel. *The Book of Salsa: A Chronicle of Urban Music from the Caribbean to New York City.* Trans., Frances Aparicio and Jackie White. Chapel Hill: The University of North Carolina Press, 2008.

Russell, Ross. *Bird Lives: The High Life and Hard Times of Charlie (Yardbird) Parker.* New York: Charterhouse, 1973. Reprint, New York: Da Capo Press, 1996.

_____. *Jazz Style in Kansas City and the Southwest.* Berkeley: University of California Press, 1971.

Schafer, William J., with Richard B. Allen. *Brass Bands and New Orleans Jazz.* Baton Rouge: Louisiana State University Press, 1977.

Schuller, Gunther. *Early Jazz: Its Roots and Musical Development.* New York: Oxford University Press, 1968.

_____. "Sonny Rollins and the Challenge of Thematic Improvisation." *Jazz Review,* November 1958, pp. 6–11. Reprinted in *Musings: The Musical Worlds of Gunther Schuller,* by Gunther Schuller. New York: Oxford University Press, 1986.

_____. *The Swing Era: The Development of Jazz 1930–1945.* New York: Oxford University Press, 1989.

Shapiro, Nat and Nat Hentoff, eds. *Hear Me Talkin' to Ya: The Story of Jazz as Told by the Men Who Made It.* New York: Rinehart, 1955. Reprint, New York: Dover, 1966.

Shipton, Alyn. *A New History of Jazz.* New York: Continuum, 2002.

Sidran, Ben. *Talking Jazz: An Oral History*. New York: Da Capo Press, 1995.

Smith, Willie "The Lion," with George Hoefer. *Music on My Mind: The Memoirs of an American Pianist*. Garden City, NY: Doubleday, 1964. Reprint, New York: Da Capo Press, 1984.

Solis, Gabriel. *Thelonious Monk Quartet with John Coltrane at Carnegie Hall*. New York: Oxford University Press, 2013.

Southern, Eileen. *The Music of Black Americans*. 2nd ed. New York: Norton, 1983.

Starr, Frederick S. *Red and Hot: The Fate of Jazz in the Soviet Union*. New York: Oxford, 1983.

Stearns, Marshall. *The Story of Jazz*. New York: Oxford University Press, 1958. Reprint, 1970.

Stewart, Alex. *Making the Scene: Contemporary New York City Big Band Jazz*. Berkeley: University of California Press, 2007.

Stewart, Rex. *Jazz Masters of the Thirties*. New York: Macmillan, 1972. Reprint, New York: Da Capo Press, 1982.

Strayhorn, Billy. "The Ellington Effect." *Down Beat*, November 5, 1952, pp. 4 ff.

Stuckey, Sterling. *Slave Culture: Nationalist Theory and the Foundations of Black America*. New York: Oxford University Press, 1987.

Sturm, Fred. *Changes Over Time: The Evolution of Jazz Arranging*. Rottenburg, Germany: Advance Music, 1995.

Sudhalter, Richard M. *Lost Chords: White Musicians and Their Contribution to Jazz 1915–1945*. New York: Oxford University Press, 1999.

Szwed, John. *So What: The Life of Miles Davis*. New York: Simon and Schuster, 2002.

Tackley, Catherine. *Benny Goodman's Famous 1938 Carnegie Hall Jazz Concert*. New York: Oxford University Press, 2012.

Tallmadge, William. "Blue Notes and Blue Tonality." *The Black Perspective in Music* 12, no. 2 (Fall 1984), pp. 155–164.

Taylor, Art. *Notes and Tones: Musician-to-Musician Interviews*. Liège, Belgium: Taylor, 1977. Reprint, New York: Da Capo Press, 1993.

Teachout, Terry. *Duke: A Life of Duke Ellington*. New York: Gotham Books, 2013.

———. *Pops: A Life of Louis Armstrong*. New York: Houghton Mifflin Harcourt, 2009.

Thompson, Robert Farris. "Kongo Influences on African-American Artistic Culture." In *Africanisms in American Culture*, ed. Joseph E. Holloway. Bloomington: Indiana University Press, 1990.

Tirro, Frank. *The Birth of the Cool of Miles Davis and His Associates*. Hillsdale, New York: Pendragon Press, 2009.

Tucker, Mark. *Ellington: The Early Years*. Urbana and Chicago: University of Illinois Press, 1991.

———, ed. *The Duke Ellington Reader*. New York: Oxford University Press, 1993.

Tucker, Sherrie. *Swing Shift: "All-Girl" Bands of the 1940s*. Durham and London: Duke University Press, 2000.

van de Leur, Walter. *Something to Live For: The Music of Billy Strayhorn*. New York: Oxford University Press, 2002.

Walser, Robert. *Keeping Time: Readings in Jazz History*. New York: Oxford University Press, 1999.

Washburne, Christopher. "The Clave of Jazz: A Caribbean Contribution to the Rhythmic Foundation of an African-American Music." *Black Music Research Journal* 17, no. 1 (Spring 1997), pp. 75 ff.

Waters, Keith. *The Studio Recordings of the Miles Davis Quintet, 1965–68*. New York: Oxford University Press, 2011.

Williams, Martin. *The Art of Jazz: Essays on the Nature and Development of Jazz*. New York: Oxford University Press, 1959. Reprint, New York: Da Capo Press, 1979.

———. *Jazz Masters of New Orleans*. New York: Macmillan, 1967. Reprint, New York: Da Capo Press, 1979.

Wilson, Olly. "The Significance of the Relationship Between Afro-American Music and West African Music." *Black Perspective in Music* 2, no. 1 (Spring 1974), pp. 3–22.

Wilson, Teddy, with Arie Ligthart and Humphrey van Loo. *Teddy Wilson Talks Jazz*. London: Cassell, 1996.

Woideck, Carl. *Charlie Parker: His Music and Life*. Ann Arbor: University of Michigan Press, 1996.

Selected Discography

Chapter 1

The Greatest in Country Blues. Vol. 1. 1201 Music 70022.

The Greatest Ragtime of the Century. Biograph BCD 103.

Johnson, Robert. *Robert Johnson: King of the Delta Blues*. Columbia/Legacy CK 65746.

Joplin, Scott. *Scott Joplin: His Greatest Hits*. Richard Zimmerman, piano. Legacy International CD 316.

Ragtime. Vol. 1: 1897–1919. Jazz Archives No. 120 159052.

Ragtime to Jazz. Vol. 1: 1912–1919. Timeless Records CBC 1-035 Jazz.

Smith, Bessie. *The Essential Bessie Smith*. Columbia/Legacy C2K 64922.

Chapter 2

Note: *The first three listings are a series of recordings reissued as CDs that encompass most of the artists of the 1920s and 1930s, as well as many artists of the 1940s.*

The Best of Jazz. A good introductory series in which each CD is devoted to a given artist and includes many of the artist's best or best-known recordings.

Classic Records. This series contains hundreds of CDs that treat the major jazz artists' work in chronological order. CD covers are color-coded to make identification easier. A drawback to the series is that it does not include alternate takes, but only principal (master) recordings.

Média 7 Masters of Jazz. This series is like the Classic Records in that major artists' works are presented in chronological order, but there is a critical difference: every known recording is included. That is, these CDs contain all takes from each recording session, live recording (irrespective of recording quality), and radio/TV broadcasts. In instances where previous reissues have already exhaustively covered an artist in question for a given period, the series purposely avoids duplication.

Bechet, Sidney. *The Best of Sidney Bechet*. Blue Note CDP 7243 8 28891 2 0.

Oliver, King. *King Oliver's Creole Jazz Band 1923–1924*. Retrieval RTR 79007 Jazz.

Chapter 3

Armstrong, Louis. *Louis Armstrong and His Orchestra 1929–1930*. Classic Records 557.

_____. *Louis Armstrong: The 25 Greatest Hot Fives and Hot Sevens*. ASV CD AJA 5171.

Beiderbecke, Bix. *Jazz Me Blues*. AAD JHR 73517.

Jazz the World Forgot: Jazz Classics of the 1920s. Yazoo (Shanachie Entertainment Corporation) 2024.

Morton, Jelly Roll. *Jelly Roll Morton and His Red Hot Peppers*. Vol. 1. Jazz Archives No. 110 158942.

Chapter 4

Ellington, Duke. *The Best of Early Ellington*. Decca GRD-660.

Henderson, Fletcher. *Tidal Wave—The Original Decca Recordings*. Decca GRD-643.

Johnson, James P. *An Introduction to James P. Johnson—His Best Recordings 1921–1944.* The Best of Jazz 4035.

Waller, Fats. *Turn on the Heat—The Fats Waller Piano Solos.* Bluebird 2482-2-RB.

Chapter 5

Basie, Count. *Count Basie: The Complete Decca Recordings.* Decca GRD-3-611.

Ellington, Duke. *In a Mellotone.* RCA 07863 51364-2.

Goodman, Benny. *Benny Goodman: Sixteen Classic Performances.* Camden (BMG) CAMCD 192.

The Real Kansas City of the '20s, '30s, and '40s. Columbia/Legacy (Sony) CK 64855.

Chapter 6

Carter, Benny. *Benny Carter.* Vol. 3. Média 7 MJCD 39.

Hawkins, Coleman. *In the Groove, 1926–1939.* Indigo Records IGOCD 2037.

Hines, Earl. *An Introduction to Earl Hines—His Best Recordings 1927–1942.* The Best of Jazz 4047.

Holiday, Billie. *Greatest Hits.* Columbia/Legacy CK 65757.

Tatum, Art. *The Quintessence.* Frémeaux & Associés FA 217.

Wilson, Teddy. *An Introduction to Teddy Wilson—His Best Recordings 1935–1945.* The Best of Jazz 4044.

Young, Lester. *Lester Young.* Vol. 1, 1936–1942. Blue Moon BMCD 1001.

Chapter 7

Gillespie, Dizzy. *Dizzy Gillespie 1940–1946.* Jazz Archives No. 99 158182.

Monk, Thelonious. *The Best of Thelonious Monk—The Blue Note Years.* Blue Note CDP 7 95636 2.

Parker, Charlie. *The Complete Savoy and Dial Studio Recordings.* Savoy 92911-2.

———. *Complete Live Sessions on Savoy.* Savoy Jazz SVY-17021-24.

Powell, Bud. *The Complete 1946–1949.* Roost/Blue Note/Verve Swing Masters. Definitive Records DRCD 11145.

Chapter 8

Blakey, Art, and the Jazz Messengers. *Moanin'.* Blue Note 7243 4 95324 2 7.

———. *Ugetsu.* Original Jazz Classics OJCCD 090-2.

Brown, Clifford and Max Roach. *Brown and Roach, Inc.* EmArcy 814 644-2.

Brubeck, Dave. *Time Out.* Columbia CK 65122.

Davis, Miles. *Birth of the Cool.* Capitol CDP 7243 4 94550 2 3.

———. *Kind of Blue.* Columbia CK 64935.

Giuffre, Jimmy. *Free Fall.* Columbia 65446.

Modern Jazz Quartet. *Concorde.* Original Jazz Classics OJCCD 002-2.

Chapter 9

Coleman, Ornette. *Change of the Century.* Atlantic 7 81341-2.

———. *The Shape of Jazz to Come.* Atlantic 1317-2.

Coltrane, John. *Giant Steps.* Atlantic 1311-2.

———. *A Love Supreme.* Impulse! GRD 155.

Dolphy, Eric. *Out to Lunch!* Blue Note CDP 7 46524-2.

Taylor, Cecil. *Unit Structures.* Blue Note CDP 7 84237 2.

Chapter 10

Adderley, Cannonball. *Mercy, Mercy, Mercy.* Capitol CDP 7 72438 29915 2 6.

Davis, Miles. *ESP.* Columbia CK 65683.

———. *Nefertiti.* Columbia CK 65681.

Evans, Bill. *Portrait in Jazz.* Original Jazz Classics OJCCD 088-2.

Fitzgerald, Ella. *The Jazz Sides.* Verve 314 527 655-2.

Getz, Stan. *Getz/Gilberto.* Verve UDCD 607.

Hancock, Herbie. *Maiden Voyage.* Blue Note CDP 46339 2.

Henderson, Joe. *Inner Urge.* Blue Note CDP 7 84189 2.

Hubbard, Freddie. *Hub Tones.* Blue Note CDP 84115 2.

Jarrett, Keith. *Arbour Zena.* ECM 1070.

Lloyd, Charles. *Forest Flower.* Soundtrack. Atlantic/Rhino 71746.

Tyner, McCoy. *The Real McCoy.* Blue Note 7243 4 97807 2 9.

Chapter 11

Corea, Chick. *Light as a Feather.* Verve 314 557 115-2.

Coryell, Larry. *Spaces.* Vanguard VMD79345.

Hancock, Herbie. *Headhunters.* Columbia CK 65123.

Mahavishnu Orchestra. *The Inner Mounting Flame.* Columbia CK UDCD 744.

Weather Report. *Heavy Weather.* Columbia CK 65108.

———. *Weather Report.* Columbia CK 48824.

Williams, Tony, and Lifetime. *Emergency!* Verve 314 539 117-2.

Chapter 12

Hancock, Herbie. *Gershwin's World.* Verve 314 557 797-2.

Hancock, Herbie. *River: The Joni Letters.* Verve B0010063 02.

Iyer, Vijay; Prasanna; and Mitta, Nitin. *Tirtha.* ACT 9503-2-LC 07644.

Lincoln Center Jazz Orchestra. *Portraits by Ellington.* Columbia CK 53145.

Marsalis, Wynton. *Jump Start and Jazz.* Sony SK 62998.

Medeski Martin & Wood. *Last Chance to Dance Trance (Perhaps).* Gramavision GCD 79520.

Redman, Joshua. *Freedom in the Groove.* Warner Brothers 9 46330-2.

Schneider, Maria. *Evanescence.* Enja ENJ-8048 2.

Washington, Grover, Jr., *Strawberry Moon.* Columbia Records CK 40510.

Zorn, John. *Spy Versus Spy—The Music of Ornette Coleman.* Elektra/Musician 9 60844-2.

Selected Jazz DVDs and Videos

We recommend **http://ejazzlines.com** *as the source to obtain these DVDs and videos. All are available on DVD format unless otherwise noted. Please note that availability may be limited.*

Adventures in the Kingdom of Swing

This historic documentary is a compilation of interviews, photographs, and performances that provides an interesting and informative look at Benny Goodman and his music. There are discussion and clips of the early days of swing, as well as a focus on Goodman's role in helping break down racial barriers.

Directed by Oren Jacoby; Sony (2000). 60 min.

Art Ensemble of Chicago: Live from the Jazz Showcase

This great film documents the avant-garde group Art Ensemble of Chicago in performance, featuring Lester Bowie, Joseph Jarman, Roscoe Mitchell, Malachi Favors Maghostut, and Famoudou Don Moye. Filmed at the Jazz Showcase on November 1, 1981.

Rhapsody Films (1990). 60 min.

At the Jazz Band Ball

At the Jazz Band Ball brings together some of the greatest hot music, song, and dance captured at the height of the Jazz Age and in the early days of sound film (1925–1933). Included are some of the giants of the period in their very best early performances: Duke Ellington's Cotton Club Orchestra in clips featuring solos and a floor show; a youthful Louis Armstrong; Harlem's William "Bo Jangles" Robinson doing his famous step dance; Bessie Smith's only screen performance; a rare clip of the Boswell Sisters harmonizing on an Armstrong classic; and an instrumental from the Dorsey Brothers band. Among the many other clips is a 1925 De Forest sound film of Ben Bernie's Orchestra in which underappreciated reedman Jack Pettis contributes what is probably the first jazz solo on film.

Yazoo Video (1993). 60 min.

Bix: Ain't None of Them Play Like Him Yet

This is the first accurate portrayal of jazz great Bix Beiderbecke, whose story is told through photographs, historic film footage, interviews with contemporaries, and his moving cornet playing. Unlike the biographical Hollywood movie *Young Man with a Horn*, this DVD is true to Beiderbecke's life and captures his spirit on film.

Directed by Brigitte Berman; Playboy Video (2001). 116 min.

Buddy Rich: At the Top

This performance was recorded at the Top of the Plaza in Rochester, New York, on February 6, 1973, and captures drum legend Buddy Rich in his prime. It includes definitive versions of "Love for Sale," the odd time signature–laden "Time Check," his famed "Norwegian Wood," "Basically Blues," and the closer "West Side Story." The film also features a rare bonus clip: a fine unaccompanied drum solo not seen since its broadcast in May 1978.

Directed by Bruce Klauber; Hudson Music (1973; DVD release 2002). 65 min.

The Coltrane Legacy

This DVD features interviews with John Coltrane's bandmates and contemporaries, including Elvin Jones, Jimmy

Cobb, and Reggie Workman. Early 1960s television footage captures moving performances of "Alabama," "Afro-Blue," and "Ev'ry Time We Say Goodbye."

Video Arts (1987). 60 min.

David, Moffett and Ornette

Director Dick Fontaine set out to catch the music, thoughts, and personalities of Ornette Coleman's mid-sixties trio during two days in Paris while they worked on scoring a film. There is a complete and memorable performance of Coleman's "Sadness," one of the best jazz performances ever captured on video.

Directed by Dick Fontaine; Rhapsody Films (1988). 30 min.

Ella Fitzgerald: Something to Live For

Writer-director Charlotte Zwerin's documentary on jazz vocal icon Ella Fitzgerald was originally produced for public television's American Masters series. The 1999 film showcases Fitzgerald through archival footage of early performances and television appearances. There is discussion of her "discovery" at the Apollo Theater and her subsequent rise to stardom during the swing era. Tony Bennett's narration adds to the film's success.

Directed by Charlotte Zwerin; WinStar Home Video (1999). 86 min.

Greatest Jazz Films Ever

This two-DVD set includes clips from *Sound of Jazz, Sound of Miles Davis, Jammin' the Blues,* and *Jazz at the Philharmonic,* among other great performances. (See individual descriptions of featured titles.)

IDEM Home Video (DVD release 2004); 130 min.

Great Jazz Performances

This long-overdue DVD includes all the existing footage of Charlie Parker, including *Jammin' the Blues,* a classic studio short film documenting a jam session with Lester Young, Harry Edison, Illinois Jacquet, Sid Catlett, Barney Kessel, Jo Jones, and others; *Hot House,* the only Parker television appearance; *Jazz at the Philharmonic,* a great studio short film offering five clips with Parker, Coleman Hawkins, Lester Young, Harry Edison, Hank Jones, Ray Brown, Buddy Rich, Flip Phillips, Ella Fitzgerald, and others; and *Sound of Miles Davis,* a television program featuring the Miles Davis Quintet with John Coltrane, Wynton Kelly, Paul Chambers, and Jimmy Cobb, with the Gil Evans Orchestra.

IDEM Home Video (2003). 60 min.

Jammin' the Blues

This 1944 short was filmed as a jam session. Noteworthy performers included Lester Young, Red Callender, Harry Sweets Edison, Barney Kessel, Illinois Jacquet, and Sid Catlett. (See *Great Jazz Performances* DVD above.)

Directed by Gjon Mili; IDEM Home Video (1944; DVD release 2003). 60 min.

Jazz at the Philharmonic

Filmed in 1950, this great studio short film offers clips of Coleman Hawkins, Charlie Parker, Lester Young, Harry Edison, Hank Jones, Ray Brown, Buddy Rich, Flip Phillips, and Ella Fitzgerald. (See *Great Jazz Performances* DVD.)

IDEM Home Video (1950; DVD release 2003). 60 min.

Jazz Casual Series

Hosted by noted author and critic Ralph Gleason, the 1960s *Jazz Casual* TV series presented some of the biggest names in jazz. Featuring a combination of commentary, interviews, and live in-studio performance footage, this show was well conceived and produced. All twenty-eight episodes are noteworthy for attention and homage paid to jazz. Showcased artists include John Coltrane, Dave Brubeck, Sonny Rollins, Mel Torme, the Modern Jazz Quartet, B. B. King, Louis Armstrong, Jimmy Rushing, Carmen McRae, Count Basie, Woody Herman, Cannonball Adderley, Dizzy Gillespie, and more. The entire series has been reissued on three- and four-episode DVDs.

Directed by Ralph Gleason; IDEM Home Video (DVD release 2003). Each episode 30 min.

Jazz on a Summer's Day

This film captured the 1958 Newport Jazz Festival in its heyday. Featured performers include Louis Armstrong, Anita O'Day, Thelonious Monk, Mahalia Jackson, and Dinah Washington.

Directed by Bert Stern; Galaxy Productions (1959). 85 min.

Keith Jarrett Trio: Live at Open Theater East

This excellent concert footage features the Keith Jarrett Trio at the peak of their creativity. Songs include "In Your Own Sweet Way," "Butch and Butch," "Basin Street Blues," "If I Were a Bell," "Oleo," "Bye Bye, Blackbird," "The Cure," "I Thought About You," and more.

Image Entertainment (1993). 130 min.

Ken Burns Jazz

Ken Burns celebrates the achievements of jazz from its origins in blues and ragtime through swing, bebop, and fusion. Six years in the making, this series blends 75 interviews, more than 500 pieces of music, 2,400 still photographs, and more than 2,000 rare and archival film clips. The ten-part musical journey spotlights many of America's most original, creative—and tragic—figures, including Louis Armstrong, Jelly Roll Morton, Bix Beiderbecke, Duke Ellington, Benny Goodman, Billie Holiday, Charlie Parker, and Miles Davis.

Directed by Ken Burns; PBS Home Video (2000). 19 hours.

Lady Day: The Many Faces of Billie Holiday

This is a fine documentary on the art of Billie Holiday, featuring rare TV and movie clips and commentary by a stellar group of jazz instrumentalists and singers who knew her well: Carmen McRae, Annie Ross, Buck Clayton, Harry "Sweets" Edison, and Mal Waldron. It includes excellent performance clips of "Strange Fruit," "What a Little Moonlight Can Do," "Please Don't Talk About Me When I'm Gone," "Fine and Mellow," and others.

Kultur Video (1991). 60 min.

Last Date

This informative documentary of Eric Dolphy uses as its focal point his legendary final recording session in Hilversum on June 2, 1964. The video also covers Dolphy's formative years, his time as a member of Charles Mingus's group, and his innovative work on alto saxophone and bass clarinet. Available on VHS only.

Directed by Hans Hylkema; Rhapsody Films (1991). 92 min.

Legends of Jazz Guitar, Vol. 1

This swinging collection presents four legends of jazz guitar: Wes Montgomery, Joe Pass, Barney Kessel, and Herb Ellis. These four artists demonstrate fine command of the fingerboard alongside explorations of standards, blues, and ballads.

Vestapol (1995). 60 min.

Legends of Jazz Guitar, Vol. 2

The high-wire act of balancing virtuosity and musicality meets its match in the remarkable artists featured in the second volume of *Legends of Jazz Guitar*: Wes Montgomery, Kenny Burrell, Joe Pass, Barney Kessel, Charlie Byrd, and Grant Green.

Vestapol (1995). 60 min.

Memories of Duke

This loving tribute, filmed at Mexico City's Palacio de Bellas Artes as well as in Guadalajara, captures the Ellington band on their 1968 Mexican tour. The DVD includes historic scenes from early films; interviews with Cootie Williams, Russell Procope, and others; the previously unreleased "Mexican Suite"; plus many classics, such as "Satin Doll," "Mood Indigo," "Black and Tan Fantasy," and "Take the A Train."

Directed by Gary Keys; A*Vision (1968). 85 min.

Miles Davis Story

This film, featuring classic performances from all eras of Davis's career, includes insightful interviews with Herbie Hancock, Ron Carter, Clark Terry, Joe Zawinul, and many others. Special features include a bio from award-winning French jazz writer Francis Davis, album profiles of virtually every important Davis record, interactive menus, and chapter selections.

Directed by Mike Dibb; Columbia Video (2001). 120 min.

Mingus

Most of this film takes place in Charles Mingus's cluttered New York loft, where he is awaiting eviction over legal tangles. Although performance footage is included, most of this black-and-white film is a harrowing look at the great composer and jazz bassist surrounded by the clutter of his life and his art. While they wait for the police to evict him, director Thomas Reichman tosses out a few questions; even in his distraction, Mingus speaks passionately and at length about politics, family, education, "sex as a source of survival," and the politics and consequences of racism.

Directed by Thomas Reichman; Rhapsody Films (1968). 60 min.

Piano Legend

Hosted by Chick Corea, this documentary celebrates the lives and the music of some of America's most talented jazz pianists. It features rare footage of Art Tatum, Duke Ellington, Count Basie, Fats Waller, McCoy Tyner, Thelonious Monk, Willie "The Lion" Smith, Meade "Lux" Lewis, Earl Hines, Mary Lou Williams, Oscar Peterson, Marian McPartland, Teddy Wilson, Bud Powell, Horace Silver, Mal Waldron, John Lewis, Lennie Tristano, Dave Brubeck, Bill Evans, Keith Jarrett, and Cecil Taylor.

Video Arts (1987). 60 min.

Satchmo

This fine documentary reconstructs Louis Armstrong's life, using never-before-seen home movies, clips from stage shows, and excerpts from some of his films. Many of Armstrong's songs are featured, including "West End Blues," "Potato Head Blues," "Weather Bird," "On the Sunny Side of the Street," "When You're Smiling," and "Mack the Knife."

Directed by Gary Giddins; Sony (1990). 87 min.

Saxophone Colossus

This documentary about Sonny Rollins combines performances (from 1986) and interviews, as well as archival footage. There is a short clip of Rollins's appearance on Ralph Gleason's *Jazz Casual* television show in the early 1960s. The film features Rollins's working quintet and a performance with an orchestra in Japan, "Concerto for Saxophone and Orchestra."

Directed by Robert Mugge; Rhapsody Films (1986). 101 min.

Sound of Jazz

This historic episode from *The Seven Lively Arts* CBS television series features some of the giants of classic and modern jazz. With Emmett Berry, Doc Cheatham, Red Allen, Rex Stewart, Joe Newman, Joe Wilder, Roy Eldridge, Vic Dickenson, Benny Morton, Dicky Wells, Pee Wee Russell, Coleman Hawkins, Lester Young, Ben Webster, Gerry Mulligan, Count Basie, Freddie Green, Jo Jones, Jimmy Rushing, Thelonious Monk, Abdul Malik, Osie Johnson, Jimmy Giuffre, Jim Hall, and others.

Directed by Jack Smight; IDEM Home Video (1957; DVD release 2003). 70 min.

Sound of Miles Davis

This exemplary television program was filmed in 1959 and features the Miles Davis Quintet with John Coltrane, Wynton Kelly, Paul Chambers, and Jimmy Cobb. Davis's group is augmented by the Gil Evans Orchestra. (See *Great Jazz Performances* DVD.)

IDEM Home Video (1959; DVD release 2003). 60 min.

Straight, No Chaser

This excellent documentary about the life of Thelonious Monk features new interviews, archival photos, studio footage, and live performances. The film tells the story of a groundbreaking pianist who was at once an important composer, improviser, and innovator.

Directed by Christian Blackwood and Charlotte Zwerin; Warner Brothers (1988). 90 min.

Stéphane Grappelli: A Life in the Jazz Century

This historic DVD features rare and unedited archival performance clips, still photos, and research notes. It also contains all known film footage of Django Reinhardt, including seven minutes of the Quintette du Hot Club de France, never before seen and newly restored. The DVD also features a two-hour feature-length documentary plus one hour of special features, including a Quintette du Hot Club "family tree."

Music on Earth Productions (2001). 120 min.

Story of Jazz

Tracing the foundation and the subsequent evolution of jazz, this film consists of interviews, rare and archival footage, performance video, and photographs. It includes performances by Charlie Parker, Duke Ellington, Willie "The Lion" Smith, Ella Fitzgerald, Dizzy Gillespie, Jimmie Lunceford, Louis Armstrong, Count Basie, Billie Holiday, Miles Davis, Thelonious Monk, John Coltrane, Charles Mingus, Gil Evans, and Sarah Vaughan.

BMG Home Video (1991). 90 min.

Sun Ra: A Joyful Noise

This interesting and sometimes weirdly amusing documentary about jazz legend Sun Ra includes concert clips and footage of Sun Ra composing.

Directed by Robert Mugge; Rhapsody Films (1980). 60 min.

Universal Mind of Bill Evans

Composer and pianist Bill Evans discusses the meaning of jazz through interviews and live performances. Filmed as an informal conversation between Evans and his brother, a professor of music at Louisiana State University, this documentary features in-depth discussion of Evans's repertory as well as his process of song interpretation and improvisation. Evans uses the song "Star Eyes" to illustrate his conception of solo piano and how to interpret and expand on the melody and the underlying chord structure.

Directed by Louis Carvell; Rhapsody Films (1966). 60 min.

World According to John Coltrane

One of the few documentaries to feature Coltrane's background, this film delves into his beginnings, starting with his childhood in North Carolina. It also showcases live performances, including the songs "My Favorite Things," "So What," and "Naima." Narration is provided by such close friends and peers as Roscoe Mitchell and La Monte Young.

Directed by Robert Palmer and Toby Byron; BMG Home Video (1993). 60 min.

Credits

1. **Kasuan Kura**
(Traditional)
Master Drummers of Dagbon
(P) 1990 Rounder Records Corp.
Courtesy of Concord Music Group

2. **Daniel**
(Traditional)
Willis Proctor and group
Courtesy of Concord Music Group

3. **Dere's No Hidin' Place Down Dere**
(Traditional)
Marian Anderson
Originally released 1941. All rights reserved
    by Sony Music Entertainment

4. **Maple Leaf Rag**
(Scott Joplin)
Scott Joplin
Courtesy of Shout! Entertainment a division
    of Retropolis LLC

5. **Maple Leaf Rag**
(Scott Joplin)
Ferdinand "Jelly Roll" Morton
Courtesy of the Jelly Roll Morton Estate

6. **Love In Vain**
(Robert Johnson)
Robert Johnson
Originally released 1937. All rights reserved by
    Sony Music Entertainment

7. **Backwater Blues**
(Bessie Smith)
Bessie Smith
Originally released 1927. All rights reserved
    by Sony Music Entertainment

8. **Tiger Rag**
(Nick LaRocca)
Original Dixieland Jazz Band
Originally released 1918. All rights reserved
    by Sony Music Entertainment

9. **Dippermouth Blues**
(Joe Oliver)
King Oliver's Creole Jazz Band
Courtesy of Concord Music Group

10. **Grandpa's Spells**
(Jelly Roll Morton)
Jelly Roll Morton's Red Hot Peppers
Originally released 1926. All rights reserved
    by Sony Music Entertainment

11. **Cake Walkin' Babies (From Home)**
(Clarence Williams - C. Smith - H. Troy)
Clarence Williams's Blue Five
Originally released 1925. All rights reserved
    by Sony Music Entertainment

12. **West End Blues**
(Clarence Williams - Joe Oliver)
Louis Armstrong and His Hot Five
Originally released 1928. All rights reserved by
    Sony Music Entertainment

13. Singin' The Blues
(J. Russell Robinson - Con Conrad - Samuel Lewis
  – Joseph Young)
Frankie Trumbauer and His Orchestra, featuring
  Bix Beiderbecke
Originally released 1927. All rights reserved by
  Sony Music Entertainment

14. Carolina Shout
(Art Hodes - James P. Johnson)
James P. Johnson
Originally released 1921. All rights reserved by
  Sony Music Entertainment

15. Tiger Rag
(Nick LaRocca)
Art Tatum
Originally released 1933. All rights reserved by
  Sony Music Entertainment

16. East St. Louis Toodle-Oo
(Duke Ellington)
Duke Ellington and His Orchestra
Originally released 1927. All rights reserved by
  Sony Music Entertainment

17. Tiger Rag
(Nick LaRocca)
Django Reinhardt and the Quintet du Hot Club
  deFrance
Courtesy of Concord Music Group

18. Down South Camp Meeting
(Fletcher Henderson)
Fletcher Henderson and His Orchestra
Courtesy of The Verve Music Group, under license
  from Universal Music Enterprises

19. Mary's Idea
(Mary Lou Williams)
Andy Kirk and His Twelve Clouds of Joy
Courtesy of The Verve Music Group, under license
  from Universal Music Enterprises

20. Every Tub
(Count Basie - Eddie Durham)
Count Basie and His Orchestra
Courtesy of The Verve Music Group, under license
  from Universal Music Enterprises

21. Down South Camp Meeting
(Fletcher Henderson)
Benny Goodman and His Orchestra
Originally released 1936. All rights reserved by
  Sony Music Entertainment

22. Ko-Ko
(Duke Ellington)
Duke Ellington and His Famous Orchestra
Originally released 1940. All rights reserved by
  Sony Music Entertainment

23. Swing That Music
(Horace Gerlack - Louis Armstrong)
Louis Armstrong and His Orchestra
Courtesy of The Verve Music Group, under license
  from Universal Music Enterprises

24. Vi Vigor
(Maurice King)
International Sweethearts of Rhythm
Originally recorded 1946. All rights reserved by
  Sony Music Entertainment

25. Body and Soul
(Johnny Green - Robert Sauer - Edward Heyman -
  Frank Eyton)
Colman Hawkins and His Orchestra
Originally released 1939. All rights reserved by
  Sony Music Entertainment

26. Swing to Bop (Topsy)
(Ensemble Improvisation)
Charlie Christian
Courtesy of Concord Music Group

27. Body and Soul
(Johnny Green - Robert Sauer - Edward Heyman -
  Frank Eyton)
Billie Holiday and Her Orchestra
Originally released 1940. All rights reserved by
  Sony Music Entertainment

28. Salt Peanuts
(Dizzy Gillespie - Kenny Clark)
Dizzy Gillespie and His All Stars
Courtesy of Savoy Label Group

29. Koko
(Charlie Parker)
Charlie Parker's Reboppers
Courtesy of Savoy Label Group

30. Manteca
(Dizzy Gillespie - Walter Fuller - Chano Pozo)
Dizzy Gillespie and His Orchestra with Chano
  Pozo
Originally released 1947. All rights reserved by
  Sony Music Entertainment

31. Tempus Fugit
(Bud Powell)
Bud Powell Trio
Courtesy of The Verve Music Group, under license
  from Universal Music Enterprises

32. Four In One
(Thelonious Monk)
Thelonious Monk Quintet
Courtesy of The Verve Music Group, under license
  from Universal Music Enterprises

33. Jeru
(Gerry Mulligan)
Miles Davis and His Orchestra
Courtesy of The Verve Music Group, under license
from Universal Music Enterprises

34. Versailles (Porte de Versailles)
(John Lewis)
Modern Jazz Quartet
Produced under license from Atlantic Recording Corp.

35. Blue Rondo a la Turk
(Dave Brubeck)
Dave Brubeck Quartet
Originally released 1959. All rights reserved by
Sony Music Entertainment

36. The Girl From Ipanema
(Antonio Carlos Jobim - Vinicius de Moraes -
Norman Gimbell)
Stan Getz and Joao Gilberto with Astrud Gilberto
Courtesy of The Verve Music Group, under license
from Universal Music Enterprises

37. Moanin'
(Art Blakey - Horace Silver)
Art Blakey and the Jazz Messengers featuring
Horace Silver
Courtesy of The Verve Music Group, under license
from Universal Music Enterprises

38. Powell's Prances
(Richie Powell)
Clifford Brown - Max Roach Quintet
Courtesy of The Verve Music Group, under license
from Universal Music Enterprises

39. Hora Decubitus
(Charles Mingus)
Charles Mingus and His Orchestra
Courtesy of The Verve Music Group, under license
from Universal Music Enterprises

40. So What (excerpt)
(Miles Davis)
Miles Davis Sextet
Originally released 1958. All rights reserved by
Sony Music Entertainment

41. Street Woman
(Ornette Coleman)
Ornette Coleman Quartet
(P) 1972 Sony Music Entertainment

42. Acknowledgement from *A Love Supreme*
(John Coltrane)
John Coltrane
Courtesy of The Verve Music Group, under license
from Universal Music Enterprises

43. Ghosts: First Variation (excerpt)
(Albert Ayler)
Albert Ayler Trio
Courtesy of ESP Records

44. Take The A Train
(Billy Strayhorn)
Ella Fitzgerald and Duke Ellington
Courtesy of The Verve Music Group, under license
from Universal Music Enterprises

45. Lullaby of Birdland
(George Shearing - George David Weiss)
Sarah Vaughan with Clifford Brown
Courtesy of The Verve Music Group, under license
from Universal Music Enterprises

46. Corner Pocket
(Freddie Greene)
Count Basie Orchestra
Courtesy of The Verve Music Group, under license
from Universal Music Enterprises

47. Sunset and the Mockingbird
(Duke Ellington)
Duke Ellington
Courtesy of Concord Music Group

48. E.S.P.
(Wayne Shorter)
Miles Davis Quintent
Originally released 1965. All rights reserved by
Sony Music Entertainment

49. Autumn Leaves (excerpt)
(Joseph Kosma - Jacques Prevert - Johnny Mercer)
Bill Evans Trio
Courtesy of Concord Music Group

50. The Windup
(Keith Jarrett)
Keith Jarrett
(P) 1974 ECM Records GmbH
Courtesy of ECM Records GmbH

51. Mercy, Mercy, Mercy
(Joe Zawinul)
Cannonball Adderley Quintet
Courtesy of The Verve Music Group, under license
from Universal Music Enterprises

52. James and Wes (excerpt)
(Jimmy Smith)
Jimmy Smith and Wes Montgomery
Courtesy of The Verve Music Group, under license
from Universal Music Enterprises

53. It's About That Time / In A Silent Way (excerpt)
(Joe Zawinul - Miles Davis)
Miles Davis
Originally released 1969. All rights reserved by
Sony Music Entertainment

54. Phenomenon: Compulsion
(John McLaughlin)
John McLaughlin
(P) 1978 Sony Music Entertainment

55. Birdland
(Joe Zawinul)
Weather Report
(P) 1977 Sony Music Entertainment

56. Express Crossing
(Wynton Marsalis)
Wynton Marsalis Ensemble
(P) 1994 Sony Music Entertainment

57. Hang Gliding (excerpt)
(Maria Schneider)
Maria Schneider Orchestra
(P) 2000 Maria Schneider
Courtesy of Maria Schneider Enterprises

58. Softly, As In A Morning Sunrise
(Sigmund Romberg - Oscar Hammerstein II)
George Benson
(P) 2003 The Verve Music Group, a division of
    UMG Recordings, Inc.
Courtesy of The Verve Music Group, under license
    from Universal Music Enterprises

59. Guataca City (To David Amram)
(Paquito D'Rivera)
Paquito D'Rivera
(P) 1987 Sony Music Entertainment

60. Salt Peanuts
(Dizzy Gillespie - Kenny Clark)
Steve Coleman and Five Elements
(P) 1994 Sony Music Entertainment

61. Solitude
(Edgar De Lange - Duke Ellington - Irving Mills)
Herbie Hancock
(P) 2007 The Verve Music Group, a division of
    UMG Recordings, Inc.
Courtesy of The Verve Music Group, under license
    from Universal Music Enterprises

62. Falsehood
(Prasanna)
Vijay Iyer with Prasanna and Nitin Mitta
(P) 2011 ACT Music + Vision GmbH & Co. KG
Courtesy of ACT Music + Vision GmbH & Co. KG

Index

Note: Photographs are indicated by page numbers in italic type.

AABA song form, 30
  See also 32-bar AABA song form
aab blues form, 8–9, 49
ABAC song form, 30
Abercrombie, John, 330
Abrams, Muhal Richard, 280
"Abstractions," 263
Abstractions, 273
"Abyss," 278
Accents, 10
Acid jazz, 362
"Acknowledgement," 269–271
Acoustic bass, 16, *16*
Acuna, Alejandro, 338
Adams, Pepper, 230
Adam's Apple, 318
Adderley, Julian "Cannonball," 237, 254,
    255, 298, 300, 309, 312, 313, 326, 336,
    361, 363
Adderley, Nat, 312, 313
Aebersold, Jamie, 349
Africa/Brass, 269
African American music
    early, 31–36
    nineteenth century, 23–29
African music, 25–28
Afro-Cuban music, 208–209, 307, 364
"After You've Gone," 150, 180, 182
Aiken, Gus, 169
"Ain't Misbehavin'," 96, 112
"Airegin," 248, 253
"Air Mail Special," 183
Akiyoshi, Toshiko, 345, *356*, 363
"Alabamy Bound," 119
Alfie (film), 249
Ali, Rashied, 272

"All Blues," 254
"All Coons Look Alike to Me," 40
Allégresse, 357
Allen, Ed, 69
Allen, Geri, 363–364, 368
Allen, Henry, 137
Allen, Lewis, 187
Allen, William Francis, 35
Allen, Woody, 127
All-girl bands, 130, 171–172, 363
"Alligator Crawl," 112
"All My Loving," 325
All Seeing Eye, The, 318
All Stars, 168, 170
"All the Things You Are," 200
Alone, 305
Alone (Again), 305
Altschul, Barry, 281, 308
Ameen, Ramsey, 279
Amen cadence, 243
American Federation of Musicians (AFM), 197
American Garage, 341
American in Paris, An, 117
Ammons, Gene, 198, 218
Amram, David, 365
Anatomy of a Murder (film), 296
Anderson, Ivie, 133
Anderson, Laurie, 263
Anderson, Marian, 34, 107
Anderson, Wes, 351
Anderson, William "Cat," 160, 287, 297
Andrews Sisters, 291
Andy Kirk's Twelve Clouds of Joy, 142–144
Ansermet, Ernest, 88, 124
"Anthropology," 220
Antiphony, 136

"Any Old Time," 168
Apex Club, 93
"Apple Honey," 219
"April in Paris," 293
April in Paris, 293
Arbour Zena, 311
Archey, Jimmy, 169
Arista Records, 281
Arlen, Harold, 287
"Armando's Rhumba," 336
Armstrong, Joe, 29
Armstrong, Louis, 47, 59, 62, 64, 66, 67, 69,
    70, 77, 78, *79*, 80, 81, *82*, 83, 86, *89*,
    89–96, *93*, 103, 112, *118*, 118–119, 121,
    164, 168–171, *170*, 175, 180, 181, 193,
    249, 361, 374
Arnaz, Desi, 208
Arpeggio, 12, 174
Arp synthesizer, 333
Arrangers, 31
Art Ensemble of Chicago, 280–281
Articulation, 14
"Artistry in Bolero," 239
"Artistry in Rhythm," 239
Art Landry and His Call of the North
    Orchestra, *141*
Ascension, 266, 271–272, 275, 317
"Ascension," 271
As Falls Wichita, So Falls Wichita Falls, 341
As If It Were the Seasons, 280
Association for the Advancement of Creative
    Musicians (AACM), 280
Astoria Kids, 126
At Fillmore, 328
"A-Tisket, A-Tasket," 166, 286
Atonality, 241

A train, *157*
Austin High Gang, 97, 150
"Autumn Leaves," 303–305, 309
"Autumn Sequence," 309
"Avalon," 182
Avant-garde, 260
　　See also Free jazz
Ayler, Albert, 271, 275–276, 281
"Azure," 278

Bach, Johann Sebastian, 231, 239, 311, 367
Bacharach, Burt, 366, 367
Backbeat (change-step), 263, 323
Back catalog, 347
Back phrasing, 187, 286
"Backwater Blues," 9, 52
Bacon, Louis, 169
Bacquet, George, 64, 68
Badrena, Manalo, 338
"Bags' Groove," 216, 253
Bailey, Benny, 209
Bailey, Buster, *118*, 118–119, 137, 150
Baker, Chet, 223, 225, 229–230, *230*, 243, 303, 363
Baker, David, 349
Baker, Dorothy, *Young Man with a Horn*, 101
Baker, Harold "Shorty," 287, 296
Baker, Josephine, 127
Balance, 136
Ballard, Jeff, 357
Ballard, Red, 153, 174
"Ballin' the Jack," 106
Ballou, Dave, 357
Banana, Milton, 237
Band, The, 327
Band-within-a-band, 150
Banjo, 29, 36
Bar, 5
Baraka, Amiri (aka Leroi Jones), *Blues People*, 274
Barbarin, Paul, 80, 169
Barber, Bill, 228
Barlines, 10
Barnet, Charlie, 173
Barons of Rhythm, 146
Barron, Kenny, 237, 354
Bartók, Béla, 154, 277
　　Second Piano Concerto, 132
Bartz, Gary, 328
Basie, William "Count," 46, 116, 131, 134, 140–143, *145*, 145–150, 178, 179, 227, 289, 292–295, 325, 345, 356
Basie's Beatle Bag, 325
"Basin Street Blues," 95, 155
Bass, *67*, 67, *139*
　　See also Acoustic bass; Walking bass
Bass (F) clef, 11
Bass drum, 16, 67
Battle, Kathleen, 334
Battle of the bands, 140–142
Bauer, Billy, 219, 238, 239
Bauza, Mario, 209, 364
Bayron, Grace, *171*
"Beale Street Blues," 48
Beat, 4–5
Beatles, 325, 338, 366
Beat movement, 223, 274
"Beau Koo Jack," 95

Beaux Arts String Quartet, 233
Bebop era, 19, 190–220
　　big bands of early 1940s, 197–198
　　big bands of late 1940s, 219–220
　　characteristics, 191, 194–196
　　Gillespie, Dizzy, 207–208
　　Goodman, Benny, 153
　　Gordon, Dexter, 217–218
　　Herman, Woody, 219
　　Johnson, J. J., 217
　　Latin jazz, 208–210
　　melodic features, 220
　　Monk, Thelonious, 213–217
　　Navarro, Fats, 217
　　origins, 180, 184, 192–194, 196–199
　　Parker, Charlie, 199–207
　　Powell, Bud, 210–213
　　Thornhill, Claude, 219–220
Bechet, Sidney, 59, 62, 63, 66, 67, 68, 70, 81, 83, *85*, 86, 88–89, *89*, 91, 103, 107, 110, 124, 127, 156, 198, 316
"Begin the Beguine," 168
Beiderbecke, Leon Bix, *73*, 81, 83, 96–101, *98*, *99*, 103, 114, 136, 140, 150, 176
Bellson, Louie, 295, 297
Ben Harney's Ragtime Instructor, 39, 40
Benjamin, Joe, 290
Bennett, Tony, 305
Benny Goodman Quartet, 182
Benny Goodman Trio, 182
"Benny Rides Again," 153
Benson, George, 4, 316, 359
Bent pitch, 330
Berg, Alban, 126
　　Violin Concerto, 132
Berigan, Bunny, 134, 152
Berkeley, Busby, 151
Berlin, Edward A., 44
Berlin, Germany, 125–126
Berlin, Irving, 11, 38, 126, 215, 367
Berliner, Emile, 74
Bernstein, Leonard, 262
Berrett, Joshua, 123
Berroa, Ignacio, 365
Berry, Chuck, 325
Berry, Leon "Chu," 164, 176, 187
Berton, Vic, 150
"Better Git It in Your Soul," 250
Bigard, Barney, 66, 80, 122, 155, *156*, 158, 160, 249
Big Bad Voodoo Daddy, 362
Big bands
　　Basie, Count, 293–295
　　bebop era, 197–198, 219–220
　　defined, 118, 133
　　early 1940s, 197–198
　　Ellington, Duke, 120–124, 295–298
　　Henderson, Fletcher, 118–120
　　late 1940s, 219–220
　　1950s and 1960s, 292–298
　　origins, 117–124
　　rhythm section, 139–140
　　swing era, 135–140
　　Thad Jones–Mel Lewis Big Band, 298
"Big Boy," 98
Big Broadcast, The, 164
Bill Evans Trio with Symphony Orchestra, 305
"Billie's Bounce," 203, 253

Billy Berg's, 205
"Bird Calls," 250
"Bird in Igor's Yard, A," 241
"Birdland," 336, 338–339
Birdland Jazz Emporium, *206*, 207, 241
Birds of Fire, 331
Birth of the Cool, 225, 227, 229, 239, 240, 247, 253
Bitches Brew, 324, 326–327
"Bitches Brew," 328
Bix and His Gang, 99
Bjork, 366
Black, Brown and Beige, 120, 155, 160, 240, 298, 352
Black activism, 273–275, 277
"Black and Blue," 112
Black-and-tan clubs, 71, 151
"Black and Tan Fantasy," 122
"Black and White Rag," 106
Black Artists Group (BAG), 281
"Blackbird," 338
"Black Bottom Stomp," 86
Black Fire, 318
"Black Jazz," 166
Blackman, Cindy, 363
Black Market, 337
Black Panther Party, 274–275
"Black Saint and the Sinner Lady, The," 250
Black Swan Records, 118
Blackwell, Ed, 261–262, 272
Blair, Lee, 169
Blake, Charlotte, 44
Blake, Eubie, 41, 103, 107, 109, 116, 120
Blakey, Art, 198, 215, *243*, 243–245, 248, 299, 300, 306, 308, 316–317, 345, 350, 353, 356
Blanchard, Terence, 353
Bland, James, 37
Blanton, Jimmy, 156–157, 158, 160, 182–183, 196
Blaue Engel, Der (The Blue Angel), 126
Bley, Carla, 357
Bley, Paul, 249, 300, 308, 364
Block-chord style, 238
Blood, Sweat & Tears, 325
Blood on the Fields, 350
Bloom, Jane Ira, 363
"Blowing the Blues Away," 198, 218
"Blue Bossa," 318
Blue Devils. *See* Original Blue Devils
Blue Friars, 98
"Blue in Green," 254
Blue Interlude, 350
"Blue Light," 158
Blue Monday, 117
"Blue 'n' Boogie," 253
Blue Note (club), 362
Blue Note Records, 213, 214–215, 218, 278, 299, 306, 316–318, 330
Blue notes, 18, 35, 95
"Blue Rondo à la Turk," 234–236, 240
Blues, 46–54
　　boogie-woogie, 53–54
　　Delta blues, 49–51
　　form, 48–49
　　Handy, W. C., 47–48
　　origins, 46–47
　　Smith, Bessie, 51–52

Blues, 46–54 (*Continued*)
vocal style, 53
"Blue Seven," 248
Blues form, 8, 17–18, 48–49
Blues harmony, 9
"Blues in Thirds," 181
"Blue Skies," 215
Blues on Bach, 231
Blues scale, 18, 19
"Blue Suede Shoes," 53
Blue Train, 267, 317
Bluiett, Hamiet, 281–282
Bobo, Willie, 307
Bocage, Peter, 63
"Body and Soul," 132, 150, 175–177, 182, 188, 199, 266
Bolden, Charles "Buddy," 63–64, 70
Boogie-woogie, 53–54
"Boogie Woogie Waltz," 337
Book, 136
Bossa nova, 209, 237
Bostic, Earl, 266
Boswell Sisters, 291
Botti, Chris, 361
Bowie, David, 330
Bowie, Lester, 280, 281, 345
"Bowl of Pop Corn, a Radio, and You, A," *133*
"Boy Meets Horn," 155
Brackeen, Joanne, 237
Braddy, Pauline, 172
Brass bands, 61
Brasses, 15
Braud, Wellman, 67, 85, 121, 123
Braxton, Anthony, 281, 308, 311
Brazilian music, 209, 237, 289, 334
Brazilian Romance, 289
Breaks, 19, 64–65
Brecker, Michael, 246, 330, 341–342
Brecker, Randy, 330, 341–342
Brecker Brothers, 339, 341–342
Brecker Brothers, The, 341
Breezin', 316, 359
Brewer, Gage, 141
Brian Setzer Orchestra, 362
Bridge, 6, 30, 146
Bridge, The, 249
Briggs, Pete, 93
Bright Size Life, 338, 341
Brilliant Corners, 217
Britain, 125
British Broadcasting Corporation, 186
Broadway Melody, 72
Brookmeyer, Bob, 230, 298, 357
"Brother, Can You Spare a Dime?," 131
Brown, Clifford, 217, 244, 246–247, 272, 290, 317
Brown, James, 324, 326, 333
Brown, John, 209
Brown, Lawrence, 34, 155, 158, 295
Brown, Marion, 271, 279
Brown, Paul, 360
Brown, Ray, *194*, 196, 211, 230, 242, 287
Brown, Sidney, 70
Brown Brothers, 69
Brown v. Board of Education, 273
Brubeck, Chris, 236
Brubeck, Danny, 236
Brubeck, Darius, 236

Brubeck, Dave, 225, 227, 230, 233–236, *234*, 240, 243, 277
Bruce, Jack, 330
Brunswick, 168, 187
Buckinghams, 313
Buckner, Milt, 238, 241, 312
Buckshot LeFonque, 361
Buddhism, 333
"Bu-Dee-Daht," 199
"Budo," 227
Burns, Dave, 209
Burns, Ken, 350
Burns, Ralph, 219
Burnside, Violet, *171*, 172
Burrell, Kenny, 315, 316
Burton, Gary, 311, 326, 330, 341
Bushell, Garvin, 125–126
Buttercorn Lady, 308
Butterfield, Don, 250
"Butterfly," 334
Butts, Jimmy, 200
Byard, Jaki, 250, 272
Byas, Don, 149, 197–200, 206, 210
"Bye Bye Blackbird," 106
BYG Records, 280
Byrd, Donald, 243, 299, 306, 327
Byrd, Ima Belle, 172
Byron, Don, 277

Cabin and Plantation Songs, 26
Cabin in the Sky, 168
Cadence, 6
Cafe Bohemia, 314
Cafe Society, 187
Cage, John, 281
Caine, Michael, 249
Caine, Uri, 367
Cakewalk, 37–38, *38*, 124
"Cake Walking Babies (from Home)," 89, 91–93
"Caldonia," 219
Caldwell, Albert "Happy," *85*
Call-and-response, 19, 26, 33, 137
"Call for All Demons, A," 279
Calloway, Cab, 156, 163–164, *165*, 193, 207
Camel Caravan (radio program), 152
Candid Records, 272, 278
"Candlelights," 100
"Cantaloop (Flip Fantasia)," 361
"Cantaloupe Island," 361
Capitol Records, 225, 227, 229, 292, 313
"Caprice Rag," 109
"Caravan," 155, 156
"Careless Love," 70
Carey, Mutt, 66, 70
Caribbean music, 62–63, 364
Carisi, Johnny, 227
Carmichael, Hoagy, 97
Carmichael, Stokely, 274
Carnegie Hall Jazz Band, 349
Carney, Harry, 121, 123, 156, 158, 230, 287, 296, 297
"Carolina Shout," 110–112
Carpenter, Richard, 253
Carr, Mancy, 93, 94
Carrington, Terri Lynn, 363
"Carry Me Back to Old Virginny," 37

Carter, Benny, 119, *127*, 135, 136, 156, 166, 167, 173, 175, 180, 181, 186–187, 293, 345, 363
Carter, Betty, 327, 355, 363
Carter, James, 354
Carter, Jimmy, 278
Carter, Regina, 363
Carter, Ron, 272, 299, *299*, 301, 306, 318, 330, 334, 350
Casa Loma Orchestra, 134, 166
"Casa Loma Stomp," 166
Casino, 335
Cassavetes, John, 250
Cassidy, Hopalong, *222*
Castle, Irene and Vernon, 73
Catlett, Sidney, 201
Cavallaro, Johnny, 168
Celestial Hawk, The, 311
Celestin, Oscar "Papa," 69, 70
"Ceora," 317
Chair, 89, 136
Challis, Bill, 95, 98, 99
Chaloff, Serge, 230, 239
Chambers, Jack, 266
Chambers, Joe, 318
Chambers, Paul, 253, 255, 299
"Chameleon," 333, 337
Chandler, Dee Dee, 64
Change of the Century, 261, 262
Channel, 30
"Chant, The," 86
Chaput, Roger, 128
Charles, Dennis, 278
Charles, Ray, 226, 311, *312*, 314, 336
Charles, Teddy, 249
Charles Lloyd Quartet, 308–309
"Charleston, The," 109–110, 126
"Charleston Rag," 109
Charlie Parker with Strings, 206
Chart, 96
Chase, Gilbert, 19
"Chase, The," 218
"Chasin' the Bird," 211
Cheatham, Adolphus "Doc," 125, 345
"Chelsea Bridge," 157
Chernoff, John Miller, 28
"Cherokee," 195, 199, 203
Cherry, Don, 249, 261–264
"Cheryl," 211
Chestnut, Cyrus, 355
Chevalier, Maurice, 122
Chicago (band), 325
"Chicago Breakdown," 93
Chicago jazz, 70, 72, 96, 280–281
Chick Corea's Elektric Band, 336
"Chimes Blues," 89
Chinmoy, Sri, 331
Chocolate Kiddies, 125, 126
"Choo Choo (I Gotta Hurry Home)," 121
Chord, 4, 7
Chord progression, 13
Chorus, 8, 18
Chorus reverberation, 340
Christensen, Jon, 309
Christian, Bud, 64, 91
Christian, Charlie, 152, 183–186, 197, 323
Christy, June, 289
Chromatic scale, 307

Church cadence, 243
Ciccarone, Rock, 357
Circle, 281, 308
Circle: The Paris Concert, 334
City of Glass, 241
Civilization: A Harmolodic Celebration, 263
Civil Rights Act (1964), 273
"Clap Hands, Here Comes Charlie," 166
Clarinet, 16, *16*, 66, 66–67, 153–154
"Clarinet à la King," 153
"Clarinet Lament," 155, 156
"Clarinet Marmalade," 99
Clark, Dick, 153, 174
Clark, Petula, 330
Clark, Sonny, 213
Clarke, Kenny, 183, 184, 193, 196, 197, 199,
    200, 209, 217, 230, 247, 253, 368
Clarke, Stanley, 325, 334–336, *336*
Classicism, 347–358
Classics in Jazz: Cool and Quiet, 225
Claves, 208
Clayton, Buck, 147, 178
Clayton-Thomas, David, 325
Clef Club Orchestra, 120
Cless, Rod, 97
Clifford Brown–Max Roach Quintet, 246–248
"Clothes Line Ballet," 112–113
Clouds of Joy, 140, 142–144
Club Alabam, 118
C-melody saxophone, 98
Coates, John, 308
Cobb, Jimmy, 255, 299
Cobham, Billy, 330–332
Coburn, Richard, 195
Cohn, Al, 179, 225, 236
Cohn, Joey, 362–363
Coker, Henry, 293
Coker, Jerry, 349
Colaiuta, Vinnie, 370
Cold war, 223
Cole, Bob, 38, 106
Cole, Nat "King," 114, 242
Cole, William Randolph "Cozy," 183
Coleman, George, 280, 300
Coleman, Ira, 330
Coleman, Ornette, 249, *261*, 261–265, 268,
    271, 272, 281, 299, 300, 303, 306, 308,
    311, 317, 341, 345, 350, 363, 367
Coleman, Steve, 367, *368*, , 374
Collective improvisation, 60
Collier, James Lincoln, 133
Collins, Booker, 144
Collins, Junior, 228
Collins, Wallace, 63–64
Coltrane, 267
Coltrane, Alice, 272
Coltrane, John, 176, 217, 218, 224, 253–255,
    265, 265–275, 279, 281, 297, 298, 309,
    315, 317, 318, 342
Columbia Records, 77, 120, 198, 253
"Come On, Come Over," 338
"Come Sunday," 160
Coming About, 357
Comping, 19, 196, 300
Complete Live at the Plugged Nickel, The, 300
Complete reissue, 347
Components, 318
Concert by the Sea, 242

Concertino for Jazz Quartet and Orchestra,
    233, 241
Concert in the Garden, 357
Concert Jazz Band, 230
Concerto, 155
Concerto for Billy the Kid, 241, 302
"Concerto for Cootie," 155, 156
Concert of Sacred Music, 297
Concerto in F, 117
Concerto Retitled, 337
Concierto de Aranjuez, 334
"Concorde," 231
Condon, Eddie, 79, 96, 97, 183
Conference of the Birds, 311
"Confirmation," 205
Connection, The, 218
Connie's Inn, 96
Conniff, Ray, 168
Connor, Chris, 289
Connors, Bill, 335
Conquistador, 278
Contemporary Records, 261
Contrafact, 195
Conversations with Myself, 303
Cook, Willie, 287
Cook, Will Marion, 38, 107, 120, 124–125
"Cool Blues," 362
Cool Heat, 289
Cool jazz, 220, 224–225, 227–239
    Brubeck, Dave, 233–236
    Davis, Miles, 227–229
    Getz, Stan, 236–238
    melodic styles, 257
    Modern Jazz Quartet, 230–233
    Tristano, Lennie, 238–239
"Copenhagen," 119
Copland, Aaron, 107, 154
    Appalachian Spring, 192
Corea, Chick, 217, 237, 281, 302, 306–308,
    308, 311, 326–328, 334–336
"Cork 'n' Bib," 239
Cornbread, 317
"Corner Pocket," 293–295
Cornet, *15*, 15, 65–66, *66*
"Cornet Chop Suey," 92
Coryell, Larry, *329*, 329–331
Cosby, Bill, 307
Cotton Club, 103, 105, 120–122, 151, 164
Cotton Club Orchestra, *156*
"Cotton Tail," 156
Coulson, Vic, 197
Count Basie Band, 142, 176, 178
Count Basie Orchestra, 356
Countermelody, 30, 78, 79
Counterpoint, 27, 225
"Country Preacher," 312, 337
Cox, Billy, 331
"Crawdad Blues," 143
Crawford, Jimmie, 165
Crayton, Pee Wee, 261
"Crazeology," 195, 205
"Crazy Blues," 47
"Crazy Chords," 236–237
"Crazy Walk," *135*
Cream, 325, 330
Creative Construction Company, 281
Creole Jazz Band, 59, 64, 66, 70, 71,
    76–80, *79*, 89

"Creole Love Call," 122
"Creole Rhapsody," 121, 122
Creoles of Color, 62
"Crescendo in Blue," 155
"Criss Cross," 215
Cron, Rosalind "Roz," *171*
Crosby, Bing, 291
Crosby, Bob, 134, 173
Crosby, Stills, and Nash, 327
Crosby, Stills, Nash & Young, 366
Crosscurrents, 305
Crosse, Gay, 266
Crossings, 331
Crossover music, 347
Cross-rhythms, 27, 238
"Crossroads," 50
Crouch, Stanley, 349
"Cubana Be/Cubana Bop," 207
Cubop, 209, 364
"Cucumber Slumber," 337
Cugat, Xavier, 208
Culley, Wendell, 293
Cup mute, *15*
Cutting contest, 108
Cymbals, 67
Cyrille, Andrew, 278

"Daahoud," 246
Da Costa, Paulinho, 360
Dagomba, 28
Dameron, Tadd, 195, 217
"Daniel," 29
Danielsson, Palle, 309
Darlings of Rhythm, 171
"Darn That Dream," 229
"Dat Dere," 244
Dave Brubeck Quartet, 227
Davis, Art, 271
Davis, Eddie "Lockjaw," 149
Davis, Ernestine "Tiny," 172
Davis, Jerome, 29
Davis, John, 29
Davis, Leonard, 169
Davis, Lew, 125
Davis, Meyer, 59
Davis, Miles, 98, 197, 203, 205–207, 214,
    217, 220, 224, 225, *227*, 227–229, 234,
    239, 240, 243, 247, 248, 252–256,
    265–269, *275*, 298–302, 306–309, 312,
    318, 324–330, *328*, 334, 335, 337, 342,
    350, 353, 355, 359, 363
Davis, Peter, 29
Davis, Richard, 272
Davis, Steve, 268
Davison, William "Wild Bill," 96
"Dawn of the Century," *54*
Day in the Life, A, 315, 325
"Dead Man Blues," 86
Debussy, Claude, 157, 216, 303, 305
Decca Records, 146, 147, 198
Decoding Society, 368
"Dee Dee," 263
Deep South Suite, 160
De Faut, Volly, 150
DeFrancesco, Joey, 355
DeFranco, Buddy, 239
DeJohnette, Jack, 309, 311, 328, 341, 342
Delta blues, 49–51

De Lucia, Paco, 331, 335
De Paris, Sidney, *85*
DePew, Bill, 153, 174
Depression, 131–133
"Dere's No Hidin' Place Down Dere," 34
"Desafinado," 209
Desmond, Paul, 179, 233–234, *234*, 281
Dett, R. Nathaniel, 36
Devotion, 331
Dexter, Jacqueline, 172
Dial Records, 205, 266
Dickerson, Carroll, 93, 96, 180–181
"Dicty Blues," 175
Dietrich, Marlene, 126
Digable Planets, 361
Digital delay, 340
Digital technology, 359
"Digression," 238
"Dill Pickles Rag," 106
Di Meola, Al, 324, 331, 335, 340
"Diminuendo and Crescendo in Blue," 296
"Diminuendo in Blue," 155
"Dippermouth Blues," 77–80, 119
Dirty Boogie, The, 362
"Disc Jockey Jump," 219
"Dis Here," 244
"Disorder at the Border," 199
Diva, 363
Dixieland, 47, 60, 70, 224, 345
"Dixie(land) Jass Band One Step," 73–74
Dixie Rhythm Girls, 172
Dixie Syncopators, 70, 80
Dixon, Bill, 275
"Dizzy Atmosphere," 200
Dodds, Johnny, 66, 68, 69, 70, 77, 78,
    79, 80, 92, *93*
Dodds, Warren "Baby," 61, 62, 63, 68, 70, 76,
    77, 78, *79*, 80, 93
Doin' Alright, 218
Dollar Brand (aka Abdullah Ibrahim), 364
"Dolores," 300
"Dolphin Dance," 305, 307
Dolphy, Eric, 250, 262, 269, 272–273,
    306, 317, 318
Domino Theory, 340
"Donna Lee," 211, 220, 253, 338
Donnelly, Ted, 144
"Do Nothin' Till You Hear from Me," 155, 160
"Don't Be That Way," 150, 166
"Don't Explain," 187
"Don't Get Around Much Anymore," 155, 158
"Don't Jazz Me–Rag (I'm Music)," 43
doo bop, 329
Doors, 325
Dorham, Kenny, 243, 318, 353
Dorsey, Jimmy, 99, 167, 176
Dorsey, Tommy, 99, 134, 135, 143, 165,
    167, 183
Dotted rhythms, 43, 44
Double drumming, 68
Double-necked guitar, 331
*Double Rainbow: The Music of Antonio
    Carlos Jobim*, 318
Douglas, Aaron, 107
Douglas, Dave, 362, 367
Downbeat, 193
Down Beat (magazine), 347

"Down-Hearted Blues," 51
"Down South Camp Meeting," 137–138,
    150, 153–154, 174, 183
"Doxy," 248, 253
Draper, Ray, 272
"Dreamland Blues," 141
Dreamland Cafe, 71, 89, 90
Dreams, 330, 331
Dream Weaver, 309
"Dreamy Blues," 122
Dred Scott decision, 277
Dreyer, Flo, 172
D'Rivera, Paquito, 364
Dropping bombs, 196
Drum Is a Woman, A, 296
Drums, 16, 67
Drum set, 16–17, *17*, 30, *67*, 67–68, 121
Du Bois, W.E.B., 273
Duke, George, 324, 331, 335
Dunn, Johnny, 120
Duple meter, 5
Durante, Jimmy, 76
Durham, Eddie, 141, 143, 147, 165, 178, 184
Duster, 330
Dutrey, Honore, 66, 70, 77, 78, *79*, 80
Dynamics, 14

Eagle Band, 60
Earland, Charles, 314
"Early Autumn," *219*, 237
Early jazz, 57–81
    band, evolution of, 64–65
    Chicago, 70, 72
    Creole Jazz Band, 77–80
    exodus from New Orleans, 68–70
    improvisation, evolution of, 80–81
    instruments, 64–68
    New Orleans, 60–64
    northern migration, 70–72
    Oliver, King, 77–80
    ragtime in relation to, 44–46, 57, 59–60
    recording, 72–77
    singing, 53
"East of the Sun," 309
"East St. Louis Toodle-Oo," 121–124, 368
"Echoes of the Jungle," 121
Echoplex, 337
Eckstine, Billy, 181, 197–198, 200, 207, 217,
    218, 243, 252, 288
ECM Records, 281, 311
Edison, Harry "Sweets," 147, 178
Edwards, Eddie "Daddy," 74, 75
Edward VII, king of England, 38
Egan, Mark, 341
"Egg, The," 307
Eicher, Manfred, 311
Eighth notes, 10
80/81, 341
Eisenhower, Dwight D., 170
Elastic meter, 303
Eldridge, Roy, 168, 180, 181, 187, 188, 197,
    200, 207, 262
Electric guitar, 140, 183–184, 186, 323
Electric piano, 300, 331, 336–337
    See also Fender Rhodes electric piano
Electronic organ, 312
Electronic wind instrument (EWI), 342

Elegant Gypsy, 335
"Elephant's Wobble," 143
Eleventh House, 330
Elias, Eliane, 342, 355, 363, 364
Eliot, T. S., *The Wasteland*, 72
Elizabeth II, Queen of England, 296
Elizalde, Fred, 125
Elizalde, Manual, 125
Elling, Kurt, 356
Ellington, Edward "Duke," 43, 46, 67, 103,
    105, 107, 110, 114, 116, 117, 119–124,
    120, 126, 127, 131, 133, 134, 136, 143,
    151, 154–160, *156*, 182–183, 226, 240,
    250, 253, 277, 278, 279, 287, 295–298,
    325, 349, 350, 353, 356, 370, 374
Ellington, Mercer, 353, 356
Ellington '66, 325
Ellis, Herb, 242
Elman, Misha, 349
Emergency!, 330
Empyrean Isles, 306, 317
Enigmatic Ocean, 331
"Entertainer, The," 43
"Epistrophy," 197
Epitaph, 252
Erskine, Peter, *337*, 339
Erskine Tate Orchestra, 90, 93
Ervin, Booker, 250
Erwin, Pee Wee, 153, 174
Escalator over the Hill, 357
"E.S.P.," 300, 301
"Ethiopia Rag," 43
Ethnomusicology, 20
Europe, 124–129, 155
Europe, James Reese, 73, 76, 103, 120,
    124, 127
"European Echoes," 263
European music, nineteenth century, 29–31
European Rhythm Machine, 363
Evanescence, 357
Evans, Bill (pianist), 237, 241, 254, 255, 299,
    302–306, 308, 311, 335
Evans, Bill (saxophonist), 328
Evans, Gil, 220, 227, 229, 256, 298, *302*, 307,
    329, 334, 357, 364
Evans, Herschel, 140, 147, 149, 176, 178, 217
Everybody Digs Bill Evans, 302
"Everyday People," 325
"Every Tub," 147–149, 178–179
"Excerpt from the First Movement to Heavy
    Metal," 335
Existential Dred, 277
Expectations, 311
"Express Crossing," 351–353
Expression, 272
Extended chord tones, 195
Extensions, 14
Extrapolation, 330
Eye on You, 368

"Fables of Faubus," 250
Facing You, 311
Faddis, Jon, 349
Fairfax, Frankie, 207
False start, 347
Famous Door, 193
"Fantasy," 239

Far Cry, 272
Far East Suite, The, 122, 296
"Farewell Blues," 97
Farlow, Talmage "Tal," 249
Farmer, Art, 268, 299
Farrell, Joe, 334, 336
Farrell, Larry, 357
Fat Albert Rotunda, 307
Fate Marable, 182
Fats Waller and His Buddies, 151
Faubus, Orval, 170, 250
Fauré, Gabriel, 305
Favors, Malachi, 280, 281
Feedback, 323
Feel the Spirit, 289
Feldman, Victor, 299
Feminism, 363
Fender Rhodes electric piano, 300, 307, 307–308, 313, 331
Fenner, Thomas P., 25, 26
Fenton, Nick, 196
Ferguson, Maynard, 306, 317, 336, 338
Festivals, 226
"Fever," 289
"Fidgety Feet," 98
Field hollers, 35
Field recording, 28
Fields, Jackie, 177
"Fiesta, La," 334
52nd Street, *198*, 198–199
"57 Varieties," 181
Figueroa, Sammy, 365
Filles de Kilimanjaro, 302, 326
Film, 135
"Fine and Mellow," 188
"Fingers," 298
Fire Music, 274
"Fireworks," 93
Fishkin, Arnold, 238
Fisk Jubilee Singers, 34
Fitzgerald, Ella, 166, 171, 180, 224, 242, 286–287, *287*, 363
Fitzgerald, F. Scott, *The Great Gatsby*, 72
Five Pieces 1975, 281
Five Spot, 217, 262, 267, 272, 278
"Flamenco Sketches," 254, 269
Flanagan, Tommy, 213
"Flashes," 100
Flat, 11
Fleet, Biddy, 199
Fletcher Henderson Orchestra, 119, 175, 177–178, 180
Flintstones theme song, 8
Flock, The, 331
"Florida Stomp," 180
Flowering, The, 309
Floyd, Samuel, 107
Floyd, Troy, 140–141, 147
Flugelhorn, 15, *15*
"Flying Home," 183
Flynn, George, 357
"Fly Right," 197
Focus, 237
"Footloose," *105*
"Footprints," 300
For Alto, 281
Ford, Henry, 71

Foreign countries, contemporary jazz in, 364–365
"Foreigner in a Free Land," 263
"Forest Flower," 309
Form, 4–9
  32-bar AABA, 5–8
  aab blues form, 8–9
Formula, 64, 178, 205
For Trio, 281
Fortune, Sonny, 328
"42nd Street," 106
Foster, Al, 328
Foster, Frank, 293, 295, 356
Foster, Pops, 61, 169
Foster, Stephen, 37
"Four Brothers," 240
Four Brothers, 219, 225, 236, 240
Four for Trane, 275
4/4 time, 5
"Four in One," 215–216
Fourth Way, 330
Fowlkes, Charlie, 293
Freak In, 367
Free jazz, 217, 238, 259–282, 345
  Art Ensemble of Chicago, 280–281
  Association for the Advancement of Creative Musicians, 280
  Ayler, Albert, 275–276
  Black Artists Group, 281
  characteristics, 282
  Coleman, Ornette, 261–265
  Coltrane, John, 265–272
  Creative Construction Company, 281
  Dolphy, Eric, 272–273
  Shepp, Archie, 274–275
  Sun Ra, 279–280
  Taylor, Cecil, 277–279
  World Saxophone Quartet, 281–282
Free Jazz, 262, 271, 272, 299, 303, 306, 317
Freeman, Bud, 97
Freeman, Russ, 229
Free Spirits, 330
Freiberg, Daniel, 365
Frenchies Bar, *46*
Friar's Inn, 97
Friar's Society Orchestra, 97
"Friday Miles," 328
Frink, Laurie, 357
Frisell, Bill, 361, 367
"Frog Legs Rag," 43
Front-line instruments, 17, 29
Frye, Carl, 188
Fugue, 231
"Fugue," 241
"Fugue on Bop Themes," 234
Full-chord style, 238
Fuller, Curtis, 244, 318
Fuller, Gil, 207
Function, 13
Functional music, 35
Funerals, 62
Funky jazz, 226, 243–246, 311–316
  Adderley, Cannonball, 312
  Blakey, Art, 243–244
  blues, 312
  guitar, 315–316
  Silver, Horace, 245–246

Smith, Jimmy, 312, 314
"Funny Paper," 282
Further Explorations, 246
Fusion, 321–342
  Brecker Brothers, 341–342
  characteristics, 321, 342
  Corea, Chick, 334–336
  Coryell, Larry, 329–330
  Davis, Miles, 326–329
  Hancock, Herbie, 331, 333–334
  Lifetime, 330
  Mahavishnu Orchestra, 330–331
  Metheny, Pat, 340–341
  origins, 323–326
  Steps, 342
  Weather Report, 336–340
FUTURE2FUTURE, 334
Future Shock, 334

G, Kenny, 345, 359, 361, 374
Gadd, Steve, 336
Gage Brewer's Versatile Radio Orchestra, *141*
Gandee, Al, *73*
Garbarek, Jan, 309, 311, 364
Gardner, Ava, 168
Garland, Red, 253, 266
Garner, Erroll, 241, 266, 289
Garrett, Kenny, 353
Garrison, Jimmy, 266, 268–270
Garrison, Lucy McKim, 31–32
Gaskin, Victor, 313
"Gathering Sky, The," 341
Gay Crosse and His Good Humor Six, 266
Gayles, Joe, 209
Gee, Lottie, 126
Gelber, Jack, 218
Gem Dance Folio, 60
Gennett Records, 76, 77, 86, 98, 151
Gentry, Bobbie, 305
George Morrison Orchestra, 141
"Georgia on My Mind," 311
Georgia Sea Island Singers, 29
Germany, 125–126
Gershwin, George, 8, 41, 105, 106, 117, 126, 195, 240, 253, 287, 298
Gershwin, Ira, 8, 287
Gershwin's World, 334
Getz, Stan, 179, 209, 219, 223, 225, *236*, 236–239, 242, 307, 363
Getz/Gilberto, 237
Ghost bands, 356
Ghosts, 275
"Ghosts," 275–276
"Giant Steps," 265–266, 269
Gibson, Rob, 349
Gifford, Gene, 166
"Giggin'," 261
Gil, Gilberto, 364
Gilberto, Astrud, 237
Gilberto, João, 237
Gillespie, John Birks "Dizzy," 143, 164, 176, 180, 183, *190*, 193, 195–210, 213, 214, 217, 219, 239, 242, 243, 246, 252, 253, 266, 287, 288, 364, 368
Gillette, Bob, *73*
Gilmore, Buddy, 124–125
Gilmore, John, 271, 279

Ginsberg, Allen, *Howl*, 223
"Girl from Ipanema, The," 237–238
"Girl Talk," 293
Gisbert, Greg, 359
Gitler, Ira, 265
Giuffre, Jimmy, 179, 219, 225, 236, 240, 241, 289, 305, 357
Give Me the Night, 359
Glaser, Joe, 168
"Glass Enclosure," 213
Gleason, Patrick, 307
Glen Island Casino, 167
Glissando, 16, 65
"Gloomy Sunday," 187
Go, 218
"God Bless America," 11
"God Bless the Child," 187
"Godchild," 227, 229
Goines, Victor, 351
Going Places, 168
Goin' Out of My Head, 315
Goin' Up, 317
Golden Rule Band, 64
Goldkette, Jean, 98, 135, 140, 166
Gold Whispering Band, 69
"Go 'Long Mule," 118
Golson, Benny, 244, 353
Gomez, Eddie, 303, 305, 336, 342
Gongons, 28
Gongs East, 272
Gonsalves, Paul, 287, 296, 297
"Good Bait," 217
"Goodbye Pork Pie Hat," 250
"Good Jelly Blues," 198
Goodman, Benny (clarinetist), 67, 107, 119, 131, 134, 135, 137, 140, 143, 146, 150–154, 151, 166, 167, 173–175, 180–183, 187, 219, 236, 289, 303
Goodman, Benny (violinist), 57
Goodman, Harry, 153, 174
Goodman, Jerry, 331
"Goodnight Sweetheart," *182*
Gordon, Dexter, 198, 210, 213, 217, 217–218, 243, 266, 306, 363
Gordon, Wycliffe, 351
Gottlieb, Danny, 341
Grace Cathedral, San Francisco, 297, *298*
Graettinger, Robert, 241
Graham, Bill, 293
Graham, Larry, 325
"Grandpa's Spells," 59
Grand piano, 17
Grand Terrace Ballroom, 181
Granz, Norman, 114, 194, 206, 242
Grappelli, Stéphane, 127–129, 363
Grateful Dead, 327, 366
Gray, Wardell, 153, 218, 266
Great Depression, 131–133
Great Migration, 70–71
Green, Charlie, 119
Green, Freddie, 146, 147, 178, 184, 293
Green, Grant, 317, 318
Greer, Sonny, 120, 121, 123, 158, 295
Griffin, Chris, 153, 174
Griffin, Johnny, 243, 280, 345
Grimes, Henry, 278
Grimes, Lloyd "Tiny," 114, 200
"Groovin' High," 195, 200, 207

Grossman, Steve, 328
Grubbs, Naima, 266
Gryce, Gigi, 216
Guarnieri, Johnny, 116
"Guataca City (To David Amram)," 364–365
Guest of Honor, A, 41
Guitar, 16, *16*, 67, 140, 315–316
    See also Electric guitar
"Gulf Coast Blues," 51
Gurtu, Trilok, 364
Gushee, Lawrence, 59, 77, 249
"Gut Bucket Blues," 92
Gutbucket sound, 120–121
Guy, Fred, 121, 123, 158
Guy, Joe, 177, 196

Habanera rhythm, 208
Hackett, Bobby, 101, 167–168, 180
Haden, Charlie, 261–264, 309, 311, 331, 341, 357, 363
Haffer, Dick, 250
Haig, Al, 201, 228
Haig, The, 229, 239
Hakim, Sadik. *See* Thornton, Argonne
"Half Nelson," 253
Half notes, 10
Hall, Edmond, 61
Hall, Jim, 186, 249, 305, 341, 367
Hallucinations," 227
Hamilton, Foreststorn "Chico," 229, 240, 272, 309
Hamilton, Jimmy, 160, 287, 296
Hammer, Jan, 331
Hammond, John, 146, 152, 181–182, 183, 187
Hammond organ, 312
Hampton, Lionel, 149, 150, 151, 152, 182, *187*, 218, 241, 246, 249
Hampton, Paula, 171
Hampton Normal and Agricultural Institute, 26
Hancock, Herbie, 254, 299–301, 305, *306*, 306–307, 312, 317, 318, 324–328, 330, 331, 333–334, 340, 342, 350, 361, 362, 366, 370, 374
"Handful of Keys," 112, 181
Hand on the Torch, 361
Handy, William Christopher (W. C.), 47–48, 106, 118, 208
"Hang Gliding," 357–358
"Hang Up Your Hangups," 334
Haque, Farreed, 365
Hard bop, 224, 226, 243–252, 316–318
    Blakey, Art, 243–244
    Blue Note Records, 316–318
    Clifford Brown–Max Roach Quintet, 246–247
    Henderson, Joe, 318
    Hubbard, Freddie, 317
    melodic styles, 257
    Mingus, Charles, 249–252
    Morgan, Lee, 317
    Rollins, Sonny, 247–249
    Shorter, Wayne, 317–318
    Silver, Horace, 245–246
Hard Bop, 243
Hardin, Lillian "Lil," 68, 77, 78, *79*, 80, 89, 90, *93*, 171, 180, 363
Hardman, Glenn, 312

Hardwick, Otto, 120, 123, 158
Hardy, Earl, 177
Hargrove, Roy, 354
"Harlem Airshaft," 155, 160
"Harlem Congo," 166
Harlem Play-Girls, 172
"Harlem Rag," 40
Harlem Renaissance, 106–108, 121
"Harlem Strut," 110
Harlem Symphony, 110
Harmolodic theory, 263
Harmonic substitution, 13
Harmonic superimposition, 267
Harmon mute, *15*, 253, 329
Harmony, 4, 7, 12–14, 31
Harrell, Tom, 354
Harrington, John, 144
Harris, Barry, 213
Harris, Benny, 195, 198
Harrison, Donald, 330, 353
Harrison, James Henry "Jimmy," 119, 166, 170
Hart, Billy, 307
Hart, Clyde, 200
Hart, Lorenz, 287
Hartwell, Jimmy, *73*
"Hattie Wall," 282
"Havona," 338
Hawkins, Coleman, 114, 118, *118*, 119, 140, 142, 147, 156, 163, 167, 175–177, *176*, 180, 198, 199, 206, 214, 217, 248, 266, 289, 363
"Hawk Variations," 176
Haynes, Roy, 272, 290, 307, 336

Head, 6, 30
Head arrangement, 31, 118, 139
Headhunters, 307, 324, 333–334
"Heartland," 341
Heath, Jimmy, 299
Heath, Percy, *230*, 230–231, 253
Heath, Ted, 125
Heavy Weather, 336, 338–339
"Heckler's Hop," 180
"Heebie Jeebies," 92, 166
Hefti, Neal, 219, 293
Heliocentric Worlds of Sun Ra, The, 279
"Hello, Dolly," 171
Hemphill, Julius, 281–282
Henderson, Fletcher, 47, 59, 89, 95, 99, 103, 105, 106, 107, *118*, 118–120, *134*, 134–137, 150, 153, 156, 174, 175, 177, 186, 243, 279
Henderson, Joe, 318
Henderson, Michael, 328
Henderson, Scott, 340
Hendricks, Jon, 291, 297
Hendrix, Jimi, 323, 325, 326, 328, 330, 338
Hentoff, Nat, 229
Herbert, Arthur, 177
Herman, Woody, 135, 207, 219, *219*, 225, 236, 237, 239, 240, 298, 306, 325, 354
Hersch, Fred, 355
Hickman, Art, 118, 125, 135
Hickory House, 193
Higgins, Billy, 249, 261–264, 317, 341

"High Society," 77
Hi-hat, 16, 67–68, *139*, 139–140
Hilaire, Andrew, 87
Hill, Alex, 95
Hill, Andrew, 217, 318
Hill, Teddy, 180, 207
Hindemith, Paul, 154
Hines, Earl, 92–96, 116, 143, 168, 180–181, *181*, 186, 197–198, 200, 207, 241, 336–337
Hinton, Milt "The Judge," 164
Hipsters, 193
"Hiroshima: Rising from the Abyss," 357
Histoire du soldat, L', 124
Hitler, Adolf, 71, 126, 131
Hodes, Art, 150
Hodges, Johnny, 122, 155–156, *156*, 158, 180, 181, 186, 266, 287, 295–296
Hogan, Ernest, 38, 40
Holder, Terence T., 140, 142
Holiday, Billie, 53, 150, 168, 171, 176, 179, 181, *187*, 187–189, 219, 223, 248, 267, 370
Holland, Dave, 281, 308, 311, 326, 328, 363, 364, 370, 374
Hollywood Cafe, 120
Hollywood Hotel, 151
Holman, Bill, 239
Holmes, Charlie, 169
Holmes, John Clellon, *Go*, 223
Holmes, Richard "Groove," 314
Honegger, Arthur, 105
"Honeysuckle Rose," 112, 199, 205
"Honky Tonk Train Blues," 53
"Hootie Blues," 199
Hope, Elmo, 217
Hopkins, Claude, 127
"Hora Decubitus," 250–251, 272
Horne, Lena, *165*
Horner, Tim, 357
Hot bands, 72, 134
Hot Chocolates, 96, 112, 121
Hot Club, 127
Hot Five, 90, 92–95, *93*, 180
"Hot House," 195, 206
Hot Seven, 93, 95
"Hotter Than That," 93
Howard Theater, 120
"How Deep Is the Ocean," 132
"How High the Moon," 198
Hubbard, Freddie, 243, 244, 271, 306, 309, 317, 334, 353, *353*
Hub Cap, 317
Hub Tones, 317
Hudson, Will, 165
Hughes, Bill, 293
Hughes, Langston, 72, 107
Humair, Daniel, 363
"Humpty-Dumpty," 336
"Hunky-Dory," *36*
Hunter, Alberta, 112
Hunter, Charlie, 361
Hurston, Zora Neale, 107
Hutcherson, Bobby, 318
Hutton, Ina Ray, *130*, 171
Hylton, Jack, 175
Hyman, Dick, 206
Hymn of the Seventh Galaxy, 335

"I Ain't Got Nobody," 181
Ibarra, Susie, 363
Ibrahim, Abdullah (aka Dollar Brand), 364
Idut, 279
"I Fall in Love Too Easily," 328
"I Feel Good," 324
"I Got Rhythm," 8, 132, 194, 195, 205, 298
"I'll Keep Loving You," 211
"I'll Remember April," 241, 248
"I Love Paris," 278
"I Loves You Porgy," 303
Imaginary Voyage, 331
"I'm an Old Cowhand," 248
"I'm Beginning to See the Light," 158
Imperial Band, 60
Imperial Orchestra, 65
"Impressions," 269
Impressions, 273
Impressions of the Far East, 296
Improvisation, 7–8, 11, 80–81, 134, 189
Impulse Records, 275
"In a Little Spanish Town," 166
In All Languages, 263
"In a Mist," 100, 114
"In a Sentimental Mood," 155
In a Silent Way, 324, 326–327, 330
"In a Silent Way," 337
Inception, 268
Incognito, 361
"In Crowd, The," 313
In Dahomey, 124
Indent, 278
"India," 269, 272
"Indiana," 239
Inner Mounting Flame, The, 331
Inside, 95, 175
Inside Hi-Fi, 239
Instrumental music, 4
Instruments
    early jazz, 64–68
    percussion, 16–17
    piano, 17
    string, 16
    wind, 15
Intermodulation, 305
International Association for Jazz Education, 349
International Sweethearts of Rhythm, *171*, 171–172
Internet, 362
Interstellar Space, 272
Interval, 10
"In the Afterglow," 350
"In the Dark," 100
In the Light, 311
"In the Mood," 53, 168
In This House, On This Morning, 350
Intonation, 136
Introduction, 6
"Intuition," 238
"In Walked Bud," 215
"I Only Have Eyes For You," 106
"I Remember Clifford," 244
Irreplaceable, 359
Irvis, Charles "Charlie," 91, 121
Irwin, Cecil, 181
I Sing the Body Electric, 337
"Island Blues," 309

"Israel," 227
Israels, Chuck, 303
"I Stay in the Mood for You," 198
"It Don't Mean a Thing (If It Ain't Got That Swing)," 133, 156
"It Gets Better," 328
"It's About That Time," 328
"It's About That Time/In a Silent Way," 326–327
"It's a Wonderful World," 361
It's Gotta Be Funky, 246
"It's Like That," 362
"It's Magic," 289
"I Want Jesus to Walk with Me," 110
"I Want to Hold Your Hand," 325
"I Want to Take You Higher," 325
Iyer, Vijay, 370–373, *372*
Izenzon, David, 263

"Jackass Blues," 126
Jackson, Greig "Chubby," 219
Jackson, Herman, 360
Jackson, Mahalia, 226, 311
Jackson, Milt, 215, *230*, 230–231, 233, 242, 253
Jackson, Quentin, 250, 287, 296
Jackson, Ronald Shannon, 279
Jackson, Rudy, 121, 123
Jackson in Your House, A, 281
"Jack the Bear," 156–157, 182
Jaco Pastorius, 338
Jacquet, Jean-Baptiste "Illinois," 149, 195, 217, 218
Jamal, Ahmad, 253, 280
James, Bob, 361
James, Elmer, 137
James, Harry, 134, 135, 150, 152, 173
"James and Wes," 315–316
"Japanese Sandman," 117
Jarman, Joseph, 280, 281
Jarrett, Keith, 243, 306, 308–311, 328
Jassamine, 110
Jazz (television documentary), 350
Jazz, origins of word, 59
Jazz Abstractions, 263
Jazz Advance, 278
Jazz at Lincoln Center, 349, 353
Jazz at the Philharmonic, 183, 186, *194*, 206, 242
Jazz at the Plaza, 302
Jazz chair, 136
Jazz Composers' Workshop, 249
Jazz Education Network (JEN), 349
Jazz Exchange, 239
Jazz-funk fusion. *See* Fusion
Jazz Gallery, 268
Jazz Hounds, 175
Jazz Kings, 127
"Jazz Me Blues," 98, 99
Jazz Messengers, 243, 299, 300, 306, 316–318, 350
"Jazznocracy," 165
Jazz pedagogy, 348–349
Jazz: Red, Hot, and Cool, 225
Jazz repertory movement, 347, 349–350
Jazz-rock fusion. *See* Fusion
Jazz Samba, 237
Jazz Singer, The, 71, *72*

Jazz singing, 53, 285–286
  See also Vocalists
"Jeep's Blues," 156
Jefferson, Eddie, 289, 291
Jefferson, Hilton, 137
"Jelly, Jelly," 198
"Jelly Roll Blues, The," 208
"Jelly Roll Soul," 250
Jelly's Last Jam, 86
Jenkins, Freddie, 122
Jenkins, Leroy, 281
Jensen, Ingrid, 357, 363
Jerome H. Remick & Company, 106
"Jeru," 228, 229
Jeter-Pillars Orchestra, 182
Jet Set Six, 362
"Jig Walk," 126
Jimmy Giuffre Clarinet, The, 240
Jimmy's Chicken Shack, 199
Jobim, Antonio Carlos, 209, 237
Johnson, Alphonso, 325, 337
Johnson, Bill, 68, 77, 78, 79, 80
Johnson, Budd, 199
Johnson, Bunk, 70
Johnson, Dewey, 271
Johnson, Eldridge, 74
Johnson, George, 73
Johnson, Howard, 209
Johnson, James P., 8, 41, 43, 46, 47, 52,
  86, 103, 107–113, *109*, 117, 121, 126,
  316, 349
Johnson, James Weldon, 38
Johnson, Jimmy, 296
Johnson, J. J., 149, 217, 225, 248, 253,
  268, 329
Johnson, Keg, 137
Johnson, Marc, 305
Johnson, Pete, 142
Johnson, Robert, 9, 47, 49–51, 325
Johnson, Walter, 137, 139
Jolly Time Popcorn, *133*
Jones, A. M., 35
Jones, Bessie, 29
Jones, Billy, 125
Jones, Claude, *85*, 137
Jones, Dolly, 171
Jones, Eddie, 293
Jones, Elvin, 266, 268–270, 272, 298
Jones, Hank, 213, 241, 268, 298
Jones, Helen, 172
Jones, Henry, 169
Jones, Jimmy, 290
Jones, Jo, 139, 146, 147, 149, 178, 183
Jones, Jonah, 164
Jones, Joseph Rudolph "Philly Joe," 253, 266
Jones, Leroi (aka Amiri Baraka), *Blues
  People*, 274
Jones, Norah, 356
Jones, Quincy, 293
Jones, Rae Lee, 172
Jones, Reunald, 293
Jones, Thad, 268, 293, 298, 345, 356, 357
Jones, Tom, 330
Jones, Wallace, 158
Jonny spielt auf, 126
Joplin, Scott, 38–43, *40*, 109, 208, 240, 349
Jordan, Duke, 205
Jordan, Kent, 351

Jorgensen, Johnny "Spider," *152*
"Joshua," 299
Jost, Ekkehard, 271, 281
Joyce, James, *Ulysses*, 72
"Joy Spring," 246
"Jubilee," 168
Jukeboxes, 134
"Jumpin' at the Woodside," 145
"Jumpin' Blues, The," 199
"Jungle Nights in Harlem," 121
Jungles Casino, 109
Jungle sound, 120–121, 127
"Jungle Waterfall," 335
"Just Friends," 206
"Just the Way You Look Tonight," 234
Juvenile Protection Agency, 72

Kadleck, Tony, 357
Kaminsky, Max, 90, *206*
Kansas City, 139, 142–143
"Kasuan Kura," 27, 28
Katché, Manu, 364
Kay, Connie, *230*, 230–231
"Keep a Song in Your Soul," 186
"Keep off the Grass," 110
Keep Shufflin', 112
Kelly, Chris, 70
Kelly, Ted, 209
Kelly, Wynton, 299, 315
Kelly's Stables, 193
Kenney, William Howland, 76
Kenton, Stan, 236, 239–241, 289, 298,
  325, 354
Kentucky Club, 120–121
Keppard, Freddie, 63–68, 70, 73
Kerouac, Jack, *On the Road*, 223
Kessel, Barney, 186, 303
Key, 13
Keyes, Lawrence "88," 199
Kilduff, Gerald, 275

Kimbrough, Frank, 357
Kind of Blue, 254, 267, 299, 302, 303,
  306, 312
King, Jackie, 172
King, Martin Luther, Jr., *273*
King Crimson, 325–326
King of Jazz, 135
"King of the Zulus," 180
"King Porter Stomp," 59, 86, 119,
  136–137, 150
Kirby, John, 166, 210
Kirk, Andy, 131, 141, 142–144, *144*, 156
Kirk, Roland, 308
Kisor, Ryan, 354
Klein, Manny, 153, 174
Klugh, Earl, 361
Knitting Factory, 362, 367
"Knock Me a Kiss," 180
Koenigswarter, Pannonica de, 207, 217, 245
Kofsky, Frank, *Black Nationalism and the
  Revolution in Music*, 275
"Ko-Ko," 158–160
"Ko Ko," 195, 203–205, 253
Kolax, King, 266
Köln Concert, 311
Konitz, Lee, 179, 220, 225, 228, 229, 238,
  239, 281, 305

Krall, Diana, 355
Krenek, Ernst, 105, 126
Krupa, Gene, 134, 140, 150–153, 173, 174,
  180, 182, *183*, 183, 219, 289
Krupyshev, Boris, 126
Kuhn, Steve, 268
Kula se Mama, 272

LaBarbera, Joe, 305
Lacy, Steve, 278, 363
LaFaro, Scott, 262, 303, 304
Laird, Rick, 331
Lake, Gene, 368
Lake, Oliver, 281–282
Lamb, Joseph, 40, 43
Lambert, Dave, 291
Land, Harold, 246
Landry, Art, 141
Landsberg, Georgi, 126
Lang, Eddie, 99, 105, 106, 140, 184
Lannigan, Jimmy, 97
LaRoca, Pete, 268
LaRocca, Dominic James "Nick," 73–74,
  75, 76
"Larry LaRue," 272
Laswell, Bill, 324
Latin jazz, 208–210, 364–366–
  See also Spanish tinge
LaVerne, Andy, 237
Lawson, Harry, 144
Lead, 4
Lead instruments, 17
Lead player, 136
Lead trumpet, 136
Lee, Gene, *Cats of Any Color*, 277
Lee, Peggy, 135, 289
Legato, 14, 66
Leibrook, Min, *73*
"Lemon Drop," 219
Leningrad Jazz Orchestra, 126
"Lester Leaps In," 147, 179
"Let Me Off Uptown," 180
Let's Dance (radio series), 150, 152
Letter from Home, 341
Lewis, Ed, 147, 178
Lewis, George, 66
Lewis, John, 209, 227, 229–231, *230*, 240,
  261, 262
Lewis, Meade "Lux," 53
Lewis, Mel, 298, 345
Lewis, Ramsey, 313, 329
Lewis, Ted, 150
Liberation Music Orchestra, 357
Liberian Suite, 160
Library, 136
Lick, 64, 178, 205
Liebman, Dave, 328, 331, 341
Lifetime, 330
Light as a Feather, 334–335
Lighthouse, 239
"Light My Fire," 325
"Li'l Darlin'," 293
Lincoln Center Jazz Orchestra, 349, 354
Lincoln Gardens, 71, 77, 96
Lincoln Theatre, 112
Lindbergh, Charles, 71
Lindsay, John, 87
Lindsay, Tommy, 177

Lining out, 33
Lion, Alfred, 215, 317
Listening Guides
    "Acknowledgement," 270–271
    "Autumn Leaves," 304–305
    "Backwater Blues," 52
    "Birdland," 338–339
    "Blue Rondo à la Turk," 234–236
    "Body and Soul," 177, 188
    "Cake Walking Babies (from Home),"
        91–93
    "Carolina Shout," 111–112
    "Corner Pocket," 293–295
    "Daniel," 29
    "Dere's No Hidin' Place Down Dere," 34
    "Dippermouth Blues," 78–79
    "Down South Camp Meeting," 137–138,
        153–154, 174
    "East St. Louis Toodle-Oo," 123–124
    "E.S.P.," 301
    "Every Tub," 147–149, 178–179
    "Express Crossing," 351–352
    "Falsehood," 373
    "Four in One," 215–216
    "Ghosts," 276
    "Girl from Ipanema, The," 237–238
    "Grandpa's Spells," 87–88
    "Guataca City (To David Amram),"
        364–365
    "Hang Gliding," 357–358
    "Hora Decubitus," 250–251
    "It's About That Time/In a Silent Way,"
        326–327
    "James and Wes," 315–316
    "Jeru," 228
    "Kasuan Kura," 28
    "Ko-Ko," 158–159
    "Ko Ko," 203–205
    "Love in Vain," 50–51
    "Lullaby of Birdland," 290–291
    "Manteca," 209–210
    "Maple Leaf Rag," 41–42, 45
    "Mary's Idea," 144–145
    "Mercy, Mercy, Mercy," 313–314
    "Phenomenon: Compulsion," 332–333
    "Powell's Prances," 247–248
    "Salt Peanuts," 201–202, 368–369
    "Singin' the Blues," 99–100
    "Softly, As in a Morning Sunrise,"
        360–361
    "Solitude," 370–371
    "So What," 255–256
    "Street Woman," 264–265
    "Sunset and the Mockingbird," 296–297
    "Swing That Music," 169–170
    "Swing to Bop (Topsy)," 184–186
    "Take the A Train," 287–288
    "Tempus Fugit," 211–213
    "Tiger Rag," 75, 115–116, 128–129
    "Versailles," 231–233
    "Vi Vigor," 172–173
    "West End Blues," 94–95
    "Windup, The," 309–310
Liston, Melba, 171
Little, Booker, 272, 280
"Little Jazz," 168
"Little Joe from Chicago," 143
"Little Pixie II," 298

"Little Willie Leaps," 253
Live at the Golden Circle, 263
Live at the Village Vanguard (Caine), 367
Live at the Village Vanguard (Coltrane), 273
Live in Europe, 336
Live in Montreux, 303
Live in Zurich, 282
"Livery Stable Blues," 48, 73
Livingston, Joseph "Fud," 125
Liza, 107
"Liza," 166
Lloyd, Charles, 308–309
Locked-hands style, 238
Lofty Fake Anagram, 330
Lomax, Alan, 29, 86
Lombardo, Guy, 134
"Lonesome Nights," 186
"Lotus on Irish Streams, A," 331
Louisiana Five, 76
Lovano, Joe, 354
"Love for Sale," 242, 278
Love-In, 309
"Love in Vain," 50–51
"Lover Man," 187, 288
Love Supreme, A, 265, 266, 269, 271
LP, 226
Lucie, Lawrence, 85, 137, 188
"Lucky Number," 168
"Lullaby of Birdland," 241, 289–291
Lulu, 126
Lunceford, Jimmie, 127, 134, 141, 163,
    165, 167
"Lush Life," 157
Lush Life, 318
Lydian Chromatic Concept of Tonal
    Organization, 241
Lyons, Jimmy, 278, 279

"Mabel's Dream," 77
Mabern, Harold, 280
Macero, Teo, 249, 326
Machito (born Frank Grillo), 206, 208,
    208–209, 364
Mad Hatter, 336
Madison, Bingie, 169
Magnolia Band, 60
Mahalakshmi, 331
Mahara's Minstrels, 48
Mahavishnu Orchestra, 324, 328,
    330–331, 335
Mahler, Gustav, 367
Mahogany, Kevin, 355
Maiden Voyage, 307, 317
Mainieri, Mike, 342
Majesty of the Blues, The, 350
Major key, 13
Makowicz, Adam, 364
Malachi, John, 198
"Malcolm, Malcolm, Semper Malcolm," 274
Malcolm X, 274–275
Malik, Raphé, 279
"Mallets," 240
"Mamanita," 86, 208
Manchild, 334
"Mandy, Make Up Your Mind," 89
Mangelsdorff, Albert, 363
Mangione, Chuck, 243, 308, 361
Manhattan Transfer, 291, 339

"Man I Love, The," 253
Mann, Herbie, 290
Manne, Shelly, 194, 239, 240
"Manteca," 207, 209–210, 364
Man with the Horn, The, 328
"Maori," 208
"Maple Leaf Rag," 39, 40, 41, 45, 86, 109
Marches, 39
Margitza, Rick, 357
Maricle, Sherrie, 363
Marsala, Joe, 150
Marsalis, Branford, 350, 353, 361
Marsalis, Ellis, 350
Marsalis, Wynton, 334, 345, 349, 349–353
Marsalis Standard Time, 350
Marsh, Warne, 238, 239, 305
Marshall, Thurgood, 273
Martin, Sara, 112
"Mary's Idea," 143, 144–145
Masada, 367
Masekela, Hugh, 364
"Masqualero," 300
Mathis, Johnny, 242
"Matrix," 307
Matthews, Artie, 40, 43–44
Maupin, Bennie, 307, 326, 333, 334
May, Billy, 292
Mayer, John, 361
Mayhew, Virginia, 363
Mays, Lyle, 341
M-Base concept, 368
McBee, Cecil, 309
McBride, Christian, 341
McCarthy, Joseph, 223
McClure, Ron, 309
McCurdy, Roy, 313
McDuff, "Brother" Jack, 314, 316
McEachern, Murray, 153, 174
McFerrin, Bobby, 355
McGhee, Nora Lee, 172
McGriff, Jimmy, 314
McIntyre, Ken, 278
McKee, Andy, 356
McKenna, Dave, 116
McKenzie, William "Red," 97, 183
McKibbon, Al, 209, 215
McKinley, Ray, 356
McKinney's Cotton Pickers, 119,
    166–167, 186
McLaughlin, John, 325, 326, 327, 330–333,
    335, 340, 364
McLean, Jackie, 243, 282, 317, 330
McLean, Richard "Abba Labba," 108
McNeely, Jim, 298
McPartland, Dick, 97
McPartland, Jimmy, 79, 97, 98, 101
McPartland, Marian, 303
McPherson, Charles, 354
McShann, Jay, 197, 199
"Mean Music," 134
"Mean to Me," 289
Measure, 5
Medeski Martin & Wood, 361
Mehldau, Brad, 354
Mellotron, 333
Melody, 4, 10–12
"Memphis Blues," 48
Mendelssohn, Felix, 40

"Men Who Live in the White House, The," 263
Mercer Ellington Orchestra, 353
"Mercy, Mercy, Mercy," 312–314, 326, 337
Merlin, Enrico, 328
Merritt, Jymie, 244
Mertz, Paul, 99
Metcalf, Louis, 123
Meter, 5, 27
Metheny, Pat, 263, 311, 338, *340*, 340–342, 361
Metric displacement, 214, 303
Metronome All-Star Band, 239
Metronomic sense, 25
Mezzrow, Mezz (born Milton Mesirow), 97, 150
Michelle, 325
Microtones, 260
MIDI. *See* Musical Instrument Digital Interface
Midnight Sons, The, 102
Midnight Special, 315
Miles, Buddy, 331
Miles, Jason, 329
Miles Ahead, 229, 256
Miles Davis All Stars, 217
Miles Davis at Carnegie Hall, 299
Miles in the Sky, 300, 302, 326, 331
Miles in Tokyo, 300
"Miles Runs the Voodoo Down," 328
"Milestones," 253
Milestones, 254, 312
Miley, James "Bubber," 120–121, 122, 123, 136
Milhaud, Darius, 105, 107, 233
Mili, Gjon, 206
Miller, Earl, 144
Miller, Glenn, 134, *167*, 167–168, 356
Miller, Marcus, 325, 328, 329
Miller, Mulgrew, 330, 356
Mills, Irving, 122, 156
Milne, Andy, 368
"Mind and Time," 261
Mingus, 252
Mingus, Charles, 213, 225, *249*, 249–252, 272, 273, 297, 354
Mingus, Sue, 252, 356
Mingus Big Band, 252, 356
Mingus Dynasty, 252, 356
"Minnie the Moocher," 164
Minor, Dan, 147, 178
Minor key, 13
Minstrelsy, 36–38, 151
Minton's Playhouse, 180, 184, 193, 196–197, 200, 207, 210, 214
"Mirrors," 311
Missourians, 164
"Misty," 242, 289
Mitchell, George, 87
Mitchell, Grover, 356
Mitchell, Joni, 252, 334, 370
Mitchell, Louis, 127
Mitchell, Richard "Blue," 307
Mitchell, Roscoe, 280, 281
MJT + 3, 280
"Moanin'," 243–244
Mo' Better Blues, 353
Mobley, Hank, 243, 244, 299, 317, 353
Modality, 13
Modal jazz, 254
Mode for Joe, 318

Modernism, 224
Modern Jazz Quartet, 225, 227, 229–233, *230*, 241, 243, 248
Moffett, Charles, 263
Moldy figs, 193
Mole, Irving Milfred "Miff," 170
Molvaer, Nils Peter, 362, 364
"Moment's Notice," 267
Monder, Ben, 357
Money Jungle, 297
Monk, Thelonious Sphere, 176, 183, 196–197, 210, 213–217, *214*, 248, 253, 267, 277, 279, 316, 336
"Monk's Mood," 215
Monroe's Uptown House, 193, 197, 199, 200
Monterey Pop Festival, 325
Montgomery, Wes, 186, 315–316, 325
Montreux Jazz Festival, 353
Montuno, 364
"Mooche, The," 121, 123–124
"Mood Indigo," 122, 156
"Moon Dreams," 227
"Moonglow," *130*, 152, 182
"Moonlight Bay," 106
"Moon Shines on the Moonshine, The," 125
Moore, Eustis, 177
Moore, Sam, 338
Moore, Vic, *73*
"Moose the Mooche," 205
Moran, Gayle, 336
Moran, Jason, 368
Morehouse, Chauncey, 99
Moreira, Airto, 331, 334, 337, 364
Morello, Joe, 234, *234*
Morgan, Lee, 243, 244, 312, *317*, 317, 318, 353
Morgan, Sam, 69, 70
"Morning Glory," 305
Morrell, Marty, 305
Morrison, George, 57, 141
Morrison, Henry, 29
Morrow, George, 246, 247
Morton, Benny, 147, 178
Morton, Ferdinand Joseph "Jelly Roll," 45, 59, 62, 63, 64, 66, 68, 76, 81, 83, *85*, 85–88, 103, 150, 151, 208, 250, 349
Moses, Bob, 341
Mosley, Snub, 169
Moten, Bennie, 142, 143, 146, 147, 156
"Moten Swing," 143, 199
Motian, Paul, 303, 304, 309, 311, 363
Motive, 90
Motivic cells, 269
Mourning of a Star, The, 311
Mouzon, Alphonse, 337
Movies, 135
Moye, Don, 281
Mraz, George, 364
Mr. Gone, 339
"Mr. Jelly Lord," 76, 86
"Mrs. Parker of K.C.," 272
Mulligan, Gerry, 179, 219, 220, 223, 225, 227–230, *229*, 243
Multiphonics, 271
Mundy, Jimmy, 181
Murphy, Jeanette Robinson, 32
Murray, Albert, 295, 349
Murray, Colleen, 172

Murray, David, 281–282
Murray, Sunny, 276, 278
Musical Instrument Digital Interface (MIDI), 359
Musical theater, 38, 121
Music Corporation of America (MCA), 146
Music for Six Musicians, 277
MusicMagic, 336
Music notation, 11
Music staff, 10, 11
"Musieu Bainjo," 36
Mutes, *15*, 65
Mwandishi, 307, 331
"My Favorite Things," 266, 269
"My Funny Valentine," 229, 240, 299
My Goal's Beyond, 331
"My Old Kentucky Home," 37
Mysterious Traveller, 337

Nance, Ray, 160, 287, 296
Nanton, Joe "Tricky Sam," 121, 122, 123, 158, 160
Nascimento, Milton, 364
Natchez (paddleboat), *69*
National Aeronautics and Space Administration (NASA), 363
National Association of Negro Musicians, 107
Navarro, Theodore "Fats," 153, 217
Nazi Party, 126
"Nefertiti," 300, 370
Nelson, Louis "Big Eye," 60, 64
Nelson, Oliver, 272
Neo-swing, 362
Nesbitt, John, 167
Nettl, Bruno, 35
New Age music, 311
New Jazz Conceptions, 302
Newman, Jerry, 197, 214
Newman, Joe, 149, 293
New Orleans, 60–64
New Orleans Feetwarmers, 89
New Orleans jazz, 60, 62, 70
   See also Dixieland
"New Orleans Joys," 208
New Orleans Rhythm Kings (NORK), 69, 76, 97, 98, 151
Newport Jazz Festival, 226, 253, 278, 296, 314
New Standard, The, 334, 366
New Testament Band, 293
New Thing, 260
   See also Free jazz
New World a-Comin', 160, 298
"New York, New York," 302
New York City, 103, 105–124, 198–199
New York Fall 1974, 281
New York Philharmonic Orchestra, 263
New York R&B, 278
New York Voices, 291
"Nica's Dream," 245
Nice Guys, 281
Nichiren Shoshu Buddhism, 333
Nicholas, Albert, 66, 80, *85*
Nicholas, George "Big Nick," 209
Nichols, Ernest "Red," 98, 101, 105, 106, 125, 140, 150, 170
Nichols, Herbie, 217
Nicholson, Stuart, 340
Niedlinger, Buell, 278

"Night in Tunisia, A," 205, 207
1920s, 103–129
Nirvana, 366
Noble, Ray, 195
"No Blues," 299
"Nobody Knows the Trouble I've Had," 35
Nock, Mike, 330
"No Figs," 239
No Mystery, 335
"Non-cognitive Aspects to the City," 280
Nontempered intonation, 260
Noone, Jimmie, 67, 69, 70, 93, 150, 181
"No One Else But You," 95
NORK. *See* New Orleans Rhythm Kings
Norris, Walter, 261
North, Dave, 97
North Atlantic Treaty Organization
    (NATO), 192
"Northwest Passage," 219
Norvo, Red, 249
"Nostalgia in Times Square," 250
Notes, 4
Now He Sings, Now He Sobs, 307, 336
"Now's the Time," 203, 253
Nu Blaxploitation, 277
Nu jazz, 362
Numbers 1 and 2, 280
"Numb Fumblin'," 112

Obama, Barack, 277
Obbligato, 30
O'Brien, Floyd, 150
Occasional songs, 35
Octave, 10
O'Day, Anita, 180, 289
"Ode to Charlie Parker," 272
ODJB. *See* Original Dixieland Jazz Band
O'Farrill, Chico, 153
Offramp, 341
"Oh, Lady Be Good," 178, 199
"Oh Dem Golden Slippers," 37
"Oh! Susanna," 37
Okeh/Phonola Records, 47, 77
Okeh Records, 90, 112
"Old Black Joe," 37
"Old Folks," 299
"Old Folks at Home" (aka "Swanee River"), 37
Old Testament Band, 293
"Oleo," 248, 253
Oliver, Joe "King," 59, 62, 64, 67–71, 76–80,
    79, 89, 96, 103, 119, 177
Oliver, Sy, 136, 165, 167
Olympia Band, 60
Olympia Orchestra, 65
Om, 265, 272
1 + 1, 340
"One Finger Snap," 306–307
"One-Note Samba," 209
"One O'Clock Jump," 53, 145
Onward Brass Band, 62, 65
Onyx Club, 193, 198–199, 207
"Open Country Joy," 331
"Opus de Funk," 245
"Opus in Pastels," 239
"Opus One," 165
O'Quinn, Keith, 357
Orange Blossoms, 166
"Orbits," 300

Orchestra World, 119
Organ, 312, 314
"Organ Grinder's Swing," 165
Original Blue Devils, 141–142, 146, 177, 183
Original Creole Band, 68
Original Dixieland Jazz Band (ODJB), 48,
    59, 67, 68, 70, 73–76, 74, 97–99, 105,
    125, 126
Original Jazz Library, 347
"Original Jelly Roll Blues," 86
Original New Orleans Jazz Band, 76
Original Tuxedo Jazz Orchestra, 69
Origins (band), 336
"Ornette," 280
Ornette on Tenor, 268
"Ornithology," 198
Orpheus Chamber Ensemble, 334
Orwell, George, *1984*, 192
Ory, Edward "Kid," 66, 69, 70, 80, 87, 89,
    92, *93*
Osby, Greg, 368
Ostinato, 269
"Ostinato," 307
"Ostrich Walk," 99
"Our Man Higgins," 317
Out-chorus, 65
Out Front, 272
"Outlaw, The," 246
Outside, 95, 271, 272
Out to Lunch, 272
Outward Bound, 272
Overdubbing, 226
Owens, Thomas, 266

Pace-Handy Music Company, 118
Page, Oran "Hot Lips," 141, 143, 197, *206*
Page, Walter, 141–142, 146, 147, 149, 177,
    178, 183
Page One, 318
Palmieri, Eddie, 364
Palomar Ballroom, 152
Panassié, Hugues, 127
"Papa's Got a Brand New Bag," 324
Paramount Records, 77
"Pardon My Rags," 311
Paris, France, 127
"Parisian Thoroughfare," 213
Parker, Charlie, 114, 179, 181, 193, 195,
    197–207, *206*, 210–211, 213, 217, 220,
    229, 241, 243, 247, 250, 252–253, 266,
    272, 288, 347, 354, 362
Parker, Evan, 364
Partial, 97
"Pastime" rags, 43–44
Pastorius, Jaco, 325, 336–341, *337*
Pat Metheny Group, The, 341
Patterson, Don, 314
Patting juba, 27
Pattitucci, John, 336
Patton, Charley, 47, 48, 49
Payne, Cecil, 209
Payne, Sonny, 293
Payton, Nicholas, 354, 374
"Peace Piece," 335
Peacock, Gary, 276, 300, 311
"Pearls, The," 86
Pedagogy, 348–349
Pedal point, 158

Pendergast, Tom, 142
Pentatonic scale, 160, 268
"People," 303
Pepper, Art, 224, 239–240
Percussion, 4, 16–17
Perez, Manuel, 62, 63, 65
"Perfect Rag," 86
Perkins, Walter, 250, 280
Perry, Rich, 357
Person, Houston, 314
Peterson, Oscar, 114, 242–243, 356, 364
Petit, Buddy, 66
Pettiford, Oscar, 160, 193, 196, 198–199, 207
Peyton, Benny, 124–125, 126
"Phase Dance," 341
Phase shifter, 337
"Phenomenon: Compulsion," 332–333
Philco radio, *153*
Phish, 361
Phonograph, *48*
Phrases, 5
Pianists, 241–243, 302–311
    Blake, Eubie, 41, 103, 107, 109, 116, 120
    Corea, Chick, 307–308
    Evans, Bill, 302–306
    Garner, Erroll, 241–242
    Hines, Earl, 92–96, 116, 143, 168,
        180–181, *181*, 186, 197–198, 200, 207,
        241, 336–337
    Jarrett, Keith, 308–311
    Johnson, James P., 8, 41, 43, 46, 47, 52,
        86, 103, 107–113, *109*, 117, 121, 126,
        316, 349
    Peterson, Oscar, 242–243
    Powell, Earl "Bud," 207, 210–213, *213*,
        215, 217, 227, 241, 245, 248, 302, 307,
        336, 361
    Shearing, George, 241
    Waller, Thomas "Fats," 41, 46, 86, 96, 103,
        107, 110, 112–113, *113*, 145, 150, 151,
        167, 181, 198, 241, 312
    Wilson, Teddy, 114, 116, 146, 150–151,
        151, 181–182, *182*, 187, 241
Piano, 17, 68, 189
Piano Improvisations, 308, 334
Piano-Rag-Music, 124
Piano rolls, 41, 109
Piano trio, 7
"Picasso," 176
Picasso, Pablo, *Guernica*, 132–133
Pickup, 174
Pick Yourself Up, 289
Picou, Alphonse, 62, 64, 66, 70, 77
Pilgrimage, 342
Pillow, Charles, 357
Pilobolus, 363
"Ping Pong," 244
Pinkard, Maceo, 107
Piron, A. J., 77, 118
"Pirouette," 240
Pitch, 10
"Pitter Panther Patter," 156
Place Congo, New Orleans, 33
Plagal cadence, 243
Plantation Cafe, 71, 80
Player piano, 41, *43*, 109
Plunger, 120
"Poco Loco, Un," 213

Pointer Sisters, 331
Point of Departure, 318
Pollack, Ben, 150, 167
Pollock, Jackson, 261
Polyphony, 27, 64, 225
Polyrhythms, 26, 238
Ponce, Daniel, 365
Ponomarev, Valery, 364
Ponty, Jean-Luc, 331, 336
"Pop Goes the Weasel," 206
"Popo," 240
Popular jazz, 359–363
Porgy and Bess, 117, 229, 256, 298
Porter, Cole, 168, 195, 278, 287
Porter, Lewis, 178, 269
Portrait in Jazz, 303
Postmodernism, 352, 367
"Potato Head Blues," 93
Potter, Tommy, 205
Powell, Benny, 293
Powell, Earl "Bud," 207, 210–213, *213*, 215,
  217, 227, 241, 245, 248, 302, 307, 336
Powell, Jimmy, 188
Powell, Mel, 152, 153
Powell, Richie, 246, 247
"Powell's Prances," 247–248
Powers, Ollie, 89
Pozo, Chano, 207, 209
Prairie View Co-Eds, 171
Praise-song, 28
Prater, Dave, 338
Prayer Meetin', 314
"Prelude," 234
Preludes for Piano, 117
"Prelude to a Kiss," 155
Preminger, Otto, 296
Preservation Hall, New Orleans, 70
Preservation Hall Jazz Band, 70, 345
Presley, Elvis, 167
Prestige Records, 248, 253
Preston, Eddie, 250
Previn, André, 240
"Prezervation," 236
Priester, Julian, 307
Prime, 6
Prime Time, 263
"Prince of Wails," 143
Printup, Marcus, 351
Prisoner, The, 307, 318
Procession, 340
Procope, Russell, 137, 287, 296
Proctor, Willis, 29
Progressions, 13
Prohibition, 71, 132
"Psalm," 269
Puente, Tito, 209, 364
Purim, Flora, 334, 364
"Purple Haze," 325, 338
"Pursuance," 269
"Put It There," 167

Quarter notes, 10
Queen's Suite, The, 122, 155, 296
Quiet Nights, 256
Quinichette, Paul, 290
Quinquaginta Ramblers, 125
Quintette du Hot Club de France, 127, 128
Quotations, 206

Race, 60, 71, 76, 86, 105, 150–151, 170–172,
  273–275, 277
Race records, 47
Rachmaninoff, Sergei, 305
Radio, 133–134, 362–363
Radiohead, 366
Raeburn, Boyd, 173, 207
Ragas, Henry, 74, 75
Ragtime, 38–46
  defined, 38
  history of, 39–40
  jazz in relation to, 44–46, 57, 59–60
  Joplin, Scott, 40–43
  syncopation, 38
Ragtime Dance, 41
Ragtime for Eleven Instruments, 124
Ragtime form, 9
"Ragtime Nightingale," 43
"Ragtime Oriole," 43
Rainey, Gertrude "Ma," 47, 51, 118
"Rainy Nights," 121
Ramblers, 175
Ramey, Gene, 199
Ramsay, Ben, 29
Ramsey, Fred, *Jazzmen*, 70
Randolph, Irving, 137
Rank, Bill, 99
Ravel, Maurice, 105, 124, 157, 305
Ray, Carlene, 172
Ray, James Earl, 273
"Ray's Idea," 190
Razaf, Andy, 96, 112
RCA Victor, 156
Reaching Fourths, 268
Real McCoy, The, 318
"Rebirth of Slick (Cool Like Dat)," 361
"Recorda Me," 318
Recording, 72–77, 197–198, 226, 347–348
"Recuerdo," 308
"Red Cross," 200
Redd, Vi, 171
Red Hot Peppers, 85–87
Redman, Dewey, 309, 311, 341
Redman, Don, 95, *118*, 118, 119, 135, 136,
  143, 167
Redman, Joshua, 354
Red Onion Jazz Babies, 91
Reed, Eric, 351
Reed, Lou, 263
Reeds, 15
Reese, Harold "Pee Wee," *152*
Reeves, Diane, 356
Reharmonization, 196
Reinhardt, Jean Baptiste "Django," 127–129,
  140, 175, 363
Reinhardt, Joseph, 128
Reisenweber's Restaurant, 74, 105
Reissue of recordings, 347–348
Rejoicing, 341
Release, 30
"Remark You Made, A," 339
Remastering, 347
Remick, Jerome, 106
Remick Song Shops, 106
"Reminiscing in Tempo," 155
Reno Club, 142, 146
Rent parties, 107
"Resolution," 269

Return to Forever, 324, 328, 334–336, *335*
Return to Forever, 334
Reuss, Allan, 153, 174
Revue Nègre, La, 127
Rhapsody in Blue, 117, 240
Rhythm, 4, 10, 30
Rhyth-mania, 121
Rhythm Boys, 291
Rhythm changes, 8, 146, 147, 200
Rhythm section, 17, 29, 136, 139–140,
  146–147
Rich, Buddy, 166
Richardson, Jerome, 250
Rickey, Branch, 151
Riddle, Nelson, 292
Ride cymbal, 16
Ries, Tim, 357
Riff, 19, 119
"Riffin' the Scotch," 150
Riis, Thomas, 36–37
Riley, Herlin, 351
Ring shout, 27, 29, 33
Rio, Rita, 171
Riverboats, *69*
Rivers, Sam, 300, 311
"Riverside Blues," 77
Riverside Records, 312, 315
River: The Joni Letters, 334, 370–372
Roach, Max, 176, 196, 197, 198–199, 203,
  205, 210, 211, 213, 228, 234, 239,
  246–247, 272, 297
Roaring Twenties, 71–72
Roberts, Luckey, 107, 108, 110, 116, 120
Roberts, Marcus, 355
Robeson, Paul, 107
Robichaux, John, 60
Robinson, Bill "Bojangles," *165*
Robinson, Clarence, 121
Robinson, Fred, 93, 94
Robinson, Jackie, 151, *152*
Robinson, Scott, 357
Robinson, Ted, 144
"Rock Around the Clock," 53
"Rocker," 229
"Rockin' Chair," 180
"Rockit," 334, 362
Rodgers, Gene, 177
Rodgers, Richard, 287
Roditi, Claudio, 365
Rodrigo, Joaquín, 256, 334
Rogers, Shorty, 240
Rolling Stones, 325
Rollini, Adrian, 125
Rollini, Art, 153, 174
Rollins, Sonny, 176, 216, 218, 223, 247–249,
  253, 265, 266, *267*, 268, 280, 303,
  305, 362
"Romantic Warrior," 335
Romantic Warrior, *335*, 335
"Rondo," 234
Roney, Wallace, 334, 353, 362
Roosevelt, Franklin, 132
Rose, Vincent, 195
Roseland Ballroom, 118
"Roseland Shuffle," 147
Rosnes, Renee, 363, 368
Rosolino, Frank, 219
Ross, Annie, 291

'*Round Midnight*, 218
"'Round Midnight," 197, 215, 253, 303
"Round Trip/Broadway Blues," 341
Roy, Badal, 331
Roy, Harry, 125
Roy, Sid, 125
Royal, Marshal, 149, 293
"Royal Garden Blues," 91, 98, 99
Royal Gardens Cafe, 71
Royal Roost, 227, 253
Rubalcaba, Gonzalo, 364
Rubato, 114
"Ruby My Dear," 197, 215
Rudd, Roswell, 275
Rugolo, Pete, 225, 239
Running the changes, 196
Runnin' Wild, 107, 110
Rupp, Franz, 34
Rushing, Jimmy, 141, 142, 289
Russell, Bill, *Jazzmen*, 70
Russell, Charles "Pee Wee," 98
Russell, Curley, 201, 203, 210
Russell, George, 168, 207, 225, 241, 302, 357
Russell, Luis, 169
Russell, Ross, 205
Russo, Bill, 239

Sacred Concerts, 155
Sadin, Robert, 351, 353
"Sailboat in the Moonlight, A," 187
Saine, Helen, *171*
"Saint Louis Blues," 48, *49*, 208
Sales, Grover, *Jazz*, 349
Salsa, 364
"Salt Peanuts," 200–202, 206, 207, 368–370
Samba, 209
Sam Morgan Jazz Band, 69, 70
Samplers, 323
Sampson, Edgar, 150, 166
Sanborn, David, 361
Sanchez, Antonio, 341
"Sanctuary," 328
Sanders, Farrell "Pharoah," 271, 272, 275
Sanders, John, 287, 296
Sandoval, Arturo, 364
"Sandu," 246
Santamaria, Mongo, 306, 307
Santana, 327
"Sassy," 289
Saturday Night Live (television program), 279
Saunders, William, 142
Sauter, Eddie, 136, 152–153, 237
Savannah Syncopators, 80
"Save It, Pretty Mama," 95
Savoy Ballroom, Harlem, 80, 127, 166, 186, 199
"Savoy Blues," 93
Savoy Hotel, London, 125
Savoy Orchestra, 93
Savoy Records, 203, 252–253, 347
Saxophone, *15*, 16, 29, 64
Saxophone Colossus, 248
Sbarbaro, Antonio "Tony," 68, 74, 75
Scale, 10–11
Scat singing, 51, 92, 286, 287
Schafer, William J., 61
Scherr, Tony, 357
Schertzer, Hymie, 153, 174

Schiller's Cafe, 74
Schneider, Maria, 357–358, *357* 363
Schoebel, Elmer, 96
Schoenberg, Arnold, 241
Schoepp, Franz, 67, 150
Schonberger, John, 195
"School Days," 335
Schuller, Gunther, 57, 180, 225, 231, 233, 240–241, 249, 252, 262, 263, 273, 349
Schulman, Joe, 228
Schumann, Robert, 367
Scofield, John, 328, 361
Scott, Bud, 80
Scott, James, 40, 43
Scott, Kermit, 188
Scott, Shirley, 314
Scott, Tony, 308
"Scrapple from the Apple," 205
Scriabin, Alexander, 305
Search for the New Land, 317
Second Herd, 219
Second Sacred Concert, 298
Secret Story, 341
Section, 5, 118, 136
Senior, Milt, 181
"Señor Blues," 245
"Sepian Bounce," 199
"Sepia Panorama," 155
Sermon, The, 314
Setzer, Brian, 362
"Seven Come Eleven," 183
Seven Steps to Heaven, 299
Seventh chords, 12
Sextant, 331
Sextet, 336
"Shadowland Blues," 141
Shadows (film), 250
Shakespeare, William, 296
Shakti, 331
"Shanghai Shuffle," 118
Shank, Bud, 239
Shape of Jazz to Come, The, 261, 262
Sharp, 11
Shavers, Charlie, 197, 200
Shaw, Artie, 107, 168, 180, 187, 325
Shaw, Woody, 318
Shearing, George, 113, 127, 238, 241, 290
Sheets of sound, 265, 267
"Shelby Steele Would Be Mowing Your Lawn," 277
Shepherd, Adaline, 44
Shepp, Archie, 271, 274–275, 278
Shepperd, William, 209
Shields, Lawrence "Larry," 74, 75
Shihab, Sahib, 215
"Shoe Shine Boy," 178
Shorter, Wayne, 243, 244, 254, 300–301, 317–318, 326, 327, 334, 336–340, *337*, 353, 363, 367, 372
Shostakovich, Dmitri, 311
Shout chorus, 65
Show Girl, 122
Shuffle, 244
Shuffle Along, 107, 109
Sideman, 136
"Sidewinder, The," 312, 317
Silent Tongues, 278
Silva, Alan, 278

Silver, Horace, 243, 245–246, 253, 277, 299, 302, 307, 316–318, 331, 353, 354
Simeon, Omer, 66, 87
"Similau," 168
Simon, George, 325
Sims, John Haley "Zoot," 179, 219, 225, 230, 236, 239
Sinatra, Frank, 135, 167, 224, 243, 267, 292, *292*, 293
"Sing, Sing, Sing," 152
Singing. *See* Jazz singing
Singing Kid, The, 164
"Singin' the Blues," 98–101, 176
Singleton, Zutty, 68, *85*, 93, 94
"Sippin' at Bells," 253
Sirone (born Norris Jones), 279
Sissle, Noble, 107, *107*, 109, 120
Sixteenth notes, 10
Sketches of Spain, 229, 256, 298, 334
Skies of America, 263
"Skip the Gutter," 93
Sky Blue, 357
Sky Dive, 309
Slap bass, 325
Slap-tonguing, 175
Slash notation, 13, 31
Slave Songs of the United States, 31, 35
"Sly," 333
Sly and the Family Stone, 325, 326, 333, 366
"Smashing Thirds," 112
Smith, Bessie, 8, 38, 47, *51*, 51–52, 110, 118, 171
Smith, Buster, 140, 199
Smith, Chris, 106
Smith, Cladys "Jabbo," 180
Smith, Cricket, 127
Smith, Edna, 172
Smith, Jimmy, 266, 312, 314, *314*, 315, 318
Smith, Joe, 47, 118
Smith, Leo, 281
Smith, Mamie, 47, 175
Smith, Russell, 137
Smith, William Oscar, 177
Smith, Willie "The Lion," 107, 108, 116, 165, 168
Smithsonian Jazz Masterworks Orchestra, 349
Smokin' at the Half Note, 315
Smooth jazz, 4, 324, 345, 359, 361
"Snake Rag," 66, 77
"Snaky Blues, The," 48
Snare drum, 16, 67
Snow, Valaida, 171
Snowden, Elmer, 120
Social Security Act, 132
Society Orchestra, 73, 76
Socolow, Paul, 365
"Softly, As in a Morning Sunrise," 4, 8, 360
Soft Machine, 325
"Solace–A Mexican Serenade," 208
"S.O.L. Blues," 93
Soli, 169, 170
"Solitude," 155, 370–371
Solo breaks, 19
Solo Concerts, 311
Solo Monk, 217
Someday My Prince Will Come, 299
"Someday Sweetheart," 150
"Some Other Time," 305

"Some Skunk Funk," 341
Something Cool, 289
Something Else!!!!, 261
"Sometimes I'm Happy," 150
"Somewhere Over the Rainbow," 10
So Near, So Far (Musings for Miles), 318
Songbooks, 287
"Song for My Father," 245, 318
"Song Is You, The," 132
Song of Singing, 308, 334
Song pluggers, 43, 106
Song X, 263, 341
Sonny Meets Hawk, 249
"Sophisticated Lady," 155, 156
"Sophistifunk," 335
Souchon, Edmond, 80
Soul Gestures in Southern Blue, 350
Soul jazz. *See* Funky jazz
Soul on Soul, 367
Sound fields, 271
Sound Grammar, 265
Sound modules, 323
"Sound of Jazz" (television show), 188
Sound of Joy, 279
Sounds and Forms for Wind Quintet, 263
"Sounds of Africa," 109
Sousa, John Philip, 39, 61
Southern Syncopated Orchestra, 107, 120, 124
Soviet Union, 126–127
"So What," 255–256, 267, 269, 306
Spaces, 330
"Spain," 334
Spanier, Muggsy, 150
Spanish tinge, 63, 86, 208
   See also Latin jazz
Speakeasies, 71
Speaking of Now, 341
Speak Like a Child, 307
Speak No Evil, 318
"Spectrum," 330
Sphere, 217
Spikes' Seven Pods of Pepper, 69
Spirituals, 33
Spiritual Unity, 275
"Splatch," 329
Sportin' Life, 340
Spotlite, 193
"Squeeze Me," 112
Staccato, 14, 66, 118
Stacy, Jess, 152, 153, 154
"Stampede, The," 175
Stances à Sophie, Les, 281
Standards, 77, 140, 298, 370
Stan Getz and the Cool Sounds, 225
Stanko, Tomasz, 364
Stanky, Eddie, *152*
Stansbery, Johnnie Mae "Tex," 172
"Star Dust," 168, 183
Stark, John, *41*, 41–43
Star People, 328
"Star-Spangled Banner, The," 11–12, 13, 40, 325
St. Cyr, Johnny, 64, 67, 72, 87, 92, *93*
Steinbeck, John
   The Grapes of Wrath, 133
   Sweet Thursday, 296
"Stella by Starlight," 299, 300
Step connection, 176, 303

Steps, 11, 342
"Steps," 307
Steps Ahead, 342
Stepwise notes, 11
Stern, Mike, 328, 342
Stewart, Leroy "Slam," 114
Stewart, Rex, 98, 101, 119, 155, 158, 180
Still, William Grant, 107
Still Life Talking, 341
Sting (musician), 361
Sting, The (film), 43
Stitt, Sonny (born Edward Boatner Jr.), 266, 299, 314
Stitzel, Mel, 86
St. Louis Shoes, 368
Stock arrangements, 119
Stockhausen, Karlheinz, 281
"Stockyards Strut," 66
Stokes, Nellie W., *44*
"Stompin' at the Savoy," 150, 166
"Stomp Off, Let's Go," 90
Stone, Jesse, 141–142
"Stop It," 109
"Stop Kidding," 167
Stop time, 19, 65
Stories of the Danube, 340
Stormy Weather, 164, *165*, 186
Storyville, 60
"Straight, No Chaser," 214, 215, 267
Straight mute, *15*
Strains, 38, 41
"Strange Fruit," 187
Strange Liberation, 367
Straphangin', 342
"Stratosphere," 165
Stravinsky, Igor, 124, 241, 277
   Pulcinella, 353
   The Rite of Spring, 206
Strayhorn, Billy, 157, 253, 287, 296, 318
Streckfus, John, 69
Street, The, *198*, 198–199
"Street from Hell, A," 279
"Street Woman," 264–265
Stretto, 233
Stride piano, 45–46, 86, 108–116
String instruments, 16
"String of Pearls," 168
Strong, Jimmy, 93, 94
Strophic, 9
Strozier, Frank, 280
"Struttin' with Some Barbecue," 93
"St. Thomas," 248, 249
Stuckey, Sterling, 33
Stuttgart Symphony, 233
Subject, 231
Such Sweet Thunder, 296
Sudhalter, Richard, *Lost Chords*, 277
"Sugar Foot Stomp," *80*, 80, 119
Suite, 122
Suite Thursday, 296
Sullivan, Joe, 150
"Summer Breeze, A—March and Two Step," 43
Summers, Bill, 333
"Summertime," 256
Sun Bear Concerts, 311
Sun Ra, 271, 279–280, 336
"Sunset and the Mockingbird," 296–297
Sunset Cafe, Chicago, 71, 93

Sunset Club, Kansas City, 142
Sun Song, 279
Superior Band, 60
"Surrey with the Fringe on Top," 249
Sutton, Ralph, 116
Sweatman, Wilbur, 120
Sweet and Lowdown, 127
"Sweet Baby," 335
Sweet bands, 72, 134
"Sweet Clifford," 246
"Sweet Lorraine," 214
"Sweet Lovin' Man," 68
Sweetnighter, 336, 337
Sweet Rain, 307
Swell, 314
Swing-bass, 146, 182, 184, 185
Swing era, 86, 130–189
   all-girl bands, 130, 171–172
   Armstrong, Louis, 168–171
   Basie, Count, 143, 145–150
   big bands, 135–140
   Blanton, Jimmy, 182–183
   Calloway, Cab, 163–164
   Carter, Benny, 186–187
   Casa Loma Orchestra, 166
   Christian, Charlie, 183–186
   defined, 133
   Dorsey brothers, 167
   Eldridge, Roy, 180
   Ellington, Duke, 154–160
   features of music, 189
   Goodman, Benny, 150–154, 173–175
   Hawkins, Coleman, 175–176
   Hines, Earl, 180–181
   Holiday, Billie, 187–189
   Jones, Jo, 183
   Krupa, Gene, 183
   Lunceford, Jimmie, 165
   McKinney's Cotton Pickers, 166–167
   Miller, Glenn, 167–168
   overview, 133–135
   Shaw, Artie, 168
   territory bands, 140–143
   Webb, Chick, 165–166
   Wilson, Teddy, 181–182
   Young, Lester, 176–180
Swingin' Affair, A, 218
"Swinging on a Star," 242
"Swinging the Blues," 147
"Swingmatism," 199
"Swing That Music," 168–170
"Swing to Bop (Topsy)," 184–186
Symphony in Black, 120
"Symphony in Riffs," 186
Synclavier, 341
Syncopation, 10, 26, 35–36, 38
Synthesizer, *322*, 322–323, 333

Tabackin, Lew, 356
Tag, 65
Tailgate trombone, 66
Take 5, 234
"Take Five," 234
"Take Me Out to the Ball Game," 10, 11
"Take the A Train," 157, 287–288
Takin' Off, 306
Tangents in Jazz, 240
Tate, Erskine, 90, 93, 181

Tate, Grady, 315
Tatum, Art, 113–114, *114*, 181, 196, 198, 199, 211, 241, 242
"Tautology," 238
Taylor, Art, 325
Taylor, Cecil, 263, 275, *277*, 277–279, 309, 318
Taylor, Eva, 91
Tchicai, John, 271
"Tea for Two," 113
Teagarden, Jack, 134, 135, 150, 151, 170, 180, 236
"Teen Town," 338
Television, *222*
Tempo, 5
"Tempus Fugit," 211–213
"Tenderly," 272, 289
Tensions, 195
Teplitsky, Leopold, 126
Terence T. Holder and His Clouds of Joy, 140
Terminal vibrato, 90
Terrasson, Jacky, 355
Territory bands, 140–143
Terry, Clark, 287, 296
Teschemacher, Frank, 97
Texture, 4, 14
Thad Jones–Mel Lewis Big Band, 298, 345
That Misty Miss Christy, 289
Theatre Owners Booking Association (TOBA), 145
Thematic cells, 269
"Theme, The," 328
"There Is No Greater Love," 308
"There's a Riot Going On," 325
"These Foolish Things," 179
Thigpen, Ben, 144, 242
"Things to Come," 207
"Third Stone from the Sun," 338
Third-stream music, 231, 240–241, 263
Third Stream Music, 233
32-bar AABA song form, 5–8
This Is This, 340
"This Masquerade," 316
Thomas, Gary, 368
Thompson, Lucky, 253
Thomson, Earl, 144
Thornhill, Claude, 219–220, 227, 239
Thornton, Argonne (aka Sadik Hakim), 203
Three Compositions, 281
Three Deuces, 180, 193, 200
369th Infantry ("Hell Fighters") Band, 73, 124
Three Quartets, 336
"Three Windows," 231
"Thriving on a Riff," 203
Thrust, 334
"Tiger Rag," 75–76, 98, 114–116, 128–129, 195
Timbre, 14
Time (magazine), 217, 233
Time Out, 234
Time signature, 10
Timmons, Bobby, 243–244
Tinney, Allen, 197
Tin Pan Alley, 47, *106*, 106, 137
"Tin Roof Blues," 76
Tio, Lorenzo, Jr., 62, 63, 66, 67
Tio, Lorenzo, Sr., 66
Tizol, Juan, 121, 122, 155, *156*, 158, 160
"TNT," 118

"Toby," 143
Tomorrow Is the Question, 261
Tom-toms, 67
Tonality, 13
Tones, 4
Tones for Joan's Bones, 307
Tonic, 11
"Touchic," 282
Tough, Dave, 97, 193, 219
Tracks, 242
Trading solos, 19
Trading twos/fours/eights, 19, 146, 290
Traditionalism, 345–358
Transcribe, 24
Transcriptions, 23–24, 31–32
"Transformation," 241
Transposition, 12–13
Travick, Julia, 172
Treadwell, George, 197
Treble (G) clef, 10, 11
Treemonisha, 42–43, 240
Trends, 363, 372
Trent, Alfonso, 140
Triad, 12
"Trial, The," 336
Trice, Clarence, 144
Trill, 184
Trimmings, 32
Trio Music, 336
Triple meter, 5
Tristano, Lennie, *206*, 229, 238–239, 243, 277, 302
Tritone, 201, 202
Tritone substitution, 14
Trombone, *15*, 15–16, 66, *66*, 170
"Troubador Rag," 43
Truffaz, Erik, 362, 364
Trumbauer, Frank, 97, 98, 99, 140, 176
Trumpet, *15*, 15, 65
"Try Me," 330
Tsfasman, Alexander, 126
Tuba, 67
Tucker, Mark, 121
Tucker, Sherrie, *Swing Shift*, 171
Tumbao, 364, 365
"Turkish Mambo," 238
"Turnaround," 341
Turner, Big Joe, 142
Turner, Lana, 168
Turn It Over, 330
Turntablists, 362
Turpin, Tom, 40
Turre, Steve, 355
Turrentine, Stanley, 314
Tutu, 329
Tutu, Desmond, 329
Tuxedo Brass Band, 62
"Tuxedo Junction," 168
12-bar aab blues form, 8
Twelve Clouds of Joy, 131
Twelve-tone composition, 241
Tyler, Will, 208
Tynan, John, 269
Tyner, McCoy, 254, 266, *268*, 268, 270, 272, 307, 318, 354, 366

"Undecided," 286
Undercurrent, 305

"Undercurrent Blues," 153
"Underneath the Harlem Moon," *108*
"Under the Bamboo Tree," 106, 208
Underwood, Lee, 324
United Nations, 192
Unit Structures, 278, 318
Unity, 318
"Unity Village," 341
"Up and at 'Em," 126
Uptown/downtown theory, 62
Urban Bushman, 281
Us3, 361

"Valentine Stomp," 112
Vally, Roberto, 360
"Valse Hot," 248
Vamp, 34, 112
Van de Leur, Walter, 157
Van Gelder, Rudy, 317
Vanguard Jazz Orchestra, 298
Van Heusen, Jimmy, 367
Varèse, Edgard, *Density 21.5*, 273
Vasconcelos, Nana, 341
Vaudeville, 38, 151
Vaughan, Sarah, 171, 198, 252, 287–291, *289*, 331, 363
V-discs, 197–198
Veal, Reginald, 351
"Vendome," 231
Vendome Theater, 93
"Venus de Milo," 229
Venuti, Joe, 105, 140
"Versailles," 231–233, 240
Vertical improvisation, 176
Verve Records, 213, 287, 289, 348
Very Cool, 225
Vibrato, 67
Victor Records, 73, 198, 213
Victor-Victrola, *74*
Vincent, Edward, 64
Vinson, Eddie "Cleanhead," 266
"Violets for Your Furs," 267
"Viper's Drag," 112
Vitous, Miroslav, 307, 336, 337, 364
"Vi Vigor," 172–173
Vocalese, 289, 291
Vocalists, 285–292
  cool singing, 289
  Fitzgerald, Ella, 286–287
  Jones, Norah, 356
  Sinatra, Frank, 292
  Smith, Bessie, 8, 38, 47, 51, 51–52, 110, 118, 171
  Vaughan, Sarah, 287–289
  vocalese, 289, 291
  Washington, Dinah, 336
  Williams, Joe, 289
  Wilson, Cassandra, 355, 368
Voice leading, 176, 303
Vola, Louis, 128
Voynow, Dick, *73*
V.S.O.P., 330, 334
"Vulcan Worlds," 335

"Wagon Wheels," 248
Wah-wah pedal, 328
Waldron, Mal, 272
Walker, Junior, 342

"Walkin,'" 253
Walking bass, 139
Waller, Thomas "Fats," 41, 46, 86, 96, 103, 107, 110, 112–113, *113*, 145, 150, 151, 167, 181, 198, 241, 312
Wallington, George, 198, 219
"Walter L.," 330
Walton, Cedar, 243, 244, 353
Walton, Greely, 169
"Waltz for Debby," 303
Ward, Helen, 150
Warner Bros., 106
Warren, Earl, 147, 178
Washburne, Christopher, 63
Washington, Dinah, 336
Washington, Grover, 361
Washington, Jack, 147, 178
Washington, Reggie, 368
Washingtonians, 120–121
"Washington Post March," 61
Watanabe, Sadao, 364
Watercolors, 341
Waterman, Richard, 25–26
"Watermelon Man," 306, 312, 333
Waters, Ethel, 110, 118
Waters, Keith, 7
Waters, Muddy, 325
Watkins, Doug, 243
Watson, Bobby, 353
Wayburn, Ned, 105
Way out West, 248
"Weather Bird," 96
"Weather Bird Rag," 96
Weather Report, 313, 324, 336–340, *337*, 363
Weather Report, 337
Weather Update, 340
Webb, Chick, 150, 165–166, *166*, 286
Weber, Eberhard, 311
Webern, Anton, 367
Webster, Ben, 137, 140, 143, 156, 158, 160, 164, 176, 181, 242, 266
Webster, Freddie, 252
Weckl, Dave, 336
"Wedding March," 40
"Wednesday Night Prayer Meeting," 250
Wein, George, 226
Weintraub, Stefan, 126
Weintraub Syncopators, 126
Weiss, Julius, 40
Welles, Orson, *Citizen Kane*, 192
"We'll Have Peace on Earth and Even in Berlin," *56*
Wells, Henry, 144
Wellstood, Dick, 116
Wess, Frank, 293
Wesseltoft, Bugge, 362

West, Harold "Doc," 188, 200
West Africa, *26*
West Coast jazz, 239–240
"West End Blues," 93, 94–95
Weston, Randy, 217
Westray, Ronald, 351
"What'd I Say," 311
"What Is This Thing Called Love?," 195
"What Love," 272
Wheeler, Kenny, 281, 368
"When It's Sleepy Time Down South," 168
"When Lights Are Low," 187
Where Have I Known You Before, 335
Whetsol, Arthur, 120
"Whispering," 117, 195
"Whisper Not," 244
White, Gonzelle, 146
White, Lenny, 335
White, Sonny, 188
"White Christmas," 11
"White Heat," 165
Whiteman, Paul, 98, 103, 105, 107, 117, 118, 125, 135, 140, 165, 291
Whiteman, Wilberforce, 165
Whitfield, Mark, 355
Whitlock, Bob, 229
"Who," 150
Whole notes, 10
Whole-tone scale, 100, 216
"Wiggle Waggle," 307
Wilcox, Eddie, 165
Wilderness, 330
"Wild Man Blues," 86
Wilkins, Ernie, 290
William Morris Agency, 106, 156
Williams, Bert, 37–38, 124, *125*
Williams, Buster, 307, 333
Williams, Charles "Cootie," 122, 142, 155, *156*, 156, 158, 160, 197, 210
Williams, Clarence, 60, 68, *89*, 89, 91
Williams, James, 356
Williams, Joe, 289
Williams, John, 144, 188
Williams, Martin, 81
Williams, Mary Lou, 131, 142–144, *143*, 171, 243, 363, 367
Williams, Richard, 250
Williams, Todd, 351
Williams, Tommy, 237
Williams, Tony, 299–301, 306, 326, 327, 330, 334, 350, 357
"Willow Weep for Me," 113
Wilson, Cassandra, 355, 368
Wilson, Dick, 144
Wilson, Teddy, 114, 116, 146, 150–151, 151, 181–182, *182*, 187, 241

Winburn, Anna Mae, 172
Windham Hill Records, 311
Winding, Kai, 217, 228, 239
Wind instruments, 15
"Windup, The," 309–310
"Witch Hunt," 318
"Wolverine Blues," 76, 86
Wolverines, *73*, 98
Women in Jazz festival, 363
Women-only bands, 130, 171–172, 363
Wonder, Stevie, 328, 333, 334
Wong, Willie Mae, *171*, 172
Woode, Jimmy, 287, 296
Wooding, Sam, 125, 126
Woodman, Britt, 250, 287, 296
Woods, Phil, 345, 354, 363
Woodstock, 325
Woodyard, Sam, 287
"Woody n' You," 199, 207
Word of Mouth, 340
"Working Man Blues," 77
"Work Song," 312
Work songs, 35
World of Cecil Taylor, The, 278
World Saxophone Quartet, 281–282
World's Columbian Exposition (Chicago, 1893), 38, *39*
World Tour, 340
World War II, 131, 135, 171, 192
Wright, Elmon, Jr., 209
Wright, Eugene, *234*, 234
Wynton Marsalis, 345, *349*, 349–353

Yamekraw, 110
Yancey, Jimmy, 53
"Yardbird Suite," 220
Yellowjackets, 361
"You Don't Know What Love Is," 248, 272
Young, Larry, 318, 325, 330
Young, Lester, 98, 101, 140, 141, 147, 149, 156, 167, 176–181, *179*, 187, 188, 199, 200, *206*, 217, 219, 225, 236, 239, 242, 250, 266, 340
Young, Myrtle, 172
Young at Heart, 330
"Your Mother's Son-in-law," 150

Zadeh, Aziza Mustafa, 364
Zawinul, Josef, 300, *302*, 312, 313, 326, 327, 336–340, *337*, 363
Zawinul Syndicate, 340
Ziegfeld, Florenz, 122
Ziegfeld Follies, 125
Zodiac Suite, 143
Zoot-suit riots, 194
Zorn, John, 366, *367*, 367